Rebels and Renegades

A Chronology of Social and
Political Dissent in the United States

Rebels and Renegades

A Chronology of Social and Political Dissent in the United States

Neil A. Hamilton

Routledge
Taylor & Francis Group

NEW YORK AND LONDON

© 2002 by The Moschovitis Group, Inc.

Published in 2002 by
Routledge
29 West 35th Street
New York, New York 10001
www.routledge-ny.com

Published in Great Britain by
Routledge
11 New Fetter Lane
London EC4P 4EE
www.routledge.uk.co

Routledge is an imprint of the Tayor & Francis Group.
Printed in the United States of America on acid-free paper.

Produced by The Moschovitis Group, Inc.
339 Fifth Avenue
New York, New York 10016
www.mosgroup.com

Publisher	Valerie Tomaselli
Executive Editor	Hilary W. Poole
Editorial Coordinator	Sonja Matanovic
Design and Layout	Annemarie Redmond
Production Assistant	Rashida Allen
Photo Research	Gillian Speeth
Copyediting	Carole Campbell
Proofreading	Adams Holman
Index	Barber Indexing

10 9 8 7 6 5 4 3 2 1

Library of Congress Cataloging-in-Publication Data
Hamilton, Neil A., 1949–
    Rebels and renegades : a chronology of social and political dissent in the
United States / by Neil A. Hamilton.
        p.   cm.
    Includes bibliographical references and index.
    ISBN 0-415-93639-X (hardcover : alk. paper)
    1. Radicalism—United States—History. 2. Radicals—United States—History.
3. Social reformers—United States—History. 4. Protest movements—United
States—History. 5. United States—History.   I. Title.
HN90.R3H354 2002
303.48'4—dc21   2002008916

Contents

Introduction

Through the traces of their lives, America's rebels and renegades still speak to us about society's injustices and their own hopes:

> Anarchism alone stresses the importance of the individual, his possibilities and needs in a free society. Instead of telling him that he must fall down and worship before institutions, live and die for abstractions, break his heart and stunt his life for taboos, anarchism insists that the center of gravity in society is the individual—that he must think for himself, act freely, and live fully.
>
> —Emma Goldman, early 1900s

> We believe that this racist government has robbed us, and now we are demanding the overdue debt of forty acres and two mules. Forty acres and two mules was promised 100 years ago as retribution for slave labor and mass murder of black people. . . . The Germans murdered 6 million Jews. The American racist has taken part in the slaughter of over 50 million black people; therefore, we feel that this is a modest demand that we make.
>
> —Huey Newton and Bobby Seale, 1966

Most Americans would classify these rebels and renegades as extremists. Their discontent with society was so strong that they called for a drastic overhauling of laws, practices, and public and personal relations. In so doing, these dissidents proposed a radical alternative to mainstream thought and actions. Their voices are the ones heard most often in this book, though our congregation of "rebels and renegades" goes beyond radicals to include more moderate reformers, along with reactionaries who defended conservatism and sought to roll back liberal developments.

"Radical" has been and remains a difficult word to define. At what point does a person fit the criteria of being a radical rather than merely a reformer? The *Oxford English Dictionary* defines radical in the political sense as a person "advocating 'radical reform'. . . or any thorough political and social change; representing or supporting the extreme section of a political party." But who fits this category resides in the eyes of the beholder, an assessment determined not only by personal opinion, but also by context and time period. A person or event that might appear to be moderate within a radical era may appear to be radical within a moderate one. For example, early twentieth-century suffragists who demonstrated outside the White House on behalf of enfranchising women were considered outrageous by many at the time, but they were quaint by the standards of 1960s feminists, who themselves would be considered antiquated by the "riot grrls" of today.

Controversy arises also over whether a discussion of radicals should include reactionaries. Many academics view radicalism as the exclusive territory of the left. But these days the label "radical right" has become shorthand for a radicalism that emerges as a reaction to leftist ideas and developments. A danger exists, of course, in applying the word radical to both liberals and reactionaries in that it could blur the distinction between them. If the word "radical" is too inclusive—if it covers too many people—it is diluted into meaning little more than those persons making a different proposal from one that already exists. Worries about dilution of meaning, however, are less important than an understanding of how rebels and renegades have been classified as radicals and reactionaries by their contemporaries and by historians since their time. The entries in this book attempt to show classification by example.

DO RADICALS MATTER?: HISTORICAL INTERPRETATIONS

Some historians deny that radicals and reactionaries, that rebels and renegades, have played any important role in the history of the United States; others insist that they have been crucial to society's development. As it turns out, the place of radicals in historical works has changed as history has been interpreted and reinterpreted.

Writing mainly between 1910 and 1945, Progressive historians moved radicals and reformers into the spotlight. These historians believed that for democracy to advance, the "have-nots," or the lower classes, had to do battle with the "haves," or the upper classes. Consequently, the Progressive historians argued that America's history should be told in terms of momentous struggles between conservatives and liberals. In this schema, conservatives and their supporters were the "haves" who disdained democratic advances and defended the status quo, while liberals and their supporters were the "have-nots" who fought for democracy and a more egalitarian society.

These battles can be divided into historical periods. According to the Progressive interpretation, in each period dissidents challenged entrenched conservatives and brought about reform, and the conservatives then challenged the reforms and brought about reaction, although not enough to undo all of the liberal advances. In 1939, historian Arthur Schlesinger, Sr. described the development: "A period of concern for the rights of the few has been followed by one of concern for the wrongs of the many."

Charles Beard, among the most prominent of all the Progressive historians and a tremendous influence on others who wrote history prior to World War II (and even later), claimed in his *An Economic Interpretation of the Constitution* (1913) that the founding document was a conservative reaction to the populism of the Revolution. The authors of the Constitution wanted it to constrain the liberalism that had been unleashed before and during the Revolution; toward that end, they worked to protect their property and property in general. In several other books Beard portrayed U. S. history as propelled by class conflict, with economic issues the most important.

Progressive historians wrote during an era of reform in the United States called Progressivism. They supported that effort to remake society and thought that by portraying U.S. history as a struggle between reformers and conservatives, with reformers as the agents of enlightenment and progress, they could further the reform agenda. In that sense, they reflected the times in which they wrote.

Those times, though, changed in the late 1940s and 1950s as the United States entered a more conservative and conformist era. With the Cold War under way, and with the expanding American economy creating higher levels of prosperity, support for—rather than the questioning of—existing institutions and practices became the order of the day. As a result, most historians began reinterpreting the past as one in which conflict played a minor role, and the country's rebels and renegades were considered to be insignificant specks of discontent in an overwhelmingly contented, middle-class country.

Because they saw Americans both past and present as being largely in agreement with the direction of society, these historians were called consensus historians. In *Interpretations of American History: Patterns and Perspectives* (1987), George Athan Billias and Gerald N. Grob describe consensus historians as those who believed that "The cement that bound American society together throughout most of its history was a widespread acceptance of certain principles and beliefs." Even conservatives and liberals agreed on basic principles, hence any differences between these two groups were minor and merely over details. Rather than the Progressive view of history as delineated by periods, the consensus historians saw the past of the United States as characterized by continuity.

Two such consensus historians were Daniel Boorstin and Louis Hartz. In the *Genius of American Politics* (1953), Boorstin insisted that the American Revolution was less a "revolution" than a colonial war for independence. Forget any struggle within the colonies between the haves and have-nots; forget any radical desire to attack the elite or frame bold, new governments. According to Boorstin, not much changed as a result of the upheaval, except that the British monarchy had been expelled from the colonies, and the colonists had founded a separate, republican government rooted in principles and practices they had established earlier. In *The Liberal Tradition* (1955), Hartz joined Boorstin in portraying the American Revolution as distinctly moderate. Unlike revolutions in Europe, Hartz observed, Americans lacked a feudal past whose overthrow would have required radical measures.

Looking beyond the Revolution, Boorstin characterized Americans as nonideological, a people given less to theorizing than to practical and pragmatic actions. Even the Puritans, he wrote in *The Americans: The Colonial Experience* (1958), "made the Calvinist theology their point of departure, they made it precisely that and nothing else. From it they departed at once into the practical life." In emphasizing pragmatism and consensus, he almost completely ignored such powerful dissident voices as the religious separatist Roger Williams and the Puritan critic Anne Hutchinson. Consensus historians turned America into a quiet land, or as Billias and Grob state, a land in which there was "no longer a history marked by extreme group conflicts or class distinctions." For consensus historians, a book detailing the significant role played by rebels and renegades in America's development would be an exercise in exaggeration.

But the writing of history changed again in the 1960s as society experienced the tremendous upheaval of the civil rights and black power movements, protests over the Vietnam War, and the sustained campaign for women's liberation. Because these protests brought previously ignored groups to the fore, historians reacted by taking more notice of the role played by minorities in the past. The disadvantaged and the dissidents began to have their day.

New Left historians, much like the Progressive historians, emphasized conflict between the haves and the have-nots. But where the Progressives saw such conflict as resulting in more democracy—progress overcoming conservative resistance—the New Left saw the battle between haves and have-nots as ultimately resulting in victories for the oppressive elite because Americans never took the crucial step of engaging in successful revolutionary change.

Like the Progressives, the New Left emphasized social and economic conflict, and they insisted that historians must address social problems such as racism, militarism, imperialism, and economic inequality. History, they said, should be written from the standpoint of the disadvantaged and inarticulate, or from the "bottom up." Invariably, New Left history retrieved rebels and renegades, at least those who qualified as left-wing radicals, from the dustbin of consensus history. As Billias and Grob note, the New Left believed that by focusing on the masses "scholars would discover the radicalism inherent in the American past." Howard Zinn's *A People's History of the United States* (1980) provided a compelling survey of U.S. history from the New Left perspective.

At the same time New Left history was gaining popularity, the 1960s ferment encouraged New Social history. These historians joined the New Left in studying those people previously ignored in the writing about America's past—including blacks, Native Americans, women, and the poor. The New Social historians, however, focused more on changes in social structure over time and more on the development of social groups than they did on individuals. They discounted ideology as a driver for change and instead stressed population patterns, geography, economics, and technology.

Despite the preference of New Social historians for social groups rather than individuals, their outlook complemented the New Left historians to the extent that they provided a greater recognition of radicals. Once again these dissidents along with other rebels and renegades could be seen as important contributors in shaping the United States through its major historical periods. Although now more than 30 years have passed since its inception, New Social history remains dominant in the writing of history.

ERAS OF RADICALISM

The periods that many historians use to divide America's past are used in this book to understand the actions of rebels and renegades. We begin in chapter one with the Colonial period, when European ideas encountered the American environment. While Boorstin insisted that practicality characterized the era; experimentation was also the order of the day, encouraged by a setting in which many European restraints no longer mattered. From the earliest moments rebels and renegades were an important part of the Colonial scene, from the peaceful efforts in the 1630s of Roger Williams, who preached the separation of church and state, to the violent rebellion in 1676 led by Nathaniel Bacon, who briefly overthrew the government of Virginia. According to Zinn, Bacon's "Declaration of the People" displayed a hatred for Native Americans but also a "populist resentment against the rich." As such, Bacon and his followers threatened the rule of that colony's elite planters.

Chapter two covers the period of the American Revolution and nation building. The Revolution involved more than complaints about British taxation: it unleashed an internal class conflict as evident in the protests staged by the Jack Tars; and it produced the Declaration of Independence, a document of ideals that radicals, reformers, and reactionaries would refer to time and again for the philosophical support of their causes—namely life, liberty, and the pursuit of happiness. Zinn observes that "town mechanics, laborers, and seamen, as well as small farmers, were swept into 'the people' by the rhetoric of the Revolution." The ideals of the Declaration, in fact, caused blacks to press for their freedom from slavery and led in 1800 to Gabriel's Rebellion in Virginia.

The period of expansion and reform, covered in chapter three, also saw blacks try to win their freedom, as evident by the actions of author David Walker and rebel leader Nat Turner. At the same time, white abolitionists such as William Lloyd Garrison and Frances Wright came forward. No more powerful testament to the influence of the Declaration of Independence can be found than in the abolitionist crusade. This period was also one in which abolitionism combined with new-born industrialization and the rise of cities to spark a variety of reform efforts, including the 1848 women's rights convention at Seneca Falls, New York.

As chapter four on the Civil War and Reconstruction reveals, the abolitionist crusade continued into the 1850s, as did the increasing awareness by women that they, too, should no longer be denied full social and political participation. These activities ranged from Sojourner Truth's speech at a women's rights convention in Ohio in 1851, to John Brown's raid on Harper's Ferry in 1859—a violent and failed attempt to stir a slave rebellion. The abolitionist crusade produced its own reaction among southerners who defended slavery, for example, George Fitzhugh's publication in 1857 of *Cannibals All! Or Slaves Without Masters*, and later with South Carolina's secession from the Union.

The period of postwar industrialization presented in chapter five reveals how the new economy and the growth of yet bigger cities stimulated another wave of radical and reform activity, some of it quite extreme—anarchism's assault on all government, including the capitalist state, for example—and some of it quite violent. Laborers launched a series of strikes in 1877; a bomb exploded at Chicago's Haymarket Square in 1886; Mother Jones organized the United Mine Workers in 1890; anarchist Alexander Berkman shot the general manager of the Carnegie Steel Company in 1892; Eugene V. Debs converted to socialism after the Pullman Strike of 1894; and W. E. B. DuBois helped organize a civil rights group in 1909 that evolved into the National Association for the Advancement of Colored People. The urban environment had clearly proved conducive to a wide array of activism.

World War I and the Roaring Twenties, covered in chapter six, are often thought of as a conservative era, when loyalty to country and to the mighty dollar were more important than social critique. Nevertheless, the peace movement thrived as the war raged, while black nationalist and separatist Marcus Garvey gained prominence, Margaret Sanger opened her birth control clinic, and Alice Paul intensified the women's suffrage movement.

As chapter seven reveals, the Great Depression and World War II posed unprecedented challenges for U.S. society that led to many radical proposals. With the economy on the skids and capitalism near collapse, communists and socialists pushed their alternatives and workers demonstrated a strong resolve to unionize—the 1936 Great Flint Sit-down against General Motors being just one example. The war ultimately helped spark the modern civil rights movement, with widespread protests against the court martial of the Port Chicago Fifty in 1944.

The emergence of the Cold War, covered in chapter eight, raised concerns linked to U.S. involvement in overseas actions and pressure for conformity at home in light of the threat from the Soviet Union and other communist enemies. At the same time, the U.S. economy prospered and the Baby Boom produced a younger population, both of which set the stage for dissidents to question the justice and direction of society. What ignites eras of protest is always a matter of debate, but it is generally agreed that the presence of a large number of young people can be a stimulus to change—because of their discontent with the traditional practices of older generations. The restlessness of the Baby Boom generation mixed with the controversy of the Vietnam War and the activism of the civil rights movement to produce social and political ferment and change.

Indeed, the civil rights movement was the catalyst to many other reform efforts because it revealed injustice on a massive scale and demonstrated the potential effectiveness of protest. Nowhere was this more evident than in the Montgomery (Alabama) Bus Boycott of 1955. The formation of Students for a Democratic Society and the Student Non-Violent Coordinating Committee in 1960 presaged the stirring of the country's college campuses, and the explosion of a kaleidoscope of reform was evident in actions that ranged from Betty Friedan publishing *The Feminine Mystique* in 1963, to Timothy Leary founding the League for Spiritual Discovery in 1966, to Reies Lopez Tijerina challenging Anglo land claims in 1967, to Native Americans occupying Alcatraz Island in 1969.

The final chapter surveys the rebels and renegades in the contemporary United States, from the 1970s to today. Those decades witnessed an extreme reactionary backlash against the liberal reforms of the 1960s. For example, in 1978 William Pierce wrote his racist, right-wing *The Turner Diaries*, a book worshipped by the far radical right; shortly afterward, the militia movement came to prominence. Soon U.S. newspapers were covering a new racist ideology called Identity Christianity and the antigovernment and racist group called Posse Comitatus, along with a shoot-out in 1983 in Medina, North Dakota, involving Gordon Kahl, and the blowing up of the Alfred P. Murrah Federal Building in Oklahoma City in 1995 by Timothy McVeigh.

At the same time, the reach of a global economy produced a backlash on the left against globalization that eventually stirred protests in Seattle, Washington, in 1999 against the World Trade Organization. In 2001 terrorism struck the United States on a previously unheard of scale when hijackers connected to extreme fundamentalist Islam crashed two jet airliners into New York City's World Trade Center, and a third into the Pentagon. The World Trade Center collapsed and the Pentagon was severely damaged. More than 3,000 people were killed. The attack, and the subsequently enforced domestic policies meant to prevent additional attacks, along with the launching of a war overseas to destroy terrorist groups, raised difficult questions regarding the role of dissent and protest—and with them the expression of radicalism—in a country seeking security.

USING THIS BOOK

Each chapter in *Rebels and Renegades* is introduced by a brief essay intended to place the individual entries within a broader historical picture. Each entry focuses on a specific development; each entry is also designed to take the reader backward and forward in time in order to provide greater context for the topic under discussion and to show both the roots and results of the event. This book quotes extensively from rebels and renegades on all sides of the political spectrum; as a result, it contains statements that today's readers might find antiquated, or controversial, or even offensive. I cite these statements not to endorse a point of view but rather to convey the spirit of the era and of the individuals involved in the making of history.

It would be impossible in a book this size, or even in several books this size, to discuss all the rebels and renegades who have shaped America's history. So I have concentrated on those who had the greatest impact; those most interesting; those most representative of the periods covered here. Throughout, I have attempted to emphasize the character of the individual, and I have tried to make this a lively presentation, one that will draw the reader into the complex and exciting world in which these rebels and renegades offered their alternatives to accepted ideas and practices. I hope these entries will whet the reader's appetite to pursue these stories further—perhaps through the Further Reading suggestions included with each entry—and to discover the lives of others who do not appear in these pages but who deserve the attention of those committed to recognizing the diversity of America's past.

Neil A. Hamilton
May 2002

CHAPTER ONE

Colonization and Settlement

When the British began settling in North America in the 1600s they arrived with great hopes and expectations. Whether it was the materialistic pursuit of gold in Jamestown or the effort to establish a godly "city upon a hill" in Boston, the settlers thought they could free themselves from the limitations that shackled them in Europe. This hope for a fresh start in a land of many possibilities encouraged rebels and renegades to challenge authority where it existed, or to build their own alternative societies.

Several developments encouraged Europeans to explore the Americas and settle there. As with so many new eras, technological changes were crucial—during the fifteenth and sixteenth centuries, improved ships and navigation made it possible to sail longer distances, and more accurate firearms made it possible to more easily dominate and conquer other peoples.

At the same time, the rise of nation states stimulated nationalism and competition among countries such as Portugal, Spain, England, and France for overseas land and wealth. The pursuit of riches was an extension of the more sophisticated banking and credit system that had developed by the late fifteenth century. Investors knew how to make money, and they wanted to make more of it; fortunes

> "Religious matters are to be separated from the jurisdiction of the state not because they are beneath the interests of the state, but . . . because they are too high."
>
> Isaac Backus "An Appeal to the Public for Religious Liberty," 1773

acquired prior to the conquest of the Americas served as a weapon with which to exploit the new land.

As the Europeans arrived in the Americas, they brought with them plans for settlement—some formulated by governments, others by individuals. To varying degrees those plans unraveled in the challenging surroundings of their new land. Spain intended to establish an absolutist system whereby the settlers would be closely ruled by the country's monarchy, but the monarchy found its rules defied by those who controlled Indian labor and amassed large landholdings. France intended a feudal system in Canada, one in which peasants would work for lords, but the feudal system collapsed as settlers found they could claim land for their own and escape into the wilderness.

In 1607, those who founded Jamestown in Virginia, the first permanent English settlement in North America, intended to find gold and return to their homeland. Much to their dismay, they discovered neither gold nor any other easy route to riches. Instead, the colony floundered and was rescued by the planting of tobacco, which brought with it the tragic consequence of black slavery in the new land.

Time and again plans were changed, and the cultural characteristics that the colonists brought with them across the Atlantic were altered by the environment and the lessons learned. One historian has noted that America acted toward European cultural practices much as a prism does toward light; it refracted those practices, never completely eradicating them, but bending them and changing them in ways neither planned nor expected.

Today, when Americans think of the Colonial Era, they tend to see it as an unvarying period, when little changed prior to the Revolution. But the colonies underwent notable developments from the sixteenth to the seventeenth centuries. The Chesapeake colonies of Virginia and Maryland, for example, became much more stable. What had been a largely single, male settlement became more family-based, and the plantation agricultural system produced a more stratified society.

In Massachusetts Bay, the Puritan community mission gave way to a greater degree of individualism. A perfect example is the town of Dedham, which was founded in the 1630s as a closed, covenanted community. The settlers wrote and signed an agreement committing themselves to living together in harmony and brotherly love with unquestioning obedience to God. They built their town as a nucleated one, meaning a town in which everyone lived near or around a common and were drawn to the common for their activities and sense of togetherness. To further community, they distributed land in a manner that made it impossible for just a few families to dominate the fertile soil; the settlers had to share in rich and rocky terrain alike.

But most of that changed in the 1700s. Farmers began enlarging their landholdings and moving away from the commons to live on the outskirts of town. As some farmers bought land from their neighbors, those with more money acquired the better soil and grew wealthier. Whereas a limited concentration of wealth had existed in Dedham in the 1600s, in the 1700s that increased. At the same time, more non-Puritans moved into town, and they disregarded the original covenant. A commercial economy appeared with trade, as opposed to the earlier subsistence pursuits. These developments stopped short of destroying community, but they pushed it into the background; society became more individualistic, driven by a bolder material pursuit that encouraged people to think more about what was best for themselves rather than what was best for Dedham as a whole. To varying degrees, this change occurred in most other New England towns; to use historian Richard Bushman's phrase, the entire colony of Connecticut, once the most stalwart of Puritan settlements, went from "Puritan to Yankee."

Over the sixteenth and seventeenth centuries, the plentitude of land and the distance from British authorities encouraged many colonists towards social experimentation. These experiments were characterized by such diverse efforts as the Pilgrims, who attempted to build a Puritan commonwealth at Plymouth Bay; William Penn, who founded a "holy experiment" in Pennsylvania; the Labadists, who began a commune in Maryland based on mystic ideas; William Gottlieb Priber, who promoted a secular communal utopia in South Carolina; and Jacob Weber, who, in the same colony, founded a religious cult that deteriorated into delusion and murder.

As much as geography and distance inspired experimentation, these factors contributed also to instability. The British colonies, for example, were anything but smooth-running. Bacon's Rebellion erupted in 1676 and momentarily overthrew the royal governor in Virginia; in 1689 Jacob Leisler seized power in New York.

For blacks, the founding of the colonies meant, by the late 1600s, enslavement. With that came efforts by dissident African-Americans to escape to freedom or overthrow the slave system altogether. Maroons fled into the backwoods, where they started communities that threatened the white-run plantations. In 1739 the bloody Stono Rebellion jeopardized slavery in South Carolina.

Such were the European settlements founded by the Spanish, French, and British in the Americas—born in hope, instability, and the oppression of one race by another. And those who pursued their dreams and endured exploitation often gave vent to their own radical alternatives that challenged the status quo.

Building A Holy Commonwealth: The Pilgrims Arrive in America

In December 1620, the Pilgrims founded Plymouth in present-day Massachusetts and dedicated themselves to building a covenanted community where they could freely practice their religion. Their beliefs challenged not only the prevailing Anglican church but also the power of the English monarchy. With their arrival in New England, the Puritans set the stage for the nation's role as a refuge for dissidents and their social experiments.

Emerging from the religious disputes that spread across Europe in the sixteenth century, the Pilgrims were part of a larger group of dissenters in England called the Puritans. These religious rebels challenged the monarchy when they condemned the Anglican church, or the Church of England, for what they viewed as corrupt practices. To the Puritans, the church hierarchy headed by the king made local congregations powerless, while elaborate ceremonies laden with Roman Catholic influences robbed the church of any true spiritual commitment. To make matters worse, in extending membership to all English citizens, the Anglican church admitted sinners, thus polluting a supposedly godly sanctuary.

Following the ideas laid out by John Calvin (1509–64), a Swiss Protestant theologian, the Puritans believed in predestination—that God had predetermined whether or not an individual was "saved" and would enter paradise. God, they claimed, wanted them to reform the Anglican church and restrict baptism to those with an unquestioning faith. Furthermore, God wanted an end to the degeneracy in society with its gambling, swearing, and Sabbath-breaking. For their beliefs, the Puritans earned the enmity of the British monarchs, who persecuted them with fines, imprisonment, and even executed two Puritans in 1593.

The signing of the Mayflower Compact. (Library of Congress)

Although most Puritans thought they could achieve reformation by working within the Anglican church, separatists among them decided that salvation required a new church and society. Consequently, in 1608, shortly after King James I labeled the Puritans subversives and vowed to "harry them out the land," one such group from the town of Scrooby immigrated to the Netherlands. In the 1580s, the Netherlands had declared independence from Spain and its Roman Catholic king, Philip II, and it tolerated many religious beliefs. The Pilgrims from Scrooby saw in that country a refuge where they could build a community covenanted to each other and to God.

But Amsterdam, where the Pilgrims first settled, and then Leyden, the walled city to which they later relocated, posed problems. The Pilgrims disliked the loss of English ways and culture among their children, and the intrusion of secular and other religious views, including Arminianism—a belief that denied the Calvinist view that God had designated certain people as "chosen." As the Pilgrims had separated from the Church of England, and then England altogether, they now decided to separate from Europe.

In September 1620, after obtaining financial backing from English investor Thomas Weston, some of the Pilgrims sailed from Plymouth, England, on the tiny *Mayflower*, bound for North America. Of the nearly 100 passengers on board, only 41 were Pilgrims; the others, called "Strangers," were laborers and craftsmen needed to build a colony.

The Pilgrims sighted New England on November 19, 1620. Years later William Bradford (1590–1657), who served the Pilgrims as governor for several decades, described the bleak scene: "For summer being done, all things stand . . . with a weather-beaten face, and the whole country, full of woods and thickets represented a savage hue." Bradford called the land a "hideous and desolate wilderness."

On board ship, the Pilgrims and Strangers signed the Mayflower Compact, affirming they would establish a civil government with officials elected annually by all the adult males. In December 1620, the Pilgrims began to build Plymouth, their settlement adjoining Cape Cod Bay. They arranged their economy so that all the settlers held property in common, and they pursued their goal of building an independent congregational church, the Church of Plymouth. Historian John Demos stated that for the Pilgrims Puritanism was an ethos—it explained everything and shaped all conduct.

Disease killed half the settlers that first winter, but the Pilgrims survived when they received help from two Native Americans, Samoset, who taught them about nearby tribes, and Squanto, who showed them how to plant corn and where to hunt and fish. The Pilgrims reaped their first harvest in October 1621 and invited the nearby Indians, under chief Massasoit, to a thanksgiving feast.

Before long, the Pilgrim settlement began to change. While it maintained largely harmonious relations with the native peoples, it became more militaristic after Miles Standish (1584?–1656), a Stranger embraced by the Pilgrims for his military prowess, killed the chief of the Massachusetts tribe. In 1623, the colony resorted to a private economy, with land assigned to each household. The population expanded, but so did crime, making necessary a law in 1624 that established criminal trials by jury.

In the 1630s, the Church of Plymouth fragmented, and, as trade expanded, the colony lost some of its distinctiveness, though its system of town-based congregational churches continued. Plymouth remained an independent colony until 1691, when it was annexed by Massachusetts.

Writing in the 1640s, Bradford deplored Plymouth's decline in morals and spirituality, and he labeled the Pilgrim mission a failure. He said:

And thus was this poor church left like an ancient mother grown old and forsaken of her children . . . her ancient members being most of them worn away by death, and those of later time being like children translated into other families, and she like a widow left only to trust in God. Thus, she that had made many rich, became herself poor.

In building their short-lived separatist community, the Pilgrims contributed to making America a land of possibilities, a potential most often embraced by those pursuing material gain, but sometimes by radicals striving to achieve their own religious, social, or ideological goals. In the colonial period, other religious radicals would soon follow, each trying to fulfill their own idea of how a godly people should live. These included everyone from Roger Williams and Anne Hutchinson—who challenged the very legitimacy of the Puritans in Massachusetts Bay and thus became dissenters against the original dissenting movement—to those such as the followers of Johann Beissel, whose communal practices shocked followers of mainstream religion.

Further Reading

Demos, John. *A Little Commonwealth: Family Life in Plymouth Colony.* 2d ed. New York: Oxford University Press, 1999.

Langdon, George D., Jr. *Pilgrim Colony: A History of New Plymouth, 1620–1691.* New Haven, Conn.: Yale University Press, 1966.

Roger Williams Advocates the Separation of Church and State 1644

A devout Calvinist, Roger Williams advanced religious freedom inadvertently: intending to protect the purity of his faith, his ideas led to a political system that separated church and state.

The son of James Williams, a merchant tailor, and Alice Pemberton, Roger Williams (1603–83) was born in London. He graduated with a bachelor's degree from Cambridge in 1627 and married Mary Barnard in 1629. That same year, he attended a conference of Puritans and decided to join their migration to America. By the end of 1630, about 2,000 settlers had arrived at Massachusetts Bay (dwarfing the number of separatist Puritans, called Pilgrims, who had settled at Plymouth); by 1640, the number had increased to about 20,000, building a Puritan culture that would dominate New England.

Puritan theology may have contained a "democratic dynamic," as some historians have argued, with its independent churches based on local congregations, but the Puritans expected conformity to their views—even though most of the settlers at Massachusetts Bay were not Puritans. They used the state to enforce their orthodoxy.

Williams, who arrived at Massachusetts Bay in 1631, immediately challenged the colonial leadership. He criticized the Salem Church congregation for failing to formally declare itself completely separate and independent from the Church of England. His separatism was at odds with most Puritans, who claimed they were still working within the Church of England with the goal of reforming it.

Although William agreed in 1633 to preach at Salem, he called for all of the churches in Massachusetts Bay to embrace religious separatism. Further, he declared the colony's charter invalid because the king had violated the sovereignty of the Indians. To Williams, only land *bought* from the Indians could be considered legitimately English. "James has no more right to give away or sell [Chief] Massasoit's lands," Williams said, "than Massasoit has to sell King James' kingdom."

In 1635, Williams claimed that the colony's leaders had transgressed when they punished persons who had violated the Ten Commandment strictures against Sabbath-breaking, idolatry, blasphemy, and heresy. He said that whenever the state enforces religion, it substitutes government edict for spiritual faith. By that year, Williams fit the description of him presented by Puritan leader Cotton Mather, that he was the "first *rebel* against the divine *church-order* established in the wilderness."

The Massachusetts General Court placed Williams on trial for his beliefs in 1636 and banished him to England, but he and his wife fled to Narragansett Bay in Rhode Island. There he bought land from the Narragansett Indians and founded the town of Providence in June 1637. Two years later he organized the Baptist church, though he soon left it, claiming no church could really be a church of true believers until apostles appeared to herald a rebirth of religion.

During a trip to England in 1644, Williams wrote *Queries of Highest Consideration,* in which he questioned the right of government to establish a state church. In his *Bloudy Tenet of Persecution,* written the same year, he asserted that all countries since ancient Israel were "merely civil," meaning without any religious basis, and he argued for a tolerant polity. "The doctrine of persecution for cause of conscience is proved guilty of all the blood of the souls crying for vengeance under the altar," he intoned.

Williams insisted: "All civil states with their officers of justice in their respective constitutions and administrators are proved essentially civil, and therefore not judges, governors or defenders of the spiritual or Christian state and worship." And he added: "God requireth not a uniformity of religion to be enacted and enforced in any civil state; which enforced uniformity . . . is the greatest occasion of civil war, . . . [the] persecution of Christ Jesus and his servants, and of the hypocrisy and destruction of millions of souls."

Before Williams died in Providence in 1683, Rhode Island had developed a government based on liberty, equality, and tolerance, with a political system that, like others in New England, employed frequent elections. Yet as much as Williams's belief in a populist state later became a beacon for democracy, he never embraced liberty for the sake of liberty itself, nor did he express a modern libertarian concept of free will. Rather, he sought to create a godly society uncorrupted by government.

America, the Land of Radical Opportunities

The Americas were conquered and colonized by bloody conquest, led by Europeans seeking land, gold, and other forms of wealth. Christopher Columbus displayed the materialistic motive in his exaggerated description of the Caribbean islands, made during his first voyage in 1492: "Hispaniola is a miracle. Mountains and hills, plains and pastures, are both fertile and beautiful. . . . The harbors are unbelievably good and there are many wide rivers of which the majority contain gold. . . . There are many spices, and great mines of gold and other metals."

Under Queen Elizabeth I in the mid-1500s, England sought to develop settlements in North America that would serve as bases from which its ships could plunder the gold-laden ships of Spain. The great sixteenth-century promoter of English colonization, the geographer Richard Hakluyt, stressed the economic benefits of establishing colonies, when, in stating one of his three primary goals, he had in mind, he used the words, "to trafficke."

Yet for all the brutality in killing Indians and worshipping mammon, another motivation coursed through the settlement of what would become the United States—the belief that a better society could be built, one superior to that which existed in Europe, a continent wracked by disease, dissolution, and war. When Sir Humphrey Gilbert sailed across the Atlantic in 1583, he carried with him not only a charter from Elizabeth, which was a practical necessity, but also a copy of Thomas More's *Utopia* (1516), which laid out an ideal society governed by reason. When the Puritans considered founding a colony in New England, one of their leaders, John Winthrop, listed religious and moral reasons ahead of material desires as the rationale for their mission. Puritans, he said, will be serving "the Church of great consequence to carry the Gospell into those [parts] of the world," and will escape the "generall callamitie" facing a Europe "brought to desolation or sinnes."

In short, alongside an economic drive there existed a hope that in this "new land," as Europeans saw it, nobler dreams could be realized. This hope would resonate throughout America's history and contribute to the popularly held sense of mission and superiority, and the belief that a higher calling must be fulfilled. Here, then, the sources of the cries for liberty in the Revolution of 1776, the striving for freedom in the abolitionist drive to end slavery, the fight for equality in the feminist crusade to advance women's rights, and onward . . . radical movement followed by radical movement, into the twenty-first century.

Further Reading

Gaustad, Edwin S. *Liberty of Conscience: Roger Williams in America.* Valley Forge, Penn.: Judson Press, 1999.

Miller, Perry. *Roger Williams: His Contribution to the American Tradition.* Indianapolis, Ind.: Bobbs-Merrill, 1953.

Morgan, Edmund S. *Roger Williams: The Church and the State.* New York: Harcourt, Brace, and World, 1967.

Anne Hutchinson Claims That God Has Revealed Himself to Her

1637

In Massachusetts Bay, Anne Hutchinson held religious meetings that assaulted the Puritan practice of relegating women to the role of "man's helper." At the same time, her ideas promoted the importance of individual conscience, none more so than when, on trial for her beliefs, she declared that she alone could determine whether God had entered her soul.

Anne Hutchinson was born Anne Marbury in 1591 in Alford, Lincolnshire, England to Bridget Dryden and Francis Marbury, a dissenting Anglican clergyman. Exposed to theology at an early age, she became conversant in the ongoing turmoil between the Church of England, also called the Anglican church, and the Puritans, who thought the Anglicans morally corrupt and spiritually bankrupt.

In the years after she married William Hutchinson, a merchant, in 1612, Anne Hutchinson gravitated toward the preaching of John Cotton, a Puritan. When Cotton immigrated to Massachusetts Bay in 1633, she convinced her husband they should do likewise, and in 1634 the couple, along with several of their children (she had 13 altogether), journeyed across the Atlantic. Because William Hutchinson was wealthy and prominent, he received a large plot of land in Boston for his family's house, a practice in keeping with a complex distribution system in which the amount of land a Puritan received was related, in part, to his standing in society. William Hutchinson continued to prosper as a merchant and served in public office.

Anne Hutchinson, meanwhile, further committed herself to John Cotton's theology, finding it more spiritually fulfilling than any taught by other Puritan preachers. Puritans had for years debated the differences between two religious concepts, the covenant of grace and the covenant of works, and the relative value of each. According to the covenant of grace, only complete faith in God could possibly bring salvation; according to the covenant of works, the doing of good deeds could assist in bringing salvation. Cotton took a position halfway between these two doctrines, stating that while works could *prepare* a person for salvation, only faith could actually open the doors to it.

Soon after Cotton began complaining that the Puritan ministers in Massachusetts Bay were emphasizing the covenant of works, Hutchinson began holding meetings at her house. Initially, she merely led discussions relating to Cotton's sermons. Later, rumors circulated that she had accused the ministers of teaching *only* the covenant of works. Such an accusation assaulted the heart of the Puritan beliefs, that faith mattered most. To accuse the Puritan ministers of teaching a covenant of works was to accuse them of being no better than the Church of England, against which the Puritan movement had originally begun as an alternative to Anglican "faithlessness." Hutchinson's charge struck at the power of the colony's leaders; the ministers did not hold public office, but they wielded enormous political power and to portray them as being on the wrong path implied they should be replaced. Consequently, her claims divided the Puritan community, and in 1636 those who supported her succeeded in electing Henry Vane as the colony's governor. Vane, the 24-year-old son of a British government official, had attended Hutchinson's meetings.

The following year, however, the orthodox Puritans defeated Vane and elected John Winthrop. These Puritan leaders felt enormous pressure to maintain conformity in Massachusetts Bay, for they had settled the colony intending to build a harmonious and godly society superior to that which existed anywhere else—a "City Upon a Hill" for the rest of the world to emulate. To dissolve into bickering fac-

Anne Hutchinson preaching. (Library of Congress)

tions would disgrace Puritanism, invite God's punishment for violating His design for them, and produce failure.

Consequently, Winthrop and his orthodox colleagues acted to end Hutchinson's influence, first by banishing or disenfranchising her most prominent allies, and then by placing her on trial in Newton, a town where she had few supporters. They formally charged her with sedition, not against the civil magistrates, but against the ministers, an indictment that revealed the close relationship between church and state and how it was believed that to undermine one was to undermine both. Pregnant and ill, she underwent intense questioning. At one point Winthrop referred to the biblical origins of the colony's laws when he accused her of violating the fifth commandment to "honor thy father and thy mother," meaning she had defied authority. At another, he attacked her for teaching men—a clear violation of Puritan society's standards that women refrain from exerting leadership.

Hutchinson denied she had ever said the ministers were preaching only the covenant of works. Nevertheless, she said, "When they preach a covenant of works for salvation, that is not truth." Strong and assertive, Hutchinson made a startling claim in her testimony to the court: "I bless the Lord," she said. "He hath let me see which was the clear ministry and which the wrong."

"How do you know that was the spirit?" the court asked her.

"How did Abraham know that it was God that bid him offer his son, being a breach of the sixth commandment?" she replied.

"By an immediate voice," the court said.

"So too me by an immediate revelation," she responded.

"How! An immediate revelation," the court said.

"By the voice of his spirit to my soul," she insisted.

Thus Hutchinson had claimed that God had revealed Himself directly to her, a stance that violated the Puritan doctrine that revelation had ended with the Bible. Orthodox Puritans labeled Hutchinson a blasphemer and an antinomian, a person who believed that commands came only from God and that salvation freed an individual from the laws of church and state. As Jean Cameron notes in *Anne Hutchinson: Guilty or Not?* (1994), to the Puritans, "if a Christian heard voices telling of God's intentions, that was not allowable; any assurances of a specific nature must come out of scripture." Such ideas as Hutchinson's opened society to potential disorder, should everyone assert that they could determine God's revelations, and with them, God's directions, for themselves.

The court read its verdict: "Mrs. Hutchinson . . . you are banished from out of our jurisdiction as being a woman not fit for our society." She next underwent a church trial, during which John Cotton abandoned her and rejected her claims that she had repented. She was subsequently excommunicated.

Hutchinson then settled in Rhode Island, along with her husband and children, as well as dozens of followers. When she suffered a miscarriage, rumors spread in Boston that God had punished her by causing her to give birth to a "monster." In 1642, William Hutchinson died and in 1643, after having moved near to New York City, Anne Hutchinson was killed by Indians who attacked her and her children. In his memoirs, Winthrop called it a fitting end—yet another sign of God's retribution.

Anne Hutchinson's radicalism manifested itself in several ways. Her religious meetings had promoted the power of the laity. At the same time, when she instructed men she challenged the male power structure. Finally, she had expressed ideas compatible with religious freedom and the concept that individual conscience mattered most. Both of these remained severely circumscribed for decades, yet the dispute raised by Hutchinson portended a colony more diverse in its outlook.

Further Reading

Battis, Emery. S*aints and Sectaries: Anne Hutchinson and the Antinomian Controversy in Massachusetts Bay Colony.* Chapel Hill: University of North Carolina Press, 1962.

Hall, David D., ed. *The Antinomian Controversy, 1636–1638: A Documentary History.* 2d ed. Durham, N.C.: Duke University Press, 1990.

Williams, Selma R. *Divine Rebel: The Life of Anne Marbury Hutchinson.* New York: Holt, Rinehart & Winston, 1981.

Plockhoy Founds a Mennonite Community 1663

In July 1663, Pieter Plockhoy and 41 other Dutch settlers arrived at the Delaware River, bringing with them their Mennonite faith and a desire to found a communitarian settlement dedicated to economic sharing, toleration, and open discussion.

Historians have long debated where to find the roots of modern American society. If one of those roots is democracy, its traces can be found in a radical group that began a short-lived communitarian settlement in seventeenth-century Delaware under Pieter Corneliszoon Plockhoy (1620?–1700?).

Plockhoy came from Zierikzee in the Netherlands and was a member of the Mennonites, a Protestant group that emphasized a spiritual life in which individuals are guided by their own consciences. The Mennonites believed in the Bible as the only religious authority, and they advocated loving their enemies and opposing war and military service.

Plockhoy was connected to the Mennonite Collegiant movement, a group from different denominations that met to discuss religious issues. The Collegiants embraced free thought and tolerance for different views, and they considered reason to be superior to any unquestioning faith in tradition.

In the late 1650s, Plockhoy visited England, where he tried to convince Oliver Cromwell, the country's revolutionary leader, to establish a universal church tolerant of all Christians. After having failed in his mission, he published *A Way Propounded to Make the Poor in These and Other Nations Happy* (1659), which presented his plan for building a commune dedicated to virtue, brotherly love, and social harmony. He founded his community on Dutch territory in North America as part of a campaign by political leaders in Amsterdam to populate the land along the south Delaware River, a region remote from New Amsterdam (present-day New York City). Plockhoy and his followers departed the Netherlands in May 1663, and in July he and 41 others settled at New Amstel, near the mouth of the Delaware.

The plans he developed for his communitarian settlement were at odds with the mainstream in several ways. He proposed, for example, the common ownership of buildings, land, ships, and tools. Yet he stopped short of a truly communistic economy and said that the settlers could otherwise own private property. To those who thought him a leveler (a believer in complete social equality), he responded:

> We hope that nobody will be so naïve, much less malevolent, as to think . . . that we are attempting to remove all differences between persons. . . . We on the contrary believe that to be impossible as that our fingers would be the same length; for every human being, because of his natural characteristics and special qualities, comprising a universe in himself, will always remain different from others.

The economy he proposed, Plockhoy said, would flourish through an arrangement similar to a cooperative. "Meat, drink, and all other things will cost us the less," he insisted, "because we buy a great quantity at once."

In addition to his economic program, Plockhoy sought to apply the principles he had advocated in the Collegiant movement. These included a separation of church and state—for while he believed in promoting the universal church, he thought that political leaders too often used religion toward their own ends. "Suffer by no means . . . that any Confession of Faith be set upon the Throne, as equal with the holy scripture," he advised. "Assist not with the sword, or money of the Common-wealth any sect, or person in particular." In addition, he preferred a republican form of government with widespread political participation.

Plockhoy's settlement lasted only one year. He apparently instituted his reforms with success, but in late 1664, the English, as part of their conquest of New Amsterdam, destroyed the Dutch colonies along the Delaware, including New Amstel. Plockhoy then largely disappeared from the historical record and likely died at age 80 while living in Pennsylvania.

Mennonite immigration to America continued after the English triumph, with about 100 Mennonites from the Lower Rhine in Europe settling in the Quaker village of Germantown, north of Philadelphia, from 1683–1705. For the most part, they resembled Plockhoy in their attachment to open discussion, tolerance, and diverse ideas—all essential elements in the establishment of a democratic system, the outline of which Plockhoy had brought with him to America.

Further Reading

Harder, Leland, and Marvin Harder. *Plockhoy from Zurik-zee: The Study of a Dutch Reformer in Puritan England and Colonial America.* Newton, Kan.: Board of Education and Publication, 1952.

1676 Bacon's Rebellion Shakes Virginia

In the summer of 1676, Nathaniel Bacon turned his rebel army on the colonial capital at Jamestown, Virginia, forcing Governor William Berkeley to flee. The insurgents aspired to redress grievances held by those living on the western frontier.

The seeds of Bacon's Rebellion were sown by economic hardship and the accompanying tension between the gentry and the propertyless. Tobacco prices plummeted in the 1660s and 1670s while Virginia Governor William Berkeley and his entourage grew richer by collecting moneys from various license fees and tributes extracted from the beaver trade with the Indians. At the same time, the House of Burgesses, the colony's legislature, relied on a head tax that fell disproportionately on the poor and rejected a land tax that would have shifted the tax burden to the wealthy.

Adding to these economic problems, a cattle plague in 1672 and 1673 killed more than half the colony's livestock, and in 1675 a drought decimated its crops. Berkeley only made matters worse when, for several years, he refused to call the Burgesses into session.

Conflict with the Indians ignited the rebellion. Berkeley had tried to keep the peace when he set up land reservations in the west for Native Americans and forts from which soldiers patrolled the countryside. But in the 1670s this system buckled under the pressure of English settlers who wanted land and of Indians who were moving from the northern colonies to the southern ones in pursuit of the fur trade.

When a colonist killed several Indians in a dispute over the ownership of some hogs, widespread fighting erupted. Berkeley refused to dispatch a large army to quell the disturbances and instead relied on his protective system of forts.

Landholders in the west, however, had suffered from Indian attacks and wanted revenge. Among them was Nathaniel Bacon (1647–76), who owned a plantation on the frontier where his overseer had been killed in an attack. Bacon, described as "young, bold, active of an inviting aspect and powerful elocution," had arrived in Virginia from England in 1674 with money and connections to the gentry that obtained for him a seat on the colonial council. Nevertheless, he disliked the way many of the wealthy obtained privileges through their special relationship with Berkeley.

Acting on their own, planters along the upper James River chose Bacon in April 1676 to lead a force against the Indians. He did so with complete ruthlessness, slaughtering about 150 Native Americans, including those friendly to the settlers. More dead Indians, of course, meant more vacant land for the colonists. Resenting this independent action, Berkeley removed Bacon from the colonial council. But the governor relented on his resistance to calling the House of Burgesses into session, thus allowing for an election that resulted in Bacon winning a seat in that body.

There followed a rapid shifting of fortunes between Bacon and Berkeley. Bacon headed to Jamestown to assume office, and Berkeley's army captured him and dragged him before the Burgesses, where he was forced to get on his knees and beg forgiveness for the Indian slaughter. That done, Berkeley restored him to the council, thinking he could better control him from that position than from the Burgesses.

But Berkeley refused Bacon's request for a military commission that would have enabled the young insurgent to legally attack Indians, whereupon Bacon gathered about 100 frontiersmen and at gunpoint, while the same Burgesses who earlier had watched him beg looked on, he forced the governor to relent. "God damne my Blood," Bacon shouted, "I came for a commission, and a commission I will have before I goe." To which Berkeley replied: "For God's sake, . . . forebear a little, and you shall have what you please." Shortly thereafter, Berkeley declared the commission void, and as Bacon gathered some 1,300 men, the governor pronounced him a rebel.

In July 1676 Bacon and his followers issued their Declaration of the People, which accused Berkeley of favoritism and condemned the system of unjust taxes, Berkeley's failure to defend the frontier, and the monopolizing of trade with Indians. Bacon demanded that Berkeley surrender as a traitor. According to one contemporary account, the rebel said: "I am confident it is the mind of this colony and of Maryland as well as Carolina, to cast off their governors." Whether Bacon truly envisioned the independence of Virginia from British rule remains unclear.

In August, Bacon's army plundered estates owned by those loyal to Berkeley. The rebels then captured Jamestown, at one point forcing the wives of the loyalists onto the capital's ramparts and daring the governor's men to open fire. When Bacon marched back to the frontier to once again fight Indians, Berkeley regained the capital. Bacon returned in September and burned Jamestown to the ground, forcing the governor and his retinue to flee.

Many gentlemen supported Bacon, as did many militia officers, indicating he had won the support of some within Virginia's leading families frustrated by Berkeley's frontier policies and excluded from the governor's clique. Bacon was also popular with other colonists and appealed to the poor when he proclaimed that he would free those servants and slaves of the loyalists who joined his fight.

The rebellion received a fatal blow, however, on October 26, 1676, when Bacon died suddenly from dysentery. The rebel army quickly disintegrated, and by the following January it was no more.

Berkeley dealt severely with the rebels, executing 23 and seizing much of their property. His actions stunned King Charles II, who said, "That old fool has hanged more men in that naked country than I did for the murder of my father." Charles had sent 1,100 soldiers to Virginia to crush Bacon's rebellion. They arrived too late, but with them came Herbert Jeffreys, who, in the summer of 1677 replaced Berkeley as governor.

When Nathaniel Bacon led his rebels through the colonial Virginia countryside—"only the Rascality and meanest of the people," one opponent called them—he expressed westerners' discontent with eastern rule and the lower orders' dismay at the power of the landed class. For years scholars have debated Bacon's Rebellion: was it largely a sectional conflict or a class one? Did Bacon seek personal power or liberal reform? Historian Edmund S. Morgan has said that Bacon's Rebellion was "with abundant causes but without a cause: it produced no real program of reform, no revolutionary manifesto, and not even revolutionary slogans." Indeed, although the House of Burgesses passed a series of acts that, among other things, allowed all freemen to vote and prohibited dual office holding, it later repealed most of these acts.

Writing in *The Southern Colonies in the Seventeenth Century* (1949), Wesley Frank Craven observes that Bacon's Rebellion was "a protest rooted in sectional interest broadened into a general attack on special privilege and on abusive political power." Like many other reform movements, Bacon's Rebellion went in directions its originator never intended, taking on a larger significance that later generations interpreted for themselves. Reformers in following decades have held up the banner of Bacon's Rebellion as an uprising of the have-nots against the haves, imbued with the spirit of America's radical legacy.

Further Reading

Washburn, Wilcomb E. *The Governor and the Rebel: A History of Bacon's Rebellion in Virginia.* Chapel Hill: University of North Carolina Press, 1957.

Webb, Stephen S. *1676: The End of American Independence.* New York: Knopf, 1984.

Wertenbaker, Thomas Jefferson. *Torchbearer of the Revolution.* 1940. Reprint, Gloucester, Mass.: P. Smith, 1965.

1681 William Penn Begins a Holy Experiment in Pennsylvania

In 1681, William Penn obtained a charter from the king of England to found a colony called Pennsylvania. From the start, he determined it would not only welcome Quakers and others but also abide by the Quaker faith in tolerance.

William Penn (1644–1718) was the son of Admiral William Penn, who, during the second Dutch War in 1655, captained a fleet that captured Jamaica for England. Penn the younger was born in London, went to school in Essex, and in 1660 entered Oxford. His matriculation was brief; he opposed a rule that all students must attend Church of England services, and he objected to the prayer book because it mandated a uniform religious view in support of the church. As a result, he was expelled.

While managing his father's estate in Ireland, Penn listened to the preaching of Quaker Thomas Loe and in 1667 converted to the faith. Soon thereafter, he wrote *No Cross, No Crown* (1669), a work that landed him in the Tower of London, the first of several prison terms he served for expressing his ideas. In *No Cross, No Crown*, Penn audaciously (for that day and age) claimed that all religion came from the soul rather than the church and that people should be guided by the "inner light," rather than ecclesiastical dictum.

The Quakers, or the Society of Friends, as they were formally called, believed in the individual's direct communication with God—it was said that their bodies sometimes quaked with the Holy Spirit. Since they believed that each person carried God within, they rejected any form of priesthood; they opposed war and the bearing of arms, because to kill meant destroying God. Furthermore, they refused to take oaths; to them, the swearing of oaths implied a double standard for truth, one while under oath and one for the rest of the time. The Quakers opposed ceremonies, emphasized the basic goodness of everyone, and embraced equality. One leader, John Woolman, said, "I believed that Liberty was the natural Right of all Men equally."

Within England, the Quakers were labeled enemies of the state for their complete rejection of the Anglican church and for their egalitarianism that challenged the social hierarchy. Many conservatives were appalled when the Quakers used the pronoun "thou," rather than, for example, "sir" or "my lord," to refer to others—a defiant and outrageous word because it ignored rank—"thee" (and "thou") were "familiar" forms of address.

In 1681, the rebellious William Penn received his land grant from the king to establish the colony of Pennsylvania. The grant satisfied a debt that the king owed William's father and would, the monarch hoped, encourage other Quakers to leave England. Penn recognized this when he wrote a friend: "The government at home was glad to be rid of us at so cheap a rate as a little parchment to be practiced in a desert 3,000 miles off."

Penn energetically promoted his colony and personally recruited settlers from Europe. His newspaper ads extolled the availability of cheap land—100 acres for five pounds. And he guaranteed religious freedom to all "who hold themselves obliged in conscience, to live peaceably and justly in civil society." No doubt, Penn expected to enrich his family fortune by selling land, but, as he intended as well, his principled toleration for religious groups attracted pietist Dutch, Germans, and Welsh, and, most prominently, Quakers. By the end of 1683, 60 ships had brought 4,000 settlers to Pennsylvania.

Penn's land stretched across wooded plains, rolling hills, and verdant mountains, west from the Delaware River to the Great Lakes, bounded by New York to the north and Maryland and Virginia to the south. No other person had ever been granted such a large part of America from the British king. Where others

*William Penn. (Bettmann/*Corbis*)*

Quakers, the Radical Faithful

The radicalism of the Quakers is rooted in the beliefs expressed by the sect's founder, George Fox, that anyone can achieve "that righteousness and holiness that Adam was in before he fell," and "that every man was enlightened by the divine Light of Christ." With the potential of every person thus evident, and with the equality of every person before the eyes of God thus established, Quakers have committed themselves to a struggle for social justice that will help individuals and advance society.

As a result, Quakers have a long history of involvement in humanitarian and peace projects. When slavery existed in America, most Quakers opposed it and advocated its end. In the 1750s, John Woolman convinced Philadelphia Quakers to promise they would never own slaves or trade in them. Nearly 100 years later, Levi Coffin helped so many slaves escape from the South he was called the "president of the underground railroad." About the same time, Benjamin Lundy published an antislavery newspaper.

Another Quaker abolitionist, Susan Brownell Anthony, organized the women's suffrage movement in an effort to gain for women the right to vote. In the late 1800s, Jane Addams founded Hull House, a settlement house in Chicago dedicated to helping poor immigrants. During the Franco-Prussian war (1870–71), Quakers formed the Friends War Victims Relief Committee, and hundreds of Quakers assisted towns and villages destroyed in the fighting. In 1947, the American Friends Service Committee received the Nobel Peace Prize for its humanitarian work.

Despite some wayward Quakers, such as President Richard Nixon, who expanded the Vietnam War and lied about the Watergate affair, modern Quakers continue to be involved in peace organizations, a commitment reaffirmed in the 1990s when the Friends World Committee for Consultation urged all Quakers to "recognize our personal and corporate potential for being more effective peace builders."

---

might have seen the grant as first and foremost a gold mine of economic opportunity (the king himself expected a share of any mineral wealth), Penn saw it as a promising site for a "holy experiment." Committed to the Quaker faith, he said: "I eyed the Lord in the obtaining of it . . . and desire to keep it; that I may not be unworthy of His love; but . . . serve His Truth and people."

Like Roger Williams in Rhode Island, Penn believed in buying land from the Indians rather than simply taking it from them. He told the Delaware chiefs: "I am very sensible of the unkindness and injustice that hath been too much exercised toward you by the people of [England]. . . . But I am not such a man. . . . I have great love and regard towards you." The treaties he signed with the Delaware and with other tribes cemented a close and generally cooperative relationship.

The government of Pennsylvania underwent several changes, but in 1701 A New Charter of Privileges established a unicameral, or one-house, legislature elected by white male property owners. With this republican political system, plentiful land, and widespread toleration, Pennsylvania thrived. Penn's egalitarianism had its limits, though; while many Quakers opposed slavery, Penn himself owned slaves and even broke up a marriage when he sold a husband and wife to different masters.

Enthusiastic Quakers in Pennsylvania and other colonies sought converts so fervently that they often sacrificed themselves as martyrs. When, for example, in 1659 the Puritans in Massachusetts Bay banished Mary Dyer upon threat of execution should she return, she reappeared the following year, whereupon the Puritans kept their word and hanged her. "In obedience to the will of the Lord God I came," she said at the scaffolding, "and in His will I abide faithful to death."

Indeed, as David S. Lovejoy shows in *Religious Enthusiasm in the New World* (1985), many other Christians joined the Puritans in condemning Quakers as delusional for their belief in salvation "with little outward help from Scripture, books, teaching, or even professional clergy." The Puritan minister Ephriam Pagitt pointed out "that Quakers believe that their people can be so possessed of the light that they become 'prophets, Christs, or Saviours,' and what they speak and write is really a declaration of the word and mind of God." To Pagitt, "any one of the 'pernicious tenets' was subversive of true religion; together they were notoriously heretical and destructive of church order."

Penn lived in Pennsylvania for a total of only four years. In 1692, the colony was placed under royal control, but it was restored to Penn in 1694. Beset by legal and financial problems, he was intending to sell Pennsylvania to the crown in 1712 when a stroke felled him; he died six years later.

By that time, Pennsylvania had changed considerably. Quakers made up only a small part of Philadelphia's population; Scotch-Irish colonists were settling the western lands. Factional fights were tearing the Quakers apart, and in the mid-1700s as the westward push of settlers ignited wars with the Indians, the Quakers relinquished their political leadership rather than compromise their pacifist principles.

As a result, Quakers passed from the scene of colonial political prominence, but only after having established a religiously tolerant society in an era when narrow-mindedness and orthodoxy prevailed. At the same time, their martyrdom displayed a tenacity other social protesters would emulate far into the future.

Further Reading

Geiter, Mary K. *William Penn.* New York: Longman, 2000.

Peare, Catherine Owens. *William Penn.* Philadelphia: Lippincott, 1956.

Soderlund, Jean R. *William Penn and the Founding of Pennsylvania: A Documentary History.* 1983. Reprint, Philadelphia: University of Pennsylvania Press, 1999.

The Labadists Found a Separatist Commune

1684

In 1684 followers of Jean de Labadie settled 3,750 acres in Maryland. Part of the seventeenth-century pietistic movement that wanted to restore spirituality to Protestantism, the Labadists pledged themselves to live apart from a world filled with sin and materialistic excess and to build an egalitarian society in which each person sacrificed personal gratification for the communal good.

Jean de Labadie (1610–74) began his religious life in the Roman Catholic church and entered the Jesuit order; after experiencing what he described as a vision, he left the Jesuits in 1639 and in 1644 founded several societies based on his mysticism. The Labadists claimed that Christ revealed Himself through prophecies, revelations, and appearances. They insisted that any church should consist only of true believers—much as did John Calvin, the foremost influence on the Pilgrims and the other Puritans who settled New England—and that it must be kept pure. Historian Bartlett Burleigh James describes Labadism as "teaching supreme reliance upon the inward illumination of the Spirit."

Soon after Labadie's death, two of the mystic's followers, Petrus Sluyter and Jasper Dankarts, obtained land in Maryland; part of a tract called Bohemia Manor, it was a donation from wealthy landowner Augustine Herrman. (Herrman later broke with the Labadists and tried to revoke the grant, but the Labadists took him to court and obtained title to the land.) They chose Maryland because of its reputation for religious tolerance—a sharp contrast from Europe, where Labadie had been persecuted for his ideas and forced to seek sanctuary in a Mennonite settlement, and where his followers had experienced similar treatment. Now bound for America, they believed they could pursue their faith in peace.

The approximately 100 Labadists who arrived in Maryland came from Wieuwerd in Friesland (the Netherlands). At the head of Chesapeake Bay, they established a settlement in which they held all property in common. The Labadists began each of their meals with chants and ended them with prayers. Committed to avoiding any activity that might pollute their souls or divert them from their worship, they allowed marriages only between Labadists, and they practiced celibacy, with men and women living apart in matrimony. Their separateness in marriage reinforced their economic system; as separate entities, each man and woman, acting as individuals rather than couples, had as much right to the communal property as did any other, and as much responsibility to the communal welfare. One Quaker visitor, Samuel Bownas, noted: "The women ate by themselves and the men by themselves, having all things in common respecting their household affairs, so that none could claim any more right than another to any part of their stock, whether in trade or in husbandry."

The Labadists made linen from flax and grew corn, hemp, and tobacco, dividing their work routine and assigning each member specific duties, such as field work, cooking, and caring for the sick. Extreme in their asceticism, they even counted the pieces of bread and butter eaten at each meal to make sure no one crossed the line into indulgence. An observer, Peter Dittleback, reported: "This friend told me that [Petrus] Sluyter would not allow them to have any fire in order to harden them and to mortify and subdue the sins of the body, while there was so much wood there that they were obliged to bury it in the fields to get it out of the way."

Dittleback went on to say, though, that "Sluyter had his own hearth well provided night and day." Indeed, the settlement looked like anything but an egalitarian experiment. Sluyter looked out for his comforts by making sure he was the group's major landholder. Other violations of Labadist principles occurred: when the settlers raised tobacco, they contributed to smoking, a vice they deplored, and they used slave labor, which breached their egalitarianism. In addition, some Labadists held political office in the colonial government, a practice that went against their separatist commitment.

In 1698, Sluyter divided his landholdings, and several Labadists acquired some of his property. He retained a considerable amount, however, and grew wealthier. Now that more Labadists owned land, the commune weakened and, with it, the devotion to a pietistic life. Consequently, just five years after Sluyter's death in 1722, the settlement collapsed. Writing in *Religious Enthusiasm in the New World* (1985), David S. Lovejoy argues, "Had it not been for selfish leadership, the Labadists' colony in Maryland might very well have survived, at least for a time."

Despite the collapse, historian Harry M. Ward labels the Labadist effort a notable countercultural experiment that challenged mainstream colonial practices. But while the Labadist example encouraged others to build communal settlements, most notably Johann Conrad Beissel, the founder of Ephrata (see entry, 1732), Sluyter's selfishness provided warnings that existence outside the mainstream might prove no more loftier than that found elsewhere in society.

Further Reading

James, Bartlett Burleigh. *The Labadist Colony in Maryland.* 1899. Reprint, Baltimore, Md.: Johns Hopkins Press, 1973.

Lovejoy, David S. *Religious Enthusiasm in the New World: Heresy to Revolution.* Cambridge, Mass.: Harvard University Press, 1985.

Saxby, T. J. *The Quest for the New Jerusalem: Jean de Labadie and the Labadists, 1610–1744.* Dordrecht, Netherlands: Martinus Nijhoff Publishers, 1987.

1689   "The Heart of a Traitor": Jacob Leisler Leads a Revolt in New York

A man of wealth who was opposed to leveling—a seventeenth-century term for establishing complete social equality—Jacob Leisler nevertheless led a rebellion against the colonial leadership that attracted many New Yorkers who felt oppressed and that resulted in a more competitive political system.

The rebellion led by Jacob Leisler (1640–91) followed several disturbing developments that had caused widespread discontent within New York's diverse population. The Dutch settlers, for instance, detested the recent conquest of the colony by the English and with it the expansion of English culture. New Englanders, who had moved into the colony, complained about the lack of a representative assembly. And many New Yorkers resented the economic monopoly held by a handful of leading families, namely the Bayards, Livingstons, and Schuylers.

On top of these rumblings there occurred in England the Glorious Revolution (1688–89), which overthrew the Roman Catholic King James II and replaced his rule with that of the Protestants William and Mary. In New York, political turmoil erupted when the highest ruling British official, Francis Nicholson, refused to immediately recognize the new monarchs. Rumors spread that Nicholson intended to establish a Roman Catholic government. With that, protesters in New York City took to the streets and many demanded that militia captain Jacob Leisler take over the colonial government.

With the protests intensifying and the city's militia members declaring themselves loyal to William and Mary, Nicholson fled, whereupon a Committee of Safety took control. The committee, in turn, chose Leisler as commander-in-chief for the entire colony. In short order he assumed Nicholson's old post as lieutenant governor.

Leisler was a wealthy man. He had served as an officer in the army that had wrested New Amsterdam from the Dutch and brought it under English control in 1660, making it New York. He then developed a thriving merchant business, dealing in furs and tobacco, earning so much money he ranked among the richest men in New York City. Despite his success, the uppermost elite families barred him from the inner sanctum of merchant rule, probably because of some squabbles he had with the Bayards and because of his ardent Calvinism.

Supporters of Leisler came from many backgrounds. They included wealthy landowners and merchants who, like Leisler, resented the elite for having used the colonial government to monopolize the economy. Others were craftsmen and laborers who demanded a greater political voice. Closest to Leisler was Jacob Milborne, an advocate of ideas that went so far beyond those held by Leisler that he truly fit the definition of the word "radical." Milborne called for popular rule and social equality, an extremism that caused a resentful Nicholas Bayard to describe the Leislerians as "poor ignorant and senseless people who suffer them[selves] to be ruled and hectored by about twenty or thirty ill drunken sots."

With Leisler in command, the Committee of Safety expanded popular power by making the offices of justice of the peace and militia captain elective. Class tensions ran high as Leislerians physically attacked wealthy persons, and anti-Leislerians attacked Jacob Leisler himself, setting upon him while shouting "Kill him, kill him!" and forcing him to draw his sword in order to escape.

In 1690, Leisler directed that an assembly be popularly elected. When it met, though, he kept its most extreme members in check, and as a result it failed to make any radical proclamations about liberty, or even to substantially address the colony's economic problems. Leisler was no revolutionary philosopher; moreover, he was preoccupied with having to defend upstate New York from attacks launched by the French Canadians and their Indian allies.

Leisler ruled New York for less than two years. Prominent merchants were able to convince the English monarchy that Leisler should be prosecuted as a rebel, and the king sent troops to New York City. In January 1691, Leisler reinforced his image as a rebel when he refused to surrender the city's fort to the royal soldiers. But when the newly appointed governor, Henry Sloughter, arrived, he relented and capitulated.

Severe retribution followed. The government indicted Leisler, Milborne, and several other Leislerians for treason. Most served prison terms and lost their property; Leisler and Milborne were hanged. According to one report, after Leisler's body was cut free from its noose, the executioner removed Leisler's heart and gave it to a spectator who held it up and shouted, "Here is the heart of a traitor!" To others, though, Jacob Leisler was no traitor: in their minds he had defended colonial New York from Roman Catholic oppression, and his revolt promised more power for the common people.

The long-term effects of the revolt were mixed. On the one hand, the power of the elite and the old economic monopolies suffered a setback, and New York retained its representative assembly. On the other, the elite kept the Leislerians from enacting radical reforms, despite the movement's often extreme voice. The repercussions from Leisler's revolt continued to be felt for years, heightening factional fights and contributing to the development of a more competitive and democratic political system.

Further Reading

Andrews, Charles M., ed. *Narratives of the Insurrections, 1675–1690*. New York: Barnes & Noble, 1943.

McCormick, Charles H. *Leisler's Rebellion*. New York: Garland, 1989.

Reich, Jerome R. *Leisler's Rebellion: A Study of Democracy in New York, 1664–1720*. Chicago: University of Chicago Press, 1953.

1706 Francis Makemie Creates the First American Presbytery

Francis Makemie fought the attempt by British authorities to make the Church of England the established church in the North American colonies; his court case struck a blow for religious tolerance.

Born near Ramelton, Ireland, to Scottish parents, Francis Makemie (1658?–1708) attended Glasgow University in 1682 and was ordained in the Presbytery of Laggan. He then decided to begin missionary work in America, partly because he disliked the restrictions imposed on Presbyterianism in Ireland.

Makemie arrived in Virginia in 1683 and traveled as an itinerant minister in that colony and in Maryland, Delaware, and Barbados, where he lived for several years during the 1690s. Presbyterians adhered to the ideas of John Calvin, including his outline for church organization, which they adopted in slightly modified form. Whereas Congregationalist Calvinists, such as the Puritans who settled Massachusetts Bay, believed in largely independent churches, the Presbyterians believed that churches needed to be coordinated. They invested this power in a *presbytery*, consisting of the ministers in a given district and elders from the congregations.

Sometime during the late 1680s or 1690s, Makemie married Naomi Anderson, and on the death of her father, the couple inherited a large estate. When he was not preaching, Makemie was engaging in trade and managing his large plantation in Accomack County, Virginia. He owned more than 5,000 acres and 33 slaves, ranking him among the colony's wealthiest citizens. He voiced his business concerns in his book *Plain and Friendly Persuasive* (1705), in which he advocated that Virginia and Maryland establish towns and commercial centers.

Fearing that the Church of England, also known as the Anglican church, would establish itself as the official church throughout the colonies, in 1706 he organized the first American presbytery, or governing body, consisting of seven ministers, and served as its moderator. Soon thereafter, he traveled to New York to build a presbytery there. At that point, the colonial governor, Edward Hyde (Lord Cornbury), a promoter of the Anglican church, threw him into jail for engaging in itinerant preaching without permission.

At his ensuing trial, Makemie argued that the 1689 Toleration Act protected him; he also argued that he was free to preach as he pleased because the Church of England lacked authority in the American colonies. A jury acquitted Makemie, and Puritan minister Cotton Mather called him a "brave man" for having stood up to the Anglican authorities. In 1707, Makemie wrote his *Narrative*, a strong defense of the rights of dissenters and an early libertarian voice in America. He died in 1708, likely at or near his home in Accomack.

Writing in *The Transformation of Virginia* (1982), Rhys Isaac asserts that Presbyterians created "considerable commotion" in the colony; and a contemporary reported that the preachers spoke "pretty freely of the degeneracy of the [Church of England] clergy." With his *Narrative*, and with his earlier argument in the New York court case, Makemie established precedents that later colonial dissenters appealed to in defending their causes, and Presbyterianism, boosted by the Great Awakening of the 1740s, continued to challenge the Anglican religious establishment for years to come.

Further Reading

Boyd, Stanley, ed. *The Life and Writings of Francis Makemie, Father of American Presbyterianism.* Lewiston, N.Y.: E. Mellen Press, 1999.

Hanzsche, William Thomson. *Forgotten Founding Fathers of the American Church and State.* Boston: Christopher Publishing House, 1954.

Isaac, Rhys. *The Transformation of Virginia, 1740–1790.* New York: W. W. Norton, 1988.

Johann Conrad Beissel Founds Ephrata

1732

A successful bread maker in Heidelberg, Germany, Johann Conrad Beissel immigrated to America and founded Ephrata, a religious commune in Pennsylvania. There his charisma and commitment attracted disciples who lived in worldly denial so that, as Beissel said, they could "walk perfectly in a pure and clean spirit."

Johann Conrad Beissel (1691–1768) was born in Eberbach, located in the Electoral Palatinate of today's German state of Baden-Württemberg. While Beissel was still an infant, his father, Matthias Beissel, died; his mother, Anna Beissel, died when he was only eight or nine. Apprenticed to a baker in Eberbach, Beissel began attending Pietist meetings. The Pietists criticized what they called "dispassionate Protestantism" and emphasized inner devotion. Some of them, the Inspirationists, engaged in exaltation and prophecy. They believed they were infused with the Holy Spirit and claimed to have had visions. These Pietists believed in miracles and spoke in tongues. Beissel was one of them.

Because Beissel suffered persecution for his beliefs, when he heard stories about mystics living in the American wilderness he decided to make his home there. In 1720, he arrived at Germantown, Pennsylvania, where he sought out religious hermits on the frontier, only to find that a retreat they had founded no longer existed. At the same time, he learned about the pious Labadist commune in Maryland (see entry, 1684) and admired it for its spiritual unity and simplicity. He may have visited it.

In 1722, Peter Becker organized the German Baptist Brotherhood in Pennsylvania, a group known as the Dunkers or Dunkards from the German *dunken*, meaning to dip, as in the process of immersion that accompanied baptism. The Dunkards baptized Beissel in Pequea Creek, and he became Becker's assistant.

As Beissel traveled from one frontier cabin to another, spreading the word, his revivalist enthusiasm and charismatic personality attracted a following. In the late 1720s, however, financial disputes with his supporters caused him to end his missionary work and seek seclusion in the backwoods.

Historians disagree as to whether, at that point, Beissel secretly coveted a large following or whether settlers flocked to him against his wishes. Whatever the case, the Camp of the Solitary, situated near a stream called Cocalico, grew around his home. About 1732, this settlement evolved into Ephrata (the pre-Israelite name for Bethlehem), a commune devoted to Beissel's religious ideas and social principles, including those that dictated all cabins be of the same size and that private property be considered contrary to spiritual devotion.

Beissel attracted many Dunkards from nearby settlements, and in one instance convinced the entire Dunkard congregation at Falckner's Swamp to relocate to Ephrata. Beissel divided his community into three orders. Two of them, the brotherhood and sisterhood, required their members to live celibate lives

The Ephrata Cloister in Ephrata, Pennsylvania. (G.E. Kidder Smith/CORBIS)

in a cloister of log and stone buildings. A third order, the householders, consisted of married couples who lived nearby. The communards at Ephrata wore plain white hooded cloaks and lived in small rooms, with wood benches for beds and solid wooden blocks for pillows. They would allow no comfort to obscure their worship of God, and they would use every discomfort to prove their unwavering faith.

In the late 1730s, Beissel led Ephrata's missionary work. His disciples entered frontier settlements with their heads bowed, their bodies covered by their cloaks, and their feet bare as they proceeded single-file along dirt roads. Their appearance must have startled more than one cabin dweller, and it certainly drew attention to Ephrata.

At the same time, Beissel intensified the communal arrangements at Ephrata. He produced what historian E. G. Alderfer calls "a communism of intentional poverty aimed at defeating the calls of the flesh and heightening the claims of the spirit."

Nevertheless, Ephrata prospered in the early 1740s as the communards raised wheat, flax, millet, and hemp, and operated a linseed oil mill, paper mill, and two sawmills. Ephrata expanded when it attracted immigrants from Europe who had learned of Beissel's work and when Beissel's own missionary zeal drew a larger following. In 1750, the population reached about 300.

Beissel, however, disliked Ephrata's commercialism and countered it by calling for more meditation and prayer. In addition, he encouraged the writing of hymn-poems, a practice begun earlier. Alderfer states that Beissel developed "his own unique, even magical system of harmony and composition, to perform wonders in training the Ephrata singers, and to compose hundreds, perhaps a thousand, poems and pieces of music for them."

Although the paper mill and a print shop continued to operate, Beissel redirected the economy toward subsistence practices. The Ephratans worked all day. They pulled carts, rather than use draft animals, and carried heavy loads on their backs, all to deny comfort to the flesh. They ate sparsely and confessed their sins weekly in public. Beissel even wrote his own catechism:

Neither the heights nor depths are yet measured; but he who thinks little of himself has seen both

All wickedness is sin, but none is as great as separation from God.

There are many souls who wish to change their outward state, but they themselves remain unchanged in their hearts. This is because their appearance is commonly directed to their own concerns rather than to God.

Over the years, Ephrata suffered several debilitating problems. While Beissel's followers considered him to be divine—and he never dissuaded them from thinking so—he ruled like a despot. One critical history states that "Beissel inhabited a celestial world in which there were many mountains, and the loftiest of these, a giddy isolated peak, was reserved for him. It was his private high-place, a temple designed for self-adoration."

Despite Beissel's firm rule, factional fights erupted. Along with these, unproven but damaging rumors circulated about Beissel's sexual transgressions—about how he supposedly "caressed" members of the sisterhood while they were sleeping.

By the mid-1760s, Beissel and many of his disciples were aging while Ephrata was attracting fewer young recruits. Beissel died on July 6, 1768, and disputes over land soon shattered the communal organization. Then came the American Revolution, during which George Washington's troops received medicine, blankets, foodstuffs, and other supplies from the Ephratans that depleted the settlement's resources. In the 1830s, a visitor reported that only a handful of Ephratans remained and their buildings had fallen into disrepair. Even the communes that appeared during that decade ignored Ephrata.

Ephratans had sought, and failed, to build an alternative society that would outlast the corrupt one that surrounded it and would serve as a beacon for change. Yet evident in words Beissel wrote late in his life to a friend, he never regretted founding Ephrata: "I did not forsake my calling, because all carnal or world-minded people are still my enemies, just the same as at the time when I first entered upon this road."

Further Reading

Alderfer, E. G. *The Ephrata Commune: An Early American Counterculture.* Pittsburgh, Penn.: University of Pittsburgh Press, 1985.

Erb, Peter C. *Johann Conrad Beissel and the Ephrata Community: Mystical and Historical Texts.* Lewiston, N.Y.: E. Mellen Press, 1985.

Klein Walter C. *Johann Conrad Beissel: Mystic and Martinet, 1690–1768.* 1942. Reprint, Philadelphia: Porcupine Press, 1972.

Slaves Rebel in South Carolina

1739

The Stono Rebellion of 1739 was the largest uprising by slaves in colonial America. Despite its failure, and the subsequent retribution, it served notice that blacks would not accept their bondage without resistance or permit their freedom to be lost while whites enjoyed theirs.

In the early part of the eighteenth century, the colony of South Carolina had developed an intensive slave labor system; focused largely on rice production, the slaves worked long hours, usually in large gangs, often standing knee-deep in disease-laden water. As the planters imported more slaves from Africa, entire parishes (governmental units often known as counties) in the coastal lowlands became heavily black. St. James Goose Creek reached 79 percent slave, St. Philip's, 75 percent, and St. James Santee, 74 percent. So great were the numbers, that one observer stated, "Carolina looks more like a negro country than like a country settled by white people."

Several events set South Carolina on edge shortly before the Stono Rebellion. For one, some blacks had engaged in a series of plots to gain their freedom, producing more instability in the slave system than at any other time in the colonial period. Other slaves had fled to Spanish-held Florida, where they lived as fugitives in St. Augustine. As early as 1688, Major William Dunlop had been sent by the authorities in South Carolina on a mission to recover runaway slaves. He had been instructed "to demand the delivery up to you of those English fugitive Negroes and others who have fled from this province."

An outbreak of yellow fever in 1739 made South Carolinians anxious about their colony's survival. Anxiety came as well when the legislature passed the Security Act, requiring all white men to carry firearms to church on Sunday to protect against a black uprising. At the same time, war broke out between England and Spain, bringing the prospect of a foreign invasion from the south. These developments may well have motivated the slaves to revolt, realizing that amid the general unrest they might stand a better chance of succeeding.

On Sunday, September 9, 1739, some 20 slaves gathered near the western branch of the Stono River, a few miles from Charlestown (today Charleston). Led by a slave named Jemmy, they broke into a white-owned store, stole some guns, and then killed the two store owners. To send a gruesome message to other whites, they decapitated the bodies of the store owners and left their heads on the front steps.

The slaves then marched onward, ransacking houses and killing more whites. Some slaves along the route were forced to join the rebels; others joined voluntarily. By late morning, the group numbered more than 50. But the white planters rallied quickly, put together a force, and engaged the slaves in battle near the Edisto River. They killed at least 14 blacks, and in retaliation for what had happened to the store owners, they beheaded their slave victims and placed the skulls on mileposts as a reminder of what awaits black rebels.

One white planter later reported: "By the Blessing of God the Negroes were defeated, the greatest Part being killed on the Spot or taken, and those that then escaped were so closely pursued and hunted Day after Day that in the End all but two or three were [killed or] taken and executed. That the Negroes would not have made this Insurrection had they not depended on St. Augustine for a Place of Reception afterwards was very certain."

The Struggle against Slavery

Although the Stono Uprising represented the most violent antislavery rebellion in colonial America, African-Americans engaged in numerous other acts of defiance to protest their bondage. Often the rebellions took on a quiet, but effective, nature. For example, in the slave quarters, parents taught their children ways to circumvent their master; in the fields, slaves purposely damaged farm implements as an act of sabotage.

Some runaway slaves formed maroon communities, illegal settlements hidden in the swamps or backwoods of places like Louisiana. From these communities, they raided plantations for food or to destroy crops. Several African-Americans who fled to the North in the early 1800s joined the abolitionist movement, most notably Frederick Douglass (see entry, 1861), a former slave instrumental in exposing the cruelties of human bondage and in building a bridge between whites who dominated the abolitionist movement and the blacks who exclusively inhabited slavery. Others who were legally freed took up the abolitionist cause. Sojourner Truth (see entry, 1851), for one, traveled throughout the Midwest in the 1850s speaking to large crowds about the evils of slavery. When the Civil War broke out, she helped gather supplies for black volunteer regiments.

Do these acts qualify as radical? Does an individual slave teaching children how to push a master to the limit compare with the collective act of the Stono Rebellion? In magnitude, perhaps not; but the struggle for freedom against oppression, itself a radical act, begins with the first person who in individual acts challenges the status quo. For that person, actions necessary to survival can very well accumulate into actions fundamental to change.

In fact, many of the slaves continued to resist for weeks. That December, a merchant in Charlestown claimed that whites still had to maintain their guard "on [account] of a Conspiracy," and he stated, "We shall Live very Uneasie with our Negroes, while the Spaniards continue to keep Possession of St. Augustine."

The Stono Rebellion had substantial repercussions. The colonial legislature passed laws that took away informal liberties from the slaves, such as freedom of assembly and the freedom to raise their own food and earn their own money. Greater surveillance resulted, and white masters who showed leniency faced stiff fines. Other laws provided rewards for slaves who acted as informants and, in an attempt to control the racial imbalance between whites and blacks, required there be at least one white person present for every ten slaves on a plantation.

In short, the Stono Rebellion unleashed a severe white repression of blacks. Yet it had been a momentous uprising for freedom that nearly shattered the colony's slave system. Peter H. Wood claims in *Black Majority*, the slaves "brought South Carolina closer to the edge of upheaval than historians have been willing to concede." The Stono Rebellion provided an example of resistance for black Americans suffering under the slave master's lash.

Further Reading

Wood, Peter H. *Black Majority: Negroes in Colonial South Carolina from 1670 through the Stono Rebellion.* New York: Norton, 1974.

Moravians Found an American Bethlehem 1741

With the failure of a short-lived experiment in founding a religious settlement in Georgia in the 1730s, a group of Moravians founded Bethlehem in Pennsylvania in 1741, complete with a communal economy and a grouping of people according to their stages in life as a way to purify their souls.

Moravians traced their roots to a religious reform movement that emerged in Moravia and Bohemia as far back as the fifteenth century. By the beginning of the Reformation, they had founded several hundred churches committed to Protestantism, the movement that rejected Roman Catholicism's claim to be the one true church. Consequently, in an era when religious toleration was practically unknown, they suffered persecution from Roman Catholic authorities. In the 1720s, Count Nicholas Ludwig von Zinzendorf gave the Moravians sanctuary on his estate in Saxony.

Concurrent with the Moravians developing a vibrant missionary organization, Zinzendorf acquired land in Georgia in 1734 for a settlement. Under August Gottlieb Spangenberg, the Moravians built a community in America dedicated to converting Indians to Christianity, but disease and the hostility of nearby settlers, who disliked Moravian pacifism, doomed the experiment, and it collapsed a few years later.

Some Moravians then volunteered to help evangelist George Whitefield build a school in Pennsylvania for African-Americans. Whitefield, however, split with them over their refusal to accept predestination, the belief that God determined who was saved and who would face eternal damnation. At that point, the Moravian church in Europe instructed its brethren in Pennsylvania to found a community in that colony that would, as in the Georgia effort, serve as a base from which to Christianize the Indians and as a commune where Moravians could purify their souls. As a result, the American Moravians founded Bethlehem in 1741.

Zinzendorf came to Bethlehem to oversee its initial development, but Spangenberg was the settlement's true leader. He devised goals for the Moravians while directing the building of structures and guiding the social and economic arrangements.

The Moravians believed that a person could attain eternal life by recognizing his or her own depravity and by developing complete faith in Christ. They viewed purification of the soul as a long process best achieved by grouping people together according to their life stages. As a result, at Bethlehem the Moravians divided society into Choirs, with each Choir comprising people of similar ages, gender, and marital status. There was, for example, a Singles Choir and a Married Choir divided into male and female groups. (Although many Moravians married, large numbers of them did not.) Children were brought up with other children in a Nursery Choir, which necessitated removing them from their parents at 18 months of age.

The Moravians believed that the Choirs would keep the settlement focused on God as opposed to families or sexual relationships. The social arrangement gave women considerable influence. Responsible for the moral and spiritual development of girls, they participated substantially in the commune's decision making. Yet they never stood on an equal footing with men: For example, finances were directed by the males, who were considered to be socially superior.

At Bethlehem the Moravians followed a rigid daily routine that dictated certain times for their activities. Work on the communal farm or in the settlement's small shops was set for 7 A.M. to 12 P.M., followed by a half hour for lunch, and then a return to work until 6 P.M. At night, a watchman sang a hymn every hour on the hour.

Under Spangenberg, Bethlehem grew from 72 settlers in 1742 to 600 in 1759. Historian Beverly Prior Smaby, writing in *The Transformation of Moravian Bethlehem* (1988), states that in the early 1740s "the excitement the new settlers felt as they developed their . . . community fairly jumps off the . . . pages of the Bethlehem Diary, the official account of events in Bethlehem."

In the late 1740s, Bethlehem deteriorated economically when, under the influence of Zinzendorf, a "Sifting Period" forced Spangenberg from office and directed the settler's efforts to mystical worship at the expense of more practical concerns, such as economic development. Spangenberg resumed leadership in 1751 and completely rebuilt the economy to again make it self-sufficient. He instructed the settlers to sign a Brotherly Agreement that committed them to a communal system prohibiting private property.

Bethlehem once again prospered, but it suffered from heavy debts incurred during the Sifting Period, and pressure grew to end the communal system. Spangenberg reluctantly agreed, and, beginning in 1762, Bethlehem started to change: not only were the settlers allowed to own private property, but children were to be raised by their parents and families were to live in individual housing. With the communal economy dissolved, moneys from the treasury were divided equally among the settlers. Despite the changes, economic restrictions remained, including limits on wages and prices and a prohibition against monopolies.

The American Revolution also greatly affected Bethlehem, much as it did Moravians in nearby Nazareth and other settlements. Some Moravians supported the British, others the American colonists; differences erupted between those who adhered to the Moravian tradition of pacifism and those who believed in taking up arms for their side. According to Smaby, when the Revolution ended, it unleashed a powerful individualistic spirit that undermined church attendance and devastated community strictures. Internal bickering increased, as did irreligious behavior.

Finally, after 1820 the development of coal mining nearby and the intrusion of an industrial economy brought in many non-Moravians, and, by the mid-1840s, Bethlehem had lost its religious mission, making the town indistinguishable from many others. The experience of the Bethlehem Moravians raises the question, faced time and again by radicals of all stripes, as to how long a commitment to founding ideals and principles can be maintained when society at large exerts enormous pressure to conform to mainstream practices.

Further Reading

Smaby, Beverly Prior. *The Transformation of Moravian Bethlehem: From Communal Mission to Family Economy.*
Philadelphia: University of Pennsylvania Press, 1988.

Christian Gottlieb Priber Proposes a Secular Utopia

1743

Religion permeated American colonial society, shaping the many proposals for communes and other alternative communities. But William Gottlieb Priber thought in secular terms; his proposed settlement would be based on liberty and equality and the living together in peace of both whites and Indians, a proposition that challenged racial assumptions in the colonies and called for a Herculean effort at tolerance.

Amid the many plans that radicals formulated in the colonial period for religious communities, Christian Gottlieb Priber (1697–1744) offered one for a secular utopian settlement he called Paradise. An immigrant from Saxony, Priber settled in South Carolina in 1734 or 1735. Attracted to Native American culture, he lived among the Cherokee Indians in 1737 and assumed substantial power within their society. One observer described him thusly: "Priber, as to his person, was a short dapper man, with a pleasing, open countenance, and a most penetrating look. His dress was a deerskin jacket, a flap before and behind his privities, with . . . deerskin pumps, or sandals, which were laced in the Indian manner on his feet and ankles." Accused by white traders of interfering with the Indian trade, Priber was seized by the military and confined to barracks at Fort Frederica. It was there that he was found to have in his possession a manuscript he had written, titled "Kingdom of Paradise."

In it, Priber outlined his vision of utopia, which appeared to be an effort to combine the best of Native American and white society—a highly unusual blend in an era when few colonists considered Native Americans to be anything more than savages. A newspaper article described the manuscript's contents as consisting of plans for a town and its government. Priber proposed that there be no marriage contracts and that children be raised by the community. Women would have the same rights as men, and private property ownership would be prohibited, with liberty and equality the foundation for the society.

Priber wanted to build his community near the mountains, within territory occupied by the Cherokee and Creek Indians. He hoped to attract settlers from both the British colonies and the Indian tribes. Governor James Oglethorpe of Georgia said in a report that Priber wanted "to make a town or settlement in that part of Georgia which lies within ye Cherokee nation, & to settle a Town there of fugitive English, French, Germans & Negores."

The British colonial authorities reacted to his plans by labeling him dangerous. Priber's project, they claimed, would attract the downtrodden and the troublemakers in Indian and white society; "Criminals, debtors, and slaves," they said, would seek refuge, allowing them to avoid justice or to escape from their masters.

Priber never had a chance to put his utopian plan into action; he died around 1744 while being held prisoner at Fort Frederica. Previously, the *South Carolina Gazette* said of his "Kingdom of Paradise": "The Book is drawn up very methodically. . . . It is extreamly wicked, yet has several Flights full of Invention; and it is a Pity so much Wit is applied to so bad Purposes." Yet Priber's manuscript offered a utopian model geared to the American environment, a Thomas More in the wilderness, that showed how the frontier could encourage a contemplation of extraordinary possibilities.

Further Reading

Mellon, Knox, Jr. "Christian Priber's Cherokee 'Kingdom of Paradise.'" *Georgia Historical Quarterly.* Vol. 57, 1973.

Strickland, Rennard. "Christian Gottlieb Priber: Utopian Precursor of the Cherokee Government." *Chronicles of Oklahoma* 48, no. 3 (1970): 264–279.

Ward, Harry M. *Colonial America, 1607–1763.* Englewood Cliffs, N.J.: Prentice Hall, 1991.

1756 Jacob Weber's Religious Cult Deteriorates into Hysteria and Murder

A Swiss immigrant, Jacob Weber heard voices and experienced visions that convinced him he was a savior chosen to lead people to the promised land. The sect he founded in 1756 shocked the sensibilities of South Carolinians and threatened to unleash widespread disorder.

No stranger or more violent a proselytizer appeared in colonial America than Jacob Weber (?–1761). Born in Switzerland, Weber settled in the South Carolina frontier at age 14 and in the mid-1750s promoted his unusual ideas among the colony's Swiss and German settlers in Dutch Fork and Saxe Gotha.

Weber experienced what he called an infusion of the divine spirit that led to his becoming a preacher. As he attracted an increasing number of followers to his Sunday sermons, he added his own passages to the Bible; he made two of his followers, John Smithpeter and a black man named Dauber, his disciples. Smithpeter carried the title of "The Son" and Dauber "The Holy Spirit," while Weber claimed for himself the title of "God the Father."

Despite such grandiose claims, Weber showed no signs of the violence into which his movement would degenerate. Like many a zealous preacher, he spoke from and with emotion, and his followers embraced his enthusiasm and passion. Then came the Cherokee War of 1760–61, which caused widespread destruction on the frontier. The war unleashed so much bloodshed and destroyed so many livelihoods that it caused many settlers to despair. They began looking for someone or something that promised them a better way of life, and salvation in the afterlife—to a few, Weber offered it. Historian Richard Maxwell Brown states in *The South Carolina Regulators* (1963), that the Indian raids affected the Weberites to the point that "the hitherto harmless cult degenerated into a homicidal craze."

Weber developed a frightening hold on his congregation; this was evident when a Lutheran preacher, Christian Theus, appeared among them and denied that Weber was the savior. At that point Weber, Smithpeter, and Dauber "sentenced" Theus to death. When they asked the congregation how Theus should be killed, the Weberites enthusiastically answered that he be drowned. Fortunately for Theus, he was able to flee his attackers by making his way to a nearby river and escaping by boat.

As the "Weber heresy" spread during 1760 and early 1761, disagreements flared between God the Father and his disciples, and Weber and Smithpeter decided to get rid of Dauber. They recruited the congregation to dig a pit and place a mattress in it. Then the Weberites shoved Dauber into the pit, piled other mattresses on top of him, and pressed down on them until Dauber smothered.

True to his egomania, or dementia, Weber next turned on Smithpeter and told the congregation to kill him. Again they obeyed, tying Smithpeter to a tree and beating him with sticks. Then they untied him and trampled him to death.

Weber's excesses shocked the colony, and when word of them reached the authorities in Charlestown, he was charged with murder, captured, and placed on trial. He later said he had been possessed by the devil. Weber was hanged in April 1761.

Weber's form of extreme separation from the established churches raised the issue of how society could ever be stable. If he could claim himself as leader, judge, and jury through his "special" relationship with God, then what was to prevent others from doing the same and establishing their own rules?

Weber's movement was an extreme representative of a general upheaval on the frontier. The backcountry loosened attachments to traditional institutions while sending its settlers into a search for stability and the social accoutrements that made them feel they had carved civilization out of the wilderness. Thus observers spoke of the rampant immorality of the frontier settlers while also noting the spread of dissenting religious congregations that tried to bring discipline to society. Brown notes that, "Practically all shades of doctrine were found in the region," including Presbyterians, Baptists, Lutherans, Quakers, Methodists, and Congregationalists. Weber represented the fanatical side, a delusional radicalism taken to the extreme in the search for moral guidance.

Further Reading

Brown, Richard M. *The South Carolina Regulators*. Cambridge, Mass.: Harvard University Press, 1963.

Isaac Backus Advocates the Separation of Church and State

1756

At a time when Massachusetts required all of its citizens to support the Congregational church, Isaac Backus called for religious liberty and in the 1770s attacked the tax system that perpetuated what he called an oppressive arrangement.

Born on January 9, 1724, in Norwich, Connecticut, to Samuel Backus and Elizabeth Tracy, Isaac experienced an intense religious event in 1741 when the Great Awakening, an evangelical movement then sweeping through the northern and southern colonies, reached Norwich. In New England, the evangelicals, called "New Lights," attacked the dominant Congregational church, which they called the "Old Lights," for its dry, passionless sermons and for its practice of admitting as members those who had failed to experience God's grace. On hearing preacher James Davenport inveigh against the Old Lights and call for a spiritual rebirth, Backus realized his own depravity. "As I was . . . alone in the field . . . ," he later recounted, "all my past life was opened plainly before me, and I saw clearly that it had been filled with sin."

Backus attended evangelist George Whitefield's sermons in 1745, and subsequently withdrew from the Norwich Congregational church. A few months later, he began preaching, and in April 1748, he was ordained a minister at the insistence of some residents near Middleborough, Massachusetts who asked him to write a covenant and organize a church.

About that time Backus married Susanna Mason; in 1749, he bought a farm at Middleborough, where he lived the rest of his life. In 1751, Backus antagonized his congregation when he rejected infant baptism and adopted the position, held by Baptists, that immersion should be restricted to true believers old enough to realize their commitment to God. As a result, his congregation excluded him, and he organized the First Baptist church in Middleborough in January 1756 and became its pastor, a position he held for 50 years. The earliest Baptist church in North America had been established by Roger Williams in Providence, Rhode Island, in 1639. Others soon followed, but the churches splintered and attracted little following beyond Rhode Island until five of them organized the Philadelphia Baptist Association in 1707 and began missionary work. It was not until the Great Awakening, however, that the Baptist church expanded widely, and as pastor at Middleborough, Backus traveled extensively, taking the evangelical message to other towns.

Backus left his greatest imprint, however, with his principled call for religious liberty and the separation of church and state. Massachusetts required that each town form and maintain a Congregational church (the descendant of the seventeenth-century Puritan church), to be led by an academically trained minister and funded through taxes paid by the local residents. Refusal to pay the tax exposed the violator to loss of property and imprisonment. Any attack on this relationship did more than undermine a religion; it threatened the power structure whereby the political elite helped the ministers financially, and the ministers used their sermons to instruct their congregations on the proper way to vote.

In the early 1770s, Backus headed the Grievance Committee of the Warren Association, a group of Baptist churches. In that capacity he petitioned the Massachusetts legislature to repeal the tax law that had created the official state church.

With America's crisis with Britain intensifying in December 1774, and the colonies moving closer to revolution, Backus stood before the First Continental Congress in Philadelphia and, on behalf of his fellow Baptists, declared: "We claim and expect the liberty of worshipping God according to our consciences." Those strong words reinforced his earlier stand on behalf of the separation of church and state. Although Backus was radical for the time, he was not alone: His views were similar to those held by some other colonists, most notably Thomas Jefferson of Virginia.

In 1775 Backus offered a resolution to the Massachusetts assembly that said "for a civil Legislature to impose religious taxes is, we conceive, a power which constituents never had to give; and is therefore going entirely out of their jurisdiction." He continued: "We are persuaded that an entire freedom from being taxed by civil rulers to religious worship, is not a mere favor, from any man or men in the world, but a right and property granted us by God."

Backus opposed Article III of the 1780 Massachusetts constitution, which continued the state-supported church. He supported the colonial fight for independence from Britain, and served as a delegate to the Massachusetts convention of 1788 that considered whether to ratify the federal Constitution. While most of the Baptist delegates opposed the document for expanding the power of the national government and making more possible the threat of political intervention in church matters, he voted for it because, he said, it excluded "any hereditary, lordly power . . . and . . . any religious test."

When Backus died in Middleborough on November 20, 1806, he left behind several written works, among them the published sermon "An Appeal to the Public for Religious Liberty" (1773), which championed those who stood against government intervention in religion: "Religious matters are to be separated from the jurisdiction of the state not because they are beneath the interests of the state," Backus argued, "but, quite to the contrary, because they are too high and holy and thus are beyond the competence of the state." In the continuing debate over how sturdy the wall should be between church and state, Backus favored the tallest and strongest one possible. In time, his ideas came to occupy the center of American political thought—partisans continue to battle over how much separation between church and state is best for society.

Further Reading

Grenz, Stanley. I*saac Backus, Puritan and Baptist: His Place in History, His Thoughts, and Their Implications for Modern Baptist Theology.* Macon, Ga.: Mercer University Press, 1983.

McLoughlin, William Gerald. *Isaac Backus and the American Pietistic Tradition.* Boston: Little, Brown, 1967.

McLoughlin, William Gerald, ed. *The Diary of Isaac Backus.* 3 vols. Providence, R.I.: Brown University Press, 1979.

CHAPTER TWO

Revolution and Nation-Building

The American Revolution was a powerful stimulant to radical attacks on existing political, social, and economic practices. Well before the British and the colonists fired the first shots in the battles at Lexington and Concord in 1775, groups were forming to challenge policies passed by Parliament. They were stimulated to do so by a complex interaction of forces, each one important in contributing to the outbreak of the Revolution.

For one, the colonists chafed under an increasingly rigid mercantilist system. Under this arrangement, regulations restricted trade to within the British Empire, forbidding the colonists, for example, from shipping tobacco directly to French or Spanish territory. Other regulations forbade the colonists from developing manufacturing, such as making iron, which might compete with industries in England. Yet other laws levied duties on colonial trade in an attempt to channel it and keep it within the British Empire. The Molasses Act of 1733 imposed a high duty on sugar and molasses from the French and Spanish Caribbean islands while allowing those items to be traded freely within the Empire.

Because most of this legislation was loosely enforced prior to the end of the French and Indian War in 1763, the colonists engaged in widespread smuggling of restricted goods and, on a small scale, developed their own industries that competed with those in the mother country. When the war ended, however, Parliament decided to plug the holes in the mercantilist system, and the stricter enforcement of the rules infuriated colonial merchants and others accustomed to the previous laxity.

A particular ideology—or what historian Bernard Bailyn has called an "intellectual circuitry"—also motivated the colonists and drew them towards revolution. This ideology consisted of several parts. Many of the educated colonists had read the writings of ancient Romans in which it was argued that a republic was superior to an empire. As British policies became more intrusive and burdensome, more and more colonists came to agree with this view—empire was a grave threat to republican institutions.

They also read Enlightenment works, especially the writings of John Locke, in which the British philosopher argued that, in a state of nature, human beings possessed life, liberty, and property, and that governments were obligated, through a contract between the rulers and the ruled, to protect and secure each of these. Locke asserted that if a government failed to fulfill its obligation, then its subjects had the right, even the duty, to alter or abolish it. Such a change, particularly in the radical form of a revolution, should come only after a long train of abuses. In time, as Parliament levied taxes and passed burdensome legislation

> "Nothing of reform in the political world ought be held improbable. It is an age of revolutions, in which everything may be looked for."
>
> Tom Paine, *The Rights of Man*, 1791

in the 1760s and 1770s, the colonists concluded that the monarchical British government needed to be abolished.

The colonists believed in the theory that power threatened liberty, that power was aggressive and was always seeking to erode liberty. Government officials in particular could never be trusted to protect it—only a vigilant populace could do so.

This concept of power versus liberty coincided with the thinking of early eighteenth-century radical English writers John Trenchard and Thomas Gordon, who were widely read in the colonies. These two men attacked British society as corrupt, as evident in high taxes, huge deficits, and the existence of a standing, or permanent, army. In this setting liberty, they argued, was being crushed by power-hungry men.

Trenchard and Gordon's ideas resonated with the colonists in 1765 when Parliament passed the Stamp Act, a measure that raised yet another element in the outbreak of the Revolution, namely the constitutional issue of taxation. The colonists insisted that they were Englishmen and entitled to all of the rights therein, including representation in any legislature that levied taxes. Thus the Stamp Act caused the colonists to declare, "No taxation without representation."

The radical Sons of Liberty reacted to the Stamp Act with precisely that cry, and a colonial boycott of British goods forced Parliament to rescind the measure. Parliament followed in 1767 with the Townshend Acts, taxes on imports, but once again a boycott forced the repeal of all but one—the tax on tea. The 1770 Boston Massacre convinced many colonists that the British army was an oppressor rather than a protector. Following a three-year period of relative calm between the colonies and the mother country, residents of Boston protested the Tea Act of 1773—legislation that was intended to entice the colonists to buy tea sold by the British East India Company and in the process inveigle them into accepting the tax on tea—by confiscating chests of tea from British ships and dumping their contents into Boston Harbor.

The revolutionary impulse went beyond challenging British policies, as evident in the action of the Jack Tars, the impoverished seamen discussed in this chapter. There was, importantly, an underlying tension between the elite and the poor in the Revolution. Indeed, many of the elite opposed the use of mobs in protesting British policies for fear that "the rabble" might get carried away and aim their wrath not only at the royal government and its supporters but also at wealthy colonists who dominated the economy and the political system.

Historian J. Franklin Jameson has noted that the Revolution was like an engorged stream that overflowed its banks and carved a broad path, sweeping away practices and traditions previously thought to be permanent. When the Declaration of Independence pronounced the principle that "all men are created equal," it combined with the anti-authoritarian spirit of the Revolution to spark protests and uprisings against slavery, the formation of Democratic Societies to protect individual rights, and a Whiskey Rebellion in western Pennsylvania to assert local authority against the power of the newly-formed national government.

The Revolution would long serve as a beacon for rebels and renegades. Its spirit and ideals; the refrain of egalitarianism; the pursuit of life, liberty, and property (or "happiness," the broader phrase used by Thomas Jefferson in the Declaration of Independence); the fear that governmental power might trample liberty—all would echo through radical and reactionary movements into the twenty-first century.

The Sons of Liberty Take to the Streets

When the British Parliament passed the Stamp Act (which placed a tax on printed material such as deeds) in 1765, the colonists demonstrated their opposition to this new tax by boycotting British goods and engaging in protests that ranged from peaceful demonstrations to violent attacks. From this uprising came the Sons of Liberty, an organized resistance group intent on repealing the Act. The Sons of Liberty initiated many of their fellow colonists into the issues of revolution and the passions of protest.

Formed in 1765, the Sons of Liberty was the first radical intercolonial group in America born from the turmoil surrounding the Stamp Act and aimed at getting the act repealed. Although, as historian Edward Countryman states, the leadership of the Sons of Liberty fell somewhere between "the elite and the plebeians," in the demonstrations and violence that marked the group's existence it reached into the lower class, tapping into the anger about conditions that went beyond the Stamp Act itself.

In addition to the Stamp Act, the formation of the Sons of Liberty relied on two other developments. First was the use of mob action prior to the Act. The colonies had experienced numerous tumults, everything from roving gangs in the cities to armed rebels along the frontiers. The Sons of Liberty built on this tradition, even borrowing the ceremonies, such as the street marches that accompanied the anti-Catholic "Pope's Day," and using the leaders who had been involved in earlier street demonstrations.

Second, the Sons of Liberty emerged only after other individuals and groups, largely disorganized, had begun protesting the Stamp Act. The colonists hated the act, as it was a tax passed by a government in which they had no representation. On the night of August 26, 1765, a mob in Boston descended on the home of Lieutenant Governor Thomas Hutchinson. Thinking him responsible for having recommended passage of the Stamp Act (he actually opposed it), and worried that documents in his possession might reveal the names of colonists involved in smuggling, the mob smashed the door to his house, tore the wainscoting from its walls, stole all his furniture and clothing, and chopped down his fruit trees. Hutchinson later said, "Such ruins were never seen in America." The following day, protesters in Newport, Rhode Island, burned pro-British figures in effigy and over the next several days engaged in riots that destroyed the homes of two residents who supported the Stamp Act.

A mob in New York City took to the streets on November 1, 1765, spurred on by stories that Acting Governor Cadwallder Colden possessed a supply of stamps; the mob destroyed his gilded coach. Historians are unsure whether the mob was organized by the Sons of Liberty. It was led by Isaac Sears, John Lamb, and others who were emerging as New York's Sons of Liberty, but it is possible they did not formally organize as a group until November 6. In Boston, a club called the Loyal Nine had formed in August 1765 to lead protests but did not call itself the Sons of Liberty until some time in December.

The Sons of Liberty took their name from a speech in Parliament by Issac Barre, a member sympathetic to the colonial cause. In reply to Charles Townshend's argument in favor of the Stamp Act, Barre said, "As soon as you began to care about [the colonists], that care was exercised by sending persons to rule over 'em in one department or another, who were . . . sent to spy out their liberty, to misrepresent their actions and to prey upon 'em: men whose behavior on many occasions had caused the blood of these sons of liberty to recoil within them."

At first, the Sons of Liberty drew its leadership and members mainly from artisans, intellectuals, and intercolonial merchants. Intellectuals included Samuel Adams of Massachusetts, who wanted to make his colony an austere Christian community. The artisans came primarily from those whose shops suffered from the importation of British goods, individuals such as the silversmith Paul Revere and the shoemaker George Hewes. The intercolonial merchants were those with few ties to the transatlantic trade. Neither rich enough

A cartoon depicts the Sons of Liberty battling British soldiers. (Bettmann/CORBIS)

to be part of the elite nor poor enough to be part of the lower class, the Sons of Liberty represented a middling sort with close ties to the common people, the very segment essential in winning independence from Britain.

By spring 1766, the Sons of Liberty existed in every colony from South Carolina to New Hampshire, and many of them corresponded with one another. In the eyes of British officials, the Sons of Liberty were dangerous radicals. Historian John C. Miller observed that, "Crown Officers and stamp masters alike believed that the Sons of Liberty had begun a reign of terror in which every supporter of British sovereignty would be crushed by the patriot mob." Whatever the tactics and wherever they took action, Sons of Liberty sought to disrupt any attempt to use the tax stamps.

Initially, they neither desired to overthrow the existing colonial governments nor radically alter them. The New York City Sons of Liberty declared: "[We] are not attempting . . . any change of Government—only a preservation of the Constitution." The various Sons of Liberty aimed their complaint mainly at Parliament, and on several occasions they affirmed their loyalty to the king; the New London, Connecticut group declared its "most unshaken faith and true allegiance to his Majesty King George the Third."

Nevertheless, as they broadened their base of support, evolving from a secret group to a public one, even printing the proceedings of their meetings in newspapers, they reached into the lower orders for members. As they did so, they plunged into class issues. In New York, the Sons of Liberty protested unemployment, high rents, and high prices. Edward Countryman says, "For both the leadership and the people of New York, domestic issues were part of the crisis."

The Sons of Liberty disbanded when Parliament repealed the Stamp Act in 1766. But several of them reorganized to protest Parliament's passage of the Townshend Acts in 1768, which sought to impose taxes on imports. They continued in existence until the American Revolution ended in 1783. Whether proclaiming the more moderate goal of repealing the Stamp Act, engaging in the more extreme acts of violence, or supporting the overthrow of British authority during the revolution, the Sons of Liberty provided a radical leadership crucial in winning American independence.

Further Reading

Countryman, Edward. *The American Revolution.* New York: Hill and Wang, 1985.

Maier, Pauline. *From Resistance to Revolution: Colonial Radicals and the Development of American Opposition to Britain, 1765–1776.* New York: W. W. Norton, 1991.

Anthony Benezet Calls for an End to Slavery 1766

In 1766, Anthony Benezet published A Caution and Warning to Great Britain and Her Colonies on the Calamitous State of the Enslaved Negroes, *in which he condemned slavery as cruel and inhumane and called for its end. His frequent writings made him the most widely read of America's early abolitionists.*

Anthony Benezet was born on January 31, 1713, in Saint-Quentin, France, to Jean Etienne Benezet and Judith de la Mejenelle Benezet, wealthy Huguenot (Protestant) parents. To escape the French government's persecution of the Huguenots, Benezet's family fled in 1715 to Rotterdam before settling a short time later in London. There young Anthony attended school and apprenticed to a merchant. At age 14 he joined the Quakers.

In 1731, the Benezet family moved to Philadelphia, Pennsylvania, and Anthony founded a merchant business with his brothers. Five years later, he wed Joyce Marriott, beginning a happy marriage that would last until her death, 48 years later. Benezet was unhappy with his merchant career, however, and quit it to become a manufacturer in Wilmington, Delaware. Feeling that he had a more humanitarian calling, and convinced that education held the key to reforming society, in 1742 he began teaching at the Germantown Academy, and then at the Friends' English Public School in Philadelphia. He would typically teach Quaker students in the day, and tutor African-Americans at night.

In 1754, he resigned his teaching post to establish the first secondary school for girls in Pennsylvania. At the same time, Benezet was developing his antislavery beliefs. His own reading, along with his friendship with fellow Quaker John Woolman, who traveled through the South and reported about the harsh conditions suffered by blacks, prompted Benezet to begin writing newspaper essays and pamphlets calling for abolition.

Benezet took an even more pioneering stand when he argued blacks are the intellectual equals of whites. In 1762, in his pamphlet *A Short Account of That Part of Africa Inhabited by the Negroes*, he denounced the widely held belief that blacks were inferior. Soon thereafter, he wrote that as a "teacher of a school . . . for many years, [I have] had the opportunity of knowing the temper and genius of the Africans."

Suffering from poor health, Benezet retired in 1766 to Burlington, New Jersey. That same year, he published *A Caution and Warning to Great Britain and Her Colonies on the Calamitous State of the Enslaved Negroes*, with its more pointed criticism of slavery and its call for an end to the oppressive institution; it sold widely in Britain. The Philadelphia Yearly Meeting of Friends approved it, thus giving it the official support of the Quakers. Although a few Quakers had earlier denounced slavery—most notably a group at Germantown in 1688, and such individuals as John Hepburn in 1715 and John Woolman in 1754—*A Caution and Warning* was written at a time when other Quakers owned slaves and almost no one outside the Quaker community had written anything condemning slavery.

In 1768 Benezet returned to teaching, writing, and speaking out against slavery and other social problems. In the early 1770s he founded a school for African-American children, and some of its graduates became leaders in Philadelphia's black community. In 1771, he published his *Historical Account of New Guinea*, which presented facts about the slave trade. On its cover appeared a drawing of a black man, kneeling and bound in chains, along with the motto, "Am I not a man and a brother." One British abolitionist later called the way Benezet's book awoke Britons to the evils of the slave trade unprecedented.

Benezet issued a call in 1775 for the first meeting of the Pennsylvania Society for Promoting the Abolition of Slavery (see entry, 1775), and he convinced the Philadelphia Quaker Yearly Meeting in 1776 to expel Quakers who trafficked in slaves. Into the 1780s, he wrote letters to political leaders in the United States and overseas calling for an end to slavery. At the same time, he campaigned against the excessive drinking of alcohol, writing an essay that gave momentum to the temperance movement.

Benezet's concern for society's oppressed extended beyond African-Americans to include Native Americans. In a letter written to a friend in 1783, he complained about "the prevailing prejudice in the back settlements against all Indians," a prejudice ignited, he said, by recent writings that threatened to lead to the slaughter of the Indians. Shortly before he died he wrote *Some Observations on the Situation, Disposition, and Character of the Indian Natives of This Continent*, published in 1784.

Benezet died on May 3, 1784. More than 400 black Philadelphians turned out for his funeral, a tribute to his beneficence toward their community, but also a recognition of the radical views he held about slavery and black abilities in an era of extensive racism.

Further Reading

Brookes, George S. *Friend Anthony Benezet.* Philadelphia: University of Pennsylvania Press, 1937.

1771 The Regulators Engage in Pitched Battle at Alamance

Beginning in the late 1760s, westerners in North Carolina and South Carolina organized into extralegal groups called Regulators, intent on bringing order to their regions and redressing wrongs they suffered at the hands of eastern-dominated colonial legislatures. Similar to Bacon's Rebellion in 1676, for some the uprising became a way to attack the wealthiest and most powerful colonists.

In the mid-1700s, the western regions of Britain's North American colonies were in great turmoil. In South Carolina, lawlessness spread throughout the "frontier hinterland," unleashed by the bloody Cherokee War of 1760–61. The Regulator movement began late in 1767 as an attempt by small farmers to establish order by "regulating" their own local societies and governments. Numerous skirmishes between outlaws and the Regulators caused the governor of South Carolina to label the Regulators an illegal group.

The Regulators then presented a list of grievances to the colonial legislature. Foremost among their complaints was the lack of an adequate court system. But the document revealed a greater frustration: using severe language, the Regulators attacked lawyers for draining them of their money under the slightest pretenses. They said South Carolina was "harder rode at present by Lawyers, than Spain or Italy by Priests." The severity of the language antagonized the lawmakers, but in November 1767 they passed an act to establish circuit courts, and they organized the Regulators as a legal body called Rangers.

For all practical purposes, the South Carolina Regulators ran the colony's backcountry for three years. One of the group's supporters claimed, "The Country was purged of Villains. The Whores were whipped and drove off. Tranquility reigned. Industry was restor'd." In enforcing order, the Regulators resorted to violence equal to that of the outlaws, but they were more vigilante than revolutionary in ideology.

In North Carolina, the Regulator movement took a more drastic turn. Like their brethren in South Carolina, the North Carolina group complained about lawyers. But unlike South Carolina, the North Carolina Regulators concluded that lawyers were part of a larger problem involving domination of the West by the eastern elite. They complained about unfair taxes and underrepresentation in the colonial legislature. In Orange County, the Regulators tried to prevent the collection of taxes, and 700 of them, bearing arms, forced the release of two of their group who had been arrested for their protests. In Anson County, 100 Regulators disrupted court proceedings.

West Versus East

Today, Americans look at the East and West coasts of their country and see different attitudes and ways of thinking, both socially and politically. Similarly, there were sectional differences in early America. For more than 150 years, the North American colonies that stretched from New England to Georgia experienced tension between eastern and western settlements that sometimes erupted into violence. The root cause of this animosity was the easterners' desire to retain control of colonial legislatures.

Toward that end, easterners only slowly organized the western parts of the colonies into counties, and in several instances made the counties, and with them the legislative districts, so large that they limited the number of representatives from the region. On top of that, the colonial governors appointed easterners (or relatives of easterners) rather than locals as sheriffs and justices of the peace. Westerners fumed at such tactics, as they did at the refusal of easterners in the legislatures to lower taxes harmful to the west, or to levy taxes that would help the West, particularly those needed for roads and other internal improvements.

The West took up arms against the East as early as the 1670s with Bacon's Rebellion in Virginia (see entry, 1676). Closer to the time of the Regulator movement, westerners in Pennsylvania, angry with the failure of the Quaker-dominated colonial legislature to appropriate money for fighting the Indians, rallied near the town of Paxton. These "Paxton Boys" formed their own army, massacred hundreds of Indians, and in 1764 marched on the capital at Philadelphia to demand the removal of all Native Americans from western lands. They returned home only after Benjamin Franklin defused the crisis by promising that the assembly would consider their complaints. There followed the Regulator movements in the South, born of sectionalism but containing within them class discontent, as westerners voiced a more egalitarian outlook than did colonists in the East.

The Regulators never identified with the colony's slaves or the most downtrodden of its poor, but they did reflect the discontent and protests of small landowners. They saw their movement as involved in a struggle against the very wealthy and described themselves as oppressed "labourers" who were fighting "rich and powerful . . . designing Monsters."

The North Carolina legislature reacted to the uprising with little more than minor reforms—along with an act clearly aimed at containing the Regulators. In May 1771, Governor William Tryon, who had decreed a cooling-off period that would allow the Regulators to peacefully disassemble, treacherously ordered the colonial militia to attack them at Alamance. Regulator Richard Henry Lee reported that "before the allowed time was elapsed, [Tryon] fell upon the unsuspecting multitudes and made great slaughter with his Cannon." The Regulators lost the battle and six of them were hanged. Many of them then left North Carolina to settle farther west, on land that would become Tennessee. The encounter at Alamance defused the Regulator movement while the colonial disputes with Britain overwhelmed the issues dividing east and west.

Historians disagree about whether most Regulators supported the American Revolution or whether, out of resentment toward the colonial legislatures, they refused to join the fight for independence. Clearly the Regulators presented a mixed bag of extremism, with the North Carolina movement more class conscious and more far reaching in its desire for change than that in South Carolina. Irrespective of the details, the uprisings displayed the extreme form sectionalism could take, a possibility more violently revealed in the dispute between North and South—also involving conflict over how to develop the West—in the years leading up to the Civil War.

Further Reading

Brown, Richard M. *The South Carolina Regulators*. Cambridge, Mass.: Harvard University Press, 1963.

Ekirch, A. Roger. *"Poor Carolina": Politics and Society in Colonial North Carolina, 1729–1776*. Chapel Hill: University of North Carolina Press, 1981.

1773 Reforms for a Better Nation: Benjamin Rush Advocates the End to Slavery

A doctor by profession, Benjamin Rush embraced a wide range of social reforms. His activism reflected the questioning of social rules and practices that occurred in the wake of the libertarian American Revolution.

Born on a plantation in Byberry, Pennsylvania, on December 24, 1745, Benjamin Rush grew up in nearby Philadelphia, where his father, John Rush, had moved his family to pursue his trade as a gunsmith. Benjamin Rush graduated from the College of New Jersey in 1760 and studied medicine, first under Dr. John Redman, from 1761 to 1766, and then under prominent physicians in Edinburgh, Scotland. He obtained his medical degree in 1768, trained for a year at St. Thomas's Hospital in London, and then returned to Philadelphia. In 1770, he wrote the first American chemistry text, *A Syllabus of a Course of Lectures on Chemistry.*

Amid the events that moved the colonists toward revolution, Rush supported the patriot side and developed friendships with Tom Paine, John Adams, and Thomas Jefferson. His reformist zeal extended to other conditions in 1773, when he wrote *An Address to the Inhabitants of the British Settlements in America, upon Slave-keeping.* Rush owned a slave; nevertheless, he said that "slavery is so foreign to the human mind, that the moral faculties, as well as those of the understanding, are debased and rendered torpid by it."

He insisted that blacks were the intellectual equals to whites, that slavery was holding them back. His solution: end the importation of slaves, teach young blacks to read and write, and provide for their gradual emancipation. In a statement directed at the Pennsylvania legislature, which was then considering a measure that would restrict the importation of slaves, Rush said, "Remember, the eyes of all Europe are fixed upon you to preserve an asylum for freedom in this country, after the last pillars of it are fallen in every other quarter of the globe." Recognizing his own fault, he agreed to manumit his slave. In 1774, Rush helped organize the Pennsylvania Society for Promoting the Abolition of Slavery.

In 1776, the same year Rush married Julia Stockton, he was elected to the Continental Congress, where he signed the Declaration of Independence. He was appointed the surgeon general for the Middle Division of the Continental Army in 1777. Rush resigned from the military in 1778 and resumed his medical practice. In 1783, he joined the staff at the Pennsylvania Hospital in Philadelphia. His observations concerning the plight of the poor and the post–Revolutionary War

Benjamin Rush. (Library of Congress)

spirit of social change caused him to engage in more reforms. In 1786, he established the first free dispensary to help the poor. The following year, he campaigned for adoption of the Constitution and served in the Pennsylvania ratifying convention. When the Constitution went into effect, he said proudly and with nationalistic fervor, "I am now a citizen of every state."

Rush condemned capital punishment and worked for prison reform. He so strongly promoted temperance that he became known as the "father of the American temperance movement." His *An Enquiry into the Effects of Spirituous Liquor Upon the Human Body, and their Influence upon the Happiness of Society* (1785) included a vivid description of a drunk: "He opens his eyes and closes them again—he gapes and stretches his limbs—he then coughs and pukes. . . ." Rush advocated education for girls, the establishment of a national university, and changes in pedagogy to teach children science and subjects they could apply to their lives, rather than a classical education. In 1793, he risked his life by staying in Philadelphia to help those afflicted by a yellow fever epidemic while most of the city's doctors fled.

In 1803, he was elected president of the Pennsylvania Society for Promoting Abolition of Slavery. His work with the insane at the Pennsylvania Hospital displayed a compassion toward their condition that was unusual for the time. He was the first to use a rudimentary form of psychoanalysis.

During these years and later, he continued to advance his medical career. In 1787, he helped organize the Philadelphia College of Physicians, and in 1789, he was appointed chair of theory and practice of medicine at the University of Pennsylvania. Three years later, he was appointed professor of that college's institutes of medicine and clinical practice. He was by far the most prominent physician of his time, and students flocked to his classes, which increased in size from about 45 annually in 1790 to about 3,000 in 1812.

Rush died in Philadelphia on April 19, 1813. Some contemporaries criticized Rush's moral certitude; others marveled at the scope of his reform activities. One compared him to a fictional character who "attacks without mercy all the giants, hydras, hobgoblins, etc." Rush was committed to building a better nation by fighting injustice in its multiple guises.

Further Reading

Binger, Carl Alfred Lanning. *Revolutionary Doctor: Benjamin Rush, 1746–1813.* New York: Norton, 1966.

D'Elia, Donald J. *Benjamin Rush, Philosopher of the American Revolution.* Philadelphia: American Philosophical Society, 1974.

Hawke, David Freeman. *Benjamin Rush: Revolutionary Gadfly.* Indianapolis, Ind.: Bobbs-Merrill, 1971.

The Boston Tea Party

1773

In December 1773, the Boston Tea Party signaled a new phase of the American colonists' crisis with Britain. More than the law had been defied; property had been destroyed on a massive scale, and radicals who wanted revolution had gained the upper hand.

The Boston Tea Party was the culmination of a series of political skirmishes between Massachusetts and the British authorities in London. One of these involved the Townshend Acts. In 1767, Chancellor of the Exchequer Charles Townshend convinced Parliament to tax a wide range of goods imported by colonies from Britain. The colonists protested this move as another effort at "taxation without representation" by boycotting trade with the British, an action that forced Parliament to end all of the taxes except the one on tea.

As a relative calm settled over the colonies in the early 1770s, events tied to the British East India Company converged to create an explosive situation. The company, an economic giant, neared financial collapse. It was especially hurt by a huge tea surplus, resulting in part from American colonists buying lower-priced tea smuggled from the Netherlands rather than buying British tea, which bore the tea duty.

To save the company, British Prime Minister Lord North proposed a Tea Act. Under its terms, the East India Company could bypass colonial middlemen and sell tea directly to its own consignees in the colonies, and it could ship tea directly from India to the colonies, thus dispensing with the customary stop in England where it sold tea to English middlemen, who then sold it to the colonists. Historian John C. Miller has observed that "by eliminating the middleman—the English merchants who bought tea at the company's auctions in London and then resold it to American merchants—the company was able to sell tea in the colonies cheaper than in England itself." North was certain the colonists would find the company's tea so attractive in price they would buy it despite the tax, which remained in effect. Although he primarily considered his measure a means to save the East India Company, North relished the thought of enticing the colonists into paying the tax and thus recognizing Parliament's right to tax them.

While North was convincing Parliament to pass the Tea Act, Boston's radicals acquired several private letters written in the late 1760s by Massachusetts Governor Thomas Hutchinson to Thomas Whately, a bureaucrat in London. The radicals jumped on a statement of Hutchinson's—he declared that if the colonies were to remain in the British Empire there would have to be "an abridgement of what is called English liberty." The Hutchinson-Whately letters converged with the Tea Act to convince many Americans that nothing less than a plot was under way to destroy their rights and enslave them.

Parliament passed the Tea Act, and matters only worsened when the East India Company picked as its consignees in America those who had been loyal to the monarchy during previous protests. That move further antagonized the colonists, and the provisions of the Tea Act, which, in effect, granted the company a monopoly in America, drew many merchants to the radical cause because they feared a monopoly in tea would be followed by similar arrangements for other British companies. Miller states, "The menace of monopoly united virtually all businessmen whether smugglers or honest traders—in opposition to the East India Company."

On November 28, 1773, the *Dartmouth* arrived at Boston harbor carrying 114 chests of tea, soon followed by two other ships, also with cargoes of tea. Governor Hutchinson, steeled in his resolve by the controversy over his letters, determined that the tea must be brought ashore, despite the radicals' demand that it stay on the ship. He believed that giving in to the radicals would be conceding "to a lawless and highly criminal assembly," and would destroy British authority. Besides, several of the consignees were his sons.

When the radicals insisted that the *Dartmouth* and its two sister ships be sent to England, Hutchinson refused. He knew that if he sent the ships to London he would violate British trade regulations. He also knew that by law if the cargo sat in the harbor for more than 20 days, it could be unloaded under the protection of British troops and sold at auction, a move that would likely cause the tea to wind up in colonial shops.

The radicals knew this, too, and wanted to avoid any possibility that the tea would be landed. On December 16, several thousand Bostonians rallied to protest the possible unloading of the tea, but Hutchinson refused to meet with their representative. The Bostonians gathered again that night at Faneuil Hall. Samuel Adams addressed the crowd, and on a prearranged cue—the words "I do not see what more Bostonians can do to save their country"—several dozen men disguised as Indians let out a whoop and headed for Griffin's Wharf. Over the course of three hours, as a large crowd watched silently and protected them, they hacked open the chests aboard the ships and threw the tea into Boston Bay, 342 chests in all.

One radical compared the destruction of the tea to the philosophical rationale offered by John Locke, who said that after suffering many transgressions a people have the right to change their government, even overthrowing it, if it failed to protect liberty. Another called the Tea Party "an act of absolute moral and political necessity."

Other tea parties followed: in 1774, a mob boarded a ship in New York City and destroyed its tea; another group in Greenwich, New Jersey, boarded the Greyhound and did the same; yet another in

Class and Radicalism: Jack Tars in the American Revolution

The American Revolution radicalized large segments of the colonial population by making apprentices, landless farm boys, women, and slaves all think they should have a voice in society. No group was more politically activated than the sailors—Jack Tars— aboard colonial merchant ships.

To society's "better sort," the Jack Tars represented the lowest form of life. These poorly paid laborers dressed shabbily, appeared dirty, frequented prostitutes, and spent money and wasted hours in grog shops. Yet they had one of the most serious complaints against British rule: the practice of impressment. The Royal Navy, suffering a constant shortage of sailors, often raided colonial seaports and forced men into service. Once in, the Jack Tars endured horrendous conditions that included low pay and frequent whippings.

The Jack Tars hated this assault on their liberty, and, as other colonists protested British tax policies, the sailors eagerly joined them, expressing a grievance that went well beyond the constitutional cry of "no taxation without representation." Historian Jesse Lemisch asserts in *Jack Tar vs. John Bull* (1997), that these sailors were resisting British tyranny "based not on the rights of Englishmen—for to be an Englishman was not to be free of impressment—but on the rights of man."

The revolutionary elite—John Adams, John Hancock, and the like—worried lest the Jack Tars and others in the lower orders, who were in many ways oppressed as much by the indigenous wealthy as by the British, turn their anger on them, those who dominated the colonial money and power. They worked hard to keep channeling mob actions toward Britain. Overall, they succeeded; but the Revolution left behind more than the recognition that the British had assaulted liberty; it left behind the scent of class differences that had been camouflaged, rather than addressed, by the mutual fight to win independence.

Charleston, South Carolina, dumped tea into the nearby river. Boston held a second tea party in March 1774, when the "Indians" again went to work.

A furious Lord North and Parliament retaliated against Massachusetts by enacting what the colonists called the Coercive Acts. They closed the port of Boston, restricted town meetings, and required local authorities to provide housing for troops. A military leader, General Thomas Gage, replaced Hutchinson as governor. These moves convinced Bostonians that Britain was out to crush their liberty.

The Boston Tea Party reinvigorated a revolutionary movement that had lost its momentum. A pleased Samuel Adams called the Tea Party "the perfect crisis," and, indeed, it moved the colonists much closer to a rebellion against British rule. At the same time, the Tea Party cost the colonists much support in England, where even moderates condemned the action. The Boston Tea Party gave birth to an even larger radicalism, the Revolution of 1776, that included among its many features a commitment to a republican government—a bold political system in a world dominated by monarchs.

Further Reading

Labaree, Benjamin Woods. *The Boston Tea Party*. New York: Oxford University Press, 1964.

A Shaker Community Is Established in New York

1774

Believing in the Second Coming of Christ and in the purging of sin, the Shakers founded societies based on communal property and beliefs in celibacy and the equality of all human beings.

Any story about the Shakers must acknowledge the important role played by Ann Lee, led the group to America. She was born on February 29, 1736, in Manchester, England at a time when that city was experiencing religious questioning and revivals that challenged the Church of England, or the Anglican church. In 1759, her father joined a breakaway group of Quakers, led by Jane and James Wardley. Like the Quakers, members of this group would pray until the Holy Spirit caused the body to quake; in this case, though, the more frenetic motions caused observers to add "shaking" to their descriptive word "quaking," and the sect became known as the Shaking Quakers. These religious enthusiasts claimed that they could communicate with the Holy Spirit, whose power resulted in speaking in tongues. They believed also that they could predict events and heal the sick, and they believed in the Second Coming of Christ, who would appear in the form of a woman.

Ann Lee joined this group, which suffered persecution for its beliefs. Disruptive to the point of being antagonistic, she and other Shakers sometimes interrupted Anglican services by bursting out in their speaking in tongues. On several occasions, Ann Lee was mobbed, and once she was stoned by an angry crowd.

In 1762, she married Abraham Stanley, apparently reluctantly, and over the next few years gave birth to four children, none of whom lived beyond infancy. In 1770, while imprisoned for one of her outbursts during an Anglican service, she claimed to have had a vision of Christ, who revealed to her "the very act of transgression committed by the first man and woman in the garden of Eden." Since, according to this vision, Adam and Eve had engaged in sexual intercourse out of lust, she advocated celibacy as essential to the deliverance from sin. She told a small group of her adherents about her vision, and they began calling her "Ann the Word" and "Mother Ann." Soon thereafter, she experienced another vision that told her to immigrate to America.

Mother Ann arrived at New York in August 1774. Presently her husband left her, and she joined her followers in 1776 at their settlement in Watervliet, near Albany. The Shakers, formally called the United Society of Believers in Christ's Second Appearing, converted many.

During the American Revolution, the Shakers held to their belief in pacifism and opposed the taking of oaths, positions that caused Ann Lee to be arrested for treason. Between 1781 and 1783, she toured New England, seeking converts. She died at Watervliet on September 8, 1784.

Fortunately for the Shakers, other talented members stepped forward to provide leadership. Beginning in 1787, James Meacham refined the Shaker laws and Shaker theology. His *A Concise Statement of the Principles of the Only True Church According to the Gospel of the Present Appearance of Christ* (1790) outlined "in what manner we find acceptance with God." Meacham recruited Lucy Wright to help him lead the Shakers, and together they organized 11 Shaker societies with 1,400 members. The Shakers continued to expand in the early-to-mid-1800s, with more than 1,500 members in 1810; 2,000 in 1820; and around 2,500 in 1840. Shaker societies appeared in several New England states and in the Midwest, Kentucky, Georgia, and Florida.

The Shaker settlements consisted of one or more "families" of about 30 persons each. Men and women lived together in the same buildings; to maintain celibacy among the members, the buildings were divided between the sexes, and men and women were prohibited from worshipping or eating together. Any children brought in by converts were separated from their parents.

The Shakers operated their settlements based on their belief, radical at the time, in complete sexual, ethnic, and racial equality. To them, men and women were equal in both the spiritual and temporal world, and they welcomed Jews and blacks in an era when both suffered widespread discrimination in society.

Early on, the Shakers engaged in mortification of the flesh, inflicting pain on themselves in a form noted by one 1812 observer: "They often dance with vehemence through the greatest part of the night . . . they would by way of further penance, lie down upon the floor on chains, ropes, sticks." They later dropped self-flagellation and instead emphasized dances with complex movements. The Shakers stressed the celibate life, justifying it by Christ's example. Regarding marriage, they said the rest of the world can "direct its churches to wink at the worse than brutish lusts exercised behind them, we nevertheless declare the flesh to be an abomination in the sight of God."

The Shakers believed that they could communicate with the dead, and they rejected both the Trinity and physical resurrection. They held all property in common and strove to make their communities prosperous, neat, and orderly. They considered hard work virtuous in the eyes of God. Consequently, although their communities were largely agricultural, they engaged in fine craftsmanship, producing furniture known for its sparse, sharp lines. One observer said that "the peculiar grace of a Shaker chair is that it was made by someone capable of believing that an angel might come and sit on it."

Beginning in the late 1800s, Shaker communities went into decline; one after another, they began disappearing, partly a result of the practice of celibacy, partly a result of the failure of the Shakers to win converts from a larger society that had embraced industrialization, materialism, and a more secular existence. Today, one active Shaker community remains, a settlement of seven persons at Sabbathday Lake, Maine. Despite the collapse of so many Shaker settlements, the extended vibrancy of the movement stands as testament to the ability of a communistic, Christian-based community to survive over a long period.

Further Reading

Campion, Nardi Reeder. *Mother Ann Lee: Morning Star of the Shakers.* Hanover, N.H.: University Press of New England, 1990.

Francis, Richard. *Ann, the Word: The Story of Ann Lee, Female Messiah, Mother of the Shakers, the Woman Clothed with the Sun.* New York: Arcade, 2001.

Quakers Form Pennsylvania Abolition Society

1775

With Americans began moving closer toward declaring their independence from Britain, Quakers in Philadelphia took seriously the talk about freedom and liberty, and they organized the Pennsylvania Society for Promoting the Abolition of Slavery.

In 1775, Quaker leader Anthony Benezet (see entry, 1766) issued the call for the first meeting of what was officially named the Pennsylvania Society for Promoting the Abolition of Slavery, for the Release of Negroes Unlawfully Held in Bondage, and for Improving the Condition of the African Race. The first formally organized antislavery society, it represented the religious impulse that undergirded the abolition movement. To these Quakers, slavery was a sin for which God would one day administer harsh punishment. The group concentrated on stopping the importation of slaves and trying to assure that free African-Americans enjoyed the same civil rights as did whites.

After the Revolutionary War, the society attracted as members such prominent men as Thomas Paine and Benjamin Franklin, who served as its president. Paine and Franklin pressured the Pennsylvania legislature to pass a bill in 1780 that called for the gradual abolition of slavery. In the late 1700s and early 1800s, the society tracked the activities of slave vessels and protested the landing of their human cargo.

The society so vigorously challenged slavery that many whites considered it to be a subversive group. Looking back on the eventual end of slavery, the society can be hailed as highly successful, but prior to the 1840s it struggled. In 1817, the society complained that "those actively engaged in the cause of the oppressed Africans are very small."

The Pennsylvania Society eventually extended membership to women, and in the mid-1800s, it admitted blacks, including some involved in the Underground Railroad, a series of safe houses that encouraged slaves to run away from their masters and escape to freedom in the North. After the Civil War, with slavery eliminated, the society concentrated on improving the conditions in which African-Americans lived. For example, it established schools for blacks in Philadelphia and raised money for black colleges. Today the society continues to provide aid to African-Americans.

Further Reading

Soderlund, Jean R. *Quakers and Slavery: A Divided Spirit.* Princeton, N.J.: Princeton University Press, 1985.

1776 Thomas Paine's *Common Sense* Rallies the Revolutionary Cause

A revolutionary of the world, Thomas Paine wrote several pamphlets, among them Common Sense, *that encouraged Americans to declare their independence from Britain. His later work stimulated Britons into pushing for reforms within their own country, defended the French Revolution, and criticized Christianity.*

Thomas Paine was born on January 29, 1737, in Thetford, England. His father, a Quaker staymaker (a person who made whalebone stays for corsets), and his mother, the daughter of a local attorney, raised him in modest surroundings. At age 13, Paine quit grammar school and apprenticed in his father's trade.

Paine worked as a staymaker for several years before signing on as an excise tax collector in Alford, Lincolnshire in 1762. There followed a long period in which Paine failed at nearly everything. In 1765, he was fired from his job for neglect of duty. He then taught school for awhile before resuming work as a tax collector, this time in Lewes, Sussex. But in 1773, he was fired again for inciting his fellow tax collectors to demand higher salaries. Soon thereafter, he and his second wife separated. (His first wife had died several years earlier.) During this tumult, Paine earned little money and experienced firsthand the plight of the poor in the towns of southeastern England. As a result, his writings would frequently address the problem of poverty, and his language would be that of the commoner rather than the educated elite.

In 1774, Paine sailed for America, determined to start life anew. He arrived at Philadelphia in November and obtained a job as editor of *Pennsylvania Magazine.* Just weeks earlier, the First Continental Congress had met and voted to ban all trade with Britain in the wake of Parliament's passage of the Coercive Acts, legislation aimed at punishing rebellious Boston, Massachusetts.

While socializing with artisans in local taverns and engaging in debates between fall 1775 and January 1776, Paine wrote a 47-page pamphlet, *Common Sense.* In vivid language, he criticized the British system as flawed and advocated a republican government founded on broad manhood suffrage. In promoting republicanism and independence, his words rang clear as a liberty bell, rallying common people and leaders alike; they carried with them a sharp rejection of Britain, showing the colonial disgust with being treated as second-class citizens. "There is something absurd in supposing a continent to be perpetually governed by an island," he wrote. "France and Spain never were, nor perhaps ever will be, our enemies as Americans, but as our being the subjects of Great Britain." In effect, Paine was arguing for a fortified American identity, and he posed a startling question: did America need Britain? "I challenge the warmest advocate for conciliation to show a single advantage that this continent can reap being connected with Great Britain."

More than 100,000 copies of the pamphlet were sold in three months; John Adams, the Massachusetts patriot, disliked Paine's political excesses, but said of him: "Without the pen of Paine the sword of Washington would have been wielded in vain." Paine's pamphlet helped lessen fears that the colonists would stand no chance of winning a war against Britain, and, more important, it inspired the colonists to see themselves as Americans rather than Britons. Writing in *Tom Paine and Revolutionary America* (1976), Eric Foner claims that *Common Sense* did something else, that in extolling a republican government, "Paine literally transformed the political language. 'Republic' had previously been used as a term of abuse in political writing; Paine made it a living political issue and a utopian ideal."

During the Revolution, Paine supported Pennsylvania radicals who established the most democratic of all the new state governments, but he was mainly involved in national affairs. In 1776, he was

Tom Paine: His Revolution Continued

For Tom Paine, his *Common Sense* and participation in the American Revolution was just the beginning of his radical activity. In 1791, Paine published the first part of his *Rights of Man* in response to Edmund Burke's attack on the French Revolution. Where Burke had stressed the wisdom and stability of the British government as derived from tradition, Paine responded: "Every age and generation must be free to act for itself, in all cases, as the ages and generations which preceded it."

In *The Rights of Man, Part Second* (1792), he presented a radical plan to end poverty through welfare. *The Rights of Man* sold widely in Britain, and Paine became a hero to radical societies then emerging as part of a reform movement in that country. It sold well in the United States, too, and convinced many Americans to support the French Revolution.

In September 1792, the year he arrived in Paris, Paine was elected to the revolutionary French National Convention, but he angered a radical faction when he opposed the beheading of King Louis XVI, and they had him arrested. While in prison from December 1793 to November 1794, he wrote part one of the *Age of Reason*, in which he presented his deist philosophy, arguing that revelations, miracles, and divine inspiration found in the Bible were invalid in the face of reason. In 1797, Paine wrote *Agrarian Justice*, in which he called for governments to implement inheritance taxes as a way to lessen disparities in wealth.

Paine returned to the United States in 1802, but Americans either ignored or abhorred him. There were several reasons for this, most notably his radical economic ideas and his attacks on orthodox religion. Quite likely Paine suffered retribution because he had appealed to the common people, a heresy among America's elite.

Thomas Paine died on June 8, 1809, in New York City; only a handful of people attended his funeral. Forgotten at death, he would be remembered by radical labor groups in the mid-1830s who honored him as a friend of the masses. And that he was—when he wrote many of his works he had their oppression in mind, along with the possibility of effecting great social and economic change. "From what we now see, nothing of reform in the political world ought be held improbable," he wrote in *The Rights of Man*. "It is an age of revolutions, in which everything may be looked for."

---

appointed aide-de-camp to General Nathanael Greene in New Jersey. Later that year, he wrote *The American Crisis*, which may well have contributed to the victory of the Continental Army over the Hessian soldiers at the Battle of Trenton. Before crossing the Delaware River to launch the attack, General Washington (1732–99) ordered that the pamphlet be read to his soldiers. The work's stirring sentiments lifted their spirits, as it did those of other revolutionaries. "These are the times that try men's souls," Paine wrote. "The summer soldier and the sunshine patriot will, in this crisis, shrink from the service of their country; but he that stand it now, deserves the love and thanks of man and woman." Tom Paine stood resolutely for republicanism embodied in an independent America.

Further Reading

Foner, Eric. *Collected Writings of Thomas Paine*. New York: Library of America, 1995.

———. *Tom Paine and Revolutionary America*. New York: Oxford University Press, 1976.

Fruchtman, Jack, Jr. *Thomas Paine, Apostle of Freedom*. New York: Four Walls Eight Windows, 1994.

Hawke, David Freeman. *Paine*. New York: Harper & Row, 1974.

Kaye, Harvey J. *Thomas Paine: Firebrand of the Revolution*. New York: Oxford University Press, 2000.

Keane, John. *Tom Paine, A Political Life*. Boston: Little, Brown, 1995.

Thomas Jefferson Writes the Declaration of Independence

1776

In a room on the second floor of a brick house in Philadelphia, at the corner of Market and Seventh streets, Thomas Jefferson surrounded himself with his papers and, from June 13 to June 28, 1776, wrote the Declaration of Independence. Even though the Continental Congress ultimately changed its wording, the document still embodied his idea, one held by many Americans, that liberty required a republican government for its survival.

For more than a year before Congress approved the Declaration of Independence, the American colonists had been in a state of war with Britain. In April 1775, British troops and colonial militiamen had exchanged shots at Lexington and Concord in Massachusetts. By the spring of the following year, the colonists had attacked Canada, and the British were assaulting colonial seaports with their navy.

Relations had deteriorated to the point where, on May 10, 1776, the Continental Congress, meeting in Philadelphia, advised the colonies to form new governments whose legitimacy would be based on the people as their source of authority, rather than the king. Then on June 7, Richard Henry Lee, a delegate from Virginia, introduced a resolution into the Congress stating:

That these United Colonies are, and of right ought to be, free and independent States, that they are absolved from all allegiance to the British Crown, and that all political connection between them and the State of Great Britain is, and ought to be, totally dissolved.

A debate ensued, but because there was much opposition to passing Lee's resolution—partly because the British had announced their willingness to discuss a plan for peace—the issue was postponed until July 1. In the meantime, Congress formed a committee to prepare a declaration of independence to which it named Roger Sherman of Connecticut, Robert R. Livingston of New York, Benjamin Franklin of Pennsylvania, John Adams of Massachusetts, and Thomas Jefferson of Virginia.

The document was largely written by Jefferson, with only minor changes by the other committeemen. Jefferson worked quickly. He later said that he labored without any books or pamphlets in hand, but he did have his draft of the new constitution for Virginia, which he had recently written, and a copy of the Virginia Declaration of Rights, which had been written largely by George Mason. The ideas and phrases from both of these appeared in Jefferson's Declaration of Independence.

Jefferson's opening paragraph used eloquent words to describe the formation of the United States as a monumental event. There followed his history-altering sentence, "We hold these truths to be self-evident; that all men are created equal; that they are endowed by their Creator with inherent and inalienable rights, that among these are life, liberty, and the pursuit of happiness." Jefferson next listed the "long train of abuses and usurpations" committed by King George III. He concluded the Declaration by stating that the colonies were "independent states" and that the congressional delegates, in support of the Declaration, "mutually pledge to each other our lives, our fortunes, and our sacred honor."

Congress received Jefferson's draft on June 28, 1776. Peace attempts having failed, on July 2, it affirmed the independence of the colonies; then it met as a committee of the whole and rewrote the document. Sensitive to criticism, Jefferson sat in anguish as Congress made its revisions. Sometimes the editing was slight, as in changing "inherent and inalienable rights" to "certain inalienable rights." At other times, Congress reworked entire passages, such as when it deleted Jefferson's condemnation of the king for "captivating and carrying" Africans into slavery. Jefferson later said the passage was stricken because delegates from South Carolina and Georgia complained about it, supported by northern states that participated in the trade. But there may have been another reason: the delegates recognized the contradiction between continuing slavery and fighting for liberty and wanted to avoid calling attention to their enslavement of fellow human beings.

In *American Scripture* (1997), Pauline Maier shows how the Declaration of Independence conformed to precedents. Jefferson borrowed heavily from British philosopher John Locke (1632–1703), with his reference to natural rights, and from the English Declaration of Rights, written in 1689, whose content every educated colonist knew. The Declaration of Rights, adopted by both houses of Parliament, had ushered in the reign of William and Mary by condemning the wrongdoings of King James II, such as raising and keeping a standing army in a time of peace without legislative approval. Jefferson's Declaration of Independence had been preceded in 1776 by more than 90 similar declarations passed by the states and towns. Thus, Maier argues, Jefferson offered nothing new.

But in other ways, the Declaration of Independence was truly radical. Where Locke had waxed philosophical, Jefferson applied the concept of natural rights on a scale never before attempted. Furthermore, he took Locke's insistence that all men are endowed with "life, liberty, and property" and changed it to "life, liberty, and the pursuit of happiness." That phrase expressed a more individualistic and subjective goal. Historian Cecelia Kenyon states: "If happiness is really an end of government, and if all men have by nature an equal right in pursuit of it, then it follows logically that every man should have a voice in the determination of public policy."

Above all else, where Locke maintained that natural rights could be protected within an authoritarian political system, Jefferson insisted that it required a republican one. Clearly, the Declaration of Independence was declaring more than *independence*; it was pronouncing a republican government in an era of monarchies. Although Congress struck the passage pertaining to slavery, the Declaration stood as a principled statement upholding human rights, establishing ideals against which future generations would measure the fulfillment of liberty, or the failure to protect it. Consequently, activists and reformers of many persuasions during various times would look not to the legalistic Constitution for inspiration and guidance but to the morally uplifting Declaration of Independence.

Further Reading

Becker, Carl Lotus. *Declaration of Independence: A Study in the History of Political Ideas.* New York: Vintage Books, 1958.

Maier, Pauline. *American Scripture: Making the Declaration of Independence.* New York: Knopf, 1997.

Wills, Garry. *Inventing America: Jefferson's Declaration of Independence.* New York: Random House, 1979.

Abigail Adams Speaks for the Rights of Women 1776

John Adams considered his wife, Abigail Adams, indispensable to his own political success; in fact, she provided everything from emotional support in his career to financial leadership in running the family farm. Society, however, considered her always his helpmate and never his equal, and in recognizing this restriction, both for herself and other women, she boldly urged her husband and others to work for a legal system more fair to wives.

Born on November 11, 1744, in Weymouth, Massachusetts, to Elizabeth Quincy Smith and William Smith, the minister of the North Parish Congregational church, Abigail Adams grew up reading extensively and learning the domestic skills expected of women, such as sewing and cooking. On October 25, 1764, she married John Adams, then a young lawyer, nine years her senior. While he built his law practice in Boston and became involved in the political crisis with Britain that would lead to the American Revolution, she managed the family farm in Braintree (later renamed Quincy), making it profitable and contributing to the financial support of their family, which by then included two children.

In the late 1760s and early 1770s, Abigail gave birth to four children in little more than five years. She continued to manage the Braintree farm for long periods during the Revolution, a time when her husband served as a delegate to the Continental Congress in Philadelphia and as a diplomat in France.

The same revolutionary leaders who protested the British infringements on liberty showed little concern for the restrictions society placed on women. In Massachusetts, women were prohibited from voting, holding political office, or even attending town meetings. Abigail Adams, however, rejected the dictum that women should remain silent in politics; instead, she and her husband shared a lively discourse on the issues of the day. She read widely, including the classical literature that influenced John

Adams and other revolutionary leaders, and strongly supported the resistance to Parliament's authority. In 1774, she told the British author Catherine Macaulay that "the only alternative which every American thinks of is Liberty or Death."

By late 1775, she was eager for the colonies to separate from Britain and in a letter to her husband criticized the Continental Congress for moving too slowly. She received a copy of Thomas Paine's pamphlet *Common Sense*, and praised it, saying, "I have spread it as much as it lay in my power, every one assents to the weighty truths it contains."

On March 31, 1776, the Continental Congress moved closer to declaring independence, and Abigail wrote a letter to John Adams that in later years would become much-quoted. In it she urged that the status of women be considered in any governmental change. She said:

I long to hear that you have declared an independancy—and by the way in the new Code of Laws which I suppose it will be necessary for you to make I desire you would Remember the Ladies, and be more generous and favourable to them than your ancestors. Do not put such unlimited power into the hands of the Husbands. Remember all Men would be tyrants if they could. If particular care and attention is not paid to the Ladies we are determined to foment a Rebellion, and will not hold ourselves bound by any Laws in which we have no voice, or Representation.

Abigail Adams. (Library of Congress)

She called men "naturally tyrannical," but said that "Men of Sense in all Ages abhor those customs which treat us only as the vassals of your Sex." She asked: "Regard us then as Beings placed by providence under your protection and in immitation of the Supreem Being make use of that power only for our happiness."

Abigail Adams was not issuing a clarion call for full equality between men and women. Prior to the Revolution, the colonies had been moving closer to English laws that more severely restricted women, and Adams saw independence as a way to stop that drift and liberalize the existing legal system. She wanted laws that would balance the power held by husbands in marriage. In general, she wanted to make it easier for married women to take court action against abusive husbands and for women to enjoy a greater share in the material rewards that came from couples working together.

John Adams replied to her in a joking vein, trying to deflect her criticism. Still, Abigail pressed her ideas, and at one point, in a letter to the author Mercy Otis Warren, she suggested that a petition be sent to the Continental Congress. Abigail was aware that after the Revolution, mothers would have to instill republican values in their children if the republic were to survive. She accepted this role but insisted it required "learned women," meaning that women should be permitted an education.

The American Revolution failed, in the short term, to liberate women. Admittedly, the crisis itself caused some women, such as Abigail, to assume larger roles in society, and some laws respecting women were liberalized, but during the late 1700s and early 1800s the "cult of true womanhood" took hold, a belief that women should live domestic lives and submit to their husbands. When women did launch a fight for greater rights, in efforts ranging from the Seneca Falls Convention of 1848 to the women's liberation movement of the 1970s, they employed the words of Abigail Adams to show that sexism—and resistance to it—had long been a part of marriage and the male domination of society.

Further Reading

Akers, Charles W. *Abigail Adams: An American Woman.* New York: HarperCollins, 1980.

Gelles, Edith. *Portia: The World of Abigail Adams.* Bloomington: Indiana University Press, 1992.

Keller, Rosemary Skinner. *Patriotism and the Female Sex: Abigail Adams and the American Revolution.* Brooklyn, N.Y.: Carlson Publishing, 1994.

Levin, Phyllis. *Abigail Adams: A Biography.* New York: St. Martin's Press, 1987.

Withey, Lynne. *Dearest Friend: A Life of Abigail Adams.* New York: Free Press, 1981.

Judith Sargent Murray Argues for Equality of the Sexes

1790

Judith Sargent Murray used her writing to present radical ideas to the American people about the relationship between men and women. She advocated education for women, and in her article "On the Equality of Sexes," (1790) she declared women equal in intelligence to men.

Judith Sargent Murray was born Judith Sargent on May 1, 1751, in Gloucester, Massachusetts. Her father, Winthrop Sargent, was a prosperous merchant. While still a younster, Judith showed her discontent with the social strictures that relegated females to a secondary status. In an era when even the girls of elite families—such as Judith's—were not expected to receive an education, she learned only to read and write and sew. She wanted desperately to learn more, especially to attend classes in Latin, but her parents refused her request. Later she complained about her limited education and claimed she grew up "wild and untutored."

Yet she read extensively and was particularly attracted to women writers. Inspired by their works, she contemplated becoming a writer herself. In 1769, she married John Stevens, a merchant who experienced declining fortunes. Then in the mid-1770s, her discontent with social strictures reappeared when she deserted her family's Puritan congregational religion for Universalism. She liked the egalitarianism espoused by the Universalists, their belief that men and women were spiritually related and that both would be saved.

In 1782, John Murray, the founder of the first Universalist Church in America (located in Gloucester, Massachusetts) read some of Judith's writings and began showing them to friends. He urged her to continue her writing, and she became excited about the prospect of developing a readership for her works. In 1782, she wrote a Universalist catechism. In the preface, she recognized the unusual path she was pursuing. "When a female steps without the Line in which Custom hath circumscribed her," she said, "she naturally becomes an Object of Speculation." She continued: "The public Eye is very incompatible with the native Modesty in which our Sex are inshrined."

By 1784, her poems and essays were appearing in New England literary magazines. Her essay "Desultory Thoughts Upon the Utility of Encouraging a Degree of Self-Complacency Especially in Female Bosoms," (1784) expressed her belief that women's intellectual ability equaled that of men. Such ideas appeared amid

Indians and the American Revolution

The American Revolution greatly affected Indians living east of the Mississippi River, mostly for the worse. When the fighting began, their loyalties were divided. Some Indians remained neutral in the conflict; others favored the revolutionaries in the hope that Indian land would be spared from the grasping settlers then spilling across the Appalachians. Many more sided with the British because they were angry at the way the colonists had treated them in the past, and because they believed the British posed less of a threat to their lands. In several instances, the war caused a deep rift among Native Americans: the Iroquois Confederacy, for example, split apart as the Mohawks supported the British and smaller contingents sided with the Americans.

Regardless of which side they chose, the Indians fought with determination. In July 1778, 500 Iroquois joined 400 British Loyalists in an attack along Pennsylvania's Susquehanna River, destroying more than 1,000 houses; in November of that year, Loyalists and Mohawks, numbering about 700 in all, burned the American settlement at Cherry Valley, west of Albany, New York.

When the war ended in 1783, the United States invoked the Treaty of Paris to assert its claim to Indian lands west of the Appalachians. The Indians rejected this ploy, reminding the Americans they had not signed the treaty. Yet the new U.S. government and the state governments used a variety of tactics, including bribery and coercion, to force treaties on the Indians that resulted in the tribes losing millions of acres. Even those Native Americans who had supported the revolutionaries, such as the Oneida and Tuscarora, lost most of their lands. Clearly the U.S. government, like the Colonial ones before it, continued patterns that in years to come would cause Native Americans to be conquered, killed, and relegated to ever smaller enclaves.

much post-Revolutionary debate in the United States about the status of women and whether they could or should participate in politics and other affairs outside the family and home. The American Revolution actually did little to liberate women, but at least it encouraged some to question society's strictures.

In 1787, John Stevens died, and in 1788, Judith married John Murray. Two years later, her essay "On the Equality of Sexes" appeared in *Massachusetts Magazine*. "Is it upon mature consideration we adopt the idea, that nature is thus partial in her distributions?" she asked. "Is it indeed a fact, that she hath yielded to one half of the human species so unquestionable a mental superiority? I know that to both sexes elevated understandings, and the reverse, are common."

In 1798, she published *The Gleaner*, a collection of her poems and essays covering such subjects as politics, religion, morals, and manners. Some critics hated the book; President John Adams praised it. She told an acquaintance: "It is written with the care and in the highest style of elegance, propriety of diction, and chastity of sentiment, which I could command."

Then, for reasons unclear, her literary production declined. She may have been preoccupied with caring for her daughter or for her husband, who became seriously ill, or she may have been disappointed with those who attacked her writing. In 1808, she complained about "repeated mortifications and rebuffs."

Judith Sargent Murray had a strong conservative streak. She defended the Federalist Party as best able to control the masses and fight disorder. And while she promoted the intellectual equality of women with men, she never advocated that women shape their lives as men did; she accepted the importance to women of marriage and motherhood (though she insisted women should not *have* to marry) and said God and nature intended such a role for them. Nevertheless, she stated that women must be educated to be good wives and mothers, and she insisted that women must have the right to make certain choices. These views put her well ahead of mainstream society and pointed the way to the women's rights movement of the nineteenth century.

Further Reading

Skemp, Sheila A. *Judith Sargent Murray: A Brief Biography with Documents.* New York: St. Martin's Press, 1998.

Daniel Shays Leads a Revolt by Farmers in Massachusetts

1786

In 1786, Daniel Shays led a rebellion of farmers against high taxes and deteriorating economic conditions in Massachusetts. These Shaysites resorted to the violence that had been used in the American Revolution to protect liberty.

Shays's Rebellion began during widespread economic distress and intense instability. While Americans today take for granted the continued existence of their country, such was not the case in 1786. At that time, the United States was only 10 years old, and many forecast that the republic would not last long in a hostile world dominated by monarchies.

Economic problems encouraged the gloomy predictions and ignited the rebellion. Postwar depression gripped the country, causing farmers to suffer from falling prices for their crops. At the same time, creditors wanted them to pay their debts in hard currency rather than less valuable paper money. In Massachusetts, the legislature increased taxes to eliminate the state's Revolutionary War debt; consequently, between 1783 and 1786, taxes on land rose 60 percent. With that, farmers in many parts of the state, but especially in the west, began demanding reduced levies and stay laws that would prevent property foreclosures. The lower house responded by passing relief measures, but the upper house, under the influence of eastern creditors, rejected them.

Amid a worsening economic crisis, the legislature announced in July 1786 that it would adjourn until January 1787. Many farmers felt frustrated and held town conventions where they wrote down their grievances. But with the legislature refusing to meet, they concluded that the Massachusetts government was as unresponsive in 1786 as had been the British Crown in 1776.

In the east, armed mobs formed. One operating in Northampton in August 1786 prevented a court from meeting. In September, mobs under the direction of Job Shattuck disrupted court sessions in Concord. In late November, however, government troops arrested Shattuck and quelled the disturbances.

In the west, though, insurrection spread throughout the Berkshires as farmers gathered in armed groups, including those organized under Daniel Shays (1747–1825). At that time 39 years old, Shays had worked before the Revolutionary War as a farm laborer. During the war, he earned a reputation for bravery at Bunker Hill and in 1779 was promoted to captain. In the months preceding the insurrection, he was plagued with debt and drawn into the protest by radicals who met near his farm.

Some 1,500 farmers organized under Shays; they marched on the courts to prevent mortgage foreclosure hearings and broke into jails to release debtors. A contemporary observer outlined the reasons for the protest: "the present expensive mode of collecting debts, which, by reason of the great scarcity of cash, will of necessity fill our gaols with unhappy debtors"; a second, "a suspension of the writ of Habeas Corpus, by which those persons who have stepped forth to assert and maintain the rights of the people, are liable to be taken and conveyed even to the most distant part of the Commonwealth, and [are] thereby subjected to an unjust punishment."

A leader of the Massachusetts elite, Benjamin Lincoln, observed that "the proportion of debtors run high in this State. Too many of them are against the government. The men of property . . . are generally abettors of our present constitution, but few of them have been in the field, and it remains quite problematical whether they will in time fully discover their own interests . . . [and] lend for a season out of their property for the security of the remainder." Despite Lincoln's doubts, they did "lend for a season out of their property" when eastern creditors provided the money for the state to raise an army, with the troops commanded by Lincoln. On January 25, 1787, Shays tried to capture the arsenal at Springfield but was turned back by an artillery barrage, and on February 4, 1787, the uprising effectively ended when Lincoln's army defeated Shays's force at Petersham.

Shays and 13 of his followers were condemned to death; at a trial for four of the rebels, Massachusetts Chief Justice William Cushing said they had tried "to overturn all government and order," and that they had given in "to the power of the most restless, malevolent, destructive, tormenting passions." Daniel Shays avoided trial by fleeing to New Hampshire and then Vermont, before settling in western New York. The Massachusetts government eventually pardoned him and all of the rebels.

Shays's Rebellion shook the political system. In Massachusetts, the voters threw out the conservative leadership in spring 1787, electing one more representative of farmers. The legislature subsequently passed several reforms, including a law that exempted clothing, household goods, and tools of trade from impoundment for debt.

In the country as a whole, Shays's rebellion stunned conservatives and others concerned with order who called it an instance of the unlettered gaining too much power and threatening anarchy. One member of the elite said, "The natural effects of pure democracy are already produced among us. It is a war against virtue, talents, and property carried on by the dregs and scum of mankind." Those discontent with the upheaval acted to form a stronger national government that could contain democratic impulses and secure order by righting the economy and, if necessary, using military force. In 1787, they met in Philadelphia, where they discarded the Articles of Confederation and replaced them with the Constitution.

Daniel Shays died in poverty and obscurity at age 78. Many Americans, including the revolutionary leader Samuel Adams, thought that Shays had gone too far and had threatened to unleash lawlessness and even class warfare, but Shays and his followers saw themselves as acting within the precedents set out by the American Revolution. Thomas Jefferson said in defense of Shays's Rebellion: "The tree of liberty must be refreshed from time to time with the blood of patriots and tyrants. It is its natural manure." That, indeed, was the radical alternative Daniel Shays had provided.

Further Reading

Szatmary, David P. *Shays's Rebellion: The Making of an Agrarian Insurrection.* Amherst: University of Massachusetts Press, 1990.

1792 African-American Benjamin Banneker Challenges White Racism

A free African-American, Benjamin Banneker challenged racist views in 1792, when he compiled an almanac. Through his work as a mathematician and astronomer, he intended to raise questions about slavery and the racial assumptions behind it.

Benjamin Banneker (sometimes spelled Bannaker) was born on November 9, 1731, near Baltimore, Maryland, the son of a former slave named Robert, and of Mary Banneky, a free mulatto. He had little formal education but was taught to read by his grandmother. Self-taught thereafter, he worked on his parents' land raising tobacco.

Banneker showed an interest in mechanics, and in 1753 he studied the inside workings of a pocket watch and built a wooden clock that kept accurate time for 40 years. In 1788, George Ellicott, a member of a prominent white family, was so impressed with Banneker's abilities that he lent him four books on mathematics and astronomy, a telescope, and several other astronomical instruments. With these Banneker began computing ephemeredes, tables that showed the location of celestial bodies.

In 1792, Banneker compiled his almanac, titled *Benjamin Banneker's Pennsylvania, Delaware, Maryland, and Virginia Almanack and Ephemeris, for the Year of Our Lord, 1792.* As was customary for almanacs of the time, most of its text came from other sources, while Banneker supplied the astronomical calculations.

He intended his almanac to challenge white views about African-American inferiority. The publication stated:

> The editors . . . feel themselves gratified in the Opportunity of presenting to the Public . . . what must be considered an extraordinary effort of Genius—a complete and accurate EPHEMERIS . . . calculated by a sable descendant of Africa, who, by this Specimen of Ingenuity, evinces, to Demonstration, that mental Powers and Endowment, are not the exclusive Excellence of white People, but that the Rays of Science may alike illumine the Minds of Men of every Clime, (however they may differ in the Colour of their Skin) particularly those whom Tyrant-Custom hath too long taught us to depreciate as a Race inferior in intellectual capacity.

The almanac included a letter from prominent political leader James McHenry (who later served as President John Adams's secretary of war) attesting to Banneker's background as a free black man who had developed an interest late in life for astronomy, a result of Banneker having benefited from the books provided by George Ellicott. McHenry assured the readers that when Ellicott gave Banneker the books he did so without "either hint or instruction that might further his studies. Or lead him to apply them to any useful result." He went on to say that "whatever merit is attached to his present performances, is exclusively and peculiarly his own." McHenry said that accomplishments such as those of Banneker's must lead in time to the weakening of slavery "should no check impede the progress of humanity."

Shortly before the almanac was published, Banneker sent a manuscript copy of it to Thomas Jefferson, along with a letter that challenged assumptions about black inferiority and that criticized Jefferson for supporting slavery. Banneker said that although African-Americans "have long been considered rather as brutish than human, and scarcely capable of mental endowments . . . one universal Father hath given being to us all; and that he hath not only made us all of one flesh, but that he hath also, without partiality, afforded us all the same sensations and endowed us all with the same faculties." He added these lines from Jefferson's own Declaration of Independence: "We hold these truths to be self-evident, that all men are created equal."

Jefferson answered by stating that "nobody wishes more than I to see such proofs as you exhibit, that nature hath given to our black brethren talents equal to those of the

Banneker's (also spelled Bannaker) Almanac. (Bettmann/CORBIS)

other colours of men & that the appearance of a want of them is owing merely to the degraded condition of their existence both in Africa and America." He said that he longed to see a system established to educate blacks, and he advised Banneker that he had "taken the liberty" to send the almanac to the Marquis de Condorcet, secretary of the Academy of Science at Paris and an advocate of racial equality, to challenge those who doubted black intelligence.

Several years later, though, Jefferson ridiculed Banneker. In 1807, he told a visitor to the White House that Banneker's letters had been "childish and trivial." In 1809, he wrote to his friend Joel Barlow that Banneker knew trigonometry enough to compile almanacs but was likely helped in his work by George Ellicott. "I have a long letter from Banneker," Jefferson said, "that shows him to have had a mind of very common stature indeed."

Banneker published his almanacs until 1797, when he discontinued them for unknown reasons. In his last years, he was able to maintain himself through the sale of his farmland. He died on October 26, 1806. Some called him the "first Negro man of science," and the appellation carries with it much truth, but it provides only part of the story. Banneker took a bold stand in expressing his views about African-American capabilities at a time when there were few free blacks in the South and when every utterance that implied racial equality risked complete condemnation.

Further Reading

Bedini, Silvio A. *The Life of Benjamin Banneker: The First African-American Man of Science.* 2d ed., revised and expanded. Baltimore: Maryland Historical Society, 1999.

1793 Democratic Societies Form to Protect Republican Government

In 1793, Americans who were discontented with the policies of the federal government formed Democratic Societies to protect republicanism from what they called monarchical power. Moderate in goals, the societies nevertheless represented the spirit of revolution.

Imagine a new nation with an unstable political system and a republican form of government, one without a monarch and based on the people electing their representatives, one that many observers predicted would be short-lived. That was the United States in 1793, the year the Democratic Societies first appeared. They were organized in the wake of a visit to the United States by Edmund-Charles Genet (1763–1834). Genet, a diplomat sent by the French revolutionary government, was on a mission to defy President Washington's proclamation of neutrality in the war then underway between Britain and France. His goal was to rally Americans in support of the French cause.

Critics of the Democratic Societies claimed that Genet had organized them, but in fact he could be directly linked to only two of the 37 societies. These societies were clearly children of the American and French Revolutions, representing the spirit of protest and republican principles those wars exemplified. But more than revolutionary influences propelled their formation. They were organized in reaction to policies of the Washington Administration, as promoted by Washington's secretary of the treasury, and the leader of the emerging Federalist Party, Alexander Hamilton (1755/7–1804). Those policies, such as the formation of a national bank, favored a wealthy elite.

The Democratic Societies aligned themselves with Hamilton's two chief opponents, Thomas Jefferson (1743–1826) and James Madison (1751–1836). Consisting primarily of craftsmen with some merchants, slaveowners, and laborers, the societies organized voters. While expressing complete loyalty to the Constitution, they voiced their support for the French Revolution as an extension of America's own fight for liberty and distributed copies of Thomas Paine's radical publication, *The Rights of Man* (1791).

The Democratic Societies represented popular participation in politics, fighting against an elite they saw as intent on destroying republicanism and instituting a monarchy. In 1793, the Democratic Society of Philadelphia proclaimed:

> The Rights of Man, the genuine objects of Society, and the legitimate principles of Government, have been clearly developed by the successive revolutions of America and France. Those events have withdrawn the veil which concealed the dignity and happiness of the human race, and have taught us, no longer dazzled with the adventitious pleasure, or awed by antiquated usurpation, to erect the Temple of Liberty on the ruins of Palaces and Thrones.

However moderate the societies were in working within the political system, Hamilton fumed about them. He considered their sympathies for the French Revolution dangerous—as far as he was concerned, anyone who supported France embraced anarchy over order and rule by a mob over rule by educated leaders. He feared that the societies would emulate the violence of the French Revolution with its beheading of monarchs and noblemen.

His fears intensified when the Whiskey Rebellion erupted in western Pennsylvania (see entry, 1794). He blamed the uprising on the societies. Other prominent Federalists agreed, and one of them, Oliver Wolcott, Jr., said that "[they] speak the sentiments of certain demagogues, and . . . consist of hot-headed, ignorant, or wicked men, devoted entirely to the views of France." With anti-Federalist and anti-Washington protests erupting in several cities, President Washington waded into the controversy surrounding the Democratic Societies when he denounced them on November 19, 1794, calling them "self-created societies"—meaning unconstitutional ones. He asked the people to determine whether the Whiskey Rebellion "had not been fomented by combinations of men who, careless of consequences and disregarding the unerring truth that those who rouse cannot always appease civil convulsions, have disseminated, from ignorance or perversion of facts, suspicions, jealousies, and accusations of the whole government?"

Washington's denunciation enraged Jeffersonians in Congress, who labeled it a blatant attempt to silence political dissent. Thomas Jefferson criticized Washington for having "permitted himself to be the organ of such an attack on the freedom of discussion, the freedom of writing, printing and publishing." With Washington lending his prestige to the assault on the Democratic Societies, they rapidly collapsed, and by 1795, they had passed from the scene. The newly organized Jeffersonian Republican Party, however, absorbed the Democratic Societies, and in that way they continued to influence politics and contributed to Jefferson's election as president in 1800.

Without a doubt, large segments of America's ruling elite had concluded that the Democratic Societies were dangerous and would radically alter the political system. Washington later said: "If these societies were not counteracted (not by prosecutions, the ready way to make them grow stronger) or did not fall into disesteem from the knowledge of their origin . . . they would shake the government to its foundation."

Further Reading

Smith, James Morton. *Freedom's Fetters: The Alien and Sedition Acts and American Civil Liberties.* Rev. ed. Ithaca, N.Y.: Cornell University Press, 1989.

New York Printers Unite as a Trade Union   1794

In 1794, the New York Typographical Society organized as one of the earliest trade unions in reaction to changing conditions in the workplace.

When New York printers organized the New York Typographical Society in 1794, they were part of a trend in that decade to form trade unions. This development came in part from the influence of the American Revolution, which through example encouraged protest against oppression and which through ideology encouraged the idea that "all men are created equal," and thus should have just reward for their labors.

The formation of trade unions was also an outgrowth mutual aid societies. Printers, carpenters, hatters, tailors, and bricklayers all had founded such organizations through which their members could help one another in times of need. But now, with the gradual change in the workplace to larger units of production, and with the effects of Britain's Industrial Revolution lapping against America's shores, workers believed they needed to protect themselves from employers determined to limit pay and dictate working conditions.

The first "authentic strike" took place in the United States in 1786, when journeymen printers in Philadelphia refused to work for any printing business that paid less than six dollars a week. That strike and several others in the early 1790s were led by temporary organizations. The New York Typographical Society, however, and other trade unions like it formed with the intention of becoming permanent groups, though many lasted only a short time. The Typographical Society, for one, collapsed after little more than a decade. Yet it shaped an important characteristic of the union movement when it denied membership to those representing employers. In 1809, its constitution stated: "As the interests of the journeymen [printers] are separate and in some respects opposite to that of the employers, we deem it improper that they should have any voice or influence in our deliberations." Here was the radicalization of the labor movement, as it saw employers and employees divided into two camps, sometimes cooperative, but often antagonistic.

Unlike modern unions, these trade unions were at first local in their reach, meaning they did not have contact with unions in other cities (or even with unions within the same city representing different workers). The unions fought to protect their skilled jobs from the intrusion of unskilled labor—a losing battle as mechanization took hold in the 1800s. They fought also for a closed shop—only union members were allowed to work in a shop. Again the Typographical Society set the standard when in 1809 it stated about closed shops, "We conceive it to be *the duty* and the interest of every journeyman printer in the City to come forward and unite with his fellow-craftsmen in promoting an object which has as its end the benefit of the whole."

These early trade unions were pioneers in pursuing collective bargaining, demanding a minimum wage and collecting strike funds. They advanced worker solidarity, which most employers considered radical and dangerous. Such associations, it was charged, were affronts to American individualism.

The unions met with mixed results, but according to historian Philip S. Foner, some gains were made. Wages for carpenters in Massachusetts, for example, increased from 74 cents a day in 1791 to $1.13 in 1820; and those for painters from $1.15 a day in 1800 to $1.34 in 1820. "Persevere in your laudable struggle," said one trade union to striking workers in the early 1800s. The workers' struggle, as it turned out, was just beginning, with its radicalizing roots begun in the early trade union movement.

Further Reading

Foner, Philip S. *History of the Labor Movement in the United States: From Colonial Times to the Founding of the American Federation of Labor.* New York: International Publishers, 1947.

1794   Whiskey Rebellion Erupts in Pennsylvania

In 1794, westerners in Pennsylvania took up arms to prevent the collection of an excise tax on whiskey. This showdown involving the power of the federal government to enforce its laws and the degree to which the people could resist them contained within it a power struggle between the elite and the masses. After the settlers attacked revenue agents, the federal government declared them dangerous insurrectionists and determined to crush them.

The Whiskey Rebellion erupted as part of a long conflict in the United States over taxes. The issue had, of course, been crucial in the outbreak of the Revolution; under the Articles of Confederation, taxes imposed by a central government were so unpopular that the United States lacked the power to levy them. Then, under the Constitution and during the presidency of George Washington, the government acted to enforce an excise tax on whiskey and other items.

Washington and his aggressive treasury secretary, Alexander Hamilton (1755/7–1804), knew that a tax on whiskey would generate protest, but in 1791, they convinced Congress to enact it as a way to raise money needed to support federal programs and to show that the national government had the authority and will to collect such a levy.

Along the frontier, though, whiskey served as a means of exchange, and in western Pennsylvania farmers refused to pay the tax, which they considered oppressive. Opponents of Washington and Hamilton—a group called the Republicans then organizing around Thomas Jefferson and James Madison—denounced the tax and stirred westerners against it. The battle over the excise tax became larger than money—it became an issue of the common people versus the elite. The Republicans said, "The fate of the excise law will determine whether the powers of the government of the United States are held by an aristocratic junto or by the people. The free citizens of America will not quietly suffer the *well born few* to trample them under foot."

In July 1793, about 500 frontiersmen attacked and destroyed the house of excise collector John Neville and killed an armed guard. Beginning in summer 1794, westerners forced revenue collectors to resign their offices, sometimes at gunpoint. For his part, Hamilton purposely antagonized the people on the frontier. Only hours before a new federal law that forbade the government from forcing people in remote locations to travel long distances for trials went into effect, he ordered that writs be served on 75 distillers to appear in Philadelphia. For most of them, the city was far from their homes. In retrospect it is clear that Hamilton *wanted* to foment armed rebellion; he wanted an excuse to use the military so he could show the government's power.

At a cabinet meeting, President Washington called the protests a threat to law and order; he later claimed "the most spirited and firm measures were necessary: if such proceedings were tolerated there was an end to our Constitution." He subsequently decided to send an army into western Pennsylvania,

---

Citizens Versus Uncle Sam

On its surface, the Whiskey Rebellion seemed to be a limited complaint by a few people against a specific tax. But the rebellion was a manifestation of a deeper distrust of the national government, part of citizens' desire to protect individual rights against encroachment. Over the years, Americans have expressed ambivalent feelings about their country. On the one hand, they have exhibited intense nationalism, a pride in the United States and what it has accomplished. On the other, they have frequently complained about the power and reach of the national government.

Protests against centralized power have ranged from peaceful proposals pursued in Congress and through other legitimate political channels to armed uprisings. The formation of the Democratic Party in the 1820s was in part a reaction against plans by the ruling party to expand national government programs; so too was the conservatism of Ronald Reagan's Republican Party crusade in the 1980s.

Protests turned violent with the secession of the South in 1860–61 in a fight to protect that region's institutions, including slavery, from federal interference. Extremists advocated violence when they directed some of the militias of the 1990s to attack government facilities and turn back a threat, as they saw it, to individual rights, such as gun ownership.

Of course, other Americans have at various times looked to the national government to defend and promote liberties, as evident with the fight for civil rights and women's rights. Yet the tendency to distrust government power will likely continue, a result of the principles on which the United States was founded during the war against another centralized system, the British Crown, back in 1776.

and for that purpose Hamilton raised a militia of more than 12,000 men. James Madison called the action an excuse to "establish the principle that a standing army was necessary for *enforcing the laws*."

President Washington led the army a short distance and then left it in Hamilton's hands. But when they reached the frontier, they discovered that the frontiersmen who supported armed action had already scattered. Rather than facing armed revolutionaries, Hamilton faced derision in newspapers and in Congress when little in the way of a rebellion could be found.

Still, Hamilton sought to capture enough insurrectionists so he could make an example of them. He rounded up 150 men, but few could be legitimately classified as rebels. Ultimately, two men were convicted of treason and sentenced to die, one of whom, Hamilton admitted, was "little short of an idiot." Washington pardoned both, with Hamilton's approval.

Hamilton rejected those critics who called his expedition a folly. Instead, he said his actions had shown that the government could restore order and maintain a republican political system against a disloyal rabble. That certainly was one interpretation; another would be to see the Whiskey Rebellion as standing for republicanism and liberty against government oppression. Certainly the whiskey rebels saw it that way—a resort to arms that defended the principles of the American Revolution.

Further Reading

Boyd, Steven R., ed. *The Whiskey Rebellion: Past and Present Perspectives.* Westport, Conn.: Greenwood Press, 1985.

Slaughter, Thomas P. *The Whiskey Rebellion: Frontier Epilogue to the American Revolution.* New York: Oxford University Press, 1986.

1800 The Most Extensive Slave Revolt in American History: Gabriel's Conspiracy

Twenty-six slaves were hanged after a thunderstorm washed out a bridge and prevented rebels under the leadership of Gabriel from marching on Richmond, Virginia, and unleashing a violent attack on whites in August 1800.

Gabriel, a slave owned by Thomas Prosser, was born around the year 1776 on his master's plantation in Henrico County, Virginia. While he was growing up, high ideals and unsettling political turmoil swept across Europe and the Americas: the American Revolution declared that "all men are created equal" and pursued liberty through a war against Britain; during that war, Britain's Lord Dunmore offered slaves in Virginia their freedom if they agreed to fight against the rebels, and several thousand did so and were liberated; the French Revolution of 1789 proclaimed "liberty, equality, and fraternity!" and resorted to beheading that country's monarchs; a violent slave uprising in Haiti in 1791 struck at white rule and led to an independent black nation. Added to these developments, tension arose in the United States when two political parties, the Federalists and Republicans, vied for power in the 1790s.

Gabriel understood the arguments for liberty, the methods used to secure it, and recognized the political division within white society, divisions he intended to exploit. In his youth, he learned to read, and he worked as a blacksmith. He was hired out, and was able to associate extensively in the local taverns with other blacks and with whites, particularly other mechanics. According to historian Douglas Egerton, Gabriel developed an understanding of the exploitation all mechanics suffered in Virginia society, and he began to think that he could put together an interracial force that would strike a blow for liberty beyond the slave community; in short, Gabriel developed a class consciousness to complement his awareness of racial oppression.

Gabriel had felt the "justice" of white society when he was convicted and sentenced to death for having bitten off part of a white man's ear in a dispute over a stolen pig. Although Gabriel's life was spared—he was jailed and branded instead—such treatment may have inclined him toward rebellion.

In 1800, the Virginia legislature tabled a motion to gradually abolish slavery, and Gabriel began plotting his uprising. He recruited followers from several counties in southern and eastern Virginia with the intention of marching on Richmond, capturing the arsenal, and abducting Governor James Monroe. Gabriel wanted to hold Monroe hostage in order to force him to free Virginia's slaves. His plan included slaughtering Richmond's white population—sparing Methodists, Quakers, and others who stood against slavery—and forming a new state with himself as ruler. Despite the anticipated bloodshed, he expected poor whites to rally to his cause. In so doing, he failed to recognize that class anger among whites paled in comparison to their widespread support of slavery.

Gabriel set August 30, 1800, as the day for the uprising. About 1,000 slaves armed themselves and readied to assault Richmond, when suddenly a tremendous storm swept through the region and washed away a bridge leading into the city. Confusion then took hold, and before Gabriel could regroup, fellow slaves revealed the plot to whites. Mosby Sheppard of Richmond sent an urgent note to Governor Monroe, in which he stated:

> I have Just been informed that the Negroes were to rise . . . in the neighbourhood of Mr Tho: H. Prossers and to kill the neighbours . . . from thence they were to proceed to Town where they would be joined by the Negroes of this place (Richmond) after which they were to take possession of the Arms and ammunition and then take possession of the Town.
>
> Here they [the informants] stopped; appearing much agitated. I then asked them two questions viz: When was it to take place! Ans to Night! Who is the principal Man! Ans Prossers Gabriel.

Another Virginian, William Mosby, told Governor Monroe of a female slave who had revealed details of the conspiracy to him. "I asked her how many she understood were to meet there," he recalled. "She said 'three or four hundred,' some from town & some from the Country and there were to be a number of them mounted on horseback. . . . [They] were to go at a distance & kill and destroy all as they went . . . to kill them in their beds & that the main body were to move on to Richmond."

As a militia rounded up the conspirators, Gabriel fled. Monroe, however, offered a $300 reward for the fugitive's capture, and Gabriel was again betrayed by a fellow slave who turned him in. A trial ensued at which additional details of the plot came out. One witness said that "The lower part of [Richmond] . . . was to be fired, which would draw forth the Citizens. . . . This would give an opportunity to the negro's to seize on the arms and ammunition." He continued: "The prisoner [Gabriel] and Gilbert concluded to purchase a piece of Silk for a flag on which they would have written *death or liberty*, and that they would kill all . . . unless they agreed to the freedom of the Blacks, in which case they would at least cut off their Arms." The "death or liberty" slogan was clearly a variation on Patrick Henry's call to revolution, "Give me liberty, or give me death!" And in yet another reference to the American Revolution one of the accused slaves said, "I have nothing more to offer than what General Washington would have . . . had he been taken by the British and put on trial."

Gabriel was hanged on October 10, 1800. Additional trials resulted in more convictions, and 26 slaves were executed, while one apparently committed suicide in his jail cell. Others were transported out of the state.

Gabriel's conspiracy had two immediate effects. First, in 1801, Sancho, one of Gabriel's slave conspirators, took up the fight and put together his Easter Plot—an uprising to occur on Good Friday or Easter Monday of 1802. This conspiracy spread through Halifax and other counties but was destroyed when a disloyal slave divulged it to white authorities.

Second, the Virginia legislature passed laws greatly restricting the movement of blacks. So severely did whites react to Gabriel's conspiracy that all hope of them abolishing slavery came to an end. In that sense, Gabriel's violent radicalism, which struck at slave society's heart, worked against blacks; but in another sense, it proclaimed that the desire for liberty was too strong to be denied, and that future generations would have to confront this oppression.

Further Reading

Egerton, Douglas R. *Gabriel's Rebellion: The Virginia Slave Conspiracies of 1800 and 1802.* Chapel Hill: University of North Carolina Press, 1993.

Sidbury, James. *Ploughshares Into Swords: Race, Rebellion, and Identity in Gabriel's Virginia, 1730–1810.* New York: Cambridge University Press, 1997.

1805 From Harmony to Economy, the Rappites Begin a Religious Utopia

Self-styled prophet George Rapp founded the Harmony Society in 1805 to establish a commune in western Pennsylvania. There and at two other settlements, Rapp and his followers awaited the Second Coming of Christ.

George Rapp was born on November 1, 1757, in Iptingen, in the European duchy of Wurttemburg, Germany, to Adam Rapp, a farmer, and Rosine Berger Rapp. He obtained an elementary school education and learned weaving as a craft.

While George Rapp was growing up, Germany was being swept by a pietistic movement that sought to counteract rationalism with religious zeal. In 1785, two years after Rapp had married Christine Benzinger, he quit the Lutheran church to pursue his own pietistic ideas. "I am a prophet and called to be one," he said in 1791, and he established a community where people could live in harmony and prepare for the Second Coming of Christ, which he believed would occur soon. In the late 1700s and early 1800s, however, unrest affected Germany in the wake of the French Revolution and the Napoleonic Wars, and the Lutheran church and civil officials worked to maintain stability by persecuting dissenters such as Rapp.

Attracted by plentiful land and religious toleration in the United States, Rapp decided to relocate his settlement across the Atlantic. In 1804, he bought a 3,000-acre tract about 25 miles north of Pittsburgh, Pennsylvania. There he and his followers built the town of Harmony.

Rapp prohibited ownership of private property, and, beginning in 1807, he enforced celibacy. The 800 Harmonists were divided into work branches headed by superintendents. The settlers made and sold shoes, hats, harnesses, barrels, farm implements, wine, beer, and whiskey.

They prospered, but Rapp sought a new location to further expand the economy and to revitalize the Harmonist religious commitment. In 1814, the Rappites moved to the Wabash Valley in Indiana, where they re-established Harmony (sometimes spelled Harmonie and sometimes called by the settlers "New Harmonie"). They raised their own food but emphasized manufacturing, using some of the first steam engines in the West to mill flour and produce other items.

Once again, though, Rapp decided to relocate, and in 1825, he sold Harmony to the utopian Robert Owen (see entry, 1825). The settlers then headed back to Pennsylvania, this time founding Economy on 3,000 acres of land along the Ohio River, 18 miles below Pittsburgh. Reasons for the exodus remain unclear, but the Rappites likely suffered from persecution by their neighbors in Indiana and, as pacifists, wanted to get away from the requirement of Indiana law that all men serve in the militia.

For a third time, the settlers prospered. Economy was at its height from 1825 until 1847 during which time the Rappites worked 12-hour days with an efficiency that allowed them to withstand the national economic depression of the late 1830s. Rapp ruled as a theocrat, using a combination of kindness and austerity that won him widespread loyalty and respect. In 1832, however, a dispute caused one-third of Rapp's followers to leave Economy and settle at nearby Monaca.

The Rappites lived simply yet still had their enjoyments. They ate well and pursued music, painting, and poetry. Despite their many accomplishments, Economy declined, owing to the failure of the Rappites to proselytize, the practice of celibacy, and the death of George Rapp on August 7, 1847. By 1900, fewer than 10 Rappites remained, and five years later Economy dissolved.

Economy and Rapp's two previous settlements never had a great spiritual impact, but they represented a radical attempt to obtain religious purity, live harmoniously, and operate without the private ownership of property, which the Rappites believed only promoted selfishness.

Further Reading

Arndt, Karl John Richard. *George Rapp's Harmony Society, 1785–1847.* Philadelphia: University of Pennsylvania Press, 1965.

Prophetstown and Confederation: The Prophet and Tecumseh Seek Indian Rebirth and Unity

1808

In the early 1800s, white settlers moved into Indian territory and, as was customary, slaughtered Native Americans. In reaction, two Shawnee Indians, the Prophet and Tecumseh, promoted religious and political reform to protect tribal culture and lands.

Like other Shawnee, the Prophet (1778–1837), who was born Lalawethika, experienced the degradation of being forced by whites from tribal lands in Pennsylvania (under the 1795 Treaty of Greenville) and made to settle in the Old Northwest (the present-day Midwest). As whites continued to move westward, the Shawnee suffered additional encroachments on their land and the destruction of the game vital to their hunting. Despondent, Lalawethika took to whiskey and sank into drunkenness.

In 1805, though, he claimed he had experienced a religious vision in which he had died and been reborn. He then took a new name, Tenskwatawa (He-Who-Opens-The-Door), but was called the Prophet. Much as many white dissidents pursued religious communes as an escape from an individualistic and materialistic society, the Prophet attempted to revitalize Indian spirituality and community in the face of white intrusion. He advocated that the Shawnee return to their old ways; that they give up whiskey and reject all white goods; and that they hunt with bows and arrows.

He promoted peaceful relations among the Shawnee and condemned ownership of private property as harmful to traditional communal values. The Prophet advised his fellow Shawnee to avoid intermarriage with whites, and he said that Indian wives of white men should leave their husbands and return to the tribe. He claimed he could perform miracles; after he announced that the sun would stand still on June 16, 1806, and a solar eclipse did,

Watercolor portrait of Tecumseh. (Library of Congress)

in fact, occur that day, his reputation spread even further. In 1808, he established a settlement in Indiana called Tippecanoe, or Prophetstown, where the Shawnee could live under his direction. The Prophet's message spread among other Indian tribes in the surrounding regions and then into the South, causing whites to worry that Tenskwatawa might unify the Indians into an effective force.

The Prophet told the Shawnee:

> There are two kinds of white men. There are the Americans, and there are the others. You may give your hand in friendship to the French, or the Spaniards, or the British. But the Americans are not like those. The Americans come from the slime of the sea, with mud and weeds in their claws, and they are a kind of crayfish serpent whose claws grab in our earth and take it from us.

Meanwhile, the Prophet's older brother, Tecumseh (1768–1813), offered a political and military solution to the white encroachment. He advocated Pan-Indian unity, whereby Indian tribes would form a centralized government. Tecumseh was able to bring several tribes together in the Old Northwest, a significant accomplishment considering he had to surmount tribal hostilities and the traditional reliance on village-centered societies.

But he encountered trouble when he tried to join forces with tribes in the South. Some Indians in that region had yet to feel pressure on their land from the whites, and the Choctaw and Chickasaw had long been at odds with several northern tribes. Tecumseh could not overcome those obstacles.

In 1810, Tecumseh repudiated Indian land cessions under the Treaty of Fort Wayne, negotiated the previous year. He told Indiana's governor, William Henry Harrison, that all Indians must "unite in claiming a common and equal right in the land, as it was at first, and should be yet."

In August 1811, Harrison, recently appointed a military general, received orders to march with 1,000 soldiers through the Wabash River Valley. He was told to meet with the Indians and to arrange a peaceful settlement; if the Indians refused, he was to attack and destroy their confederation. With Tecumseh away, Harrison led his men toward the Prophet's encampment. On November 6, he negotiated an armistice with the Prophet's messenger and camped out along the Tippecanoe River.

Tecumseh had warned the Prophet about the danger of fighting Harrison, but the Indians attacked anyway. Harrison's men barely withstood the assault. "Indians were in the Camp before many of my men could get out of their tents," Harrison later reported. Nevertheless, his troops repelled the attack with a bayonet charge, and swords, tomahawks, muskets, and battle axes all clashed in a fierce engagement. The following day, his men entered the Prophet's encampment and burned it to the ground. The Prophet escaped and fled to Canada. He returned to the Old Northwest in 1826, but was forced with other Shawnee to relocate west of the Mississippi River in 1837.

Because of the Battle at Tippecanoe, Tecumseh joined the British in the War of 1812 to fight against the Americans. In 1813, he was killed at the Battle of the Thames in Canada. On his death, his Indian confederacy collapsed. Yet the Prophet and Tecumseh had offered an alternative that involved an unprecedented restructuring of Indian society so that it might be saved from the white invasion, and the spirit of their resistance has provided a source of pride and determination for Indian culture.

Further Reading

Drake, Benjamin. *Life of Tecumseh and of his Brother the Prophet.* Salem, N.H.: Ayer, 1988.

Eckert, Allan W. *A Sorrow in Our Heart: The Life of Tecumseh.* New York: Bantam, 1992.

Edmunds, R. David. *The Shawnee Prophet.* Lincoln: University of Nebraska Press, 1983.

CHAPTER THREE

Expansion and Reform

In the 1990s, Americans pondered the rise of a new Internet or dot.com economy that had the potential of changing society in unprecedented ways. These developments, however, paled in comparison to the social changes wrought in the early 1800s, at the dawn of the Industrial Revolution. The shift from agricultural to industrial societies that had begun first in Europe was, says historian Stephen Thernstorm, "the most profound change in living and working patterns since man learned to cultivate crops and domesticate animals 10,000 years earlier." In the United States, the rise of industry stimulated a new wave of rebels and renegades who questioned the equity of the modernizing society.

In the early 1800s, about six million people populated the United States, compared to 15 million in Britain and 27 million in France. Of these six million, about 1.5 million were slaves. Prior to the Louisiana Purchase of 1803 the western boundary of the United States ended at the Mississippi River; most of the nation's land was untamed, with virgin forests and minerals that lay undisturbed. The entire population between the Mississippi and the Appalachian Mountains numbered below 500,000; Buffalo, New York was an outpost in a forest wilderness.

By the 1820s, however, industrialization was bringing about the rise of cities of substantial population and size. At that time no cities in the United States remotely approached those in Europe, but by the time of the Civil War, several numbered more than 100,000.

Improvements in technology and organization made possible an industrial revolution. Historian W. Elliott Brownlee has written that for the United Sates the economic change "began in the textile factories of New England. By 1800, an array of machines were in use to clean and fluff raw cotton fibers and to prepare the fibers for weaving." The biggest change in textile manufacturing, he notes, came with the invention of the spinning jenny, which mechanized the manufacture of thread. Brownlee states that with the spread of technology "by 1830, virtually all the processes involved in the manufacture of cotton cloth had been mechanized in the United States." The profits that came from this change led to mechanization in other industries. "The industrial revolution," Brownlee claims, "had seized the American imagination."

In earlier years, merchants had been the dominant elite group in the North; now power shifted to industrialists. With that, a new class arrangement emerged with an urban society marked by distinct housing districts: the poor living near the factories, the middle-class living farther out, and the rich living in fashionable neighborhoods.

> "I am in earnest—
> I will not equivocate—I
> will not excuse—I will
> not retreat a single
> inch.—AND I WILL
> BE HEARD."
>
> William Lloyd Garrison, 1831

Industrialization went hand-in-hand with improved transportation. Roads were expanded, and the National Road connected Cumberland, Maryland, with Vandalia, Illinois. Even more important was the building of canals. Construction of the Erie Canal began in 1817 and lasted six years. The 280-mile-long canal linked Buffalo, New York, with Albany, thus providing a quick route between the Great Lakes and the Hudson River and connecting the entire interior of New York State, Ohio, Indiana, and Illinois with New York City. As freight rates between Buffalo and Albany dropped from $100 a ton to $15, and as travel time decreased from 20 days to eight, New York City boomed as a port of departure for produce from the Midwest and a port of entry for manufactured goods from the East Coast and Europe.

Beyond industry, fewer Americans farmed the land as commercial agriculture expanded, and improvements in farming methods and technology lessened the reliance on manual labor. Some of the rebels and renegades who gained prominence in this era expressed the discontent of these rural communities, for example, those connected with the 1839 anti-rent war in New York state. But the larger dynamic came from industry as workers challenged the business class. In 1829 laborers in New York City formed the Working Men's Party, and in 1834 women employed in the textile mills at Lowell, Massachusetts, went on strike. One year later, the Locofocos appeared as a radical labor organization in New York City. The tension in urban America caused by industrialization was further evident in 1837 when discontented and unemployed workers in New York City began a food riot, during which a mob destroyed barrels of flour. According to one account, "the mayor ordered out a military force, which with . . . other measures adopted, kept the rioters in check."

Industrial and agricultural advances were greatest in the northern states, but the South experienced its own economic growth. The westward movement of settlers across the Appalachians brought cotton agriculture into Alabama, Mississippi, and Texas. Slavery intensified and plantations prospered—so much so that between 1840 and 1860 per capita income in the South grew faster than for the country as a whole. Investments in slavery brought a substantial return, with planters making profits in the 1840s and 1850s that averaged 10 percent a year, a rate that exceeded the best New England textile factories.

Yet some blacks vigorously rebelled against slavery. In 1829 David Walker published his *Appeal*, a call to abolish the institution and bring about racial equality. Two years later, Nat Turner, a black preacher in Virginia, led a slave uprising. Whites joined the protests—in 1833 Lydia Child demanded the end to slavery, and in 1837 Angelina and Sarah Grimké, two wealthy southern women, toured New England to promote abolition.

At the same time, in the Jacksonian era politics emphasized the voice of the common people. A new style of campaigning that used slogans, parades, and mass rallies, and that depended on expanded white manhood suffrage, advanced the concept of democracy. Previously disdained as pandering to the unlettered masses, democracy had become a practice to be promoted and praised. Jacksonian politics combined with the demographic and economic changes under way to encourage the belief that individuals could liberate themselves from the past, while at the same time industrialization produced a sense of oppression through its regimented practices and uneven benefits.

Although the democratic impulse most strongly advanced the status of white men, it became entwined with modernity's attack on tradition to stimulate the women's rights movement. In 1848 the first women's rights convention was held in Seneca Falls, New York; this initial meeting inaugurated a struggle for woman's suffrage and other reforms that would continue for more than 70 years.

Industrialization and urbanization radicalized a new generation whose activism produced what historian James A. Henretta has called a "wave so strong" that it "spilled out of the conservative channels first carved by business-class reformers . . . to challenge some of the basic premises of American society."

Free Love, Free Education, and Free Blacks: Frances Wright Founds Nashoba 1825

When Frances Wright stood before audiences to lecture, even her appearance inspired a controversy. She wore a white tunic and pants in an era when no "respectable woman" wore anything other than dresses. When she launched into her speech, the controversy only intensified, for she attacked almost everything sacred to mainstream society. In an attempt to end slavery, she founded a settlement in Tennessee called Nashoba that failed miserably and brought her yet more criticism.

Frances Wright (sometimes known as "Fanny") was born on September 6, 1795, in Dundee, Scotland. Both of her parents died when she was young, and she was raised by relatives. She first traveled to the United States in 1818, and, through a book she wrote, *Views of Society and Manners in America* (1821), she established a friendship with the Marquis de Lafayette. When General Lafayette toured America in 1824, Wright joined him. Convinced that slavery was evil, she developed a plan to end it. Wright took much of the considerable fortune she had inherited from her parents and in 1825 founded Nashoba, deep in the wilderness of southwestern Tennessee.

She intended Nashoba to be a place where she could implement several of her radical ideas; it would function as a commune free of what she called the "tyrannies" of marriage, religion, and capitalism. In addition, she intended to buy slaves to work at Nashoba under conditions that, within five years, would allow them to pay off their servitude and gain their freedom.

Wright believed that if she were able to do this, other slaveowners would follow her example and slavery would, in time, come to an end. She coupled this with her belief in racial intermarriage; the children of those unions would form a bridge between the races, and thus create an environment hostile to slavery. She claimed that slavery resulted from the education "stamped" on the "minds and hearts" of the slaveholders. As a result, she insisted, "we must come to the slaveholders . . . not in anger, but in kindness, and when we ask him to change his whole mode of life, we must shew [sic] him the means by which he may do so, without the complete compromise of his ease and of his interests."

Trouble besieged Nashoba from its start. The commune was poorly financed and poorly led. Understandably, blacks at Nashoba distrusted Wright and the other whites, who they believed would never set them free.

Wright, meanwhile, continued to speak out on social issues. In that day, women were supposed to abide by a set of ideas called the "cult of true womanhood," whereby they were to leave all public issues to men. Her appearances in front of mixed audiences of men and women generated enormous criticism. On top of that, she attacked religion as oppressive and advocated women's rights. In addition, she called for an end to marriage as a legal institution. Couples, she said, should be united and remain united on their own terms, without the strictures of society or the state.

Wright returned to Scotland in 1827 and trouble overwhelmed Nashoba. The managers she left in charge there mistreated the slaves, and scandal erupted when one manager admitted he was living with a female slave. Wright returned to the United States and in 1829 bought the Ebenezer Baptist church in New York City, which, in a direct assault on religion, she converted into a Hall of Science. The following year, she accompanied William Phiquepal, a Frenchman, in transporting the slaves from what was by then a defunct Nashoba to Haiti, where they could live in freedom. During the voyage, she conceived a child with Phiquepal. In July 1831 she married him, but they shortly divorced.

Back in the United States in 1835 after another trip to Europe, Wright resumed her controversial lectures in which she advocated women's rights, birth control, and a more equitable distribution of property. She insisted that the state should hold all capital and everyone should be employed by the state.

Wright became a leader of the New York free thinkers. Among their many ideas, this group advocated free education as a way to enlighten people about the gap that existed between the theory of politics and the way government actually operated. About education she said, "By fostering the good, and repressing the evil tendencies . . . and cultivating the peculiar talent or talents of every child . . . all human beings . . . might be rendered useful and happy." Pushing her ideas to the extreme, she proposed that children be taken from their parents at a young age and sent to boarding schools where their minds could be liberated.

Wright joined the short-lived Working Men's Party (see entry, 1829) and in 1830 talked about class warfare in an article for the *Free Enquirer.* "What distinguishes the present from every other struggle in which the human race has been engaged," she said in recognizing the spread of industry, "is, that the present is . . . a war of class, and that this war is universal."

By the mid-1830s, mainstream society considered Wright a dangerous person, and she had to endure several mob assaults. Conservative Americans applied the term "Fanny Wrightism" to discredit reform causes, and even women's rights advocates criticized her, claiming that her extremism only gave credence to the argument that women liberated meant America corrupted. Women's rights advocate Catherine Beecher said of Wright: "There she stands with brazen front and brawny arms, attacking . . . all that is venerable and sacred in religion. . . . I cannot perceive any thing in the shape of woman, more intolerably offensive and disgusting."

Fanny Wright died on December 13, 1852, in Cincinnati, Ohio. Near the end of her life she said that she felt like "a being fallen from a strange planet among a race whose senses and perceptions are all different from my own." She was placed in that position by her radicalism, which one modern historian has said challenged "every assumption about womanhood."

Further Reading

Bartlett, Ann. *Liberty, Equality, Sorority: The Origins and Interpretation of American Feminist Thought.* Brooklyn, N.Y.: Carlson Publishing, 1994.

Eckhardt, Celia Morris. *Fanny Wright, Rebel in America.* Cambridge, Mass.: Harvard University Press, 1984.

1825 Robert Owen Founds Utopian New Harmony

In founding New Harmony, a utopian settlement in Indiana, Robert Owen relied on reason rather than religion to challenge the capitalist ethic and promote community.

Robert Owen once said, "I know that society may be formed to exist without crime, without poverty, with health greatly improved, with little, if any, misery, and with intelligence and happiness increased a hundredfold; and no obstacle whatsoever intervenes . . . except ignorance to prevent such a state of society from becoming universal." The son of a shopkeeper, Owen was born on May 14, 1771, in Newtown, Wales; by age 18 he had risen from working as a clerk to managing one of the largest textile mills in Manchester, England. In 1799 he and several partners pooled their experience and money to buy textile mills located at New Lanark, Scotland.

Disturbed by the working conditions at New Lanark, Owen determined to make changes. For the factory's 2,000 laborers he renovated housing, established safety procedures, provided insurance plans through payroll deductions, and founded schools. But Owen was in a quandary. He had made tremendous money in industry, but he disliked the degrading conditions produced by an industrial economy that extended far beyond New Lanark. Owen viewed industrialization as a blight on English society, encouraging competition and brutality. He decided that society must be changed.

Where other reformers turned to religion for guidance, Owen was preeminently a rationalist. On the masthead of a newspaper he published appeared the words, "The character of a man is formed for him, not by him," and in that spirit Owen believed that the environment exerted the primary influence in shaping people's actions. In *A New View of Society* (1813), he advocated that the government institute programs to change surrounding conditions and help those living in ignorance and poverty.

Around 1815, Parliament rejected his proposals for unemployment benefits and relief for the poor, causing Owen to lose his faith in government. He then began to advocate the formation of villages where workers would live in comfortable housing, with good schools, and a cooperative environment. His proposals profoundly affected American reformers, including Josiah Warren (see entry, 1851), causing them to see the value of his environmental argument and the limitations to their own belief in individualism.

In 1824 the Harmony Society, operating the Harmony commune in southern Indiana, contacted Owen about selling its property to him. He bought the nearly 20,000 acres and 200 buildings and called it New Harmony. Owen arrived in the United States in November 1824 with grand plans to apply his progressive ideas to the settlement. His program excited reformers and mainstream Americans alike; he even addressed Congress twice and met with President James Monroe and president-elect John Quincy Adams. Here, after all, was a man with an alternative to the industrial hardship that had overwhelmed England and that now threatened the United States, whose agricultural economy was being gradually supplanted by factories.

Years later, Owen's son, Robert Dale Owen, described the scene at New Harmony as his father began his social experiment: "The land around the village, of which three thousand acres were under cultivation, was of the richest quality of alluvial soil, level . . . and in good farming order. . . . The village had been built on the bottom land, quarter of a mile from the [Wabash] River. . . . Several large buildings

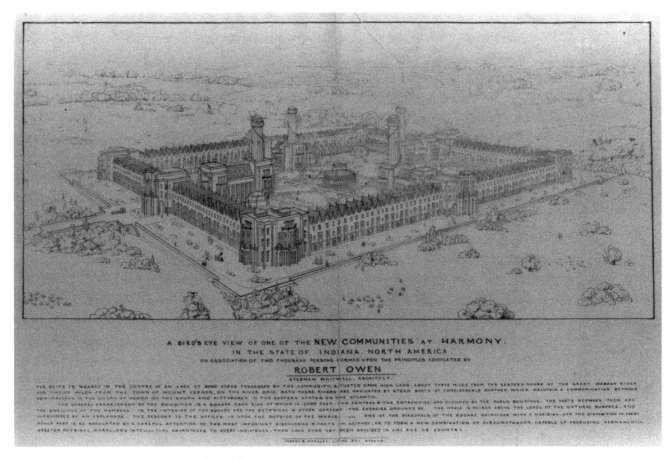

A photograph of the original plan for New Harmony. (CORBIS)

stood out . . . of which a spacious cruciform brick hall . . . was the chief. There was also a church, a steam mill, a woolen factory and several large boardinghouses."

As fertile as the land was, Owen's plans grew only brambles. At first New Harmony seemed destined for greatness. About 800 settlers arrived in 1825, among them renowned intellectuals and activists, including William Maclure, president of the Philadelphia Academy of Sciences. But most of the settlers shared little commitment to Owen's ideas. Writing in New Harmony's newspaper, the *Gazette*, Robert Dale Owen stated, "Our opinion is that Robert Owen ascribed too little influence to the early anti-social circumstances that had surrounded many of the quickly collected inhabitants of New Harmony before their arrival there." In short, Owen had failed to screen his initiates.

Other problems bedeviled the settlement: Owen saw the institution of the family and the concept of private property as barriers to community, yet he never completely decided how they should be handled. Reacting to his own private ownership of New Harmony, some of the settlers pressured him to turn it into a true commune, whereby all of them would hold the property in common. Speaking in 1827, Owen recounted that "it was proposed, that a community of common property and equality should be formed from among the members of the preliminary society" *most fully* committed to his ideas. But, he said, "this intention was frustrated by a motion . . . that *all* the members of the preliminary society should be admitted members of the community."

Owen contributed to New Harmony's problems by failing to provide effective leadership. He spent little time at the settlement, relying too much on his son to communicate his ideas through the *Gazette*.

Owen's experiment encouraged the formation of 16 Owenite communities in the United States between 1825 and 1829. All lasted only a short time, and New Harmony itself failed in 1828. Back in England by that year, minus about $200,000 he had lost in the collapse of New Harmony, Owen continued to pursue reforms that would help the working class. He died in Newtown on November 17, 1858.

Despite New Harmony's short existence, Robert Owen had challenged the industrial capitalist ethic with ideas that stressed community over selfishness. Significantly, where other reformers had previously attempted utopian communities in America, they had usually done so by relying on religion; Owen looked instead toward reason, infused with an idealistic vision, as a beacon for the rest of humanity.

Further Reading

Harrison, J. F. C. *Robert Owen and the Owenites in Britain and America: The Quest for the New Moral World.* London: Routledge and K. Paul, 1969.

Leopold, Richard William. *Robert Dale Owen: A Biography.* New York: Octagon Books, 1969.

Royle, Edward. *Robert Owen and the Commencement of the Millennium: A Study of the Harmony Community.* New York: St. Martin's Press, 1998.

1828 William Ladd Forms the American Peace Society

For his founding of the first national peace organization in the United States and for his untiring effort to spread pacifist ideas, William Ladd earned a reputation as the "apostle of peace." He envisioned a body of nations that would work to lessen armaments and encourage arbitration in place of war.

An outgoing and friendly man, William Ladd came to the peace movement in middle age. He was born on May 10, 1778, in Exeter, New Hampshire, the son of a wealthy sea captain. While still a young man, he took to the sea and, after graduating from Harvard, commanded a brig based in Portsmouth, New Hampshire.

In 1813, he and his wife settled in Minot, Maine, where he owned and operated a farm of several hundred acres dedicated to scientific agriculture. Six years later, he stumbled across the peace movement through the influence of Jesse Appleton, the president of Bowdoin College. Appleton had dedicated himself to the movement, then only a few years old, and told Ladd about the various peace societies beginning to form. According to Ladd, "This was almost the first time I ever heard of them. The idea then passed over my mind as the day-dream of benevolence." Ladd stated that his reading on the subject added to his interest, riveting his attention "in such a manner as to make it the principal object of my life to promote the cause of Peace on earth and good-will to man."

Ladd wrote "Essays on Peace and War" that began appearing in the *Christian Mirror* of Portland, Maine, in 1823 and were published as a book in 1825. He originated the idea for a national peace society and in 1827 convinced the peace societies of Maine, Massachusetts, and New Hampshire to pass resolutions supporting his effort. Finally, on May 8, 1828, the American Peace Society was organized, with Ladd as chairman of its board of directors. The group's goal was educating the public to the "evils of war" and showing how best to abolish war. Most of the local peace societies were soon absorbed by the national group.

When Ladd formed the American Peace Society, he avoided the controversial issue of whether pacifists should condemn defensive wars. If anything, he at first supported such conflicts. But he changed his mind as he realized that some of the world's greatest aggressors had portrayed their battles as defensive ones. To Ladd, all wars were immoral and to accept one meant accepting all. The American Peace Society never had more than a few hundred members, nevertheless it printed and distributed many tracts. Ladd traveled widely, promoting the society, giving lectures, and raising money. He wrote articles for newspapers and magazines, and edited the society's periodical, *Calumet*.

Moreover, Ladd promoted the idea for a Congress of Nations and in 1832 wrote a pamphlet on the subject. In an 1840 essay Ladd broke new ground by advocating that his proposed Congress of Nations be divided into two parts: a Congress of Ambassadors that would devise plans for preserving peace and a Court of Nations that would arbitrate disputes between countries. It was his intent to answer critics who said that any international court would invariably be controlled by self-interested diplomats. In words that reflected the separation of powers in the U.S. governmental system, Ladd said his plan would divide "the diplomatic from the judicial functions." He stated, "I consider the Congress as the legislature, and the Court as the judiciary, in the government of nations." Although the U.S. Congress refused to adopt Ladd's plan, it served as an outline for the later World Court, League of Nations, and United Nations.

Ladd continued his campaign for peace right up to his death. On April 8, 1841, he spoke to a group in Boston. The following day, he died, partly from exhaustion that had worsened his declining health.

In a time of "manifest destiny," when Americans aggressively sought more territory and were willing to fight for it, Ladd offered a bold alternative. That he was speaking in a wilderness—a society where peace organizations were few—attested to the radicalism of his ideas and the work needed to popularize them. Later peace groups owed much to his efforts and honored him as an "apostle of peace."

Further Reading

Call, Arthur D. *William Ladd, Peace Leader of the Nineteenth Century: A Centenary Review of Certain Realities in the Anti-war Movement.* Washington, D.C.: American Peace Society, 1940.

Ziegler, Valarie H. *The Advocates of Peace in Antebellum America.* Bloomington: Indiana University Press, 1992.

The Working Men's Party Calls for Equal Property and Equal Privileges   1829

As poverty and the inequality of wealth worsened in the United States during the 1820s, and as a democratic spirit took hold, artisans in New York City and elsewhere formed the Working Men's Party whose proposals ran from the moderate call for public schools to the more extreme pronouncements that everyone should enjoy equal property.

The Working Men's Party was formed as Americans of many persuasions were lamenting what they considered to be a disturbing development: an increasing amount of poverty and the increasing disparity between the poor and the rich in the growing cities. The country's urban centers appeared well on the road to the class stratification and the grinding poverty found in Europe.

The first Working Men's Party, and thus the first labor party in the United States, formed in Philadelphia in 1828, followed by another in New York City in 1829. The "Workies," as their members were called, consisted mainly of craftsmen and skilled journeymen. In New York City, the party emerged after workers held mass meetings in spring 1829, concerned about reports that business owners intended to extend the work day. That October, a Committee of Fifty, formed at the rally, issued a report that shocked conservatives with its call for equality. The conservatives called the party's candidates "a ticket got up openly and avowedly in opposition to all banks—in opposition to social order—in opposition to the rights of property." Conservatives experienced another shock when the party elected a carpenter, Ebenezer Ford, to the state legislature and ran competitively for other seats in the November elections—this despite having had less than a month to organize.

George Henry Evans, who helped found the New York party, published the *Working Man's Advocate*, the first labor newspaper, under a masthead that proclaimed, "All children are entitled to equal education; all adults to equal property; and all mankind to equal privileges." In an editorial Evans stated, "The working classes have taken the field and never will they give up the contest until the power that oppresses them is annihilated."

Those who emerged as leaders of the New York Working Men's Party included the utopian Robert Dale Owen (see entry, 1825) and one of the country's most outspoken women, Frances Wright (see

A Vote for James Birney Is a Vote for James K. Polk: Something Different from America's Third Parties

Americans are frequently told that casting their vote for a third party is like casting their vote to the wind. A sampling of third parties active today would seem to confirm that lesson: there are the Common Good Party, the New Liberty Party, the Working Families Party, the Freedom Socialist Party, the United States Pacifist Party—all largely ignored by the public—not to mention the even more obscure VAMPS, a party whose leader says he wants to "revive the government from the dead."

Over the years, however, several third parties have reshaped national politics by offering proposals with such strong appeal that one or both of the major political parties have adopted them. They have also forced major party nominees to address third-party concerns and have sometimes determined the election between presidential candidates. The Prohibition Party (formed in 1869) caused Congress and the states to enact the eighteenth amendment to the Constitution in 1919, making illegal the manufacture, sale, and distribution of alcoholic liquors. With Theodore Roosevelt as the Progressive Party's presidential standard-

bearer in 1912, and with the large number of votes won by him, the federal government was compelled to consider more vigorous reform measures, such as the direct election of United States senators. In the year 2000 presidential election, the Green Party forced Democratic Party candidate Al Gore to take a more liberal stand on some issues than he otherwise might have, and observers argue that the Greens were a factor in Gore's loss to George W. Bush.

For the expansion and reform period of the mid-nineteenth century, the case for influential third-party movements can be found in the rise of the Liberty and Free Soil Parties. James G. Birney's run for the presidency in 1844 as the Liberty Party candidate so affected the vote in New York that it made Democrat James K. Polk president. Just as important, Birney's emphasis on abolition pressured the major political parties to consider the issue rather than bury it. A few years later, the Free Soil Party, which opposed slavery in the territories, led directly to the formation of the Republican Party and the election to the White House of Abraham Lincoln.

entry, 1825). Wright gave numerous lectures and in so doing challenged society's strictures that women should not address men, speak in public, or in any way lead a political movement.

The New York Working Men's Party demanded establishment of the 10-hour work day, the abolition of imprisonment for debts, a ban on monopolies, the founding of free public schools, and an easing of laws requiring militia service. In a more radical appeal it issued "The Working Men's Declaration of Independence," which made considerable reference to the Declaration of Independence of 1776, and made clear the extent to which class consciousness and divisions existed in American society and that the growth of business combinations threatened the sanctity of the individual. It pronounced:

> We hold these truths to be self evident that all men are created equal; that they are endowed by their creator with certain inalienable rights; that among these are life, liberty and the pursuit of happiness; that to secure these rights against the undue influences of other classes in society, prudence as well as the claims of self defence, dictates the necessity of the organization of a party, who shall, by their representatives, prevent dangerous combinations to subvert these . . . fundamental privileges.

The Working Men's Declaration continued: "The laws and municipal ordinances and regulations… have heretofore been ordained on such principles, as have deprived nine tenths of the members of the body politic, who are *not* wealthy, of the *equal means* to enjoy '*life, liberty, and the pursuit of happiness*' which the rich enjoy exclusively."

But despite its many grievances, the Working Men's Party displayed an underlying faith in American institutions in its call for free public education. If enacted, here would be the means for the children of craftsmen and journeymen to advance and for class distinctions to be lessened.

The formation of Working Men's Parties spread into New England, and they scored several election victories, most notably in Newark, New Jersey; Wilmington, Delaware; and New London, Connecticut. These parties, though, soon disintegrated; the New York City party collapsed in 1831 as factions warred over control. Some of the party's members formed the similarly short-lived Equal Rights Party; others joined the reformist wing of the Democratic Party. Indeed, the Democrats proved adept at defusing the Working Men's Parties by adopting several of their proposals.

Some historians claim that because Working Men's Parties attracted a diverse membership that included atheists, deists, and utopians, and even some employers and shopkeepers, they did not reflect a movement strictly geared to the interests of labor. Nevertheless, these parties should be remembered primarily as the first large-scale labor movement in the United States—a radical commentary on a society moving toward an urban, industrial, corporate future whose outlines could be glimpsed by the workers of the early nineteenth century and judged by them as threatening to individual rights.

Further Reading
Wilentz, Sean. *Chants Democratic: New York City and the Rise of the American Working Class, 1788–1850.* New York: Oxford University Press, 1984.

Walker's *Appeal* Calls for a Slave Uprising

1829

In 1829 David Walker's Appeal *shocked Americans when it called for blacks to use violence, if necessary, to destroy slavery.*

When David Walker was born on September 28, 1785, to a slave father and free mother, he was, because of the status of his mother, legally free. But as he traveled extensively through the South as a youth, slavery and the racial prejudice of whites angered him. In the 1820s he moved to Boston, where he escaped the slave environment but found racial segregation firmly entrenched. Walker opened a second-hand clothing store and joined the fight to abolish slavery and win civil rights for blacks, becoming a member of the Massachusetts General Colored Association. In 1828, he made a speech to that group, and in 1829 he published a 76-page pamphlet titled *Walker's Appeal.*

Walker held back nothing in making his revolutionary demands. The *Appeal* boldly condemned slavery and called for slaves to rebel. Walker believed that slavery was so evil and oppressive that whatever violence it took to bring about its end was justified. Many whites and blacks criticized his radicalism, but he printed two more editions of his *Appeal* in 1830, with the third one more militant than the first.

Walker began his *Appeal* by declaring that "we (coloured people of these United States,) are the most degraded, wretched, and abject set of beings that ever lived since the world began." To slavery, he said, whites have added complete humiliation. Walker asked, "Have they not, after having reduced us to the deplorable condition of slaves under their feet, held us up as descending originally from the tribes of *Monkeys* or *Orang-Outangs?* . . . Has Mr. [Thomas] Jefferson declared to the world, that we are inferior to whites, both in the endowments of our bodies and our minds?"

The American Revolution, Walker insisted, had done nothing for blacks. "I must observe . . . that at the close of the first Revolution in this country with Great Britain, there were but thirteen States in the Union, now there are twenty-four, most of which are slave-holding States, and the whites are dragging us around in chains and in handcuffs to their new States and Territories to work their mines and farms."

Whites, he said, must awaken to the libertarian principles of the Revolution and to their hypocrisy. "See your Declaration Americans! ! ! Do you understand your own language? Hear your language, proclaimed to the world, July 4th, 1776—'We hold these truths to be self evident—that ALL MEN ARE CREATED EQUAL! ! That they *are endowed by their Creator with certain unalienable rights*; that among these are life, *liberty*, and the pursuit of happiness! !' Compare your own language above . . . with your cruelties and murders inflicted by your cruel and unmerciful fathers and [by] yourselves on our fathers and on us."

Walker saw to it that his *Appeal* reached the South—a feat that has puzzled historians who are unsure how this was accomplished. He may have sewn copies of it into the lining of sailors' clothing that he distributed at his store with the intent that it be circulated below the Mason–Dixon line. However the *Appeal* was distributed, it could be found in several southern states. Although most slaves could not read, these states feared the publication's influence. The Georgia legislature quickly passed a law making it a capital offense to circulate material intended to incite slaves, and elsewhere in the South a price was put on Walker's head.

When friends suggested to Walker that for his own safety he should flee to Canada, he reportedly said, "I will stand my ground. *Somebody must die in this cause.* I may be doomed to the stake and to the fire, or to the scaffold tree, but it is not in me to falter if I can promote the work of emancipation."

Walker died on June 28, 1830. Some contemporaries said he was poisoned by his enemies, but no evidence has been found to support that charge. Despite Walker's statement that masters who released their slaves should be forgiven, his *Appeal* brooked no compromise: slavery must be ended immediately and through violence if needed. No other abolitionist had written with such bold commitment and radical courage, and for years to come black militants would absorb his words for their stark appraisal of white supremacy.

Further Reading

Aptheker, Herbert. *"One Continental Cry": David Walker's Appeal to the Colored Citizens of the World, 1829–1830.* New York: Humanities Press, 1965.

Dillon, Merton Lynn. *Slavery Attacked: Southern Slaves and Their Allies, 1619–1865.* Baton Rouge: Louisiana State University Press, 1990.

Hinks, Peter P. *To Awaken My Afflicted Brethren: David Walker and the Problem of Antebellum Slave Resistance.* University Park: Pennsylvania State University Press, 1997.

Joseph Smith Begins a New Church Based on the *Book of Mormon* 1830

When Joseph Smith claimed to have had visions in which the angel Moroni told him that all existing churches had deserted God, he founded the Mormon church, a group so radical in its faith that it was severely persecuted and Smith eventually killed.

Born on December 23, 1805, Joseph Smith was just 15 when he had his first vision in 1820, followed by two others in September 1823. At that time, with the revivalist Second Great Awakening then raging across western New York, visions were frequently reported by those coming to grips with their own sin. According to Smith, the angel Moroni "appeared to me three times in one night and once on the next day." The angel told him about gold plates on which were inscribed revelations in an ancient language. "I immediately went to the place and found where the plates were deposited," he said. The place was an ancient Indian mound near Palmyra, New York.

To translate the plates' inscriptions, Smith had to use special glasses provided to him by the angel; he claimed also a "miraculous" intervention. Smith published his interpretation in 1830 as the *Book of Mormon*, so named after the author of the golden plates, Mormon, who supposedly had written them in the fourth century. The *Book of Mormon* tells of a Lost Tribe of Israel who had come to America and established a Christian civilization, but were wiped out by Indians. (The story of such a lost tribe had long circulated; Thomas Jefferson and many others thought it might be true.) Smith claimed he had received a charge from God to reestablish the true church; so, in April 1830 he founded the Church of Jesus Christ of Latter-Day Saints, or Mormon church, in Fayette, New York.

Seeking to build a new society, Smith and his small group of followers settled at Kirtland, Ohio, in 1831. There they began a commune, with all property held by the church. This development was in line with a wave of commune-founding during a vibrant reform era as Americans struggled to reconcile their expanding urban economy and individualistic values with traditional practices. In 1833, Smith published his "Words of Wisdom," which prohibited Mormons from using tobacco or drinking alcohol. But controversy enveloped Smith over the handling of church finances, forcing him to escape arrest by fleeing to Missouri, where some of his followers had already relocated.

The Mormons were chased from Missouri, however, amid accusations by their neighbors that the religious group was inciting slaves against whites, a charge linked to the Mormon belief in abolitionism. The governor of Missouri said the Mormons "had to be exterminated, or driven from the state."

In 1839, Smith and his fellow Mormons settled at Commerce, Illinois, which they renamed Nauvoo. They built a thriving community, and, after Smith pitted the Democrats against the Whigs, enticing each with the possibility of Mormon votes, he obtained from the state legislature a charter that granted Nauvoo a semiautonomous status and even allowed him to raise a militia, the 2,000-strong Nauvoo Legion.

Nauvoo grew quickly; within a short time it boasted 15,000 residents, making it the largest city in Illinois. A stone temple towered over the town, and one observer sympathetic to the Mormons described Nauvoo's homes as "almost all of them brick, built in New England style, neat as well as substantial, surrounded by garden plats . . . and without any of the temporary *makeshift* appearance that characterizes the settlements of the West."

Smith wielded enormous power at Nauvoo, for the Mormons revered him as a prophet. In 1843, he caused a split within the church when he announced his revelation that Mormons should practice polygamy, whereby husbands would have more than one wife. As Smith prepared to run for president of the United States in 1844, his opponents within the church attacked him in a newspaper, the *Nauvoo Expositor*. They disliked his ruling regarding polygamy and called his power excessive. He retaliated by ordering the paper's printing press destroyed. At the same time, residents near Nauvoo persecuted the Mormons and condemned Smith for his beliefs. Smith's destruction of the printing press caused the governor to have him arrested for inciting a riot.

Smith surrendered peacefully to the state militia and, on June 27, 1844, was placed in jail. Hours later, an angry mob, which included some members of the militia, broke into the jail and shot and killed Smith and his brother, Hyrum.

Why did so many people hate the Mormons? Part of the answer resides in Nauvoo's prosperity— many non-Mormons envied the thriving community and disliked the economic competition it provided. Others judged Smith to be an extremist, seeing his plans and ideas as a threat to accepted practices. They particularly objected to Mormon communalism and abolitionism, the acceptance of polygamy, and the claim that the *Book of Mormon* stood on the same level as the Bible as holy scripture.

The Mormons left Illinois in 1845 and founded Salt Lake City, Utah, under the leadership of Brigham Young. Their problems with the outside world would continue, however, and soon they would be embroiled in an intense showdown with the federal government, called the Mormon War (see entry, 1857). From their base in Utah, the Mormons continued to proselytize, making their church one of the fastest-growing in the world in the twentieth century.

In their early years, the Mormons appealed strongly to those seeking both economic and spiritual salvation. According to one convert, "In [Nauvoo], there is a prospect of receiving every good thing both of this world and that which is to come." The poet John Greenleaf Whittier said about the Mormons, "They speak a language of hope and promise to weak hearts, tossed and troubled." Smith and his followers presented a radical spiritual alternative that was at once Christian in accepting the Bible but unique in announcing a new prophet bearing the *Book of Mormon*. In 2002 the Church of Jesus Christ of Latter-day Saints had some 11 million members worldwide.

Further Reading

Anderson, Robert D. *Inside the Mind of Joseph Smith: Psychobiography and the Book of Mormon.* Salt Lake City, Utah: Signature Books, 1999.

Compton, Todd. *In Sacred Loneliness: The Plural Wives of Joseph Smith.* Salt Lake City, Utah: Signature Books, 1997.

Draper, Maurice L. *The Founding Prophet: An Administrative Biography of Joseph Smith, Jr.* Independence, Mo.: Herald Publishing House, 1991.

1831   Nat Turner Leads a Bloody Slave Revolt

The slave Nat Turner thought he could divine the heavens, and after seeing what he took to be blood on corn and an eclipse of the sun, he launched his raid on several plantations in Southampton County, Virginia. As he and his followers butchered their victims, he intended nothing less than to incite a general slave uprising.

Nat Turner, who like many slaves adopted the last name of his master, was born on October 2, 1800, on the plantation of Benjamin Turner in Southampton County, Virginia, to Nancy, a slave woman, and a father he never knew. Nat was later described by a white person as "from childhood . . . very religious, truthful, and honest."

In 1822 the South was shocked when it was revealed that a free black, Denmark Vesey, and slave artisans had plotted an uprising in Charleston, South Carolina. The plot was crushed and 37 African-Americans were executed. At the same time, economic hardship gripped the South, and Benjamin Turner's son, Samuel Turner, who had inherited Nat, tried to compensate for declining cotton prices by working his slaves especially hard. At one point, after a flogging by a brutal overseer, Nat Turner fled into the swamps and hid there for a month. He had earlier thought himself divinely inspired and during his defection experienced prophetic revelations that led him to contemplate rebellion. He later stated: "I began to direct my attention to this great object, to fulfill the purpose for which . . . I felt assured I was intended—Knowing the influence I had obtained over the minds of my fellow servants . . . by the communion of the Spirit whose revelations I often communicated to them, and they believed and said my wisdom came from God."

The omens continued to appear as he worked in the fields, including one, as he later described it, of "white spirits and Black spirits engaged in battle." In 1825, Nat Turner was sold to Thomas Moore, another harsh master, and the prophetic slave began leading religious meetings as a self-styled preacher.

In this role, Turner traveled along the dirt roads of Southampton County—Moore allowed him to do so—making friends with fellow slaves and free blacks and developing a following. Around 1825 Turner "discovered drops of blood on the corn, as though it were dew from the neighborhood" and told others of it. "I then found on the leaves in the woods hieroglyphic characters and numbers," he recalled, "with the forms of men in different attitudes, portrayed in blood, and representing the figures I had seen before in the heavens." He experienced an intense vision in May 1828 that told him he should attack white slave owners by using their very own weapons against them. Turner later stated:

I heard a loud noise in the heavens, and the Spirit instantly appeared to me and said the Serpent was loosened, and Christ had laid down the yoke he had borne for the sins of men, and that I should take it on and fight against the Serpent, for the time was fast approaching when the first should be last and the last should be first.

Was Turner a "dangerous religious lunatic," as the novelist William Styron said about him in the 1990s, or "a highly intelligent man who [found] it impossible to accept the status quo and discover[ed] his rationalization for his rebellious feeling in religion," as Herbert Aptheker wrote in *Nat Turner's Slave Rebellion* (1966)? Perhaps the truth lies somewhere in between: Clearly madness did not drive Turner to violence, the slave master's whip did. And rather than a rationalization, it seems likely that Turner's visions were a manifestation of a world he was conditioned to see as evil because it robbed blacks of their liberty.

Later in 1828 Turner became the slave of Joseph Travis, whom he described as a "good master." Then in 1831 Turner witnessed a solar eclipse, which he deciphered as a sure sign to begin an uprising. He told four coconspirators that July 4 would be the day for action, an indication that he saw his own plan as linked to the freedom pronounced in the Declaration of Independence.

On that day, however, Turner became ill—perhaps from anxiety about the uprising—and the rebellion was canceled. Then on August 13, he saw a spot on the sun. To him it was yet another omen: a black hand signaling the time had come to act. He set August 21 as the new date for the uprising. His followers gathered that night, and early on the morning of August 22 they attacked his own master's plantation. Turner brandished an axe and struck Joseph Travis in the head. The blow, however, failed to kill Travis, and others in the party finished him off and killed his wife and children. "There was a little infant sleeping in a cradle, that was forgotten," Turner recalled, "until we had left the house and gone some distance, when Henry and Will returned and killed it."

From there Turner and his fellow rebels attacked other plantations in Southampton County. They descended without warning, galloping on horses and running through the fields, armed with guns, axes, swords, clubs, and pikes. By mid-morning, Turner's band had expanded to 40; at its height, the group numbered about 60. In one raid Turner killed Margaret Whitehead, the daughter of a planter. "Miss Margaret, when I discovered her, had concealed herself in a corner, formed by the projection of the cellar cap from the house," Turner said. "On my approach she fled, but was soon overtaken, and after repeated blows with a sword, I killed her by a blow on the head, with a fence rail."

Turner hoped to ignite a larger slave uprising, but whites counterattacked later in the day on August 22, and he was forced to retreat and decided to go into hiding. A brutal white retribution followed, in which more than 200 black men, women, and children were killed. Turner was captured near the Travis plantation on October 30, tried on November 5, and hanged on November 11. His body was skinned. The deposition he had given to his lawyer, Thomas Gray, was published as the *Confessions of Nat Turner* (1831) and quickly sold more than 50,000 copies, mainly to whites attracted by the gory details and fearful of another uprising.

Prior to Turner's rebellion, the Virginia legislature had been debating the future of slavery. The uprising destroyed all hope it would be ended peacefully. One legislator said, "We're going to lock the niggers in a cellar and throw away the key." Many Southerners, their skittishness intensified by slave uprisings in the Caribbean, blamed the rebellion on abolitionists (no link between the two has ever been proved), and they tightened the laws governing slavery. In the short run, Nat Turner's rebellion made slavery more repressive, but it made clear the black hope for freedom and added to the stories of slave resistance that blacks knew so well and whites feared so deeply.

Further Reading

Aptheker, Herbert. *Nat Turner's Slave Rebellion.* New York: Humanities Press, 1966.
Oates, Stephen B. *The Fires of Jubilee: Nat Turner's Fierce Rebellion.* New York: Harper, 1990.

1831   *The Liberator*: William Lloyd Garrison Declares Abolitionists Will Be Heard

For William Lloyd Garrison there could be no compromise with slavery or slaveholders. He repudiated the Constitution as a contract with the devil and advocated that the North secede from the Union as a way to destroy slavery.

Born on December 12, 1805, in Newburyport, Massachusetts, to Abijah Garrison and Frances Maria Lloyd Garrison, William Lloyd Garrison entered the field of journalism in 1826 when he bought the *Essex Courant* from a friend and renamed it the *Free Press.* He owned it only a short while but earned a reputation as an eloquent fighter for his political views.

Garrison was greatly influenced by Boston's religious and intellectual ferment. He listened to Lyman Beecher's sermons, which, combined with the alcoholism of Garrison's father and one of his brothers, led him into the temperance movement.

He acquired the *National Philanthropist*, a temperance paper, in 1827, and insisted he would "raise the moral tone of the country." In 1828, he took a more radical reformist turn after he met Benjamin Lundy, a Quaker who published a newspaper calling for the abolition of slavery and who based his antislavery stance on the Bible and the Declaration of Independence. Lundy's beliefs convinced Garrison to speak out against slavery. He then read *The Book and Slavery Irreconcilable*, written in 1816 by Rev. George Bourne, and converted to "immediatism," meaning he wanted slavery ended without delay; other abolitionists were "gradualists," believing that slavery should be ended in stages. Writing in *All on Fire* (1998), Henry Mayer states that "Garrison's embrace of immediatism completed his equivalent of a religious conversion. He felt purged of sin, ready to testify about his convictions, and eager to exhort others to repentance."

In fall 1829, Garrison began editing Lundy's newspaper, *Genius of Universal Emancipation*, in Baltimore, but criticized his friend's belief in colonization, a proposal that blacks be freed and resettled in Africa or Latin America. To force blacks to leave the United States, he said, would violate their rights.

Garrison unloosed his pen in searing attacks against merchants who engaged in the slave trade. His criticism of Francis Todd caused a Baltimore grand jury to indict Garrison for libel. Found guilty, he entered jail in April 1830. The abolitionist responded, "The court may shackle the body, but it cannot pinion the mind."

His release came 49 days later, whereupon he returned to Boston and lectured against slavery, stating it must be ended through the power of the Gospel. On January 1, 1831, he published the first edition of his newspaper, *The Liberator*. In an article, Garrison extolled the principles of the Declaration of Independence and called gradualism timid, unjust, and absurd. He declared: "I am in earnest—I will not equivocate—I will not excuse—I will not retreat a single inch.—AND I WILL BE HEARD." Part of what he wanted heard was that the North should leave the Union. He believed doing so would weaken slavery by depriving it of economic sustenance received from the North and the military protection received from the federal government; moreover, he thought that northerners must purge their souls of sin by completely disassociating with human bondage.

In addition to advocating abolition, *The Liberator* promoted civil rights for African-Americans. The circulation of *The Liberator* was never much more than 3,000, yet it raised southern anger; when one issue reported rumors of a slave uprising in the Carolinas, a grand jury in Raleigh, North Carolina, reacted by indicting Garrison for "distributing incendiary matter."

In 1832, Garrison formed the New England Anti-Slavery Society, the first organization dedicated to immediatism. Later that year, he founded the American Anti-Slavery Society, and wrote its declaration: "We plant ourselves upon the truths of Divine Revelation and the Declaration of Independence as upon the EVERLASTING ROCK."

In the 1840s Garrison pursued the principle found on *The Liberator*'s masthead: "No Union with Slaveholders." Calling the Constitution an agreement with the devil because of its proslavery content, he burned a copy of it at a Fourth of July celebration. The Compromise of 1850, which permitted slavery in New Mexico (should the territory's residents vote for it) and strengthened the fugitive slave laws, convinced many abolitionists that Garrison was right about the futility of seeking a political solution.

Nevertheless, Garrison antagonized many fellow abolitionists with his crusade for other reforms, particularly his advocacy of women's rights. Some abolitionists opposed Garrison's stands on principle; many others feared that by engaging in so many reforms, he would antagonize mainstream Americans and divert attention away from abolitionism itself.

In 1859 the radical abolitionist John Brown raided the federal arsenal at Harper's Ferry, Virginia (see entry, 1859), in an attempt to ignite a slave rebellion, and Garrison rushed to Brown's defense. Garrison preferred nonviolence, but he portrayed Brown's fanatical act as an extension of the American revolutionary fight for liberty. When the Lower South seceded late in 1860, Garrison supported the war against the Confederacy (despite his earlier advocacy that the North and South should separate) because it was being waged against slavery.

In the late 1860s, Garrison toured Europe, lecturing about his work as an abolitionist. In 1868, he began writing articles for the *New York Herald*. He died on May 24, 1879, in New York City. For Garrison, there could never be compromise or tolerance of anyone who supported compromise. "I have need to be all on fire," he said, "for I have mountains of ice about me to melt."

Further Reading

Kraditor, Aileen S. M*eans and Ends in American Abolitionism: Garrison and His Critics on Strategy and Tactics, 1834–1850.* Chicago: I. R. Dee, 1989.

Mayer, Henry. *All on Fire: William Lloyd Garrison and the Abolition of Slavery.* New York: St. Martin's Press, 1998.

Merrill, Walter. *Against Wind and Tide: A Biography of William Lloyd Garrison.* Cambridge, Mass.: Harvard University Press, 1963.

Stewart, James Brewer. *William Lloyed Garrison and the Challenge of Emancipation.* Arlington Heights, Ill.: Harlan Davidson, 1992.

Thomas, John L. *The Liberator, William Lloyed Garrison: A Biography.* Boston: Little, Brown, 1963.

1833   Lydia Maria Francis Child Demands an End to Slavery and Calls for Racial Equality

A novelist, poet, and essayist, Lydia Maria Child stunned her reading audience in 1833 when she published Appeal in Favor of That Class of Americans Called Africans, *a stirring attack on slavery. Over the ensuing years she wrote additional abolitionist works and advocated women's rights.*

Lydia Maria Child (née Francis) was born on February 11, 1802, in Medford, Massachusetts. She received little formal education yet read extensively, and in 1824, at the age of 22, published her first novel, *Hobomok*, which portrayed intermarriage between an Indian man and a white woman.

Hobomok sold widely and, coupled with her second novel, *The Rebels* (1825), earned her a national reputation as a writer. She began a magazine for children, *Juvenile Miscellany*, in 1826 and wrote children's stories. In 1828 she married David Lee Child, a lawyer, state legislator, and editor of the *Massachusetts Journal.* He was a friend of abolitionist William Lloyd Garrison (see entry, 1831), and he and Garrison converted Lydia to the cause. About Garrison, Lydia Child said, "He got hold of the strings of my conscience and pulled me into reform. . . . Old dreams vanished, old associates departed, and all things became new."

Child stunned many of her readers in 1833 when she published *Appeal in Favor of That Class of Americans Called Africans.* Although several future abolitionists credited the book with convincing them to join the fight against slavery, it caused many of Child's regular readers to desert her. In *Appeal* she not only condemned slavery but also attacked racial discrimination, including laws that prohibited racial intermarriage. In agreement with the Garrison wing of the abolitionist movement, she called for the immediate end to slavery.

Lydia Maria Child. (Library of Congress)

Similar to other women engaged in the abolitionist movement, Child fought for women's rights. She admitted that differences between men and women meant they would often have distinct roles, but she disliked societal restrictions on women based solely on their gender. She said, "The word and act of every reflecting woman should show that she considers herself an individual, responsible being—not the passive tool, or sensual plaything, of man."

A woman, Child insisted, should be able to apply her talents as an editor, writer, teacher, or in whatever occupation she found rewarding. And she believed that as a reformer, her effort against slavery would help women. "It is best not to talk about our rights," she argued, "but simply go forward and *do* whatsoever we deem a duty. In toiling for the freedom of others, we shall find our own."

In addition to *Appeal*, Child wrote other abolitionist works, most notably an anthology, *The Oasis* (1834). She stressed moral abolitionism, saying it was essential to change people's minds about slavery; political abolitionism, she complained, sought to push change before consciences had been awakened. That tactic, she said, would only lead to war.

Child had contradictory views about race. On the one hand, she maintained that "the races of mankind are different, spiritually as well as physically." But she added: "It is the differences between the trees of the same forest, not as between trees and minerals." Advocating black rights, she nevertheless believed in the superiority of white civilization. At one point she said, "Similar influences [to those enjoyed by Caucasians] brought to bear on the Indians or the Africans, as a race, would gradually change the structure of their skulls and enlarge their perceptions of moral and intellectual truth."

Sympathetic to John Brown's raid at Harper's Ferry (see entry, 1859), Child began a correspondence with him that was later reprinted as a pamphlet and sold more than three million copies. When the Civil War ended, she advocated programs to help former slaves. She fought for black suffrage and land redistribution, and attacked racism and discrimination, including laws that prohibited marriage between the races. In 1868, she wrote *An Appeal for the Indians,* and in the 1870s, she wrote articles promoting civil service reform and the eight-hour day for workers. Lydia Child died on October 20, 1880, having used her pen to present bold insights about the place of blacks and women in American society.

Further Reading

Baer, Helene Gilbert. *The Heart is Like Heaven: The Life of Lydia Maria Child.* Philadelphia: University of Pennsylvania Press, 1964.

Clifford, Deborah Pickman. *Crusader for Freedom: A Life of Lydia Maria Child.* Boston: Beacon Press, 1992.

Meltzer, Milton. *Tongue of Flame: The Life of Lydia Maria Child.* New York: Crowell, 1965.

Venet, Wendy Hamand. *Neither Ballots nor Bullets: Women Abolitionists and the Civil War.* Charlottesville: University Press of Virginia, 1991.

Women Strike in Lowell, the "City of Spindles"   1834

In 1834 and again in 1836, women workers at the textile mills in Lowell, Massachusetts, went on strike to protest wages and working conditions. In so doing, they challenged not only the factory owners but also the social strictures that said women should refrain from public activism.

For several decades prior to the 1820s, the making of cloth in the United States was accomplished commercially through the "putting out" system, whereby capitalists would hire workers to labor in their homes. Shortly before 1820, however, a group of investors, led by Francis Lowell, formed the Boston Manufacturing Company and bought land in the Merrimack River Valley, where they built textile factories. Lowell, Massachusetts, became the "City of Spindles."

The company hired young women as workers and developed the Lowell System, which was hailed as an improvement over the grimy and morally bankrupt industrial environment in England. Women in their teens and early twenties came from the New England countryside and found employment in the mills. Most stayed only a short time, trying to earn enough money for a dowry that would enable them to follow the traditional route of marriage and family.

These young women lived together in boardinghouses, closely supervised by the factory managers to protect morals. The women sang the "Song of the Spinners":

Now we sing, with gladsome hearts,
The theme of the spinner's song,
That labor to leisure a zest imparts,
Unknown to the idle throng.

As the demand for cloth grew, and as competition among the mills intensified, the managers began forcing the workers to increase output and to "stretch-out," or increase the number of machines they worked. On top of that, they lowered wages and raised room rents. The women worked from early morning until the evening in rooms that were hot in summer and cold in winter. For supper, they often received only bread and gravy. The hopes for a factory system more humane than that of Europe quickly faded.

When the Lowell mills announced a 15-percent wage cut in the winter of 1834, some 800 women out of a labor force of 2,400 went on strike, or "turned out." The women marched, held rallies, and made speeches. One of them, Harriet Hanson, said: "When the girls in my room stood irresolute, uncertain what to do . . . I . . . became impatient, and started on ahead, saying . . . 'I don't care what you do, I am going to turn out . . .,' and I marched out, and was followed by the others. As I looked back at the long line, that followed me, I was more proud than I have ever been since." In a petition the striking women proclaimed, "We will not go back into the mills to work unless our wages are continued. . . . None of us will go back, unless they receive us all as one."

That the women lived together in boardinghouses and came from similar backgrounds created a sense of community that translated into a developing sense of solidarity. The strikers linked their walkout to the ideals found in the American Revolution and the Declaration of Independence; they saw their oppression as more than economic, equating it with a loss of liberty. In one of their poems, they stated, "Yet I value not the feeble threats/Of Tories in disguise/While the flag of independence/O'er our noble nation flies." Many outside the mills considered the strike to be outlandish, even scandalous: women were supposed to leave politics and economics to men. One business leader called it an "amizonian [sic] display."

The strike, though, lasted less than a month and failed to bring about any changes. The pay cut remained in effect, and most of the women gave up and returned to work, while others quit their jobs and left town. In 1836, faced with stiffer competition and declining profits, the mill owners announced additional wage cuts and increases in room and board that caused another turnout. This time more women participated, some 2,000 of them, and the strike lasted several months. The women achieved minor gains when the mills agreed to roll back the increases in rents, but the strikers once again failed to get the wage cuts rescinded.

The activism of the 1830s led to the formation of the Ten Hour Movement in the 1840s, whereby women petitioned the legislature to mandate a reduction in work hours from the typical 12-to-17-hour day. The legislature, however, refused, and in the 1850s the mill owners switched to employing largely Irish immigrant women who would work for yet lower wages. Nevertheless, the protests of the

1830s and 1840s raised class consciousness, causing the women to see themselves as workers who were distinct from the managers. Gone were the joyful refrains of the "Song of the Spinners"; they were replaced with lyrics sung in 1836:

> Oh! Isn't it a pity, such a pretty girl as I
> Should be sent to the factory to pine away and die?
> Oh! I cannot be a slave, I will not be a slave,
> For I'm so fond of liberty,
> That I cannot be a slave.

Further Reading

Dublin, Thomas. *Women at Work: The Transformation of Work and Community in Lowell, Massachusetts, 1826–1860.* New York: Columbia University Press, 1979.

Striking a Match for Labor Rights, the Loco-Focos Organize in New York — 1835

Writing in The Age of Jackson, *the historian Arthur M. Schlesinger, Jr. called the era of Jacksonian Democracy one of class conflict. Evidence for that claim can be found in the Loco-Foco Movement, which sought to protect the rights of workers in an increasingly industrial age and in the process advance unionism.*

The Loco-Focos derived from a split within the Democratic Party of New York. In 1835, workers protested the party's domination by pro-banking leaders at Tammany Hall, the headquarters of the Democratic political machine. In general, the workers wanted more say in the party; specifically, they wanted controls placed on banks (if not an end to banks altogether), which they considered to be a tool of the wealthy. They complained that the banks were driving up inflation and eroding workers' wages by using paper notes rather than coins. And, they opposed imprisonment for debt and advocated laissez-faire economics, meaning an end to government privileges that favored some economic interests over others, which was at that time a liberal reform. Historian Lee Benson states in *The Concept of Jacksonian Democracy* (1961) that the Loco-Focos wanted to "allow every man to pursue his own self-interest, unrestricted by government unless he trespassed upon the 'natural rights' of other men."

At a meeting in October 1835, Tammany leaders tried to force probank candidates on the party; in response the workers, recently organized as "Equal Rights Democracy," refused Tammany's choice for chairman. When the Tammany supporters walked out of the room and tried to end the meeting by turning off the gas lights, the workers struck matches called Loco-focos (that lit by using friction rather than sulfur) and continued their meeting. Newspapers called their slate of candidates the Loco-Foco ticket; workers embraced the term, and it stuck. The ensuing election resulted in the Tammany candidates defeating the rival Whigs, but Loco-Foco votes reduced their opponents' margin of victory.

At about the same time, a legal ruling stunned the workers when the New York Supreme Court called unionism a conspiracy that ruined employers by forcing them to pay high wages. The combination of workers, said the court, amounted to "a statutory offence because such practice was injurious to trade and commerce."

Outraged workers and their supporters expressed their anger at rallies and in writings. The poet John Greenleaf Whittier wrote: "So then it has come to this, that in a land of equal rights a laborer cannot fix the amount of his wages in connection with his fellow laborer, without being charged as a criminal before our courts of law." Yet, he said, merchants could fix prices, lawyers fees, and manufacturers wages.

Workers spread handbills, one proclaiming: "THE RICH AGAINST THE POOR!" and held a mass rally attended by 27,000 in New York City. They linked their cause to the Declaration of Independence when they called the court ruling a "concerted plan of the aristocracy" to take from the workers "that *Liberty* which was bequeathed to them as a sacred inheritance by their revolutionary sires."

In September 1836, a Convention of Mechanics, Farmers and Working Men met in Utica, New York, and formed the Equal Rights Party as part of the movement generally called Loco-Focoism. An economic depression in 1837 added momentum to the Loco-Focos after banks suspended specie payments, meaning they refused to redeem paper notes for hard money. The workers demanded resumption of specie payments and viewed the state banking system as a "hydra-headed monster" that threatened human rights. As Loco-Focism spread to Pennsylvania, Massachusetts, and other northeastern states, the workers demanded that the national government begin a public works program to help the unemployed and reform banking practices to end speculation.

The Democrats responded to the Loco-Focos in a limited way when President Martin Van Buren pushed for an independent treasury intended to reduce the use of paper bank notes and to lower inflation. Van Buren's actions led to many Loco-Focos returning to the Democratic Party. In 1842 the Massachusetts Supreme Court ruled that workers could form unions, the first time a state supreme court had recognized this right.

The Loco-Focos never amounted to an anticapitalist movement; numerous small businessmen and lawyers joined the workers as they saw fewer government restrictions as the answer to their own particular problems. But in fighting against banks and seeking to establish a stable currency, the Loco-Focos advanced the workers' cause in forming unions that could counteract privilege and the power of business combinations. They realized that political democracy could not be achieved without economic democracy.

Further Reading

Wilentz, Sean. *Chants Democratic: New York City and the Rise of the American Working Class, 1788–1850.* New York: Oxford University Press, 1984.

1836 Ralph Waldo Emerson Proclaims an American Creed

In 1836 Ralph Waldo Emerson published Nature, *one of his works of rebellion against conformity, materialism, and organized religion. He condemned the church as irrelevant, thus raising the ire of conservatives.*

Ralph Waldo Emerson broke with the rationalism of his era, particularly the doctrine of the Unitarian church, to proclaim a birthright of individualism. In this period, the onslaught of industry and the expansion of slavery worked to tighten social conformity. The poet Walt Whitman proclaimed that "I was simmering, simmering; Emerson brought me to a boil." Such was the case for many intellectuals influenced by Emerson's beliefs, and the case for many other Americans as well, who sought alternative philosophies in a changing world.

Born on May 25, 1803, in Boston to William Emerson and Ruth Haskins Emerson, Ralph Waldo was a bookish child influenced by his father's literary pursuits and religiosity. The elder Emerson preached at the First Church, a congregational church. When Ralph Waldo was eight years old, his father died, leaving the young man and his five siblings to be raised by their mother and an aunt, Mary Moody Emerson.

Emerson graduated from Harvard as class poet in 1821, and taught for awhile, but, dissatisfied, he returned to Harvard and entered the divinity school, where he prepared for the ministry. From 1826 until 1832 he preached as a Unitarian minister, while filled with doubt about his vocation and faith. By 1832 Emerson was in full revolt against the teachings and strictures of his church, and his emerging philosophy was expressed in his final sermon, titled "The Genuine Man." To his congregation he said that the genuine man "leaves all thought of private stake . . . and in compensation he has in some sort the strength of the whole. . . . His heart beats pulse for pulse with the heart of the Universe." In other words, the church and other institutions serve only to confine humankind.

Emerson then journeyed to Europe—a trip that, despite all his subsequent talk about being a son of New England, helped to shape his intellect. In the Old World he met three persons he had long admired: the poets Samuel Coleridge and William Wordsworth, and the historian Thomas Carlyle. Emerson returned to Massachusetts inspired by the transcendental ideas being discussed among English essayists. Transcendentalists disagreed over specifics, but they agreed that truth should derive from a mystical contact with nature rather than from authority and that the meaning of these experiences could only be determined by the individual.

Emerson settled in Concord in 1834, married a second time in 1835 (his first wife had died several years earlier), and in lectures attracted an ever-larger following. During that year, his six talks on biography were received enthusiastically by audiences in Boston. In 1836, he published *Nature*, in which he asserted that by contemplating the natural world, man could learn the heavenly dimensions of God. "The greatest delight which the fields and woods minister," he said, "is the suggestion of an occult relation between man and the vegetable."

Building on this idea, Emerson presented a speech, "American Scholar," before the Phi Beta Kappa Society at Harvard in August 1837; in it he called on Americans to free themselves from the dead hand of European culture. He said, "Our long dependence, our long apprenticeship to the learning of other lands draws to a close. Events, actions arise, that must be sung, that will sing themselves." The statement paralleled his belief that persons go through a period of apprenticeship before they achieve greatness— Emerson saw in larger events the projection of the individual.

Emerson insisted that all power and wisdom came from nature and stated that while the past should influence the present, it should never be allowed to dictate actions. He urged individuals to be true to themselves, saying that only through this commitment could there be personal and social harmony.

Speaking before the graduating class of Harvard's Divinity College in 1838, Emerson drove home the ideas he offered in *Nature* and assailed orthodox Christianity. He declared the church dead for hav-

Speak Softly and Carry a Big Idea: Philosophy and Radicalism

In his multivolume work *The Americans*, historian Daniel Boorstin argues that the United States has never been a deeply philosophical country. Ideas—let alone philosophical constructs—have played less of a role in its development than has practical necessity. This could be seen from the start—the Puritans never debated theology in the abstract so much as they applied it to the building of their communities, whose rough-hewn foundation they squared with their environment.

Yet radicalism has often contradicted this picture, likely because radical movements are generated by someone's ideas about how to build a better society. A march through the antebellum radical landscape shows, for example, that communes owed their existence to John Humphrey Noyes's concept of "complex marriages" and to the European phi-

losophy of Fourierism. On the rocky ground of Puritanism was born, at least on the American side of the Atlantic, transcendentalism. Here the philosophers, the denizens of an intellectual otherworld, advocated individualism and a respect for the freedom of the individual that sprang up and flourished in a garden of reform.

In the end, philosophies are bent and shaped to meet particular conditions—and in this sense they run smack into Boorstin's practical necessities. As used in building communes, Fourierism, for example, took on a different shape from the way it appeared in Fourier's book. Still, the ideas of the philosophers were the first weapons for fighting entrenched practices and established power and have the ability to resonate across time and cultures far beyond their originating point and the initial attempts to apply them.

ing neglected the soul and said that individuals should rely on intuitive experience. His comments brought a virulent attack from newspapers, and Harvard disowned him.

Nevertheless, his speech earned him a larger audience for his lectures, and in 1840, he helped found a publication, *The Dial*, that in its brief four-year existence served as the voice of New England transcendentalism. Emerson edited *The Dial* from 1842 until its demise in 1844. In the meantime, he issued his *Essays* in two series, one in 1841 and another three years later.

Emerson once said about industrial labor that "the incessant repetition of the same handwork dwarfs the man, robs him of his strength, wit, and versatility." In such thoughts could be found his objection to black slavery. He spoke out publicly against human bondage in 1844, condemned the Fugitive Slave Act of 1850, and in 1855 called for the raising of money to free slaves. He admired the radical abolitionist John Brown and supported him financially.

Emerson died on April 27, 1882. Over the years, countless numbers of Americans had listened to his belief that virtue and happiness came from balancing the contradictory characteristics found in human beings: to become one with the world and harmonious with it yet to remain unique as an individual. Emerson's creed represented a sharp challenge to conservative thought and spawned numerous reform efforts that ranged from the formation of communes to the advocacy of abolitionism.

Further Reading

Firkins, Oscar W. *Ralph Waldo Emerson.* New York: Dover Publications, 2000.
McAleer, John. *Ralph Waldo Emerson: Days of Encounter.* Boston: Little, Brown, 1984.
Porte, Joel, ed. *Ralph Waldo Emerson: Essays and Lectures.* New York: Library of America, 1983.
Richardson, Robert D., Jr. *Emerson: The Mind on Fire.* Berkeley: University of California Press, 1995.

1836 Two Plantation Women Stun the South: Angelina and Sarah Grimké Fight against Slavery and for Women's Rights

In 1836, Angelina and Sarah Grimké publicly announced their opposition to slavery and their belief that women should lead the crusade. Their stand was all the more surprising given that they had grown up on a plantation, where slavery and traditional gender roles were considered to be bedrock social values.

Sarah Moore Grimké, born on November 29, 1792, and Angelina Grimké, born on February 20, 1805, were daughters of Mary Smith Grimké and John Grimké. Sarah and Angelina were raised in comfort; their father was a planter and lawyer who owned many slaves in South Carolina.

Overcome by loneliness, and feeling alienated from a Southern society that relied on slavery, Sarah Grimké started attending Quaker meetings in Charleston. Mystical experiences followed, in which she heard inner voices telling her to join the religious group. In 1821, she made a momentous decision: she would leave Charleston for Philadelphia, where she could live within the Quaker community and cleanse herself of all attachment to slavery. In 1823 she was accepted as a member of Philadelphia's Society of Friends.

Meanwhile, Angelina had her own unsettling experiences with slavery. She witnessed the cruelties of the workhouses, places where masters sent their slaves for punishment, and, repulsed by what she saw, she criticized human bondage whenever she could.

In 1829, Angelina followed Sarah to Philadelphia, and in 1831 she too joined the Quakers. In 1834, Angelina began reading *The Emancipator* and *The Liberator*, abolitionist newspapers. Sarah said that Angelina "found to her surprise that their principles were her principles."

Abolitionism extolled the traditional belief in women as society's moral guardians, yet such claims encouraged some women to break through the strictures about their proper place being in the home.

They concluded that they should actually take the lead in fighting slavery. Several abolitionists, including the Grimkés, classified men as sexually predatory and oppressive by their nature.

In the mid-1830s, Angelina Grimké began making speeches on behalf of the American Anti-Slavery Society. Founded in Philadelphia in 1833, the society advocated the immediate emancipation of slaves, along with the setting up of schools to educate them and the passage of laws to protect their civil rights. An interracial organization, the society believed blacks should have an equal standing with whites in the abolitionist movement itself.

In 1836 Angelina wrote *An Appeal to the Christian Women of the South,* in which she called for women to use their moral qualities and to challenge the social strictures against entering the political arena. She said, "Try to persuade your husband, father, brothers, and sons that slavery is a crime *against God and man.*" That same year, Sarah published *An Epistle to the Clergy of the Southern States.* "What an appalling spectacle do we now present!" she stated. "With one hand we clasp the cross of Christ, and with the other grasp the neck of the down-trodden slave!"

In 1836, and again in 1837, the sisters toured New England and other northern states where they advocated the end to slavery and more: an end to the oppression of women. Angelina spoke most forcefully against slavery, Sarah most forcefully for women's rights.

Discontented with Quaker moderation and angered by the reprimand they had received for having sat on the "colored bench" at a Quaker meeting, the Grimkés left the Society of Friends in 1837. That same year they attended the Anti-Slavery Convention of Women in New York City and offered the controversial view that race prejudice must be fought in the North as much as in the South. To those who said that women should keep quiet on social and political issues, Angelina wrote her *Appeal to the Women of the Nominally Free States*, published by the convention. In it she said, "The denial of our duty to act in this case is a denial of our right to act; and if we have no right to act, then may we well be termed 'the white slaves of the North,' for like our brethren in bonds, we must seal our lips in silence and despair."

The following year Sarah wrote *Letters on the Equality of the Sexes,* an appeal for women's rights in which she asserted that God had created women as man's equal. In the eyes of the public, the Grimké sisters had become the leading proponents of abolitionism and women's rights as a linked movement, two of the more radical and, for most Americans, unconscionable threats to traditional values.

As pacifists, Angelina and Sarah endorsed the Civil War only reluctantly while they continued to push for the immediate emancipation of all slaves. With the war over, they collected money and clothing for former slaves. Often given to spiritualism and dream interpretation, Sarah lived her last days with her sister and her sister's husband, the abolitionist Theodore Weld, caring for the couple's children at their home near Boston. Sarah died at the age of 81 on December 23, 1873; Angelina died on October 26, 1879. At Angelina's funeral, abolitionist Wendell Phillips stated, "No man who remembers 1837 and its lowering clouds will deny that there was hardly any contribution to the anti-slavery movement greater or more impressive than the crusade of the Grimké sisters through the New England States." Add to that their contribution to women's rights, and the tribute is complete.

Further Reading

Browne, Stephen H. *Angelina Grimké: Rhetoric, Identity, and the Radical Imagination.* East Lansing: Michigan State University Press, 1999.

Ceplair, Larry, ed. *The Public Years of Sarah and Angelina Grimké: Selected Writings, 1835–1839.* New York: Columbia University Press, 1989.

Lerner, Gerder. *The Grimké Sisters from South Carolina: Rebels Against Slavery.* Boston: Houghton Mifflin, 1967.

Lerner, Gerder, ed. *The Feminist Thought of Sarah Grimké.* New York: Columbia University Press, 1998.

Lumpkin, Katharine DuPre. *The Emancipation of Angeline Grimké.* Chapel Hill: University of North Carolina Press, 1974.

1839 Farmers in New York Rebel against Landlords

Ever since colonial days, many of New York's farmers had worked their land through a leasehold system where-by they paid rent to landlords who owned vast acreage. In 1839, they rose up to change that, using arms and politics to end their oppression.

For generations some 3,000 farmers had been paying rent on land near Albany, New York, owned by Stephen Van Renssalear. Each year, he required they provide him with 10 to 14 bushels of wheat per 100 acres, along with a contribution of fowl and a day's work on his estate. These terms were actually milder than those found elsewhere; landlords varied in their demands, but many required a monetary payment. Around 1840 the typical tenant owed $32 in yearly rent. This might seem a small sum today, but tenant farmers only raised about $300 worth of produce annually and consumed two-thirds of their crops, leaving a mere $100 worth to be sold at market. Most were heavily indebted to shopkeepers and had to pay them from whatever profits they earned.

The rents had a psychological impact as well. Historian David M. Ellis insists that "The status of tenant rankled in the minds of many farmers. The leasehold seemed an anachronism in a country of independent farmers. Time and again the tenants insisted that it was incompatible with our republican institutions."

Meanwhile, reform ignited the traditionally conservative countryside. This was the era of the common man, when Jacksonian democracy took an anti-elite turn and those discontented with societal developments crusaded for temperance, women's rights, and abolition.

Farmers in central New York's hill country worked lands of marginal quality and thus could not readily participate in commercial agriculture and its greater profits; they were the ones who carried the heaviest burdens from the rents they had to pay. This was most true in the Helderberg townships of western Albany County.

When Stephan Van Renssalaer died in 1839, his heirs attempted to collect $400,000 in back rent from the farmers of Helderberg. The farmers refused to pay, and when sheriffs tried to evict them for nonpayment, the tenants donned disguises, some covering their faces with masks of lamb skin and others dressing as Indians—a device reaching back to the Boston Tea Party (see entry, 1773). Using such scare tactics, they were able to stay on the land.

Governor William H. Seward then mobilized the militia, and the Helderberg uprising ended. But the quiet lasted only a short while. Farmers in large numbers still refused to pay their rents, and sheriffs could not evict all the culprits. More highly organized than before, the farmers formed anti-rent associations, and protests spread to other parts of central New York. In August 1844, "Indians" tarred and feathered a sheriff passing through the town of Renssalaerville.

The following year, several protestors tried to shoot the horse out from under a sheriff in Delaware County, but they missed and instead killed him. The sheriff's death prompted Governor Silas Wright to declare the county in a state of insurrection. The incident even appalled many dissident farmers and allowed moderates to regain control of the anti-rent protest from extremists.

Acts of defiance continued, but the anti-rent movement shifted its emphasis to political reform. The associations played an instrumental role in getting John Young elected governor in 1846, whereupon New York enacted a constitutional amendment, which was followed by court decisions, that ended the leasehold system. The pressure from dissident action, both violent and political, had brought about the change.

Further Reading

Ellis, David M. *Landlords and Farmers in the Hudson-Mohawk Region, 1790–1850.* Ithaca, N.Y.: Cornell University Press, 1946.

James G. Birney Declares against Slavery and Runs for President under the Liberty Party Banner

In 1840, James G. Birney ran for president as a candidate of the Liberty Party. Despite his failure to win many votes, his campaign heightened the tension over the issue of slavery and made more prominent those abolitionists who advocated the use of politics to end slavery.

James G. Birney was one of those rare Southerners who owned slaves yet committed himself to ending human bondage. He was born on February 4, 1792, to one of the wealthiest men in Kentucky, a slaveholder who nevertheless favored emancipation. His 1810 marriage brought Birney several slaves; in 1818 he moved to Huntsville, Alabama, where he owned a plantation, worked as a lawyer, and held local political office. At the same time, he experienced the religious revivals that were part of the Second Great Awakening, and that were calling America to the doctrine of salvation through faith and good works. A Presbyterian, he engaged in several reform movements, among them temperance.

As a lawyer Birney represented the Cherokee Indians against the encroachment of white people on their lands. His work for them in 1824, coupled with his religious conversion and his father's influence, caused him to question slavery. He began to consider it an evil that needed to be ended. Yet he believed its demise had to be accompanied by a plan to send former bondsmen to Africa—free blacks and whites, he concluded, could never live together in peace. Consequently, in 1832 he traveled the South spreading that message for the American Colonization Society. To a friend he wrote, "I cannot but trust . . . that the Sun of prosperity is about to break out with great warmth and brilliancy upon the cause of unhappy Africa, and that this cause so intimately connected with the progress of Truth and its triumph in the world will be signally blessed."

Later that year, he relocated to his home state of Kentucky, and in 1834, he granted his slaves their freedom, a move that publicly branded him an abolitionist. Increasingly, he embraced antislavery as a moral movement, and in 1835, he helped form the Kentucky Antislavery Society. It was a stunning development: a former slaveholder, a Southerner, a member of the ruling class taking a stand against slavery. He was so hated, and received so many threats of violence, that he decided to move to Ohio. There in 1836 he published the *Philanthropist*, an abolitionist newspaper.

In 1837 Birney attended the convention of the New England Antislavery Society in Boston. By this time he had moved away from his insistence on colonization and embraced "immediatism," as it was called—the belief that slavery should be ended without delay. A gradual approach, he said, diluted any moral appeal and could not, he claimed, "lay hold of mens consciousness." He wanted abolitionists to denounce and agitate. "Do you not think it probable," he wrote to a friend, "that very gentle and calm measures would not have been sufficient to rouse up from its torpor the public sentiment of this nation and make it, in spite of itself, look steadfastly at the sin and injustice of Slavery?"

To those who supported slavery, or thought it best ignored, Birney's ideas meant nothing less than radicalism. Yet some within the abolitionist movement thought him too moderate, and the disagreements between Birney and extremists led by William Lloyd Garrison revealed a serious split among the reformers. Where Garrison rejected the Constitution as a pro-slavery pact with the devil, Birney thought slavery could be ended by amendment.

In 1840 Birney moved to New York on his election as executive secretary of the American Antislavery Society. That same year, after calling the North a "conquered province" for having succumbed to Southern policies pushed through Congress, he accepted the presidential nomination of what soon became known as the Liberty Party. Again, he split with Garrison, who insisted that as a moral crusade abolitionism must operate outside of the political system, lest it be compromised by slaveholders. Yet

Birney's radicalism revealed itself when he supported the right of slaves to violently rebel against their masters. "Those who approve of the conduct of our fathers in the American Revolution," he said, "must agree that the slaves have at least as good a natural right to vindicate their rights by physical force."

Birney won fewer than 8,000 votes in the election, but the Liberty Party nominated him again for another presidential run in 1844. The party platform reflected Birney's evolving views; he now distanced himself from the Constitution. The Liberty Party swore its allegiance to the founding document, but it renounced those parts of it that in any way lent support to slavery, such as the three-fifths compromise and references to the fugitive slave law.

This time Birney won more than 62,000 votes, concentrated in New England, New York, New Jersey, Pennsylvania, Ohio, Illinois, Indiana, and Michigan. He finished a distant third to the Democratic and Whig candidates, but the 15,000 votes he won in New York contributed to preventing the Whig nominee, Henry Clay, from winning, and threw the election to the Democrat, James K. Polk. Unfortunately for the abolitionists, Polk supported the acquisition of Texas as slave territory, and his war against Mexico amounted to expanding slavery westward. Despite Birney's loss, the ideas of the Liberty Party lived on when it merged with the Free Soil Party in 1848, whose members eventually joined the Republican Party.

Birney retired from public life in 1845 after a fall from a horse left him partially paralyzed. He died on November 25, 1857. Birney's journey toward radicalism had been marked by a change from supporting gradual emancipation tied to colonization, to immediate abolition through political action; with it he made abolitionism a more vibrant movement, a voice that insisted it would be heard in elections until slavery itself came crashing down.

Further Reading

Fladeland, Betty. *James Gillespie Birney: Slaveholder to Abolitionist.* Ithaca, N.Y.: Cornell University Press, 1955.

1841 In the Oneida Community "Complex Marriages" Means the Sharing of Husbands and Wives

Relatives concluded that John Humphrey Noyes was mad; but he saw himself as imbued with the holy spirit. He insisted that he had risen above sin and reached a perfect state; by founding a commune at Oneida he invited others to join him in his thralldom.

John Humphrey Noyes was born on September 3, 1811, in Brattleboro, Vermont, to John and Polly Noyes. In his youth, Noyes was closest to his mother, a deeply religious woman who taught him to fear the Lord. After graduating from Dartmouth College in 1830, he studied and practiced law in New Hampshire. He intended to return to Vermont and join his uncle's law firm in Brattleboro, but in 1831, he experienced a religious conversion that convinced him to study theology.

In 1833, Noyes joined a small Congregational church in New Salem, New York, as its pastor. He believed that even a person who had lived a wicked and sinful life could start anew, provided that person surrender completely to God. Beginning in 1834, Noyes sank into despair over his own faults, until finally he experienced a vision. He later explained: "On my bed [one] night, I received the baptism which I desired and expected. Three times in quick succession a stream of eternal love gushed through my heart and rolled back again to its source." There followed such a complete breakdown that Noyes's relatives thought him deranged. Noyes insisted, however, that spiritual growth required suffering.

In search of answers to social problems, some Americans embraced perfectionism, a belief that moral or spiritual perfection could be achieved by individuals or groups. Perfectionism took different forms, such as the striving for an immediate end to slavery. For Noyes, it meant proclaiming he had reached a state without sin and that others could do the same. (Once perfect, a person was incapable of sinning.) He said that "men were either totally pure and perfect in Christ or they were sinners," and he placed himself among the pure. With that, the Congregational church expelled him.

Noyes began proclaiming that the millennium had occurred in 70 A.D. and, as a result, no one had any need to fear sin. "The kingdom of Heaven," he declared, "could be realized on earth." In 1837, Noyes wrote a letter in which he outlined his views about sex and marriage. He stated that a higher morality would develop once sex was "elevated to spirituality," and said that in a godly community sexual intercourse should be no more restrained by law than "eating and drinking should be—and there is as little occasion for shame in the one case as in the other."

In 1838, Noyes married, and he then founded a perfectionist community in Putney, Vermont, where some 30 followers operated two farms and a store. He instructed his adherents to study the Bible three times a day, and said to one: "I would much rather that our land should run to waste than that you should fail of a spiritual harvest."

Over the next few years, all but one of Noyes's five children were stillborn; these tragedies led to his concept of male continence. He insisted that the human sex drive must be controlled to avoid moral collapse and painful childbirth for women. Since men were morally superior to women, he said, they must take the lead in exerting sexual self-control, but since sex was not to be restrained, he stated that during intercourse the male should maintain an erection and reach orgasm while avoiding ejaculation. To those who called the practice impossible, he proclaimed he had accomplished it through willpower that had come from God.

Noyes formulated what he called his concept of "complex marriage" in 1846, after he and his wife engaged in sex with another couple. Noyes, who concluded that monogamous marriages produced jealousy and selfishness, saw his idea as a compromise between traditional marriage and free love, declaring that "the human heart is capable of loving more than one at the same time." Under his plan, men and

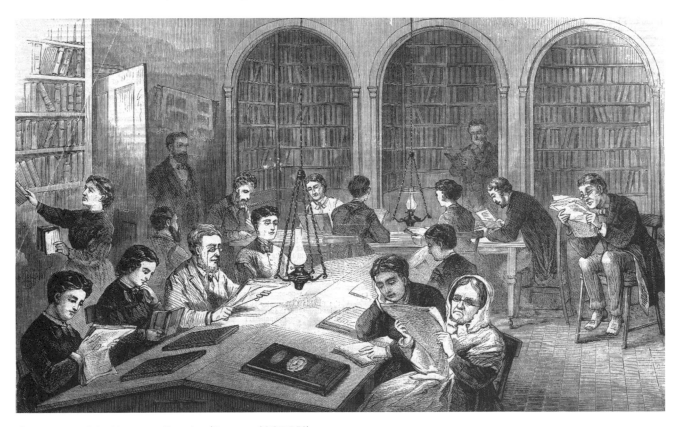

Illustration of the library at Oneida. (Bettman/CORBIS)

A Fond Farewell: Radical Community

Communes have been a part of the American landscape since colonial times, but they were most numerous during two great reform periods: the Jacksonian era of the mid-1800s and the countercultural era of the 1960s. In both periods communes represented a radical alternative to mainstream life but differed widely in structure.

In Jacksonian America, communes ranged from the secular experiment at New Harmony, to the religious planning at Oneida, to the transcendentalist construct and, later, Fourier economic society at Brook Farm. Each offered an escape from the social ills besetting society, in this case the exploitation found in an industrializing economy in the North and a slave economy in the South.

Communes in the 1960s also formed from discontentment with mainstream society. In this case, communards, often young, rejected the barbarity and brutishness reflected in the oppression of African-Americans, women, and other groups, and in the Vietnam War. One communal resident said that in forming alternative societies, reformers were "saying, as we progress, a fond farewell to the system, to Harvard, Selective Service, General Motors, Bank of America, IBM, A&P, BBD&O, IRS, CBS, DDT, USA, and Vietnam."

As in Jacksonian America, diversity characterized radicalism in the 1960s. Some communes developed around free love, others around religion, still others around black power and women's liberation. Some followed anarchistic arrangements, while others developed highly structured routines. In both Jacksonian and 1960s America, most communes lasted only a short time, but communards often measured their success not in longevity but in having experienced radical proposals in real living terms as their way of saying "a fond farewell to the system."

---

women could have multiple partners because all adults in the commune were declared as being married to one another. He linked complex marriage to ascending and descending fellowship, in which spiritually advanced members were to associate with those less spiritually advanced.

The authorities, however, thought Noyes's association was nothing less than adultery, and they indicted him for it. He and his group subsequently fled Putney and in 1848 founded the Oneida Perfectionists in Oneida, New York. They built a biblically based communist economic system in which no one person owned property, and they engaged in farming, sawmilling, blacksmithing, and silk production. Most of their money, though, came from making steel traps used by hunters in the beaver trade. When that trade declined, they turned to making silverware.

Despite the group's initial prosperity, dissension grew, and in 1879 the commune's members abandoned their system of complex marriage. Presently, Noyes moved to Canada to escape legal action, and the Oneida Perfectionists disbanded in 1881 to form the Oneida Community, a joint stock company that thrived by continuing to make silverware.

Noyes died in Niagara Falls, Ontario, Canada, on April 13, 1886. Through his concepts of sex, marriage, and economics he had challenged the foundation of mainstream society; his ideas proved so radical that in time even those who lived at Oneida abandoned them.

Further Reading

Klaw, Spencer. *Without Sin: The Life and Death of the Oneida Community.* New York: Allen Lane, 1993.

Parker, Robert Allerton. *A Yankee Saint: John Humphrey Noyes and the Oneida Community.* New York: G. P. Putnam's, 1935.

Thomas, Robert David. *The Man Who Would Be Perfect: John Humphrey Noyes and the Utopian Impulse.* Philadelphia: University of Pennsylvania Press, 1977.

1841 New England Communes: Hopedale and Brook Farm

Two communes begun in the same year offered two different visions of alternative living. According to Adin Ballou, a Universalist minister, salvation could be obtained by fighting for social justice, and that was what he intended in his founding of a commune at Hopedale. The founders of Brook Farm, on the other hand, sought to build a commune that would liberate the individual through transcendental practices.

Adin Ballou ascribed lofty ideas to Hopedale. When he founded it in 1841 on 600 acres near Milford, Massachusetts, he dedicated it to "liberty, equality, fraternity"—the principles of the French Revolution—and said it would be a society without prejudice. Thirty settlers broke ground, tilling the land and raising buildings. By 1851 the number had reached 175. Ballou declared:

> It is a Church of Christ . . . based on a simple declaration of faith in the religion of Jesus Christ . . . All members are free, with mutual love and toleration, to follow their own highest convictions of love and toleration, to follow their own highest conviction of truth and religious duty.

But he said certain requirements must be met, among them "supreme love to God and man" and "total abstinence from . . . all unchastity; all intoxicating beverages; all oath-taking; all slave-holding and proslavery compromises; all war and preparations for war; all capital and other vindictive punishments; all insurrectionary, seditious, mobcratic and personal violence against any government, society, family, or individual."

Hopedale's communards participated extensively in the larger society, using their settlement as a basis from which to go into the surrounding communities and push for women's rights, temperance, and abolition. Ballou even served as president of a peace group, the New England Non-Resistance Society.

Despite his having declared Hopedale a "socialistic Community . . . promulgating practical Christian socialism," the settlers never came to grips with the issue of property ownership. Ballou organized Hopedale as a joint-stock venture and allowed some individuals to acquire more interest in it than others, and with that he inadvertently sowed the seeds of the commune's destruction. Hopedale collapsed in 1856 after Ebenezer and George Draper used their majority stock holding to take over the commune's assets and turn it into a business. Ballou observed: "We lacked the Christlike wisdom and virtue necessary to the successful prosecution and final triumph of such an undertaking."

Like Hopedale, Brook Farm represented the reform impulse pervasive in New England as that region struggled in its shift from agriculture to industry. Two Unitarian ministers, William Ellery Channing and George Ripley, founded Brook Farm in 1841 near Boston. They tried to wed intellectual work with manual work by stipulating that everyone labor with his or her hands but in a mentally stimulating atmosphere. One observer reported that "the weeds were scratched out of the ground to the music of [the poets] Tennyson and Browning." In more prosaic terms, Nathaniel Hawthorne, who stayed at Brook Farm briefly and based his novel *The Blithdale Romance* (1852) on his experience, disparagingly recounted his task of shoveling a pile of manure. Assignments were rotated, and everyone was paid at the same rate, regardless of activity.

Discipline proved difficult, however, because the transcendentalist beliefs that prevailed on the commune prized individualism. Brook Farm provided free education for its children—its school earned a widespread reputation for innovation and quality—and sought to help those who could not help themselves due to ill health or infirmity. But its humanitarian impulses suffered when private property ownership took precedence. Finally, in 1844, Brook Farm reorganized as a "Phalanx" under the Fourier movement, a socialist experiment.

According to historian Ronald G. Walters, Brook Farm and Hopedale failed because they were too moderate; they needed to separate themselves more from the mainstream, particularly on the issue of property ownership. Still, outsiders found both to be unorthodox in intent and methods and radical at least in their social organizations.

Further Reading

Holloway, Mark. *Heavens On Earth: Utopian Communities in America, 1680–1880.* London: Turnstile Press, 1951.

Walters, Ronald. *American Reformers: 1815–1860.* New York: Hill and Wang, 1978.

1842 Albert Brisbane Advocates Phalanxes to Liberate the Individual

In 1842, Albert Brisbane began promoting the establishment of new societies based on the radical ideas of a Frenchman, Charles Fourier. Seeking to liberate the individual through regimentation and to walk a fine line between socialism and capitalism, Fourierism offered a peculiar alternative to both mainstream society and the current communal experimentation.

Albert Brisbane came across Fourier's ideas accidentally. A wealthy young man from upstate New York, in 1832 Brisbane was given a book written by Fourier, whose works included *Theory of the Four Movements and General Destinies* (1808) and *Treatise on Domestic and Agricultural Association* (1822). The idea of forming a new society by unleashing human potential through the enjoyment of work immediately attracted Brisbane, but he had to sort through Fourier's complex proposals and often incredible assertions.

Fourier wanted labor to be divided between groups, with each group bound together in a Series, such as a horticultural Series, a livestock Series, and so on. Each Series would, in turn, be bound together into a Phalanx of between 1,600 and 1,800 individuals living together in harmony. A Phalanx was to cover several square miles consisting of fields, orchards, gardens, and a three-story communal building called a Phalanstery.

Workers were to move from job to job as fit their passion. Fourier believed this would prevent boredom. Each member of a Phalanx was to receive shares of stock in it with profits divided among the members based on a formula that favored those who did the work over those who provided the money for projects, and which provided for the most pay to be allocated to those doing the most disagreeable jobs, such as collecting garbage.

Fourier filled his writings with fanciful notions. For example, he believed that the Earth was headed for an age of harmony, during which a polar crown would form and emit a perfumed dew, the sea would turn to lemonade, and wild beasts would be replaced by their becalmed "antidotes," such as anti-lions and anti-sharks.

Fourier's European followers tried to establish communities according to his plan in the mid-1830s, but they failed. In the United States much excitement followed Brisbane's publication in 1840 of his Fourierist-inspired book, *Social Destiny of Man.* Horace Greeley, the editor of the *New York Tribune*, enthusiastically supported Brisbane and, beginning in 1842, allowed him space in the newspaper for presenting his ideas.

Some readers embraced Brisbane's Fourierism so enthusiastically that they formed Phalanxes without adequate capital or land. These communities suffered also from incompatible members. One Fourierist observed: "There were philosophers and philanthropists, bankrupt merchants and broken-down grocery-keepers; officers who had retired from the Texan army on half-pay; and some who had retired from situations in the New York ten-pin alleys. There were all kinds of ideas, notions, theories and whims; all kinds of religions; and some persons without any. There was no unanimity of purpose, nor congeniality of disposition."

Among the most successful of the Phalanxes was the North American, located near Red Bank, New Jersey. Begun in 1843, it lasted 12 years and at its height had some 100 residents. During that time it prospered with an orchard and crops of wheat, melons, and vegetables. The settlers followed much of the Fourier plan, including dividing profits according to formula. But infighting over religion and a fire that destroyed several mills in 1854 brought the Phalanx to an end.

Fourierists formed 28 Phalanxes in America between 1841 and 1858. Each relied on investors getting some kind of return from their capital, yet each considered labor to be a form of capital and entitled to a return higher than capital itself, making the Phalanxes neither corporations nor true communes, but hybrids. They represented a search for community amid America's industrialization and sectional tension; they strove to alleviate poverty and derive meaning and even enjoyment from work.

Further Reading

Holloway, Mark. *Heavens On Earth: Utopian Communities in America, 1680–1880*. London: Turnstile Press, 1951.
Walters, Ronald. *American Reformers: 1815–1860*. New York: Hill and Wang, 1978.

Millerites Proclaim the Second Coming of Christ Is Near 1843

In an era when perfectionists were claiming they had cleansed themselves of all sin and when religious revivals were sweeping through large areas of the country, William Miller offered a startling prophecy: the end of the world would come in 1843.

William Miller showed no attachment to evangelical religion in his youth; just the opposite: he was a deist who believed in an impersonal God. Born on February 15, 1782, in Pittsfield, Massachusetts, to a Revolutionary War captain, also named William Miller, and Paulina Phelps Miller, young Miller grew up in modest surroundings.

In 1803, he married Lucy P. Smith and moved to Pultney, Vermont. Nine years later, he joined the army to fight against the British in the War of 1812. With the war over he settled in Hampton, New York, and experienced a religious conversion some historians ascribe to his dismay over the carnage he saw in combat, but others link to his belief that God had directed the United States to stand up to the British. In 1815, Miller joined the Baptists, saying of his conversion: "God by his Holy Spirit opened my eyes. I saw Jesus as a friend, and my only help. And the Word of God as a perfect rule of duty."

In 1823 Miller predicted the second coming of Christ "on or before 1843," based on his own study of the Bible and calculation of dates within it. By the early 1830s, he was publicly claiming that God had spoken to him, telling him to spread a message of impending doom. Beginning in 1831, he lectured on this cataclysmic theme in front of ever-larger audiences attracted by his powerful personality. He said, "Graves will open, Christ will reappear. There will be signs in the heavens. The dead will rise."

Licensed to preach by the Baptists in 1833, he continued his jeremiads at the Baptist, Methodist, and Congregational churches that invited him to speak. Three years later he published his sermons as *Evidence from Scripture and History of the Second Coming of Christ about the Year 1843*.

Then in 1839, Joshua V. Himes, a Christian activist, convinced Miller to more fully spread the word about the impending end of the world. Hines and Miller traveled about the northeast, and beneath a large revival tent the preacher beseeched his listeners. Many fellow preachers criticized Miller; they believed in a second coming, but not until sin had been ended, a prerequisite Miller chose to ignore. Reformers also opposed him for encouraging passivity; his followers, after all, were more concerned with the second coming than with improving current social conditions.

When a comet appeared in the sky early in 1843—an omen, some said, of the prophecy soon coming true—thousands more people flocked to Miller. Some gave away their homes as they prepared to ascend to heaven. One story claimed that a Vermont farmer had sewn "ascension robes" to be worn by his cows so they could go to heaven with him.

When the first prophecy failed, some of Miller's followers deserted him. But he revised his date to October 21, 1844—the day of Atonement on the Hebrew calendar—and new converts heeded his call to the point that, while the date approached, they left crops untended and shuttered their businesses. With this prediction also failing, Miller's followers dwindled to a small core. Miller later said he had miscalculated the date.

From the Millerite movement came the formation of the Adventist churches, in which Miller played only a minor role, preferring, instead, to retire to his farm. Miller never intended to form a new sect, but from the start he had been a strong voice in shaking up existing churches and offering hope and a revived religiosity to Americans besieged by a changing society in which materialism was taking precedence over spirituality.

Further Reading

Knight, George R. *Millennial Fever and the End of the World: A Study of Millerite Adventism.* Boise, Idaho: Pacific Press, 1993.

Numbers, Ronald L., and Jonathan M. Butler, eds. *The Disappointed: Millerism and Millenarianism in the Nineteenth Century.* 2d ed. Knoxville: University of Tennessee Press, 1993.

1848 The Seneca Falls Convention Declares Equal Rights for Men and Women

In 1848, delegates met at Seneca Falls, New York, and declared they would fight against society's continued oppression of women. All laws that placed women "in a position inferior to that of men," they proclaimed, "are contrary to the great precept of nature, and therefore of no force or authority."

A contemporary cartoon of the Seneca Falls meeting. (Library of Congress)

Elizabeth Cady Stanton

In the mid-1800s, it was common for abolitionists and women's rights advocates to crusade hand-in-hand. Such was the case for Elizabeth Cady Stanton. Born in Johnstown, New York, on November 12, 1815, she became a feminist while still a child after her father, a judge, ruled that women had no legal recourse against mistreatment by their husbands and fathers. At the same time, under the influence of a cousin, she became interested in the antislavery movement.

In 1840, she married Henry B. Stanton, a prominent abolitionist, and that same year, she attended the world antislavery convention held in London. Though she spent much of her time raising her five children, she spoke out on women's issues while condemning slavery. Stanton organized the women's rights convention at Seneca Falls, New York, and then took the controversial stand that once blacks were free, reformers should work to gain the right to vote for both African-Americans and women. Others thought it wrong to link the two causes, that to fight for both would detract from each. In May 1869, Stanton was chosen president of the National Woman Suffrage Association, and after that group merged with another in 1890 to form the National American Woman Suffrage Association, she was chosen president of it.

In the 1880s Stanton joined Susan B. Anthony and Matilda Joslyn Gage to write the three-volume *History of Woman Suffrage* (1881–86). Stanton devoted her later years to pushing for changes in divorce laws. She died in New York City on October 26, 1902.

Outside the subjugation of women itself, no greater catalyst existed for the rise of the women's rights movement than abolitionism. Through the fight against slavery, women developed a greater sense of their own oppression and mustered the fortitude to do something about it. Abolitionist Abby Kelly said about women and their effort to free the slaves that in "striving to strike his irons off, we found most surely, that we were manacled *ourselves.*"

More pointedly, events at the world antislavery convention in London in 1840 motivated Elizabeth Cady Stanton and Lucretia Mott to organize the Seneca Falls meeting. Stanton was appalled when she and other women were denied seating as delegates to the convention, and while in London she met and became good friends with Mott, who was also frustrated with discrimination against women. According to Stanton, she and Mott "resolved to hold a convention as soon as we returned home, and form a society to advocate the rights of women."

At that time, women suffered a second-class status in America's male-dominated society. They were prohibited from voting; had no legal control over their property; could obtain no formal education beyond the elementary level; and if divorced had to relinquish custody of their children to their husbands.

Events delayed Stanton and Mott in fulfilling the resolve they had made at London, but in July 1848, they at last brought together more than 200 women and men at Seneca Falls. At this convention the delegates adopted a Declaration of Sentiments, written by Stanton and Mott, that followed the format and the spirit of the Declaration of Independence. "We hold these truths to be self-evident," the Seneca document stated, "that all men are created equal; that they are endowed by their Creator with certain inalienable rights; that among these are life, liberty, and the pursuit of happiness." The document continued: "The history of mankind is a history of repeated injuries and usurpations on the part of man toward woman, having in direct object the establishment of absolute tyranny over her."

The document resolved "that woman is man's equal—was intended so by the Creator, and the highest good of the race demands that she should be recognized as such." The reference to equal voting rights raised the most controversy at the convention, but still 100 of the delegates signed the Declaration of Sentiments.

The Seneca Falls convention led to other women's rights meetings in the 1850s, most notably the "first national convention" at Worcester, Massachusetts, in 1850, and the Ohio Women's Rights

Convention at Akron in 1851, at which the former slave Sojourner Truth spoke (see entry, 1851). The states, however, enacted few reforms for women prior to the Civil War, and it wasn't until 1869 that Wyoming became the first state to grant women the right to vote.

Still, Seneca Falls brought men and women together in a quest to reshape American society by ending oppression based on sex. The convention in upstate New York laid the groundwork for the modern women's rights movement.

Further Reading

DuBois, Ellen Carol. *Feminism and Suffrage: The Emergence of an Independent Women's Movement in America, 1848–1869.* Ithaca, N.Y.: Cornell University Press, 1978.

Stanton, Elizabeth Cady. *Eighty Years and More.* New York: European Publishing, 1898.

Weatherford, Doris. *A History of the American Suffragist Movement.* Santa Barbara, Calif.: ABC–CLIO, 1998.

1849 Henry David Thoreau Defends Individual Moral Conscience in "Civil Disobedience"

With his essay "Civil Disobedience," Henry David Thoreau criticized the state as a purveyor of force rather than of liberty. The defense of liberty, he insisted, relied on the individual willing to take a moral stand, even if it meant imprisonment.

Most Americans best remember Henry David Thoreau for his two-year sojourn on the banks of Walden Pond. He advocated simplicity, and in physically distancing himself from society he earned a reputation in his lifetime as a misanthrope. But Thoreau felt a deep commitment to others, which he developed through his relationship with nature.

Born on July 12, 1817, in Concord, Massachusetts, the site of Walden Pond, to John Thoreau, a shopkeeper and pencil maker, and Cynthia Dunbar Thoreau, Henry David loved the outdoors. As a boy, he hunted and fished and closely observed the wooded habitat. He graduated from Harvard College in 1837, learning within its walls the mechanics of English and the beauty of poetry, but his real school remained nature itself.

In 1841, he lived in the home of fellow Concordian Ralph Waldo Emerson (see entry, 1836), and the two men developed a friendship that brought Thoreau into contact with prominent transcendentalists and their emphasis on spiritual reality. Thoreau thereupon decided he would live in a cabin beside Walden Pond, on land owned by Emerson, as a means to meditate and experience a simpler life.

He began his residence on July 4, 1845, and remained there until September 6, 1847. It was during his first summer there that the local authorities arrested him for refusing to pay his state poll tax. He was jailed, though only for a day—much to his disappointment, a relative paid his fine. Thoreau's refusal to pay the tax was a protest against the Mexican War, which he saw as a fight to extend slavery. He told the story about his protest in his essay "Resistance to Civil Government," later called "Civil Disobedience," which was published in 1849.

"That government is best which governs least . . . ," Thoreau said, though he continued, "Unlike those who call themselves no-government men, I ask for, not at once no government but *at once* a better government." Then he expressed his specific dissent when he stated:

How does it become a man to behave toward this American government to-day? I answer that he cannot without disgrace be associated with it. I cannot for an instant recognize that political organization as *my* government which is the *slave's* government also.

He went on to urge abolitionists to withdraw their support from the Massachusetts government. Speaking in words that resonated beyond the slavery issue, with meaning for protest movements in all times, he insisted, "Under a government which imprisons men unjustly, the true place for a just man is also in prison." As an existentialist who worshipped the free spirit, Thoreau stated that "the State never intentionally confronts a man's sense, intellectual or moral, but only his body, his senses. It is not armed with superior wit or honesty, but with superior physical strength."

A decade later, in 1859, Thoreau expressed his support for the abolitionist John Brown (see entry, 1859), who tried but failed to foment a slave rebellion by capturing the federal arsenal at Harper's Ferry, Virginia. In describing Brown's martyrdom, Thoreau resorted to a naturist's metaphor when he said, "In the moral world, when good seed is planted, good fruit is inevitable, and does not depend on our watering and cultivating. . . . When you plant, or bury, a hero in his field, a crop of heroes is sure to spring up. This is a seed of such force and vitality, that it does not ask our leave to germinate." He denied that John Brown was mad; the madness, he said, resided in slavery. He likened Brown's hanging to the crucifixion of Christ—"two ends of a chain which is not without its links," Thoreau said, and added: "He is not Old Brown any longer; he is an angel of light."

Thoreau died on May 6, 1862, as the Civil War moved President Abraham Lincoln closer to ending slavery. "Civil Disobedience" has since lived on as a powerful inspirational document for protestors around the world, a thundering effect from the quiet of a cabin at Walden Pond. Which person concerned with social justice, and willing to sacrifice for it, could fail to find inspiration in Thoreau's essay? "I think that we should be men first, and subjects afterward," Thoreau wrote. "The only obligation which I have a right to assume is to do at any time what I think right." "Civil Disobedience" resonated in the pen of Russia's Leo Tolstoy, the *satyagraha* of India's Mohandas Gandhi, and the integrationist vision of America's Martin Luther King, Jr. It continues to resonate among countless others engaged in social protest.

Further Reading

Harding, Walter Roy. *The Days of Henry Thoreau: A Biography.* 2d ed. New York: Dover Publications, 1982.

Salt, Henry Stephens. *Life of Henry David Thoreau.* Urbana: University of Illinois Press, 1993.

Sayre, Robert F., ed. *Henry David Thoreau: A Week on the Concord and Merrimack Rivers/Walden; Or, Life in the Woods/The Maine Woods.* New York: Library of America, 1985.

Withrell, Elizabeth Hall. *Henry David Thoreau: Collected Essays and Poems.* New York: Library of America, 2001.

CHAPTER FOUR

Civil War and Reconstruction

The Civil War is one of the great defining moments of U.S. history—the nation torn asunder, its very existence threatened. Abolitionists played a powerful role by pointing out the injustice of slavery. Such dissent from what was the country's "norm" heightened the tension between North and South. Ultimately abolitionism raised questions about the morality of nearly all institutions as it asked Americans to rid their country of evil. From the abolitionists came an intense revulsion against injustice and a belief that religious moral commitment and militant tactics could remake society. This mentality, in turn, stoked a reform spirit that transcended the Civil War and carried into the succeeding Reconstruction period. The deepening sectional crisis, however, not only emboldened the abolitionists and encouraged reformers, it also produced a conservative reaction among southerners that caused South Carolina to secede from the Union in December 1860.

> "I John Brown am now quite certain that the crimes of this guilty land: will never be purged away; but with Blood."
>
> John Brown, 1859

About half of all the slaves in the South lived on small farms, but large plantations dominated the region economically, socially, and politically. Overseers supervised the slaves, and a leading southern journal, *De Bow's Review*, advised them to create the impression that they stood alongside their slaves, rather than above them, in a common effort to till the land:

Nothing more reconciles the Negro to his work than the overseer's sharing with him. If they shuck corn at night, let him be present until the last moment; if the sun shines hot, let him stand in it as long as they do; if it rains, let him take his share of it; if it is cold, let him not go to the fire oftener than they do.

Yet overseers regularly exerted their authority; they often used the whip, and it was the harsh physical treatment meted out by them and by the slaveowners that added fervor to the abolitionist movement. Slaves considered disobedient or troublesome, especially those who attempted to run away, suffered a wide variety of tortures, including branding; ear removal, often called "ear cropping"; castration; and imprisonment in coffin-like containers known as "nigger boxes."

As abolitionists attacked slavery for its many cruelties, many southern planters reacted with reforms to eliminate the worst abuses. The changes were limited, and they were inspired less by humanitarian concern than by a need to quiet the demands to end slavery. Planters worked hard to crush any vestiges of abolitionist thought in the South, and they worked to prevent northern abolitionist ideas from gaining a foothold in the region. A long war of words preceded the fighting on the battlefields. On the abolitionist side, Harriet

Beecher Stowe's *Uncle Tom's Cabin* (1852) enflamed opinion, while on the southern side George Fitzhugh's *Cannibals All!* (1857) defended slavery on practical and philosophical grounds.

In the 1850s, the Free Soil movement, which attempted to prevent slavery from expanding into western territories, gained the support of northerners at the time they were developing an industrial and commercial economy different from the southern plantation system. Free Soilers wanted the western lands then being settled to be closed to slavery. Morality motivated some—many believed slavery was evil—while economics played the larger role. Free Soil advocates believed slavery in the West would create a hostile environment for industry, trade, and farms based on wage labor and individual initiative.

The debate between Free Soil and pro-slavery advocates tore apart the Whig Party, one of the two major political parties in the early 1850s, and led Free Soilers to form the Republican Party, which embraced their idea as an uncompromising principle: slavery must be kept out of the western lands. In the mid-1850s, Free Soil and pro-slavery forces took up arms in Kansas and fought to command that territory, turning it into "Bleeding Kansas."

In 1857, the Supreme Court's Dred Scott decision shocked northerners. In that ruling, the Court, headed by Chief Justice Roger Taney, a pro-slavery Virginian, held that a slave was property and a slave owner could take his property wherever he wanted. Hence no law could keep slavery out of the western territories. The decision infuriated the North while striking at the heart of the Republican Party.

Southerners called Republicans "Black Republicans" for their anti-slavery views, even though most Republicans did not argue for abolition and promised to allow slavery to continue where it already existed. Southerners feared that Republicans were abolitionists *in effect*, because Free Soil ideology would prevent the plantation system from expanding to new lands and would, as a consequence, cause it to wither and die. Southerners disliked other parts of the Republican platform: tariffs to protect industry from foreign competition; federal aid to railroads; legislation to provide free homesteads to farmers; and measures to promote foreign immigration. The Republican platform would, they feared, foster an industrial future at the expense of the southern way of life.

The greatest stumbling block between the North and the South, though, was race. Abraham Lincoln was right; the United States could no longer exist half slave and half free. When southerners defended states' rights, they espoused a strategy meant to protect slavery and maintain white supremacy; when northerners supported Free Soil, they advocated an ideology meant to ultimately relegate slavery to history's trash heap.

To southerners, the threat to slavery and to southern civilization intensified in 1859 when John Brown launched his raid on the federal arsenal at Harper's Ferry, Virginia (today West Virginia). Exaggerated reports swept through the South; some of them claimed that Harper's Ferry had been attacked by hundreds of revolutionaries; others that Brown possessed a map marked with "X's" indicating centers of planned revolution in the South. Harper's Ferry was thought to be just the beginning of a great abolitionist plot to free blacks through a cataclysmic bloodbath.

The election of Abraham Lincoln to the White House in November 1860 threatened to tilt the national government toward the industrial and Free-Soil side and strengthen the abolitionist cause. South Carolina quickly called a special state convention, and on December 20, 1860, the state became the first to secede from the Union. Other Deep South states followed, and, 10 days before Lincoln's inauguration in March 1861, they formed the Confederate States of America. The Upper South hesitated, but found the president's call for troops in the wake of the first shots being fired at Fort Sumter intolerable and, in April 1861, joined the Confederacy.

The South misjudged northern unity, and for northerners secession made the burning sectional issue primarily that of preserving the Union, a cause that they could more readily rally around than one to help blacks. For the South, race and fear dominated everything else. Confederate vice president Alexander Stephens insisted:

> Slavery with us is no abstraction—but a <u>great</u> and <u>vital fact</u>. Without it our every comfort would be taken from us. Our wives, our children made unhappy—education, the light of knowledge—all, <u>all</u> lost and our <u>people ruined</u>

forever. <u>Nothing short of separation from the Union can save us</u>.

When the Civil war ended, radical Republicans took charge of Reconstruction and, exhibiting an abolitionist-like fervor to purge the country of evil, and a vengeful desire to punish transgressors, they proposed to remake the South by confiscating land and distributing it to former slaves. As discussed in this chapter, congressman Thaddeus Stevens expressed this view most forcefully, to the point that he risked his own political future by his advocacy.

With slavery eliminated and some civil rights extended to blacks through the Fourteenth Amendment and congressional legislation, the Ku Klux Klan, one of the reactionary groups among rebels and renegades, came to the forefront of the southern fight to maintain white supremacy and prevent northern values from shaping the region. The Civil War had repercussions in American society well into the twentieth century; in the 1950s, reformers concluded that the protection of black civil rights required yet another assault on white supremacy— a Second Reconstruction.

1851 Anarchy for the Modern Times Commune

Many observers of New Harmony, Robert Owen's Indiana commune (see entry, 1825), blamed its failure on the lack of a strong central authority. But Josiah Warren, a musician, lamp manufacturer, and utopian idealist, concluded just the opposite: With his own commune, Modern Times, he set out to prove that a society organized around maximum individual freedom could succeed.

Josiah Warren (1798–1874) began Modern Times in 1851 amid the farmland of Suffolk County on New York's Long Island and based it on his concept of the "sovereignty of every individual." He said that society "must avoid all combinations and connections of persons and interests . . . which do not leave every individual at all time at liberty to dispose of his or her person, and time, and property in any manner in which his or her feelings or judgement may dictate, WITHOUT INVOLVING THE PERSONS OR INTERESTS OF OTHERS."

He screened all potential settlers to make sure their way of thinking would be compatible with his philosophy. He particularly wanted them to accept his idea of a "time store," which he believed liberated the individual from the constraints found in the larger economy. In 1827 Warren had opened a time store in Cincinnati, Ohio, and it prospered under a peculiar system: Shoppers paid cash for items whose prices were set to cover the cost of the items and some basic overhead, such as store rent. But the prices did not reflect the amount of time Warren had to spend in helping the shopper; to cover that cost, the shopper would agree to "pay" Warren by providing him with a service. A watchmaker, for example, might agree to work on one of Warren's watches without charge for a set number of minutes.

Warren established a time store at Modern Times and, extending that idea further, sought to have all goods and services exchanged by barter. He stipulated that none of the land or buildings at Modern Times could ever be sold for a profit, but unlike many contemporary communes, he allowed each of the settlers to own land—a practice that would ultimately be Modern Times's undoing.

True to the highly individualistic environment, Modern Times attracted a wide assortment of people engaged in any number of reforms. They gathered at the commune's public hall and discussed abolition, women's rights, vegetarianism, and other experimental ideas. At one point free love advocate Mary Gove Nichols settled there, annoying many of her fellow communards when she insisted that everyone at Modern Times accept her philosophy. As it turned out, nearly all of them rejected free love and instead entered into traditional marriage.

One Modern Times resident later said about his fellow settlers: "They were flush in Enthusiasm. . . . They were willing to sacrifice much in building an Equitable village which should be an example of Harmony and Justice; which should be a bright and shining light to all the world." But left largely to their own devices, they began selling land for a profit and acting in economically similar ways as the larger society.

Frustrated and disappointed, Warren quit Modern Times in 1862. Two years later, its residents adopted the name of Brentwood for the settlement, and it became another of the many satellite towns near New York City. "Man seeks freedom as the magnet seeks the pole or water its level," Warren once wrote, "and society can have no peace until every member is really free." Ironically, it was precisely such freedom that brought about the demise of Modern Times.

Further Reading

Wunderlich, Roger. *Low Living and High Thinking at Modern Times, New York.* Syracuse, N.Y.: Syracuse University Press, 1992.

Sojourner Truth Declares for Women's Rights

Born into slavery and abused as a child, Sojourner Truth developed a deep spirituality that encouraged her commitment to abolition and women's rights. Along with Harriet Tubman, she is remembered today as one of the two most prominent African-American women of the nineteenth century.

Sojourner Truth stood six feet tall and spoke in a low strong voice with clipped diction that revealed a Dutch accent and told vividly about her experiences as a slave. She was born with the name Isabella in Ulster County, New York, 90 miles north of New York City, around the year 1797, to John and Elizabeth, slaves owned by Colonel Johannis Hardenbergh. In that part of the country, Dutch farmers, such as Hardenbergh, dominated the economy, and they used slaves to work large landholdings. About 10 percent of the total population in Ulster was black.

In the early 1800s, Isabella was sold to an Englishman, John Neely, separating her from her parents and her brother. The Neely family treated her cruelly, often administering terrible beatings. Shortly thereafter, she was sold to a fisherman in Kingston, New York, and then to John J. Dumont, who owned a plantation nearby. Once again she suffered physical and sexual abuse when she was assaulted by her mistress, Sally Dumont.

In 1827, about the same time the New York legislature passed a bill to emancipate all slaves, Isabella ran away from the Dumonts, who had indicated they would be slow to comply with the new law. She eventually made her way to New York City, where she worked as a domestic and began following a self-proclaimed prophet by the name of Matthias, formerly Robert Matthews. Matthias said he had purged his soul of all sin and that the Holy Spirit had spoken to him and warned that judgment day would soon come.

Isabella joined a commune founded by Matthias in the early 1830s at Sing Sing, New York, and worshipped him as a messiah, even though those close to her warned her that he was a fake. After 1835, however, the two drifted apart. Around 1840, Isabella changed her name to Sojourner Truth. She claimed that God told her to take the name "Sojourner," as part of her calling to preach, and that she took the name "Truth" on her own, to indicate what she would be preaching.

Sojourner Truth began spreading the word of God in 1843 at a time when evangelical movements proliferated in the North. She preached beneath the big tents at camps set up by the numerous Millerites—those who warned that the end of the world was near. She never officially joined them, yet they received her warmly and directed her to the

Sojourner Truth. (Library of Congress)

Northampton Association, a commune in western Massachusetts run by abolitionists. Truth later said that at the commune she enjoyed complete "liberty of thought and speech."

Truth lived at Northampton for several months before joining the ranks of antislavery feminists, and, in the late 1840s, traveling as an abolitionist speaker and a crusader for women's rights. This activity earned her some money, as did the publication of her *Narrative of Sojourner Truth* (1850), written by abolitionist Olive Gilbert, which presented Truth's experiences as a slave. Writing in *Sojourner Truth: A Life, A Symbol* (1996), Nell Irvin Painter describes Truth at this stage of her life as "a singing evangelist whose religion is joyous, optimistic, and at times ecstatic."

Truth spoke before the national women's rights meeting in Worcester, Massachusetts, in 1850, where she expressed her faith in God, a conviction, she said, necessary to bringing an end to evil. She observed that women had "set the world wrong by eating the forbidden fruit" but that she would now set it right. At another meeting at Akron, Ohio, in 1851, Truth asked permission to speak and according to one reliable report said,

> I am a woman's rights. I have as much muscle as any man. . . . I have plowed and reaped and husked and chopped and mowed, and can any man do more than that? . . . I have heard the Bible and have learned that Eve caused men to sin. Well if woman upset the world, do give her a chance to set it right side up again.

A later, exaggerated account had her stating these words before a hostile audience and using the phrase "Ain't I a woman?" (or "Ar'n't I a woman?"). As documented by Painter in *Sojourner Truth*, that account doesn't hold up, but the essence of Truth's comments lives on: to insist that women could do the same work as men; that the Bible did not relegate women to a secondary status; and that, as a result, women should be extended equal rights. Truth expressed the link between women's rights and economics when, at another point, she said to a male audience, "When we get our rights, we shall not have to come to you for money, for then we shall have money enough in our own pockets and may be you will ask *us* for money."

Truth settled in Battle Creek, Michigan, in the mid-1850s and from there continued her campaign against slavery and for women's rights. During that decade she met the abolitionist author Harriet Beecher Stowe, and in 1863, Stowe wrote about Truth in an article for *Atlantic Monthly* titled "Sojourner Truth, the Libyan Sibyl." Filled with as much myth as fact, the article paid tribute to Truth but also condescended to her. Stowe told about Truth's supposed hymn: "'There is a holy city . . . ' [Truth] sang with the strong barbaric accent of the native African. . . . Sojourner, singing this hymn, seemed to impersonate the fervor of Ethiopia, wild savage, hunted of all nations, but burning after God in her tropic heart."

During the Civil War, Truth collected food and clothing for black soldiers, and she met with Abraham Lincoln at the White House. After the war, she continued to advocate women's rights and urged the government to provide land in the West for former slaves. She wanted the wording of the Fourteenth Amendment changed so that it would enable women to vote. Truth died in a sanatorium in Battle Creek on November 26, 1883.

Feminist Elizabeth Lukins described Truth in 1851 in these words: "Her heart is as soft and loving as a child's, her soul as strong and fixed as the everlasting rocks, and her moral sense has something like inspiration or divination." Truth served as inspiration for African-Americans and women of both races in her time, as she continues to do today—a bold voice for equal rights.

Further Reading

Bernard, Jacqueline. *Journey Toward Freedom: The Story of Sojourner Truth.* New York: Feminist Press at the City University of New York, 1990.

Fitch, Suzanne Pullon. *Sojourner Truth As Orator: Wit, Story, And Song.* Westport, Conn.: Greenwood Press, 1997.

Painter, Nell Irvin. *Sojourner Truth: A Life, A Symbol.* New York: W. W. Norton, 1996.

Amelia Bloomer Advocates Dress Reform in *Lily* 1851

Amelia Bloomer was a leading advocate for women's rights, especially voting rights, but her name has come down through history attached to a derided form of female clothing called bloomers that, oddly enough, fit her desire to liberate women.

Amelia Bloomer was born on May 27, 1818, in Homer, New York, as Amelia Jenks. In 1840, she married Dexter C. Bloomer, a Quaker and reformer. Eight years later she attended the Woman's Rights Convention at Seneca Falls, New York, and in 1849 she founded a temperance newspaper, *Lily*, that within a few months carried articles devoted to women's rights. Many women reformers liked the newspaper, and in short order its circulation grew from a few hundred to about 4,000.

Bloomer made her proposal to change women's clothing in an article published in *Lily* in 1851. At that time, society prescribed outfits that were considered attractive, yet protective of a woman's body and her morals: tight corsets, several layers of petticoats, and full-length dresses. The whalebone corsets were highly restrictive, making women feel imprisoned like latter-day Jonahs; the dresses dragged on the ground and collected dirt; and the ensemble weighed some 15 pounds.

As an alternative, in her article Bloomer advocated a loose bodice, along with baggy ankle-length pantaloons and a dress hemmed at the knee. She did not invent the design—a few other women, such as English actress Fanny Kemble, had been wearing these outfits for years—but she argued for it so strongly that it became called the "Bloomer Costume," or, simply, "bloomers." Amelia Bloomer wore bloomers until the late 1850s. She was joined in her sartorial revolution by suffragists such as Elizabeth Cady Stanton and Susan B. Anthony, which led to the clothing ensemble becoming strongly identified with the women's rights movement.

Mainstream America derided the outfit, calling it odd and indecent. To tradition-minded Americans, bloomers became the symbol of women undermining social values. So strong was the outcry (while at the same time the curious flocked to see Amelia Bloomer in dress and pantaloons as she lectured for women's rights) that by 1860 the bloomer costume had been relegated to the storage chest of history.

Bloomer continued her campaign for women's rights long after the clothing controversy. In 1855, she and her husband moved to Council Bluffs, Iowa, and although she ceased publishing *Lily*, she lectured and wrote extensively. From 1871 until 1873, she served as president of the Iowa Woman Suffrage Association. And, she arranged for Stanton, Anthony, and others to speak in Iowa on women's issues.

Bloomer was particularly forceful in her advocacy of women's suffrage. She said, "I hold, not only that the exclusion of woman from the ballot-box is grossly unjust, but that it is her duty . . . to go to it and cast her vote along with her husband and brother; and that, until she shall do so, we can never expect to have a perfectly just and upright government under which the rights of the people—of all the people— are respected and secured."

Bloomer's dress reform was not a complete failure. Women's clothing in the late 1800s adopted some of the bloomer look, and more important, for all of their differences, the promoters and critics of bloomers had a valid point: Clothing says something about social values. Amelia Bloomer recognized that to accept more liberated clothing for women meant accepting a more liberated woman.

Further Reading

Bloomer, Dexter C. *Life and Writings of Amelia Bloomer.* 1895. Reprint, New York: Schocken Books, 1975.

1852 The Sting of the Lash: *Uncle Tom's Cabin* Inflames North and South

Angered by congressional passage of the Fugitive Slave Act in 1850, Harriet Beecher Stowe wrote Uncle Tom's Cabin, *an antislavery novel that so inflamed passions in both the North and the South it contributed to the outbreak of the Civil War.*

Harriet Beecher, who was born on June 14, 1811, in Litchfield, Connecticut, grew up in a strict Calvinist family awash in moral fervor. Her father, the Congregationalist Rev. Lyman Beecher, expected his sons to become preachers and his daughters to marry preachers. In 1832, Lyman was appointed head of Lane Theological Seminary in Cincinnati, Ohio, and Harriet moved there with her family. She began writing magazine articles and in 1836 married Calvin Ellis Stowe, a Lane professor.

Living near the Ohio River, just across from slave territory, Harriet Beecher Stowe heard many stories about slavery and visited a plantation in Kentucky. From one of her brothers, who traveled to New Orleans, she absorbed more tales about slavery and the abolitionist sentiment of the seminary.

When Congress passed the Fugitive Slave Act (1850), which gave southern slaveholders wide power to hunt down and recover runaway slaves, Stowe—like abolitionists everywhere—reacted with disgust. That same year, she moved back to New England, and the vibrant abolitionist spirit she found there influenced her all the more. Her brother Edward, a preacher in Boston, urged her to write something that would take slavery to task.

Stowe penned *Uncle Tom's Cabin, or Life Among the Lowly* as a serial that appeared in an abolitionist paper, the *National Era*, from June 1851 to April 1852. Later that year she expanded it into a book that sold 10,000 copies in its first week and 300,000 in its first year. Some 1.5 million pirated copies sold in England over a short period.

The hero of the book is Uncle Tom, a slave owned, at various times, by three different masters, including Simon Legree. With dramatic effect, she portrays Tom as a martyr and adds to his story the death of a child, Eva, and the flight of the slaves George and Eliza from their master to Canada. Through Tom, she depicts the physical and mental cruelty of slavery. At one point in the novel, Legree tells Tom that he will one day make him a slave driver.

"I beg Mas'r's pardon," said Tom; "hopes Mas'r won't set me at that. It's what I an't used to,—never did,—and can't do, no way possible."

"Ye'll larn a pretty smart chance of things ye never did know, before I've done with ye!" said Legree, taking up a cow-hide, and striking Tom a heavy blow across the cheek, and following up the infliction by a shower of blows.

Stowe was the first American author to make a black man the hero of a novel, and she portrays Tom as a brave and pious figure, one who tries to improve himself against insurmountable odds. Stowe displays her own religiosity when, in another scene, she has Tom again raise Legree's ire by still adamantly refusing to take on the slave driver's job:

"Mas'r Legree," said Tom, "I just can't do it. . . ."

"Yes, but ye don't know what may come. . . . How would ye like to be tied to a tree and have a slow fire lit up around ye;—wouldn't that be pleasant,—eh, Tom?"

"Mas'r," said Tom, "I know ye can do dreadful things; but,"— he stretched himself upward and clasped his hands,—"but, after ye've killed the body, there an't no more ye can do. And O, there's all ETERNITY to come, after that!"

Legree's hatred for Tom only intensifies, and the sneering master eventually whips Tom to death. For all of Tom's refusal to be a slave driver, Tom always "turned the other cheek" against indignities and on many occasions tried to please Legree, a part of his character that was later emphasized in the insulting use of the name "Uncle Tom" to mean blacks who acted obsequiously toward whites.

Many abolitionists applauded the novel; others criticized it as too mild, and with good reason. For example, Stowe shows one master as kindly to his slave, Scipio, and portrays Scipio as so appreciative of his master that he refuses his offer to be given his freedom; instead, he becomes a docile, obedient servant.

Many years after *Uncle Tom's Cabin* appeared, the critic Edmund Wilson wrote that the novel "if anything leans over backwards in trying to make it plain that New Englanders are as much to blame as the South and to exhibit Southerners in a favorable light." The character Simon Legree, in fact, wasn't even a native of the South; he originally came from Vermont. Stowe was doing more than trying to make her story more palatable to southerners; she was trying to show how slavery corrupted everyone, northerners and southerners alike.

Stowe used racial stereotypes and distorted the facts to dramatize her story. When so many critics called her claims inaccurate, she published the nonfiction *A Key to Uncle Tom's Cabin* (1853) to refute their charges. The *Key* showed that she had relied heavily on Theodore Dwight Weld's abolitionist tract, *Slavery As It Is, the Testimony of a Thousand Witnesses* (1839) for information—while writing the novel she supposedly had the work with her day and night and slept with it under her pillow—but the Key failed to quiet her critics.

Uncle's Tom's Cabin sold widely in the North, but it angered the South. Many southerners considered it to be nothing less than seditious. Whatever the veracity of *Uncle Tom's Cabin*, it brought slavery

LITTLE EVA READING THE BIBLE TO UNCLE TOM IN THE ARBOR. Page 63.

Illustration of a scene from Uncle Tom's Cabin. *(Library of Congress)*

Literature and Radicalism

The relationship between political writing and radical reform—between Karl Marx's *Communist Manifesto*, say, and socialist revolution—is often clear, but such is not always the case with novels. Yet America has a rich tradition of protest fiction that has stimulated change. Harriet Beecher Stowe's *Uncle Tom's Cabin* is but one example, and a pointed one at that. Often, the literary protest is more subtle but no less effective. John Steinbeck's *The Grapes of Wrath* (1939) exposed class oppression and in so doing encouraged some Americans to think about restructuring their society.

Many a countercultural youth in the 1960s related to the life-is-absurd and antiwar themes found in the novels of Kurt Vonnegut, Jr. His *Slaughterhouse Five* (1969) so

effectively revealed the inhumanity of the Allied bombing of Dresden, Germany, in World War II that it fed the peace movement. More recently, black writers like Alice Walker in *The Color Purple* (1985) and Toni Morrison in *Beloved* (1987) have stimulated readers into thinking about issues of gender and race.

While none of these authors presented a detailed program for reform, they raised consciousness about social issues and, more important, made it easier for readers to identify with the plight of those oppressed—developing an empathy that the turgid prose of the *Communist Manifesto* could never accomplish. In that way, these works supplied the spark needed for radical action.

---

into the homes of thousands of people who otherwise had little contact with servitude. The book contributed to northerners and southerners viewing each other simplistically, and it heightened the emotion and hatred between the regions as the issue of slavery dominated national politics.

Soon after publishing *Uncle Tom's Cabin*, Stowe traveled to England, where she was feted and hailed. In 1856, she published a second antislavery novel, *Dred, A Tale of the Great Dismal Swamp.* She remained a prolific writer, averaging a book a year and producing many works for *Atlantic Monthly* and other magazines. She spent most of her later years in Florida and died on July 1, 1896.

Because of *Uncle Tom's Cabin*, Stowe obtained an audience during the Civil War with President Abraham Lincoln. Legend has it that he summed up the impact of the book in one short sentence when, on meeting her, he said, "So you're the little woman who wrote the book that made this great war."

Further Reading
Gerson, Noel Bertram. *Harriet Beecher Stowe: A Biography.* New York: Praeger Publishers, 1976.
Hedrick, Joan D. *Harriet Beecher Stowe: A Life.* New York: Oxford University Press, 1994.
Stowe, Harriet Beecher. *Uncle Tom's Cabin.* With an introduction by Alfred Kazin. New York: A. A. Knopf, 1995.

1854 Republican Party Forms under the Banner of "Free Soil, Free Men!"

To a southerner in the 1850s, no greater political poison existed than the Republican Party. To accept its free soil principles would mean death to slavery and ultimately to the South's civilization.

Although, in the long term, it was the years of slavery in the South and the growth of commercial agriculture coupled with industry in the North that gave birth to the Republican Party, the immediate cause was the Kansas–Nebraska Act, passed by Congress in 1854. Senator Stephen A. Douglas of Illinois, a Democrat and the sponsor of the act, thought it would resolve the issue of slavery in the western territories and lessen sectional tension; instead, it caused an explosive reaction in the North. By applying the concept of popular sovereignty—meaning the settlers in Kansas and Nebraska would vote on whether to permit slavery within territorial borders—the act ended the nearly sacrosanct Missouri Compromise of 1820, which had prohibited slavery north of latitude 36° 30'. This opened the door to the expansion of slavery throughout the unorganized lands of the West.

Several towns in the North and the Midwest held "anti-Nebraska rallies" to protest Douglas's act. The first to apply the name "Republican" to a meeting was most likely the rally held at the Congregational church in Ripon, Wisconsin, on February 28, 1854. Those who met there called for a new political party based "on the sole issue of the non-extension of slavery." In the terminology of the day, they stood for free soil, the position that slavery should be banned from all the western territories.

Michigan was the first state party to formally organize a Republican Party on July 6, 1854. Later that year, and into 1855, other state Republican parties appeared as the Whig Party dissolved and many of its former members joined the new political entity. The effect of the Kansas–Nebraska Act on the North could be seen in the 1854 congressional elections, when 66 of 91 incumbent Democrats, all of them from the free states, went down to defeat.

The Republican Party consisted of diverse elements, ranging all the way from abolitionists—considered radical by northerners and southerners alike—to conservative businessmen. According to historian David Donald, "The force that cemented them . . . was common opposition to the further extension of slavery in the territories."

Republican opposition grew even more adamant in the wake of the Supreme Court's Dred Scott decision in 1857, which said that the Missouri Compromise—recently superseded by the Kansas–Nebraska Act—had been unconstitutional all along. The court said that Congress had no authority to deny a slave owner the right to take his slave wherever he wanted, for a slave was property, pure and simple. Many a Republican feared that the Court would next rule that no *state* could prohibit slavery, a move that would reopen the North to the slave system. Republican comments poured forth in anguished tones, describing the Dred Scott decision as "a new and atrocious doctrine," "a deliberate iniquity," and "willful perversion."

One conservative claimed that the typical Republican free-soil speech was one-third repeal of the Missouri Compromise, one-third disorder in Kansas, and "one-third disjointed facts, and misapplied figures, and great swelling words of vanity, to prove that the South is, upon the whole, the poorest, meanest, least productive, and most miserable of creation." To nearly every southerner, no greater radicals existed. Abraham Lincoln and his fellow Republicans could insist that they stood only against slavery in the territories, not where it already existed; but to southerners, the Republicans ultimately wanted to end slavery. They reasoned that to contain slavery would strangle it. And after all, were there not abolitionists in the Republican ranks?

Moreover, Southerners pointed to the Republican platform that backed high tariffs and in other ways expressed sympathy for the North's industrial and commercial economy rather than the South's agricultural one. Indeed, the Republicans envisioned the future America as the North writ large.

The Republican dedication to free soil should not necessarily be interpreted as dedication to African-Americans and their rights. Many Republicans believed blacks were inferior to whites, and when they called for free soil their main desire was to reserve the West for white settlement in a society where independent farmers and small businessmen would prevail.

Lincoln expressed the Republican belief in mobility when he said about the North that "there is no permanent class of hired laborers among us." In other words, many Republicans saw slavery as abominable less for what it did to blacks than what it did to whites. In short, slavery was bad for business. It gave excessive power to a few white masters, denigrated labor, and restricted opportunities for other whites. David Davis, Lincoln's adviser, displayed Republican racist thought when, to soothe anxieties among whites that Republicans stood for racial equality, he advised party candidates to "distinctly and emphatically disavow *negro suffrage*, negroes holding office, serving on juries, and the like."

Whatever motivated the Republican free soilers, as the 1860 national election approached—the last one, as it turned out, before the outbreak of the Civil War—they showed no willingness to compromise.

They vowed they would remake the Supreme Court with free soil appointments. The *Chicago Tribune*, a Republican newspaper, said, "The remedy is . . . the ballot box. Let the next President be Republican, and 1860 will mark an era kindred with that of 1776."

Lincoln won the presidency, and on December 11, 1860, wrote a letter to a congressman in which he insisted: "Entertain no proposition for a compromise in regard to the *extension* of slavery." This was to southerners as revolutionary a challenge to the existing order as anyone could imagine, or fear.

Further Reading

Foner, Eric. *Free Soil, Free Labor, Free Men: The Ideology of the Republican Party Before the Civil War.* New York: Oxford University Press, 1995.

1854 George Fitzhugh Advocates Slavery for North and South

Capitalism unfettered is greedy and destructive; those people who are poorer and less educated than others must be helped—these statements sound like prescriptions for liberal reform. But they came instead from a conservative, the southerner George Fitzhugh, who in his Sociology for the South *(1854) and* Cannibals All! *(1857) wrote a strident defense of slavery that many northerners interpreted as an example of southern extremism.*

George Fitzhugh (1806–81) was born in Prince William County, Virginia, received little formal education, and, by most accounts, was more of a derivative than original thinker. He wrote articles for the *Richmond* (Virginia) *Examiner* and, between 1857 and 1867, for the influential southern magazine, *De Bow's Review.* His reputation, however, is based on his two books, *Sociology for the South* and *Cannibals All! Or Slaves Without Masters.* Historian David Donald states that with regard to slavery, by the 1850s "Southerners ceased being apologists for a dying institution and became fervent defenders of a beneficent system justified on historical, Biblical, scientific, economic, and sociological grounds." Fitzhugh primarily argued the economic and sociological points.

The beauty of slavery, according to Fitzhugh, was its paternalism; whereas in the North competition led to selfishness and greed, in the South slavery led to those with wealth caring for those who had little. Extolling his vision of tranquil plantation life, Fitzhugh observed in *Sociology for the South*, "The competitive system is a system of antagonism and war; ours of peace and fraternity. The first is the system of a free society; the other that of a slave society."

He claimed that in the North, the capitalist system left laborers fending for themselves in search of shelter, food, clothing, and in times of sickness, care; while in the South, masters handled all such matters for their slaves, making the lives of the laborers more comfortable and secure. Within capitalism, "The poor man is burdened with the care of finding a home, securing employments, and attending to all domestic wants and concerns. Slavery relieves our slaves of these cares altogether." In that way, he said, slavery is a form of socialism, but superior to the "isms" of Europe, which were bred amid urban and industrial decay.

Furthermore, slavery best suited the South with its large black population, for it provided education, guidance, and jobs to African-Americans who were inferior to whites and doomed to failure without white institutions. Fitzhugh wrote:

> It is clear the Athenian democracy would not suit a negro nation, nor will the government of mere law suffice for the individual negro. He is but a grown up child, and must be governed as a child. . . . The master occupies towards him the place of a parent or guardian. . . . The negro is improvident; will not lay up in summer for the wants of winter; will not accumulate in youth

for the exigencies of age. . . . The negro race is inferior to the white race, and living in their midst, they would be far outstripped or outwitted in the chase of free competition.

In *Cannibals All!* Fitzhugh continued his theme of providence from slavery, showing how the system went beyond benefiting blacks to helping even the lowliest of whites. "It elevates those whites," he insisted, "for it makes them not the bottom of society, as at the North—not the menials, the hired day laborer, the work scavengers, and scullions—but privileged citizens, like Greek and Roman citizens, with a numerous class far beneath them. In slave society, one white man does not lord it over another; for all are equal in privilege, if not in wealth. . . . The menial, the exposed and laborious, and the disgraceful occupations, are all filled by slaves."

Northerners reacted to Fitzhugh's works with sharp criticism and disdain. His views threatened their society as much as any abolitionist view threatened southern society and proved to many northerners the aggressive nature of slaveholders. Particularly galling was Fitzhugh's claim that slavery should be applied to white laborers as well as black, that it would save them from the cruelties found in capitalism.

Fitzhugh did agree with abolitionists on one point: the institution of slavery was a zero-sum game. In *Sociology for the South*, Fitzhugh predicted: "One set of ideas will govern and control after awhile the civilized world. Slavery will every where be abolished, or every where be re-instituted." No one could doubt which one he thought should prevail. "The Southerner is the negro's friend, his only friend," he concluded. "Let no intermeddling abolitionist, no refined philosophy, dissolve this friendship."

Further Reading
Genovese, Eugene D. *The World the Slaveholders Made: Two Essays in Interpretation.* New York: Pantheon Books, 1969.
Loewenberg, Robert J. *Freedom's Despots: The Critique of Abolition.* Durham, N.C.: Carolina Academic Press, 1986.
Wish, Harvey. *George Fitzhugh, Propagandist of the Old South.* Baton Rouge: Louisiana State University Press, 1943.

Mormons in Utah Engage Federal Troops in a Showdown   1857

Soon after the Mormons settled Utah in an attempt to escape persecution, they found the U.S. army descending on them while easterners concluded that the emigrants wanted nothing less than to form their own country.

The Mormons first arrived in Utah in July 1847, seeking a distant land that would isolate them from the persecution they had experienced in Missouri and Illinois. Their leader, Brigham Young, had heard about the valley of the Great Salt Lake from the journal kept by explorer John C. Fremont and from Lansford W. Hasting's *The Emigrants' Guide to Oregon and California.* As the Mormons passed through the Wasatch Mountains and descended into the valley, they sighted what one of them called "a broad and barren plain . . . blistering in the burning rays of the midsummer sun . . . the paradise of the lizard, the cricket, and the rattlesnake." This was their new home.

Young built a theocracy. To survive and prosper in the hostile environment, he ordered that the church direct everything: where people could live, the size of landholdings, the layout of Salt Lake City. He supervised the building of an irrigation system that changed the brown plain into a green oasis.

The Mormons even founded a state government—they called their settlement Deseret—not as an attempt to usurp the U.S. government, but as a way to provide a political system where Congress had yet to take action. In July 1849, the Mormon legislature asked Congress to accept Deseret as a state. Congress didn't go that far, but in 1850, it did establish the territory of Utah with Young as governor. In the meantime, the Mormons continued to attract settlers; their missionary work led to 33,000 immigrants arriving from England, while others came from elsewhere.

To eliminate the possibility of persecution, Young ordered that Mormons gain ownership of all the good land, mineral deposits, and forests—no one, he insisted, must ever wield economic power over the church. When he arranged the judicial system in a way that would leave any federal courts powerless, trouble ensued.

Three judges sent to Utah by the federal government returned East with exaggerated reports about how the Mormons intended to defy national authority. At the same time, it was widely rumored among non-Mormon settlers that the Mormons were planning to kill all nonbelievers in Utah and that they were allying with the Indians to accomplish that goal. Many of these non-Mormons disliked the theology of the Mormon church and its practice of men having multiple wives. At that point, in May 1857 President James Buchanan declared Utah to be in open rebellion, and he ordered 2,500 soldiers into the territory as a symbol of federal power.

The troops approached Utah just as a religious revival was encouraging Mormons to rededicate themselves to their original cause and to reject all compromises with non-Mormons. When the Mormons heard about the troop movement, they concluded that the army was being sent to crush them. They frantically formed militias and sent men out to scorch the earth ahead of the troops, leaving the invaders with little food for themselves or fodder for their animals.

Amid these events, a group of 134 immigrants, called the Fancher Company, was passing through southern Utah on its way to California. They stole from the Mormons and let their cattle trample Mormon land, whereupon a group of Mormons in Cedar City arranged for the Ute Indians to attack them. The Indians killed a few and then laid siege to the rest. At that point, the Mormons decided to kill the remaining immigrants and, together with the Indians, they attacked the group on September 11, 1857, slaughtering all but the youngest children in what became known as the Mountain Meadows Massacre.

The Mormons blamed the massacre on the Indians, but few in the East believed them, and President Buchanan ordered more troops to Utah. Some panic-stricken Mormons burned their houses and fled, while others gathered arms; Brigham Young, however, decided that an exodus or a war would devastate the Mormon church. Consequently, he accepted the appointment of a new territorial governor and the presence of troops in Utah, though with the stipulation they be kept away from Salt Lake City. In April 1858 President Buchanan pardoned all Mormons who agreed to accept the authority of the federal government.

The "Mormon War" had really been no war at all, but it showed how threatened Mormons felt by the federal government and that easterners thought the Mormons a danger to accepted religious practices and national unity. In the end, the settlement between the Mormons and the federal government did little to weaken Mormon authority; Brigham Young still ruled the territory through the church that remained Utah's dominant force.

Further Reading

Billington, Ray Allen. *The Far Western Frontier, 1830–1860.* New York: Harper, 1956.

Cook, Lyndon W., and Donald Q. Cannon, eds. *The Exodus and Beyond: Essays in Mormon History.* Salt Lake City, Utah: Hawkes Publishing, 1980.

1859   Fifteen Killed as John Brown Leads Raid on Harper's Ferry

John Brown's life was consumed with the issue of slavery and his burning desire to eliminate it. In the 1850s, he turned to bloodshed, first at Potawatomie, Kansas, and then at Harper's Ferry, Virginia, where he staged a spectacular raid to purge the land of the evil institution and the sin attached to it.

Contemporaries and historians have debated the question of whether John Brown was a madman. Brown was born on May 4, 1800, in Torrington, Connecticut, to Owen Brown and Ruth Mills Brown. His mother was insane, as was his maternal grandmother. His mother's sister also died insane, and insanity struck others in the family line.

Brown held various jobs, but mainly plied his father's trade as a tanner. He moved frequently, lived in constant debt, and at one point declared bankruptcy.

Brown made his first public statement against slavery in 1837, when he rose in the back of a church in Ohio and said, "Here before God, in the presence of these witnesses, I consecrate my life to the destruction of slavery." In the 1850s, he was drawn deeply into the antislavery battle after five of his sons settled in Kansas, which was then embroiled in an intense dispute between proslavery and antislavery groups, each of which was trying to gain control of the territory. A letter from John Brown, Jr., to his father in June 1855 depicted the showdown: "The storm every day thickens; its near approach is hourly more clearly seen by all. . . . The great drama will open here, when will be presented the great struggle in arms, of Freedom and Despotism in America. Give us the arms, and we are ready for the contest."

Brown responded by raising money in the East, loading a wagon with guns and ammunition, and heading for Kansas. An attack by proslavery forces on antislavery settlers at Lawrence, Kansas, sent Brown into action. In the spring of 1856, he led four of his sons and two other followers on a massacre of six proslavery settlers at Pottawatomie Creek. According to affidavits filed by eyewitnesses, who were the relatives of Brown's victims, at separate cabins Brown and his followers hauled four men into the dirt and as the wives and children of the victims trembled in fear, they hacked the men to death with broadswords; they killed one of them by gashing open his head and cutting off his arms. (The murderers were never prosecuted.)

Brown went back East in summer 1856, to raise money for his crusade in Kansas with the help of several prominent Massachusetts abolitionists, among them Theodore Parker, Samuel Gridley Howe, and Thomas W. Higginson. Historians still debate the extent to which these abolitionists knew about what had happened at Pottawatomie. Evidence indicates that they knew a good deal, and that when they provided money for Brown's antislavery activity they also provided him with arms, realizing they would be backing bloodshed. Some who met Brown, however, thought him crazed; businessman John Murray Forbes thought he had detected in Brown "a little touch of insanity." Brown returned to Kansas and engaged a proslavery force in battle at Osawatomie, during which his son Frederick was killed.

Early in 1857, Brown began putting together his plan for invading the South. He intended to incite a slave uprising and form a free state under his leadership. In April 1858, he sent John, Jr., to Harper's Ferry, where a federal arsenal was located, to reconnoiter the small town tucked away in Virginia's western mountains. At a meeting in Chatham, Canada, his followers endorsed the plan and his proposed state constitution, which called slavery "a most barbarous, unprovoked, unjustifiable war of one portion of citizens upon another portion."

In 1859, Brown rented a farm five miles north of Harper's Ferry. He recruited 16 whites and five blacks to participate in his raid. On the overcast night of October 16, Brown and his men entered Harper's Ferry. They cut the telegraph wires and quickly gained control of the bridges and the armory with its arsenal. As bells tolled, signaling what Virginians thought was a slave uprising, several slaves joined Brown's group. But whites quickly rallied, and a militia trapped Brown and his men in the armory engine house. On the night of October 17, marines under the command of Colonel Robert E. Lee arrived. Brown refused to surrender, and they stormed the engine house. One marine thrust a sword into Brown, severely wounding him.

Sources of Radicalism: The Old and the New

The radicals of the mid-1800s exhibited a mix of the old and new that was the basis for their movements. Time and again radicals reached back to the American Revolution for ideas and inspiration. The belief that "all men are created equal," as asserted in 1776, found expression among abolitionists, who argued that slavery violated natural rights. Women's rights advocates extended the concept beyond the noun *men* and argued that all *men and women* were created equal. On the issue of women's suffrage, they pointed to the Revolution's credo "no taxation without representation." Women were taxed, and in other ways legislated for, but they could not vote for their representatives.

Radicals reached back as well to the moral content of Puritanism with its emphasis on building a better society. They were influenced by the evangelical spirit of reform found among Congregationalists and Baptists, a sense that every person could be improved and society could be cleansed of sin.

Radicals were also heavily influenced by the new individualism found in the democratic spirit emanating from the Jacksonian era and in the philosophical movement of transcendentalism. Many no longer felt they had to rely on the elite to show them what to do or to lead the way. Whether it was Sojourner Truth speaking out or John Brown firing rifles, many radicals expressed a democratic spirit.

Brown was quickly put on trial for treason against Virginia, and for conspiracy with slaves and first-degree murder. He offered no defense and on November 2 was found guilty. On December 2, he rode to his hanging, perched atop his own coffin. Prior to his execution, Brown had slipped a note to his jailer stating: "I John Brown am now quite certain that the crimes of this guilty land: will never be purged away; but with Blood."

Seventeen affidavits had been sent to Virginia's governor attesting to Brown's insanity, but the governor ignored them. Political leader Salmon P. Chase said about Brown: "How sadly misled by his imaginations! How rash—how mad—how criminal." Yet Brown's plan had received the endorsement of several abolitionists, and his use of violence was no greater than that employed by others in an era when congressmen were regularly carrying knives into the Capitol.

Brown was reviled throughout the South; Virginian John Wilkes Booth attended Brown's hanging and said, "I looked at the traitor and terrorizer, with unlimited undeniable contempt." Many northerners viewed him as a martyr. Poet Walt Whitman waxed eloquent about Brown, and women's rights advocate Lydia Maria Child declared, "His soul is marching on."

Abraham Lincoln thought little of Brown's raid. "That affair, in its philosophy," he said, "corresponds with the many attempts . . . at the assassination of kings and emperors. An enthusiast broods over the oppression of the people till he fancies himself commissioned by Heaven to liberate them. He ventures the attempt, which ends in little else than his own execution." The black abolitionist Frederick Douglass (see entry, 1861), though, measured the raid at Harper's Ferry quite differently. In extremism he found success. He said: "Did John Brown fail? . . . John Brown began the war that ended American slavery and made this a free Republic."

Further Reading

Boyer, Richard O. *The Legend of John Brown: A Biography and a History.* New York: Knopf, 1972.

Keller, Allan. *Thunder at Harper's Ferry.* Englewood Cliffs, N.J.: Prentice-Hall, 1958.

Oates, Stephen B. *To Purge This Land with Blood: A Biography of John Brown.* New York: Harper & Row, 1970.

Quarles, Benjamin, ed. *Allies For Freedom: Blacks on John Brown.* New York: Da Capo Press, 2001.

1860   The Union Dissolved—South Carolina Secedes

On December 20, 1860, delegates attending a special state convention in Columbia, South Carolina, unanimously passed an ordinance declaring that "the union now subsisting between South Carolina and the other

States, under the name of the 'United States of America,' is hereby dissolved." As stated in a Declaration of Causes passed on December 24, at the heart of South Carolina's reason for leaving the Union was the election of a president, Abraham Lincoln, "whose opinions and purposes are hostile to slavery."

South Carolina, and later the other future Confederate states, seceded for several reasons, but first and foremost because of slavery. When in 1859 the radical abolitionist John Brown attacked the federal arsenal at Harper's Ferry, Virginia, in an attempt to foment a slave rebellion, his action sent shock waves through South Carolina. Writing in *Crisis of Fear* (1974), historian Steven A. Channing observes that "John Brown struck at the deepest and most intimate anxieties of the white South."

Secessionist agitators, called fire eaters, excited South Carolina well before Harper's Ferry. They wanted South Carolina to quit the Union, and they drew on deep-seated social anxieties in a state where vigilance committees and slave patrols worked to keep blacks in check and guard against white outsiders who might spread antislavery ideas.

With the raid at Harper's Ferry, rumors circulated that Brown had in his possession a map that targeted South Carolina for insurrection. In various statements the fire eaters fulminated:

Men of the South! Think of your threatened firesides, your menaced wives and daughters, and beware of this useless strife. . . . We believe [southern civilization] to be the best ever devised. But it has enemies by the thousands and hundreds all over Christendom.

Our Negroes are being enlisted in politics. . . . If Northern men get access to our negros to advise poison and the torch we must prevent it at every hazard.

The election of [Abraham Lincoln] will be a virtual subversion of the constitution of the United States, and . . . submission to such a result must end in the destruction of our property and the ruin of our land.

In late 1860, South Carolinians feared that with Abraham Lincoln and the Republicans in the White House, slavery would be dismantled, and their economy ruined. Gone, too, would be the white supremacy that maintained civilization as they knew it.

South Carolina, the first state to secede, was also the blackest of all the states. That blackness—some lowland counties were 90 percent African-American—caused white South Carolinians to react to any antislavery sentiment, and even any criticism of their society, with an intense fervor akin to the anticommunist witch hunts of the 1950s. Channing observes that in the final six weeks before passage of the secession ordinance, "the pitch of excitement in the state rose to an incredible level, and with it rose the fear of slave insurrection."

Other issues were indeed involved in South Carolina and elsewhere in the South: states' rights, the tariff, the desire to show that the South could stand on its own apart from the North; but the fundamental and galvanizing issue was slavery and, linked to it as it always had been, white supremacy. One southern planter commented, "It is insulting to the English common sense of the race which governs here to tell them they are battling for an abstract right common to all humanity. Every reflecting child will glance at the darkey who waits on him & laugh at the idea of such an abstract right." And Confederate vice president Alexander Stephens stated:

Slavery with us is no abstraction—but a *great* and *vital fact*. Without it our every comfort would be taken from us. Our wives, our children, made unhappy—education, the light of knowledge— all lost and *our people ruined forever. Nothing short of separation from the Union can save us.*

South Carolina's secession was a reactionary effort to protect existing institutions rather than to engage in revolutionary beginnings; an action extreme in its goal to tear apart the nation and risk, as every South Carolinian knew it did, the possibility of war.

To northerners, South Carolinians had taken a treasonous path: an overthrow of the federal government made all the more dangerous when other Deep South states followed South Carolina's course and when, in April 1865, rebel forces fired on federal troops at Fort Sumter. For most northerners the fight became one to save the Union from extremists intending to replace democracy with slaveholding despotism.

Further Reading

Channing, Steven A. *Crisis of Fear: Secession in South Carolina.* New York: Simon & Schuster, 1970.

Sinha, Manisha. *The Counterrevolution of Slavery: Politics and Ideology in Antebellum South Carolina.* Chapel Hill: University of North Carolina Press, 2000.

1861 Frederick Douglass Proposes that African-Americans Fight in the Union Army

When African-American abolitionist Frederick Douglass advocated that blacks be allowed to fight in the Union army during the Civil War, most white northerners considered his proposal to be absurd. For these northerners, blacks should never be allowed to fight because they were so inferior to whites that they would fail in combat; more than that, to allow them to fight would imply they were equal to whites.

Under President Abraham Lincoln, the federal government initially excluded African-Americans from serving in the Union army. Lincoln's decision came partly from his racial prejudice against blacks, but also partly from his fear that to allow blacks to fight would drive the slaveholding border states, then tenuously clinging to the Union, over to the Confederate side. Lincoln took this position despite African-Americans having fought in the Revolutionary War and in the War of 1812, and having served in the navy from the beginning of the Civil War.

Frederick Douglass, a former slave, objected to Lincoln's policy. In an editorial he wrote for his newspaper, *Douglass' Monthly*, in September 1861, he said, "Men in earnest don't fight with one hand, when they might fight with two, and a man drowning would not refuse to be saved even by a colored hand."

In referring to the previous black experience, Douglass said sarcastically in February 1862, "Colored men were good enough to fight under Washington. They are not good enough to fight under [General] McClellan. They were good enough to fight under Andrew Jackson. They are not good enough to fight under General Halleck. They were good enough to help win American Independence, but they are not good enough to help preserve that independence against treason and rebellion."

By early 1863, Lincoln had changed his mind and, shortly after issuing the Emancipation Proclamation, he

Frederick Douglass. (Library of Congress)

began supporting the use of black troops. He did so because of the impression made on him by whites willing to command black regiments and because of the need for manpower. To a fellow politician he said, "I thought that whatever Negroes could be got to do as soldiers leaves just so much less for white soldiers to do, in saving the Union."

The reaction of northerners to Lincoln's decision was mixed. "I see by late papers that the governor of Massachusetts had been autheured to raise nigar regiments . . . ," stated one Union soldier. "The feeling against nigars is intensely strong in this army. . . . They are looked upon as the principal cause of this war." Another, however, said in reference to blacks and Copperheads—those northerners who opposed the war—that "I think more of a Negro Union soldier than I do of all the cowardly Copperhead trash of the north and there is no soldier but what approves of the course of the present administration and will fight till the Rebels unconditionally surrender and return to their allegiance."

From the army, blacks faced discrimination, sometimes based on their lack of experience, but more often based on race. All black regiments were to be led by white officers, and, until 1864, black privates received less pay than white ones. Furthermore, blacks were most often relegated to support duties, such as digging trenches, rather than being allowed to fight.

Meanwhile, blacks faced enormous retribution from the enemy. In battle, Confederate soldiers were particularly vengeful toward blacks, sometimes mutilating them. African-American prisoners of war were mistreated, and on more than one occasion black captives were killed. The Confederacy announced a formal policy of executing captured black soldiers or re-enslaving them. (Lincoln responded by promising that for every Union soldier killed in violation of the laws, a rebel soldier would be put to death, and for every Union soldier enslaved, a rebel one would be sent to hard labor.)

Several battles convinced white northerners that African-Americans could fight effectively. On May 27, 1863, two black regiments from Louisiana took part in the assault on Port Hudson, just below Vicksburg, Mississippi, and showed their courage. A few days later, black soldiers at Milliken's Bend, just above Vicksburg, beat back a Confederate offensive. One Washingtonian said, "I heard prominent officers who formerly in private had sneered at the idea of negroes fighting express themselves after that as heartily in favor of it." On July 18, 1863, the black Massachusetts 54th Regiment staged a daring attack on Fort Wagner in South Carolina. The *New York Tribune* reported, "It made Fort Wagner such a name to the colored race as Bunker Hill had been for ninety years to the white Yankees."

By October 1864, the Union army had 58 black regiments, and northerners more often welcomed than condemned them. The *New York Times* proclaimed that year:

> There had been no more striking manifestation of the marvelous times that are upon us than the scene in our streets at the departure of the first of our colored regiments. . . . Eight months ago the African race in this City were literally hunted down like wild beasts [during race riots]. . . . How astonishingly has all this been changed. The same men who could not have shown themselves in the most obscure street in the City without peril of instant death . . . now march in solid platoons . . . and are everywhere saluted with waving handkerchiefs, with descending flowers, and with the . . . plaudits of countless beholders.

By war's end about 186,000 African-Americans had served in the army, 134,000 of them from the slave states. About 3,000 had been killed in battle. Unfortunately, despite their sacrifices in the war, blacks remained second-class citizens. With the spread of racial segregation, the majority of Americans forgot that blacks had fought in the Civil War. Yet Douglass had a point when, in 1863, he claimed: "Once let the black man get upon his person the brass letters, U.S.; let him get an eagle on his button, and a musket on his shoulder and bullets in his pocket, and there is no power on earth which can deny that he has earned the right to citizenship."

African-Americans would fight in World War I and World War II, and in both they won the grudging admiration of whites, some of whom concluded that keeping blacks oppressed at home contradicted the goal of fighting for democracy overseas. African-Americans came to the same conclusion; thus, the experience of war provided a powerful impetus to the modern civil rights movement.

Further Reading

Donald, David Herbert. *Lincoln*. New York: Simon & Schuster, 1995.

McFeely, William S. *Frederick Douglass*. New York: Norton, 1991.

Quarles, Benjamin. *Frederick Douglass*. Washington, D.C.: Associated Publishers, 1948.

1864   The Radical Democracy Demands Equality for All

For much of the Civil War prior to the summer of 1864, when the Union effort took a turn for the better, widespread criticism of President Abraham Lincoln was heard in the North. Radical abolitionists in particular thought him incompetent and too lenient toward the South. They decided to stop his reelection, and toward that end they formed a short-lived political party that proposed protecting black civil rights.

In May 1864, a group of 400 disaffected Republicans from 16 states, joined by some Democrats, met in Cleveland, Ohio, to found a third party and promote an alternative candidate for that year's presidential election. Never an impressive group in terms of prominent political names, the delegates nevertheless attracted a number of abolitionists to their cause, among them Wendell Phillips and Elizabeth Cady Stanton.

They quickly nominated the famous explorer and general, John C. Fremont, as their standard-bearer. Fremont, who had run unsuccessfully as the Republican presidential candidate in 1856, neither sought nor coveted the nomination, but the delegates thought him more radical than Lincoln, and he accepted their decision. Prominent abolitionist William Lloyd Garrison, who disdained political routes toward ending slavery (see entry, 1831) showed the division within antislavery ranks when he belittled the entire procedure. "General Fremont, as yet," he said, "has not shown a single state, a single county, a single town or hamlet in his support. Who represents him from Massachusetts, on the call for the Cleveland Convention? Two men . . . neither of [whom] has a particle of political influence." And the pro-Lincoln *New York Times* described the meeting as "a congregation of malcontents . . . representing no constituencies, and controlling no votes."

Nevertheless, the delegates wrote a platform notable for two radical proposals. First, they called for all rebel lands to be confiscated and divided among active soldiers and among settlers in the South. Second, they proposed a constitutional amendment abolishing slavery and guaranteeing everyone "absolute equality before the law." The delegates denounced Lincoln for his "civil and military failure," and for supporting a reconstruction policy so lenient toward the South that it would be "more disastrous to liberty than even disunion."

But the Radical Democracy, as the malcontents called their new party, stumbled. Republicans distrusted the presence of Democrats in its ranks, thinking that all they really wanted to do was disrupt the Republican Party, and Fremont rejected the call for confiscating rebel properties. The *New York Times* called the convention "a precious piece of foolery."

Still, Lincoln worried that Fremont might pull enough votes away from the Republicans to enable the Democrats to win the White House. To appease the Radical Democracy and other critics, the president removed Postmaster General Montgomery Blair from his cabinet. Blair had denounced abolitionists and opposed harsh treatment of the South. In September, Fremont, who rejected any type of a deal, withdrew from the race because he thought Lincoln's reelection would be less damaging to the country than a victory by the Democrats. He offered, however, harsh words for Lincoln, stating, "I consider that his Administration has been politically, militarily, and financially a failure, and that its necessary continuance is a cause of regret for the country."

Even though the Radical Democracy collapsed, some of the ideas it embraced, ideas expressed by others in Congress and elsewhere, eventually came to fruition. The Thirteenth Amendment, ratified in 1865, abolished slavery, and the Fourteenth Amendment, ratified in 1868, stipulated that no state "shall . . . deprive any person of life, liberty, or property, without due process of law"—a step toward the equality Radical Democracy had demanded.

Further Reading
Waugh, John C. *Reelecting Lincoln: The Battle for the 1864 Presidency.* New York: Crown Publishers, 1997.

Ku Klux Klan Spreads Terror in the South 1866

The riders wore white hoods that cut through the darkness of night in such ghostly fashion that onlookers stood petrified by fear. Such was the Ku Klux Klan (KKK), organized in Pulaski, Tennessee, first as a fraternal group and then as a secret terrorist band intent on crushing Republican Reconstruction and maintaining white supremacy.

The Civil War had just ended and Republican Reconstruction had just begun when southern whites formed the KKK in 1866. On the whole, the Reconstruction measures passed by Congress were only mildly punitive toward a region that had sought to overthrow federal authority, but many in the South thought them harsh. Conditioned by the racist attitudes long a part of the now-defunct slave system, they opposed citizenship rights being extended to blacks. To see blacks voting and holding public office, such as sitting in state legislatures, appalled these whites. They determined white supremacy must prevail.

More than 24 former Confederate generals and colonels joined together to become leaders of the KKK, with General Nathan Bedford Forrest serving as Grand Wizard, though he never admitted it and quit the post after a short while. By 1868, the KKK consisted of sheeted, night-riding terrorists who would keep blacks and their white Republican allies from the polls—and otherwise keep them in line—by burning down their houses, by beating them, and by lynching them.

The Klan took to its lawlessness in an atmosphere made all the more explosive by the Democratic Party, intent on winning control of the national government by building a solid base of support in the South. The Democratic platform for 1868 called the Reconstruction Acts "unconstitutional, revolutionary, and void." Frank Blair, a Missourian and the party's vice-presidential candidate, used a blatant racist appeal to win the southern white vote. He called the Republican Reconstruction governments "bastard," and said, "The white race is the only race in the world that has shown itself capable of maintaining free institutions for a free government." He claimed that southern whites were being "trodden under foot by an inferior and barbarous race."

With the 1868 elections approaching, Nathan Bedford Forrest said he intended to kill radical Republicans—those responsible for Reconstruction—and vowed that "if trouble should break out, none of them would be left alive." He added: "If they send the black men to hunt those confederate soldiers they call kuklux, then I say to you, 'Go out and shoot the radicals.' "

Most active in Arkansas, Georgia, Louisiana, South Carolina, and Tennessee, the KKK's reign of terror against blacks and their white supporters was so effective that in fall 1868, 11 Georgia counties cast no votes for Republicans. In Louisiana, 21 parishes that had cast over 26,000 Republican votes in the April 1868 state elections cast only 501 that November, and in the same time period, the state went from a Republican majority of 58 percent to a Democratic majority of 71 percent. During these months, 1,000 Louisianans, mostly blacks, had been killed.

Republican governors tried to fight the Klan but ran into so many obstacles that their efforts proved futile. When they called out the militia, they could never trust its members, white men who generally hated blacks. Sheriffs pursued the Klan found their own homes attacked and their families threatened—and even if they arrested a Klansman, where could they find a jury that would return a guilty verdict?

Amid the violence, Congress belatedly passed three force acts in 1870 and 1871 that made it a federal offense to violate a person's civil or political rights and that gave the president the power to enforce the law by using the army and suspending the writ of habeas corpus. President Ulysses S. Grant sent the cavalry into several South Carolina counties and suspended the writs in nine of them.

In 1871, federal marshals arrested thousands of Klansmen throughout the South, and federal grand juries indicted more than 3,000 people. The authorities obtained more than 600 convictions. Additional arrests and trials continued into 1872; the Klan survived—and would experience a resurgence soon after World War I—but terrorism declined.

Yet other forms of intimidation continued, and southern blacks would have to wait until the 1960s civil rights movement to regain the suffrage and liberties they had enjoyed immediately after the Civil War. Whatever restraints were placed on the KKK, its radicalism filled with racial hatred left a powerful and lasting mark on the social landscape.

Further Reading

Chalmers, David Mark. *Hooded Americanism: The History of the Ku Klux Klan.* 3rd ed. Durham, N.C.: Duke University Press, 1987.

Swinney, Everette. *Suppressing the Ku Klux Klan: The Enforcement of the Reconstruction Amendments, 1870–1877.* New York: Garland, 1987.

The Acceptance of Radical Ideas

From revolutionary republicanism in the 1770s to abolitionism in the 1860s and onward into the twenty-first century, radical ideas have at times found acceptance in American society, "turning those who opposed them, formerly members of the mainstream, into reactionaries." There is, however, no easy formula to determine why some radical ideas gain such endorsement while others do not.

During the American Revolution, republicanism—formerly deemed an aberration with no chance of surviving in a monarchical world—obtained legitimacy after British actions reached a point that confirmed the revolutionary argument that the political system produced oppression. Northerners, who formerly rejected abolition as too extreme, accepted it after the pressures of the Civil War made the freeing of the slaves necessary to defeat the South, and after the slave system was shown to hurt whites and oppress blacks. Women's rights, civil rights, environmentalism, and gay rights experienced the same evolution. Each once stood starkly apart from the social norm, only to have at least some of their ideas incorporated into the mainstream. So, too, has been the case for right-wing radicals who, for example, found their antigovernment ideology partly adopted by the Republican Party in the 1980s and later.

Yet over the years, many other radical ideas have failed to gain widespread acceptance. The defeats for alternative proposals are many: free love, pacifism, socialism, and a host of others. Who can tell where radicalism in the future will take hold?

Radicals Seize Control of Reconstruction 1866

When Abraham Lincoln was president, he proposed measures that would heal the wounds from the Civil War and reconstruct the South on lenient terms. Even at that early date, a small group of Radical Republicans in Congress wanted to go further. After Lincoln's assassination, they wrested control of Reconstruction from the White House and imposed their own harsher, yet more libertarian, measures.

Andrew Johnson, the former Tennessee governor who succeeded Abraham Lincoln as president, inadvertently provided the fuel for the Radical cause. When southern state conventions met in 1865, they were expected to recognize slavery's end, nullify the secession ordinances, and repudiate Confederate debts. But these measures were not always carried out.

Making matters worse, the South sent to Congress four Confederate generals, five colonels, and Alexander Stephens, the former vice president of the Confederacy, while conservatives and secessionists filled the state legislatures.

Southerners made it clear that with slavery gone, a new system would oppress African-Americans, namely black codes that allowed freedmen to hold and sell property but prohibited them from serving on juries, testifying against whites in court, and, in South Carolina, from engaging in anything except farm labor. Most southern states passed laws stipulating that blacks arrested as vagrants could be hired out to landowners. Johnson saw nothing wrong with the black codes or with the decision by southern states to exclude freedmen from voting. And he did nothing when Mississippi refused to ratify the Thirteenth Amendment, which outlawed slavery.

To many northerners, the South's actions, and Johnson's acquiescence, were nothing less than an attempt to reestablish the South as it had existed before the Civil War, with only nominal changes. They wondered why they had fought the war and shed so much blood. Northern congressmen fumed about the rebels being back in power, the resistance reborn, the black codes passed. When Congress convened in December 1865, it was determined to take charge.

Historians have called 1866 the "critical year"—when President Johnson could have built a bridge to Congress, then dominated by moderates, had he been willing to compromise. But he refused, and his obstinacy allowed Radicals to work skillfully to gain the upper hand for their agenda: a more punitive reconstruction of the South, combined with asserting Republican power and advancing the rights of blacks, all directed by Congress rather than the president.

Johnson first showed his inflexibility when he vetoed a bill to extend the Freedmen's Bureau, which supervised labor contracts for former slaves and protected their civil rights. His veto caused many moderates to support the Radicals; but an even larger number turned against the president when he vetoed a civil rights bill, despite his entire cabinet advising him to sign it. Johnson said the bill violated states' rights.

Congress then sent the Fourteenth Amendment to the states to be ratified. Moderates prevented the Radicals from including in it a proposal to guarantee black suffrage, but it stipulated that "no state shall . . . deprive any person of life, liberty, or property, without due process of the law." Because it was a constitutional amendment, Johnson could not veto it, but he encouraged the southern states to reject it, and when they did, the amendment stalled. Moderate and Radical northerners alike, in and outside Congress, berated this intransigence and the president's contribution to it.

Then in July 1866, a race riot erupted in New Orleans, and the bloodshed combined with the unratified Fourteenth Amendment created the leading issue for the 1866 congressional races. As a result, the Republicans increased their majority to more than two-thirds in both the House and the Senate. A

Radical-dominated Congress now seized full control of Reconstruction; it determined which states could be represented and as a result set the requirements for rebuilding the Union.

The Radicals divided the South into five military districts under federal commanders and stipulated that blacks be allowed to vote in choosing delegates to state constitutional conventions. Additionally, they said that any new state constitution must protect the black franchise and disqualify Confederate leaders from voting, and that the state legislature must ratify the Fourteenth Amendment. Congress might then allow a state to regain its representation.

Johnson vetoed all the Radical bills, and in each instance Congress overrode him. Yet Congress stopped short of an even more extreme measure. A small group within the Radical contingent, led by Representative Thaddeus Stevens of Pennsylvania, realized that blacks could never really be free until they owned property. These Radicals wanted Congress to confiscate land from southern plantation owners and redistribute it to landless freedmen. Among blacks, "Forty acres and a mule!", a slogan that preceded Stevens's proposal but that was encouraged by it, became a rallying cry. Combining concern for African-Americans with punishment for former Confederates, Stevens stated, "Strip a proud nobility of their bloated estates, send them forth to labor . . . and you will thus humble the proud traitors."

But in the end, property confiscation was too extreme for Congress. Wealthier Americans feared where such a policy would take the United States: would demands to confiscate other property to help other poor and dispossessed people soon follow? Where would the line be drawn?

Ultimately, Stevens was right. Without property and some economic clout, blacks could not protect the civil rights granted them under Radical Reconstruction. Those rights would, by and large, remain an empty promise until after World War II and the birth of the modern civil rights movement.

Further Reading

Brodie, Fawn M. *Thaddeus Stevens: Scourge of the South.* New York: Norton, 1959.

Cullent, Richard N. *Old Thad Stevens, A Story of Ambition.* Madison: University of Wisconson Press, 1942.

McPherson, James. *Ordeal by Fire: The Civil War and Reconstruction.* 2d ed. New York: McGraw-Hill, 1992.

Trefousse, Hans Louis. *Thaddeus Stevens: Nineteenth-century Egalitarian.* Chapel Hill: University of North Carolina Press, 1997.

1869   "One for All, All for One!" The Knights of Labor Challenge Big Industry

Organized in 1869 as a secret order of workers, the Knights of Labor became in the 1880s the largest union in America to that time and one that challenged the very foundation of the emerging capitalism of corporations.

The Knights of Labor, officially the Noble and Holy Order of the Knights of Labor, was organized by Uriah Stephens (1821–82) and several other tailors in Philadelphia. Originally trained for the ministry, Stephens condemned the long working hours, then common for industrial laborers, as ungodly.

At first the Knights grew slowly, but discontent among railroad workers in the late 1870s led to a surge in membership. Cuts in wages, the use of child labor, and the exploitation of immigrants in various industries caused workers to search for an organization that would stand up to big business and, at the same time, offer laborers a sense of community in an increasingly impersonal urban society. "The Secret Order of Labor has taken a deep hold on the workingmen of this country," declared the *National Labor Tribune* in 1875. "The Order is spreading silently, like the rising of a tide. . . . It is labor's coming salvation. . . . The door is open to all good men, and they are welcomed as brothers by the brotherhood of toilers, who are making the elevation of Labor their religion."

An 1878 convention of the Knights at Reading, Pennsylvania, captured the discontent when it declared that the "alarming development and aggressiveness of great capitalists and corporations unless checked, will lead to the pauperization and hopeless degradation of the toiling masses." The Knights called for the arbitration of labor disputes and for an eight-hour work day. At a time when many labor activists ignored the plight of women, the Knights declared they wanted women to receive the same pay as men for the same jobs. And in an era when capitalism promoted private property as untouchable, the Knights called for the end to the "evil of monopoly" through the government ownership of telegraphs, telephones, railroads, and banks.

The Knights originally kept their organization secret, fearing retaliation from their employers. But this led to charges that they were plotting to overthrow the government, so in the early 1880s, under the leadership of Terence V. Powderly (1849–1924), the union opened itself up. That move, along with economic hardship from a recession, led to a dramatic growth in membership. The Knights gained 600,000 members in 1885–86 alone.

The Knights rejected exclusivity and formed mixed local assemblies that brought together skilled, semiskilled, and unskilled workers. They included in their ranks immigrants, southern blacks, and women, groups largely excluded by other unions. They even shook up racial attitudes in the South when they formed several integrated assemblies. This formidable grouping was accompanied by words that set business leaders on edge: "We declare an inevitable and irresistible conflict between the wage system of labor and republican system of government."

Business leaders reacted by using the police to crush strikes and the courts to restrict union activities. During a steel strike in Cleveland, Ohio, a pro-business newspaper called the union members "ignorant and degraded whelps" and "Communistic scoundrels."

With the motto "One for All, All for One!" everything about the Knights stressed labor solidarity: the common goals, the socials, the meeting halls with cooperative stores on the first floor. One historian has observed that "The Knights helped create an alternative cultural world, a world that unmistakably belonged to the producing classes."

The Knights pushed hard for an eight-hour work day in an era when 12- and 14-hour days prevailed. That demand, and one for wage increases, caused the Knights to strike the Southwestern Railroad and other companies in 1886. When the Knights lost these walkouts, its reputation suffered— as did that of the entire union movement when a demonstration of workers at Chicago's Haymarket Square in May turned violent.

At that point the Knights of Labor quickly unraveled, declining to only 100,000 members in 1890. In addition to the repercussions from 1886, the Knights suffered from tension between its skilled and unskilled members, disputes between its leaders who disliked strikes and its members who saw them as a crucial weapon, and competition from the American Federation of Labor, which attracted craftsmen. Yet in its short life the Knights had demonstrated a worker solidarity that exposed deep class divisions in American society and the oppression that reflected and created them. The labor movement owes a debt of gratitude to the Knights for exposing the pitfalls in organizing workers, showing the potential for creating unions, and stirring workers into action. From this experience emerged the labor crusades of the late 1800s and early 1900s, ranging from socialist activism to giving the workers a greater say in corporate boardrooms.

Further Reading

Fink, Leon. *Workingmen's Democracy: The Knights of Labor and American Politics.* Urbana: University of Illinois Press, 1983.

Phelan, Craig. *Grand Master Workman: Terence Powderly and the Knights of Labor.* Westport, Conn.: Greenwood Press, 2000.

Voss, Kim. *The Making of American Exceptionalism: The Knights of Labor and Class Formation in the Nineteenth Century.* Ithaca, N.Y.: Cornell University Press, 1993.

1872 Victoria Woodhull Advocates Free Love, Women's Rights, and Socialism

Controversial and provocative, Victoria Woodhull went from telling fortunes to advocating some of the more radical ideas of her era, among them free love, women's rights, and socialism.

Contemporary accounts universally describe Victoria Woodhull's parents, Reuben Buckman Claflin and Roxana Hummel Claflin, as "eccentric." Victoria Woodhull was born Victoria California Claflin in Cleveland, Ohio, on November 20, 1853, and while still a child claimed, like her mother, to be clairvoyant. Her father, willing to do almost anything to make money, put together a traveling spiritualist show in which Victoria and her sister, Tennessee (sometimes spelled Tennie C.), told fortunes.

At age 15, Victoria married Canning Woodhull, a Cleveland doctor who was an alcoholic. She left her father's show but continued to tell fortunes. In 1864, she divorced Woodhull. Two years later, she married Colonel James Harvey Blood, but kept her first husband's name. She was divorced from Blood in 1868 (they later remarried and divorced again), moved to New York City, where she ingratiated herself with the railroad and shipping magnate Cornelius Vanderbilt, himself an enthusiastic spiritualist. With Vanderbilt's money, she and her sister opened a stock brokerage office; with his investment advice they accumulated a substantial amount of money.

In 1870, Victoria and Tennessee began publishing *Woodhull and Claflin's Weekly*, in which she advocated socialism, equal rights for women, and free love. At that time, she became the leader of the New York section of Karl Marx's Second International. Regarding free love, she said in 1871, "I am a free lover. I have an inalienable, constitutional and natural right to love whom I may."

That same year, she testified on behalf of women's suffrage before the Judiciary Committee of the House of Representatives. In November she said in a lecture that "public opinion is against Equality, but

Illustration of Victoria Woodhull testifying before Congress. (Library of Congress)

it is simply from prejudice, which requires but to be informed to pass away. No greater prejudice exists against equality than there did against the proposition that the world was a globe. . . . I declare it as my candid belief that if women will do one-half their duty . . . Congress will be compelled to pass such laws as are necessary to enforce the provisions of the XIV and XV Articles of Amendments to the Constitution, one of which is equal political rights for all citizens."

On the then much-discussed topic of prostitution, Woodhull called it in her *Weekly* a "social evil," but at various times advocated its regulation and at other times its legalization. "Palliatives and curatives," she said, "will never remove a moral disorder whose causes lie deep in human instincts, and whose growth is festered by poverty and ignorance."

In 1872, the small Equal Rights Party nominated her for president of the United States; during the election she tried but failed to overturn the law that banned her and other women from voting. Her candidacy called attention to the political and social oppression of women, as did the many lectures she gave that year and in following years advocating women's rights.

Where Woodhull's ideas generated controversy, her charges against the renowned Henry Ward Beecher, pastor of Brooklyn's Plymouth church, produced a sensation. She claimed that Beecher was having an affair with Elizabeth Tilton, the wife of Theodore Tilton, a member of the editorial board of the religious publication, *Independent*. At the same time, she revealed her own sexual relationship with Theodore Tilton. Beecher was put on trial for adultery but acquitted. Woodhull was then tried for publishing an obscene work but, after spending seven months in prison, was acquitted. The episode sullied the suffrage movement for many Americans, confirming the conservative warning that liberated women, such as Woodhull, were licentious and would ruin the country's morals.

Woodhull moved to England in 1877 and in 1883 married John Biddulph Martin, a wealthy English banker. She continued to lecture and in 1892 began publishing a magazine, the *Humanitarian*. She died on June 10, 1927.

Her extreme challenge to conventional ideas was evident in her "firsts"—the first woman to appear before a congressional committee and the first to be nominated for president of the United States—and her extremism. Woodhull's contemporaries and some historians have argued that she damaged the women's rights movement; others see her efforts as having drawn attention to the cause and making reform more possible. Most likely it was a mixture of both, repelling some and awakening others.

Further Reading

Goldsmith, Barbara. *Other Powers: The Age of Suffrage, Spiritualism, and the Scandalous Victoria Woodhull*. New York: Knopf, 1998.

Meade, Marion. *Free Woman: The Life and Times of Victoria Woodhull*. New York: Knopf, 1976.

Underhill, Lois Beachy. *The woman who Ran for President: The Many Lives of Victoria Woodhull*. Bridgehampton, N.Y.: Bridge Works, 1995.

Susan B. Anthony Arrested for Voting

1872

In November 1872, Susan B. Anthony brought her campaign for women's suffrage to a head when she defied existing laws by registering to vote and actually voting. She was arrested, and a high-profile trial ensued, filled with confrontation and controversy.

By the time of her arrest, Susan B. Anthony had been fighting for women's suffrage for years. She was born on February 15, 1820, in Adams, Massachusetts, to Quaker parents dedicated to social causes. Her first major encounter with sex discrimination came in the 1840s, when she began teaching school in upstate New York and discovered she was being paid much less than her male colleagues. When she complained, the district school board fired her.

She held other teaching jobs, but in 1850 she left education. At her home in Rochester, New York, she met some of the leading reformers of the day, including abolitionists William Lloyd Garrison, Wendell Phillips, and Frederick Douglass. In 1851, she met Amelia Bloomer and Elizabeth Cady Stanton at a temperance convention in Seneca Falls, New York. She and Stanton developed a lasting friendship and collaboration.

Anthony was drawn to the temperance movement by the stories she had heard of drunken husbands beating their wives. In 1852, she served as a delegate to the Sons of Temperance meeting in Albany. When the group's leaders prevented her from speaking because she was a woman, she formed the Woman's State Temperance Society of New York. She continued to speak for temperance and encountered more hostility toward women participating in public debates, whereupon she gravitated to the women's rights movement. And like many other women reformers who began as temperance advocates, she joined the abolitionist cause and supported William Lloyd Garrison's demands for the immediate end to slavery.

Anthony traveled and lectured almost constantly; Stanton, who had a husband and children, could not tour as much and saw Anthony as the great proselytizer for women's rights. "I forged the thunderbolts and she fired them," she said.

In 1863, Anthony and Stanton formed the Woman's Loyal National League, which sent to Congress a petition bearing 400,000 signatures calling for a constitutional amendment to abolish slavery. While Congress debated the Fourteenth Amendment, which was designed to extend full citizenship to former slaves, Anthony urged that its wording be changed to specifically guarantee women's right to vote. Congress refused, and a schism appeared in the suffrage movement as some activists insisted that the issue of women gaining the ballot should take priority over blacks gaining the right to vote. Others believed that extending the vote to blacks could be used as a foundation for extending voting rights to women.

Anthony thought blacks should wait. She criticized the push for the Fifteenth Amendment, which would prohibit denying a person the right to vote based on race, and said that as voters, black men would join white men in oppressing women. Many of her comments denigrated African-Americans, and in 1868 she began publishing *The Revolution*, a women's rights journal that took an editorial stand for "educated suffrage," which was essentially code for "whites only."

In 1869, Anthony and Stanton formed the National Woman Suffrage Association (NWSA) to promote the ballot for women as a movement separate from the larger issue of women's rights. Anthony chaired the group's executive committee. At various times Anthony advocated a Sixteenth Amendment to guarantee women's voting rights; at other times the NWSA pursued congressional laws to implement what it saw as the voting rights already existing in the Fourteenth Amendment.

On November 1, 1872, Anthony and several other women entered a barbershop, a traditional male bastion, in Rochester. Anthony demanded that she be allowed to register to vote. Taken aback, the male registrars, or inspectors, did not know what to do; as they hesitated, Anthony told them she had suffrage rights under the New York constitution and the Fourteenth Amendment. She warned that if she were refused, she would sue the inspectors. They debated among themselves for another hour, before finally agreeing to register her. Newspapers then vilified them for having done so; the *Rochester Union and Advertiser* said, "Citizenship no more carries the right to vote than it carries the power to fly to the moon. . . . If these women in the Eighth Ward offer to vote, they should be challenged, and if they take the oaths and the Inspectors receive and deposit their ballots, they should all be prosecuted to the full extent of the law."

On November 5, Anthony cast her vote (as did about 50 other women). She wrote Stanton, "Well I have been & gone & done it!!—positively voted the Republican ticket—strait this a.m. at 7

Oclock. . . . If only now—all the women suffrage women would work to this end of enforcing the existing constitution—supremacy of national law over state law—what strides we might make this winter—But I'm awful tired—for five days I have been on the constant run—but to splendid purpose—So all right—I hope you voted too."

Two weeks later marshals arrested her for voting illegally in a federal election. In the months before her trial she lectured extensively around Rochester, arguing that women had the right to vote and urging juries "to fail to return verdicts of 'guilty' against honest, law-abiding, taxpaying United States citizens for offering their votes at our elections." She swayed so many people that Judge Ward Hunt arranged for a change of venue from Monroe County to Ontario County, whereupon Anthony began speaking there.

At Anthony's trial, which began in June 1873, Hunt stunned the jury when he announced he was dismissing it and handing down a verdict of guilty. Amazingly, he had written the verdict before the trial had even begun. "The Fourteenth Amendment gives no right to a woman to vote," Hunt said, "and the voting by Miss Anthony was in violation of the law." That night, Anthony wrote in her diary that the trial was "the greatest judicial outrage history has ever recorded!"

Anthony remained defiant. At her sentencing, when Judge Hunt asked her if she had anything to say, she launched into a long declaration. The judge interrupted her several times, ordering her to sit down, but she refused. "Robbed of the fundamental privilege of citizenship," she told the court, "I am degraded from the status of a citizen to that of a subject; and not only myself individually, but all of my sex, are, by your honor's verdict, doomed to political subjection under this, so-called, form of government."

Judge Hunt fined Anthony $100. She declared that she would never pay it, and she never did. Anthony continued to fight for women's rights, and from 1892 until 1900, she served as president of the National American Woman Suffrage Association. She died on March 13, 1906. Anthony did not live to see passage of the Nineteenth Amendment, which finally guaranteed women's right to vote in 1920, but her strenuous efforts for suffrage in the face of hostile audiences did much to advance the cause, and suffrage activists pointed to her trial in 1872 as an example of the extent to which authority would be used to oppress women.

Further Reading

Barry, Kathleen. *Susan B. Anthony: A Biography of a Singular Feminist.* New York: New York University Press, 1988.
Sherr, Lynn. *Failure Is Impossible: Susan B. Anthony in Her Own Words.* New York: Times Books, 1995.

Hutterites Found Collective Farms in South Dakota 1874

Persecuted for years in Europe, the Hutterite Brethren immigrated to the United States and established collective farms based on their religious beliefs.

The Hutterites who came to the United States were descended from the Anabaptists of the sixteenth-century Protestant Reformation. They originated in Switzerland, Germany, and the Tyrol region of northern Italy and southern Austria. The Hutterites began living communally in 1528 under Jacob Weiderman. Five years later, Jacob Hutter emerged as their leader, but he was burned at the stake in Innsbruck, Austria, in 1536 for refusing to renounce his faith.

Hutterite beliefs—adult baptism, separation of church and state, and pacifism—antagonized European governments; so too did the Hutterite stand against private property and their desire to live apart from the rest of society.

The Hutterite immigrants, about 900 in number, brought these beliefs with them when they settled in South Dakota in 1874. They established groupings of farms, which they called "colonies," with about

100 people living in each under a strictly regulated system. According to their interpretation of the teachings of Jesus, all private property was forbidden and all money made from their farming was to be used by the entire community, with distribution based on need. The Hutterites lived in shared buildings with common dining rooms.

Under their patriarchal arrangement, the men held all authority, with the women prohibited from any leadership role. The family was central to Hutterite life; everyone was expected to get married and have children. Everyone was required as well to worship God faithfully and diligently. In addition to church services every Sunday, the Hutterites attended daily prayer meetings.

Despite intermittent persecutions by their neighbors and the shift in America from an agricultural to an urban society, the Hutterite colonies, what one historian has called "a radical experiment in communal living," continue in South Dakota, Montana, and Canada, now with about 35,000 members. No other group in modern Western history has maintained communal living for such a long period. The colonies have their problems, but divorce, crime, drug use, and many of the other ills found in modern society are practically nonexistent among the Hutterites. They are proof that a communal, collectivist society can succeed, in this case based on intense dedication and submersion of individualism to the will of the group.

Further Reading

Hostetler, John. *Hutterite Society.* Baltimore, Md.: Johns Hopkins University Press, 1997.
Hostetler, John, and Gertrude Enders Huntington. *The Hutterites in North America.* New York: Harcourt, Brace, 1996.

CHAPTER FIVE

Industrialization and the Progressive Era

Between the Civil War and 1900," historian Howard Zinn writes, "steam and electricity replaced human muscle, iron replaced wood, and steel replaced iron." The industrialization that had begun in the antebellum period increased its pace, and so did urban expansion. More immigrants entered the United States; unlike earlier immmigrants who had come mostly from northern Europe, they hailed from Italy, Greece, Poland, Russia, and other countries located in that continent's southern and eastern regions.

Increasing industrialization, the rapid growth of cities, and the great rise in the number of immigrants contributed to problems including political corruption, slum housing, abusive child labor, oppressive factory conditions, environmental destruction, and the rise of a plutocracy that threatened to destroy republican government. In reaction, the Progressive reform movement was born; it was a middle-class movement intended to cure society's ills while preserving the newly formed corporate capitalist economy. President Theodore Roosevelt most prominently expressed the Progressive outlook and program in this era of smokestacks and big cities. Other reformers and reform movements either fit the Progressive mold or showed the influence of Progressivism; these included the American Union Against Militarism, Roger Baldwin and the American Civil Liberties Union, Margaret Sanger and the birth control campaign, the Women's Peace Party, and the effort to enfranchise women, all discussed in this chapter.

Now that factories, machines, and railroads dominated the United States; by 1899, manufacturing produced more than half of the country's commodity output—in 1869, manufacturing accounted for only one-third of the nation's goods. During the same 30-year period, the gross national product increased six-fold.

Where canals had provided the new infrastructure for America's industrial growth before the Civil War, railroads did so after it. The amount of track increased from 53,000 miles in 1870 to 167,000 in 1890. In 1914, track mileage passed the 250,000 mark, an astonishing figure given that it exceeded the total for the rest of the world. The growth in railroads involved more than just laying track; it required combining the various railroad lines into an efficient network. Furthermore, because building the railroads required a tremendous amount of capital, their founders organized them into corporations, thus taking the lead in the rise of a corporate economy.

The railroads consumed a tremendous amount of iron and steel; thus, the production of these metals took

> "We urgently call upon the wage-earning class to arm itself in order to be able to put forth against their exploiters such an argument which alone can be effective: Violence."
>
> The Central Labor Union, 1885

on an importance not seen earlier in U.S. history. Steel undergirded skyscrapers, trolley lines, and subways, and it provided the pipelines needed to transport oil, gas, water, and sewage. Steel allowed for the building of a powerful, modern navy, and it made possible the production of the automobile and many other consumer products. So important and pervasive was the metal that the era has been called the Age of Steel.

As industry came to rule the economy, and as the consumer market expanded based on a larger population tied to high birthrates and immigration, more corporations appeared. Businesses sought to grow bigger, stronger, and more profitable. One way they did so was through vertical integration, whereby they aimed to dominate resources, processing, and distribution. Gustavus F. Swift was the innovator: He developed refrigerated cars for shipping meat long distances, operated butcher shops, and opened packing houses in stockyard centers, including Chicago, Kansas City, Fort Worth, and Omaha.

John D. Rockefeller pursued a similar route with oil. He began as a processor, or refiner, and as new oil fields opened in the Midwest, he dominated them. He soon gained the upper hand in distributing oil, first by arranging deals with railroads, and later by controlling most of the country's pipelines.

Rebels and renegades in this era functioned within this new urban, industrial environment, a transitional setting from the previous era of agriculture. The growth of industry and big business substantially affected labor and stimulated union organizers, socialists, and other activists who made up the rebels and renegades of the late 1800s and early 1900s. Several economic depressions caused workers to suffer wage cuts while they continued to work long hours, often under dangerous conditions. Beyond that, workers felt a declining sense of usefulness. With skilled labor giving way to semiskilled and unskilled jobs, such as operating a machine or performing a repetitive function on an assembly line, workers felt less and less attached to their work—what Karl Marx called the "alienation of Labor." The workers felt as if they were mere cogs; expendable and replaceable. That status, as much as low wages, stirred their discontent and caused them to turn to unions and more radical proposals that involved socialism and even anarchy.

Some of the rebels and renegades covered in this chapter fall within the Progressive category; they angered conservatives with their demands for more federal government involvement to protect the interests and rights of the average person. For other rebels and renegades, however, Progressivism failed to go far enough; these activists concluded that no reform of the corporate system could end the oppression of the masses.

Because these activists saw society in terms of a class conflict between the workers and the elite, they wanted to destroy corporate capitalism and replace it with a more equitable system. These radicals included socialist leaders Eugene V. Debs and Elizabeth Gurley Flynn; socialist writer Upton Sinclair, whose novel *The Jungle* revealed oppressive conditions in the meat-packing industry; anarchist Alexander Berkman; and the newly formed union, the Industrial Workers of the World, which sought revolutionary change not just in labor-management relations but in society as a whole. Consequently, socialists, communists, and anarchists joined Progressives, labor organizers, and civil rights advocates to pressure for change, adding to the cacophony that made the late 1800s and early 1900s a tumultuous period.

The Great Upheaval

Beset by an economic depression, declining wages, and an increasing divide between the wealthy and the masses, the United States experienced a wave of labor unrest in 1877 that spread from the country's railroads to other industries. Suddenly everything seemed violent and chaotic as society struggled to come to grips with the dark side of the Industrial Revolution.

Any attempt to understand the Great Upheaval of 1877 must begin with the hardship facing industrial workers in the preceding months. The United States was suffering from an economic depression; and industries were cutting wages and firing workers, aggravating the already bleak conditions in the soot-filled factories and rundown neighborhoods.

Laborers reacted by organizing and striking. In August 1875, workers at the textile mills in Lowell, Massachusetts (see entry, 1834), walked out after the owners announced a 10-percent wage cut. But the strikers sank into poverty, and they were forced to march on City Hall to demand bread for their children. They were met, not by sympathy, but by the militia and police, who turned them away. In October, the strike ended with the workers cowed into submission.

That same year, coal miners in Pennsylvania's anthracite district suffered a crushing defeat. They went on strike after coal operators slashed wages 10 to 20 percent. The walkout lasted several weeks, until starvation forced the workers back into the mines at the reduced pay and with their union shattered.

Some of the miners continued to meet in a secret Irish fraternity called the Ancient Order of the Hibernians. The mine owners crushed this group, too; they called it the Molly Maguires, and they hired spies from the Pinkerton Detective Agency to destroy it. Moreover, the owners paid armed vigilantes to kill and terrorize miners. Based on perjured testimony in a series of trials from 1875 to 1877, several "Molly Maguires" were convicted of murder and hanged.

With these victories, the company bosses thought the workers had been silenced. But the grievances led to the upheaval of 1877.

By that year, the wages for railroad workers had declined to an average of $10–15 a week; brakemen typically made $1.75 a day for 12 hours of labor. And the work was dangerous; in Massachusetts alone, 42 railroad workers died each year in accidents. In the spring, several railroads colluded to cut wages even more—while still paying dividends to stockholders—and on June 1, the Pennsylvania Railroad announced its cuts would be applied to other lines. In addition, the company said it would require each train to pull 36 rather than 18 cars, thus increasing the load for each worker and reducing the number of jobs.

On July 16, firemen and brakemen struck the Baltimore and Ohio Railroad, which had declared a 10-percent wage cut, and prevented the freight trains from moving. In short order, firemen and brakemen in Martinsburg, West Virginia, joined the walkout, taking control of the local depot. The police arrested several of their leaders, but a mob freed them. On July 19, President Rutherford B. Hayes sent federal troops into Martinsburg, the first time the regular army had been used to crush a strike in a time of peace. J. P. Morgan and other financiers bankrolled the pay for the army's officers.

Still, the strike spread to other railroads, and beyond the railroads to other industries: miners, canal boatmen, and ditchdiggers all began striking and marching. The railroad strikers used the tactic of blocking the rails with their bodies, allowing passenger and mail trains to pass, but stopping the freight trains vital to industry.

Violence erupted, usually instigated by the industrialists and their minions. At Cumberland, Maryland, a militia fired into a crowd of workers, killing 12 and wounding 18. In Pittsburgh, the Pennsylvania Railroad requested that the militia be called out, and the governor complied—despite no signs of violence by the protesters. When the troops arrived, they encountered a hostile crowd that threw rocks at them.

The militia then fired into the crowd, killing 20 people, including a woman and three children. One newspaper reported that "Women and children rushed frantically about, some seeking safety, others calling for friends and relatives." (Later, a grand jury called the act "an unauthorized, willful, and wanton killing . . . which the inquest can call by no other name than murder." Nevertheless, no soldiers were prosecuted.)

Miners and factory workers joined the railroad strikers. A mob surrounded the soldiers and drove them into a roundhouse, where the trains were repaired and housed. Suddenly the roundhouse and other railroad property exploded into flames, causing the troops to withdraw. No one ever determined who set the fires, but the following day, violence continued in the streets of Pittsburgh, and 20 residents and five militiamen were killed.

Chicago turned especially violent. The socialist Working Man's Party rallied the workers, and when the mayor ordered the police to fire into the crowds, warfare erupted in the streets. On July 26, a cavalry unit charged into a march and, brandishing swords, killed 12 protesters while wounding many others.

In St. Louis, Missouri, the strikes crossed the color line when African-Americans and whites joined forces. One black steamboat worker said to a largely white crowd, "Will you stand with us regardless of color?" "We will!" the crowd shouted. The workers demanded an eight-hour day, wage hikes, and laws to prohibit the employment of children.

Disgusted with the railroads' involvement in stock fraud, land manipulation, bribery, and high shipping rates, the public at first sided with the strikers. The *New York Tribune* reported: "It is folly to blink at the fact that the manifestations of Public Opinion are almost everywhere in sympathy with the insurrection."

Most politicians, businessmen, and newspapers, however, decried the strikers as dangerous and as communists. As violence erupted, support for the strikers began to weaken. Within a month, the strikes ended, crushed by the financial and political strength of big business and by military power.

The strikes taught the workers that they needed better organization and more money to tide them over during walkouts. And they revealed to Americans that their society was not beyond the class divisions of Europe.

In his classic work *Democracy in America* (1848), Alexis de Tocqueville argued that Americans in the early 1800s considered their society to be middle class—despite the existence of slavery and stratification among urban workers. Apparently, the widespread ownership of land in a mainly agricultural society encouraged this view and assured that there would be no revolution; as Tocqueville said, among the middle class "the idea of giving up the smallest part of [their property] is insufferable to them. . . . Hence the majority of citizens in a democracy do not see clearly what they could gain by a revolution."

Even though industrial development in the later 1800s stripped away the economy's agricultural base, the old Tocquevillian view of society remained rooted in the public consciousness. But the Great Strikes of 1877 were not led by a middle class; they revealed a socioeconomic divide lurking just beneath the surface of American society. In shaking up the traditional view of America as the land of equality, they indicated the dawning of perilous times.

Further Reading
Bruce, Robert V. *1877: Year of Violence.* Chicago: I. R. Dee, 1989.
Foner, Philip Sheldon. *The Great Labor Uprising of 1877.* New York: Monad Press, 1977.
Stowell, David O. *Streets, Railroads, and the Great Strike of 1877.* Chicago: University of Chicago Press, 1999.

1879   Henry George Proposes a Single Tax

To Henry George something was wrong with a United States in which a few people lived in splendor and many others lived in want. He believed the country needed to distribute its wealth more equitably and widen opportunity. Toward that end he wrote Progress and Poverty *(1879) and proposed a single tax.*

Radical Finance

Monetary issues have long stirred radical movements. In the 1790s, the federal government's establishment of a national bank that favored the wealthy added to the discontent of the common people, which in turn expressed itself in the formation of Democratic Societies and in the outbreak of the Whiskey Rebellion (see entry, 1794). The bank issue, and what it meant to the value of money and who would have money, reared its head again in the 1820s and radicalized workers.

After the Civil War, as the American economy industrialized and experienced uneven growth and wrenching economic depressions, some reformers turned to monetary issues as the answer to the country's problems. In the 1860s and 1870s, they wanted to keep in circulation paper money, called greenbacks, that had been issued by the federal government during the Civil War. When the war ended, the federal government started calling in the greenbacks; with fewer of them available,

debtors were required to pay off their loans in more valuable gold. The debtors complained that they had obtained their loans in greenbacks and now were being forced to repay them with a higher valued specie. Some saw in the government's decision a plot by creditors to enrich themselves.

Others who favored the greenbacks argued that cheap money would boost the economy. More money in circulation, they said, would lower interest rates and make loans more available for farmers and small businessmen.

In 1874, a Republican-dominated Congress passed the Resumption Act, quickening the pace for retiring the greenbacks. Those who wanted cheap paper money formed the Greenback Party, but in 1876, its presidential candidate received only 80,000 votes. The cheap money interests, though, refused to fade; they returned in the 1890s, advocating silver coinage over gold and pushing their agenda through the People's Party (see entry, 1892).

Brought up in a poor family, Henry George (1839–97) thought that hard work would lead to success. But try as he might, as a newspaperman he encountered only setbacks. Then came the depression of the 1870s, and George concluded that opportunity for millions of Americans had been destroyed. He reasoned that the country needed a structural change in its economy, and in 1879 he wrote *Progress and Poverty*.

"The present century has been marked by a prodigious increase in wealth-producing power," he claimed, that was expected to "make real poverty a thing of the past." Instead the majority had reaped only disappointment. He continued: "The gulf between the employed and the employer is growing wider; social contrasts are becoming sharper; as liveried carriages appear, so do barefooted children."

George bemoaned the loss of the frontier and the public domain, which in the past had provided cheap land and a chance to live independently. There existed, he said, only a finite amount of land, and with population growth it was becoming more expensive and unavailable to the working people. Landowners, he claimed, were getting more of the country's wealth, while small business owners and laborers were getting less.

George proposed a "single tax," a 100-percent tax on increased values of land, with the money collected to be used for the social welfare. For example, should a tract of land valued at $500 increase in value to $600, the $100 would be taxed at 100 percent, meaning the entire $100 would go into the public coffers, and the owner of the land would never realize more than his original investment. With such a levy, the country would need no other taxes—hence the name "single tax"—and would have no need to resort to more extreme measures, such as confiscating property or replacing capitalism with communism.

George believed his tax was fair because land increased in value as a result of the community growing up around it, so the community as a whole should enjoy the profits. His tax, he claimed, would discourage people from speculating in land; on the other hand, because capital and wages would be untaxed, they would increase and therefore poverty would end.

Within a year *Progress and Poverty* sold millions of copies, and its readership extended overseas. One union, the Knights of Labor, claimed, "No man has exercised so great an influence upon the labor movement of to-day as Henry George." Writing in the *American Journal of Economics and Sociology* in October 1997, Michael Perelman states that "Henry George's stance was decidedly radical" because it challenged traditional economic theory and embraced the "strongly held beliefs of working people."

Americans formed single-tax clubs, and in 1886, George ran for mayor of New York City, losing by a narrow margin. George never envisioned starting a single-tax colony, but one was founded, in 1894, when proponents of his idea settled the town of Fairhope along Mobile Bay in Alabama.

By the time George died in 1897, his single-tax idea was out of favor and soon largely forgotten. It was, after all, a curious attempt to solve urban problems by emphasizing a commodity tied to the rural past, namely land. Obviously, land remained important in America's development, but the industrial economy focused less on its availability than on the availability of jobs, and on working conditions and the regulation of capital itself. Even economic radicals ignored George; they thought his single tax irrelevant and turned instead for reform to unions, anarchism, socialism, and other ideas and devices better attuned to the cities and factories.

Further Reading

Barker, Charles A. *Henry George.* New York: Oxford University Press, 1955.

Cord, Steven B. *Henry George: Dreamer or Realist?* Philadelphia: University of Pennsylvania Press, 1965.

Wenzer, Kenneth C., ed. *An Anthology of Henry George's Thought.* Rochester, N.Y.: University of Rochester Press, 1997.

1881 In *A Century of Dishonor* Helen Hunt Jackson Condemns America's Treatment of Indians

No other speech moved Helen Hunt Jackson as did the one given by Chief Standing Bear of the Ponca tribe in Boston in 1879. The Chief spoke about the injustices perpetrated against Native Americans; Jackson listened to his story and determined to write one of her own, a scathing criticism of America's treatment of Indians since the late eighteenth century that she titled A Century of Dishonor.

In discussing Helen Hunt Jackson, one magazine said about her in her thirties: "Up to this time she had given absolutely no signs of literary talent. She had been absorbed in her duties as wife and mother, and had been fond of society, in which she was always welcome because of her vivacity, wit, and ready sympathy."

She was born Helen Maria Fiske on October 15, 1830, in Amherst, Massachusetts, where her father taught college. In 1852, she married Edward Bissell Hunt, a soldier who became a major in the Army Corps of Engineers. Tragedy led her to writing. In 1863, her husband died in an accident while testing a submarine; two years later, her young son died. In 1866, she moved to Newport, Rhode Island, where she wrote a poem that appeared in *The Nation.*

She followed that with other poems and romance stories. In 1873, while living in Colorado Springs, Colorado, she met William Sharpless Jackson, a banker, financier, and railroad executive. They married in October 1875.

Four years later, Helen Hunt Jackson attended Chief Standing Bear's lecture in Boston. She heard him tell of the forced removal of the Ponca from Nebraska to the Indian Territory (today Oklahoma), and how they suffered from disease, starvation, and sorrow. She then engaged in a long period of research at the Astor Library in New York City before publishing *A Century of Dishonor* (1881). She intended it to influence public opinion and cause Congress to change federal policies concerning the Indians.

The book was published at a time when the wars against the Indians were coming to a close. (The last battle, actually a massacre of Sioux by the U.S. Army, would occur at Wounded Knee, South Dakota, in 1890.) With the surviving Indians slipping into despair, liberals were trying to stir the American conscience. *The Nation* had lamented in 1876 the horrid plight facing Indians in the taking of their lands by whites, calling the development "shocking . . . [with] nothing in our religion, or manners, or laws, or tradition, or policy, to give it any countenance or support."

Jackson fully intended to further stir that conscience; her book detailed the treatment of seven tribes: the Cheyenne, Cherokee, Delaware, Nez Perce, Ponca, Sioux, and Winnebago. In some passages she unleashed a straightforward barrage. She wrote:

It makes little difference . . . where one opens the record of the history of the Indians; every page and every year has its dark stain. . . .

The history of the Government connections with the Indians is a shameful record of broken treaties and unfulfilled promises. The history of the border white man's connection with the Indians is a sickening record of murder, outrage, robbery, and wrongs.

In other passages she presented a poignant, but no less assertive, account, such as when she presented testimony provided by Cheyenne Indians to a government committee:

When asked by Senator Jon T. Morgan, "Did you ever really suffer from hunger?" one of the chiefs replied, "We were always hungry; we never had enough. When they that were sick once in awhile felt as though they could eat something, we had nothing to give them."

"Did you not go out on the plains sometimes and hunt buffalo without the consent of the agent?"

"We went out on a buffalo-hunt, and nearly starved while out; we could not find any buffalo hardly . . . we had to kill a good many of our ponies to eat, to save ourselves from starving."

Jackson's prescription to help the Indians relied in part on ending the U.S. government's habit of "cheating, robbing, and breaking promises," but it also relied on assimilating the Indians into white culture. To a great extent, she wanted to eliminate through peaceful measures the culture others were eliminating through warfare.

Her book sold so widely that the government made her a special commissioner to investigate conditions among the Mission Indians of California. Her 56-page report was subsequently ignored by the secretary of the interior, causing her to appeal directly to the American people with a novel that would show the suffering of the Indians. She intended *Ramona* (1884) to do for Native Americans what *Uncle Tom's Cabin* (see entry, 1852) had done for black slaves; the book sold well, but most readers related to its romantic content rather than its social criticism.

Jackson died on August 12, 1885, just two years before Congress passed the Dawes Act. The legislation represented the assimilationist view that Jackson had championed; it ended Indian tribes as legal entities and divided land among individual Indians to make them property owners. The Dawes Act, which was rescinded in 1934, produced only limited assimilation, damaged Indian culture, and caused many Native Americans to lose their land through fraudulent actions by whites.

"The utter absence of individual title to particular lands deprives every [Indian] . . . of the chief incentive to labor and exertion." Jackson had written. Ironically, by trying to make Indian society more white, she subjected it to the very greed she despised.

Further Reading

Banning, Evelym I. *Helen Hunt Jackson*. New York: Vanguard Press, 1973.

Jackson, Helen Hunt. *A Century of Dishonor; A Sketch of the United States Government's Dealings with Some of the Indian Tribes*. New York, Harper & Brothers, 1881. New edition with foreword by Valerie Sherer Mates. Norman: University of Oklahoma Press, 1995.

Mathes, Valerie Sherer. *Helen Hunt Jackson and Her Indian Reform Legacy*. Norman: University of Oklahoma Press, 1997.

May, Antoinette. *Helen Hunt Jackson: A Lonely Voice of Conscience*. San Francisco: Chronicle Books, 1987.

1886 Workers Form the American Federation of Labor

Beset by a worsening economy and deserted by fellow workers in the Knights of Labor, in 1886 America's trade unions united into a new group, the American Federation of Labor (AFL), determined to win a class struggle and establish the eight-hour workday.

Before the AFL organized, a dispute erupted within the Knights of Labor (see entry, 1869). The country's largest union to that time, it was a massive grouping of both skilled and unskilled workers. Elements within the Knights, including many socialists, were opposed to trade unions, both those affiliated with the Knights and those independent of it, and wanted to see them dismantled. They asserted that trade unions, which consisted of craftworkers, had outlived their usefulness, for with the rise of industry, the crafts had lost their importance and would soon fade from the scene; and they complained that trade unions were shortsighted in campaigning for an eight-hour workday while greater issues (e.g., the need to restructure the entire economy) faced the country. Furthermore, they said that trade unions were too divided—that when one went on strike, the others still did business with the company being struck.

For their part, many trade unions disliked the Knights for its polyglot membership and unrealistic goal of creating a workers' utopia. Wages and hours, trade unions insisted, were the real issues. Meeting in Pittsburgh, Pennsylvania, in November 1881, several national trade unions formed the Federation of Organized Trades and Labor Unions, the forerunner to the AFL. A two-year economic recession, beginning in 1883, and several defeats in labor disputes with companies stunted the organization's growth, however, and it did little more than pass resolutions that few people noticed.

In 1884, the General Assembly of the Knights of Labor reacted to the Federation by declaring: "Our order contemplates a radical change, while Trades' Unions . . . accept the industrial system as it is and endeavor to adapt themselves to it. The attitude of our Order to the existing industrial system is necessarily one of war."

The dispute between the trade unions and the Knights climaxed in 1886, just as the labor movement came under harsh criticism for the violence that erupted at Chicago's Haymarket Square, a clash between police and workers that resulted in 11 deaths and more than 100 injuries (see entry, 1886). Hit with a 20-percent cut in wages in New York City, the members of the Cigar Makers' International Union, affiliated with the Knights, went on strike. When it seemed that they would win, District Assembly 49 of the Knights undercut them by reaching a wage agreement below what the International Union had been demanding, with the added requirement that the cigar makers employ only members of the socialist-dominated Progressive Union.

Some Knights complained about the agreement, calling it an example of the "Knights of Labor being victimized by the Knights of Labor in collusion with grinding, grasping bosses." The agreement outraged the trade unions, and several of them sent delegates to a meeting in Philadelphia in May 1886, where they complained that the Knights of Labor had colluded with management. They called for the autonomy of all trade unions within the Knights, a position difficult for the Knights of Labor to accept given its commitment to labor solidarity. In addition, they wanted the Knights to foreswear organizing affiliated unions, such as the Progressive Union, that competed with the existing trade unions.

The delegates presented their demands, or "treaty," to the General Assembly of the Knights when it met that month in Cleveland, Ohio. The assembly completely rejected it, however, and the head of the Knights, Terrance V. Powderly, added insult to the rebuff when he accused the trade union representatives of drunkenness at meetings.

Another General Assembly meeting in October 1886 ordered that cigar workers who were members of the International Union must quit the Knights, a move that caused the trade unionists to conclude they had no home in the Knights of Labor. Several trade union leaders then issued a call for all trade unions to send delegates to Columbus, Ohio, for a meeting in December 1886. Forty-two delegates appeared, representing national unions, local unions, and other labor organizations. On December 8, they organized themselves into the AFL. At the same time, the Federation of Organized Trades and Labor Unions met in Columbus and voted to merge with the new group. The AFL dedicated itself to forming local trade unions and uniting them through a central organization.

As with other groups, the extremism of the AFL could be measured only subjectively. Many in the Knights concluded the AFL was a conservative, reactionary group, willing to accept the new industrial order. To them, the Knights of Labor stood for radical change. Meanwhile many businessmen considered the AFL a threat to their control of labor; all unions, they claimed, were un-American. For their part, AFL members saw their union as more practical than the Knights, but no less conscious of the plight of the worker in an industrial society that robbed the laboring class of wages, dignity, and freedom. The preamble to the constitution of the Federation of Organized Trades and Labor Unions, ratified in November 1881 and later adopted almost verbatim by the AFL so that it became a declaration of principle for the new group, stated: "A struggle is going on . . . between the oppressors and the oppressed . . . a struggle between capital and labor . . . which must grow in intensity year by year, and work disastrous results to the toiling millions . . . if not combined for mutual protection."

Further Reading

Greene, Julie. *Pure and Simple Politics: The American Federation of Labor and Political Activism, 1881–1917.* New York: Cambridge University Press, 1998.

Kaufman, Stuart Bruce. *Samuel Gompers and the Origins of the American Federation of Labor, 1848–1896.* Westport, Conn.: Greenwood Press, 1973.

A Bomb Rips through Haymarket Square

1886

On May 4, 1886, a bomb exploded under mysterious circumstances during a labor rally at Chicago's Haymarket Square. The police and politicians, doing the bidding of businessmen, seized the bombing as an opportunity to destroy the union movement.

By 1886, industrial workers in Chicago and most everywhere else in the United States were caught in a vise of longer hours and lower pay. The expansive, post-Civil War economy had plunged into a depression, while the political system conspired to contain protests by the workers and protect big business. In 1886, the Supreme Court ruled that corporations were "persons," and that the Fourteenth Amendment, passed by Congress to protect black civil rights, applied to such businesses, by making regulation of state laws unconstitutional.

In this atmosphere, some workers became militant; especially among recent immigrants, socialism and, to a lesser extent, anarchism appealed. The Chicago-based International Working People's Association had connections to the European anarchist movement; at the time of the Haymarket bombing, it boasted 5,000 members.

During the early part of 1886, militant labor groups in Chicago prepared for nationwide strikes on May 1 to promote the eight-hour workday. Groups in other cities, including New York, Detroit, Cincinnati, Baltimore, Boston, Philadelphia, and St. Louis, joined in the preparations. Some 350,000 workers responded by walking off their jobs, while the largest marches, in Detroit, New York City, and Chicago, broadcast the protest message. The protesters pursued a limited demand with their eight-hour plea, yet class consciousness permeated the movement, and radicals had something more in mind when, shortly before the strike, the Central Labor Union declared: "We urgently call upon the wage-earning class to arm itself in order to be able to put forth against their exploiters such an argument which alone can be effective: Violence."

On May 3, 1886, just one day before the Haymarket bombing, a massacre occurred in front of Chicago's McCormick Harvester Company. For several months, striking workers at the firm had been locked out by management. The workers wanted an eight-hour day and wages increased to two dollars a day. The company refused to budge and instead hired strikebreakers. When they and the strikers clashed, the police fired into the crowd, killing four people. Anarchist August Spies expressed outrage in a circular that declared:

> Workingmen, to Arms!!!
>
> You have for years . . . worked yourself to death. . . . Your Children you have sacrificed to the factory lord. . . . When you ask them now to lessen your burden, he sends his bloodhounds out to shoot you, kill you!

To protest the McCormick Massacre, a rally was called for May 4 at Haymarket Square. About 3,000 workers turned out. By the time the meeting was drawing to a close, only a few hundred remained. At that point, the police moved in to break up the rally and a bomb exploded, killing seven officers and injuring several more.

Chicago's political leaders reacted by launching a massive unrestrained hunt for those involved in the bombing. The police illegally searched apartments, planted evidence, and bribed some workers to testify as witnesses.

The police arrested eight anarchists and charged them with murder, leading to a blatantly prejudiced trial. Judge Joseph E. Gary of Cook County Criminal Court ruled that anyone who had incited the explosion was as guilty as whoever threw the bomb, meaning that to get a guilty verdict, the state's lawyers had only to show that the anarchists had used incendiary words.

Gary disallowed any defense challenges to potential jurors. As it turned out, the jury was greatly tainted, with one juror related to one of the murdered policemen. In his closing argument, the state's attorney said to the jury, "Convict these men, make examples of them, hang them and you save our institutions, our society."

The jury convicted seven of the eight defendants, and they were sentenced to death. (The eighth was found guilty of a lesser charge.) Most Americans supported, the verdict, but extensive protests followed the trial, and the governor lessened two of the anarchists' sentences. A third anarchist committed suicide. The other four were hanged. The last words of one of them, Adolph Fischer, rang with defiance: "Hurrah to anarchy!"

A new governor, John Peter Altgeld, pardoned the anarchists remaining in prison, a move so controversial that it likely cost him reelection in 1896. To this day, no one knows who was responsible for the bomb. But a few years after the trial, it was revealed that the Chicago police had infiltrated anarchist groups to provoke the dissidents, and evidence indicates an agent may have planted the bomb.

The chief of police admitted that members of his force had on several occasions planted arms and ammunition at anarchist meetings. The items were then "discovered" by the police and the findings used to discredit the radicals by making them appear to be violent. Capitalists and their supporters saw such publicity as a way to contain the workers and protect their own profits and power. Such tactics damaged the entire eight-hour day and union movements.

Yet Haymarket Square emboldened and radicalized many workers. For them the words of August Spies, spoken at the gallows, rang clearest:

> If you think that by hanging us you can stamp out the labor movement . . . the movement from which the downtrodden millions, the millions who toil in want and misery—expect salvation— if this is your opinion, then hang us! Here you will tread upon a spark, but there and there, behind you and in front of you, and everywhere, flames blaze up. It's a subterranean fire. You cannot put it out.

Further Reading

Adelman, William. *Haymarket Revisited.* Chicago: Illinois Labor History Society, 1976.

Avrich, Paul. *The Haymarket Tragedy.* Princeton, N.J.: Princeton University Press, 1986.

Smith, Carl S. *Urban Disorder and the Shape of Belief: The Great Chicago Fire, the Haymarket Bomb, and the Model Town of Pullman.* Chicago: University of Chicago Press, 1996.

Edward Bellamy Looks Forward to Socialism with His Novel *Looking Backward* 1888

What could be done about the imbalance of wealth in the industrializing United States? What was the answer to the exploitation of the workers? For novelist Edward Bellamy, hope came in the form of a socialist utopia, as outlined in his novel Looking Backward, 2000–1887.

A native New Englander, Edward Bellamy (1850–98) discovered the human debris of industrial society when, at age 18, he traveled to Germany. There he was stunned by the wretched conditions in which industrial workers lived.

When Bellamy returned to the United States in 1869, he studied law in Springfield, Massachusetts, and soon thereafter opened his own legal practice. Disgusted with the profession, he left it after trying only one case and devoted his time to journalism and writing. Through his pen he expressed a moral fervor, criticizing in several articles child labor and the inequality of wealth.

In 1880, he and his brother began publishing the *Springfield Daily News.* At the same time, Bellamy wrote short stories for magazines and turned out four novels, none of which attracted much notice. He had married Sylvia Bowman in 1882, and with the birth of their second child, he began thinking in earnest about how the world could be improved for his children and future generations. He was influenced as well by Laurence Gronlund's *The Cooperative Commonwealth* (1884), a Marxist work.

At that time, the United States was experiencing a great upheaval: rapid industrialization brought with it the quick growth of cities and slums; factory laborers endured long hours and brutal workplaces; labor strikes threatened to disrupt the economy and spread disorder. Social inequality widened while some flaunted their wealth in an era called the Gilded Age.

With these conditions in mind, Bellamy wrote his novel *Looking Backward.* It sold more copies than any book previously published in the United States, with the exception of Harriet Beecher Stowe's *Uncle Tom's Cabin* (see entry, 1852). The novel tells of Julian West, who falls asleep in 1887 after being hypnotized and wakes up in the year 2000. Gone are the muddy streets, the poverty, the slums. In their place stands a utopian society, clean, prosperous, and equitable. West describes his physical surroundings: "Public buildings of a colossal size and architectural grandeur unparalleled in my day raised their stately piles on every side."

Looking Backward presents a socialist society, or what Bellamy calls a nationalist society, in which the state controls production and distribution of all goods. The result is an enlightened utopia where universal comfort, education, and art are bound together by cooperation and love. To some readers in the 1880s and 1890s, Bellamy's imaginary society presented a wondrous alternative to injustice and industrial squalor.

The book's popularity led to the formation of Bellamy Clubs, where readers discussed the virtues of the "nationalist" system. A nationalist movement promoted Bellamy's ideas in the political arena, though it soon faltered partly as a result of its siding with the farmer-based Populist movement, rather than with the city dwellers whose votes were more numerous and whose outlook was more progressive. It lost further momentum in the fervor of the Spanish-American War and the economic expansion of the late 1890s.

In 1891, Bellamy had founded the short-lived *New Nation*, a magazine devoted to utopian ideas. With the success of *Looking Backward*, he spent most of his time as a promoter and propagandist for nationalism. In 1897, he wrote *Equality*, a sequel that clarified his ideas; the book failed to gain widespread readership.

Whatever the limitations of *Looking Backward*, many reformers and radicals credited the book with changing their lives. Socialist leader Eugene V. Debs said it helped him "out of darkness into the light." Fellow socialists Norman Thomas and Upton Sinclair (see entry, 1906) credited the book with a similar influence. So, too, did the socialist novelist Jack London, the historians Charles Beard and Vernon Parrington, and the economist Thorstein Veblen. Even some New Dealers in the 1930s gave credit to Bellamy's work; Arthur Ernest Morgan, chairman of President Franklin Roosevelt's Tennessee Valley Authority, said, "Striking parallels may be drawn between *Looking Backward* and various important aspects of New Deal policy." The power of the novelist's vision influenced federal programs that affected millions of Americans and reshaped politics.

Further Reading

Bellamy, Edward. *Looking Backward, 2000–1887.* Edited with an introduction by Daniel H. Borus. Boston: Bedford Books of St. Martin's Press, 1995.

Bowman, Sylvia E. *Edward Bellamy.* Boston: Twayne Publishers, 1986.

Morgan, Arthur Ernest. *Edward Bellamy.* 1944. Reprint, Philadelphia: Porcupine Press, 1974.

1890   *How the Other Half Lives* Exposes America's Underside

With cumbersome camera and flash bar in hand, the journalist Jacob Riis combed the slums of New York City and took pictures of the immigrant poor, their work, and their habitats. Those photographs appeared in How the Other Half Lives *(1890), a book that merged text with pictures on an unprecedented scale and stimulated reformers to fight poverty.*

Jacob Riis (1849–1914) was himself an immigrant. Born in Ribe, Denmark, where he apprenticed as a carpenter and helped his father publish a weekly newspaper, he arrived in New York City in 1870. Like those whom he described in his later articles and books, he lived in poverty, often resorting to flophouses for lodging. So desperate had he become that he several times contemplated suicide. But,

Photo of "Mulberry Bend" slum in New York City, from How the Other Half Lives. *(Bettmann/CORBIS)*

ambitious and determined, he eventually used his experience at laying out pages to land a job at a small newspaper on Long Island.

In 1877, Riis found work with the *New York Tribune* as a reporter and began visiting police head-quarters near what he called the "foul core of New York's slums." He quit that job in 1888 to report for the *New York Evening Sun*, a position he held until 1899. In writing about crime and poverty he wan-dered among the poor—their streets, their shelters, their tenements.

How the Other Half Lives earned Riis a reputation in the United States and in Europe as a reformer. His narrative breathes compassion and disgust. "In the tenements all the influences make for evil," he said, "because they are the hot-beds of the epidemics that carry death to rich and poor alike; the nurseries of pauperism and crime that fill our jails and police courts; that throw off a scum of forty thousand human wrecks to the island asylums and workhouses year by year; that turned out in the last eight years around a half million beggars to prey upon our charities; that maintain a standing army of ten thousand tramps with all that that implies; because, above all, they touch the family life with deadly moral contagion."

Riis places the reader at the scene of the city's horrors:

Be a little careful, please! The hall is dark and you might stumble over the children pitching pennies there. . . . The sinks are in the hallway, that all the tenants may have access—and all be poisoned alike—by their summer stenches. Hear the pump squeak! It is the lullaby of tenement-house babes.

Six cents for his bed, six for his breakfast of bread and coffee, and six for his supper of pork and beans . . . are the rate of the boys' "hotel" for those who bunk together in the great dormitories that sometimes hold more than a hundred berths, two tiers high. . . .

Two [boys] were found making their nest once in the end of a big iron pipe up by the Harlem Bridge, and an old boiler at the East River served as an elegant flat for another couple.

Beyond Riis's words, though, the larger effect of *How the Other Half Lives* came from the photographs used to support his narrative. At that time, photography was new, only recently popularized by Matthew Brady and his Civil War pictures, and those who promoted the technology claimed it would reveal the truth, that "pictures never lie." Riis had learned from reading *Street Life in London* (1877), by John Thompson and Adolph Smith, that photographs could be used as infallible testimony, or so those authors said. Riis's photographs, then, gave his book more credibility, more power, and a wider audience.

Riis's books continued with *Out of Mulberry Street* (1898), *The Battle with the Slum* (1902), and *Children of the Tenement* (1903). His work led to the tearing down of the squalid Mulberry Bend tenement block, which was replaced with a park. He exposed corruption in the police department and contaminants in the city water supply. Reformers embraced him and several, foremost among them Theodore Roosevelt, urged him to enter politics, but he refused.

How the Other Half Lives appealed primarily to a well-to-do audience, and Riis minced no words in instilling in them the fear that without changes, the lower orders would rise up. One passage in the book describes a poor man standing on a street corner watching the carriages of the wealthy pass by. The man starts thinking about "little ones crying for bread around the cold and cheerless hearth," and with that he moves through the crowd and slashes "those around him with a knife, blindly seeking to kill, to revenge." The clear message was that the mad act of one could become the mad act of many.

Riis's concern for the poor had its limits, however. For example, the Denmark native displayed a prejudice against immigrants from southern and eastern Europe and stereotyped them in degrading ways. He described the Italians as "happy-go-lucky" and "content to live in a pig sty." Further, while he acted from altruism, it can be argued that he did so as well from a desire to impose middle-class values on others. Riis believed slums came more from personal traits than from a rapidly urbanizing and industrializing society. To him, strong doses of Christianity and stable families would cure the blight.

Whatever motivated Riis, and whatever the limits of his work, he nevertheless galvanized Progressive reformers in a book bold in its techniques and challenging in its ideas. To Riis, the conservative view, which said nothing could or should be done about poverty and slums, would only breed suffering for wealthy and poor alike.

Further Reading

Gandal, Keith. *The Virtues of the Vicious: Jacob Riis, Stephen Crane, and the Spectacle of the Slum*. New York: Oxford University Press, 1997.

Lane, James B. *Jacob A. Riis and the American City*. Port Washington, N.Y.: Kennikat Press, 1974.

Meyer, Edith Patterson. *"Not Charity, But Justice": The Story of Jacob A. Riis*. New York: Vanguard Press, 1974.

Riis, Jacob A. *The Complete Photographic Work of Jacob A. Riis*. Edited by Robert J. Doherty; with an introduction by Ulrich Keller. New York: Macmillan; London: Collier Macmillan, 1981.

1891 Mother Jones Organizes for the United Mine Workers

Wearing a full skirt, black blouse, and a black shawl, her gray hair partly covered by a bonnet, Mother Jones traveled the anthracite coal mines of Pennsylvania in 1891 organizing for the United Mine Workers. It was not her first fight for labor, nor would it be her last; in a crusade that began around 1870 and continued until 1930—when she was 100—Mother Jones stood for exploited workers throughout the United States.

Mother Jones was born Mary Harris on May 1, 1830, in Cork, Ireland, and as a young girl witnessed the clashes between British soldiers and Irish farmers; she later said, "I was born in revolution." Her father, Richard Harris, came to America and found employment on a railroad, and the rest of the family followed in the mid-1830s.

In 1860, while teaching school in Memphis, Tennessee, she married Robert Jones, an iron worker. Tragedy struck in 1867 when a yellow fever epidemic killed her husband and all four of her children. Distraught, she moved to Chicago and opened a dressmaking shop, only to be hit by another reversal in 1871 when a citywide fire destroyed her business.

Her life took a different turn when she was helped in her penniless state by her husband's friends and through them became an organizer for the Knights of Labor, the largest union in the country at that time. An effective speaker, she went from meeting hall to meeting hall calling for worker solidarity.

During a strike in December 1874 among the miners in western Pennsylvania's anthracite coal fields, the Knights sent Mary Harris into the battle to rally the workers. In 1869, the miners had succeeded in getting the mine operators to sign a contract with their union, the Workingmen's Benevolent Association. But just five years later, taking advantage of an economic downturn, Franklin B. Gowen, leader of the mine operators, determined to crush the union. It was during the anthracite coal strike that Mary Harris Jones was given the name Mother Jones for combining her stamina with a maternal concern for the workers. One labor radical later said of her:

> She might have been any coal miner's wife ablaze with righteous fury when her brood was in danger. Her voice shrilled as she shook her fist at the coal operators, the mine guards, the union officials, and all others responsible for the situation. . . . The miners loved it and laughed, cheered, hooted, and even cried as she spoke to them.

Despite her exhortations, in 1875 the strike failed and wages were cut 20 percent.

In 1877, Mother Jones participated in a railroad strike in Pittsburgh, Pennsylvania, and in the 1880s, she pushed for the eight-hour workday. Despite her later support for the Socialist Party, she usually rejected doctrinal disputes. To her, the important point was to agitate.

In 1891, Mother Jones again went into Pennsylvania's anthracite coal fields, this time at the insistence of the president of the United Mine Workers (UMW), John Mitchell, who saw in her an effective organizer. No union had existed in the region since the failed strike of more than a decade earlier, but she rallied the workers. To elude the Coal and Iron Police, assembled by the mine operators to crush all union activity, she traveled in disguise.

During a strike of miners in Arnot, Pennsylvania, in 1899–1900, she recruited the miners' wives to protest, expecting the owners would be less likely to use physical violence against them than against the men. As Mother Jones describes the scene in her autobiography: "The women kept continual watch of the mines to see that the company did not bring in scabs. Every day women with brooms and mops in one hand and babies in the other arm . . . went to the mines and watched that no one went in. And all night long they kept watch."

When the mine operators convinced the farmers nearby to withhold food from the miners, Jones traveled the countryside in a buggy, getting the farmers to change their minds. "Sometimes it was twelve or one o'clock in the morning when I would get home. . .," she said. "Sometimes it was several degrees below zero. . . . The wind whistled down the mountains and drove the snow and sleet in our faces. My hands and feet were often numb."

This time, the strike ended successfully for the workers when they received a wage increase. Jones broke with Mitchell, though, over a strike among Colorado miners in 1903. The workers were demanding the eight-hour day and payment for their labor in cash rather than company scrip. When the mine operators agreed to terms for some of their mines but not for others, Mitchell accepted the offer, calling it the best that could be worked out. Mother Jones called it a travesty to abandon some of the miners. She accused Mitchell of ingratiating himself with the rich and powerful and said that he lived in splendor while the miners were living in tents and earning 63 cents a week.

Mother Jones rejoined the UMW as an organizer in 1912—at age 82—and, in a treacherous act by the authorities in West Virginia, was arrested and sentenced to 20 years in prison. A massive public outcry caused the governor to pardon her in March 1913.

The following year, she announced that she opposed women's suffrage, saying action was more important than voting. "You don't need a vote to raise hell!" she insisted. "[Do] you need convictions and a voice? I have never had a vote and I have raised hell all over this country." Curiously, for all of her union activity, she maintained that a woman's proper place was in the home, that if the "industrial problem" were solved, men would make enough money so women could stay at home and take care of their families.

In 1930, at age 100, she appeared before the Movietone news camera and again held nothing back. "Power lies in the hands of labor to retain American liberty," she said, "but labor has not yet learned how to use it. . . . Capitalists sidetrack women into clubs and make ladies of them. Nobody wants a lady, they want women. Ladies are parlor parasites." Later that year, on November 30, she died, never having wavered in her commitment to the laborer. Ten years earlier, during a strike at the steel mills in Gary, Indiana, she had said about the managers: "I'll be 90 years old the first of May, but by God if I have to, I'll take 90 guns and shoot the hell out of them."

Further Reading

Fetherling, Dale. *Mother Jones: The Miners' Angel.* Carbondale: Southern Illinois University Press, 1974.

Foner, Philip, ed. *Mother Jones Speaks.* New York: Monad Press, 1983.

Josephson, Judith P. *Mother Jones: Fierce Fighter for Workers' Rights.* Minneapolis, Minn.: Lerner Publications, 1997.

1892 People's Party Calls for a New Economic Order

Control of the Nebraska and Kansas legislatures in the West and several legislatures in the South, governors in executive mansions and representatives in Congress—in the early 1890s, the People's Party, or the Populists, as they were more often called, challenged the Democrats and Republicans so strongly that it looked like they would displace one of them as a major party. Their message: that the emerging corporate capitalist system must be dismantled.

The Populists emerged out of the depression of 1877, when farmers in Texas organized the Farmers' Alliance with the goal of forming cooperatives that could smash the control of powerful merchants over the marketing of crops and the providing of supplies. By 1886, the Alliance counted 100,000 members, and that year it issued a request for "such legislation as shall secure our people freedom from the onerous and shameful abuses that the industrial classes are now suffering at the hands of arrogant capitalists and powerful corporations."

With the National Farmers' Alliance reaching 400,000 members in the early 1890s, the discontent crystallized into an indictment of an emergent economic system dominated by big business and big banks.

The farmers combined their financial complaint—voiced while the price of corn dropped from 45 cents a bushel in 1870 to 10 cents in 1889—with a greater one: that economic control by the few meant a loss of liberty for the many.

Many farmers embraced a conspiracy theory tied to the circulation of money. They maintained that bondholders and others who held notes on loans had gotten together to end the coining of silver so that debt payments would have to be made in gold, a commodity appreciating so rapidly that the lenders would receive more in money than the original loans were worth. Consequently, they would dominate the economy. The farmers wanted the unlimited coinage of silver. A cheaper metal than gold, if silver circulated widely it would inflate the prices for farm goods and would allow the farmers, nearly always in debt, to pay off their loans more easily.

In 1890, Alliance governors held office in Georgia and Texas, and 38 Alliance men sat in the U.S. Congress. In February 1892, several state alliance groups met in St. Louis, Missouri, and formed the People's Party, more often called the Populists. At their national convention in Omaha, Nebraska, that July, they wrote a platform with a resounding preamble: "The fruits of toil of millions are boldly stolen to build up colossal fortunes for a few, unprecedented in the history of mankind; and the possessors of these, in turn, despise the Republic and endanger liberty."

From there they proposed the unlimited coinage of silver and much more. They wanted to democratize the country through the direct election of senators (then chosen by the state legislatures), and they wanted to prohibit the president from serving more than one term. Moreover, they wanted to establish the recall—that is, force an official to stand for election before the scheduled end of his term—and the referendum—that is, require certain issues be put to a popular vote.

On the economic front, the Populists wanted to restructure the economy through a sub-treasury plan whereby the federal government would hold crops in storage until prices increased and would provide the farmers with low-cost loans. If approved, this plan would put the federal government into the banking business.

And the Populists wanted the country's railroads nationalized. They should be run, they said, on a nonprofit basis for the benefit of everyone, rather than for the few wealthy capitalists. If enacted, the sub-treasury and nationalized railroads would strike daggers into the heart of the corporate economy, causing people to rethink the boundaries between private property and community welfare.

Finally, the Populists wanted a graduated income tax that would fall most heavily on the wealthy; in trying to broaden the People's Party beyond its farm base, they added to their platform demands for the eight-hour day for industrial workers.

In the South, the Populists posed yet another threat to entrenched interests. They talked about forming racially integrated organizations—the People's Party in Texas did, in fact, include whites and blacks—to unite the poor into a powerful economic and political force. Populist leader Thomas E. Watson of Georgia said about both races: "You are kept apart that you may be separately fleeced of your earnings. . . . The accident of color can make no difference in the interest of farmers, croppers, and laborers."

The Populists nominated James B. Weaver, an Iowa congressman, for the presidency in 1892 and stunned the Republicans and Democrats by capturing one million votes and carrying four states. Yet, amazingly, the party quickly died, a result of several developments. First, despite its appeal to industrial workers, the Populists were largely a farm party, an anachronism in a country with an urban majority, and they attracted little support in the cities. Second, in 1896 the Democrats and Republicans maneuvered to defuse the Populists. The Democrats called for the unlimited coinage of silver and ran a "silver candidate" for president, William Jennings Bryan. Bryan's candidacy tore the Populists apart; they debated whether they should support him or run their own candidate. To support Bryan, they feared, would destroy their

Raising Hell: Mary Elizabeth Lease and the Populists

Mary Elizabeth Lease—famous for the thundering statement she once made to farmers: "Raise less corn and more hell!"—has been called the most effective of the Populist orators. Born in Pennsylvania, Lease (1853–1933) moved to Kansas, where she taught school, got married, and, with her husband, failed as a farmer. She then studied law and was admitted to the Wichita bar.

In 1888, she joined the Union Labor Party, a forerunner to the People's (Populist) Party, and, even though women were ineligible to vote, she ran for a county office. Four years later, she helped found the People's Party. In her fiery speeches, Lease attacked eastern money men and acknowledged the suffering experienced by farmers and city workers alike:

> Wall Street owns the country. It is no longer
> a government of the people, by the people, and
> for the people, but a government of Wall Street,
> by Wall Street, and for Wall Street. . . .

The [political] parties lie to us and the political speakers mislead us. . . . The politicians said we suffered from overproduction. Overproduction, when 10,000 little children . . . starve to death every year in the United States, and over 100,000 shop girls in New York are forced to sell their virtue for the bread their niggardly* wages deny them. . . .

We will stand by our homes and stay by our firesides by force if necessary. . . . The people are at bay; let the bloodhounds of money who dogged us thus far beware.

Lease left the People's Party in 1896 after it supported the Democratic candidate, William Jennings Bryan, for president. She moved to New York City, joined the *New York World* as a political reporter, and lectured frequently, advocating women's suffrage, prohibition, and birth control.

* *Niggardly* is a synonym for stingy and has no racial meaning.

---

party. In the end, the Populists endorsed the Democrat. For their part, the Republicans promised prosperity through a high protective tariff.

Third, the Populist emphasis on silver ignored the need for greater structural reforms and thus narrowed the Populist audience. The same can be said for the Populist belief in conspiracy—when they concluded that economic problems came from the machinations of a few, it limited their view and made them appear reactionary. Closely tied to their conspiracy theories, they conveyed an anti-Semitic message that attracted some but, again, caused others to see them as backward. Populist speaker Mary E. Lease called President Grover Cleveland "the agent of Jewish bankers," and another Populist leader said that "the aristocracy of the world is now almost altogether of Hebrew origin."

Fourth, the return of prosperity to the farms—wheat went from 72 cents a bushel in 1896 to 98 cents in 1909—soon made Populism irrelevant. Ironically, this economic recovery resulted in part from cheaper money—not through the coinage of more silver as the farmers had wanted, but through the coinage of more gold, by then plentiful and cheap because more mines had been opened.

Finally, in the South when Populists advocated racially integrated organizations, they stirred resentment among whites who hated blacks and concluded that the Populists were a "nigger party." Furthermore, the white Democratic elite used the race issue to keep whites from allying with blacks, unleashing racial demagoguery.

The Populists faded from the scene, but corporate America marched onward and consolidated its power. New challenges would emerge, but henceforth they would be urban in origin and focus, the agrarian force largely spent.

Further Reading

Goodwyn, Lawrence. *Democratic Promise: The Populist Moment in America.* New York: Oxford University Press, 1976.

Hofstadter, Richard. *The Age of Reform: From Bryan to F. D. R.* New York: Vintage Books, 1955.

Kazin, Michael. *The Populist Persuasion: An American History.* New York: Basic Books, 1995.

McMath, Robert C. *American Populism: A Social History, 1877–1898.* New York: Hill and Wang, 1993.

Alexander Berkman Tries to Kill Henry Clay Frick

1892

On July 23, 1892, anarchist Alexander Berkman (1870–1936) attempted to kill the general manager of the Carnegie Steel Company, Henry Clay Frick, in an act meant to apply "propaganda of the deed."

Violent labor strife preceded Berkman's assault. In early 1892, Henry Clay Frick, manager of the Carnegie Steel Plant in Homestead, Pennsylvania, decided to reduce workers' wages and smash their union. At the time, the plant's owner, Andrew Carnegie, was vacationing in England, and so was not directly involved in Frick's decision; nevertheless Frick's actions reflected stirred Carnegie's own disgust with the union.

Frick surrounded the steel plant with a fence three miles long and 12 feet high, and when the workers refused his wage cut, he locked them out. The workers then declared a strike, and Frick called in the Pinkerton Detective Agency to guard the plant and protect the strikebreakers he was hiring.

On the night of July 5, 1892, Pinkerton guards arrived at Homestead on river barges to find 10,000 strikers and their supporters waiting for them. When the Pinkertons refused to heed warnings and tried to leave the barges, a worker shot at them, whereupon the Pinkertons fired back. The ensuing gunfight left seven workers dead.

The Pinkertons then retreated, and the state sent in the militia and crushed the strike. Several strike leaders were charged with murder, but pro-labor juries acquitted them.

During the turmoil, Alexander Berkman, a young Russian immigrant, plotted to kill Frick. An anarchist, Berkman developed his plan with the help of his lover, the anarchist leader Emma Goldman. Some anarchists believed in "propaganda of the deed," meaning that actions spoke louder than words. The assassination of someone like Frick, Berkman believed, would reveal the oppression in society that caused violent acts and would generate support for change. It would also terrorize the upper class and avenge the killing of the union workers by the Pinkertons. Berkman said, "The killing of a tyrant . . . is in no way to be considered the taking of a life. . . . To remove a tyrant is an act of liberation, the giving of life and opportunity to an oppressed people."

On July 23, Berkman entered Frick's office and shot and wounded Frick, before guards wrestled Berkman to the ground. Convicted of attempted manslaughter, Berkman was sentenced to 22 years in prison. He served 14 years and was released in 1906. He then resumed his anarchist activities, opposing America's entry into World War I. During the Red Scare in 1919, he was deported to Russia, along with Emma Goldman and more than 200 other radicals (see entry, 1919).

Berkman's attack on Frick had the opposite result of what he had intended: he was widely condemned, even by most anarchists. No tyrants were removed and no people were liberated.

Further Reading
Berkman, Alexander. *Prison Memoirs of an Anarchist.* 1912. Reprint, New York: New York Review of Books, 1999.
Felher, Gene, ed. *Life of an Anarchist: The Alexander Berkman Reader.* New York: Four Walls Eight Windows, 1992.

Coxey's Industrial Army Marches on Washington

1894

As the worst economic collapse to hit the United States prior to the Great Depression produced massive unemployment, Jacob Coxey marched an army of jobless to the nation's Capitol to demand relief, only to be arrested and thrown into jail.

America's shift from an agricultural economy to an industrial one after the Civil War caused severe depressions struck which first in the late 1870s, again in the mid-1880s, and a third time in the mid-1890s. The depression that caused Jacob Coxey (1854–1951) to act began in 1893 with the collapse of the country's railroads. By mid-1894, more than 150 railroads had gone bankrupt, and, as they closed, the steel industry went with them. Unemployment quickly surpassed three million, with the number of homeless in New York City reaching 20,000.

Coxey's march turned out to be one of many protests during the turbulent year 1894 as the industrial masses refused to simply accept their plight. A successful businessman and a reformer who advocated the circulation of greenbacks, or paper money unsupported by specie, Coxey wanted Congress to pass his proposed Good Roads Bill. Under its provisions, the federal government would employ men to build roads. Congress, however, rejected the bill, and also rejected his call for a larger public works program, whereupon he announced that he would lead a massive army of the unemployed on a march to Washington, D.C.

Coxey—scrawny, bespectacled, and articulate—predicted that 100,000 men would join his march, but when the protest began in Massillon, Ohio, on a snowy March 25, 1894, only 86 showed up. There were 40 reporters present, though, and as the marchers started out on horses, bicycles, and foot, they received extensive newspaper coverage. By and large, the reports portrayed the protestors as misguided and potentially dangerous. The *Akron Beacon* (Ohio) described the group as "poorly clad," and said that "those who had no banners to carry marched along, their hands in their pockets, and many were shivering with cold. It would have been difficult to find among the lot one man who under ordinary circumstances would not be classed as a tramp."

As Coxey's Army moved east, it picked up recruits, and by the time it reached Pennsylvania it numbered 600. Thousands of people turned out in the towns it passed through, cheering the men on. But in Washington, tension prevailed, for in addition to Coxey's Army, many others were forming. In California, Lewis C. Fry led an army that left Los Angeles bound for the nation's capital, as did Charles T. Kelly, who organized an army in San Francisco. To make the long journey, these western groups commandeered railroads.

Coxey's army reached Washington on May 1, 1894, only to find the city police, under the orders of President Grover Cleveland, out in full force. As Coxey led his men toward the Capitol, the police directed them to the outskirts of town. Once Coxey and his men realized what was happening, they ran back to the Capitol. Mounted police quickly caught up with them.

"What do you want to do here?" the police captain asked Coxey.

"I wish to make an address," he replied.

"But you cannot do that," the captain said.

Coxey was arrested for walking on the grass and for illegally carrying a banner—in his case a button attached to his lapel. The other protesters were dispersed by force. The trial judge subsequently sentenced Coxey to 20 days in jail.

Coxey's army, joined by a few hundred men from the other armies, remained in Washington until August, when the movement disintegrated. Thousands of additional protesters were headed for the capital, but President Cleveland used court injunctions, marshals, and even federal troops to break up the advancing armies.

In the end, Congress refused to pass any public works bills. Yet Coxey had changed the course of political debate. In an era when the federal government routinely helped big business but was expected to stay away from social programs, Coxey insisted it had the duty to provide the unemployed with relief. Much later, during the Great Depression of the 1930s, his idea would be accepted. In that changed climate, Coxey returned to the steps of the Capitol on May 1, 1944, and in a ceremony to mark the fiftieth anniversary of his arrest, gave the speech he intended to give so many years before.

Further Reading

Schwantes, Carlos A. *Coxey's Army: An American Odyssey.* Lincoln: University of Nebraska Press, 1985.

Eugene V. Debs claimed that when he was locked in jail after the Pullman Strike of 1894, he became a socialist. Actually, his conversion occurred over a longer period, and unlike other socialists who traced their ideological growth to European influences, his socialism resulted primarily, from developments specific to the United States.

Born on November 5, 1855, in Terre Haute, Indiana, Eugene V. Debs came from a Midwestern town that embraced traditional values far removed from the radical cauldron of "isms"—anarchism, communism, and socialism—soon to attract many dissidents. Most people in Terre Haute considered Americans to be God's chosen people; they supported business; they thought that with hard work anyone could advance; and they believed in democracy and the autonomy of the individual.

By the 1870s, changes under way outside of Terre Haute began to infringe on the Midwestern town and challenge its interlocked views. Businesses grew in size; some became part of larger corporations directed by absentee owners; increasingly, Terre Haute's residents saw the world divided between capitalists and workers. The comfortable town boundaries shook with the arrival of the machine, and Debs's life coincided with these changes.

In 1870, Debs found a job with the Terre Haute and Indianapolis Railway, starting as a locomotive paint scraper and eventually becoming a locomotive fireman. Four years later, he lost his job during an

Eugene Debs. (Library of Congress)

economic depression and found work as a clerk in a wholesale grocery. Still wanting to remain attached to the railroad, in 1875 Debs joined the Brotherhood of Locomotive Firemen (BLF), and in 1878 was appointed editor of its *Firemen's Magazine*. In 1880, he was made the BLF's national secretary. He worked long hours, traveling the country to develop the BLF into an effective union and gaining a reputation as the defender of workingmen's rights.

By the early 1890s, recurring economic depressions, low wages, the use of machines to replace skilled labor, and decision-making from afar that made workers feel replaceable bred widespread discontent in the ranks of labor. Debs reacted by asserting that the workers should have a just share of company profits. He also wanted to enhance the unity and power of the railroad workers by bringing them together into one large union. Toward that end, in 1893 he founded the American Railway Union (ARU).

In April 1894, Debs succeeded in gaining wage increases when he led a strike against the Great Northern Railroad, a victory that helped increase ARU membership, making it the largest railroad union, with 150,000 members. After workers at the Pullman factory in Chicago—a company that made sleeping cars—went on strike, ARU's members wanted to support them. Debs advised against it, saying the union was too new for such an undertaking, but after the membership overrode him, he applied his characteristic energy to organize the workers. The refusal of the ARU to move any trains using Pullman cars shut down many railroads—including those carrying the U.S. mail—and paralyzed Chicago, the hub of the country's rail network.

The federal government then acted to crush the strike. On July 2, 1894, the government obtained an injunction against the ARU and, even though the governor of Illinois objected, sent troops into Chicago. As violence flared, Debs was arrested for conspiring to obstruct the mails and for violating the injunction, which he had ignored. In February 1895, the trial judge sentenced him and several others to six months in jail. Debs later depicted his imprisonment as an epiphany. He said: "I was to be baptized in Socialism in the roar of the conflict . . . in the gleam of every bayonet and the flash of every rifle the class struggle was revealed."

Actually, he had yet to fully embrace socialism, but he began calling for a cooperative society. When the government intervened in the Pullman strike, it defeated the workers; still on Debs's release from jail in November 1895, a jubilant crowd of about 100,000 people greeted him and listened to him criticize corporate America for assaulting individual autonomy. He said, "So long as one man depends upon the will of another or more often the whims and caprice of another for employment, he is a slave."

In 1897, Debs stated, "I am for socialism because I am for humanity," and he merged the remains of the ARU—decimated by the Pullman strike—with the Social Democratic Party of America. Debs wanted to replace the wage system with one in which the workers would own the means of production, running factories for the good of society rather than the profits of a select few; in sum, a true community held together by a commitment to the public welfare. He took traditional American ideals, born in the country's early history, and mixed them with the reality of industrial society.

An effective orator, Debs attracted large crowds to his speeches. He would lean his lanky frame into his audiences, extend his right arm, and move his forefinger about. Time and again he stressed that the true worth of a cooperative commonwealth resided in the dignity it would bring to individuals, a dignity intended by America's founding fathers. He called socialism patriotic, and he expressed his faith in democracy when he said change could be accomplished through the ballot box. With that view, he parted company with those radicals who insisted that entrenched power would always manipulate the voters to prevent any real change.

Debs ran for president in 1900 as the nominee of the Social Democratic Party and the Socialist Labor Party. In 1901, the Social Democratic Party merged with a faction of the Socialist Labor Party to form the Socialist Party of America, with Debs as its leader. He ran again for president in 1904 and 1908, and yet a fourth time in 1912, when he garnered 900,000 votes, six percent of the national total.

During World War I, Debs was imprisoned for violating the Espionage Act when he condemned the war, which he believed was sacrificing the lives of workers for the financial benefit of capitalists. While in prison in 1920, he again ran for president and recorded his highest total of 914,000 votes. In December 1921, he was pardoned by President Warren G. Harding and released.

Socialism was more than a minor movement; its power worried the governing elite, and encouraged Theodore Roosevelt and other political leaders to pursue Progressive reform lest Debs and his followers gather even greater support. Debs awakened Americans to the threat that an emerging corporate economy posed to the autonomy, dignity, and material well-being of the individual.

Further Reading

Constantine, J. Robert, ed. *Gentle Rebel: Letters of Eugene V. Debs.* Urbana: University of Illinois Press, 1995.

———. *Letters of Eugene V. Debs.* 3 vols. Urbana: University of Illinois Press, 1990.

Salvatore, Nick. *Eugene V. Debs: Citizen and Socialist.* Urbana: University of Illinois Press, 1982.

Temperance Crusader Carry Nation Begins Smashing Saloons with an Axe 1900

Through the towns of Kansas marched Carry Nation, descending on saloons with hatchet in hand, smashing paintings, mirrors, and bottles. Mentally unstable, scarred by the experience of her first marriage, stirred by religious revivalism, she intended to awaken the country to the evil of alcohol.

Carry Nation (1846–1911), born Carry Amelia Moore, grew up in an unusual household—her mother suffered from delusions that made her think she was Queen Victoria. At age 10, Carry could be called unusual, too: she experienced a religious conversion and claimed to have had visions.

In 1867, she married Charles Gloyed, a physician who preferred alcohol to doctoring. He was drunk at their wedding, and after they spent several miserable months together, she abandoned him. It would be simplistic to conclude that Gloyed's problems with the bottle caused Carry, some 30 years later, to start smashing saloons. But the experience left a scar, reminding her not only about the dangers of excessive drink but also about the many women suffering in marriages to alcoholic men.

In yet another bad choice for a mate, she married David Nation in 1877, a lawyer and minister who was nearly 20 years her senior. The couple had little in common and fought frequently.

Settling at Medicine Lodge, Kansas, with her husband in the 1890s, Nation founded a sewing circle to make clothes for the poor, and she provided meals for them at Thanksgiving and Christmas. Kansas was a dry state, and when the Supreme Court ruled in 1890 that no state could prohibit the sale of alcohol that came in its original packaging, she formed a branch of the Woman's Christian Temperance Union to protect the Kansas dry law and force saloons operating in defiance of it to close.

At first she relied on peaceful protest, but little came of it. Then in 1899, she experienced visions in which, she claimed, God told her to go to Kiowa, Kansas, and smash its saloon to pieces. "I'll stand by you," God said. On June 7, 1899, Nation entered the Kiowa saloon, presented a brief lecture on the evils of drink, and then threw rocks at the mirrors, glasses, and bottles.

In spring 1900, she attacked the saloon in Wichita's Hotel Carey, this time with a hatchet that she applied to the windows, bars, sexually explicit paintings, and bottles of liquor. Newspapers covered her crusade, and she became among the most talked-about women in the country.

Onward she marched into several other Kansas towns, and then to New York, Washington, Pittsburgh, and San Francisco. Arrested many times, she continued her violent attacks, often striking fear in saloonkeepers and patrons alike with her sharp tongue and even sharper axe wielded by her large-armed, six-foot body.

Progressives and Socialists as Reformers

In the early twentieth century, Progressive reform emerged to correct abuses under the corporate capitalist system. Progressivism addressed the use of women and child labor, long work weeks, poverty in immigrant neighborhoods, unsanitary food, corrupt political machines, and a host of other problems largely urban and industrial in origin. Most liberal reformers supported Progressivism as a way to show that capitalism could develop a social conscience.

But for other liberals, socialism had the greater appeal. Like the Progressives, the socialists disliked capitalist exploitation, the high concentration of wealth in too few hands, and the abuse of power and privilege. Unlike the Progressives, they believed that a fine-tuning of the system would placate the middle class by eliminating a few problems that affected

them directly while leaving the exploitation of the lower class intact. Beyond any economic measure, socialism had as its appeal a community of men and women united in making society more humane.

There was no magic formula that made a liberal into a socialist as opposed to a Progressive. A few learned their socialist ideas from their parents. Others learned them in the heat of industrial battle, as did Eugene V. Debs (see entry, 1895), or from the racial oppression that went hand-in-hand with economic oppression, as did W. E. B. Du Bois. Whatever the origin, unlike the Progressives, they would all agree with socialist convert Helen Keller, who observed, "Our democracy is but a name. We vote? What does that mean? It means that we choose between two bodies of real, though not avowed, aristocrats."

In time she earned some money by lecturing and by selling souvenir hatchets. She operated several short-lived publications to spread her message, including *The Smasher's Mail* and *The Hatchet*. Traditional temperance advocates disavowed Nation, partly because of her violence and partly because of her appearances at somewhat unseemly venues such as Coney Island vaudeville and in a performance called *Hatchetation*.

Carry Nation did not live to see national Prohibition take effect in 1920—she was beaten to death in a confrontation with a woman bar owner in Montana in 1910—but the memory of her sensational tactics kept the issue alive in the public's mind.

Further Reading

Grace, Fran. *Carry A. Nation: Retelling the Life*. Bloomington: Indiana University Press, 2001.

Taylor, Robert Lewis. *Vessel of Wrath: The Life and Times of Carry Nation*. New York: New American Library, 1966.

1901 An Anarchist Assassinates President William McKinley

In the 1890s, conservatives had condemned socialists, communists, and anarchists as dangerous rabble, drawn largely from the immigrants who had recently arrived in the United States and worthy of being cast aside. When the anarchist Leon Czolgosz assassinated President William McKinley, for many his act confirmed the stereotype.

Enormously popular, President McKinley toured America in 1901, and on September 5 appeared at the Pan-American Exposition in Buffalo, New York, where he laid out an important economic goal: "Commercial wars are unprofitable," he said. "A policy of goodwill and friendly trade relations will prevent reprisals."

The next afternoon, he headed for the Temple of Music, where he was scheduled to shake hands for 10 minutes. His chief aide argued against his going, saying it posed a security risk. McKinley thought otherwise: "No one would wish to hurt me," he said.

The Temple was decorated for the president's appearance with potted palms and flowers, and as a huge pipe organ provided soft music, and three guards stood nearby, McKinley began shaking hands. Only two or three minutes remained in the event when an anarchist, Leon Czolgosz, approached him.

From his hand that he had bandaged to hide a gun, Czolgosz pulled out the weapon and fired twice at McKinley. One bullet bounced off a button on the president's coat, the other went into his stomach.

One of the president's bodyguards recalled the scene:

> As the president was reaching for the hand of the assassin, there were two quick shots. Startled for a moment, I looked and saw the President draw his right hand under his coat, straighten up, and pressing his lips together, give Czolgosz the most scornful and contemptuous look possible to imagine.
>
> At the same time I reached for the young man and caught his left arm. The big negro standing just back of him, and who would have been next to take the President's hand, struck the assassin in the neck with one hand and with the other reached for the revolver.

Over the following week the president talked and joked and seemed to be recovering. But his wound had never been properly cleaned and gangrene set in. On September 13, he whispered the words "Nearer My God to Thee," and on September 14, he died.

Immediately after the shooting, the government arrested scores of anarchists and held them without bail. Angry crowds broke up anarchist meetings and clubbed and beat the radicals.

Among those arrested in the roundup was the prominent anarchist Emma Goldman, for Czolgosz had attributed his act to one of her speeches. According to the *New York Times*, Goldman said incredulously after her arrest, "Am I accountable because some crack-brained person put a wrong construction on my words?"

Indeed, Czolgosz, the son of Polish immigrants, was mentally ill at the time he shot McKinley, and after his quick trial and execution on October 29, 1901, several doctors concluded he had been "suffering from some form of mental disease for years."

As for the anarchists, they split over whether to defend Czolgosz. They thought about the words he had uttered while strapped in the electric chair: "I killed the President because he was the enemy of the good people—the good working people. I am not sorry for my crime." Most thought him more mad than anarchistic. Goldman, however, would later romanticize him, saying he had been moved to act because of society's oppression. Whatever the anarchists thought, the killing of McKinley so discredited their movement, and the standing of political radicals in society as a whole, that ultimately it played into the hands of conservatives and reactionaries.

Further Reading

Johns, A. Wesley. *The Man Who Shot McKinley*. South Brunswick, N.J.: A. S. Barnes, 1970.

LESLIE'S WEEKLY
McKINLEY EXTRA

Vol. XCIII. EXTRA NUMBER   New York, September 9, 1901   PRICE 10 CENTS

LEON F. CZOLGOSZ, THE ASSASSIN.

FIRST PHOTOGRAPH OF THE WRETCHED ANARCHIST WHO SHOT THE PRESIDENT AT FOUR P. M., SEPTEMBER 6TH, 1901, AT THE PAN-AMERICAN EXPOSITION—COPYRIGHTED BY JONES COMPANY, 1901.

Leon Czolgosz. (Library of Congress)

1905 The Industrial Workers of the World Vow to Tear Down Capitalism

In 1905, Bill Haywood, leader of the Western Federation of Miners, called to order a new union, the Industrial Workers of the World (IWW) with the following words: "Fellow workers, this is the Continental Congress of the working class. We are here to confederate the workers of the country into a . . . movement that shall have for its purpose the emancipation of the working class from the slave bondage of capitalism."

Some 200 socialists, anarchists, and radical trade unionists met that June morning in 1905 to found the IWW, whose members, for reasons unclear, were sometimes called the Wobblies. They embraced an idea then gaining favor among radicals in Europe, called anarcho-syndicalism, which meant the workers should stage massive strikes that would topple the government and the economic system, at which point the workers would gain control of industries and run them for the good of the entire society. The IWW declared strikes for more limited purposes, such as higher wages, but considered these to be mere stopgaps along the path to a greater upheaval.

Unlike the American Federation of Labor (AFL; see entry, 1886), which advocated working within capitalism and with corporate leaders to secure better pay and working conditions, the IWW wanted revolutionary change, and its members committed themselves to militancy. "Direct action," said the Wobblies, "means industrial action directly by, for, and of the workers themselves, without the treacherous aid of labor misleaders or scheming politicians. A strike that is initiated, controlled, and settled by the workers is direct action. . . . Direct action is industrial democracy."

Toward that end, the IWW sought to organize all workers in one large union and enhance labor's power by ending the conflicts that appeared when workers usually organized along the lines of particular crafts or job categories. The IWW especially sought to recruit the more unskilled and impoverished workers, the very ones largely ignored by the AFL. The editors of *Who Built America? From the Gilded Age to the Present* (1992) have called the IWW "the most egalitarian labor organization in American history" because it recruited "skilled and unskilled men and women, blacks, and Mexicans, and, in a break with tradition, Chinese and Japanese workers."

At first, the IWW suffered both from internal bickering and from harassment by the government and big business. But in 1909, it gained increased membership, a result of unskilled immigrant workers having struck the Pressed Steel Car Company in McKees Rocks, Pennsylvania, and won several concessions. A massive textile strike in Lawrence, Massachusetts, in 1912 produced widespread public support for the IWW after the police shot and killed a woman picketer and attacked children who were being sent away from the town by their parents.

But the IWW's fortunes changed in 1913 when a steel strike at Paterson, New Jersey, failed as the managers took advantage of ethnic divisions among the workers. Ideological differences also hurt the IWW as anarchists and their opponents battled for control of the union. The 1915 execution of radical agitator and songwriter Joe Hill (see entry, 1915) was a blow to the IWW. While Hill's death rallied some to the IWW cause, it dispirited others and reinforced the impression that the IWW was dangerous and should be crushed.

The heyday of the IWW quickly came and went, and after 1920 the union exerted little influence. Yet writing in *A People's History of the United States* (1980), historian Howard Zinn observes that "In the ten exciting years after its birth the IWW became a threat to the capitalist class, exactly when capitalist growth was enormous and profits huge. The IWW never had more than five to ten thousand enrolled members at any one time. . . . But their energy, their persistence, their inspiration to others, their ability to mobilize thousands at one place . . . made them an influence on the country far beyond their numbers."

Further Reading

Dubofsky, Melvyn. *We Shall Be All: A History of the Industrial Workers of the World.* Urbana: University of Illinois Press, 1988.

Kimeldorf, Howard. *Battling for American Labor: Wobblies, Craft Workers, and the Making of the Union Movement.* Berkeley: University of California Press, 1999.

Zinn, Howard. *A People's History of the United States: 1492–Present.* 1980. 20th anniversary ed. New York: HarperCollins, 1999.

Daniel De Leon Calls for Socialist Industrialism

1905

Daniel De Leon was, according to fellow socialist Arnold Peterson, "a lone Titan, battling for a great principle, surrounded by a pack of yelping human canines, who . . . were anxious to set their teeth in his flanks and, if possible, trip him and rend him." Yet, noted Peterson, De Leon's speech "Socialist Reconstruction of Society," presented on July 10, 1905, exposed the shallowness of his opponents with "a monument of Socialist science."

Daniel De Leon (1852–1914) came to socialism gradually. He earned a law degree from Columbia University in 1878, and worked briefly as a lawyer in Texas, and returned to Columbia as a lecturer, where he taught Latin American diplomacy for six years. The economic depression of the 1880s, and the attendant misery for many workers in New York City, caused him to seek social change.

At first, he supported Henry George's single tax plan (see entry, 1879) and campaigned for George when the reformer ran for mayor in 1886. Two years later, De Leon joined a union, the Knights of Labor (see entry, 1869). In 1890, he moved much further to the left when he joined the Socialist Labor Party (SLP), which had derived from the Socialist First International of 1864. He was elected editor of the party's magazine, *The People*, in 1891, and later that year ran unsuccessfully for governor of New York as the SLP candidate. (He would run again for the state assembly and for Congress, losing each time.)

Under De Leon, the SLP represented just one of many socialist ideologies. He advocated a democratic socialism, whereby all laborers would be united under a single union and, through workers' councils, control the country's industries. He opposed any government action to nationalize industries, or any attempt by a political party to take them over in the name of the workers. Such measures, he claimed, would only replace capitalist oppression with state oppression.

The SLP, De Leon insisted, should work to gain control of the government, but once having done so, the party should abolish itself and let workers' councils take over, establishing what he called an "industrial form of government." Unlike anarchists, and some socialist extremists, he opposed revolutionary violence; the SLP must win at the ballot box, he said, to avoid a reactionary slaughter by the state that violent tactics would incite, and it must win votes to establish credibility and certify its democratic credentials.

In 1895, De Leon formed the Socialist Trade and Labor Alliance, which complemented the work of the SLP and was the first union in the United States to proclaim a socialist society as its goal.

An eloquent writer, De Leon stated his views in editorials he wrote for *The People*:

The exploiting and idle class struggles upon the lines of their class interests. They aim to conserve the power they now enjoy to live in luxury without work, to ride the proletariat, to fleece the workers.

The working class of America has nothing, no economic or social powers, worth conserving. "Conservatism" can never mean the striving to conserve chains.

A corporation can do as it pleases. . . . [And if it breaks the law], all that can happen is a fine. . . . The individuals who compose it go scot free . . . ready to do it all over again. In this way, it may well be true that nine-tenths of the corporations of the country have no reason for existence than lifting someone above the law.

De Leon criticized the American Federation of Labor (AFL) for its willingness to work within the capitalist system. He said that when the AFL talks about " 'redemption of the workers from the bondage of industrial slavery,' the words are used as so much claptrap."

In 1901, many members resigned from the SLP. They accused De Leon of exerting dictatorial powers and disagreed with his ideas. The departure crippled the SLP, but De Leon continued as its leader. Four years later, he helped found the Industrial Workers of the World (IWW; see entry, 1905), which also advocated worker control of industry.

On July 10, 1905, De Leon presented his speech "Socialist Reconstruction of Society" (later published as a pamphlet) to a rally in Minneapolis, Minnesota. He declared:

> After thirty years of arduous toil; after thirty years, during which the soil of the land was literally drenched with the sweat and blood and marrow of the workingman; after thirty years during which the American working class produced more heiresses to the square inch than the working class of any other country . . . ; at the end of thirty years during which the working class . . . produced a phenomenal amount of wealth—at the end of these thirty years the American working class is just where it was thirty years before, the wretched retainer of only $20 out of every $100 worth of wealth that it produced!

Ultimately, "In the framework of the capitalist social system, the working class and the employing or capitalist class have nothing in common."

To De Leon and the IWW a "new epoch" had begun, a step toward a great labor crusade that would bring capitalism to its knees. That same year, he stated that "if the capitalists should be foolish enough in America to defeat, to thwart the will of the workers expressed by the ballot, then there will be a condition of things by which the working class can absolutely cease production, and thereby starve out the capitalist class, render their present economic means and all their preparations for war absolutely useless."

De Leon allied the SLP with the IWW from 1905 to 1908, yet the hopes of a grand march toward socialism faltered when factional disputes ended the relationship. Over the next six years of his life, he continued to promote his socialist ideas, but his industrial format found support with only the smallest of radical groups.

Further Reading

Coleman, Stephen. *Daniel De Leon.* New York: St. Martin's Press, 1990.
Seretan, L. Glen. *Daniel De Leon: The Odyssey of an American Marxist.* Cambridge, Mass.: Harvard University Press, 1979.

1906 Upton Sinclair's Novel *The Jungle* Hits the Public in the Stomach

While Upton Sinclair's novel The Jungle *caused Congress to pass a meat inspection act, Sinclair never supported the measure and never considered it substantial. He wanted something much more: the replacement of capitalism with socialism.*

Upton Sinclair (1878–1968) began writing while still in college, earning money for tuition by cranking out stories for pulp magazines. At the same time, he read widely and inquired deeply, showing an idealistic faith in the ability of individuals to improve the world. He graduated from the College of the City of New York in 1897 whereupon he turned to more serious writing, producing two nondescript novels, one in 1901 and the other in 1903.

By then, George D. Herron, a writer and lecturer, had interested Sinclair in the socialist movement. So, too, had Jack London's novel *People of the Abyss*—a story about how the author lived incognito in the East End of London, England, to study poverty—and, according to Sinclair, Christianity, with its example of Jesus as a "rebel carpenter" sacrificing for humanity. In 1902, Sinclair joined the Socialist Party. The editors of *Literary History of the United States* (1963) write that "Socialism came to him as more than an intellectual conviction; it came as a magnificent discovery, as a combined religious conversion and revelation, in the light of which he saw clearly the ends for which he might live."

With this background, Sinclair wrote *The Jungle.* The idea was first presented to him by J. A. Wayland, the editor of a socialist weekly, *Appeal to Reason*, who gave Sinclair a small advance to investigate the meatpacking industry. Sinclair spent seven weeks in Chicago researching his topic. He talked to factory workers and some government officials, but never entered a slaughterhouse or a meatpacking plant. *The Jungle* appeared first as a serial in *Appeal to Reason* and then was published as a book in February 1906.

It caused an immediate uproar, but less so for its tale of exploited workers, such as Jurgis Rudkus and other Lithuanian immigrants, than for what Sinclair had to say about meatpacking itself—an account that took only about 12 pages but that sent stomachs churning and tempers flaring over the poison being fed consumers in the guise of meat. Even today, the vividness of his passages strikes with force:

> As for the . . . men who worked in tank rooms full of steam, and in some of which there were open vats near the level of the floor, their peculiar trouble was that they fell into the vats; and when they were fished out, there was never enough of them left to be worth exhibiting—sometimes they would be overcooked for days, till all but the bones of them had gone out of the world. . . .
>
> There was never the least attention paid to what was cut up for sausage; there would come back from Europe old sausage that had been rejected, and that was mouldy and white—it could be dosed with borax and glycerine, and dumped into the hoppers, and made over for home consumption.
>
> Rats were nuisances, and the packers would put poisoned bread out for them; they would die, and the rats, bread and meat would go into the hoppers together.

Critics accused Sinclair of exaggerating, and a report in 1906 by the Department of Agriculture's Bureau of Animal Husbandry concluded he had engaged in "willful and deliberate misrepresentations of fact." But a congressional investigation supported Sinclair, and he defended his novel as factually accurate.

The Jungle created such a public outcry that in 1907 Congress passed the Meat Inspection Act. But Sinclair had wanted more; he wanted to expose the suffering by workers under capitalism. A promotion for the novel, written by Jack London and approved by Sinclair, stated in part: "Take notice and remember, comrades, this book is straight proletarian. It is written by an intellectual proletarian, for the proletarian. . . . It is to be read by the proletariat. What *Uncle Tom's Cabin* did for the black slaves *The Jungle* has a large chance to do for the white slaves of today." And in the book itself, a socialist speaker proclaims: "We shall have the sham reformers self-stultified and self-convicted; we shall have the radical Democracy left without a lie with which to cover its nakedness! Then will begin the rush that will never be checked, the tide that will never turn till it has reached its flood. Chicago will be ours!"

Disappointed by his failure to ignite a mass movement toward socialism, Sinclair said, "I aimed at the public's heart, and by accident hit it in the stomach." Actually leaders in the Republican and Democratic Parties did conclude that *The Jungle* had the potential to wreck capitalism. That possibility,

Media and Radicalism—The Muckrakers

In 1906, Theodore Roosevelt applied the name "muckrakers" to those journalists engaged in uncovering corrupt and inhumane practices in America's industrializing society. Tired of what he considered to be their harping, he likened them to the Man with the Muckrake in John Bunyan's *Pilgrim's Progress* (1678–84), "who was offered the celestial crown for his muckrake, but would neither look up nor regard the crown he was offered, but continued to rake the filth of the floor."

Muckraking journalists, mainly writing for magazines, usually rejected radical ideologies. Most of them wanted to reform capitalism rather than destroy it; and most of them wanted to make the United States more democratic and just. Ida Tarbell, who exposed the workings of the Standard Oil Company, recalled, "The things we were advocating were not advocated with a view toward overturning the capitalist system." For most muckrakers, the system was less at fault than individuals, who had the ability to commit great evils but also to advance great reforms.

McClure's emerged as the leading muckraking magazine. Within a four-month period, from October 1902 to January 1903, it printed Tarbell's articles about Standard Oil and Lincoln Steffens's article about political bosses in St. Louis and Minneapolis.

Muckraking journalists broke with the prevailing florid writing style to produce articles with the sound of urgency and to use leads that grabbed the reader's attention. Some combined their narratives with drawings and even photographs. Muckraking included the pioneering social photographers Jacob Riis (see entry, 1890), who exposed slum conditions in immigrant neighborhoods, and Lewis Hine, who sneaked into factories with his camera and exposed how industrialists exploited child labor.

In the heyday of Progressivism, muckraking boosted magazine sales while encouraging reform. With the entry of the United States into World War I, muckraking magazines suffered; *McClure's* merged with another magazine in 1929, after having deserted its reformist crusade, and others, such as *Collier's*, changed their formats.

---

as much as any desire to help society, propelled President Theodore Roosevelt to push for the Meat Inspection Act; he concluded that if capitalism failed to show it could correct its worst abuses, then socialism would indeed take over. The Meat Inspection Act was the bandage to stanch the wound Sinclair had inflicted on the system.

Sinclair went on to write many more novels, along with a series of nonfiction works, that showed how capitalism shaped the church, press, and schools to serve its ends. In addition, he stepped from behind the writer's desk and in 1906 ran for Congress as a socialist from New Jersey. He lost that race, as he did several others when he ran under the Socialist Party banner. He came closest to winning office during the Great Depression, when he sought the governorship of California as a Democrat (see entry, 1934). He won the primary under the slogan "End Poverty in California," but lost the general election to Republican incumbent Frank Merriam. In the race Sinclair was vilified by corporate leaders and MGM movie studios while the *Los Angeles Times* misrepresented his proposals and warned that a Sinclair victory would bring socialism to the state and lead to poor people from all over the country descending on California.

Sinclair's death did not still his appeal; his books continued widely in print in the United States and in many other countries. *The Jungle* serves as an example of radical ideas that led to only moderate reform; in that sense, while it brought change, it unwittingly allowed capitalism to defeat the larger cause.

Further Reading

Harris, Leon. *Upton Sinclair: American Rebel.* New York: Crowell, 1975.

Mitchell, Greg. *The Campaign of the Century: Upton Sinclair's Race for Governor of California and the Birth of Media Politics.* New York: Random House, 1992.

Sinclair, Upton. *Autobiography.* New York: Harcourt, Brace & World, 1962.

She's a rebel girl, a rebel girl
To the working class she's the strength of this world
From Newfoundland to B. C.
She's fighting for you and for me
And I'm proud to fight for freedom
With the rebel girl!

These words come from a song, "The Rebel Girl," written by labor organizer Joe Hill in 1915 for Elizabeth Gurley Flynn. To many within and outside the labor movement, Flynn was a hero, fighting for workers' rights and for the dignity of women. In the late 1930s, her radicalism took her into the Communist Party.

Raised in the Bronx in New York City, Elizabeth Gurley Flynn (1890–1964) was born into an activist family. "My father and mother," she once told an interviewer, "were socialists, were members of the Socialist Party." As a young girl, though, she thought the socialists too stodgy and wanted something bolder. "We felt a desire to have something more militant, more progressive, and more youthful," she said about herself and her friends, "and so we flocked into the . . . IWW."

She joined the IWW, or Industrial Workers of the World (see entry 1905), after having been expelled from high school for blocking traffic while giving a speech on socialism. In 1907, she became a full-time organizer. The IWW had been founded two years earlier by socialists, anarchists, and radical trade unionists who wanted to unite all of the country's workers into one union and use strikes as a weapon to topple capitalism and bring industry under the workers' control. "The IWW believed in the class struggle," she said. "They didn't believe in the brotherhood of capital and labor."

Among the several strikes that Flynn helped organize were those involving textile workers in Lawrence, Massachusetts (1912), and in Paterson and Passaic, New Jersey (1913 and 1926). During this time, Flynn wrote a pamphlet titled *Sabotage* (1915), in which she advocated "the withdrawal of efficiency" as a weapon in the fight against the capitalists. She stated: "Sabotage means either to slacken up and interfere with the quantity, or to botch in your skill and interfere with the quality, of capitalist production or to give poor service. Sabotage is not physical violence; sabotage is internal, industrial process. And these three forms of sabotage—to affect the quality, the quantity, and the service, are aimed at affecting the profit of the employer."

Flynn took the lead in fighting for free speech rights at a time when many local laws prohibited IWW members from holding public meetings. Moreover, she rallied support and collected money to defend IWW members arrested and held on dubious grounds, among them Bill Haywood and Joe Hill. "I became more and more specialized in what is called labor defense work," she said.

Flynn took an interest in organizing women and children, and she criticized the secondary status assigned to women by some of the men in the IWW. Her main concern was not with feminist issues, however; for example, she believed that women should have the vote, but she thought that the suffrage movement took focus and energy away from the real cause of oppression, namely the control of the masses by an "elite."

With American entry into World War I in 1917, she defended those prosecuted under the Sedition Act (which made it a crime to criticize the war effort), including conscientious objectors, socialists, and IWW members. That same year, she helped found the National Civil Liberties Bureau, which later became the American Civil Liberties Union (ACLU; see entry, 1920).

When the war ended, Flynn led a movement to win the release of those imprisoned under the Sedition Act, and in 1924, President Calvin Coolidge issued an amnesty. Suffering from poor health, Flynn took a break from her activism in 1926, but 10 years later she joined the Communist Party and dedicated herself to its triumph. The ACLU reacted in 1940 by removing her from its executive board, a retaliation all the more controversial given the group's commitment to free speech.

Flynn supported the fight against fascism in World War II, urging people to buy savings bonds and advocating the drafting of women into the military. After the war, the federal government arrested her for violating the Smith Act (1940), which made it illegal to call for the forcible overthrow of the U.S. government or to be a member of any group advocating such an overthrow. She was tried and convicted in 1952 and unsuccessfully appealed the verdict, before serving her prison term from January 1955 to May 1957 at the women's federal penitentiary in Alderson, West Virginia. While confined, she helped to racially integrate facilities at the prison.

On her release, she resumed her work with the Communist Party and in 1961 became its national chairman. She died on September 5, 1964, during a trip to the Soviet Union and was given a state funeral in Moscow's Red Square. In 1978, the ACLU posthumously rescinded her expulsion.

In one of her last public appearances, Flynn told a group of college students to imbibe the words of nineteenth-century Russian anarchist Peter Kropotkin, an influence in her own life, who wrote in *An Appeal to the Young* (1880): "All of us together, we who suffer and are insulted daily, we are a multitude whom no man can number, we are the ocean that can embrace and swallow up all else. When we have but the will to do it, that very moment will Justice be done: that very instant the tyrants of the Earth shall bite the dust."

Further Reading

Baxandall, Rosalyn Fradd. *Words on Fire: The Life and Writing of Elizabeth Gurley Flynn.* New Brunswick, N.J.: Rutgers University Press, 1987.

1909 Ladies Garment Workers Strike in New York City and a Tragic Fire Follows

A Yiddish newspaper described what happened at the Grand Hall of Cooper Union in New York City on November 22, 1909: "At least 2,500 men and women who work in the Ladies Waist industry [were there]. They filled up the big hall. . . . And many, many hundreds blocked up the street outside." The strike that followed was led by the International Ladies Garment Workers Union (ILGWU); it forced management concessions that, although limited, represented a large step forward for collective bargaining.

Before the strike began, months of turmoil convulsed New York City's garment industry. The ILGWU was organized in 1900 and affiliated with the American Federation of Labor (AFL). At first membership grew quickly, but by 1904, the union had stagnated as its conservative no-strike policy discouraged many workers, most of whom were young Italian and Jewish immigrant women who had been attracted to socialist ideas and militant tactics in Europe. Subject to working long hours for low wages in the United States, they wanted more than mild talk.

One garment worker, speaking in 1909, said that "the regular work pays about six dollars a week and the girls have to be at their machines at 7 o'clock in the morning and they stay at them until 8 o'clock at night, with just one half-hour for lunch." On top of this, women who made shirtwaists—long blouses fashionable at that time—at the Triangle Shirtwaist Company complained in 1909 about poor sanitary facilities, inadequate ventilation, and overcrowding. To protest this sweatshop environment, the Triangle workers went on strike; however, garment workers elsewhere remained on their jobs.

Victims of the Triangle Shirtwaist fire, 1911. (Bettmann/CORBIS)

The Triangle workers then called for a general strike to include other factories. There followed the meeting at Cooper Union, where the speakers included the head of the AFL, Samuel Gompers, who said he would support a strike but stopped short of calling for one. At that point, Clara Lemlich, a teenage Jewish immigrant from Russia previously arrested for marching in picket lines, spoke in Yiddish, declaring, "I have listened to all the speakers and have no further patience for talk. I am the one who feels and suffers from the things pictured. I move we go on strike!"

The crowd broke into cheers, throwing hats in the air and shouting "Strike!" About 20,000 workers—most of them women—walked off their jobs. The women, effectively organized by the ILGWU, endured brutal assaults on the picket lines and held out for 13 weeks, returning to work only after 350 factories agreed to a 52-hour work week and higher wages. The strikers failed, however, to gain recognition for the ILGWU.

One company that rejected the agreement was the place where the walkout had begun, the Triangle Shirtwaist Factory, owned by Max Blanck and Isaac Harris. They relied heavily on subcontractors, who paid the workers wages that were among the lowest in the garment industry.

On March 25, 1911, a fire swept through the Triangle factory, burning so quickly and so fiercely that it trapped many of the workers on the building's upper floors. More than 140 workers, mostly women, were killed by the flames or by their desperate attempts to escape them when they jumped to the street below. One reporter wrote that "as I looked up I saw a love affair in the midst of all the horror." He was referring to a young man who was helping girls leap from a window, when one of the girls "put her arms about him and kissed him. Then he held her out into space and dropped her." He immediately followed, plunging to his own doom. "Thud—dead, Thud—dead. . . . I saw his face before they covered it. . . . He was a real man. He had done his best."

A reporter for the *New York Times* wrote about the fire:

> The crowd yelled "Don't jump!" but it was jump or be burned, the proof of which is found in the fact that fifty burned bodies were taken from the ninth floor alone. . . . Of those who stayed behind it is better to say nothing except what a veteran policeman said as he gazed at a headless and charred trunk . . . hours after the worst cases had been taken out:
> "Is it a man or a woman?" asked the reporter.
> "It's human, that's all you can tell," answered the policeman.
> It was just a mass of ashes, with blood congealed on what had probably been the neck.

The Triangle factory had no fire escapes; the foreman had bolted all the exit doors to prevent the workers from leaving early; and the doors opened in instead of out. During the strike, the shirtwaist workers had complained about these conditions, but nothing had been done about them.

The fire led to New York City enacting the most progressive laws in the country regulating factory working conditions. Yet the tragedy at a company that had failed to accept the agreement with the striking workers revealed the limited gains made by labor. Sweatshops continued to operate—as they still do today—and the workers' struggle would have to continue.

Further Reading

McClymer, John F. *The Triangle Strike and Fire*. Fort Worth, Tex.: Harcourt Brace, 1998.
McCreesh, Carolyn D. *Women in the Campaign to Organize Garment Workers, 1880–1917*. New York: Garland Publishers, 1985.
Stein, Leon, ed. *Out of the Sweatshop: The Struggle for Industrial Democracy*. New York: New Times Book, 1977.
Tyler, Gus. *Look for the Union Label: A History of the International Ladies' Garment Workers' Union*. Armonk, N.Y.: M. E. Sharpe, 1995.

1909 NAACP Formed to Fight for Black Civil Rights

In 1909, prominent white and African-American liberals gathered in New York City and founded the National Association for the Advancement of Colored People (NAACP), which soon became the country's leading civil rights organization. They acted as racism intensified and white attacks on blacks escalated.

By 1896, the feeling of liberation and the march toward freedom that African-Americans had exulted in as the Civil War ended and as the states ratified the Fourteenth and Fifteenth Amendments was negated when in *Plessy v. Ferguson* the Supreme Court declared racial segregation constitutional. In the wake of *Plessy*, blacks lost more than the right to vote and hold office, and more than the possibility of equal economic and social opportunities—they lost their lives. As segregation and the concept of white supremacy spread, a pattern of violence took hold. Lynchings occurred around the country; in 1900 more than 100 African-Americans were lynched; by 1914, the total had reached 1,100. The South led in lynchings, followed by the Midwest.

Race riots also erupted: in Statesboro, Georgia, in 1904, when whites dragged two African-Americans accused of murder from their cell, burned them alive, and then went on a rampage through the black neighborhood; in Atlanta, in 1906, when whites descended on a suburb and began slaughtering blacks; in Brownsville, Texas, also in 1906, when whites claimed that blacks had "shot up the town."

A race riot in Springfield, Illinois, was the immediate inspiration for the NAACP. In August 1908, a white mob attacked African-Americans, lynching two, killing six others, and forcing 2,000 blacks to leave the city. William English Walling, a white writer and socialist, witnessed the horror, and in an article titled "The Race War in the South," published in the *Independent*, he said that "a large part of [Springfield's] white population" was engaged in "permanent warfare with the Negro race." He called for the "spirit of the abolitionists" to be revived so that blacks could achieve social and political equality with whites and the violence could be brought to an end.

Mary White Ovington, a journalist with the *New York Evening Post*, read the article and met with Walling. "I saw the article as soon as it came out," Ovington recalled in 1947. "Its description of rioting and brutality was terrible. . . . [But] what made me put down the magazine and write to Walling within the hour was the appeal to citizens to come to the Negro's aid." Together, Walling and Overton called for a general meeting to act on racial problems, and several prominent reformers answered by gathering in New York City on February 12, 1909.

The participants included W. E. B. Du Bois and other young blacks from the Niagara Movement—though at least one prominent militant, William Trotter, refused to attend because he did not trust the white reformers. As a group dedicated to immediate equality, the Niagara Movement consisted of African-Americans who disagreed with moderate black leader Booker T. Washington's accommodationist policy toward whites. "In detail our demands are clear and unequivocal. . . ." Du Bois had stated in his Niagara Address of 1906. "We want full manhood suffrage, and we want it now."

The reformers formally established the NAACP, with the goal of ending forced racial segregation, obtaining equal education for white and black children, assuring the right to vote for African-Americans, and securing enforcement of the Fourteenth and Fifteenth Amendments. Another meeting in May 1910 chose the organization's officers, making Moorfield Storey of Boston the president and Walling chairman of the executive committee. Only one African-American—W. E. B. Du Bois—was elected to office; he became director of publicity and research.

Du Bois edited and wrote articles for the NAACP magazine, *The Crisis*, which first appeared in November 1910 and by 1918 had achieved a monthly circulation exceeding 100,000. Du Bois spoke out boldly, in his Niagara Address, at one point linking the black drive for voting rights with that of women. "Every argument for Negro suffrage is an argument for women's suffrage; every argument for women's suffrage is an argument for Negro suffrage," he said. "There should be on the part of Negroes absolutely no hesitation whatever and wherever responsible human beings are without voice in their government."

The NAACP encountered considerable hostility. Publication of *The Crisis* caused Mississippi to prohibit the circulation of materials "favoring social equality." Texas began debating a bill to disband the state NAACP. And in 1910, John Shillady, the national organization's white executive secretary, was brutally assaulted during a visit to Austin. "The haters of black folk beat him and scarred him like a dog," wrote Du Bois in *The Crisis*, "because he tried to talk quiet reason to Texas."

Pursuing largely legal challenges, the NAACP scored two important victories before 1920. In *Guinn v. United States* (1915), the Supreme Court ruled unconstitutional the grandfather clauses in Maryland and Oklahoma. (These clauses had restricted suffrage to those persons whose grandfathers could vote, in effect eliminating nearly all African-Americans, whose grandfathers had been slaves, from the voter lists.) There followed *Buchanan v. Warley* (1917), in which the Supreme Court ruled unconstitutional a Louisville, Kentucky, ordinance that restricted blacks to one part of the city.

By 1921, the NAACP had more than 400 branches. In the 1960s, many young African-Americans thought the NAACP too conservative and stodgy—too much court time, not enough street time. Although it suffered from scandals and financial problems in the 1990s, the organization played an essential role in advancing black civil rights, achieving the seminal decision in *Brown v. Board of Education* (1954) that overturned *Plessy v. Ferguson*, and in intensifying the assault on racial segregation.

Further Reading

Lewis, David Levering. *W. E. B. Du Bois: The Biography of Race.* New York: Henry Holt, 1993.

———. *W. E. B. Du Bois: The Fight for Equality and the American Century, 1919–1963.* New York: Henry Holt, 2000.

Zamir, Shamoon. *Dark Voices: W. E. B. Du Bois and American Thought, 1883–1903.* Chicago: University of Chicago Press, 1995.

CHAPTER SIX

World War I and the Roaring Twenties

Radical dissenters could not have found a more hostile ground for their activities than the periods of World War I and the Roaring Twenties, the first noted for its patriotic fervor and the second for its materialistic indulgence. While significant numbers of Americans opposed the entry of their country into the war, many more, and the government itself, supported the fight as a patriotic duty, one that, as President Woodrow Wilson said, was necessary to "make the world safe for democracy." Consequently, the government arrested agitators—including women such as Alice Paul, who picketed outside the White House to gain women's suffrage—in an attempt to silence them. When Wilson, a Democrat and a Progressive, wrapped the war in democratic ideals, he made known his intent to project Progressivism on the rest of the world. Just as Progressives had worked to make the United States more democratic, they would work to make the *world* more democratic; just as Progressives had worked to make the United States more just, they would work to make the *world* more just.

Wilson's proposal for a League of Nations reflected these goals and tapped into the widespread desire in the United States to avoid another war. Even though the proposal initially represented the liberal goal for world peace, in the end its fate became a different sort of benchmark, signaling a transition to a more conservative era. With the League, Wilson wanted to establish a representative body in which delegates from many countries would deliberate international issues and resolve disputes, and maintain peace by keeping aggressors in check. It was the quintessential Progressive formula, an international city commission, so to speak, whose informed members would reflect, respond, and resolve.

At Wilson's insistence, the League of Nations was included in the Treaty of Versailles that ended World War I. But the League proposal doomed the treaty in the United States, and when it went down to defeat, the League stood no chance of working. Republicans in Congress opposed the treaty partly because they did not want Wilson to get credit for it, but also because they feared participation in the League would open the door to foreign countries intervening in U.S. domestic affairs, and would cripple U.S. foreign policy while pulling the United States into overseas wars. Senator Henry Cabot Lodge of Massachusetts argued that the League covenant, which called for collective security measures if a member nation were attacked, would infringe on the provisions in the U.S. Constitution that granted Congress the authority to declare war. In short, the League's opponents distrusted Wilson's internationalism.

For his part, Wilson rejected efforts to compromise on the treaty. Even though the Senate rejected the document, other countries ratified it, and the League was formed in the 1920s. Still, the United States refused to

> "Goodbye Bill.
> I die like a true rebel.
> Don't waste time
> mourning—organize!"
>
> Joe Hill to Bill Haywood, 1915

join the League, and Wilson's successor, President Warren G. Harding, declared: "We seek no part in directing the destinies of the world." Without the United States as a participant, the League stood no chance of surviving and, during its brief existence, was ineffective.

The failure of the League in the United States reflected a turn away from reform in America—the emergence of an environment much more hostile to those rebels and renegades intent on advancing liberal economic, political, and social change. The 1920s began in the wake of the controversy over the League and also over Attorney General A. Mitchell Palmer's crackdown on radicals during the Red Scare and evolved into a pro-business atmosphere so intense that it made traditionalism the byword of the day.

Americans believed the country's businessmen would end all poverty; with such strident faith, business became a national religion. Historian Frederick Lewis Allen has pointed out that the highest praise that could be given a clergyman was to call him a good businessman. Indeed, the book *The Man Nobody Knows* (1925) by Bruce Barton rose to the best-seller lists by equating Jesus Christ with business and advertising. Barton wrote that Jesus was not only "the most popular dinner guest in Jerusalem" but also a "great executive." Barton called Jesus' parables "the most powerful advertisements of all time" and concluded that "Jesus was the founder of modern business."

On the surface, the 1920s was an era of dazzling prosperity. The value of new construction doubled from $6 billion in 1921 to $12 billion in 1927; during the decade, the gross national product grew by 40 percent; manufacturing output increased 64 percent and worker productivity 40 percent. An automobile assembly line could produce one new car every 93 minutes, and by 1929, more than 23 million cars were using the country's roads. The making of automobiles led to road building, along with the building of gas stations, motels, and restaurants to serve motorists.

In 1919, Americans spent $2.5 billion on leisure activities; in 1929, that sum reached $4.3 billion, 21 percent of which was spent on movies, music, and sports. The number of telephones doubled, from 10 million in 1915 to 20 million in 1929. Appliances such as washing machines, vacuum cleaners, and electric toasters began appearing in more and more middle-class homes.

The economic boom occurred when Republicans occupied the White House and dominated Congress. Under Presidents Warren G. Harding, Calvin Coolidge, and Herbert Hoover, multimillionaire businessman Andrew Mellon served as secretary of the treasury. In that position, he crafted policies that sharply reduced taxes overall, but mainly for the rich.

These good times, however, had limits. Not every American could indulge in the technological inventions, with the electric iron being the one appliance owned by a majority of people. At least 50 percent of all farm and non-farm workers barely earned a subsistence income, while the top 5 percent of Americans received about 33 percent of the nation's personal income, revealing a disturbing disparity between the haves and the have-nots. Unemployment remained high throughout the 1920s, hovering between 7 and 12 percent of all non-farm workers.

In all, though, most Americans enjoyed prosperity, and while the frivolous indulged in such fads as flagpole sitting and goldfish swallowing, they put little credence in dissidents' complaints. Still, protesters appeared, determined to be more than voices in a wilderness; for example, the United Mine Workers attempted to organize miners in West Virginia, and A. Philip Randolph formed a union for black railroad porters. Randolph's work sowed the seeds for a civil rights movement that would become even more emboldened by the New Deal policies of the 1930s. The rebels and renegades of the 1920s refused to be seduced by the opiate of materialism.

Women's Peace Party Organized in Washington

Jane Addams, a Progressive reformer and pacifist, at first doubted that there would be enough support to organize an all-women's peace party, but late in 1914, she admitted, "In this case the demand has been so universal and spontaneous over the country that it seemed to me best to take it up."

In the years immediately prior to the outbreak of World War I, other peace groups were formed before the Women's Peace Party. These included the New York Peace Society, the World Peace Foundation, and the Church Peace Union. They called for arbitration of international disputes, the establishment of a world court, and the use of disarmament treaties to avoid war. None, however, declared all war evil, condemned the nation-state system, or blamed war on capitalism.

In September 1914, with World War I underway, reformers and pacifists met in Chicago to talk about the possibility of forming a women's peace group. Late that year, several women, led by Jane Addams, began the Chicago Emergency Federation of Peace Forces. This group, in turn, called for a meeting of women to be held in Washington, D.C., in January 1915. Carrie Chapman Catt was instrumental in putting together the meeting, showing the organizational genius she was known for in feminist circles.

Approximately 3,000 women showed up in Washington, D.C., and following the forceful pronouncement of Emeline Pethnick-Lawrence about World War I that "if men will tolerate this thing, women will not," they officially declared themselves the Women's Peace Party (WPP). With Jane Addams as its chairwoman, they passed a platform containing the following demands: that neutral nations meet to mediate the war; that arms be limited; that women be consulted on all issues of war and peace; that a world court be established; and that the economic causes of war be eliminated.

With the United States moving closer to fighting in the war, the WPP opposed preparedness, which would, it believed, make entry inevitable. In January 1916, Addams represented the WPP before the House Committee on Foreign Relations and said the group wanted to see an international police force established, along with a world body of nations that would deliberate and resolve international disputes.

The WPP's stand against preparedness found support among many Americans who were not pacifists but who wanted the country to stay out of the war; isolationists, for example, sided with the WPP. But once the United States entered the war, the WPP was labeled as extremist, and even un-American when it opposed the Conscription Act. Amid escalating criticism of the WPP, Addams endured considerable strain. In 1917, she complained that she was weary of being a social outcast.

Yet the WPP survived its wartime trials and in 1919 continued as the Women's International League for Peace and Freedom (WILPF). By 1937, the group had 13,000 members in 120 branches located in the United States and overseas. In the 1840s, the WILPF supported the formation of the United Nations. In the 1960s, it protested the Vietnam War; throughout the Cold War, it campaigned for nuclear test ban treaties; and in the 1980s, it opposed President Ronald Reagan's plan for a space-based missile defense system called Star Wars.

Further Reading

Levine, Daniel. *Jane Addams and the Liberal Tradition.* Westport, Conn.: Greenwood Press, 1971.

Meyer, Robert S. *Peace Organizations Past and Present.* Jefferson, N.C.: McFarland, 1988.

1915 American Union Against Militarism Opposes Military Preparedness

Among the many reforms stimulated by Progressivism in the early 1900s, none generated more controversy than the peace movement. Progressives themselves were divided over whether such a movement would threaten United States security, and they debated what form, if any, a peace movement should take. The American Union Against Militarism represented the more extreme among the peace crusaders.

To a Progressive like former President Theodore Roosevelt, peace groups were pure bunk. They would, if they had their unmanly way, leave the United States weak and vulnerable to attack by foreign countries. But other Progressives argued that they would make the United States stronger by moving the world toward disarmament and removing the threat of war. They took that stand during the Spanish American War in 1898, and with the outbreak of World War I in 1914, they criticized the rush to military preparedness as likely to drag the United States into the conflict.

Within the peace movement itself, disagreement arose over whether to accept some military preparedness, or arms buildup, or take a pure stand against it in all forms. In 1915, a group of Progressives, pacifists, and socialists, led by Lillian Wald, Oswald Garrison Villard, and Norman Thomas, organized the Anti-militarism Committee to completely oppose preparedness. In January 1916, they changed its name to the Anti-preparedness Committee, and later that year to the American Union Against Militarism (AUAM).

In November 1915, the AUAM joined the Women's Peace Party (see entry, 1915) in sponsoring the "Truth About Preparedness Campaign." The AUAM combined a moral argument against preparedness and war with an economic one: industrialists advocated preparedness so they could make money from it. The AUAM cast militarism in terms of class conflict, as a scheme whereby the rich exploited the lower orders.

The AUAM advocated strict neutrality of the United States, lobbied Congress against preparedness, opposed the draft, and condemned American imperialism in Latin America. In summer 1916, the group began a massive publicity campaign to pressure President Woodrow Wilson to remove troops he had sent to Mexico.

By that time, AUAM branches had appeared in every major American city, and AUAM speakers were touring the country. The group's theme song, "I Didn't Raise My Boy to Be a Soldier," became a hit.

When the United States entered the war, AUAM called for an early peace, formed a bureau to help conscientious objectors, and said that civil liberties must be protected. From this concern, Roger Baldwin, AUAM's secretary, and Crystal Eastman, the executive director, founded the Civil Liberties Bureau of the AUAM that soon became the American Civil Liberties Union (see entry, 1920). Obviously, the AUAM failed to prevent America's entry into World War I, yet it exposed the link between making armaments and making money and energized those who thought civil liberties precious, even in time of war.

Further Reading
Cook, Blanche Wiesen, ed. *Crystal Eastman on Women and Revolution.* New York: Oxford University Press, 1978.
Humes, D. J. *Oswald Garrison Villard: Liberal of the 1920s.* Syracuse, N.Y.: Syracuse University Press, 1960.
Lamson, Peggy. *Roger Baldwin: Founder of the American Civil Liberties Union.* Boston: Houghton Mifflin, 1976.
Thomas, Norman Mattoon. *Conscientious Objector in America.* With a new introduction by Charles Chatfield.
    New York: Garland, 1972.

Burning Crosses and Preaching Hate, the Ku Klux Klan Rides Again

Reorganized in 1915 by William Simmons, a defrocked Methodist Episcopal preacher who once said that as a boy he saw visions of Klansmen riding on their horses, the Ku Klux Klan (KKK) appealed to prejudice directed at African-Americans, immigrants, Jews, and Roman Catholics.

As William Simmons described it, he revived the KKK in a ceremony atop Stone Mountain, near Atlanta, Georgia, surrounded by a flag-draped altar bearing a Bible, a burning cross lighting the night, and initiates dressed in white robes and pointed caps.

Through the Klan, Simmons wanted to rally white Protestants against blacks, Jews, immigrants, and Roman Catholics, and the social changes they brought. The Klan's rebirth came as immigrants entered the United States in unprecedented numbers, primarily from eastern and southern Europe and overwhelmingly Catholic in faith.

The rebirth came amid intensifying bigotry. In the South, prejudice took an ugly turn in the weeks before the Stone Mountain ceremony when a mob dragged Leo Frank from an Atlanta jail—just a few miles from Stone Mountain itself—and hanged him. Frank, who was Jewish, had been convicted of raping a teenage girl. Both his trial, filled with legally questionable proceedings, and his hanging, exhibited signs of anti-Semitism. So, too, did the ranting of Georgia political leader Tom Watson, a former Populist whose speeches attacked blacks, Catholics, and Jews.

In 1915, the release of D. W. Griffith's *Birth of a Nation,* a pioneering movie in terms of its elaborate production, added to the climate of hate and bigotry. Based on Thomas Dixon's novel *The Clansman*, the movie portrayed blacks as imbecilic and dangerous, and the original KKK, formed shortly after the Civil War, as the saviors of civilization during the late 1860s and 1870s. Writing in *The Emergence of the New South* (1967), George B. Tindall says about *Birth of a Nation*, "One could hardly exaggerate its significance . . . in preparing the way for the revival of the Klan." In an intriguing bit of timing, Simmons printed his first public notice in an Atlanta newspaper about the Klan's rebirth while *Birth of a Nation* opened at theaters there.

Yet the appeal of the movie extended well beyond the South, playing to sold-out theaters from New England to California (and finding favor with President Woodrow Wilson). Around 1920, the Klan's reach extended beyond the South. To the American anxiety about blacks, immigrants, Catholics, and Jews (with the last three groups overlapping, since many immigrants were Roman Catholic or Jewish) was added the discontent with the way World War I had turned out—promoted as a war to make the world safe for democracy, it clearly had not—and dismay, at least among moral traditionalists, over open sexuality, liberated women, and the defiance of Prohibition.

Only native-born white Protestants could join the Klan. The group typically called foreigners "dirt," "scum," and "filth," and Simmons declared, "When the hordes of aliens walk to the ballot box and their votes outnumber yours, then that alien horde has got you by the throat." The Klan saved its greatest invective—at least outside the South, where it aimed mainly at blacks—for Catholics, derided as a threat to Protestant Christianity and a group likely to take orders from the pope. Combining its nativist and anti-Catholic stands, the Klan called the pope the "dago on the Tiber."

The Klan reached its peak in numbers and strength in the early to mid-1920s: membership estimates vary between three and four million. The KKK was strongest in Alabama, Georgia, Louisiana, Texas, Indiana, Ohio, Pennsylvania, and New York. It helped elect 16 senators and 11 governors; Earl Mayfield, a senator from Texas, was openly a member.

In 1925, articles in the *New York World* that detailed Klan bigotry and violence led to a congressional investigation. From the perspective of the Klan's opponents, the hearings backfired when in his testimony Simmons skillfully portrayed the KKK as the defender of American values.

Still, many people actively opposed the Klan. New York City banned the KKK from parading; Cleveland fined anyone belonging to a society promoting "racial hatred and religious bigotry," and that city's mayor said, "I cannot imagine a more vicious organization." The American Unity League, based in Chicago, infiltrated the Klan, stole its membership lists, and published the names of Klansmen, a move that exposed several prominent businessmen and politicians, including the chairman of the Indiana Republican Party. Other groups, some populated by bootleggers who disliked the Klan's call to more vigorously enforce prohibition, attacked the KKK, in one instance bombing its newspaper office in Chicago.

In the late 1920s, Klan membership declined rapidly, hastened by the conviction of a Klan leader for murder, passage of a law in 1924 restricting immigration, the failure of the Klan to show effective political leadership or widen its membership, and public disgust with Klan tactics. The KKK never again regained its size, but its bigotry, invective, and hate revived in the 1950s as the civil rights movement gained momentum.

Further Reading

Chalmers, David Mark. *Hooded Americanism: The History of the Ku Klux Klan.* 3rd ed. Durham, N.C.: Duke University Press, 1987.

Quarles, Chester L. *The Ku Klux Klan and Related American Racialist and Anti-Semitic Organizations: A History and Analysis.* Jefferson, N.C.: McFarland, 1999.

Wade, Wyn Craig. *The Fiery Cross: The Ku Klux Klan in America.* New York: Oxford University Press, 1998.

1915   Joe Hill Executed in Utah

On November 19, 1915, at 7:44 A.M., at the Utah State Penitentiary in Salt Lake City, a firing squad executed Joe Hill, a songwriter and activist with the Industrial Workers of the World. He had been found guilty of murder in a case that to many Americans was less designed to assure justice than to silence a radical.

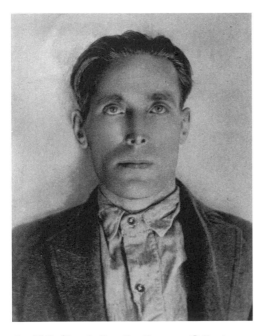

Joe Hill. (Seattle-Post Intelligencer *Collection; Museum of History & Industry: CORBIS*)

Joe Hill's past is shrouded in so much myth and legend it makes the details surrounding his arrest and conviction a true mystery. Hill was born Joel Haggland in Gavle, Sweden, in 1879 and, with his brother, immigrated to the United States in 1902. He spent some time in New York City before going out West and working as an itinerant laborer—as a longshoreman, miner, logger, and fruit picker. Between 1906 and 1910, for reasons unknown today, he changed his name to Joseph Hillstrom. Some say he was trying to alter his identity because he had engaged in petty crime; others say he was being hounded by company bosses who disliked his labor activism.

Hillstrom enrolled in the San Pedro, California, local of the Industrial Workers of the World (IWW; see entry, 1905) in 1910 and the following year joined his fellow Wobblies (the nickname for IWW members) in Tijuana, Mexico, where they plotted to overthrow the Mexican government. Back in the United States, his labor protests resulted in several skirmishes with the police, and he later admitted to having spent 30 days in the San Pedro jail for vagrancy.

By that time, Hillstrom was using "Hill" as his last name and writing songs intended to rally Wobblies as they organized and engaged in strikes. Usually, he wrote lyrics set to popular tunes of the day. Hill's songs began appearing in the *Little Red Song Book*, an annual published by the IWW, that sold for ten cents. Bearing the slogan "To Fan the Flames of Discontent," the *Little Red Song Book* exhorted workers to rise up against their company bosses. Some in the IWW criticized the resort to music as frivolous, but Hill said, "If a person can put a few cold, common sense facts into a song and dress them . . . up in a cloak of humor to take the dryness out of them, he will succeed in reaching a great number of workers who are too unintelligent or too indifferent to read a pamphlet or an editorial on economic science."

Hill's songs certainly succeeded. His "Casey Jones—The Union Scab," a parody set to another song about Jones, was widely popular with Wobblies and other workers, as was his "The Preacher and the Slave." By 1913, he had become the most frequent contributor to the *Little Red Song Book.*

That year, he went to Utah, where he may have worked briefly in the silver mines at Park City. On the night of January 10, 1914, at about 10 P.M., two men wearing dark hats and coats, and with handkerchiefs pulled up over their faces, entered a grocery store in Salt Lake City owned by John G. Morrison. When Arling Morrison, John's son, pulled out a revolver and shot at them, they fired back, killing both John and Arling. As 13-year-old Merlin Morrison rushed from a back room to see what was going on, the two men fled. Merlin later gave only vague descriptions of the two intruders.

Later that night, Joe Hill appeared at a doctor's house, bleeding from a gunshot wound. He always insisted that the wound had been inflicted during an argument with a woman. On hearing the police request for help in the killings, the doctor turned in Hill, and he was arrested.

Only circumstantial evidence existed to convict Hill. Morrison offered nothing positive; another witness who saw one of the gunmen fleeing the store said he saw a scar on the intruder's face that resembled the one on Joe Hill's face. Surprisingly, Hill refused to testify and identify the woman who he claimed had shot him. The jury deliberated for four hours before finding him guilty. Hill had his choice of execution—by hanging or by firing squad. "I'll take the shooting," he told the judge. "I've been shot a couple times before, and I think I can take it."

Had Hill been framed by enemies who wanted to eliminate a labor agitator? If he had been engaged previously in petty crime, it seems plausible that he may have resorted to robbery. Evidence indicates that at the time of his arrest, the police had no idea he was a Wobbly and so had no political motive for jailing him. Yet other facts of the case nagged at the minds of Hill's supporters. The murdered shopkeeper, John Morrison, was an ex-policeman who admitted that in his years on the local force he had angered many criminals, some of whom threatened to get him. Furthermore, the grocery store gunmen took no money, either because they panicked and forgot it or because they intended to kill Morrison rather than rob him. Finally, added to the circumstantial evidence was the feeling of the community against unions; the IWW had sponsored strikes in 1912 and 1913 at three mines. Writing in May 1914, Hill's lawyers said, "The main thing the state has against Hill is that he is an IWW and *therefore* sure to be guilty."

The IWW claimed Hill had been victimized, and it called for workers to rally behind him. Letters poured into the office of Utah governor William Spry from around the country and the world, pleading for clemency for Hill. The Swedish ambassador to the United States protested; so too as did President Woodrow Wilson, who asked that Hill's case be "reconsidered." Spry responded by asking Hill if he had anything to say in his defense, but the convicted man refused to speak.

Hill was honored by 30,000 mourners at his funeral procession in Chicago. One newspaper reporter wrote, "What kind of man is this whose death is celebrated with songs of revolt and who has at his bier more mourners than any prince or potentate?" For many workers, Joe Hill became a martyr, and his image would be resurrected numerous times in struggles against authority, including the Vietnam War in the 1960s. ("I dreamed I saw Joe Hill last night, alive as you and me," sang folk musician Joan Baez at

In November 1962, Elizabeth Gurley Flynn, former member of the Industrial Workers of the World (IWW; see entry, 1905) and member of the American Communist Party, addressed an audience of students and teachers at Northern Illinois University in Dekalb. She spoke about the IWW, what it had stood for, and what it had meant.

Flynn stressed that, unlike the American Federation of Labor (AFL; see entry, 1886), the IWW as a union envisioned a socialist future; rather than cooperate with capitalism, the IWW wanted to destroy it. Toward that end, the union used militant tactics.

An important part of her story, however, dealt with the way the IWW reached out to workers ignored by other unions. That inclusiveness attested to the IWW's desire for solidarity and its goal of providing dignity to people society considered expendable. "Now the IWW's positive side," Flynn said, "certainly it was militant, it was courageous, that it fitted the period, that it belonged to the pioneer days and that it fought for the interests of the poorest, the most lonely, the most despised, those that the AFL couldn't organize, the foreign born, the women, and as the Negroes began coming into industry, the Negroes." Only later, primarily after World War II, would the AFL bring these groups into its member unions, following what the IWW had dared to do many years before.

Woodstock in 1969.) Shortly before Hill was executed, he wrote a fellow Wobbly, Bill Haywood: "Goodbye Bill. I die like a true rebel. Don't waste time mourning—organize!"

Further Reading

Foner, Philip Sheldon. *The Case of Joe Hill.* New York: International Publishers, 1965.

Smith, Gibbs M. *Joe Hill.* Salt Lake City, Utah: Peregrine Smith Books, 1984.

1916 Marcus Garvey Arrives in the United States and Promotes Black Nationalism and Black Pride

Marcus Garvey arrived in New York City from Jamaica in 1916 with charisma, polished oratory, an established organization—the Universal Negro Improvement Association—and a list of goals: "To establish a Universal Cofraternity among the race; to promote the spirit of pride and love; to reclaim the fallen; to administer to and assist the needy; to assist in civilizing the backward tribes of Africa; to assist in the development of Independent Negro Nations and Communities."

Marcus Garvey (1887–1940) was born on the Caribbean island of Jamaica and at age 16 became a foreman printer in Kingston. In 1910, he joined the migrant wave looking for work in Central America and over the next four years traveled to South America and England. Each stop made him more aware of the suffering endured by black people in a world economically and politically dominated by whites. In London, he met Duse Mohammed Ali, a half-black Egyptian, and worked for his Pan African paper, *Africa Times.* With Garvey, Mohammed Ali shared his thoughts about the oppression of blacks in England and the decline of black culture in Africa.

As Garvey sailed back to Jamaica in 1914 he read Booker T. Washington's *Up from Slavery*, which taught him about race pride and the segregation faced by blacks in the United States. Garvey later recalled that he began asking himself, "Where is the black man's Government? Where is his King and his Kingdom? Where is his President, his country, and his ambassador; his army, his navy, his men of big affairs?" In answer, he stated, "I could not find them, and then I declared, 'I will help to make them.'"

With that, Garvey founded the Universal Negro Improvement and Conservation Association and African Communities League, usually referred to by the shortened name of the Universal Negro Improvement

Association (UNIA). He wrote his goals, or "general objects," as he called them, and in a manifesto stated that he wanted "all people of Negro or African parentage" to join his group's crusade to save the race.

In March 1916, Garvey arrived in New York City to raise money for the UNIA; he stayed for 11 years, officially relocating the UNIA headquarters to his adopted city in 1917. His message that blacks should be proud of their past and look forward to a momentous future resonated with African-Americans then struggling with white racism and turning toward their own culture for identity and guidance. Garvey arrived as Jim Crow laws gripped the South and as a black exodus from that region to northern and western cities caused a white backlash in places like New York and Detroit. Shut out from white society, African-Americans were turning to jazz and the blues—emerging from traditional black music—and to their own writers and artists. They turned to the black churches, and Marcus Garvey turned to them, appealing to their Christianity and to the greater desire for black pride. "Christ died to make men free," Garvey told African-Americans. "I shall die to give courage and inspiration to my race."

Marcus Garvey said that although God was color-blind, African-Americans must see him as black, in order to break the control whites had over his image. Garvey declared he wanted to build a black republic in Africa stretching from Liberia to Capetown. It would serve, he said, as a source of black pride and as a refuge from white oppression. Writing in *Black Moses* (1955), E. David Cronon states, "It was never Garvey's intention that all Negroes in the New World would return to Africa. . . . Rather he believed like many Zionists that once a strong African nation was established Negroes everywhere would automatically gain needed prestige and strength and could look to it for protection if necessary."

Garvey showed an impressive ability to bridge the gap between his West Indian culture and American culture, and the UNIA quickly developed a widespread following. In 1918, he founded the *Negro World* newspaper; by the early 1920s, its circulation topped 100,000; at the same time UNIA branches spread to 38 states.

In 1919, Garvey bought an auditorium in Harlem and renamed it Liberty Hall. There his followers gathered to listen to his speeches. Other Liberty Halls were soon established in Philadelphia, Pittsburgh, Cleveland, Detroit, Cincinnati, Chicago, and Los Angeles.

Garvey advocated economic independence for blacks, a separatism that reflected his belief that blacks must look out for themselves. He founded the Negro Factories Corporation to begin black-owned businesses, and in 1919, he obtained a charter to begin the Black Star Line, which he envisioned as a fleet of ships operated by and staffed only with African-Americans. To raise capital, he issued stock and declared in an advertising circular: "Now is the time for the Negro to invest in the Black Star Line so that in the near future he may exert the same influence upon the world as the white man does today."

In short order, he raised more than $600,000. At $10 a share, even poorer African-Americans could invest, look forward to making money, and contribute to a black company founded by and for black people. In November 1919, about 5,000 African-Americans gathered at New York's 135th Street pier, and, as a UNIA band played, they sent off the *Yarmouth*, the first ship of the Black Star Line.

Garvey's reputation had become almost global; millions of blacks looked to him for leadership. In 1920, he held a massive International Convention at New York's Madison Square Garden. Some 25,000 delegates attended from dozens of countries. At the meeting he demanded that whites be expelled from Africa, and the delegates approved a Declaration of Rights of the Negro Peoples of the World. "Nowhere in the world, with few exceptions, are black men accorded equal treatment with white men. . ." the Declaration claimed. There followed a long list of demands and the statement, "Be it known that whereas, all men are created equal and entitled to the rights of life, liberty, and the pursuit of happiness . . . [we] do declare all men, women and children of our blood throughout the world free citizens, and do claim them as free citizens of Africa, the Motherland of all Negroes."

Garvey's crusade generated controversy and earned him enemies. Some blacks disliked his insistence on racial purity and condemnation of mulattos. He caused an uproar in 1922 when he met with leaders of the Ku Klux Klan and told them he supported their fight against interracial marriage. To his critics, Garvey responded: "I regard the Klan . . . as better friends of the race than all other hypocritical whites put together."

The integrationist National Association for the Advancement of Colored People (NAACP) attacked Garvey's separatism. W. E. B. Du Bois, an NAACP leader, called Garvey a "lunatic." Garvey called Du Bois a "lazy dependent mulatto." The federal government spied on the UNIA, and, at the urging of several white and black leaders with the NAACP, the government prosecuted Garvey for fraud involving the Black Star Line. The charges had little merit—the shipping company's profits suffered from mismanagement rather than anything illegal—but a jury found Garvey guilty, and a judge who was a member of the NAACP sentenced him to a maximum five years in prison.

President Calvin Coolidge commuted Garvey's sentence in 1927—but ordered him deported. He returned to Jamaica, edited two newspapers, and in 1929 held another international convention. Back in the United States, the UNIA suffered from factional disputes.

To many blacks, Marcus Garvey died in 1940 a hero. Historian E. David Cronon observes that "Garvey exalted everything black and exhorted Negroes to be proud of their distinctive features and color. Negroid characteristics were not shameful marks of inferiority to be camouflaged and altered; they were rather symbols of beauty and grace." In that way, Garvey stood for the racial nationalism evident in the later Nation of Islam (Black Muslims) promoted by Malcolm X (see entries, 1948 and 1964) and the 1960s "black is beautiful" philosophy extolled by Huey Newton and Bobby Seale of the Black Panthers (see entry, 1966). Pride, independence, and unity . . . these Garvey attributes appealed to African-Americans, or in the words of the UNIA official motto: "One Aim! One God! One Destiny!"

Further Reading

Cronon, E. David. *Black Moses: The Story of Marcus Garvey and the Universal Negro Improvement Association.* Madison: University of Wisconsin Press, 1955.

Garvey, Marcus. *Philosophy and Opinions of Marcus Garvey.* 2 vols. New York: Arno Press, 1968–69.

Hill, Robert A., ed. *The Marcus Garvey and UNIA Papers.* Berkeley: University of California Press, 1983.

———. *Marcus Garvey, Life and Lessons: A Centennial Companion to the Marcus Garvey and Universal Negro Improvement Association Papers.* Berkeley: University of California Press, 1987.

Stein, Judith. *The World of Marcus Garvey: Race and Class in Modern Society.* Baton Rouge: Louisiana State University Press, 1986.

Youssef, Sitamon Mubaraka, ed. *Marcus Garvey: The F.B.I. Investigation Files.* Trenton, N.J.: Africa World Press, 1998.

1917 The Bisbee Deportation: Copper Companies Kidnap Miners

On July 12, 1917, vigilantes led by Sheriff Harry Wheeler rounded up more than 2,000 miners in Bisbee, Arizona, forced most of them into railroad boxcars caked with animal dung, hauled them to New Mexico, and dropped them in the middle of the desert. The miners' only crime: they had gone out on strike against Phelps Dodge and other mining companies.

Even before the "Bisbee Deportation," problems were brewing between management and miners. The mines in Arizona were producing nearly 50 percent of the country's copper, and profits were increasing substantially (and along with them, taxes paid to Arizona, making the companies important to the state's finances and powerful with politicians), but miners' wages were lagging behind inflation. In addition, the mining companies owned the workers' housing and charged the workers high prices at company stores.

In 1917, miners organized by the Western Federation of Mines in several Arizona towns, went on strike. At the same time, the Industrial Workers of the World (IWW; see entry, 1905) began organizing miners in Bisbee, a small town near the Mexican border that relied for its survival on the massive copper mines operated by Phelps Dodge and other smaller companies.

In 1917 the Wobblies, as the IWW members were called, demanded that the mining companies negotiate to resolve several grievances centered around inadequate wages: they demanded a minimum wage based on the quantity of copper produced rather than a flat rate; and they protested wages and job assignments that discriminated against Mexican laborers. Moreover, the IWW denounced the blacklisting of union members and dangerous working practices, including detonating dynamite in proximity to the workers. Phelps Dodge officials refused to meet with the miners, and, on June 27, 1917, the Wobblies began their strike.

From the start, Phelps Dodge portrayed the IWW as dangerous, violent, and a threat to United States security. The last charge carried considerable weight with the public, for the country had just entered World War I, which the Wobblies had long denounced as a conflict to enrich the capitalist class, and their strike threatened to disrupt the production of copper at a time the country desperately needed it. The president of Phelps Dodge charged: "I believe the government will be able to show that there is German influence behind this movement. The men had no money yet they are rich with it now. . . . The organizers spend money like drunken sailors and there is a general belief it is German money."

The mining companies consistently referred to the Wobblies as violent thugs intent on blowing up the mines. In truth, while the IWW expressed a revolutionary ideology espousing the overthrow of capitalism, it engaged in little violence in Bisbee, or anywhere else. About the IWW, historian Foster Rhea Dulles claims that "In spite of the violence of its propaganda, [it was] too cautious to be successful as a revolution. The only thing in which it fully succeeded was in arousing popular fears of violence."

Beyond discrediting the IWW with words, the mining companies infiltrated the union with undercover agents meant to disrupt its proceedings. Then the sheriff, Harry C. Wheeler, with the help of Phelps Dodge executives, began deputizing residents, forming a vigilante group. Wheeler had earlier criticized the IWW strike. "It is difficult for me to believe," he announced, "that any loyal American . . . would contemplate anything which might in the slightest degree cripple the government of our country. The closing down or hindrance of the great copper industry in this section, would prove a direct blow, and a heavy one, to the government of the United States."

Early in the morning of July 12, 1917, the vigilantes went to work. The daughter of one vigilante recalled: "A few cars went by. The sounds of horses were muted. Voices were low, words indistinguishable. Dad got up from his bed when a low tap on the front door tattooed a signal. He hushed out questions. 'Stay indoors. Keep quiet. Don't build a fire. . . .' He took his rifle down from the wall, the door opened, and he was gone."

The vigilantes captured Bisbee's telephone and telegraph lines. Then they rounded up more than 2,000 miners and marched them to a ball field. Many of the men, according to one observer, "were still in their nightshirts, many in long underwear, some apparently hadn't been given time to put on their shoes." The miners were given an opportunity to abandon the strike and go back to work. Those who refused, 1,185 in all, were forced to board the filthy boxcars. As it turned out, a substantial number of them were neither Wobblies nor strikers but workers inadvertently rounded up in the dragnet.

Under the headline THE GREAT WOBBLY DRIVE, and with a photo captioned: "All right, you goddam wobbly—you get your ass into that side-door pullman!" the *Bisbee Review*, a newspaper controlled by Phelps Dodge, crowed: "The surprise was as complete as though these deputies had descended from the heavens. The 'wobblies' reeled like drunken men. They were more than surprised; they were dazed."

The train left Bisbee for Columbus, New Mexico, but officials turned it away, saying the town lacked the facilities to handle so many men, and the miners were abandoned on the desert near Hermanas. Another train later brought them food and rations; nevertheless, they were without shelter for two days until federal troops rescued them on July 14. Back in Bisbee, mounted guards patrolled the streets to make sure none of the deportees returned, while many of the miners were detained by the federal government for several months. Needless to say, the strike was broken.

Despite his dislike for the IWW, President Woodrow Wilson ordered the Federal Mediation Commission to investigate the incident, and the commission found the mining companies at fault. No action was taken against them, however, either by the federal government or the state of Arizona. About 300 deportees filed civil suits against the El Paso Southwestern Railroad and the copper companies, but these were settled out of court.

"It was a deportation upon a staggering scale," said the *Bisbee Review*. "It was Bisbee's answer to the impudent, arrogant effort of a lawless lot of outcasts to dictate her industrial and business affairs—the greatest copper city in the world to the blackest and most infamous organization in the world." More accurately, it was the corporate answer to oppressed miners wanting their grievances redressed and their worthiness acknowledged.

Further Reading

Byrkit, James W. *Forging the Copper Collar: Arizona's Labor Management War of 1901–1921*. Tucson: University of Arizona Press, 1982.

Hanson, Rob E. *The Great Bisbee I. W. W. Deportation of July 12, 1917*. Bisbee, Ariz.: Signature Press, 1989.

1917   Margaret Sanger Jailed for Operating a Birth Control Clinic

By the 1930s, most Americans favored birth control, and in 1960, the Pill became widely available, beginning a new era in contraception. But in the early twentieth century, laws forbade the distribution of birth control devices or even birth control literature. When Margaret Sanger did both, she was arrested and imprisoned. Rather than silencing the birth control movement, the episode drew attention to its urgent pleas.

Margaret Sanger (1879–1966) was involved in radical causes well before her arrest in 1917. Born Margaret Higgins, she studied nursing in 1899 but quit in 1902 when she married William Sanger, an architect. In 1912 she moved to New York City, where she made friends with radical intellectuals; joined the Socialist Party; wrote articles for the socialist magazine, *Call*, and marched in picket lines during strikes declared by the Industrial Workers of the World (see entry, 1905), a revolutionary socialist union. She believed also that women should be liberated from suppressing their erotic desires, and she enthusiastically promoted free love.

In 1914, Sanger began publishing the *Woman Rebel*, a rabidly anticapitalist magazine that defended political assassination. Federal authorities arrested her for violating antiobscenity laws, and to avoid prosecution she fled to Europe. Sanger had already shown an interest in the issue of birth control, partly because her own health made it risky for her to become pregnant again (she had three children with William Sanger). Now Havelock Ellis, a British philosopher who became her lover, convinced her to toss aside her other issues for this one.

Sanger became convinced that women's oppression was tied to women's function as childbearer. She believed that liberation depending on women exerting greater power over whether to have children, when to have them, and how many of them to have. In short, women must determine what happened to their bodies.

That year, Sanger plunged determinedly into the birth control campaign already started by others. Obsessive and overbearing in temperament—Sanger "insisted on pursuing life strictly on her own terms," according to historian Doris Dwyer—she wanted to dominate the movement, and considered her leadership of it absolutely essential for it to succeed.

In October 1916, Sanger decided she would challenge the New York state law that made it illegal to distribute birth control devices or information. To Sanger and many other women, those laws represented an attempt by men to dictate when children would be born, and how many children a couple would have. They reasoned that if women were to gain access to birth control devices or information that would allow them to take the initiative in conception, not only would their health be protected from unwanted pregnancies—and their own families, and the country as a whole, spared the poverty that resulted from having too many children—but male authority would be aslo weakened and women liberated, both sexually and spiritually.

On October 16, 1916, in the Brownsville section of Brooklyn, Sanger, her sister Ethel Byrne, who was a registered nurse, and Fania Mindell, a Russian woman willing to serve as an interpreter for the neighborhood's immigrants, opened the Brownsville Clinic. Any woman could enter the clinic and for ten cents obtain a pamphlet written by Sanger, *What Every Girl Should Know*, along with instructions on how to use contraceptives. Handbills that advertised the clinic announced:

MOTHERS

Can you afford to have a large family?

Do you want any more children?

If not, why do you have them?

DO NOT KILL. DO NOT TAKE LIFE, BUT PREVENT.

The day the clinic opened, a long line of women waited to enter. On October 26, an undercover policewoman arrested Sanger, Byrne, and Mindell. Sanger reopened the clinic, and was arrested a second time on November 14. She opened the clinic yet again, and was arrested on November 16. This time the police forced the landlord to evict her, and the clinic closed for good.

Sex and Reform

When Margaret Sanger advocated that women use birth control, she ventured into a delicate and controversial realm for reformers: the private sex lives of Americans. This was deliberate: she saw birth control as a way for women to improve their health and to liberate themselves sexually. Sanger was not the first reformer to address the role of sex in society. In the mid-nineteenth century, for example, John Humphrey Noyes tried to liberate sex from the traditional boundaries of marriage at his Oneida Community (see entry, 1841) through his system of "complex marriages." The feminist Victoria Woodhull (see entry, 1872) espoused free love, a stand also embraced a few years later by the anarchist Emma Goldman (see entry, 1919).

Time and again women who advocated for women's rights confronted the issue of sex. In the 1960s and 1970s, liberationists argued that the oppression of women was related to society's expectation that men dominate them sexually. They called for sexual practices that would please women as much as they did men, and they argued that the personal was political—in other words, "private" attitudes and behavior carried over to how women were treated in society at large. The sexually selfish and dominant male, they claimed, produced the politically selfish and dominate male.

In contemporary times, both pro-choice and pro-life activists have had to confront the issue of sex—how their stands influenced sexual practices, either liberating or restricting them, producing healthier sexual attitudes, or damaging morals. Likewise, the gay rights movement has also raised the issue of what the advocacy of reform meant for sexual practices and public morals.

Margaret Sanger (to the left of baby) greets her supporters outside her trial. (Library of Congress)

Shortly before Sanger went to trial in January 1917, several prominent women organized the Committee of 100 to help her, Byrne, and Mindell. They raised money for lawyers and rallied public opinion. When Byrne was tried, convicted, and sent to prison at Blackwell's Island, she began a hunger strike, and the Committee of 100 held a protest rally at Carnegie Hall, at which Sanger appeared and fervently declared: "I come to you tonight from a vortex of persecution. I come not from the stake of Salem where women were once burned for blasphemy, but from the shadow of Blackwell's Island where women are tortured for so-called obscenity."

Sanger was convicted and served a 30-day sentence from February to March 1917. The New York court of appeals upheld her conviction, But it also redefined provisions in the law to make it easier for doctors to prescribe contraceptives.

Sanger continued her birth control campaign, but with some changes in outlook. She identified more closely with eugenicists who sought to control human reproduction to improve society. They advocated, for example, the sterilization of people with hereditary defects (mental illness and the like). Sanger argued that birth control should be used to prevent the working class from "overbreeding" and to limit the number of "unfit" persons. Furthermore she abandoned her support for leftists. In 1922, after divorcing William Sanger, she married James Noah Henry Slee, a wealthy oilman, and circulated in high society. His money bankrolled the American Birth Control League (ABCL) that she had founded in 1921.

Sanger opened the Clinical Research Bureau in New York in 1923, the first legal birth control clinic in the United States, and it provided contraceptive devices to women. Sanger resigned from the ABCL in 1928, and renamed the Clinical Research Bureau the Birth Control Clinical Research Bureau

(BCCRB). In 1939, the ABCL and the BCCRB merged to form the Birth Control Federation of America, which changed its name in 1942 to the Planned Parenthood Federation of America.

Sanger remained active in the birth control movement into the 1950s, when she campaigned for the federal government to fund contraceptive services. Sanger never doubted that birth control would liberate women. "The basic freedom of the world is woman's freedom," she wrote in *Woman and the New Race* (1920). "A free race cannot be born of slave mothers. . . . No woman can call herself free who does not own and control her body." Birth control has indeed challenged male authority and given women more freedom to act; yet it has also shifted responsibility for safe sex to women and may have encouraged men to expect sex from them. If so, that was not Sanger's intent. She advocated birth control for a variety of reasons—to fight poverty, to heighten women's erotic experiences, and, as she once said, to assert women's rights "regardless of all other considerations to determine whether she shall bear children or not, and how many children she shall bear if she chooses to become a mother."

Further Reading

Chesler, Ellen. *Woman of Valor: Margaret Sanger and the Birth Control Movement in America.* New York: Simon & Schuster, 1992.

Douglas, Emily Taft. *Margaret Sanger: Pioneer of the Future.* New York: Holt, Rinehart & Winston, 1969.

Gray, Madeline. *Margaret Sanger: A Biography of the Champion of Birth Control.* New York: R. Marek, 1979.

Government Brutalizes Suffragists Who Picket Outside the White House   1917

To some Americans it was a frivolous, even whimsical sight, when in January 1917 women from the National Woman's Party began picketing outside the White House for the right to vote. But the protests took on a different appearance that April, when the government reacted by arresting and brutally treating the suffragists.

The picketing represented a more militant stage in the suffrage movement, led by Alice Paul (1885–1977). Women had been campaigning for the right to vote since before the Civil War, and in the months immediately prior to the White House protest, they had staged marches in New York and Washington, D.C. They hoped to obtain from President Woodrow Wilson support for a constitutional amendment, but he rejected their appeal and, at the same time, Congress refused to act.

So they began picketing, several protesters at a time, working in shifts. Writing in *One Woman, One Vote* (1998), Marjorie Spruill Wheeler says these women "were the first . . . to picket the White House for a political cause." On January 27, 1917, the *Washington Star* reported how President Wilson had returned from playing a round of golf to find the women standing outside the White House gate; he looked at their signs and then "rewarded the pickets with his most genial smile and doffed his hat."

But Wilson's genial smile turned to rage when the United States entered World War I that April. He disliked the picketers mocking his idealistic reasons for fighting the war. They had begun denouncing the hypocrisy behind such Wilson statements as "We shall fight for the things which we have always held nearest our hearts—for democracy, for the right of those who submit to authority to have a voice in their own government." They called him "dictatorial and oppressive" toward women and chided him as "Kaiser Wilson."

Their tactic divided the suffrage movement. More moderate suffragists, such as Carrie Chapman Catt, believed that rather than agitate, the movement needed to educate, especially men. Militancy, they feared, would only make men more intransigent in their opposition to women's suffrage. Other moderates thought that the picketers were besmirching the character of women through their "unladylike" actions. Catt was less concerned with that complaint—according to historian Robert Booth Fowler, she had "a sneaking sympathy with the picketers' tactical militance"—than with the possible political damage, and in a letter to Alice Paul she labeled the picketing a "futile annoyance to the members of Congress" and "an insult to President Wilson," whose backing she wanted for a suffrage amendment.

The dispute between the moderates and the militants shows how discord among radicals can shift the very definition of what is a radical. To the militant suffragists, the moderates hardly qualified as radicals; to the suffrage opponents, both groups were radical, though different in degree. Interestingly, the work of the radicals had two effects: on the one hand, they hardened many of the suffrage opponents; on the other, by making Catt and other moderates appear less radical, they made the moderates' ideas more acceptable.

In June 1917, the government began arresting the suffragists on charges of obstructing traffic. At first, they received only minor sentences, but they kept picketing—even withstanding an assault by a mob in July—and Paul was arrested and sentenced to seven months at the Occoquan Workhouse in Virginia.

Because the government ignored her request, and those of other arrested picketers, to be recognized as "political prisoners," she and her colleagues began a hunger strike. Paul was placed in a psychiatric ward, and, when she still refused to eat, she was force fed. For Paul and the other hunger strikers, however, force feeding was more than, as the government said, an attempt to "save them"; it was painful punishment with tubes jammed down their nostrils and throats.

On November 14, the police arrested 33 more picketers, and, in what has been called a "night of terror," the women were clubbed, handcuffed to iron bars, and denied access to toilets. Later that month, a judge released Paul and the other protesters. The episode failed to intimidate or dissuade them; instead, they reacted with anger and intensified commitment. Texas suffragist Lucille Shields commented: "In jail . . . you realize more keenly the years that women have struggled to be free and the tasks that they have been forced to leave undone for lack of power to do them." They resumed picketing the White House.

Wilson finally announced his support for women's suffrage on January 9, 1918, and the next day, the House of Representatives passed a constitutional amendment granting women the right to vote. The

Suffragists outside the White House, circa 1917. (Library of Congress)

Senate did likewise in June 1919, and in August 1920, Tennessee became the thirty-sixth state to ratify the change, putting it into effect as the Nineteenth Amendment. For this progress, women's militancy must receive at least partial credit; it had provoked the government into a reaction that appalled many Americans and broke conservative resistance.

Further Reading

Barker-Benfield, G. J., and Catherine Clinton, eds. *Portraits of American Women: From Settlement to the Present.* New York: St. Martin's Press, 1991.

Becker, Susan D. *The Origins of the Equal Rights Amendment: American Feminism Between the Wars.* Westport, Conn.: Greenwood Press, 1981.

Cott, Nancy F. *The Grounding of Modern Feminism.* New Haven, Ct.: Yale University Press, 1987.

Lunardini, Christine A. *From Equal Suffrage to Equal Rights: Alice Paul and the National Woman's Party, 1910–1928.* New York: New York University Press, 1986.

Wheeler, Marjorie Spruill. *One Woman, One Vote: Rediscovering the Woman Suffrage movement.* Troutdale, Ore.: NewSage Press, 1995.

Labor Strikes and the Red Scare Sweep across the Country 1919

The United States was victorious in World War I, but in 1919, the country stood on edge, as if balanced on the sharp tip of a bayonet. Both labor and a government–business alliance went to extremes; the Red Scare discouraged free speech and led to smear tactics and deportations, among them the anarchist Emma Goldman; workers around the country went on strike, including a massive steel strike. Had World War I been won only to see America disintegrate in a great wave of intolerance and fear?

As American troops returned home from Europe in 1919, the country seemed less secure than before the war and far removed from the near-utopian notion, voiced loudest by President Woodrow Wilson, that the world would be made safe for democracy. Workers were pinched by inflation and worried about job security in an economy slowing from war production.

At the same time, many Americans feared that communist ideas emanating from the Bolshevik-led Russian Revolution would take over the United States. Big business and government fed those fears as a way to control laborers and their unions by labeling them as "commies." "The people are shivering in their boots over Bolshevism," said columnist Walter Lippman. "They are far more afraid of Lenin than they ever were of the Kaiser."

The year 1919 began with labor strikes. In January, shipyard workers in Seattle walked off their jobs, and, when workers in other industries joined them, they paralyzed the city. The mayor and corporate managers labeled the strikers "anarchists." Although the Seattle strike failed, others followed: theater actors in New York City, textile workers in New England and New Jersey, and police in Boston.

Terrorists contributed to the hysteria. They sent package bombs to the Seattle mayor and to a former senator, whose maid and wife were injured when it exploded. The police intercepted other bombs, 36 in all. On June 2, bombs planted in eight different cities exploded; in the most spectacular incident, one ripped through Attorney General A. Mitchell Palmer's house in Washington, D.C.

In September, more than 300,000 steel workers walked off their jobs. The strike ended nearly all steel production and damaged the economy. The steel companies fought back. In Pittsburgh, U.S. Steel colluded with the local sheriff to deputize 5,000 of its employees; in nearby towns, state troopers waded through crowds of peaceful strikers, clubbing them; in other towns, strikers were arrested and shot. In Gary, Indiana, the strike turned violent, federal troops reinforcing the local police, and the steel workers, deprived of income and unable to feed their families, resorting to rioting.

The companies and the government bombarded the public with propaganda about how the strikers wanted to ignite a Bolshevik revolution. They circulated stories about labor leader William Z. Foster's attachment to socialism and raised questions about the loyalty of the many immigrants among the strikers—had they brought with them un-American ideas?

In November, Attorney General A. Mitchell Palmer added to the crisis when he began arresting radicals, having 39 of them deported in what became known as the "Red Scare." The next month, the government deported 249 aliens to Russia.

Among them was anarchist Emma Goldman, a Russian émigré. She had just finished serving a prison sentence for advising young men to defy the World War I military draft, when J. Edgar Hoover, head of the General Intelligence Division of the Department of Justice (later the FBI), pursued her. Consequently, the government formally charged her under a law passed by Congress in 1918 that authorized deportation for any noncitizen immigrant who belonged to an organization that advocated revolution. In early December, a federal court ruled that Goldman did not have the United States citizenship she claimed to have acquired through marriage and could be deported to Russia. On December 21, she was placed aboard the transport *Buford*, nicknamed the "Soviet Ark," along with fellow anarchist Alexander Berkman (see entry, 1892) and the other 247 radicals. The *New York Times* said good riddance, hailing "the sweet sorrow of parting at last with two of the most pernicious anarchists, Emma Goldman and Alexander Berkman, for a generation among the most virulent and dangerous preachers and practicers of the doctrines of destruction."

In January 1920, the postwar crisis eased. Palmer launched his most extensive raid of the Red Scare when federal agents arrested 6,000 alleged communists in 33 cities—in many instances, the government failed to obtain proper warrants or allow those arrested to contact lawyers—but rather than applaud Palmer's latest raid, many Americans thought the attorney general had gone too far. So even though the Red Scare would continue to work its influence, revulsion against it had set in. Weariness with the crisis appeared evident when the public reacted with horror to the Wall Street bombing of September 1920, which killed 29 people, but also with a sense that it had been committed by a few individuals rather than by a large-scale revolutionary underground.

Radical Actions, Radical Reactions

Whether it was mine companies, local businesses, and the Colorado state government joining together in 1902 to crush striking miners in Cripple Creek, or Attorney General A. Mitchell Palmer organizing the Red Scare in 1919, many Americans realized from these confrontations with radicals a sense of their own Americanism. Comparable to the Cold War of the late 1940s through the 1980s, when portraying the Soviet Union as evil confirmed for Americans that they were good, portraying the Industrial Workers of the World (IWW) or the Socialist Party as aberrant reconfirmed for mainstream society what proper values should be.

A similar dynamic worked for the radicals. Their definition of who they were, their sense of solidarity, and their knowledge of their own rightness relied on demonizing the opposition, in this case the capitalist economy and government. Both sides, then, needed to believe the worst of the other; it confirmed their reason for being and the judgments they held to be true.

So when during World War I a congressman linked the IWW to the German Kaiser by calling it "Imperial Wilhelm's Warriors," he effectively demonized the union; and when IWW members sang "Solidarity Forever," their words echoed a view meant to vilify the capitalist opponent:

> They have taken untold millions that they never
> toiled to earn
> But without our brain and muscle not a single
> wheel can turn
> We can break their haughty power; gain our free-
> dom when we learn
> That the Union makes us strong.

That same month, the steel strike collapsed, with the workers beaten down by the combined corporate and state power. As quoted in *The Century* (1998), by Peter Jennings and Todd Brewster, John Meyerick, age 11 in 1919, recalled: "When I was growing up my father worked at the U.S. Steel Mill in Gary, Indiana. You had to work 10- and 14-hour days of dirty, hard, manual labor at that mill. Wages were very poor, but if you asked for more pay the superintendent would say, 'If you're not satisfied, you know where the gate is.'" The strike of 1919 changed none of that.

Further Reading

Allen, Frederick Lewis. *Only Yesterday: An Informal History of the 1920s.* New York: Harper & Brothers, 1931.

Coben, Stanley. A. *Mitchell Palmer: Politician.* New York: Da Capo Press, 1972.

Murray, Robert K. *Red Scare: A Study of National Hysteria, 1919–1920.* Minneapolis: University of Minnesota Press, 1955.

Nielsen, Kim. *Un-American Womanhood: Antiradicalism, Antifeminism, and the First Red Scare.* Columbus: University of Ohio Press, 2001.

Schlesinger, Arthur Meier, Jr. *The Crisis of the Old Order, 1919–1933.* Boston: Houghton Mifflin, 1957.

Victory for the Temperance Movement

1919

Even before the American Revolution, a significant campaign against the manufacture and consumption of alcohol was in place. That campaign accelerated in the early 1800s and reached its apex in 1919 when the states ratified the Eighteenth Amendment, known as the Prohibition Amendment.

Walter Lippman, a famous newspaperman himself, once called John Reed (1887–1920) the consummate journalist. Today, the ban on alcohol may seem like a violation of individual freedom. In the late 1800s and early 1900s, however, the Prohibition movement attracted a variety of reformers. Few took their protests to the fanatical level of Carry Nation (see entry, 1900); most temperance advocates were highly educated moderates, committed to uplifting America's morals.

By the twentieth century, the Anti-Saloon League (ASL) had replaced the Women's Christian Temperance Union as the leader in the fight against alcohol. To a considerable extent, those who supported the ASL came from the country's small towns; to them, banning alcohol meant containing the "evil influences" of urban society threatening to overwhelm small-town traditions. But many Prohibition supporters were cosmopolitan Progressives, including Jane Addams, the founder of Hull House; Theodore Roosevelt, the Republican president who was widely recognized as the political leader of Progressivism; and Louis Brandeis, the liberal Supreme Court justice. For some feminists, such as Susan B. Anthony (see entry, 1872) temperance was a feminist issue because men's abuse of alcohol often led to violence against women.

Critics of Prohibition said it would never work. They questioned the desirability of legislating morality on such a sweeping scale. They also called it a discriminatory attack on immigrants and ethnic groups such as German-Americans and Irish-Americans, whose beer gardens and pubs were central to their social gatherings.

The push for a constitutional amendment gathered momentum from the outbreak of World War I. The fight against Germany became a fight against German influences, breweries for example, within the United States. In a propaganda piece, the ASL linked patriotism to Prohibition, saying, "If our Republic is to be saved the liquor traffic must be destroyed."

In the end, Prohibition was a failure. All through the 1920s, Americans made and drank alcohol in widespread violation of the constitutional ban. Many argued that the law, which was intended to uplift morals, actually damaged them by encouraging an appalling increase in crime through bootlegging, and that in encouraging people to violate the law, Prohibition had led to a greater disrespect for the law in general.

The Twenty-First Amendment, which took effect in 1933, rescinded the Eighteenth Amendment, and the manufacture, sale, and consumption of alcohol again became legal. Historically, Prohibition serves as an example of urban Progressives and small towns working together in a misguided effort to improve morals in the United States.

Further Reading

Blocker, Jack S. *Retreat from Reform: The Prohibition Movement in the United States, 1890–1913.* Westport, Conn.: Greenwood Press, 1976.

Kerr, K. Austin. *Organized for Prohibition: A New History of the Anti-Saloon League.* New Haven, Conn.: Yale University Press, 1985.

Mason, Philip P. *Rumrunning and the Roaring Twenties: Prohibition on the Michigan–Ontario Waterway.* Detroit, Mich.: Wayne State University Press, 1995.

Wiebe, Robert H. *The Search for Order, 1877–1920.* Westport, Conn.: Greenwood Press, 1980.

1919 John Reed Excites Radicals with *Ten Days That Shook the World*

In 1919, John Reed shook America with his account of the Russian Revolution, Ten Days That Shook the World, *so passionate in its narrative that it encouraged leftist radicals to form John Reed Clubs and join the communist crusade.*

Walter Lippman, a famous newspaperman himself, once called John Reed (1887–1920) the consummate journalist. With his dogged pursuit of stories, his insightful mind, and his vivid, though subjective, writing, Reed certainly deserved Lippman's praise.

John Reed was born into a wealthy family and attended Harvard University, where he wrote plays and was named the college orator and poet. He graduated in 1910 and he joined the staff of *American Magazine* where he began studying the works of Progressive reform writers, particularly Lincoln Steffens and Ida Tarbell. Reed, though, traveled well to their left, and in 1913 began writing for *The Masses*, a socialist magazine.

That same year, *Metropolitan* magazine sent him to Mexico to report on Pancho Villa's peasant uprising against the dictator Victoriano Huerta. Casting all objectivity aside, he joined the fight to topple Huerta, and reported with writing that exploded across the page:

> The sharpshooter running in front stopped suddenly, swaying, as if he had run against a solid wall. . . . He shook his head impatiently, like a dog with a hurt ear. Blood drops flew from it. Bellowing with rage, he shot the rest of his clip, and then slumped to the ground and thrashed to and fro for a minute. . . . Now the trench was boiling with men scrambling to their feet, like worms when you turn over a log.

His attachment to the downtrodden affirmed, in 1914 Reed went to Russia, where his socialist views antagonized the czarist regime. He returned to Russia in 1917, arriving in the capital of St. Petersburg to witness the October Revolution that overthrew Czar Nicholas. He attended the rally at the Great Hall of the Smolny Institute, where Lenin proclaimed the founding of the "Workers and Peasants Government."

When Reed sought to return to the United States in 1918, the federal authorities, then involved in crushing dissent to maintain unity during World War I, prevented his reentry. Reed stayed in Norway and wrote *Ten Days That Shook the World*, in which he described how Lenin rallied the workers and peasants to the Bolshevik cause and how the Red mob stormed the Winter Palace. Reed's fervor for the revolution courses through his book as strongly as had his fervor for Villa, and his descriptions bring the reader to the scene:

> It was just 8:40 when a thundering wave of cheers announced the entrance of the presidium, with Lenin—great Lenin—among them. A short, stocky figure, with a big head set down in his

shoulders, bald and bulging. Little eyes, a snubbish nose, wide, generous mouth, and heavy chin; clean-shaven now, but already beginning to bristle with the well-known beard of his past and future. . . . Unimpressive, to be the idol of a mob, loved and revered as perhaps few leaders in history have been.

Reed had developed a friendship with Lenin, which enabled him to obtain inside information about political leaders and their plans; Reed even wrote propaganda for the Bolsheviks. He finally reentered the United States in 1919 and appeared before a Senate committee investigating sedition. His radicalism caused him to be expelled from the Socialist Party, and he became an organizer for the Communist Labor Party (CLP), writing its manifesto and editing its paper, the *Voice of Labor*. The CLP, however, was at odds with other leftists, who formed the Communist Party.

Reed was indicted for sedition, so he returned yet again to Russia and made numerous speeches in Moscow. But in 1920, he contracted typhus, and on October 27 he died. He was buried near Red Square; in the 1960s, the Soviet government removed his remains to a privileged spot within the Kremlin walls.

Back in the United States, *Ten Days That Shook the World* gave rise to John Reed Clubs, founded in 1929 by the Communist Party to promote its ideology through art and literature "of a proletarian character" and, as the party stated, through "agitational and propagandistic writing, art, and activities." The clubs proclaimed "Art is Propaganda" and "Art is a Class Weapon" and attracted writers such as Richard Wright, an African-American from Mississippi most noted for his autobiography, *Black Boy* (1945).

Though short-lived, more than 30 clubs were established, and several published their own magazines with articles bearing titles such as one that appeared in Milwaukee, Wisconsin: "Milwaukee Millionaires in Favor of Another World War to Make the World Safe for Democracy!" The New York City chapter founded a journal, *Partisan Review*, that broke with the Communist Party in the late 1930s but continues to publish. In September 1935, however, the Communist Party ordered the John Reed Clubs disbanded on the ground that they were too theoretical rather than practical.

John Reed died despondent that the workers in America would ever rise up against their capitalist exploiters, yet hopeful they would somehow change the system. He said, "I cannot give up the idea that out of democracy will be born the new world—richer, braver, freer, more beautiful." Even for the many radicals who rejected communism, Reed's challenge remained a beacon.

Further Reading

Baskin, Alex. *John Reed: The Early Years in Greenwich Village*. New York: Archives of Social History, 1990.
Hicks, Granville. *John Reed: The Making of a Revolutionary*. New York: Macmillan Company, 1936.
Newsinger, John, ed. *Shaking the World: John Reed's Revolutionary Journalism*. Chicago: Bookmarks, 1998.
Reed, John. *Ten Days That Shook the World*. 1919. Reprint, New York: St. Martin's Press, 1997.

Roger Baldwin Forms the American Civil Liberties Union   1920

Determined to expand his work in protecting conscientious objectors from government harassment and prosecution to include protecting all Americans from government assaults on their constitutional rights, especially free speech, in 1917 Roger Baldwin established the National Civil Liberties Bureau, which in 1920 was renamed the American Civil Liberties Union.

Roger Baldwin (1884–1981) was raised in comfortable surroundings and educated in the best of schools; he was exposed to liberal causes as a child—his mother worked in the women's rights movement, and an uncle, William Baldwin, worked in civil rights. While attending Harvard in the early 1900s, Baldwin was so affected by the Progressive reform movement that he accepted a position as head of a St. Louis settlement house, organized to help poor immigrants. In 1908, he met anarchist Emma Goldman and counted her as one of the great influences on his life, particularly with regard to pacifist ideas and the belief in individual freedom.

Like many prominent liberal reformers, Baldwin condemned the outbreak of World War I and opposed United States involvement. He declared himself a conscientious objector, and, relocating to New York City, joined the American Union Against Militarism (AUAM; see entry, 1915) as its secretary. in the wake of Congress passing the Selective Service Act in 1917, Baldwin became head of the AUAM's Civil Liberties Bureau (CLB), which he had organized. The CLB tried, but failed, to have a provision included in the act that would allow for conscientious objection. Baldwin continued to defend the rights of conscientious objectors even after the United States entered the war in April 1917. Consequently, federal authorities spied on Baldwin and called him in for questioning.

In October 1917, Baldwin and the AUAM's chair, Crystal Eastman, founded the National Civil Liberties Bureau (NCLB). They committed the NCLB to defending freedom of speech and of the press and to protecting conscientious objectors from government oppression.

The government continued to watch Baldwin. The Office of Naval Intelligence claimed that he favored "extreme radicalism and violence." In August 1918, government agents raided the offices of the NCLB, looking for evidence that the group had advised men to resist the draft. One month later, Baldwin was drafted. He refused to serve, however, and was tried and sentenced to prison. On his release in 1919, he returned to the NCLB and in January 1920 changed its name to the American Civil Liberties Union (ACLU). He would be its director for the next 25 years.

At a time when the Red Scare of 1919–20 chilled dissent, Baldwin expanded the mission of the ACLU beyond protecting free speech to defending other first amendment rights—religious freedom and the right to assemble—and to fighting for racial equality. The ACLU gained national prominence and increased support in 1925, when it hired Clarence Darrow to defend John Scopes in the "Monkey Trial" in Dayton, Tennessee (Scopes had been charged with breaking Tennessee law by teaching the theory of evolution in a public school). Even though Darrow lost, the trial rallied liberal opinion behind the ACLU.

For all of his commitment to free speech, Baldwin published *Liberty Under the Soviets* (1927), based on his recent trip to the Soviet Union, and in it called the communist government's repression necessary to further revolutionary change. But he shifted his view in 1940 when the Soviet Union signed a pact with Adolph Hitler. The ACLU, acting under Baldwin's leadership, passed a resolution that prohibited communists from serving on the organization's board, and expelled one board member, Elizabeth Gurley Flynn (see entry, 1907), for her membership in the Communist Party. Clearly, Baldwin had compromised his commitment to free speech; ironically, the ACLU resolution served as a model for similar ones used by trade unions and government agencies during the nationwide hunt for communists that violated First Amendment rights.

Because Baldwin often neglected his duties as head of the ACLU, in 1949 the organization's board pressured him to retire. The ACLU continues to defend free speech and other constitutional rights, often from a highly principled perspective that has earned it both praise for its protection of the individual and criticism for assaulting community values.

Further Reading

Lamson, Peggy. *Roger Baldwin: Founder of the American Civil Liberties Union.* Boston: Houghton Mifflin, 1976.
Walker, Samuel. *In Defense of American Liberties: A History of the ACLU.* New York: Oxford University Press, 1990.

West Virginia Mining District Erupts in Violence at Matewan and Blair Mountain

Bloodshed at Matewan, West Virginia, in 1920 and nearby Blair Mountain the following year attested to the degrading and exploitive working conditions of coal miners in the state and the determination of mine operators to maintain their advantage.

Winthrop Lane, writing for the *New York Evening Post*, described mining towns at the time of the Matewan incident: "Many . . . are unsightly, unhealthful and poorly looked after. Houses are slapped up, seldom repainted and allowed to go unrepaired. The [outhouse] is nearly everywhere in evidence; it is a prevalent cause of soil pollution and often stands on high ground back of the house, so that its contents are washed toward the bed of the creek." Historian Beverly Samosky has noted that "the average coal mining community was a dirty and depressing sight. The only reason for its existence was the removal of coal from the earth upon which it stood."

Beyond depressing, dirty, and polluted environments, miners faced other problems: they had to buy nearly all of their groceries from company-owned stores, and those stores charged high prices; they had to sign contracts in which they promised they would never join a union and that if they did, they would be fired; they had to live in company-owned housing, which they had to vacate if they lost their job; and they had to endure dangerous working conditions—West Virginia reported a higher mine death rate than any other state, a fact underscored by the explosion in 1907 at a mine in Monongah that killed 361 miners.

Beyond this, the mine owners dominated the state's politics and newspapers. Thus, by 1920, the miners in West Virginia had long suffered and long endured an oppressive system that seemed impervious to change. The end of World War I only made matters worse; a recession led to depressed coal prices that resulted in lower wages and layoffs.

When striking miners elsewhere in the country won a 27 percent wage increase, coal miners in southwestern West Virginia, angry and frustrated with being left behind, began joining the United Mine Workers (UMW). In 1920, nonunion miners in Mingo County, which included Matewan, went on strike, at which point UMW organizers convinced many of them to join the union.

The mine operators fought back with massive firings. When the mayor of Matewan, Cabel Testerman, and the town's police chief, Sid Hatfield, sided with the miners, the companies hired detectives with the Baldwin-Felts agency to evict unionized miners from their homes. Well known as a hired gun for businesses wanting to destroy strikes and crush unions, and well known for its brutal tactics, Baldwin-Felts wasted no time; Albert Felts himself arrived in Matewan in May 1920, along with 11 other detectives.

With the evictions underway, Sid Hatfield advised the townspeople to arm themselves, and he let it be known that he would arrest Felts. With striking miners looking on, Felts and his men approached Hatfield and Testerman in front of Matewan's hardware store and announced they had warrants to arrest them. "They had guns on their shoulders," Hatfield later said, "with high-powered rifles, and there were 12 or 13 of them, and they were in automobiles." Hatfield responded that he had warrants of his own, soon to arrive on train No. 16, for the arrest of Felts and his men, and that in the meantime he was going to hold them for violating a town ordinance that prohibited carrying guns. At that point, shots rang out—no one knows who fired first—and Testerman fell to the ground wounded.

The shots continued, and at one point, Hatfield chased Felts down to the post office, where the detective hid. After Hatfield yelled to him, "Come out and shoot it out like a man," they fired at each other, and Hatfield killed Felts. At that time, train No. 16 pulled into town; Hatfield retrieved the arrest warrants, stood over Felts's body, and said, "Now, you son of a bitch, I'll serve it on you."

The shootout at Matewan left seven Baldwin-Felts detectives dead, and another wounded; two miners died, along with Mayor Testerman; four other people were wounded. Miners in Mingo County reacted by joining the UMW in droves—by July, more than 90 percent of them had signed up. Over the next year, violence rocked the mountains as miners and companies engaged in bombings and gun battles.

But the UMW suffered two great losses. In August, Sid Hatfield, who had been tried for murder in the shootout and acquitted, was brought to the McDowell County courthouse in Welch to be tried on trumped-up charges involving a shooting in a mining camp. As he stood on the courthouse steps, Baldwin-Felts detectives murdered him. Hatfield's death cost the UMW one of their dynamic supporters.

Then several thousand miners led by UMW organizer Frank Keeney decided to march into Logan County, where the mine operators had crushed unionizing efforts. The governor subsequently met with Keeney and told Keeney he would be charged with treason if the march continued, whereupon Keeney ordered the miners to disband. But most of them, armed with rifles, continued marching, whereupon sheriff's forces under National Guard command assembled at the top of Blair Mountain. In the closing days of August, the miners and sheriff's men clashed, with the fighting so intense that President Warren Harding ordered federal troops to the scene. They arrived on September 3, and most of the miners surrendered, though a few continued fighting until the next day.

The defeat of the miners at Blair Mountain severely damaged the UMW; with the federal troops breaking the strike, the union's membership in West Virginia's southwestern coal fields dropped drastically. Together, Matewan and Blair Mountain rank among the bloodiest conflicts in American labor history and testify to the extremes both unions and businesses would go to—the unions in fighting oppression, the businesses in maintaining their power.

Further Reading

Dubofsky, Melvyn. *John L. Lewis: A Biography*. New York: Quadrangle, 1977.
Lunt, Richard D. *Law and Order versus the Miners, West Virginia, 1907–1933*. Hamden, Conn.: Archon Books, 1979.
Sayles, John. *Thinking in Pictures: The Making of the Movie* Matewan. Boston: Houghton Mifflin, 1987.

1921 A. J. Muste Founds Brookwood Labor College

When radical labor leader and pacifist A. J. Muste organized the Brookwood Labor College in Katonah, New York, he wanted to provide students with an education untainted by attachments to corporate interests and to prepare them for an activist fight on behalf of the working class.

Labor's battles with big business in the early 1900s convinced several union leaders that the movement needed to form schools that would provide students with advanced education while at the same time encouraging them to fight capitalist exploitation. They founded several labor colleges, the most prominent of which were Brookwood (1921–37); People's College (1904–41) in Duluth, Minnesota; and Commonwealth College (1923–41) near Mena, Arkansas.

Having joined the Comradeship, a small group of pacifists, and having led a successful textile strike in Lawrence, Massachusetts. Abraham Johannes Muste (1885–1967) directed Brookwood and served as chairman of its faculty. He disliked traditional universities for their reliance on corporate funds, for their preparing students to unquestioningly serve the corporate economy, and for their "bourgeois mentality."

As quoted in Richard J. Altenbaugh's *Education for Struggle: The American Labor Colleges of the 1920s and 1930s* (1990), Helen G. Norton, a Brookwood instructor, explained why students were coming to the college:

They're coming, in the first place, for knowledge . . . knowledge about their own unions, about the history of the labor movement in this and other countries. . . . Then they're coming to learn how to use facts after they have them—how to express their ideas so the crowd will get them and be moved to *action* by them; how to put ideas into print so people will read and understand them. They're coming to learn how people act under given conditions and why, and all the other things that psychology can teach about handling groups and individuals.

She added that "the labor college curriculum prepared students to serve the labor movement as active organizers and leaders instead of as union bureaucrats."

Housed in a large, white-pillared building in Westchester County, Brookwood offered a two-year course in history, English, sociology, economics, and speech, along with labor tactics and a survey of the working class. Using progressive techniques that relied on students taking an active part in shaping courses, Brookwood's teachers cultivated a proletarian consciousness.

The students wrote and performed their own labor plays—*Starvation Army, Mill Shadows*, and *Sit-Down*—and sang labor songs. In the late 1920s, they celebrated Marx, Lenin, and Trotsky, and Brookwood as a whole took an increasingly radical bent. Morris Lewit, a student and later a communist, recalled that Arthur W. Calhoun, "a good teacher, came from a religious socialist background, taught economics," and offered a course on Marx from a communist perspective.

Soon the American Federation of Labor (AFL; see entry, 1886), which provided funding for the school—as did a foundation sponsored by the American Civil Liberties Union (see entry, 1920)—began to complain about how the faculty promoted Marxist ideas; Brookwood faculty, in turn, criticized the AFL for being too meek. In 1929 and 1930, students from Brookwood went to the South and tried, but failed, to unionize mill workers. Then they sided with a rival to the AFL, the Congress of Industrial Organizations.

The college closed in 1937 for several reasons: the AFL withdrew its support; ideological factions erupted within the college; and big business and conservatives condemned the school as un-American. Yet Brookwood produced a number of activists who unionized workers and agitated for the left.

Further Reading

Hertoff, Nat. *Peace Agitator: The Story of A.J. Muste.* New York: Macmillan, 1963.

Howlett, Charles F. *Brookwood Labor College and the Struggle for Peace and Social Justice in America.* Lewiston, N.Y.: E. Mellen Press, 1993.

Robinson, Jo Ann Ooiman. *Abraham Went Out: A Biography of A. J. Muste.* Philadelphia: Temple University Press, 1981.

Anarchists Nicola Sacco and Bartolomeo Vanzetti Found Guilty of Murder 1921

Initially, the arrest of the Italian immigrant anarchists Nicola Sacco and Bartolomeo Vanzetti for robbery and murder attracted little notice. But the strategy of their lawyer converged with deep-rooted fears in society about their ideology and foreign background, as well as concerns about liberty and justice, to create one of the most sensational criminal cases of the twentieth century.

The crime at first looked like a typical gang heist. On the afternoon of April 15, 1920, a paymaster and his guard, Alessandro Berardelli, were walking along the main street in South Braintree, Massachusetts, carrying bags loaded with $15,000, when two men, toting guns, suddenly jumped them, grabbed the money, and in the melee mortally wounded them. The robbers then fled in a getaway car.

On May 5, the police arrested Nicola Sacco and Bartolomeo Vanzetti for the robbery and murder. The two men had pistols on them, and Sacco had in his possession an anarchist flyer. Before charging them, the police held them for hours and questioned them about their political activities—leading the men to believe they were being investigated for their anarchism.

Along with the Braintree robbery, the police charged Vanzetti with committing a holdup in nearby Bridgewater in December 1919, and he was tried for that crime first. Despite Vanzetti providing witnesses who supported his alibi, the jury found him guilty. That the witnesses were Italian immigrants who spoke little or no English, and whose testimony had to be translated, may have prejudiced the "native" jury. The judge, Webster Thayer, handed down a stiff 10–15-year prison sentence.

For the Braintree case, Sacco and Vanzetti hired Fred H. Moore, a lawyer known for his defense of labor organizers. He decided on a two-fold strategy. First, he would claim that Sacco and Vanzetti were being prosecuted for their political beliefs; second, he would rally public opinion by appealing to unions, liberals, and libertarians for help, and even to the Italian government. Toward that end, Moore used the media in ways modern publicists would admire.

Moore's tactics combined with long-standing concerns about the fairness of the American trial system together they generate a heated response. Where liberals argued that Sacco and Vanzetti weren't being so much prosecuted as persecuted, conservatives argued that Sacco and Vanzetti had committed the crime, driven to do so by their anarchistic commitment to violent acts and the immorality anarchism encouraged.

In fact, Sacco and Vanzetti were dedicated anarchistic militants who had engaged in labor strikes and, during World War I, had distributed antiwar propaganda. They supported violence to achieve revolutionary ends, and even though they had no previous criminal record, the police knew them well. The robbery and murder, conservatives argued, fit the defendants' past. The arrests, liberals countered, came because police hated anarchists.

On July 24, 1921, a jury found Sacco and Vanzetti guilty of the Braintree murder and robbery. Testimony revealed that Sacco and Vanzetti had lied extensively during questioning by the police. Crucial to the verdict, though, was the evidence provided by two forensic experts. They insisted that one of the

---

Immigrants and Radicals

In *A People's History of the United States* (1997), Howard Zinn says that "immigrants were more controllable, more helpless than native workers; they were culturally displaced, at odds with one another, therefore useful as strikebreakers." Indeed they were, but something else characterized the millions of immigrants who entered the United States in the late 1800s and early 1900s: they brought with them from Russia, Italy, and other eastern and southern European countries a familiarity with socialism and anarchism and were sometimes active in those ideological groups.

Exploitation in American industries, where immigrants were treated as "controllable" foreigners, along with the immigrants' ability to replicate Old World neighborhoods and, with them, the political and social organizations that brought them a sense of solidarity, made many of the recent arrivals receptive to radical ideas. Historian Paul Buhle says

in *Marxism in the United States* (1987), that "for the unskilled, especially those Eastern Europeans already familiar with factory life prior to immigration, Socialism spoke directly to a sense of class and national oppression."

Thus when coal miners struck against the Colorado Fuel and Iron Company in 1903, the most militant protesters came from Italian immigrants experienced in European socialist and anarchist movements. And when hod carriers, men who bore on their shoulders troughs laden with bricks, struck in 1910 in Providence, Rhode Island, the largely Italian workforce sang the Italian Royal March followed by the Socialist Anthem (and a tribute to Italian nationalist leader Giuseppe Garibaldi).

Socialism's class solutions to economic problems would, in time, be mellowed by America's aversion to class-conflict theories, but until then, immigrants helped provide socialism with a meaning that stirred militant action.

several bullets extracted from Berardelli's body matched the worn bottom part of Sacco's gun barrel. They labeled the bullet "No. III."

But much evidence contradicted the state's case. For example, while Sacco and Vanzetti did lie to the police under questioning, their lies came early in the investigation, before they had been charged with the robbery and murder. In short, they may have lied thinking they were being targeted as part of an investigation into their political activities and so wanted to protect their fellow anarchists.

As for the bullet, two forensic experts for the defense disagreed with the state's experts. Jeremiah McAnarney stated: "My opinion is that No. III bullet was not fired from the pistol given to me as Exhibit 28." Moore asked: "Kindly now explain to the jury the reasons that you have for that opinion." McAnarney responded: "The land marks on the No. III bullet do not correspond, in my best judgment, to bullets I have seen fired from this pistol."

The defense raised the possibility that the police had fired the bullet from Sacco's pistol and then claimed it had been found in Berardelli's body. Writing in *Postmortem: New Evidence in the Case of Sacco and Vanzetti* (1985), William Young and David E. Kaiser agree with this claim. They studied eyewitness accounts that said the robber who killed Berardelli stood directly over him, after he had fallen

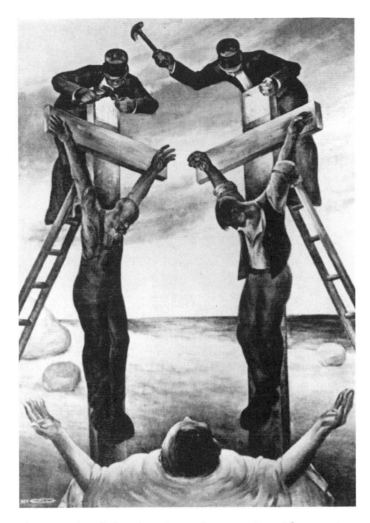

A cartoon from Labor Age *depicts the martyrdom of Sacco and Vanzetti, 1921. (Library of Congress)*

to the ground, and then fired into his body. It would be impossible for only one of the bullets extracted from the victim to have come from Sacco's gun—either they all did, or none did. Furthermore, the authors point to notes jotted down by the assistant detective, in which he states that three bullets had been fired into Berardelli, while at the trial the state claimed it had been four. The bullet entered into evidence, Young and Kaiser believe, was a plant. Yet the authors were unable to provide specific evidence showing who planted the bullet, and thus they failed to conclusively prove their thesis.

It also turns out that the gun carried by Berardelli, which Vanzetti supposedly took from him, was a .32 revolver, while the one found on Vanzetti was a .38. In any event, the defense, led by a new lawyer, pleaded for a retrial, pointing to perjury, illegal police actions, and strong evidence that a notorious gang had committed the crime. Judge Thayer heard the motions and rejected them.

One of the motions Thayer ruled against had accused him of judicial prejudice. Yet that he was prejudiced during both the trial and the appeal was clearly evident when he remarked outside the courtroom, "Did you see what I did with those anarchistic bastards the other day? I guess that will hold them for a while."

The case dragged on for six years. Near the end, Massachusetts Governor Alvan T. Fuller appointed a committee to advise him on whether to grant Sacco and Vanzetti executive clemency. The committee, headed by A. Lawrence Lowell, the president of Harvard, concluded that the trial had been fair.

As the date for the executions neared, newspapers generally supported the trial result, condemning Sacco and Vanzetti for un-American extremism. On August 23, 1927, they were electrocuted. Thousands of Bostonians protested by following the funeral cortege through the streets, and demonstrators overseas stoned United States embassies and burned American flags. To many, it was not two anarchists who had died, but justice.

In his final statement to the court, Nicola Sacco declared in broken English:

I know the sentence will be between two class, the oppressed class and the rich class, and there will be always collision between one and the other. . . . You persecute the people, tyrannize over them and kill them. We try the education of people always. You try to put a path between us and some other nationality that hates each other. That is why I am here today on this bench, for having been the oppressed class. Well, you are the oppressor.

Further Reading

Avrich, Paul. *Sacco and Vanzetti: The Anarchist Background.* Princeton, N.J.: Princeton University Press, 1991.

Montgomery, Robert H. *Sacco and Vanzetti: The Murder and the Myth.* New York: Devin-Adair, 1960.

Russell, Francis. *Sacco and Vanzetti: The Case Resolved.* New York: Harper & Row, 1986.

———. *Tragedy in Dedham: The Story of the Sacco and Vanzetti Case.* New York: McGraw-Hill, 1962.

Young, William and David E. Kaiser. *Postmortem: New Evidence in the Case of Sacco and Vanzetti.* Amherst: University of Massachusetts Press, 1985.

1921 Communists Form the Workers' Party of America

From December 23 to December 26, 1921, some 150 delegates from communist and leftist organizations around the country met at the Labor Temple on East 84th Street in New York City and founded the Workers' Party of America. They intended to take communism from the political underground, where it had existed, to the public arena of open conventions and contested elections.

Prior to the meeting, various communist groups had been formed, including the Communist Party of America, committed to the revolutionary overthrow of the United States government through clandestine activities. But these groups suffered a severe setback when Attorney General A. Mitchell Palmer raided them during the 1919–20 Red Scare, using their secretive plotting to justify his move. Palmer's agents swept down, making hundreds of arrests without warrants, and the federal government deported many immigrants simply for their belief in communism.

The raids so damaged the communists—now completely tainted by the federal authorities as un-American—that their membership ranks dropped from about 27,000 in 1919 to 8,000 in 1920. For their very survival, many in these groups decided they had to go above ground; credibility so earned, they believed, would make communism stronger.

Those groups that participated in the meeting at the Labor Temple agreed to several principles, including "to lead the working masses in the struggle for the abolition of capitalism through the establishment of a government by the working class." James P. Cannon, the meeting's temporary chairman, told the delegates he expected the new party would win over America's workers; "They will hail it as the morning star," he said. "They are looking for it. I say, comrades, they are looking for it with longing eyes."

Because the communists remained committed to militancy, and to a workers' utopia, and praised the Russian Revolution and Lenin's Soviet government, most Americans viewed the party as radical; but to more extreme communists, it had become too moderate. When the Workers' Party called itself an "open party" of communism, these extremists concluded it had abandoned its revolutionary commitment whereby a cadre would rise up and liberate the masses. When the party announced it would push for higher wages, better housing, and the like, these extremists called it "petty bourgeois."

In February 1922, a splinter group formed the United Toilers of America, which embraced the old strategies and goals. They vilified the Workers' Party, for instance calling the editor of the party's newspaper a "pusillanimous purveyor of putrid punk." Yet when Moscow completely backed the Workers' Party, the United Toilers relented, and in 1923 merged with the former enemy.

The appearance of the Workers' Party made the Communist Party a true political party rather than a subterranean clique. But the government attacks continued; as the party's second convention ended on August 22, 1922, in Bridgman, Michigan, FBI agents broke in and arrested 17 delegates, charging them with "unlawful assembly." Above ground or underground, communism would remain unacceptable to the federal government—something so radical it had to be crushed.

Further Reading

Draper, Theodore. *American Communism and Soviet Russia: The Formative Period.* New York: Viking Press, 1963.

Shipman, Charles. *It Had to Be Revolution: Memoirs of an American Radical.* Reprint, Ithaca, N.Y.: Cornell University Press, 1993.

A. Philip Randolph Organizes a Black Union

1925

"The most significant step toward the unionization of African-Americans," writes John Hope Franklin in From Slavery to Freedom *(1994), "was the organization of the Brotherhood of Sleeping Car Porters by A. Philip Randolph in 1925." Randolph saw the union as more than an economic weapon: he wanted to end racial segregation and advance black civil rights.*

Members of the Brotherhood of Sleeping Car Porters. Randolph is in the front row, third from right. (Library of Congress)

A tremendous demographic and economic shift preceded Randolph's union activity: in the early 1900s, tens of thousands of blacks were leaving the South and settling in the North, making Harlem in New York a largely African-American community; as they settled in the city, they obtained jobs in industry.

During those years, A. Philip Randolph (1889–1979) earned a following among blacks for his strident denouncement of racial segregation. Along with Chandler Owen, in 1917 he founded the *Messenger*, which they called "the only radical Negro magazine in America." And radical it was, espousing socialism, praising the Bolshevik Revolution in Russia, condemning the lynchings of blacks in the South, and during World War I, urging African-Americans to resist military service until they received equal rights.

Oddly, given his later labor leadership, Randolph thought unions incapable of helping black Americans. But in 1925, a group of porters employed by the Pullman Company—these were workers who helped passengers board trains and handled baggage, shined shoes, and cleaned cars—asked Randolph to organize them, and Randolph came to believe that a union formed outside the white labor structure could advance blacks economically and socially.

In 1925, then, he organized the Brotherhood of Sleeping Car Porters (BSCP). At first, he made little progress; the Pullman Car Company ignored him, as did the American Federation of Labor (AFL). Then in 1926 and 1929, Randolph negotiated wage agreements with the company, and in the 1930s, New Deal legislation made it easier to unionize. Finally, in 1935, the AFL granted a charter to the BSCP.

Randolph embraced socialism, but he disagreed with the argument that the oppression suffered by blacks could be solved through economic measures alone; racism, he said, defied a pure economic solution. By the 1930s, he opposed communism, saying the Bolshevik Revolution had taken the wrong path in developing a dictatorship and warning that communist influence in the BSCP would open it to charges of un-Americanism and destroy it.

Randolph supported the entry of the United States into World War II, but he threatened to hold a huge protest march against racial discrimination in Washington, D.C., unless President Franklin Roosevelt ended segregation in employment and in the military. It would be, he envisioned, an all-black protest. "We shall not call upon our white friends to march with us," he said. "There are some things Negroes must do alone." Roosevelt forestalled the march by agreeing to a limited response: he signed an executive order prohibiting the federal government from entering into contracts with businesses or unions that practiced racial discrimination.

Eventually, Randolph did stage a massive march on Washington for civil rights—this one in 1963, when 200,000 protesters gathered and heard Martin Luther King, Jr.'s "I Have a Dream" speech.

Further Reading

Davis, Daniel S. *Mr. Black Labor: The Story of A. Philip Randolph, Father of the Civil Rights Movement.* New York: E. P. Dutton, 1972.

Patterson, Lillie. *A. Philip Randolph: Messenger for the Masses.* New York: Facts On File, 1996.

Pfeffer, Paula F. *A. Philip Randolph: Pioneer of the Civil Rights Movement.* Baton Rouge: Louisiana State University Press, 1990.

CHAPTER SEVEN

The Great Depression and World War II

In October 1929, the stock market crash initiated a stunning reversal in the U.S. economy, a riches-to-rags slide from the boom of the previous decade to the Great Depression that would last for 10 years. By 1932, unemployment had risen to 12 million; the middle class, accustomed to jobs and a steady paycheck, was hit especially hard. Stories circulated about unemployed men who would don their suits and ties, leave their houses in the morning, and return home in the evening after having sat in a public park all day—simply to make their neighbors think they were going to work, that they still held jobs as any decent man of their social standing should. Such was the stigma they were trying to avoid.

The economic collapse shaped the actions of the rebels and renegades of the 1930s, strengthening their belief that the country needed radical change. The widespread concern at all levels about the economy provided then with a larger, more receptive audience for their views.

At first, President Herbert Hoover, the Republican in the White House at the start of the Great Depression, hoped businesses could work the country out of the Depression with minimal help from the government. On November 19, 1929, he met with industry leaders; this meeting, and other similar meetings, ended in pronouncements that employment and investments

> "Wake up you prisoners of hunger! The world is changing at the base, We who have been nothing will be everything!"
>
> lyrics to "The Internationale"

would be maintained. By letting business try to pull the United States out of the Depression, Hoover was relying on a strategy that reflected the unbounded faith in business that had characterized society in the 1920s. Many Americans believed that if businessmen had been capable of bringing the country so much prosperity during the Jazz Age, they would be able to revive it in the wake of the stock market crash. Yet when the business leaders who attended Hoover's conferences left Washington and returned home, they invariably encountered declining profits and the need to cut spending, and with that, jobs. Rather than hold the line, they let the deteriorating forces overwhelm them.

By September 1931, manufacturing volume in the United States had declined 50 percent from two years earlier, and steel plants were operating at only 11 percent of capacity. Despite these precipitous drops in output and demand, many experts within and outside the Hoover Administration still believed that once the economy hit bottom it would recover, and that the government should wait rather than begin extensive and expensive recovery initiatives. As a result, Hoover failed to take bolder action until the last months of his administration, and it was then too late for him politically. Democrat Franklin D. Roosevelt overwhelmed him in the 1932 presidential election.

President Roosevelt offered Americans hope with his warm speeches and firm commitment to getting the country moving again. He launched a "New Deal," an array of programs that amounted to an experiment in rebuilding the economy. The legislation passed during Roosevelt's first 100 days in office emphasized relief and recovery. The Economy Act, passed by Congress on March 20, 1933, aimed at balancing the budget and reorganizing government agencies to reduce costs. The Beer and Wine Revenue Act legalized wine, beer, and ale of a certain alcaholic content, and taxed them. On May 12, Congress created the Federal Emergency Relief Administration (FERA), and provided it with $500 million to help states establish programs for the unemployed. Other programs sought to provide jobs and help agriculture.

In the boldest legislation of the first 100 days, Roosevelt worked with Senator George W. Norris to establish the Tennessee Valley Authority (TVA), which could help ameliorate that region's chronic poverty while protecting its natural resources. Roosevelt wanted a comprehensive plan that would include power development, flood control, land reclamation, projects to stop soil erosion, and enticements to attract industry. The bill gave the TVA a mandate to build dams and power plants and to make and distribute fertilizers. Between 1933 and 1944, the government constructed nine major dams and several smaller ones and generated electricity at prices that attracted industry. Conservatives protested, claiming only private business should operate electric plants, but as a result of the TVA, the Tennessee Valley entered a new era of scientific land use, industry, and electricity.

The Emergency Relief Appropriation Act that Congress passed in 1935 established the Works Progress Administration (WPA), a large-scale program to employ the jobless. Roosevelt saw the WPA as a way to get money into the pockets of workers and start it flowing through the economy. Between 1935 and 1943, the WPA employed 8,500,000 workers at a cost of $11 billion. Critics called it wasteful and pointed to those on the government payroll whose jobs consisted of little more than "busy work" to fill time. Doubtless, waste occurred, but the WPA produced some outstanding results: paintings, public buildings, playgrounds, and some of the finest state histories ever written.

Roosevelt stunned Washington with many proposals aimed mainly at reform. One of the most important established a social security system to provide retired persons with a small pension, ranging from $10 to $85 a month, from moneys paid into a fund by employers and employees.

The National Labor Relations Act, also called the Wagner Act, created the National Labor Relations Board (NLRB). This board had the power to supervise elections called by workers to determine collective bargaining units. The NLRB could also hear testimony about unfair employment practices and issue orders to stop them. Notably, it could act against companies that fired workers for engaging in union activities. The historian Walter E. Leuchtenburg has called the Wagner Act—pro-labor and pro-union—"one of the most drastic legislative innovations of the decade." Without a doubt, it encouraged the growth of unions and stimulated labor activism. While conservative critics thought that Roosevelt was advancing the efforts of leftists among the workers, in fact the growth of unions blunted the communist appeal among laborers, an appeal discussed in this chapter, and was in line with the president's desire to keep extremists from gaining power.

To try to defuse radicals who said the government was not doing enough for the people, Roosevelt changed the New Deal in 1935 by building a welfare state with corporate capitalism as its foundation: He wanted the federal government to help those Americans that business could not or would not help. He rejected socialism and other far left ideas and thought his programs would save capitalism. But conservatives considered him, a threat to free enterprise and the profit motive.

As much as FDR tried to outmaneuver the country's rebels and renegades, they were stirred by his attack on entrenched interests and by the continued suffering wrought by the Great Depression. They, and many other Americans, reached the conclusion that something had gone terribly wrong with the corporate system—something that Roosevelt had not addressed—and they determined to organize radical movements or seek government help to ease their plight. Communists demonstrated against food shortages, and, as discussed in this chapter, they rallied thousands to unemployment marches, proclaiming "We ring the bell, comrades!" Socialists sought to remake California into a state where workers' cooperatives would prevail; in this chapter, we find Upton Sinclair proclaiming that he will end poverty in California. We learn as well that in 1934, Senator Huey Long of Louisiana proposed "sharing the wealth," through a program that would limit fortunes and provide every family with a guaranteed minimum income. In yet another response to the economic hardship, in 1936–37 the United Auto Workers staged a massive sit-down strike in Flint, Michigan, that paralyzed General Motors.

The military build-up prior to U.S. entry into World War II ended the Great Depression but brought charges from communists that it was an "imperialist" war. At the same time, discriminatory practices in the armed forces revealed that American society continued to be burdened with racism, that white supremacy oppressed blacks while the country fought a war against Nazi Germany's racist and anti-Semitic barbarism. The horrific explosion at Port Chicago most dramatically revealed the racist environment.

Yet amid the war, people lived their lives shaped by other, more personal concerns. During the war years, Malcolm X, then Malcolm Little and not yet the famous activist he would become in the 1950s and 1960s, looked in the mirror and despised his blackness because white society denigrated his race. His search for an identity and his sense of mistreatment led him to agree with those who called whites the devil. Malcolm's experience and the Port Chicago controversy foreshadowed the great social upheavals that would shake the country in the 1960s.

Together, the Great Depression and World War II shaped the actions of rebels and renegades. Economic hardship and the mobilization to fight Germany and Japan neither silenced dissidents nor made them irrelevant; quite the opposite, these two developments added urgency to their calls for change.

1929 Nudists Bare All

Americans had engaged in skinny-dipping long before 1929; for just one example, it is known that in the 1790s, President John Adams swam naked in the Potomac River. But the nation's Puritan heritage had also censored such activities as immoral; and nudism as a liberating movement, often called the naturist movement, awaited European influence in the early twentieth century.

The modern naturist movement began in Europe around 1900, when young German men and women members of back-to-nature groups took to backpacking in the forests and shedding their clothes to swim in lakes and streams. They were reacting to the constraints imposed by a newly urbanized society increasingly cut off from nature.

The naturist cause also had its roots in the Natural Healing Movement, in which German physicians recommended nude sunbathing to cure various ills. Yet another influence was Dr. Heinrich Pudor's book, *The Cult of the Nude*, published around 1900, in which the author extolled the benefits of activities without clothes.

In 1903, Paul Zimmerman founded the first nudist resort, Free Light Park, south of Hamburg, Germany, and in 1921, some Britons formed England's first nudist club, the English Gymnosophist Society.

Several rural New England communes practiced nudity as early as 1915, and according to naturist writer Lee Baxandall, "Free spirits like . . . John Reed, Eugene O'Neill, and Max Eastman talked of naked joy in New York City's Greenwich Village in the winters and lived it [during] summers in the country." The naturist movement reached the United States in 1929 by way of a German immigrant, Kurt Barthel. While living in New York City, he founded the American League for Physical Culture. Its first outing was a nude picnic, attended by 12 men and women, in the Peekskill Mountains. Within two years, the group had about 200 members. One of them, Ilsley Boone, became the leading publicist for nudism.

Many Americans considered nudity to be obscene, and into the 1950s, private, secluded nude resorts were raided by police, often at the insistence of religious groups who wanted the "sinners" locked up and their activities put to an end. As for nudity in public locations, such as on beaches, most states and localities in the year 2002 still forbade it; a few allowed for "clothing optional" beaches, such as Haulover Beach in southern Florida.

Around 1990, membership in the American Sunbathing Association, a naturist group, reached 30,000. But the group lamented that while in Europe nude vacations have become "a right," in the United States much work remained to be done "for the same kind of recognition."

The modern naturist movement offered more than shock value and something other than a sin against God, as some Christians would have it. The movement challenged constraints imposed by clothes and by society itself. It challenged what society said was shameful and recast it as a joyful experience that in effect said to social pressure: "You cannot control me."

Further Reading

Goodson, Aileen. *Therapy, Nudity, and Joy: The Therapeutic Use of Nudity through the Ages from Ancient Ritual to Modern Psychology.* Los Angeles: Elysium Growth Press, 1991.

Hartman, William E., Marilyn Fithian, and Donald Johnson. *Nudist Society: The Controversial Study of the Clothes-Free Naturist Movement in America.* Los Angeles: Elysium Growth Press, 1991.

Lester, Hugh C. *Godiva Rides Again: A History of the Nudist Movement.* New York: Vantage Press, 1968.

Communists Rally the Masses

Writing in Freedom from Fear *(1999), historian David M. Kennedy says about the early stages of the Great Depression that "what struck most observers, and mystified them, was the eerie docility of the American people, their stoic passivity as the depression grindstone rolled over them." From the start, the communists were anything but passive: tens of thousands of Americans rallied to their strikes, protests, and unemployment marches that exploded into violence in the early 1930s in New York City, in the Appalachian coal mines, and at the Ford Motor Company's River Rouge plant.*

As the Great Depression deepened, reaching bottom in 1932, Americans reacted with shock at its severity. To save money, large companies, such as General Electric, typically told employees to report to work on Monday . . . and then take the rest of the week off. Employment in the building trades dropped 80 percent; in New York City, 90 percent of the members of the Amalgamated Clothing Workers' Union were unemployed; in Philadelphia, 1,300 homes and apartment buildings were being sold each month at distress sales. The Depression took an almost inestimable physical and psychic toll on the nation.

Into the hard times stepped the Communist Party, confident it could make inroads as capitalism neared collapse. Early in 1930, the Communist International, meeting in Moscow, called for mass demonstrations around the world on March 6, what it called International Unemployment Day. Millions of unemployed workers responded by demonstrating in Paris, London, Berlin, and other European cities, demanding bread and jobs.

In the United States, 50,000 protesters turned out in Chicago and Boston; 40,000 in Milwaukee; and in New York City, nearly 100,000 protesters gathered at Union Square, near the headquarters of the Communist Party. They waited for the city to give them permission to march. But city officials refused, whereupon party leader William Z. Foster mounted a platform and declared, "Will you take that for an answer?" The crowd shouted "No!" and he pointed to City Hall and said, "Then I advise you to fall in line and proceed."

When the crowd marched onto Broadway, the police reacted violently. The *New York Times* reported that "hundreds of policemen and detectives, swinging nightsticks, blackjacks, and bare fists, rushed into the crowd, hitting at all with whom they came into contact." The protesters began running, many screaming in fear; some retaliated by throwing bricks at the police. The police unleashed tear gas and sprayed water from fire hoses. By the time the melee ended, four policemen and more than 100 protesters had been injured.

Newspapers condemned the marchers and the communist influence that, they asserted, had caused the violence. Still, the protests made the country more aware of the widespread economic misery and moved politicians to more urgent action.

That summer, the Communist Party formed Unemployed Councils, partly to pressure Congress for unemployment relief and insurance, but also to move evicted families back into their homes and to pressure the police and courts to leave the jobless alone. In December 1931, and again the following year, the councils led massive hunger marches on Washington, D.C.

The largest strike sponsored by the communists erupted in May 1931 in the Appalachian coal fields of western Pennsylvania, eastern Ohio, West Virginia, and Kentucky. That month, wage cuts at a mine near Pittsburgh caused workers to strike, and the communist National Miners Union (NMU) organized them to keep the walkout going. By July, the NMU estimated that 40,000 miners had joined the strike, though it admitted that most had done so without encouragement from the union. Foster called the protest "by far the greatest mass struggle conducted by revolutionary unionists in this country . . . a brilliant exposition . . . of the growing radicalization of the workers."

Foster himself went into the coal mines to direct the strike, hoping to broaden it into a general uprising against capitalism, and the NMU sponsored hunger marches and picketing. Violence attached to the walkout resulted in three miners being killed and more than 50 hospitalized.

As it turned out many mine operators spurned the NMU and signed contracts with the rival and less radical United Mine Workers Union (UMW). That, along with starvation among the miners, ended the strike in August 1931 and severely damaged the NMU.

The communist struggle found new life the following year, however, when the NMU led a miners' strike in Harlan County, Kentucky. The mine companies, working together with state and local authorities and with vigilante groups, waged a full-scale war against the strikers. They raided NMU headquarters, beat protesters senseless, and killed several miners and an NMU organizer. Additionally, the companies used racist attacks; they condemned the NMU for bringing whites and African-Americans together in its ranks, and they called for whites to stand up against the black influence. A communist journal, *Class Struggle*, pointed to the bravery of the striker's effort when it said, "With wives and children by their sides, the Kentucky miners Negro and white, are breaking the chains of race prejudices in a struggle for their very life."

A few weeks later, the journal said, "We ring the bell, Comrades! The [economic] contradictions have reached their climax. 1932 has become the year of head-on collision!" As in 1931, however, the NMU suffered from inadequate resources and lost out to the UMW; the strike collapsed, and the following year the NMU disbanded. The editors of *Who Built America?* (1992) have said that "of all the unemployment activities led by the Communist Party, the most dramatic was the 'Ford Hunger March.'" By 1932, Henry Ford had laid off thousands of workers at his enormous River Rouge auto assembly plant in Dearborn, Michigan. This was the same plant that in the 1920s had prided itself in paying workers an unusually high $5.00 a day and that had served as a symbol of America's industrial prosperity. On March 7, 1932, more than 3,000 protesters led by the small, communist-dominated Auto Workers' Union marched on the plant to demand jobs. When the police intervened to stop the marchers, Ford security guards began firing into the crowd; as the protesters retreated, the police sprayed them with bullets from machine guns. Four marchers were killed; more than 60 were injured.

The following Sunday, nearly 40,000 attended the funeral for the four dead men, and as the caskets were lowered into the ground, the mourners sang the "Internationale," the song of radical worker solidarity: "Wake up you prisoners of hunger!/The world is changing at the base,/We who have been nothing will be everything!"

Further Reading

Barrett, James R. *William Z. Foster and the Tragedy of American Radicalism.* Chicago: University of Illinois Press, 1999.
Green, James R. *The World of the Worker: Labor in Twentieth-Century America.* New York: Hill and Wang, 1980.
Nevins, Allan. *Ford.* 3 vols. New York: Scribner, 1954–63.

1931 Trials of the Scottsboro Boys Excite and Divide the Political Left

On March 25, 1931, two white girls from Huntsville, Alabama, looked at a lineup of nine black youths, one of whom was only 12 years old, and concluded that the youths were the same blacks who had raped them in a vicious assault while riding in a railroad boxcar. The subsequent trials of the "Scottsboro Boys" both galvanized and divided America's political left.

The crime was alleged to have occurred near Stevenson, Alabama, in the northern part of the state. At the depths of the Depression, scores of unemployed and homeless people, largely men but some women, were riding the rails as hoboes, traveling from town to town in search of jobs. Such was the case on this freight train; a group of blacks and a group of whites had sneaked aboard its boxcars. Among the whites were two girls, Victoria Price and Ruby Bates. Soon after the train left Stevenson, the whites and blacks began fighting, and when the train pulled into the town of Paint Rock, a posse greeted the blacks and hauled them off to jail in Scottsboro.

At that point, Price and Bates claimed they had been raped aboard the train by pistol- and knife-wielding blacks. Rumors quickly spread through town that the girls had been brutalized, that one of the blacks had "chewed off one of the breasts" of Ruby Bates. As happened frequently in the racially segregated South, a lynch mob appeared to string up the accused, but the National Guard intervened.

In such a racist environment, when white women accused black men of rape, the usual result was a guilty verdict and almost always a death sentence. So there appeared little hope for the nine youths. The state decided to try the them in groups and assigned them two unqualified lawyers, one of whom showed up at the first trial in Scottsboro drunk.

To no one's surprise, the trials of the "Scottsboro Boys" led to guilty verdicts, but the evidence was so flawed—and the supposed gang rape so sensational—that the case gained national attention and generated enormous controversy. Both the National Association for the Advancement of Colored People (NAACP) and the Communist Party, through its legal division, the International Labor Defense (ILD), stepped in to take over the cases on appeal. Worried that some of the Scottsboro Boys might actually be guilty, the NAACP moved perhaps too slowly; then a struggle between ILD and NAACP lawyers, including Clarence Darrow, caused the NAACP to withdraw from the case.

Many liberals and leftists objected to the behavior of the ILD, saying that the communists cared little about the black youths, that they only wanted to use the case to win favor with African-Americans in the South. The charge carried much truth: the Communist Party wanted to prove itself to the black community, and it cast the entire case as one of the peoples' fight against a capitalist system that bred racism. The communist newspaper, the *Daily Worker,* said, "Precisely because the Scottsboro Case is an expression of the horrible national oppression of the Negro masses, any real fight . . . must necessarily take the character of a struggle against the whole brutal system of landlord robbery and imperialist national oppression of the Negro people."

The communists surprised many observers, however, when they chose someone from outside the party, famed criminal attorney Samuel Leibowitz, to handle the defense. Leibowitz cared

Attorney Samuel Leibowitz with the Scottsboro defendants. (Bettmann/CORBIS)

nothing for furthering a communist agenda; he wanted above all to help the young men, whom he thought had been victimized by racism. When the Supreme Court overturned the Scottsboro convictions in 1932 on grounds that the defendants had not been accorded due process of the law, Leibowitz took over the case and in spring 1933 told the *New York Times*:

> I am not interested in the affairs of the Republican party, the Democratic party, the Socialist party, the Communist party, or any other group in the conduct of this case. I am interested solely in saving these innocent boys from the electric chair, and I will do my best to see that their case is not endangered by propaganda or agitation from any quarter. I have ordered the irresponsibles away and they must stay away.

Over the next four years, Leibowitz and the ILD defended the Scottsboro Boys through a series of retrials and appeals, during which time Ruby Bates recanted her story and Victoria Price provided testimony riddled with contradictions. One prosecution witness who placed the girls at the scene of the crime described them as having worn dresses when they actually had worn overalls; another admitted he had received spending money from the state's lead lawyer. At one of the trials, a prosecuting attorney stirred a storm of protest from Jews and many northerners when he asked the jurors "whether justice in this case is going to be bought and sold with Jew money from New York?" At another point, Judge James Horton, who presided over the retrial of Haywood Patterson in the spring of 1933, was so appalled by the jury's guilty verdict, when clearly Price had lied on the stand, that he ordered a new trial.

Leibowitz soon became infuriated with the effort by the communists' to use the Scottsboro Boys for their benefit, or what he called a "meal ticket," so in 1935, he formed his own defense committee, forcing the ILD to relinquish its exclusive role and join with the American Civil Liberties Union, the NAACP, the Church League for Industrial Democracy, the Methodist Federation for Social Service, and the League for Industrial Democracy in the defense efforts.

Ultimately, Leibowitz and the defense committee secured the release of eight of the Scottsboro boys between 1937 and 1950, either through decisions by the state to drop the prosecutions or to grant paroles. The ninth defendant broke out of jail in 1948. Even though Leibowitz kept the black youths from the seemingly inevitable electric chair, they had been forced to spend years in jail under horrendous conditions for a crime they had never committed.

The trials of the Scottsboro Boys galvanized many on the left and stimulated the Communist Party, which held numerous rallies. The Associated Press claimed that 1,700 protests had been waged by the ILD in the United States and overseas. But the trials also divided the left, causing disputes between those who believed the communists should be welcomed in defending the black youths and praised for their role in the case, and those who thought the presence of the Reds only hurt the Scottsboro Boys and branded everyone who wanted to help them as un-American extremists.

The NAACP reflected the ambivalence within the left when, in reference to the Supreme Court having struck down a second round of convictions in 1935 because blacks had been excluded from the jury lists, it claimed: "An important legal victory has been won against the lily-white jury system. . . . The whole Negro race is far ahead of where it would have been had the Communists not fought the case in the way they did." But it also asked about the Reds, "Did they have the right to use the lives of nine youths, who . . . did not know what it was all about, to make a propaganda battle . . . ?"

Further Reading

Carter, Dan T. *Scottsboro: A Tragedy of the American South.* Baton Rouge: Louisiana State University Press, 1969.
Goodman, James. *Stories of Scottsboro.* New York: Pantheon Books, 1994.

Dorothy Day and Peter Maurin Begin Publishing the *Catholic Worker*

Peter Maurin, an intellectual from France, introduced young activist Dorothy Day to the concept of apply-ing Roman Catholicism to radical social reform. Together they founded the Catholic Worker *in 1933, a newspaper that insisted Catholics must serve the poor.*

Dorothy Day (1897–1980) grew up alienated and rebellious, and these characteristics defined her life. From 1914 to 1916, she attended the University of Illinois in Urbana–Champaign and met other disaf-fected students who influenced her with their radical outlook. She had already declared herself an athe-ist; now she learned about socialism. Bored with college life and discontented with mainstream society, she quit the university and moved to New York City, where she began working for *The Call*, a socialist newspaper. She joined other protesters in picketing the White House for women's suffrage (see entry, 1917), and was arrested and jailed.

In New York she lived in Greenwich Village and again kept company with a radical crowd, among them Floyd Dell and Max Eastman, who chose her to edit *Masses*, a socialist publication like *The Call.* In need of money, and still living a rootless existence, in 1918 Day found work as a nurse at Kings County Hospital in Brooklyn. The following year, she returned to journalism as a writer for the rad-ical *Liberator.*

She then went through two disastrous relationships with men, the second of which, with Forster Batterham, led to her becoming pregnant and having an abortion. It was in 1925 that she began living with Batterham, a writer more given to drink than work. In 1927, Day bore their child, and at the end of the year she converted to Roman Catholicism. A committed atheist, Batterham left Day at the same time many of her Greenwich friends also deserted her.

In 1932, she met Peter Maurin (1877–1949), and her Catholicism found a companion to her radi-calism. Maurin was a French émigré, a former Christian Brother, and an intellectual schooled in Catholic humanism. He disliked capitalism and modern technology for undermining community; he hoped that one day people would return to a subsistence economy of agriculture and handmade production; he believed in helping the poor by living among them. In Maurin, Day saw a commitment to serving soci-ety and an attachment to individual freedom and responsibility.

To promote Maurin's vision, Day joined him in founding the *Catholic Worker*. It first appeared in May 1993, and by 1936 its circulation had surpassed 150,000. Day ran the *Catholic Worker* with a firm hand, allowing little dissent. A pacifist, she insisted that anyone who worked at the newspaper accept her antiwar view without question.

The *Catholic Worker* became the voice of the Catholic Worker Movement. Following Maurin's plan, Day established hospitality houses where the homeless could receive food, shelter, and guidance; and she founded communal farms. Day said, "We [Catholic Workers] believe in an economy based on human needs, rather than the profit motive. . . . We are not judging [wealthy] individuals, but are trying to make a judgment on the system . . . which we try to withdraw from as much as possible. . . . What is worst of all is using God and religion to bolster up our own greed, our own attachment to property, and putting God and country on an equality."

Day's pacifism ran so strongly through the movement, that when World War II began, a *Catholic Worker* headline declared, "We Continue Our Pacifist Stance." Even after the Japanese attack on Pearl Harbor, Day stood by her principles. In response to those who once asked her to define her pacifism, she said, "I can write no other than this: Unless we use the weapons of the spirit, denying ourselves and tak-ing up our cross and following Jesus, dying with Him and rising with Him, men will go on fighting, and

Radical Catholicism

The Roman Catholic Church is oftentimes thought of as a conservative institution—with its opposition, for example, to abortion rights—yet it has also exhibited a progressive reform streak evident in Dorothy Day's activities. In the 1950s and 1960s, several Catholic priests and institutions became leaders in the civil rights movement. When Martin Luther King, Jr., wrote his *Letter from a Birmingham Jail* in 1963, he noted the pioneering role played by Jesuit-run Spring Hill College in Mobile, Alabama, as the first college in the state to desegregate. King wrote, "I commend the Catholic leaders of this state for integrating Spring Hill College several years ago."

The brothers Daniel and Philip Berrigan (see entry, 1964) continued the radical tradition in the 1960s when they protested the Vietnam War. From the 1970s through the 1990s, they were at the forefront of those Catholics who campaigned for peace and against nuclear arms.

In the late 1990s and the early years of this century, Catholics marched on the School of the Americas at Fort Benning, Georgia, which they criticized for training troops from Latin America that commited human rights violations in their home countries. (The School of the Americas closed in December 2000 and reopened in January 2001 under a new name, the Western Hemisphere Institute for Security Cooperation.)

In May 2001, a federal judge sentenced several of the Fort Benning peace activists to jail for having trespassed on the army school the previous November—these included an 88-year-old Catholic nun, Dorothy Hennessey, who received a six-month term. One of the leaders of the protesters said, "This genteel Southern judge smiles and then comes the dagger. It baffles me how he can sleep at night when an 88-year-old nun is going to prison . . . when assassins and soldiers who have tortured and raped get pardons. A grave injustice has been done." Every indication was that reform-minded Catholics would do as they had done in the past and continue their fight for social justice.

---

often from the highest motives, believing that they are fighting defensive wars for justice and in self-defense against present or future aggression."

Day died on November 29, 1980, at Maryhouse, a Catholic Worker shelter for the homeless in New York City. Despite her death, the Catholic Worker Movement remained vibrant, actually growing to more than 140 houses and expanding into Australia, New Zealand, Germany, and England. Many Catholic radicals, among them Daniel and Philip Berrigan and Michael Harrington, said their moral commitment was inspired by Day. In the words of Patrick Jordan, writing in *Commonweal* in 1997, Day and the Catholic Worker Movement provided "critical voices in the midst of the capitalist state and lively antidotes to the spirit of bourgeois Christianity."

Further Reading

Day, Dorothy. *Loaves and Fishes.* 1963. Reprint, Maryknoll, N.Y.: Orbis Books, 1997.
Forest, James H. *Love Is the Measure: A Biography of Dorothy Day.* Rev. ed. Maryknoll, N.Y.: Orbis Books, 1994.
Klejment, Anne, and Nancy L. Roberts, eds. *American Catholic Pacifism: The Influence of Dorothy Day and the Catholic Worker Movement.* Westport, Conn.: Praeger, 1996.
Miller, William D. *Dorothy Day: A Biography.* San Francisco: Harper & Row, 1982.

1934   Tenant Farmers Organize

The word "farm" may bring to mind bucolic images of country living. But there was nothing bucolic about the farms worked by sharecroppers and tenants in the 1930s; farmers lived miserably, with money due them stolen by wealthy planters, while every attempt they made to gain economic benefits and dignity was met with forceful retaliation. This situation inspired the formation of the Southern Tenant Farmers' Union (STFU), which was remarkable for its interracial membership.

The STFU was begun in July 1934 in a schoolhouse amid the cotton fields of the Fairview Plantation near Tyronza, in the Arkansas delta. To an extent the Depression and President Franklin Roosevelt's New Deal contributed to the farmers' discontent, but long-term oppression and long-simmering anger were the stronger impetus for the formation of the STFU.

In 1919, black farm tenants near Elaine, Arkansas, organized the Progressive Farmers and Household Union of America to pressure their landlords for itemized statements and quicker payments. The landlords reacted by charging the union with fomenting a race war; a subsequent shooting led to whites killing more than 100 blacks in what became known as the "Elaine Massacre."

Within days of the bloodshed, a grand jury indicted 65 African-Americans; eventually, 12 were sentenced to death and the rest to prison. Rulings by the state supreme court and the U.S. Supreme Court overturned the convictions of those sentenced to death; the justices cited irregularities and a disregard for due process.

The call for economic reform went unanswered, however, and, despite some modest gains in the 1920s, by the time the Great Depression began in 1929, both white and black tenant farmers were living in wretched poverty. In 1931, the Communist Party organized the Sharecropper's Union (SCU), an African-American group, in Tallapoosa County, Alabama. The local sheriffs retaliated by raiding the farmers' meetings and firing on SCU members, who then shot back.

SCU activist Ned Cobb recalled how in 1932 his landlord reacted to the union activity of a fellow sharecropper, Clint Webster, by sending a deputy sheriff to kick Webster off the land. Cobb rushed to Webster's defense. "The deputy . . . ," Cobb said, "jumped up and told me, 'I'm going . . . to get [Sheriff] Carl Platt and bring him down here. He'll come down here and kill the last damn one of you, shoot you in a bunch.' Now a organization is a organization, and . . . if I'm sworn to stand up for myself and stand up for all the poor class of farmers, I have to do it. Weren't no use under God's sun to treat colored folks like we been treated here in the state of Alabama. . . . Work hard and look what's done to me." In the end, the deputies shot Cobb and arrested him; he subsequently spent 12 years in prison.

In 1933, Congress passed a New Deal program called the Agricultural Adjustment Act (AAA), which was intended to help farmers by paying them to leave some of their fields fallow; the intent was to decrease the glut of farm products on the market and eliminate depressed prices. In practice, the AAA hurt tenant farmers. When wealthy planters received their federal subsidies, they used the money to mechanize their farms and kick the tenants off the land. On top of that, many wealthy farmers kept the federal money they should have passed on to the tenants.

Early in 1934, in Tyronza two small businessmen who had converted to socialism invited socialist leader Norman Thomas to the delta so he could meet with several displaced white and black tenants. They listened to his attack on the AAA, and then founded the STFU. One of those at the meeting asked, "Are we going to have two unions, one for the white and one for the colored?" A black farmer who had been through the Elaine Massacre and knew the importance of interracial unity answered, "The same chain that holds my people holds your people too. If we're chained together on the outside we ought to stay chained together in the union."

Given the racism prevalent in southern society, the decision to form an interracial union was exceptional. As the STFU grew, most whites and blacks met in segregated locals, but the national convention remained integrated, and the union itself expanded to include Mexican-Americans and Native Americans.

Much as in Phillips County in 1919, the planters reacted to these development with violence. They condemned the STFU for its socialist alliance and arrested STFU activists on charges of "criminal anarchy" and violating segregationist laws. The planters and their allies shot up homes, burned down churches, and evicted STFU tenants from their lands. So brutal were the attacks—several blacks were lynched—that the STFU was forced to move its headquarters out of farm country to Memphis, Tennessee.

Still the STFU gained members, and in 1935 it staged its first strike, demanding payment from the landlords of $1.00 per 100 pounds of cotton grown, as compared to the prevailing rate of 40 to 60 cents. When Norman Thomas spoke to an STFU rally in Mississippi, a mob of planters and deputies forced him from the platform, with one planter snarling, "We don't need no Gawd-damn Yankee Bastard to tell us what to do with our niggers." The strike, though, resulted in some upward price adjustments and attracted more members. By 1938 STFU membership topped 30,000, with chapters in several states, and the strongest in Arkansas, Alabama, Missouri, Oklahoma, Tennessee, and Texas.

Other strikes in 1936 and 1938 failed to gain concessions from the planters, but the upheaval brought support from outside groups, including the American Civil Liberties Union (see entry, 1920), and generated national news stories that detailed the tenant farmers' plight. Reacting to the crisis, Roosevelt's administration made changes to the New Deal. These included loans and grants to poor farmers and programs to start cooperative farm communities that experimented with collective farming (rather than the individual ownership of land).

As the Depression wore on, Rev. Owen Whitfield, an African-American and an organizer and vice president for the STFU, led about 1,000 tenants in southeastern Missouri, mostly blacks but including whites, in a dramatic strike. In January 1939, the strikers moved their belongings from their houses and camped out in makeshift shelters along Highways 60 and 61, in the state's boot heel. One tenant said, "We're only making six bits to a dollar a day, and you can't make an honest, decent living on it. That's the reason we're out here on Highway 61."

But cold weather produced distress, and when newspaper reporters descended on the scene, the state forced the tenant farmers to relocate. Several months after the strike, in June 1939, Rev. Whitfield founded Cropperville, a communal settlement near Poplar Bluff. The 80 black and 15 white families who moved there received financial aid from the federal government, but Cropperville collapsed after 10 years.

In the late 1930s, the STFU unraveled. Mechanization spread, making tenant farmers more disposable. The union, which had affiliated with the Congress of Industrial Organizations in 1937, fell victim to internal fighting between its largely non-communist membership and a small contingent of communist organizers who sought to dominate it. In the 1950s, the STFU dissolved, leaving a legacy of interracial cooperation among the poor in the fight for economic and social justice.

Further Reading

Kester, Howard. *Revolt Among the Sharecroppers.* Knoxville: University of Tennessee Press, 1997.

Mitchell, H. L. *Mean Things Happening in this Land: The Life and Times of H. L. Mitchell, Co-founder of the Southern Tenant Farmers Union.* Montclair, N.J.: Allanheld, Osmun, 1979.

1934   Huey Long Advocates Redistributing Wealth

"Every man a king," Senator Huey P. Long of Louisiana proclaimed in the middle of the Great Depression, as he proposed a "Share Our Wealth" plan. Intended to do more than boost the nation's economy, it aspired to alter it fundamentally.

By the time Huey Long (1893–1935) made his controversial proposal, he had established himself in Louisiana as a near dictator. Emerging from rural, poverty-ridden Winn Parish with a hillbilly image—he once said that he cared only for what the folks at the "fork of the creeks" thought—he promoted a populist program that led to his election as railroad and public service commissioner and, in 1928, governor. He owned oil property but pushed through the legislature a constitutional amendment to tax the oil companies and use the revenue to build highways and fund education. The following year, he survived an attempt by the legislature to impeach him for bribery. He won election to the U.S. Senate in 1930, but retained the governor's office for two more years, an unprecedented hold on power.

Most Louisianans liked Long, even as he flashed across the state in fancy cars, white silk suits, and pink ties, and caroused in low-class bars. His appeal came partly from his ability on the stump; from the parish bottoms he scaled oratorical heights—able to gauge his crowd and switch between erudite speech that reflected his law degree and country expressions that reflected his rural upbringing.

As Long gained a following beyond Louisiana and set his sights on the White House, President Franklin Roosevelt called him one of the most dangerous men in America. He certainly became one of the most popular. At one point FDR refused to listen to Long's economic proposals, causing the Louisianan to act to end the Depression, change the country's economic structure, and fulfill his own political ambitions. So on February 23, 1934, he made a national radio address in which he announced he was founding the Share Our Wealth Society, with the slogan "Every Man a King."

The society, Long said, would advocate certain principles based on proposals he had previously offered in his Senate speeches. These principles stipulated that the federal government should impose taxes that would prevent a family from owning a fortune of more than $5 million or from earning more than $1 million a year; that these taxes should be redistributed by giving every family $5,000; and that there should be an annual guaranteed income of $2,300, or one-third the average family income. The society also sought monthly pensions for the elderly, bonuses for veterans, and payments for college students.

Long wanted to redistribute wealth to fight its concentration, which he considered not only obscene but also injurious, at the time when the Great Depression was impoverishing the vast majority of Americans and fraying the social fabric of the nation. Writing in *Huey Long* (1989), T. Harry Williams states that Long's plan was "designed to hasten recovery," but in addition, "the federal government would have assumed a larger and permanent role in directing the economy." Using religious imagery, Huey Long said to his supporters:

> God invited us all to come and eat and drink all we wanted. He smiled on our land and we grew crops of plenty to eat and wear. He showed us in the earth the iron and other things to make everything we wanted. . . . God called: "Come to my feast!" [But then] Rockefeller, Morgan and their crowd stepped up and took enough for 120,000,000 people. . . . And so many millions must go hungry and without those good things God gave us unless we call on them to put some of it back.

Long's plan might seem unusual now, but others at the time were striving to end economic misery and make society more just. Father Charles Coughlin, a Roman Catholic priest known for his radio broadcasts, for example, advocated currency inflation, and Dr. Francis Townsend, a California physician, proposed a substantial monthly pension to older people.

Long's Share Our Wealth clubs spread rapidly. Some 60,000 letters a week poured into his Senate office by April 1935, and, according to Williams, in reaction to one of Long's many radio speeches about the plan, the senator received 30,000 letters a day for 24 consecutive days. Not all of the letters supported him, but the great majority did.

Within a year of its founding, the Share Our Wealth Society, the official organization for all of the clubs, asserted it had five million members—a figure likely exaggerated, but not by much. The clubs were more regional than national; and were concentrated in the South, California, and New York.

Long, like Roosevelt, was a Democrat, but the president ordered that a close watch be kept on what a presidential friend called the "great Louisiana demagogue." FDR suspended all patronage to Long's political machine and ordered the Internal Revenue Service to investigate him. A public opinion poll conducted by the White House found that should Long run for president as a third-party candidate in 1936, he would capture a surprisingly high 10 percent of the popular vote.

In March 1935, Long did declare his candidacy for president, but that September, while walking along a corridor of the Louisiana Capitol in Baton Rouge, he was shot and fatally wounded by Carl Weiss, a physician. Long's Share Our Wealth plan died with him, but it worked its influence in pressuring Roosevelt to become bolder in his economic policy, especially with a Wealth Tax Act that placed higher levies on the rich.

Further Reading

Hair, William Ivy. *The King fish and His Realm: The Life and Times of Huey P. Long.* Baton Rouge: Louisiana State University Press, 1991.

Long, Huey. *Every Man a King: The Autobiography of Huey Long.* First Da Capo Press Edition, New York: Da Capo Press, 1996.

Williams, T. Harry. *Huey Long.* New York: Knopf, 1989.

1934   Socialist Upton Sinclair Wins Democratic Governor's Primary in California

With the Great Depression crushing California's once buoyant economy, Upton Sinclair, self-proclaimed socialist and author of the muckraking novel The Jungle, *stunned the political world in 1934 by winning the state's Democratic gubernatorial nomination. Winning the state house, however, proved another matter; conservatives and moderates alike combined in a vicious campaign to defeat him.*

Critics said that Upton Sinclair (1878–1968) failed as a politician because he was too much of a dreamer, but many people were looking for a dreamer in a nightmare landscape where refugees from Oklahoma scrambled for menial jobs picking fruit, where homeless families slept in lean-tos built from cardboard boxes and searched for food in garbage dumps, and where unemployed workers and workers decimated by wage cuts resorted to mass protests.

On July 16, 1934, Californians witnessed a paralyzing general strike in San Francisco, led by Harry Bridges, a communist and head of the International Longshoremen's Association. Strikers shut down the city's factories, and along with them laundries, theaters, restaurants, and many other shops. They blockaded highways and prevented food and fuel from reaching stores. The strike ended four days later, with the workers obtaining most of their demands, but with the population shaken and concerned that the Depression might bring class war.

From the economic hardship came ideas for radical change. Some Californians, and many people beyond the state, listened that year to Long Beach resident Dr. Francis Townsend and his proposal, first advanced in fall 1933, to remove elderly workers from the job market by having the federal government pay them a pension. Townsend said that all persons over age 60 should receive $200 each month, funded by a 2 percent value-added tax that would be levied on goods at each stage of their manufacture. According to Townsend, his plan would help the elderly, boost wages by making their jobs available to younger workers, and stimulate recovery by pumping money through the economy.

Townsend Clubs appeared, first in California and then in other states. At meetings, Townsendites gathered petitions to send to Congress, and Townsend rallied his supporters through his newsletter, the *Townsend National Weekly.* By fall 1934, more than 5,000 Townsend Clubs had been formed across the country, and more than 25 million Americans had signed his petitions.

For those seeking to go beyond a pension plan to a substantial restructuring of society, Sinclair offered a more radical alternative. In his pamphlet *I, Governor of California and How I Ended Poverty,* he presented a reform proposal written from the perspective of having already won the election and taken action to turn around the state's economy. He called his program EPIC (End Poverty in California), and described how through it the state acquired idle land and factories and transferred them to farmers and industrial workers to run as cooperatives, abolishing all want and all economic greed.

Sinclair took the EPIC idea from his pamphlet and made it the centerpiece for his gubernatorial campaign. In August 1934, he showed the strength of his appeal when he won the Democratic primary, defeating his closest opponent by nearly 150,000 votes out of 813,000 cast.

Sinclair's victory put the Democratic Party in a quandary. President Franklin Roosevelt and the party's other leaders in Washington, along with its moderate leaders in California, thought Sinclair too radical and believed that if he won the governorship, the entire party would be tainted as extremist. Yet to oppose a fellow Democrat would risk destroying the state party and would reelect Frank Merriam, a conservative Republican opposed to Roosevelt's New Deal.

Privately, Roosevelt called EPIC a harebrained idea; publicly he refused to either support or oppose Sinclair, a silence that left the Democratic candidate to the Republican wolves. Republicans launched a campaign that distorted Sinclair's statements and proposals. Shortly after Sinclair won the Democratic primary, he had supposedly said to a Roosevelt adviser, "If I am elected, half of the unemployed will come to California." The Republicans jumped on the statement to frighten Californians; they said that with Sinclair as governor a shiftless horde would descend on the state.

The pro-Republican *Los Angeles Times* pilloried Sinclair by taking statements from his many books—he had written dozens—and quoting them out of context or making them appear as if he would apply them as policy. Other Republicans jumped on Sinclair's statements that had criticized marriage as exploitive and had portrayed the Roman Catholic church as "The Church of the Servant Girls." Morality and religions, the Republicans implied, would sink beneath a socialist tide.

None other than Louis B. Mayer, whose MGM studios wielded enormous economic and political clout, produced short movies that distorted Sinclair's campaign by making it look as if communists would take over the state. These shorts were shown on screens before the feature films and helped turn public opinion against Sinclair.

Writing in *Franklin D. Roosevelt and the New Deal* (1963), Walter E. Leuchtenburg states that "in the closing days of the campaign, New Deal officials forged an alliance between Democratic conservatives and the anti–New Deal Merriam." On Election Day, Merriam swept to victory, with 1,139,000 votes to Sinclair's 880,000. (About 300,000 votes went to a third candidate),

The moderates and conservatives had turned back Sinclair's challenge. California would settle into the New Deal and, like the rest of the country, take its solutions for ending the Great Depression not from radicals but from a mainstream political party.

Further Reading

Harris, Leon. *Upton Sinclair: American Rebel.* New York: Crowell, 1975.

Mitchell, Greg. *The Campaign of the Century: Upton Sinclair's Race for Governor of California and the Birth of Media Politics.* New York: Random House, 1992.

Sinclair, Upton. *Autobiography.* New York: Harcourt, Brace & World, 1962.

Father Charles Coughlin Creates the National Union for Social Justice   1934

Using a religious radio show intended to reach members of the Roman Catholic church, Father Charles Edward Coughlin spun tales of political conspiracy and proposed that the government take over all banks. But his meteoric rise in popularity was followed by a fast and inglorious crash.

In the mid-1920s, Charles Edward Coughlin (1891–1979), who had been ordained a priest several years earlier, was assigned to found a new parish in Royal Oak a suburb of Detroit, Michigan. When he ran into difficulty raising money, he turned to a recently developed technology, the radio, to reach a greater number of people and build support for his church. He first began broadcasting in October 1926 on WJR, a Detroit station that could be heard in 20 states.

The "radio priest," as he soon became known, discussed Catholic doctrine, presented sermons for children, and attacked the anti-Catholic Ku Klux Klan (see entries, 1866 and 1915). His speaking voice fit radio—it was rich and warm, with a slight Irish brogue, what novelist Wallace Stegner said was "a voice made for promises."

During the Great Depression, Father Coughlin changed the content of his shows, making them more political. In 1930, he began broadcasting over the CBS network, and in his programs attacked bolshevism and socialism as anti-Christian. Moreover, he spun tales about an international conspiracy that had caused the Depression. Coughlin insisted that bankers had planned the economic collapse as a way to tighten and dominate the money supply in order to extract greater profits. Part of the widespread appeal of his story was that it tapped a long-held distrust of bankers and coincided with attacks by leading politicians on "concentrated wealth."

Coughlin wanted Congress to abolish the Federal Reserve, nationalize the country's banking system, and increase the money supply, though on the last point he offered no specifics. He soon left CBS and organized his own network that could be heard on 26 stations.

In 1932, Coughlin supported Democrat Franklin Roosevelt for president. He said that FDR would drive the money changers from the temple of government. But after Roosevelt won the White House and ignored Coughlin's entreaties to follow his advice, the radio priest turned on him. He attacked New

Father Charles Coughlin addresses a rally in Cleveland, 1936. (Library of Congress)

Dealers, communists, and capitalists, and, in an implausible tale, lumped them all together, saying they were involved in a secret plot to grab power for the few and enslave the many. His story found an audience with those disgusted, disheartened, and frightened by the Depression.

By 1934, Coughlin was receiving thousands of supportive letters a day, often with money enclosed. That year, he founded the National Union for Social Justice to protect the common worker and lobby the government for change. The group wielded its greatest influence when it helped to keep the United States from joining the World Court, a body it attacked for "dangerous internationalism."

In 1936, Coughlin started a weekly newspaper called *Social Justice* to endorse political candidates and elaborate on his radio sermons. And he founded the Union Party and confidently predicted that its presidential nominee, William Lemke of North Dakota, would get 10 percent of the popular vote. He actually won far less.

The loss deepened Coughlin's suspicions of conspiracy and emboldened him further. In 1938, his sermons turned blatantly anti-Semitic. He blamed Jews for just about every problem in America, called Roosevelt's New Deal the "Jew Deal," and even published portions of "The Protocols of the Elders of Zion," a virulent anti-Semitic tract, in *Social Justice.* He accused Jews of having financed the communist revolution in Russia and praised Nazi actions against the Reds.

That same year, he organized the Christian Front, whose members physically attacked Jews in several cities. With these activities, and with his radio speeches turning ever more extreme, in 1940 the National Association of Broadcasters forced him off the air.

After the Japanese attacked Pearl Harbor, Coughlin blamed the outbreak of World War II on yet another conspiracy, this one involving the British, Jews, and Roosevelt. Infuriated, the Catholic church ordered him to end his rhetoric or face defrocking. In 1942, Coughlin agreed to quit the public scene and thereafter, until his retirement in 1966, he said little beyond church sermons, which were innocuous for the most part.

Coughlin died on October 27, 1979, in Birmingham, Michigan. Historian Michael Kazin has said that Coughlin was effective because he "translated papal encyclicals about labor and poverty into American vernacular. He unraveled the complexities of banking transactions and legislation concerning the economy. He ridiculed pompous men of wealth." In a time when economic despair encouraged some people to believe the worst about others, Coughlin built a widespread appeal that quickly collapsed when the Depression ended.

Further Reading

Bennett, David H. *Demagogues in the Depression: American Radicals and the Union Party, 1932–1936.* New Brunswick, N.J.: Rutgers University Press, 1969.

Brinkley, Alan. *Voices of Protest: Huey Long, Father Coughlin, and the Great Depression.* New York: Knopf, 1982.

Carpenter, Ronald H. *Father Charles E. Coughlin: Surrogate Spokesman for the Disaffected.* Westport, Conn.: Greenwood Press, 1998.

Kazin, Michael. *The Populist Persuasion: An American History.* New York: Basic Books, 1995.

Marcus, Sheldon. *Father Coughlin: The Tumultuous Life of the Priest of the Little Flower.* Boston: Little, Brown, 1973.

Warren, Donald I. *Radio Priest: Charles Coughlin, The Father of Hate Radio.* New York: Free Press, 1996.

Auto Workers Stage the Great Flint Sit-Down

1936

On December 30, 1936, the men at the Fisher One Plant, where General Motors made auto bodies, knew they had to act or they would lose their chance to unionize the company. Railroad cars had pulled up to the loading docks, and GM was getting ready to move the dies essential in making the auto bodies to a more docile plant and thus break any resistance that could be mustered at Fisher One. With that, the men decided on a sit-down strike that paralyzed the company and won recognition for the union.

In the mid-1930s, Flint, Michigan, was a true company town, one completely dominated by GM. The mayor, chief of police, judges—all were on, or had been on, the company payroll or held shares of stock in the company. The newspaper was under GM's control, and the town relied almost exclusively on the auto company for jobs.

With the grit and grime of the factory came oppressive working conditions. Foremen treated the workers with scorn, and although GM paid a decent hourly wage, it laid off workers for long periods, meaning that their income fell below the $1,600 annual government poverty level. Added to those hardships, the company imposed the "speed-up," moving the assembly line quicker and firing workers who refused to pick up their pace. Genora Dollinger recalled how her husband, Kermit Johnson, had been "a young man grown old from the speed-up. He had come home at night . . . so tired he couldn't eat. He was wakened the next morning with his hands so swollen he couldn't hold a fork."

To prevent the workers from forming a union, GM placed spies on the assembly lines, spending nearly $1 million in 1934 alone on what it called "detective work." GM organized a group to tar and feather union activists, and it frequently fired those suspected of union activity.

To organize GM, the United Auto Workers (UAW) planned an initial strike at Flint for January 1937. The UAW realized that if it could shut down Fisher One, the heart of GM's die and chassis production, it could cripple the company. But auto workers elsewhere had jumped the gun and were already going out on strike—in Kansas City, Detroit, and Atlanta—and they were doing so with a recently developed tactic called the sit-down. First applied in the United States in 1906 at a General Electric plant in upstate

GM workers on strike at the Flint plant, 1935. (Bettmann/CORBIS)

New York, the sit-down required that workers stop all machinery, sit in place, and refuse to move. This enabled them to literally take over the plant.

Just days before the strike at Flint, workers at a GM factory in Cleveland, Ohio, started a sit-down and gained concessions. Then on December 30, 1936, the railroad cars arrived at Fisher One to pick up the dies. Emboldened by the success in Cleveland, the UAW quickly called a meeting of workers. To the chants of "Shut her down! Shut down the goddamn plant!" the strike began. All work stopped at Fisher One and at the nearby Fisher Two.

The workers barricaded the factory doors with unfinished car bodies and welded together metal sheets to cover the windows. They formed committees to stand watch and to establish contact with supporters on the outside, who provided the strikers with food. Other committees arranged entertainment to prevent boredom. The workers demanded a 30-hour week, six-hour day, time-and-a-half pay for overtime, a minimum pay rate, joint control by the union and management over speed-ups, and recognition of the UAW.

The sit-down captured the country's attention as newspapers and radio covered it extensively. GM portrayed the sit-down as the effort of "outside agitators" (some communists were involved in organizing the work stoppage), and claimed that most at the plant opposed it. The company obtained an injunction ordering the strikers to vacate the plants, but the workers ignored the legal writ, and GM temporarily lost public support when it was revealed that the judge who had issued the order owned more than $200,000 of company stock.

When GM shut off the heat to the plants, the workers threatened to build fires, and the heat returned. When GM shut off the electricity, the workers threatened to light torches, and the electricity returned. The workers sang:

> When they tie the can to a union man
> Sit down! Sit down!
> When they give 'im the sack, they'll take him back
> Sit down! Sit down!
> Sit down, just take a seat.
> Sit down, and rest your feet.
> Sit down, you've got 'em beat.
> Sit down! Sit down!

On January 11, 1937, violence erupted at Fisher Two when company guards attempted to prevent food from being passed to the strikers, and the workers attacked the guards and took their keys. The guards then called in the police, who blockaded the streets and charged a group of strikers positioned at the factory gate. When the police lobbed tear gas canisters, the strikers responded by hurling bottles and lumps of coal and spraying water from hoses. Forced back, the police retaliated by opening fire and wounding 14 strikers. Men and women gathered outside by the thousands to support the workers, and the strikers inside the plant warned that if the police assaulted them again, they would destroy the assembly lines. At that point the police retreated. The assault became known as the "Battle of Bulls Run," recalling the Civil War battle and playing on the word "bulls," which was slang for police.

Besides joining in the battle, women provided important support to the workers throughout the strike. They patrolled the streets outside the plant, and a Women's Auxiliary kept watch and alerted the community about any movement of the company guards or police.

With the strike dragging on toward February, the UAW concluded that it needed to exert more pressure by having the strikers capture the Chevy Four plant. GM, however, had stationed guards around it; to take

Labor Makes America More Democratic

An overall view of unions in the 1930s and early 1940s reveals an aversion to certain modern democratic ideals, such as sexual and racial equality. The American Federation of Labor (AFL; see entry, 1886), for example, was openly hostile to women workers and had a hard and fast rule that prohibited African Americans from joining any of its trade unions. Yet as workers rebelled against corporate bosses, they challenged the barrier of discrimination that hampered democracy both inside and outside the workplace, and they activated the entire working class to make its demands known in the political arena.

Much more than the AFL, the Congress of Industrial Organizations (CIO) reached out to African-American workers. The CIO convinced a large number of the 85,000 black workers in the steel industry to join the white-dominated Steel Workers Organizing Committee. One black worker said, "I'll tell you what the CIO has done. Before, everyone used to make remarks about . . . 'that stinkin' black bastard' . . . but you know I never hear that kind of stuff anymore. I don't like to brag, but I'm one of the best-liked men in my department."

The CIO recruited large numbers of women in the garment, textile, and electrical assembly industries. The largely female Amalgamated Clothing Workers of America climbed from 60,000 members in 1932 to over 300,000 in 1942, and membership in the International Ladies' Garment Workers' Union rose from 40,000 to 200,000. One woman union member said, "We are no longer robots. We are independent. We are strong."

In challenging racial and sexual discrimination, and in forming picket lines, staging sit-ins, and bargaining collectively, organized workers brought the democratic emphasis on popular power into the workplace and extended it back into the community as their own commitment to reform energized others. Much remained to be done—white males still dominated union leadership, while women and blacks were still largely relegated to lower-paying, more menial jobs—but working people had made their power known and expected their federal, state, and local governments to be more responsive to their needs.

---

the factory, the union let it be known to company spies that it would assault and capture the Chevy Nine plant. On February 1, a small band of strikers entered Chevy Nine, starting a fight with GM guards and the police. As the battle raged, a women's brigade, wielding baseball bats, smashed open the factory windows to let tear gas escape from inside. The diversion under way, other strikers captured Chevy Four.

To the gathered workers one union leader, Joe Sayen, declared:

We want the whole world to understand what we are fighting for. We are fighting for freedom and life and liberty. This is our one great opportunity. What if we should be defeated? What if we should be killed? We have only one life. That's all we can lose and we might as well die like heroes than like slaves.

On February 3, GM agreed to negotiate. The following week, the company capitulated to the heart of the UAW demand: that the union be recognized as the bargaining agent for the workers. On February 11, the workers left the factories in triumph. Later talks resulted in increased pay, but most important was the recognition. One worker said, "Even if we got not one damn thing out of it other than that, we at least had a right to open our mouths without fear."

Public opinion, though, turned against the sit-down strikes. Some people just tired of the turmoil; others listened to corporate propaganda that portrayed the workers as extremists. Then in 1939, in the case of *NLRB v. Fansteel Metallurgical Corporation,* the Supreme Court ruled that sit-down strikes were an unconstitutional violation of the rights of property holders.

Nevertheless, the Flint sit-down strike resulted in the UAW rapidly organizing nearly the entire auto industry. The union's membership increased 500 percent in the first six months of 1937, reaching 400,000. Writing in *Freedom from Fear* (1999), historian David M. Kennedy says that with the strike,

"Industrial unionism had established a major beachhead in a core American industry." Beyond that, it had invigorated the union movement in other industries and displayed the force of labor solidarity. To this day, workers in Flint wear white shirts every February 11 to memorialize the sit-down strike.

Further Reading

Bernstein, Irving. *Turbulent Years: A History of the American Worker, 1933–1941.* Boston: Houghton Mifflin, 1970.

Fine, Sidney. *Sit-Down: The General Motors Strike of 1936–1937.* Ann Arbor: University of Michigan Press, 1969.

Kennedy, David M. *Freedom From Fear: The American People in Depression and War, 1929–1945.* New York: Oxford University Press, 1999.

Kraus, Henry. *Heroes of Unwritten Story: The UAW, 1934–39.* Urbana: University of Illinois Press, 1993.

The Memorial Day Massacre   1937

In March 1937, the Steel Workers Organizing Committee (SWOC), part of the Congress of Industrial Organizations (CIO), scored a tremendous victory when it convinced United States Steel to recognize it as the bargaining agent for the committee's members. But other steel companies, referred to collectively as "Little Steel," refused to recognize the SWOC, and Republic Steel especially, located in Chicago, vowed to hold firm. The company recruited police to protect its plant from strikers, and on Memorial Day, the police fired at unarmed men, women, and children in a massacre captured on film by a newsreel crew.

Unlike the American Federation of Labor, which sought to unionize workers based on their craft, the CIO sought to do so by industry—all steel workers, for example, whatever their skill, were to be brought together in one union. With that goal, the CIO formed the SWOC in June 1936 and in January 1937 obtained the contract with U.S. Steel. In May, the SWOC decided to strike three of the Little Steel companies at the same time—Youngstown Sheet and Tube, Inland, and Republic. Beginning May 26, picket lines closed down most of the plants, but Republic's South Chicago factory remained open, operated by strikebreakers.

Using strikebreakers was only one part of the strategy in the offensive against unions. Ever since the sit down strike at General Motors in Flint, Michigan (see entry, 1936), businessmen and supportive politicians determined to put an end to labor's uprising. They issued propaganda about radicals; curried favor with newspapers that portrayed activists as rabble-rousers intent on forcing workers to join unions and engage in strikes; formed alliances with the police; and equipped their own private guards with nightsticks, pistols, rifles, shotguns, and tear gas grenades.

In the days before the massacre, several incidents intensified the tension between the Chicago police and the strikers. The most serious occurred on May 27, when 400 strikers and members of their women's auxiliary marched toward the Republic gate. As they wound their way through the streets leading to the plant, the marchers encountered a line of police, and when they tried to break through, fighting broke out. The police bloodied several heads with their billy clubs, and some of the policemen pulled revolvers from their holsters and fired into the air. The crowd fell back and dispersed, but uneasiness gripped the city.

On the afternoon of May 30, Memorial Day, about 1,200 strikers and some 200 women and children attended a rally, during which SWOC leaders urged them to support the right to organize. Republic's use of the Chicago police as a strikebreaking force, said one leader, violated the Wagner Act, which prohibited businesses from engaging in unfair labor practices.

The crowd then approved resolutions protesting the recent police conduct, whereupon someone moved that they march to the Republic gate. The crowd agreed and proceeded behind two American flags. They trekked along a dirt road, and headed across the prairie that stretched out before the plant, all the while chanting "CIO, CIO!" Labor sympathizer Howard Fast described the scene:

Most of the strikers felt good. Tom Girdler, who ran Republic, had said that he would go back to hoeing potatoes before he would meet the strikers' demands, and the word went around that old Tom could do worse than earn an honest living hoeing potatoes. The strike was less than a week old; the strikers had not yet felt the pinch of hunger, and there was a good sense of solidarity everywhere. Because it was such a fine summer day many of the strikers brought their children out onto the prairie to attend the first big mass meeting; and wherever you looked, you saw two-year-olds and three-year-olds riding pick-a-back on the heavy-muscled shoulders of steelworkers. And because it was in the way of being their special occasion as well as a patriotic holiday, the women wore their best and brightest. . . .

About two hundred and fifty yards from the plant, the police closed in on the strikers. Billies and clubs were out already, prodding, striking, nightsticks edging into women's breasts and groins. But the cops were also somewhat afraid and they began to jerk guns out of holsters.

"Stand fast! Stand fast!" the line leaders cried. "We got our rights! We got our legal rights to picket!"

The cops said, "You got no rights. You red bastards, you got no rights. . . ."

Grenades began to sail now; tear gas settled like an ugly cloud. Children suddenly cried with panic, and the whole picket line gave back, men stumbling, cursing, gasping for breath. Here and there a cop tore out his pistol and began to fire; it was pop, pop, pop at first, like toy favors at some horrible party, and then as the strikers broke under the gunfire and began to run, the contagion of killing ran like fire through the police.

They began to shoot in volleys at these unarmed men and women and children who could not strike back or fight back. The cops squealed with excitement. They ran after fleeing pickets, pressed revolvers to their backs, shot them down, and then continued to shoot as the victims lay on their faces, retching blood.

A later Senate investigation confirmed Fast's description of the massacre. Some of the marchers had thrown sticks at the police before the first shots were fired, but it was a largely peaceful, if determined, crowd. The police responded to the sticks by throwing tear gas bombs. Then, as the protesters retreated, an officer behind the front lines fired his pistol into the air. Other policemen then fired directly into the retreating crowd.

In all, the police killed 10 strikers and shot 30 other people, including three children. Another 28 were hospitalized with injuries delivered by billy clubs and axe handles.

The following day, a Chicago newspaper ran the headline: Reds Riot at Steel Mill, and the *New York Times* ran the less incendiary but still biased headline: 4 Killed, 84 Hurt as Strikers Fight Police in Chicago, Steel Mob Halted. Movie theaters in Chicago refused to show the newsreel of the clash for fear it might ignite a riot.

All through that summer, more strikers were assaulted across the country: eight killed in the Midwest in June, 50 injured in Hawaii at the Hilo Massacre in August. In Ohio, the governor used the National Guard to escort strikebreakers into steel plants, and the state prohibited picketing and even union meetings. One report stated, "Ohio National Guardsmen killed and wounded dozens of strikers and jailed hundreds more in the confrontations that followed."

The SWOC reeled from the violence and for the moment failed to get Little Steel to recognize the union. Adding to SWOC's woes, a resurgent depression put jobs at a premium and made strikes less attractive than job security. SWOC's leaders left 1937 chastened and ready to try a different approach. They would, in the 1940s, rely less on militant action and more on government regulatory bodies, mainly the

National Labor Relations Board (NLRB). In 1941, Republic and the other Little Steel companies reacted to an investigation by the NLRB by agreeing to end their unfair labor practices, and in 1942, they signed contracts with the United Steelworkers of America, the successor to the SWOC.

In the larger picture, the Memorial Day Massacre was the result of greater forces than just the events of 1937; radicalism, and the harsh reaction to it, had been bred in an atmosphere encouraged by the growth of corporate capitalism, one where workers and managers distrusted each other, where they worked together not as a community but as opposing groups, the exploiter and the exploited.

Further Reading

Lens, Sidney. *The Labor Wars: From the Molly Maguires to the Sitdowns.* Garden City, N.Y.: Doubleday, 1973.

Zieger, Robert. *The CIO: 1935–1955.* Chapel Hill: University of North Carolina Press, 1995.

American Communist Party Condemns World War II as Imperialist War   1939

The Communist Party, United States of America (CPUSA), followed a strange and winding road toward World War II, at first urging preparedness, then backing away and advocating that the United States stay out of the war, and then changing course again. The party was not motivated by peaceful intentions, but by the dictates of the Soviet Union.

In the mid-1930s, the CPUSA reached out to workers by forming a Popular Front, meaning that it wanted communists to cooperate with labor unionists outside the party and with liberals of many different persuasions to form a progressive coalition. In time the Popular Front in the United States developed a life of its own beyond the directives of the Communist Party, but the edict for forming it came from the Soviet-dominated Comintern (Communist International), which was creating popular fronts in many countries.

While the communists had as their goal attracting members to their ideology, the Popular Front was aimed primarily at fighting fascism, both in reference to the actual fascist ideology emanating from Europe—an ideology that prized nation and race above all else and that relied on autocratic government—and in reference to what the communists considered to be reactionary, autocratic leaders in the United States who wanted to protect capitalism against socialism. Many communists placed President Franklin Roosevelt and his allies in this last group. One CPUSA leader, William Z. Foster, warned in 1936 of fascists within Roosevelt's New Deal government. He added: "In the United States now there is a race between the fascists and the Communist Party for the leadership of the politically rapidly weakening toiling masses, [and] the fascists are at present far ahead in this race."

To fight fascism as represented by Adolph Hitler, the communists advocated that the United States prepare itself militarily for a war with Germany. But their opinion suddenly changed in 1939 when Hitler and Soviet dictator Joseph Stalin signed a nonaggression pact, promising neither would attack the other. Hitler then invaded Poland from the west, beginning World War II, and Stalin invaded Poland from the east, grabbing land for the Soviet Union. Britain and France reacted by declaring war on Germany, the Soviets causing denounce to the Allied action as imperialist and to call Britain the enemy of the working class. Clearly, though, the Soviets believed that if Hitler were defeated, their pact with him would be overturned and the land they acquired from Poland lost.

With the Soviet decree, the CPUSA fell in line, backed away from preparedness, and asserted that the United States should stay out of the war. The party labeled American efforts to help Britain and France "war-mongering." The rapid change stunned many in both the CPUSA and in the Popular Front, and the party itself lost thousands of members. Intellectuals mocked Jews in New York who had joined the Popular Front and allied with communists by shouting at them, "Heil Hitler!"

When Earl Browder, head of the CPUSA, ran for president in 1940, he did so as an isolationist. He polled only 46,000 votes in a country strongly opposed to Hitler and moving closer to war. Within the party itself, several in the leadership opposed the shift to isolation, and debates over the issue degenerated into heated arguments.

But in June 1941, Germany invaded Russia, and as quickly as the tune had changed from preparedness to isolation, it now changed back from isolation to preparedness . . . and more: advocacy that America enter the war and fight Hitler. The fight against Germany, the communists now said, was no longer imperialistic, but democratic. The Comintern called the emerging alliance between the Soviet Union and the western European countries a "just war of defense." To a small nucleus of dedicated communists, the shifting positions were pragmatic moves; to others the supposedly radical ideology had revealed opportunism at its core.

Further Reading

Draper, Theodore. *American Communism and Soviet Russia: The Formative Period.* New York: Viking Press, 1960.

Howe, Irving, and Lewis Coster. *The American Communist Party: A Critical History.* New York: Praeger, 1962.

Klehr, Harvey, and John Earl Hayne. *The American Communist Movement: Storming Heaven Itself.* Boston: Twayne, 1992.

1944   The Port Chicago Fifty

In July 1944, an explosion rocked the Port Chicago Naval Base in California, a blast so massive it sent fire and smoke 12,000 feet into the sky and shattered windows 20 miles away, and so devastating it killed 320 sailors and civilians—200 of them black. Because the navy used only African-Americans in the dangerous job of loading munitions at Port Chicago, their deaths raised questions about racist policies and provided impetus to the civil rights movement.

The blacks who had been killed were loading the *E. A. Bryan* and preparing to load the *Quinalt Victory.* They had received no training in handling explosives; nor had they been given any written safety procedures. Quoted in David M. Kennedy's *Freedom from Fear* (1999), one black sailor recalled, "We were just shown a box-car full of ammunition, wire nets spread out on the docks and the hold in the ship and told to load."

The navy's racist munitions-loading procedure was reinforced by the segregation that prevailed throughout the military. Port Chicago was so strictly segregated that black sailors were prohibited from eating in the mess hall until the white sailors had finished their meals. When no exact cause could be found for the accident, 258 blacks refused to work without guarantees for their safety. In retaliation, the military court-martialed 50 of those it suspected of being either leaders of the work stoppage or unwilling to obey all orders, and tried them in the largest mass mutiny trial in American history. Thurgood Marshall, chief counsel for the National Association for the Advancement of Colored People (NAACP; see entry, 1909), said, "This is not 50 men on trial for mutiny. This is the Navy on trial for its whole vicious policy toward Negroes. Negroes in the Navy don't mind loading ammunition. They just want to know why they are the only ones doing the loading!"

In October 1944, the Port Chicago Fifty were found guilty and punished severely, with several of them sentenced to 15 years hard labor. The verdict appalled blacks and many whites and led to protests, including mass meetings and a clemency petition campaign organized by Eleanor Roosevelt, the National Urban League, and the NAACP. Historian John Patrick Diggins writes in *The Proud Decades: America in War and Peace, 1941–1960* (1988) that "the Port Chicago trial provoked one of the largest mass campaigns in behalf of racial justice."

Historical Forces and Radicals

No person, radical or otherwise, can exist outside historical context. In the United States, radicals have been propelled into action by imperialism—as in the case of British actions leading up to the 1776 Revolution; slavery—as in the case of abolitionism; industrialization—as in the case of socialists; and so on. The 1930s provide a case where an economic depression followed a largely prosperous and quiescent decade.

Hardly anyone expected an economic depression to begin in 1929 or reach the depths that it did. Yet with the economic free fall, normally complacent people turned to radical acts that ranged from the embrace of extremist ideas to violence and rioting. In the early 1930s in Iowa, as prices dropped for farm goods, farmers declared a halt to agricultural sales. Reminiscent of Shays' Rebellion (see entry, 1786), farmers in South Dakota threatened sheriffs' deputies with violence should they evict neighbors from their homes.

In Indiana Harbor, Indiana, 1,500 jobless men laid siege to the Fruit Growers Express Company and demanded jobs to keep them from starving. In Chicago, 500 school children marched on the board of education and demanded that the school system provide them with food. The jobless in many parts of the country joined communist-sponsored Unemployed Councils to demand relief. In Pennsylvania, miners took over company property and mined and sold their own coal. In Seattle, the fishermen's union bypassed the monetary system and exchanged fish with farmers who gave them fruits and vegetables.

Sometimes the radical acts were planned; sometimes they were spontaneous. Sometimes they occurred in small ways; sometimes in ways that made people rethink the structure of their society. But in each instance, the historical force of the Great Depression caused people to act.

The NAACP Legal Defense Fund handled the appeal of the Port Chicago Fifty in 1945. At the trial, Marshall introduced evidence that black enlistees at Port Chicago were relegated to the most dangerous work, given no special training, ordered by the officers to form teams that competed with each other in loading the ships, and barred from receiving promotion. Nevertheless, the judge upheld the original conviction.

Because of the Port Chicago Fifty controversy, in August 1944 the navy began desegregating some of its crews, and by the end of 1945, it ended segregation entirely. Also late in 1945, the Port Chicago Fifty were released and granted clemency.

But the incident had more than turn the spotlight on racial segregation in the military: it promoted alliances between African-Americans and white liberals. The NAACP, for one, benefited from such an alliance and from the heightened activism. Its membership surged from 50,000 in 1940 to 450,000 in 1946. The case of the Port Chicago Fifty took a nascent civil rights movement and pushed it along, increasing momentum in the challenge to racial segregation and white supremacy that would transform American society.

Further Reading
Allen, Robert L. *The Port Chicago Mutiny.* New York: Warner Books, 1989.
Diggins, John Patrick. *The Proud Decades: America in War and in Peace, 1941–1960.* New York: Norton, 1988.

Communists Take Control of New York American Labor Party 1944

In the late 1930s and 1940s, New York's vibrant leftist politics produced a third political party, the American Labor Party (ALP), every bit as strong as the Democrats and Republicans in New York City. Communists quickly took advantage of the ALP by infiltrating it and then commandeering it as a vanguard for their own proletarian revolution.

In 1936, unions in the men's and women's garment industry, along with some smaller unions and the Social Democratic Federation (SDF)—a faction that split from the Socialist Party and opposed the communists—founded the ALP. Sidney Hillman, president of the Amalgamated Clothing Workers, and David

Dubinsky, president of the International Ladies' Garment Workers, were the masterminds behind it. Hillman had secured President Franklin Roosevelt's support to build a party that would rally to the president's re-election campaign those trade unionists and other liberals, including Republicans, who were disenchanted with New York's corrupt Democratic Party machine.

The ALP's Declaration of Principles called for a "sufficient planned utilization of the national economy so that coal, oil, timber, water and other natural resources [that] belong to the American people . . . shall be protected from predatory interests." The declaration stopped short of an explicit call to socialism but made clear that the ALP had more faith in government control than in business control of resources. The agreement among the various groups that formed the ALP stipulated that communists would be banned from the party.

With the November 1936 national elections approaching, the ALP promoted Roosevelt's New Deal program to end the Depression. The party won some 300,000 votes in New York for the president.

The ALP was stronger by far in New York City than elsewhere in the state. It thrived in the city's blue-collar, union, immigrant environment. Near the time the communists took over the ALP, about half of New York City's 2.6 million wage earners labored at manual jobs. On top of that, unions wielded considerable power, and the city's many ethnic neighborhoods attested to the heavily immigrant and first-generation American population. More than a few of these residents had been weaned on leftist politics in their homelands or within the neighborhoods.

As the ALP grew, communists saw the possibility of using it to pry unionists away from their attachment to capitalist or bourgeois values and attach them to truly Marxist principles. They wanted unionists to think in grander terms than wages and benefits, or even vague statements about protection from predatory interests; they wanted them to become a revolutionary vanguard.

So, in short order, communists violated the agreement reached in forming the ALP and began infiltrating the party. No more vibrant and attractive a leader than Vito Marcantonio, a Republican Italian-American, joined the ALP and allied himself with the communist drive. He won election to Congress in 1934, lost in 1936, and returned to his seat in 1938 with the backing of the ALP. Marcantonio denounced Republicans and Democrats, conservatives and liberals; during the year he began his second term in Congress, the Republicans booted him from their party. Yet he continued to win Republican primaries.

Marcantonio generally supported New Deal programs, but he didn't really like them; he thought them too conservative. In one instance, he chided Roosevelt for refusing to have the government take over all utilities; in another, he criticized the president's social security plan for burdening the workers with a payroll tax. Historian Gerald Meyer has called him "the closest thing to a national spokesman for the left during this period."

When World War II erupted, Marcantonio espoused the communist line that the Allies were fighting an imperialist war and the United States should stay out of it. Then when Germany invaded Russia, he voiced the communist view that the United States should prepare itself for war against the fascists.

Marcantonio was unique among congressmen in that he openly defended the Communist Party. He called it an "American political party operating in what it considers to be the best interests of the American working class and people."

Marcantonio relied on the communists and the unions for his election, and with his support, the ALP moved deeper into the communist camp. In 1944, the communists captured the legal state committee. That development split the ALP, and those who opposed the communists quit and formed the Liberal Party. The liberals called the ALP "the Communist-Labor Party."

With the departure of the liberals, the communists had achieved their goal of controlling a largely trade union party. For a time, the ALP remained effective. In 1945, it outpolled the Liberal Party in the

New York City elections; it elected candidates to the New York City council; and in 1948, it elected Leo Isaccson to Congress, while Marcantonio continued to run under its banner.

The Cold War and the Red Scare, along with bickering among the communists, ultimately destroyed the ALP. The government portrayed Marcantonio, the ALP, and any other person or organization that held leftist ideas as un-American. Marcantonio retaliated by slamming the House Un-American Activities Committee for its attacks on free speech. And he condemned President Harry Truman's decision to send American troops to fight communist forces in Korea.

New York's newspapers then launched a campaign to silence him and the ALP. Democrats, Republicans, and Liberals joined together in a powerful coalition in 1950 and nominated the same person, James Donovan, to run against Marcantonio. They defeated him, though Marcantonio still won more than 41 percent of the ballots and lost by only 14,000 votes.

Harassed by the federal government, the communists concluded in 1953 that if they stayed in the ALP, they would expose themselves to arrest. So most of them decided to leave the party, though some objected to the move, and Marcantonio's supporters tried to get the communist members to stay.

In 1954, the ALP candidate for governor won fewer than 50,000 votes; two years later the party collapsed. The ALP sealed its own fate though, when it allowed the liberals to leave in 1944. In trying to purify the party and make it into a revolutionary vanguard, the communists narrowed its base, opened it to charges of extremism, and hastened its end.

Further Reading

Meyer, Gerald. *Vito Marcantonio: Radical Politician, 1902–1954.* Albany: State University of New York Press, 1989.

Malcolm X Learns about the Nation of Islam

1948

In 1948, while in prison for burglary, Malcolm Little received two letters from his brothers, Philbert and Reginald. They told him about a religion, the Nation of Islam, which preached that whites were devils and blacks should live separately from them. Four years later, Little converted to the faith, changed his name to Malcolm X, and soon after that became the group's most prominent member.

Malcolm Little (1925–65) was born in Omaha, Nebraska, and felt the sting of racism while still in childhood. His father was a Baptist minister and organizer for Marcus Garvey's Universal Negro Improvement Association (see entry, 1916), which promoted black pride. Not long after the elder Little moved his family to Lansing, Michigan, white racists known as the Black Legionnaires set fire to the family's home. "I remember," Little recalled, "we were outside in the night in our underwear, crying and yelling our heads off. The white police and firemen came and stood around watching as the house burned down to the ground."

Racism again intruded on Little's life when he told his white junior high school teacher that he wanted to go to college and become a lawyer, and the teacher told him that job was unsuitable "for a nigger." Instead, the teacher advised that he become a carpenter.

Little finished the eighth grade and then dropped out of school. At age 17, he went to Boston and supported himself by working on a train that ran to New York City. Soon he was spending more time in Harlem, waiting on tables, shining shoes, gambling, selling bootleg liquor, and pimping. At the same time, he was swearing, drinking, and trying to look more white by dying and straightening his hair.

In 1946, Little was arrested in Boston for burglary and sentenced to 10 years in prison. He later said that he entered jail an atheist, uncouth, with a vocabulary of no more than 200 words. All of that soon changed. In 1948, he received the two letters from his brothers. He didn't fully understand what they were all about, but then Reginald came to visit him and told him how the Nation of Islam, through its spiritual leader, Elijah Muhammad, believed that God, or Allah, had created blacks as the first race, and how in ancient times Yacub, a black scientist, had rebelled against Allah by creating a devilish people with bleached skin—the white race. Whites had ruled the earth for 6,000 years, but their time was nearing an end, Reginald said; the original black race would soon give birth to a leader instilled with wisdom and unlimited power.

These ideas offered the imprisoned Little an explanation for his brutal treatment by whites and why blacks as a whole had suffered at the hands of white people. Whites were created to be that way; it was innate to them; they could be no different. "The white people I had known marched before my mind's eye . . . ," Little recalled. "The white people who kept calling my mother 'crazy' to her face and before me and my brothers and sisters, until she was finally taken off by white people to the Kalamazoo asylum . . . the white judge and others who had split up the children . . . and the teachers—the one who told me in the eighth grade to 'be a carpenter' because thinking of being a lawyer was foolish for a Negro."

His brother told Little that whites had robbed blacks of their names and their identities and had erased from their memories nearly all knowledge about their African homeland. Other relatives wrote Little and told him that they, too, had converted to the Nation of Islam, had become Black Muslims. They urged him to "accept the teachings of The Honorable Elijah Muhammad."

Through literature they sent him, Little learned about the great civilizations once built by blacks in Africa. He learned that whites had perpetrated the greatest crime ever by enslaving blacks and forcibly taking them to the Americas. He learned that whites had raped black women, and diluted the black race by creating mulattos. And he learned that Christianity equated black with evil and white with good, making blacks a people to be reviled.

Little read more than Black Muslim literature. He read classic and modern intellectual works—philosophies, histories, politics. He read so much and in such poor light in prison that his eyesight deteriorated. But he kept on reading and kept on learning: Herodotus, Harriet Beecher Stowe, Mahatma Gandhi, Will Durant, Schopenhauer. Little would leave prison a changed man—a Black Muslim in outlook, for sure, but also educated, articulate, and freed from the profanity and crime that had been his previous life. That change, in turn, would reshape the black experience in America, bringing more African-Americans into the Nation of Islam and intensifying the question of how whites and blacks should relate to each other. Should they integrate, as most activists in the civil rights movement advocated, or should they live separately?

Within weeks after being paroled in 1952, Little met Elijah Muhammad at the headquarters of the Nation of Islam in Chicago. Shortly after that meeting, he converted and replaced his last name, the one given his family by whites, with "X," representing the African name he would never know. The following summer, Malcolm X was made assistant minister of Detroit's Temple Number One.

Malcolm X organized temples in Boston and Philadelphia, and showed so much skill as a public speaker, that in 1954 Elijah Muhammad appointed him minister of Harlem's Temple Number Seven, one of the most important temples within the Nation of Islam.

The expansion of the Black Muslims in the 1950s was in great measure attributable to Malcolm X and his appeal. Other factors also contributed to the change: the general belief among blacks that they should no longer accept a second-class citizenship, the population surge among young African-Americans, and the very nature of Black Muslim belief and activities that offered African-Americans a source of pride. For the Nation of Islam was more than a religion; it provided opportunity, operating farms, bakeries, supermarkets, and restaurants—all black-owned.

In 1961, Malcolm X founded *Muhammad Speaks*, the official publication of the Nation of Islam. In a time when the civil rights movement was intensifying under Martin Luther King, Jr., Malcolm X and the Black Muslims disagreed with King's philosophy. Where King wanted integration, the Black Muslims wanted separation. They were black nationalists who believed that the devil—white people—could never be reformed and that blacks should stay away from such evil.

Malcolm X's distance from King was never more evident than when he scathingly criticized the massive 1963 March on Washington, an event organized by A. Philip Randolph but strongly supported by King and made notable by his "I Have a Dream" speech. Malcolm said the black organizers started out with the right intentions: "They were going to march on Washington, march on the Senate, march on the White House, march on the Congress, and tie it up, bring it to a halt, not let the government proceed." But King allowed the white power brokers to step in and orchestrate the protest. Malcolm claimed: "It became a picnic, a circus. Nothing but a circus, with clowns and all. . . . It was a takeover. . . . They told those Negroes what time to hit town, where to stop, what signs to carry, what song to sing, what speech they could make, and what speech they couldn't make, and then told them to get out of town by sundown."

Malcolm X's controversial statements continued that year with his observation

Malcolm X. (Hulton Archive)

that the assassination of President John Kennedy was "a case of chickens coming home to roost," meaning that the hatred bred by whites had killed him. That remark caused Elijah Muhammad to suspend him from the Black Muslims. A year later, Malcolm X split with the Nation of Islam (see entry, 1964), but his actions in the 1950s and early 1960s had already served to emphasize the racial divide between white and black America and challenged the assumption of the mainstream civil rights community that racial justice could be obtained through integration.

Further Reading

Goldman, Peter Louis. *The Death and Life of Malcolm X.* 2d ed. Urbana: University of Illinois Press, 1979.

Karim, Benjamin. *Remembering Malcolm.* New York: Carroll & Graf, 1992.

Wood, Joe, ed. *Malcolm X: In Our Own Image.* New York: St. Martin's Press, 1992.

X, Malcolm. *The Autobiography of Malcolm X.* With the Assistance of Alex Haley. 2nd ed. New York: Ballantine Books, 1999.

Smith Act Trials Shatter the Communist Party 1949

In 1940, Congress passed the Alien Registration Act, more widely called the Smith Act, after its sponsor, Congressman Howard Smith of Virginia. The Smith Act made it unlawful for any person to advocate or teach the overthrow of any government in the United States by force or violence, or to organize or become a member of any group dedicated to such a doctrine. For the first time since 1798, when Congress passed and President John Adams signed the Alien and Sedition Acts, the federal government had made it a crime to advocate ideas.

In 1949, the Justice Department charged 11 leaders of the Communist Party with violating the Smith Act. The government wanted these leaders imprisoned and the Communist Party destroyed. Those charged included Eugene Dennis and Henry Winston, leaders of the national organization; John Gates, editor of the party newspaper, the *Daily Worker*; and Gus Hall, leader of the party in Ohio. Was the prosecution of the communist leaders a violation of the First Amendment protection of free speech? That was the argument made by the defense, for in relying on the Smith Act, the government had based its charge on words and ideas—there was no evidence that any of those on trial had attempted to forcibly overthrow the federal government or had actually incited others to pick up weapons and lay waste to it. Rather, the case rested on the defendants' belief in Marxism–Leninism, their teaching of Marxist–Leninist concepts to others, and their publication and distribution of Marxist–Leninist books and other reading material.

Prosecutor John F. X. McGohey said in the government's opening statement:

It is . . . charged that the defendants would organize clubs, district and state units of their party; that they would recruit new members of their party; and that they, the defendants, would publish books, magazines, and newspapers; that they would organize classes, in all of which it was planned that there would be taught and advocated the Marxist–Leninist principles of the duty and necessity of overthrowing and destroying the Government of the United States by force and violence.

McGohey admitted that the communists were not necessarily talking about overthrowing the federal government tomorrow, but at such time as they thought it right. The deed, in other words, could be a distant one, though the danger of the ideology spreading was more immediate.

Crucial to the government's case were three books: *The Communist Manifesto* (1848) by Karl Marx and Friedrich Engels; *The State and Revolution* (1917) by Vladimir Lenin; and *Foundations of Leninism* (1932) by Joseph Stalin. When the defense attorneys objected to introducing these books as evidence because reading and discussing them was protected by the First Amendment, Judge Harold Medina overruled them. He said they were important as "part of the paraphernalia of the crime."

The judge was a professed anticommunist at a time when the Cold War had just begun and politicians were hunting for leftists. The House Un-American Activities Committee had previously launched an investigation into communist influences. Republicans and Democrats alike, though more so the Republicans, used Red baiting to win office—on the flimsiest evidence they accused their opponents of being communists or dupes of the communists. Therein, in fact, rested a good part of the reason for the Smith Act trials. Democratic President Harry Truman did not want himself and his party to be labeled by his Republican foes as "soft on communism," a phrase that many equated with being treasonous toward the United States. Consequently, he insisted that the Justice Department rigorously enforce the Smith Act.

So intense was the atmosphere generated by the Red Scare that during the trial, which lasted from January to September, 400 police surrounded the Foley Square courthouse in New York City to protect the proceedings from any violence.

In March, Louis Budenz, former managing editor of the *Daily Worker*, appeared as a government witness. He admitted that the party constitution stated that any member who conspired to overthrow any "institutions of American democracy" would be expelled from the group. But he called such provisions "Aesopian language," meaning "roundabout, protective" words like those found in Aesop's fables intended to cover up the party's true intentions, namely its commitment to revolutionary violence. "It has been stated by Lenin and Stalin," Budenz said, "the historical mission of the working class is the establishment of socialism by the violent shattering of the capitalist state."

The defense attorneys admitted that their clients adhered to controversial and radical ideas, but they had taught and advocated them with "peaceful intent." Attorney Eugene Dennis said, "When the defense puts our Communist Party constitution in evidence, the jury will see that it speaks of the duty to organize and educate the working class, and declares that Socialism should be established, not by force and violence, but 'by the free choice of the majority of the American people.' "

The largely wealthy jurors returned guilty verdicts against all 11 communist leaders, 10 of whom served five years in prison, one of whom served three. The defendants appealed their case to the Supreme Court (*Dennis et al. v. United States,* 1951), but by then the Korean War had broken out, and communist hysteria had spread further, seizing most Americans, including several of the Court's justices. Chief Justice Fred Vinson alluded to as much in the 6–2 decision that upheld the convictions when he said that "world conditions, . . . uprisings in other countries, and the touch-and-go nature of our relations with countries," produced a "clear and present danger" that communists would use Marxism–Leninism to overthrow the U.S. government.

Dissenting Justice Hugo Black strongly disagreed with Vinson. He said that the defendants suffered the worst kind of First Amendment violation: *a priori* censorship of their speech, for they had not been charged with writing anything intended to overthrow the government but rather with agreeing to talk about and publish "certain ideas at a later date."

Having won guilty verdicts against the original 11 communist leaders, the federal government obtained indictments against others. More than 160 Communist Party members were tried and found guilty. Their imprisonment, and the fear struck into anyone even remotely attached to communist principles, gutted the party. The prosecutions continued until 1957, when the Supreme Court reversed its earlier ruling and overturned most of the post-1949 convictions.

The Smith Act trials displayed the power of the government to abridge free speech and the power with which the context of the times shaped legal decisions. They showed how freedom as stipulated in the Bill of Rights exists not in some rarefied domain of permanency but in a changing world subject to social pressure. Justice Black realized this when he said, "Public opinion being what it now is, few will protest the conviction of these Communist petitioners." And few did, as security took priority over liberty.

Further Reading

Belknap, Michal. *Cold War Political Justice: The Smith Act, the Communist Party, and American Civil Liberties.* Westport, Conn.: Greenwood Press, 1977.

Kutler, Stanley. *The American Inquisition: Justice and Injustice in the Cold War.* New York: Hill and Wang, 1982.

Steinberg, Peter. *The Great "Red Menace": United Sates Prosecution of American Communists, 1947–1952.* Westport, Conn.: Greenwood Press, 1984.

CHAPTER EIGHT

Postwar United States

The Cold-War era encompassed a remarkable change in society—so much so that people living in the 1950s might well have concluded in the 1960s that they were no longer in the same country. In the 1950s, conformity ruled the nation, a result of the pressure exerted by corporate society for a malleable work force and a compliant consumer base and of the patriotic values stirred by the fight against communism.

Popular culture exhibited the conformity. Americans flocked to the speeches and writings of Norman Vincent Peale. A minister at the Marble Collegiate Reformed Church in New York City, Peale preached a feel-good Christianity devoid of any self-sacrifice or strong social consciousness. Philosopher Russell Kirk has said that it offered "little more than a vague spirit of friendliness." Peale's greatest fame came from his book *The Power of Positive Thinking* (1952). It reached the best-seller lists (and by 1974 had sold more than three million copies) based on a content that preached success through self-confidence and faith. With chapters such as "How to Get People to Like You," the book emphasized fitting in, making it a bible for 1950s conformity.

Bouyed by economic prosperity, Americans traveled more, both domestically and overseas. But as they did so, they indulged in the decade's conformist behavior. In the United States, they stayed at motel chains, most prominently Howard Johnson's and Holiday Inn. These companies prided themselves on buildings that everywhere looked the same—no surprises and no diverse experiences. Taking chances at the local eatery became less common, too, as McDonald's began to expand and offered a standardized menu at its fast-food outlets.

When Americans traveled abroad, they flew in planes staffed by women attendants called stewardesses. The airlines stressed conformity among them—they had to be young, white, and good-looking—a combination of sexual attractiveness and middle-class wholesomeness. Those who reached the ripe old age of 30 were dismissed, as were those who became overweight or pregnant. And travelers increasingly stayed at the Hilton Inn, a chain that promised that each of its hotels was a "little America."

Television broadcast programs watched by people throughout the country. It was possible to travel from one region to another and strike up a conversation with a stranger by discussing the latest episode of the hit comedy series *I Love Lucy*. Not only were Americans watching the same programs as their neighbors, they were also eating the same meals while glued to the tube—in 1953 Clarke and Gilbert Swanson introduced frozen TV dinners, and by 1955, they were selling 25 million of them a year.

Perhaps more than any other social development, suburbs bespoke the decade's conformity. In the 1940s, William Levitt and his brother acquired several thousand

> "Extremism in the defense of liberty is no vice. . . . moderation in the pursuit of justice is no virtue."
>
> Barry Goldwater, 1964

acres of farmland in Hempstead, Long Island, a short distance east of New York City, and began mass-producing houses. A two-bedroom Levittown Cape Cod sold for as low as $7,990, well within reach of middle-class families helped by low-cost, government-sponsored mortgages.

Suburban developments stretched mile after mile in sameness. The only way that Levitt and other developers could produce houses so cheaply was to make the house plans uniform—a buyer could make few, if any, changes in the house to be built, otherwise the rapid-pace construction would be disrupted and costs increased.

As much as Americans came together in a consumer community in the 1950s, they huddled together in fear of an atomic war. Fear of the A-bomb saturated popular culture, including print stories, movies, and TV shows. Fallout shelters even appeared in suburbia; *Life* magazine told of one that could be bought for $3,000. The federal government suggested that shelters could be designed to double as playrooms or family dens. Schools held regular A-bomb drills; in New York City, administrators issued millions of ID tags to students so they could be identified in the event of a nuclear attack.

In the 1950s, it was this sense of impending annihilation and smothering conformity that stimulated rebels and renegades, radicals and reactionaries. The radicals dreamed of jolting the country out of its smug conformity, of rallying it to confront social injustice, while reactionaries sought to protect "good old" American values against the radicals and against the "communist menace" of the Cold War. The civil rights movement intensified as blacks protested the contrast between the nation's vision of itself as the land of freedom and the practice of routine segregation based on race. Thus the 1955 Montgomery, Alabama, bus boycott gained national and international attention. At the opposite extreme, right-wingers such as Robert Welch attributed setbacks in the Cold War to a vast, domestic communist conspiracy and its fellow travelers, the civil-rights advocates and others who questioned society's traditional values.

The civil rights movement was the first sign of the countercultural upheaval to come in the 1960s. That young people would lead the charge became apparent on February 1, 1960, when four African-American college students began a sit-in at the F. W. Woolworth store in Greensboro, North Carolina, to protest its policy (standard throughout the South) of refusing to serve blacks at the lunch counter.

Later in the year, college students at the University of Michigan in Ann Arbor founded Students for a Democratic Society (SDS), which dedicated itself to making the United States more just through "participatory democracy." SDS gave rise to a New Left that, unlike the Old Left that had matured during the Great Depression of the 1930s, rejected ideological debates about capitalism and communism—at least until later in the 1960s. The New Left got its energy from calling attention to the contradictions within the United States, society that called itself democratic but oppressed its own citizens, a society that called itself humane but killed Asians by the hundreds of thousands in Vietnam.

In the 1960s, dissidents shook the very foundation of U.S. civil society; they protested the Vietnam War, advocated black power, pushed for women's liberation, promoted Chicano and Native American rights, and even, for an extremist few, embraced violent tactics and Marxist ideas as part of an effort to overthrow the federal government. This chapter discusses dissidents such as the Black Panthers, founded by Huey Newton and Bobby Seale in 1966; Malcolm X and his conversion from black nationalism to a more moderate civil rights program; Cesar Chavez and his campaign to organize Chicano migrant workers; Redstockings and their feminist view that male supremacy oppressed women; the Weather Underground and its revolutionary Marxism; the reactionary Minutemen who advocated violence, if necessary, to defend state's rights and individual liberty; and many others.

The challenges from the left, and the conservatives who opposed them, caused a rift between countercultural youths and mainstream society. President Richard Nixon worsened the rift when he appealed to what he called the "Silent Majority," or what *Time* magazine called "Middle Americans." *Time* defined this nebulous group as those who sported American-flag decals on their cars, wanted order in the streets, and opposed having their children bused to schools for desegregation. According to *Time*, "Middle Americans sing the national anthem at football games—and mean it." While Nixon's strategy aimed particularly at the South, it reached into all neighborhoods where Middle America reigned, primarily in suburbs across the country. As previous chapters in this book attest, dissent and protest have been integral to American society, from the Puritans who founded Massachusetts Bay to the civil rights crusaders who stood alongside Rosa Parks in Montgomery. Nevertheless, Nixon and other conservatives effectively portrayed the counterculture as an un-American rabble, an aberrant swarm intent on destroying everything that was good and decent about the United States. So intense was this feeling that when National Guard troops fired on anti-war protesters at Kent State University in Ohio in 1970, killing four of them, Nixon gave every indication that the protesters got what they had coming.

In the 1960s atmosphere of distrust, the U.S. government established a top-secret counter-intelligence program within the FBI, called COINTELPRO, to spy on protest groups, infiltrate them, and disrupt them. The government hoped that in the process it would be able to destroy these groups. COINTELPRO engaged in unethical and often illegal activities in what was a far-reaching assault on freedom of speech.

COINTELPRO leaked false information to newspapers, harassed financial contributors to various organizations, wiretapped phones, broke into homes and offices, and even encouraged and helped arrange political assassinations. But COINTELPRO was no aberration—it was part of widespread government efforts to attack and silence dissidents. Nixon, for example, had his group of "plumbers" that engaged in numerous blackbag operations, including breaking into the office of a psychologist frequented by a Vietnam War critic. And, under Conus Intel, or Continental U.S. Intelligence, the military kept dossiers on 25 million Americans.

With the conflict between dissidents and Middle America underway, the country was vastly different from 10 years earlier. So great was the change from the conformist 1950s, so extensive the turmoil, that the previous 10 years seemed much more than a decade past; it seemed like an eternity.

State Department Revokes Paul Robeson's Passport

The U.S. State Department revoked the passport of Paul Robeson, a prominent African-American singer and actor, after Robeson criticized the sending of United States troops to Korea. Authorities had been watching Robeson for years and disliked the leftward drift of his politics toward communism.

By 1950, Paul Robeson (1898–1976) had built a career marked by controversy, both on and off the stage. In 1923, he accepted the lead in a new Eugene O'Neill play, *All God's Chillun Got Wings*, a production that brought criticism for its topic of interracial marriage. Two years later, Robeson made his major singing debut in New York, performing black spirituals and folk songs; thanks to his widely acclaimed performances, he was offered a recording contract with the Victor Talking Machine Company. Even greater fame arrived in 1928, however, when he appeared in the musical *Show Boat* in London and sang "Ol' Man River."

The English loved Robeson, and in the 1930s, he made several movies for British film companies. In 1934 and again in 1936, he visited the Soviet Union and marveled at that country's lack of racism; he said that in Russia his dignity was restored. While there he studied Marxism and decided to send his son to a Russian school.

Robeson's first significant political involvement occurred in 1936, during the Spanish Civil War. Robeson declared his support for the Popular Front Republican forces fighting General Francisco Franco, who had overthrown the democratically elected Spanish government. Over the next three years, Robeson raised money for the Popular Front, only to see Franco win.

In September 1939, Robeson sang a stirring song, "Ballad for Americans," on national radio in the United States; it brought him his greatest fame and caused Americans to hail him as a true patriot. In 1946, Robeson visited with President Harry Truman and urged him to support a bill that would make the lynch-ing of blacks a federal crime. The meeting went poorly, with Robeson criticizing United States foreign policy and defend-ing the Soviet Union. That October, he appeared before the California Legislative Committee on Un-American Activities and testified that, although he was not a communist, he found much to support in their fight for equality. Several towns, including Peoria, Illinois, reacted by banning Robeson from using any of their public facilities for an appearance.

The following year, Robeson suspended his concert tours to campaign for the Progressive Party presidential can-didate, Henry Wallace. The Progressive Party adopted as its platform several proposals that historian David McCullough has labeled as "virtually no different from the Communist Party platform" in its "denunciation of the Marshall Plan, the Truman Doctrine, [and] the new draft law." Like the leaders of the Soviet Union, the Progressives called for the United States to destroy its nuclear weapons at a time when only the United States had them. In 1948, Robeson traveled through Europe and again condemned United States for-eign policy. The State Department and other government agencies began spying on him, and when he stated in 1949

Paul Robeson. (Library of Congress)

that African-Americans would never fight for the United States in a war against the Soviet Union, a barrage of criticism was heard from both whites and blacks.

As had happened earlier, Robeson's political beliefs and statements caused communities to forbid him from staging concerts, and under such pressure, the management company that handled his bookings canceled 85 of his scheduled shows. The bans became even more extensive after violence erupted at one of his outdoor concerts sponsored by trade unionists and pacifists in Peekskill, New York, in August 1949. Town residents had been greatly divided over his appearance; one who opposed letting him stage the concert had said in the *Peekskill Evening Star* that Robeson and those who were backing him were subversives, and that "if we have not forgotten [World War II], let us cooperate with the American Legion and similar veteran organizations and vehemently oppose their appearance." As events unfolded, legionnaires, joined by the Ku Klux Klan, led a rampaging mob stirred into action not only by Robeson's political views, but also by his race. One eyewitness reported that some in the mob demanded, "Give us Robeson. We'll string that nigger up!" Many cities looked at the riot that had erupted at Peekskill and feared that any show that featured Robeson would result in bloodshed.

In 1950, Robeson criticized Truman for sending troops to Korea. Speaking about African-Americans before a civil rights rally in the United States, the singer said, "They will know that if we don't stop our armed adventure in Korea today—tomorrow it will be Africa. . . . I have said it before and say it again, that the place for the Negro people to fight for their freedom is here at home." When the State Department responded by revoking Robeson's passport, a move that prevented him from traveling overseas, an official explained that "the Department considers that Robeson's travel abroad at this time would be contrary to the best interests of the United States." With the Red Scare under way, during which even mild liberal ideas could be attacked as communist, organizations were reluctant to defend Robeson or, indeed, to be even remotely affiliated with him. At the same time, the FBI intensified its surveillance of the singer, which it had begun in the early 1940s.

Under attack from the right and abandoned by most of the left, Robeson endured tremendous strain. Robeson regained his passport in 1958 when the Supreme Court declared such suspensions unconstitutional, and he staged concerts in England and other European countries. Shortly afterward, he stayed at an East Berlin sanatorium to receive treatment for physical and emotional problems. He returned to the United States in 1963 only to find that many Americans still shunned him.

The civil rights movement, however, rehabilitated his image, praising him as a fighter for freedom; in 1965, several black actors and writers held a salute in his honor. In 1973, they were joined by civil rights leaders in staging a birthday celebration for him at Carnegie Hall in New York City. Still, Robeson generated controversy. For those on the left, he had become a martyr; but for many Americans he remained saddled by his reputation as an extremist. For them, he continued to bear the Cold War label of disloyalty, a man who had sacrificed his great stage talent to an unpatriotic radicalism.

Further Reading
Duberman, Martin B. *Paul Robeson.* New York: Knopf, 1989.
Robeson, Paul. *Here I Stand.* Boston: Beacon Press, 1958.
Stewart, Jeffrey C., ed. *Paul Robeson: Artist and Citizen.* New Brunswick, N.J.: Rutgers University Press, 1998.

Puerto Rican Nationalists Try to Assassinate President Truman   1950

Gunfire erupted in Washington, D.C., on November 1, 1950, when two Puerto Rican nationalists, Griselio Torresola and Oscar Collazo, tried to kill President Harry Truman. Their attempt came amid a wave of violence by those wanting independence for Puerto Rico.

The afternoon of November 1, a Wednesday, found Truman staying at Blair House while the White House was being remodeled. It was an unusually hot day and a momentous one: Truman had just learned that Communist Chinese troops had entered the fight against U.S. troops on the Korean peninsula.

Shortly after 2:00 P.M., Torresola (1930–50), age 20, and Collazo (1914–94), age 36, both dressed in suits, approached Blair House from opposite directions. While Torresola talked to one of the guards stationed in a booth, Collazo walked up to the front steps, pulled a pistol from his pocket, and shot another guard, Donald Birdzell. Wounded in the leg, Birdzell struggled to the street so he could divert Collazo's attention away from Blair House. By then, gunfire was filling the air as the president's guards reacted. Torresola was shot through the head and died immediately; one guard, shot in the chest and the stomach, later died at a hospital. Collazo was also shot in the chest and lay face down on the sidewalk.

Some later reports stated that, on hearing the gunfire, Truman had rushed to his upstairs window to see what was happening and stayed there until someone on the sidewalk below shouted, "Get back! Get back!" But a secret service agent assigned to protect the president, Floyd Boring, discounted that story. Boring stated: "The problem is, that these fellows are never at the scene who always make up these reports, you know. They had President Truman coming to the window upstairs, and I'm supposed to have waved and told him to go back. But he never showed up there."

Torresola and Collazo were both militants who wanted their homeland to be free from U.S. rule. Their plot to kill Truman was not an isolated case of violence; other radicals launched assaults aimed at placing greater pressure on the federal government to meet their nationalist demands. On October 30, six of them had tried to shoot their way into La Fortaleza, the governor's residence in San Juan, yelling the slogan "Viva Puerto Rico Libre." Concurrently, Puerto Rican uprisings were staged in New York City. Many Puerto Rican nationalists, however, denounced the violence and called it counterproductive.

Collazo was sentenced to death for the assassination attempt and slated for execution in 1952, but Truman commuted his sentence to life in prison. In 1979, President Jimmy Carter commuted the life sentence, and Collazo was released. He died in February 1994 at 80 years of age. Many Puerto Ricans continue to aspire to independence, but in the 1950s, the movement was greatly damaged by the violence.

Further Reading

Heine, Jorge, and Juan M. García-Passalacqua. *The Puerto Rican Question.* New York: Foreign Policy Association, 1984.
McCullough, David G. *Truman.* New York: Simon & Schuster, 1992.
Raskin, Jonah. *Oscar Collazo: Portrait of a Puerto Rican Patriot.* New York: New York Committee to Free the Puerto Rican Nationalist Prisoners, 1978.

1953 *Dissent* Offers a Socialist Alternative

As Senator Joseph McCarthy launched his hunt for communists, New York intellectual Irving Howe responded in 1953 by cofounding and editing the magazine Dissent. *Socialist in outlook,* Dissent *offered the left wing an alternative to flaccid liberalism and authoritarian communism.*

Howe (1920–93) was born in New York City and earned a bachelor's degree at the City College of New York before taking graduate courses at Brooklyn College. He had been a socialist since he was a teenager; after World War II, he wrote for *Partisan Review, Commentary,* and other leftist publications. Howe believed that in the face of McCarthyism and the country's overall turn to the right in the early 1950s, intellectuals in general, and liberals in particular, had cowered and had shaped their views to the conformist times. He wrote that "intellectual freedom . . . is under severe attack and the intellectuals have . . . shown a painful lack of militancy" in standing up to McCarthy.

Yet in promoting socialism, Howe neither gave a concrete definition of the word nor expected social-ism to replace the corporate capitalist system. For him, socialism was an evolving set of ideals that he hoped would prod people to reform society. He compared it to religious ideals—no one was expected to live up to all of them all of the time, but people were expected to *strive* to live up to them.

Contributors to *Dissent* attacked the inequities of capitalist society, but they also criticized the tyran-ny overseas that often posed as socialism, for example, the dictatorial regime in the Soviet Union. Writing in *Atlantic* magazine in January 1998, Nathan Glick observed that "the position [the *Dissent* writers] took was that socialism could not be said to have failed; it had simply never been tried, because, in Howe's words, 'there can be no socialism without democracy.' "

Indeed, *Dissent* debated the possibilities of developing socialism while avoiding totalitarianism. Throughout, the magazine's writers expressed faith in democracy, and when the 1950s gave way to the revolutionary fervor of the 1960s counterculture, *Dissent* rejected the leftist extremists who embraced such communist dictators as Cuba's Fidel Castro, China's Mao Zedong, and North Vietnam's Ho Chi Minh.

Writing *The Sixties: Years of Hope, Days of Rage* (1993), Todd Gitlin states that *Dissent* was "harsh-toned" and "prided itself on its freedom from illusion, its ability to face what Howe later called the 'sheer terribleness of our time.' " In short, the magazine offered a utopian vision cast in a realistic evaluation of the era. In so doing, *Dissent* attracted younger intellectuals who formed the lifeblood of the civil rights and antiwar protests that marked the 1960s and 1970s.

Further Reading
Alexander, Edward. *Irving Howe: Socialist, Critic, Jew.* Bloomington: Indiana University Press, 1998.
Howe, Irving. *A Critic's Notebook.* Edited and introduced by Nicholas Howe. New York: Harcourt Brace, 1994.

Blacks in Montgomery, Alabama, Boycott the City's Buses 1955

The Montgomery bus boycott of 1955 did more than shake up a single city; it exposed the deep racism in American society, gave birth to a more activist civil rights movement, and propelled Martin Luther King, Jr., to the forefront of black leadership.

The bus boycott originated from a sudden but not wholly unexpected event. On the evening of December 1, 1955, Rosa Parks (1913–), a black seamstress, tired from a long day at work, boarded a Montgomery bus. Soon the front of the bus filled with whites, and the driver, James Blake, turned around and ordered the black passengers to move to the back.

Several obeyed Blake. Parks, however, remained seated, whereupon Blake demanded she move, and Parks refused. He then called the police, and they removed her from the bus. "Why do you all push us around?" Parks asked one of the policemen. "I don't know," he answered, "but the law is the law, and you're under arrest."

Parks had wanted to ride home in peace; she never intended to become the "test case" in chal-lenging the segregation law for the National Association for the Advancement of Colored People (NAACP). But she neither wanted to give in to Blake, whom she detested, nor compromise her princi-ples. She later explained:

These other persons had got on the bus after I did. It meant that I didn't have a right to do any-thing but get on the bus, give them my fare, and then be pushed wherever they wanted me. . . . There had to be a stopping place, and this seemed to have been the place for me to stop being pushed around and to find out what human rights I had, if any.

Rosa Parks being fingerprinted in Montgomery, Alabama. (Library of Congress)

The Montgomery chapter of the NAACP had earlier decided to challenge the city's segregated bus system. The indignity that African-Americans had suffered over the years by being forced to give up their seats to white riders when the "whites only" section of a bus overflowed hurt all the more with the realization that blacks made up 70 percent of the riders and were thus the economic lifeblood of the city's public transportation system.

When in March 1955 15-year-old Claudette Colvin was riding home from high school and was arrested for violating the segregation law, it looked as if the NAACP had the case it could use to challenge the city in court. But the group's leaders refused to pursue it—the girl, it turned out, was short-tempered, unwed, and pregnant. To have her stand trial would damage the NAACP in its attempt to influence public opinion. "They'd call her a bad girl," Parks recalled, "and her case wouldn't have a chance."

A few weeks later, in summer of 1955, Parks attended the Highlander Folk School, near Chattanooga, Tennessee. Founded to protest social injustice, the school taught Gandhian nonviolent resistance and encouraged blacks and whites to use such tactics in fighting for civil rights. Primed for a protest, Parks was ready to do battle, though her decision to stay in her seat on December 1, 1955, was neither planned ahead of time nor thought of by her as the beginning of a civil rights challenge.

Yet her arrest energized the black community. As her case headed for court, an even more significant development occurred: under the guidance of E. D. Nixon, the Montgomery NAACP decided to boycott Montgomery's buses.

Nixon and his colleagues recruited a young African-American Baptist preacher, Martin Luther King, Jr., to lead the boycott and formed a special organization to coordinate it, the Montgomery Improvement Association (MIA). The protesters made modest demands, stopping short of calling for complete desegregation of the buses. But the city refused them, and on February 1, 1956, the MIA said it wanted the buses integrated.

The bus boycott was perilous. Those who joined it—and nearly all African-Americans did—risked losing their jobs, being harassed by the police, and being physically attacked. King's house was bombed, and dynamite was tossed onto the lawn of Nixon's home. Parks was fired from her job, yet she persevered and helped coordinate the boycott.

On November 13, 1956, the U.S. Supreme Court declared bus segregation unconstitutional, and on December 21, the city of Montgomery complied with the ruling. The boycott achieved a milestone victory in the fight for civil rights and took the movement into a larger realm of public protest through boycotts and demonstrations.

Further Reading

Brinkley, Douglas. *Rosa Parks*. New York: Penguin Books, 2000.

Parks, Rosa, with Jim Haskins. *Rosa Parks: My Story*. New York: Dial Books, 1992.

Willis Carto Founds Anti-Semitic Organization, the Liberty Lobby

1955

A virulent anti-Semite and racist, Willis Carto founded the Liberty Lobby in 1955; he claimed that he did not hate Jews but wanted to fight Zionists. Over the next two decades, his magazine The Spotlight *reached a circulation of about 200,000.*

In the 1950s, Carto (1926–) associated with the numerous organizations and leaders then coming out of the intolerant side of the anticommunist movement, and, for a brief period, he helped edit *Right*, an anti-Semitic newsletter. Carto was greatly influenced by *Imperium*, a book written in 1949 by Francis Parker Yockey, a law graduate of Notre Dame. Yockey envisioned a future in which science would serve technology and Jews would be controlled by an authoritarian government. He called Jews the destroyers of civilization and dedicated *Imperium* to the "Hero of the Second World War," meaning Adolph Hitler. Carto sold the book through the Liberty Lobby and added a 35-page introduction to it.

The formation of the Liberty Lobby was seminal in the far-right hate movement. Many of those who monitor intolerance in the United States credit the Liberty Lobby with doing more than any other group to promote racism and anti-Semitism from the mid-1950s into the 1970s. Scholar Frank Mintz has said that "structurally the Lobby was a most unusual umbrella organization catering to constituencies spanning the fringes of Neo-Nazism to the John Birch Society and the radical right. It was not truly paramilitary in the manner of the Ku Klux Klan and Nazis, but was more accurately an intermediary between racist paramilitary factions and the recent right."

Carto accompanied his anti-Semitic rhetoric with a blistering attack on blacks. He complained in the 1950s that "only a few Americans are concerned about the inevitable niggrefication of America." In his introduction to *Imperium* he wrote: "Negro equality . . . is easier to believe in if there are no Negroes around to destroy the concept."

The Spotlight contained articles that praised the White Patriot Party for its true Americanism, attacked civil rights leader Martin Luther King, Jr., as a communist, and defended the actions of the Ku Klux Klan and neo-Nazis. In the pages of *The Spotlight*, Carto blamed the outbreak of World War II on Jews and asserted that the Nazi Holocaust had never occurred. Carto's statements provided a hate-filled litany:

If Satan himself . . . had tried to create a . . . force for the destruction of the nations, he could have done no better than to invent the Jews.

Hitler's defeat was the defeat of Europe and of America. . . . The blame . . . must be laid at the door of the international Jews.

A German victory [in World War II] would have assured that the life-span of the White world would have been extended for many centuries more than now seems likely; indeed, for the "thousand years" promised by Hitler.

The Spotlight added to these attacks a barrage of warnings about the development of a one-world government that would destroy individual liberty.

In 1966, Carto bought control of the magazine *American Mercury*, founded many years earlier, and converted it to an anti-Semitic publication, while his Noontide Press offered books crafted for a bigot's taste. *Our Nordic Race* told about "threats to Nordic survival"; *The Testing of Negro Intelligence* derided the supposedly anemic performance of blacks on IQ tests; and *The Road Back* gave instructions to "white patriots" on how to mine roads and blow up bridges.

Carto created the Institute for Historical Review (IHR) in 1979, dedicated to disproving the Holocaust. Based in California, the IHR recruited historians and the general public through materials it called "revisionist." Carto called reports of the Holocaust "atrocity propaganda," and the IHR held annual conventions that brought together anti-Semites dedicated to the organization's mission. The *Journal of Historical Review* was founded by Carto to provide the IHR with a forum that looked academic and legitimate.

Carto founded the "modern" Populist Party in 1984, taking the name of the party begun in the late 1800s, but stressing white racism and anti-Semitism. In 1988, former KKK member David Duke ran as its presidential candidate, though by that time the party was torn by factional disputes revolving around Carto's dictatorial style. Conflict continued to surround Carto in the 1990s and brought disarray to his hate empire. A controversy over his handling of stock worth several million dollars caused the IHR to turn against him and in 1993 fire him. Carto reacted by founding *The Barnes Review* (named after a Nazi sympathizer) to compete with the *Journal of Historical Review.*

In 1998 he and a partner, Todd Blodgett, acquired Resistance Records, a neo-Nazi recording company that produced white power rock, along with *Resistance* magazine, both previously operated by Tom Metzger's White Aryan Resistance. The *Washington Post* described Resistance Records as "vehemently anti-government and racist." One year later, however, Carto's continuing legal battles with the IHR forced him to declare bankruptcy and sell his shares of the Resistance Records, which was purchased by William Pierce, leader of the neo-Nazi National Alliance. Shortly thereafter, the Liberty Lobby announced it would disband—though it actually continued some activities—and in 2001 *The Spotlight* suspended publication. Several years earlier, the Simon Wiesenthal Center had called Carto "the most influential professional anti-Semite in the United States."

Further Reading

Mintz, Frank P. *The Liberty Lobby and the American Right: Race, Conspiracy, and Culture.* Westport, Conn.: Greenwood Press, 1985.

1958 Robert Welch Begins the John Birch Society to Fight a "Communist Conspiracy"

An operator of a candy company who became convinced during the Cold War that communist traitors in the United States were selling out the country, Robert Welch founded the right-wing John Birch Society in 1958 to turn back the advancing "Red Tide."

As a child, Robert Welch (1899–1985) exhibited a precocious intellect. He learned to read when he was three years old, knew basic algebra at age six, and received his high school diploma at age 12. He entered the University of North Carolina at Chapel Hill in 1912 and graduated in the top third of his class in 1916. Then began a period of searching and dissatisfaction—he served a stint at the U.S. Naval Academy and attended Harvard Law School, among others—until he entered the candy business in 1921 by buying a fudge recipe from a candy store owner. Welch operated the Oxford Candy Company from a loft in Cambridge, Massachusetts. The business was moderately successful until the Great Depression ruined it.

In 1932, Welch joined the staff of the country's largest candy manufacturer, E. J. Brach. Two years later, he quit to become sales manager and vice president of his brother's candy business, the James O. Welch Company. Under his guidance, the company's sales increased from $20,000 in 1935 to $20 million in 1956.

During that time Welch wrote *The Road to Salesmanship* (1941), and, on a visit to England, he studied and criticized socialism. With the advent of the Cold War his conservatism hardened, and he made his one and only run for public office in 1950 when he campaigned in Massachusetts for lieutenant governor as a Republican. He attracted a sizable vote but was defeated.

In 1952, Welch joined the presidential campaign of Ohio Senator Robert A. Taft, but Taft lost the Republican nomination to General Dwight D. Eisenhower. That year, Welch wrote *May God Forgive Us*, a searing criticism of President Harry Truman's decision to dismiss General Douglas MacArthur from his command of United Nations forces in Korea.

Disheartened and angered by the communist advances in China and eastern Europe, Welch blamed the reverses on traitors operating within the United States. In 1954 he wrote *The Life of John Birch*, a patriotic story whose title referred to an American military intelligence officer who had been killed by the Chinese communists 10 days after World War II had ended. Welch portrayed him as "the first casualty of World War III."

Welch retired from the candy business in 1958 to fight communism full time; at a meeting in Indianapolis, Indiana, he and 11 other men founded the John Birch Society, named for the intelligence officer and dedicated to "less government, more individual responsibility, and a better world." Welch once said that most Americans fell into one of four categories: "Communists, Communist dupes or sympathizers, the uninformed who have yet to be awakened to the Communist danger, and the ignorant."

The many accusations he made in the late 1950s and early 1960s ran the gamut of right-wing extremism. He declared President Eisenhower to be "a dedicated conscious agent of the Communist conspiracy," and said of the president's brother, Milton Eisenhower, that "the chances are very strong that [he] is actually Dwight Eisenhower's superior boss within the Communist Party." He called Secretary of State John Foster Dulles and CIA Director Allen W. Dulles "tools of Communism."

Welch opposed civil rights programs, calling them a communist plot, and for that same reason he wanted the Supreme Court's decisions ending racial segregation in public schools to be overturned by a constitutional amendment. And he wanted the United States to withdraw from the North Atlantic Treaty Organization and the United Nations. In 1960, he claimed in his monthly magazine, *American Opinion*, that 40-to-60 percent of the United States was under communist control.

The influence of the John Birch Society peaked in the mid-1960s. At that time, the organization had about 85,000 to 100,000 members in 4,000 chapters; it had 270 employees at its headquarters in Belmont, Massachusetts, and an annual budget in the range of $5-to-8 million; moreover, it had a publishing house, a radio program, and 400 bookstores. In 1964, it gained entry into the inner circles of the Republican Party with the nomination of archconservative Barry Goldwater for president.

But the more Welch's views became known, the more they were scrutinized. If free speech promotes a marketplace for ideas, then the value of Welch's ideas began to plummet. He was widely labeled as extreme, even lunatic; as a result, he was deserted by most conservative Republicans. Welch tried at one point to modify his assessment of Eisenhower, claiming that he never called him a communist, but only a dupe of the communists. Nevertheless, Welch continued propagating his fantastical theories; in the November 1966 issue of *American Opinion*, he claimed that the communist conspiracy was part of a 200-year-old plot by a secret group, called the Illuminati, to rule the world.

The John Birch Society still exists, directing its ire less toward communist threats and more toward perceived one-world government schemes that would trample the independence of the United States. Birchers want the United States to get out of the United Nations (as they have advocated for years), which they claim aims to take away guns, the military, and private property. The Society insists that "our common bond is a love for liberty and our rejection of totalitarianism in any form." But its intolerance for opposing views, especially liberal ones, bespeaks a goal less attached to liberty and more attached to an authoritarian mentality.

Further Reading

Broyles, J. Allen. *The John Birch Society: Anatomy of a Protest.* Boston: Beacon Press, 1964.

Griffin, G. Edward. *The Life and Words of Robert Welch, Founder of the John Birch Society.* Thousand Oaks, Calif.: American Media, 1975.

Hardisty, Jean. *Mobilizing Resentment: Conservative Resurgence from the John Birch Society to the Promise Keepers.* Boston: Beacon Press, 1999.

1960 Student Non-Violent Coordinating Committee Rallies Young People to the Civil Rights Movement

The Student Non-Violent Coordinating Committee (SNCC) emerged in 1960 from sit-in demonstrations begun by black college students in Greensboro, North Carolina, to protest racial segregation. Within a few short years, SNCC changed from fighting for civil rights to fighting for black power, and, as it did so, it embraced the use of violence.

On February 2, 1960, the *New York Times* reported: "A group of well-dressed Negro college students staged a sit-down strike in a downtown Woolworth store . . . and vowed to continue it in relays until Negroes were served at the lunch counter." The day before, Ezell Blair, Jr., Franklin McClain, Joseph McNeill, and David Richmond, freshmen at North Carolina Agricultural and Technical College, a local all-black school, had begun the sit-down, or sit-in. They had acted out of disgust with the racist policy at the five-and-dime store, but also out of anger that segregation remained entrenched throughout much of the South—despite several rulings by the Supreme Court, and the efforts of Martin Luther King, Jr., and others to secure civil rights.

The four young protesters stayed at the lunch counter until it closed, one hour later. They returned the next day, along with 27 other students; on day three, the number increased to 63; on day four, to 100; and by week's end some 1,000 protesters were descending on Woolworth's and the nearby S. H. Kress store. Over the next two weeks, African-Americans repeated the Greensboro strategy in 15 cities across five southern states.

As the protests spread, Ella Baker (1903–86), the 57-year-old executive director of King's Southern Christian Leadership Conference (SCLC), saw an opportunity to mobilize youths for the civil rights movement and to encourage aggressive tactics. According to Joanne Grant in *Ella Baker: Freedom Bound* (1998), "To Ella Baker it was a dream come true. Here was the beginning of the civil rights revolution which she had looked forward to."

Baker convinced the SCLC to sponsor a meeting of the protest leaders, and she arranged for her alma mater, Shaw University in Raleigh, North Carolina, to provide the facilities. The meeting began in April 1960; Baker expected about 100 students, but more than 200 attended. The students expressed impatience with the leading civil rights groups for having relied too heavily on legal proceedings; they wanted quicker results through civil disobedience, and they wanted more than token gains. They respected King, but feared that he would manipulate them.

At Baker's suggestion, they formed a Temporary Student Non-Violent Coordinating Committee with a structure separate from the SCLC. Here began what Grant calls "a new phase of the civil rights movement." She writes: "It was no longer to be controlled by a stodgy ministerial or bureaucratic presence. It was to be led by a new force."

In October, the students declared SNCC a permanent organization. While they voiced nonviolent ideas similar to those held by King, they distrusted strong leadership by any one individual and relied on their youthful enthusiasm for motivation along with an almost romantic faith in their ability to change society. SNCC thought King too stodgy, and, according to Terry Anderson in *The Movement and the Sixties* (1995), "The organization . . . aimed to revolutionize the [civil rights] struggle by inciting so many demonstrations across the South that America would realize that inequality was not just a southern problem, but a national one." SNCC's chairman, Charles McDew, expressed the group's confidence—even bravado—and its intent to proceed when he said, "Instead of sitting idly by, taking the leavings of a sick and decadent society, we have seized the initiative, and already the walls have begun to crumble."

At that time, few African-Americans in the South could vote, so in August 1961, SNCC opened its first voter registration school in McComb, Mississippi. Whites in the state reacted violently, beating blacks and their white supporters. In 1964, SNCC began a bigger campaign to register blacks, called Mississippi Freedom Summer. Many in the civil rights movement believed the effort would produce a white backlash and damage the reelection chances of President Lyndon Johnson, a man they liked because he had convinced Congress to pass strong civil rights legislation.

SNCC rejected that argument; instead, its more radical members made clear that they would challenge racism without regard for how it might affect traditional politics. During the Mississippi Freedom Summer, more than 1,000 volunteers worked on voter registration and established the Mississippi Freedom Democratic Party (MFDP) to challenge the existing, lily-white Democratic Party.

The volunteers included white college students from the North, and many blacks in SNCC soon resented them for trying to dominate the voter campaign. Within SNCC a struggle erupted between those who saw the whites as valuable, and those who believed SNCC programs should be exclusively in black hands.

The voter drive took a tragic turn when racists killed three volunteers outside Philadelphia, Mississippi—Michael Schwerener and Andrew Goodman, two white youths from New York, and James Chaney, a black youth from Mississippi—all of whom were working for another civil rights group, the Congress of Racial Equality. That the FBI only investigated the crime primarily because whites had been murdered infuriated SNCC, as did the FBI's refusal to protect civil rights workers. The failure of the summer project to register a large number of black voters added to the anger among SNCC members.

The Generation Gap and Counterculture Radicalism

Radicalism is often thought of as the province of the young; it reflects a youthful discontent with society and a drive to change that which is unjust. To a great extent, this generalization holds true for people when they first become activists—the initial foray usually occurs early in a person's life, before middle age. Numerous examples can be found in these pages, such as the working women who walked out of the textile mills in Lowell, Massachusetts (see entry, 1834); the suffragists who picketed outside the White House (see entry, 1917); and the workers who staged the Great Flint Sit-down (see entry, 1934). (There are of course numerous exceptions, as when Betty Friedan published *The Feminine Mystique* [see entry, 1963] at 42 years of age.)

The countercultural radicalism of the 1960s especially owed its development to young people, for its foundation was the enormous population of young people—the baby boom that began in 1946 and continued through 1964. In 1946 alone, 3.4 million babies were born, or one every nine seconds. The live birthrate per 1,000 women aged 15 to 44 jumped from 82.2 in 1945 to 110.1 in 1947, when total births reached a record 3,817,000. More people were born between 1947 and 1953 than in the previous 30 years, and in 1954, the number of births topped four million for the first time.

Many of the counterculture's radical leaders were born before the boom—Al Haber, the founder of SDS (see entry, 1960); Bobby Seale, cofounder of the Black Panthers (see entry, 1966); Abbie Hoffman, cofounder of the Yippies (see entry, 1967)—but they ultimately drew on the tremendous pool of young people for support. The counterculture itself was grounded in the country's infatuation with youth that extended from fashion, to rock music, to protests in the streets.

Soon, SNCC began recommending that blacks working in the voter drive arm themselves for protection. The failure of King and other civil rights leaders to back more strongly the MFDP when it tried to unseat white delegates from Mississippi at the 1964 Democratic National Convention, along with riots in the Watts ghetto of Los Angeles in 1964, the 1965 assassination of Malcolm X (see entries, 1948 and 1964), and the widening war in Vietnam, produced a sense of urgency and crisis.

In January 1966, SNCC condemned the Vietnam War; the U.S. government, SNCC claimed, was protecting an illegitimate regime in South Vietnam while doing nothing to protect blacks in America. The following year SNCC declared itself dedicated to protecting human rights throughout the world. As such, it pledged to support struggles against colonialism, racism, and economic exploitation.

By that time, SNCC had rejected its earlier commitment to nonviolence and had kicked out its white members. The group's leader, Stokely Carmichael, talked about killing police, or "offing pigs," and his successor, H. Rap Brown, talked about going to war against whites. SNCC promoted black power, an amorphous but militant movement that African-American leader Floyd McKissick defined as "putting power in black people's hands." He said, "We don't have any, and we want some."

When SNCC radicalized, mainstream civil rights groups and white financial backers deserted it. At the same time, the U.S. government infiltrated and harassed it, with undercover agents stirring it to more extreme measures. In the early 1970s, SNCC collapsed. One member recalled that the group had nurtured "a vision of a revolution beyond race, against other forms of injustice, challenging the value-system of the nation and of smug middle-class society everywhere."

Further Reading

Grant, Joanne. *Ella Baker: Freedom Bound.* New York: Wiley, 1998.

Carson, Clayborne. *In Struggle: SNCC and the Black Awakening of the 1960s.* Cambridge, Mass.: Harvard University Press, 1981.

Sitkoff, Harvard. *The Struggle for Black Equality, 1954–1980.* New York: Hill and Wang, 1981.

Zinn, Howard. *SNCC: The New Abolitionists.* Westport, Conn.: Greenwood Press, 1985.

1960 Students for a Democratic Society Forms as the Vanguard of the New Left

Centered on college campuses, Students for a Democratic Society (SDS) challenged conservatives and liberals alike in attacking social injustices and the Vietnam War. SDS developed such an intensive revolutionary consciousness that Life *magazine proclaimed: "Never in the history of this country has a small group, standing outside the pale of conventional power, made such an impact or created such havoc."*

SDS emerged in 1960 from the League for Industrial Democracy, an old liberal organization that had done battle in the 1930s on behalf of labor unions. Led by Al Haber, a student at the University of Michigan (UM), younger activists within the League founded SDS as part of a resurgent college Left. Nationally, the expanding student population provided a recruiting base for SDS, and the civil rights movement stirred social consciousness. The oppression faced by blacks and their white supporters convinced many liberal students that American society had fallen far short of the patriotic ideals that they had learned in elementary and high school.

Into 1962, the organization remained largely a two-person operation run by Haber (its first president) and Tom Hayden, editor of the student newspaper at UM. To expand its reach, SDS decided to more forcefully support the civil rights drive in the South, thus earning recognition on college campuses as a group concerned with social injustice. SDS gained additional members when President John Kennedy hesitated in his support of a black voting rights drive, causing some college students to distrust the government's leaders. These students believed that liberals differed little from conservatives in protecting a corrupt Cold War state. Hayden pronounced liberalism bankrupt and described it as little more than a smile on the face of conservatism.

In June 1962, SDS held its national meeting at Port Huron, Michigan, near Detroit. There the delegates produced the Port Huron Statement, a wordy, cumbersome document that took society to task for its moral impoverishment and oppression. The Port Huron Statement called for greater individual rights and a participatory democracy that would diminish the power of the corporate elite and government bureaucrats and place more power in local communities. The document committed SDS to building a leftist base among college students. "We are people of this generation," the statement said, "bred in at least modest comfort, housed now in universities, looking uncomfortably to the world we inherit." The statement continued:

> We would replace power rooted in possession, privilege, or circumstance by power and uniqueness rooted in love, reflectiveness, reason, and creativity. . . . We seek the establishment of a democracy of individual participation, governed by two central aims: that the individual share in those social decisions determining the quality and direction of his life; that society be organized to encourage independence in men and provide the media for their common participation.

In 1964, SDS launched its Economic Research and Action Project (ERAP) by sending dedicated SDSers into urban ghettos to help the poor. The following year, SDS participated in protests against the Vietnam War and sponsored a march on Washington that attracted 25,000 people—the largest peace demonstration in America up to that time. Consequently, SDS gained additional prominence on campuses, with more than 50 chapters and several hundred members, and moved toward using confrontation as part of its belief that power must be met with power.

SDS failed to build a strong, cohesive national structure, partly because it wanted to remain open to diverse ideologies and partly because it let local chapters take the lead in formulating agendas. At the same time, foes of the antiwar movement targeted SDS. Senator John Stennis of Mississippi proclaimed that the government needed to destroy the group and "grind it to bits." Nevertheless, by the end of 1965 SDS had expanded to 124 chapters with more than 4,000 members.

When President Lyndon Johnson announced his plan that year to end draft exemptions for college students, SDSers, who supported draft resistance, saw an opportunity to recruit yet more college students. They believed that a real chance existed to create a generation of committed radicals. In 1966, SDS organized no fewer than six sizable protests on campuses aimed at the military.

SDS took the lead in sponsoring a mass draft card burning in New York City on April 15, 1967. With the group's membership reaching 30,000, some SDS members began talking about the need for sweeping changes in U.S. institutions and saw themselves as the vanguard of a revolutionary movement. But others saw their mandate as more limited—primarily geared to ending the Vietnam War, rather than fomenting widespread rebellion—thus an already weak organizational structure came under greater pressure.

In spring 1968, an SDS chapter helped lead a student protest at Columbia University, during which 1,000 students occupied five buildings. The action stimulated a surge in student protests, even at normally quiet colleges, such as Stanford University, the University of Miami, and Northwestern University. That year, Bernardine Dohrn won election as SDS interorganizational national secretary and proclaimed herself a "revolutionary communist." Dohrn was a recent graduate of the University of Chicago law school and had represented the protesters arrested at Columbia before joining the occupation herself.

With the 1968 Democratic National Convention preparing to open in Chicago (see entry, 1968), SDS at first opposed plans by several groups to stage a massive protest. The group was more interested in diversifying beyond the war issue; its vice president said: "We must deal with questions of power rather than act out our generational alienation." Nevertheless, several current and former SDS members participated in the protest, and, when the police resorted to controlling the crowd by bashing heads, SDS membership boomed to more than 100,000. Many young people looked at the events in Chicago and concluded that those in power had declared war on them.

But SDS membership soon declined, a victim of factions fighting for control, and many members rejecting the organization's radicalism. One faction called itself Weatherman (see entry, 1969). Led by Dohrn, Weatherman sought to advance communism through violent revolution, and the group called on America's youth to escalate their struggle at home as a way of showing unity with worldwide liberation movements and creating a rearguard action against the U.S. government that would bring about its downfall.

SDS, now barely more than a skeletal organization, officially rejected Dohrn and her followers, but the formation of Weatherman, along with the infiltration and harassment of SDS by government agents, so shattered the group that in 1970 it collapsed, passing from the scene just as the decade to which it had linked its hopes came to an end.

Years later, one SDS member recalled how the group had felt at the writing of the Port Huron Statement. "It was exalting. We thought that we knew what had to be done, and that we were going to do it."

Further Reading

Gitlin, Todd. *The Sixties: Years of Hope, Days of Rage.* New York: Bantam, 1987.

Hayden, Tom. *Reunion: A Memoir.* New York: Random House, 1988.

Miller, Douglas T. *Democracy Is in the Streets: From Port Huron to the Siege of Chicago.* New York: Simon & Schuster, 1989.

Sale, Kirkpatrick. *SDS.* New York: Vintage, 1973.

1960 Robert DePugh Founds the Minutemen

Disgusted with the rise of Fidel Castro to power in Cuba and influenced by literature issued by the right-wing John Birch Society (see entry, 1958) and the ideology behind the House Un-American Activities Committee, Robert DePugh (1923–) began the Minutemen as a militia group in Norborne, Missouri.

Prior to forming the Minutemen in 1960, DePugh was a chronic failure. He had enlisted in the U.S. army during World War II, only to be dismissed for nervousness and depression. He enrolled at Kansas State University in 1946 but quit a few months later. He then skipped from one job to another until he founded a dog food supplement company in 1953. Three years later that folded; there followed a short stint at Washburn University in Topeka, Kansas, before DePugh reactivated his business in the town of Norborne, Missouri, and developed the idea to found the Minutemen.

DePugh described the Minutemen as dedicated to stopping enemies within the United States who were seeking to advance communism. In choosing the name for his group, he referred back to the American Revolution and the Minutemen militia that fought against the British at Lexington and Concord. As with other militia leaders in post–World War II America, DePugh considered himself and his followers to be true patriots, ordinary citizens willing to sacrifice their lives for the freedoms they loved, as had those gallant farmers in the Revolution.

DePugh's vision for the Minutemen was multifaceted: it was to be a guerrilla outfit ready to fight communists, a nationwide spy network reporting on treasonous activity, and a propaganda outfit distributing literature that talked about the international socialist conspiracy and showed how to make bombs and ammunition. He said that he wanted to provoke the federal government—which he considered to be under the control of communist sympathizers—into repressive measures that would, in turn, cause the people to rise up against it. He edited the Minutemen newsletter, *Taking Aim*, which in 1964 advised its readers: "If you are ever going to buy a gun, buy it now."

That same year, DePugh held a paramilitary training camp in California that attracted 50 Minutemen out of a total membership of several hundred. In 1966, he founded the Patriotic Party, a political wing of the Minutemen, intended to be a public, high-profile organization that would run candidates for office. By and large, though, the Minutemen operated in great secrecy as its members stockpiled weapons, including rifles, submachine guns, and mortars.

In his 1966 book, *Blueprint for Victory*, DePugh urged the privatization of government agencies to reduce the budget deficit, advocated a broad resistance movement to oppose leftists, charged that labor unions had been infiltrated by an international socialist movement, insisted that the federal bureaucracy would soon destroy states' rights, and urged Americans to regain their freedom by rising up against their oppressors. That same year, DePugh was arrested for violating federal firearms laws. He was convicted in November 1966 and resigned as head of the Minutemen in 1967 (though he continued as its unofficial leader). In 1968, while DePugh was free on appeal, a grand jury indicted him for conspiring to rob several banks in Washington State. DePugh fled, but FBI agents captured him in New Mexico in July 1969. He served nearly four years of an 11-year prison sentence before being paroled in February 1973.

Without DePugh, the Minutemen faded into obscurity. In the 1980s, he reentered the radical picture by adopting Identity Christianity (the belief that Jews and blacks were inferior to whites and that white Gentiles would one day inherit the world) and published a survivalist book with advice on how to handle the catastrophe that would occur after the Federal Reserve recalled all paper money. In the early 1990s, he was arrested and convicted on a morals and pornography charge involving an underage girl and on three counts of federal firearms violations.

The Minutemen revived in the 1990s, but DePugh was not among them. He had professed disgust with all politics and retired from activism, leaving a legacy of having taken up arms to fight the threat of One World socialism.

Further Reading

Jones, J. Harry. *The Minutemen.* Garden City, N.Y.: Doubleday, 1968.

Stern, Kenneth S. *A Force Upon the Plain: The American Militia Movement and the Politics of Hate.* New York: Simon & Schuster, 1996.

The Group Women Strike for Peace Seeks to End War and Nuclear Weapons   1961

Founded in 1961 to rid the world of nuclear weapons, Women Strike for Peace (WSP) protested U.S. military intervention overseas, including the Vietnam War in the 1960s.

WSP emerged during an unprecedented worldwide surge in the number of nuclear weapons; in the United States from 1953 to 1961, the number of nuclear weapons increased from 1,200 to 30,000. On November 1, 1961, some 50,000 women staged an international protest against nuclear testing, stressing in particular its adverse effect on the health of children. They carried signs saying "Let the Children Grow" and "End the Arms Race, Not the Human Race." Building on the energy generated by that event, political leader Bella Abzug, labor activist and economist Donna Allen, and several other women founded WSP. The group took the position that women were better able than men to work for peace because their maternal instincts put them more closely in touch with cooperation than with violence. During the demonstration of November 1, Allen was interviewed by a newspaper reporter who wrote:

I have noticed that so many of the nuclear bomb protest stories seem to wind up on the women's pages, creating an impression that the average American male is more concerned about building a fallout shelter than joining the "little woman" in a peace picket line. What do you think about this?

Allen said that she believed that women have a particular role in efforts to prevent war "because women are naturally more concerned about the next generation."

In 1962, Allen said that WSP had a "single-minded" program. She explained: "We stand for an end to [nuclear] testing, an end to the arms race, and for reliance upon the United Nations for preservation of the world it represents." Some observers attribute the signing of the 1963 Nuclear Test-Ban Treaty between the Soviet Union and the United States in part to the protests waged by WSP.

The federal government, however, responded to WSP's actions with investigations and attacks, portraying it as a disloyal group. In 1964, the House Un-American Activities Committee subpoenaed Allen and two other WSP leaders to testify. When they refused, Congress cited them for contempt, and in April 1965 a federal court convicted them. (A few months later an appeals court overturned the conviction.)

WSP was at the forefront of the opposition to the Vietnam War, adopting the slogan, "Not my son, not your son, not their sons." In March 1965, Alice Herz, an 81-year-old member of WSP, protested the U.S. bombing of North Vietnam by setting herself afire on a Detroit street. The following year, WSP attempted to block shipments of napalm to U.S. forces in Vietnam. In January 1967, about 2,500 WSP members marched on the Pentagon with the demand that they be allowed to speak with the generals who were sending "our sons to Vietnam." The discussions never occurred, but the resulting rise of the group's profile led to an increase in membership to more than 100,000.

In the years since the end of the Vietnam War, WSP has continued as an influential organization working against nuclear weapons and war. The group hailed the Comprehensive Test Ban Treaty in 1996 as "a triumph for citizen activism led by world peace and disarmament movements who struggled for decades to end the nuclear arms race." In the year 2000, WSP demanded that the U.S.–led embargo against Iraq be ended because of the suffering it was causing to that country's children.

Further Reading

Swerdlow, Amy. *Women Strike for Peace: Traditional Motherhood and Radical Politics in the 1960s.* Chicago: University of Chicago Press, 1993.

Taylor, Ethel Barol. *We Made a Difference: My Personal Journey with Women Strike for Peace.* Philadelphia: Camino Books, 1998.

1962   Rachel Carson Awakens the Public to Chemical Pollution with Her Book *Silent Spring*

Rachel Carson was raised on a 65-acre farm in Pennsylvania and from an early age learned about nature, often guided by her mother, with whom she was close. Moreover, she liked to write, so she combined her interests in composing Silent Spring*, which alerted the world to the dangers of pesticides and herbicides.*

With undergraduate and graduate degrees in zoology in hand, Rachel Carson (1907–64) worked for the federal government's Bureau of Fisheries and wrote newspaper articles before writing a series for the *New Yorker* magazine in 1951 that resulted in *The Sea Around Us*, a book that combined a survey of geological forces that created the oceans with a discussion of the continuing human attraction to the sea. It stayed on the *New York Times* best-seller list for 86 weeks and won the National Book Award for nonfiction.

Carson left her government job in 1952 to devote herself full-time to writing, and her *Edge of the Sea* (1955) also reached the best-seller list.

But *Silent Spring*, published in 1962, gained her the greatest notice and generated an intense reaction from the chemical industry. *Silent Spring* revealed the dangers of pesticides and herbicides, how certain types of them could be found in nearly all living things, and how they were killing fish and wildlife and endangering human beings.

In the ominously titled chapter "Elixirs of Death," she began:

For THE FIRST TIME in the history of the world, every human being is now subjected to contact with dangerous chemicals, from the moment of conception until death. In the less than two decades of their use, the synthetic pesticides have been so thoroughly distributed throughout the animate and inanimate world that they occur virtually everywhere. They have been recovered from most of the major river systems and even from streams of groundwater flowing unseen through the earth. . . . They have entered and lodged in the bodies of fish, birds, reptiles, and domestic and wild animals so universally that scientists carrying on animal experiments find it almost impossible to locate subjects free from such contamination.

She added that the chemicals could be found in most human beings and that "they occur in the mother's milk, and probably in the tissues of the unborn child."

Spokesmen for the chemical industry and scientists tied to it attacked Carson's findings with misleading reports, and even attacked her personally. (The criticism revealed another, hitherto ignored development: the selling out of many scientists, and scientific objectivity, to corporate dollars.) Yet Carson's work led to the formation of a presidential advisory commission to investigate the problem and, eventually, to laws banning many pesticides, such as DDT, and to laws restricting their use. She was a pioneer in the post–World War II environmental movement, helping to awaken a complacent America.

Further Reading

Carson, Rachel. *The Edge of the Sea.* New edition with an introduction by Sue Hubbell. Boston: Houghton Mifflin, 1998.

———. *The Sea Around Us.* New edition with an introduction by Ann H. Zwinger; afterword by Jeffery S. Levinton. New York: Oxford University Press, 1989.

———. *Silent Spring.* New edition with an introduction by Al Gore. Boston: Houghton Mifflin, 1994.

Ehrlich, Amy. *Rachel Carson.* San Diego, Calif.: Harcourt Trade Publishers, 2002.

Betty Friedan's *The Feminine Mystique* Ignites a Women's Movement 1963

When Betty Friedan's book The Feminine Mystique *appeared in 1963, it challenged the idea that women who were restricted to the home, where they were expected to take care of husband and children, were happy and fulfilled. There existed, Friedan claimed, a "problem that has no name" which had to be resolved so women could be liberated.*

Betty Friedan (1921–), born Betty Naomi Goldstein, married Carl Friedan, a theater producer, in 1947. Friedan later recalled (in what some call an exaggerated story) that when, in 1952, she requested a maternity leave to have her second child, she was fired from her job as a writer by her employer, a union publication called the *UE News.* (UE stood for United Electrical, Radio, and Machine Workers of America.) Rather than protest, she retreated to her family's home along the Hudson River and tried to follow the path that 1950s society expected of women—that of the suburban homemaker. At the same time, she wrote magazine articles in which she portrayed women as satisfied and fulfilled by their duties as house-wives. Friedan, however, realized that this theme conflicted with her own experience, and she wondered whether other suburban women were also unhappy. In 1957, she decided to find out by interviewing her former classmates from Smith College.

Friedan published her findings in *The Feminine Mystique.* This work immediately earned a wide read-ership because its theme, that many women felt frustrated with their lives, resonated with a large audi-ence, and because it coincided with a nationwide stirring of social and political activism. Friedan's phrase, "feminine mystique," referred to the idealized traditional role of the woman as wife and mother. Societal expectations, she claimed, both frustrated and oppressed many women and represented a male conspira-cy to keep them in a secondary position.

Friedan referred to "the problem that has no name" to indicate the feeling of emptiness gnawing at women. She said that "as the typical housewife made the beds, shopped for groceries, matched slipcover material, ate peanut butter sandwiches with her children, chauffeured Cub Scouts and Brownies, lay beside her husband at night, she was afraid to ask even of herself the silent question: 'Is this all?'" Friedan con-tinued: "Gradually I came to realize that the problem that has no name was shared by countless women in America. The women who suffer this problem have a hunger that food cannot fill." She insisted:

> If I am right, the problem that has no name stirring in the minds of so many American women today is not a matter of loss of femininity or too much education, or the demands of domestic-ity. It is far more important than anyone recognizes. . . . It may well be the key to our future as a nation and a culture. We can no longer ignore that voice within women that says: "I want something more than my husband and my children and my home."

Many women and men applauded Friedan for her conclusions, but some reacted negatively and opposed her for undermining middle-class values. As the debate over her book intensified, she toured the nation, making speeches and appearing on television.

Friedan decided that advancing women's liberation required political action. So in 1966, she helped found the National Organization for Women (NOW), a group devoted to obtaining equal rights by enforcing existing legislation, such as the 1964 Civil Rights Act that made discrimination in employment illegal, and by pursuing a Constitutional amendment to ban gender discrimination entirely.

Divisions within NOW hampered Friedan's efforts, however, as younger, more radical women joined the organization. Whereas Friedan sought to form alliances with men who supported the liberationist cause, these radicals considered men to be their enemies and opposed cooperating with them. Some of these radicals raised sexual issues, such as rights for lesbians, that Friedan did not want to address because she feared they might alienate many women. Meanwhile, a radical fringe completely rejected the family unit as dysfunctional and oppressive.

The discord within NOW grew so intense that in 1970 Friedan retired as the organization's presi-dent. She continued her activism, however, by organizing a rally later that year called the "Women's Strike for Equality," where participants demanded equal rights with men. The turnout in Washington, D.C., and in other cities made it the largest women's rights rally in many decades. "That was the high point of my political career," she recalled 30 years later. "The strike for equality showed us the great strength, depth, and breadth of the [women's] movement at that time."

In the 1970s, Friedan worked through the National Abortion Rights Action League, which she had founded a few years earlier, to lead the fight for safe and legal abortions. In 1971, she joined other feminists to found the National Women's Political Caucus, which encouraged women to seek public office. Over the following three decades, Friedan continued to lecture and write, but she is best remembered for *The Feminine Mystique.* "It is twenty years now since [it] was published," she observed in 1983. "I am still awed by the revolution that book helped spark."

Further Reading

Friedan, Betty. *The Feminine Mystique.* New edition with an introduction by the author. New York: W. W. Norton, 1997.

Hennessee, Judith Adler. *Betty Friedan: Her Life.* New York: Random House, 1999.

Horowitz, Daniel. *Betty Friedan and the Making of The Feminine Mystique: The American Left, the Cold War, and Modern Feminism.* Amherst: University of Massachusetts Press, 1998.

Malcolm X Experiences a Transformation at Mecca   1964

Increasingly at odds with Elijah Muhammad, the leader of the Nation of Islam, Malcolm X (see entry, 1948) made a trip to Mecca in 1964 that changed his life and transformed his political views, moving them closer to the camp of Martin Luther King, Jr., and other moderates in the civil rights movement.

When Malcolm X (1925–65) criticized the civil rights march on Washington, D.C., in summer 1963 (at which King gave his "I Have a Dream" speech) as little more than a circus under white control, he expressed the outrage many Black Muslims felt about working with whites to achieve racial integration. But his status as a rising leader in the Nation of Islam came to a halt at a rally on December 1, 1963, when he referred to President John F. Kennedy's assassination as a case of "the chickens coming home to roost," meaning that the same hatred that whites had directed at blacks had boomeranged to fell the president.

Whites and blacks decried Malcolm X's remark as insensitive, and Elijah Muhammad, leader of the Nation of Islam, ordered Black Muslims to disown the statement and prohibited Malcolm X from speaking publicly for 90 days. Muhammad's anger, though, was motivated by more than what Malcolm X had said. He feared that his protégé was becoming too popular and too powerful and needed to be contained.

For his part, Malcolm X had heard rumors about Muhammad's jealousy. Malcolm, however, was more concerned about rumors that Muhammad had engaged in extramarital affairs, a practice that to Malcolm X made the Muslim leader a hypocrite. Malcolm X was also becoming discontented with the separationist stand of the Black Muslims, which he felt did nothing to alleviate the racial discrimination blacks suffered, and which put the group in agreement with the Ku Klux Klan and other white supremacists who also said blacks and whites should live segregated from each other. Consequently, in 1964 Malcolm X quit the Black Muslims and formed Muslim Mosque, Inc. That April, he made his pilgrimage to Mecca, the holy city of Islam.

The pilgrimage, and his journeys elsewhere in the Middle East and in Africa, revealed to him how wrong he and the Black Muslims had been about the issue of race. Malcolm X still believed that whites were oppressive and that blacks must fight for their rights. But everywhere he went among Muslims he found no discrimination based on race and certainly no belief that whites were the devil. The Islamic faith, he concluded, had been corrupted in the United States by the Nation of Islam. Whites, he concluded, did evil things, but their evil was not innate—it grew from the racial prejudice rampant in Western culture and therefore could be changed.

In June 1964, Malcolm X formed the Organization of Afro-American Unity to bring together blacks of different faiths and ideologies. He called for blacks to control their economies, and he stated that in both the Third World and America, capitalistic exploitation and racist oppression relied on each other.

Malcolm X changed his name to El-Hajj Malik El-Shabazz and met with moderate black leaders, including Martin Luther King, Jr., and Rosa Parks. In so doing, he further antagonized the Black Muslims. At the same time, the FBI worried that he might prove to be a dynamic black leader able to lead African-Americans to rebel against the government, so it spied on him.

While the FBI watched Malcolm X, the Black Muslims attacked him. At Elijah Muhammad's behest, Louis X, later known as Louis Farrakhan, wrote in *Muhammad Speaks* that Malcolm had counted non-believers among his friends and that "no Muslim is a Muslim who accepts such people as his brothers." He warned: "Such a man as Malcolm is worthy of death."

Malcolm was convinced that the Nation of Islam and the federal government wanted him killed, and he had long predicted that he would die violently. That prophecy was given credence on February 14, 1965, when his home was firebombed. The following Sunday, on February 21, 1965, he was scheduled to address his followers at the Audubon Ballroom in New York City. When he began to speak, three men stood up and fired 16 shots at him. He died 90 minutes later.

Two of the three assassins were Black Muslims, but at the trial where they were sentenced to life terms, no evidence was offered that they had been ordered by the Nation of Islam to kill Malcolm. In the year 2000, however, Farrakhan, by then head of the Black Muslims, admitted to television correspondent Mike Wallace, "I may have been complicit in words that I spoke leading up to February 21."

About his trip to Mecca, Malcolm X had said it was "the first time I had ever stood before the Creator of All and felt like a complete human being." And he said, "I'm a human being first and foremost, and as such I'm for whoever and whatever benefits humanity as a whole."

Further Reading

Jenkins, Robert L., and Mfanya Donald Tryman. *The Malcolm X Encyclopedia.* Westport, Conn.: Greenwood, 2002.
X, Malcolm. *The Autobiography of Malcolm X.* With the Assistance of Alex Haley. Second Ballantine Books edition. New York: Ballantine Books, 1999.

1964 Daniel and Philip Berrigan Lead the Catholic Peace Fellowship in Agitating Against the Vietnam War

Founders of the Catholic Peace Fellowship (CPF), priests Daniel and Philip Berrigan were at the forefront of using "ultraresistance" to protest the Vietnam War.

Born to a Roman Catholic family with a union activist father, Daniel Berrigan (1921–) and Philip Berrigan (1923–) grew up in an atmosphere in which religious faith and issues of social justice were important. Daniel decided while a senior in high school to join the Jesuits (Society of Jesus) and was ordained a priest in 1952. Philip studied in the Society of St. Joseph and was ordained in 1955.

A critical turning point for Daniel occurred in 1963, when he attended the Christian Peace Conference in Prague, Czechoslovakia, and from there journeyed to Russia and South Africa. At the conference, he listened to criticism of the Vietnam War; in Russia, he witnessed Catholics bravely maintaining their faith against government persecution; in South Africa, he saw apartheid in its most brutal form. He later said his trip overseas helped him realize "what it might cost to be a Christian" and "what it might cost even at home, if things continued in the direction I felt events were taking."

Soon after he returned to the United States in 1964, Daniel plunged into the civil rights and anti-war movements. That year, he and Philip, along with several other Catholic activists, founded the Catholic Peace Fellowship to protest the Vietnam War. They were greatly influenced by Dorothy Day (see entry, 1933), who was a strong force in the Catholic pacifist movement.

The CPF advocated conscientious objection, but it also lobbied American bishops, and in New York City it picketed Cardinal Spellman's offices in reaction to Spellman having called Vietnam a "war for civilization." Daniel Berrigan gained considerable notice when he defended the actions of David Miller, a Catholic who, in October 1965, burned his draft card in front of the armed forces induction center in Manhattan—the first such burning since a new law had gone into effect imposing stiff penalties for the offense. At the same time, the CPF ran advertisements in several publications, denouncing the war as immoral.

Daniel's antiwar actions raised enormous opposition among church leaders, and they decided to silence the rebellious priest by assigning him to South America, where he reported for *Jesuit Missions*, a magazine that he edited. The move stirred Catholic liberals into response; they demanded Daniel's return, and within three months the leaders relented.

In fall 1967, Daniel Berrigan moved to Ithaca, New York, to help direct the United Religious Work Program at Cornell University. Continuing his outspoken opposition to the war, he participated in a march on the Pentagon that October and was one of several hundred demonstrators who were arrested. The following year, he traveled to Hanoi, Vietnam, with leftist professor Howard Zinn and helped gain the release of three American prisoners of war. During his stay, he was forced to hide in bomb shelters to escape attacks by American planes. Later that year, he published an account of his experience, *Night Flight to Hanoi.*

Meanwhile, Philip Berrigan had staged an antiwar protest at the customs house in Baltimore, Maryland, where he and three accomplices entered the Selective Service Office and destroyed files by pouring calves' blood over them. While awaiting sentencing for that deed, he approached his brother Daniel about staging another spectacular protest. Daniel agreed, and on May 17, 1968, the Berrigans and seven fellow protesters walked into the Selective Service Office in Cantonsville, Maryland, and startled workers by grabbing hundreds of files, putting them in trash cans, taking them outside, and burning them with homemade napalm. In a statement, the protesters said:

> We are Catholic Christians who take our faith seriously. We use napalm because it has burned people to death in Vietnam, Guatemala and Peru and because it may be used in American ghettoes. We destroyed these records because they exploit our young men and represent misplaced power concentrated in the hands of the ruling class. . . . We believe some property has no right to exist.

Known as the Cantonsville Nine (one year later Daniel wrote a play, *The Trial of the Cantonsville Nine*), the group faced charges of conspiracy and destroying government property. Their tactics caused dissension within the Catholic peace movement; some activists questioned the destruction of property—a form of civil disobedience protesters termed "ultraresistance"—as too violent.

A jury found the Berrigans guilty, but Daniel and Philip went underground, convinced they could do the most good slipping in and out of towns and spreading their protest message. Much to the embarrassment of the FBI, whose agents were pursuing them, Daniel appeared at a Methodist church on August 2, 1970, and presented a sermon in which he called for courageous actions to win the peace. Nine days later, however, the FBI captured Daniel at Block Island, Rhode Island. His was imprisoned until February 24, 1972.

Philip was also apprehended in 1970 and was sent to the federal penitentiary in Lewisburg, Pennsylvania. While incarcerated, he was charged with conspiracy to blow up government buildings and kidnap federal officials, and with exchanging concealed communications at a federal penitentiary. Philip was acquitted of the charges, and on November 30, 1972, he was granted parole.

Both Daniel and Philip Berrigan remained active in social causes, including the peace movement, and they continued their protests for justice into the 1990s. In May 1997, Daniel damaged a U.S. navy missile cruiser in Portland, Maine, and in March 2000, Philip was sentenced to 30 months in jail for vandalizing two U.S. warplanes at an Air National Guard base in Maryland. He had committed the act the previous year to protest the use of depleted uranium in missiles deployed on the planes. Their efforts in the 1960s brought considerable attention to the injustice of the Vietnam War and encouraged the recognition of pacifism as a movement within the Catholic church.

Further Reading

Polner, Murray. *Disarmed and Dangerous: The Radical Lives and Times of Daniel and Philip Berrigan.* New York: BasicBooks, 1997.

1964   Barry Goldwater Is Nominated for President by Republicans and Supports Extremism to Defend Liberty

When Vice President Lyndon Johnson, a Democrat, succeeded to the presidency in November 1963 after the assassination of President John Kennedy, liberalism accelerated when the new chief executive pushed a civil rights bill through Congress and declared himself committed to fighting a War on Poverty. In reaction, the Republican Party turned to its extreme right wing to beat back the liberal offensive and in 1964 chose Arizona Senator Barry Goldwater as its presidential candidate.

Goldwater made it clear from the start of his campaign that the choice between him and Johnson, who was seeking election, amounted to choosing between individual liberty and government tyranny. No compromise was possible; no middle ground; no varied levels of commitment or watering down of rhetoric. In his acceptance speech at the Republican National Convention in San Francisco that August he declared: "Extremism in the defense of liberty is no vice. . . . Moderation in the pursuit of justice is no virtue."

He surrounded his now-famous phrase with allusions to a losing fight against communism that had to be turned around. "The administration which we shall replace," he said, "has . . . talked and talked and talked and talked the words of freedom. Now, failures cement the wall of shame in Berlin. Failures blot the sands of shame at the Bay of Pigs. Failures mark the slow death of freedom in Laos. Failures infest the jungles of Vietnam. And failures haunt the houses of our once great alliances and undermine the greatest bulwark erected by free nations—the NATO community. Failures proclaim lost leadership, obscure purpose, weakening wills, and the risk of inciting our sworn enemies to new aggressions and to new excesses."

Goldwater mourned a perceived loss of moral leadership and order in society. "Rather than useful jobs in our country, people have been offered bureaucratic 'make work;' rather than moral leadership," he claimed. "They have been given bread and circuses, spectacles, and, yes, they have even been given scandals. Tonight there is violence in our streets, corruption in our highest offices, aimlessness among our youth, anxiety among our elders, and there is a virtual despair among the many who look beyond material success for the inner meaning of their lives."

During the campaign, Goldwater made several statements that indicated he would, if elected, turn the United States sharply to the right. He talked about using tactical nuclear weapons in Vietnam. He called for a rollback of Johnson's Great Society social programs. He opposed civil rights legislation. He suggested that social security be made voluntary rather than mandatory. He said that the Tennessee Valley Authority, the government agency created during President Franklin Roosevelt's New Deal to generate electricity and improve the economy in that region of the country, should be sold to private interests.

Democrats responded to Goldwater by saying his proposals would ruin social security and deny blacks liberty, and that if Goldwater won, he would be trigger-happy in using nuclear weapons. Goldwater insisted, though, that he was "a choice not an echo." Johnson's landslide victory showed the voters' choice—Johnson. Nevertheless, Goldwater was either prescient or premature with his conservatism; the discontent with Johnson and the liberal big government set the stage for a conservative resurgence in the 1980s under Ronald Reagan.

Further Reading

Perlstein, Rick. *Before the Storm: Barry Goldwater and the Unmaking of the American Consensus.* New York: Hill and
    Wang, 2001.
White, Theodore Harold. *The Making of the President, 1964.* New York: Atheneum, 1965.

Maulana Karenga Forms United Slaves

1965

*Shortly after the Los Angeles ghetto of Watts erupted into riots and flames, Maulana Karenga emerged as the
city's most influential black leader. He advocated cultural separatism from whites through a new organization, United Slaves (US).*

An intelligent, college-educated, charismatic figure, Karenga (1941–) was born Ronald McKinley Everett,
but took the Swahili name Maulana Karenga in 1965; he required all members of US to also adopt Swahili
names. Karenga gained a following among young blacks in Watts who felt exploited by whites and neglected by the civil rights movement. Karenga believed that the riots showed how little Martin Luther King,
Jr.'s, supporters had accomplished. To him, and many other black ghetto residents, integration—the right
to use the same facilities as whites—meant nothing when unemployment and poverty remained high.

Blacks, he insisted, needed to liberate themselves by embracing African culture, emphasizing cultural revolution before political revolution, and establishing an African-American cultural nation within the
United States. (To further these goals, he founded Kwanzaa, a black holiday celebrated annually over several days in late December. The name Kwanzaa comes from the Kiswahili word *kwanzaa*, which means
"first fruits," and refers to the event by which African communities traditionally celebrated their first harvest. The holiday stresses seven principles: unity, self-determination, collective work and responsibility,
cooperative economics, purpose, creativity, and faith.)

United Slaves, or US ("us"), advocated black self-determination, a goal similar to that of the Black
Panther Party. Karenga differed with the Panthers, however: where they argued that racism resulted from
economics, and economics must be addressed first, Karenga argued that racism transcended economics
and had become the leading international issue; and where the Panthers sought alliances with white
groups, Karenga and US rejected any such arrangements.

Through US, Karenga told blacks that to achieve liberation they must first erase their Negro mentality. He defined Negro in these terms:

The "Negro" is made and manufactured in America.
The "Negro" works on a two-fold economy. He buys what he wants and begs what he needs.
"Negroes" want to be like Jesus; blond hair, blue eyes, and pale skin.

He called for 1970 to be the year of separation from white domination, and for 1971 to be the year
of defensive guerrilla action.

Karenga directed US to educate blacks in African culture. Fluent in Swahili, he insisted that blacks
learn the language. He dressed in a "buba," a toga-like garment he thought representative of an African
style, and one that became an important symbol for US.

The founding of US occurred when many urban blacks were turning to groups outside the mainstream of
the civil rights movement. The Black Panthers and US engaged in a power struggle for influence among
African-Americans, and Karenga accused the Panthers of being a front for white leftists. "We must save ourselves," he said, "or we cannot be saved." His differences with the Panthers boiled over into violence. Early in

1969, two members of US disrupted a meeting of black students being held in a classroom at the University of California at Los Angeles and shot and killed two Black Panthers. The shooting damaged the reputation of US among blacks, as did Karenga's conviction on charges of assaulting a woman member of US (an accusation that reinforced an existing view that Karenga was a male chauvinist). The group collapsed in the early 1970s.

It should be noted that the United States government aimed its top-secret counter-intelligence program, called COINTELPRO, at US and the Black Panthers in an attempt to destroy both of them. Through COINTELPRO, agents from the FBI spread rumors and encouraged dissent. The government especially wanted the two groups to engage in a violent showdown with each other. In 1976 the U.S. Senate Select Committee to Study Governmental Operations reported:

In early May 1970, FBI Headquarters became aware of an article entitled "Karenga King of the Bloodsuckers" in the May 2, 1970, edition of the BPP [Black Panther Party] newspaper which "vilifies and debases Karenga and the US organization." Two field offices received the following request from headquarters: [s]ubmit recommendation to Bureau . . . for exploitation of same under captioned program. Consider from two aspects, one against US and Karenga from obvious subject matter; the second against BPP because, inherent in article is admission by BPP that it has done nothing to retaliate against US for killing of Panther members attributed to US and Karenga, an admission that the BPP has been beaten at its own game of violence.

In response to this request, the Special Agent in Charge in Los Angeles reported that the BPP newspaper article had already resulted in violence, but that it was difficult to induce BPP members to attack US members in Southern California because they feared US members. The Los Angeles field office hoped, however, that "internecine struggle" might be triggered through a skillful use of informants within both groups.

The Los Angeles Division is aware of the mutually hostile feelings harbored between the organizations and the first opportunity to capitalize on the situation will be maximized. It is intended that US Inc. will be appropriately and discretely advised of the time and location of BPP activities in order that the two organizations might be brought together and thus grant nature the opportunity to take her due course.

Karenga described the failure of the Black Power movement thusly: "The presumption that the people who hold power are moral rather than amoral [was] the fatal flaw. . . . [We depended] so much on the goodwill of the oppressor and [our] white allies." Ideologically, Karenga became a Marxist in the 1970s, and in 1992, he helped calm Los Angeles when rioting broke out among blacks in response to the Rodney King verdict.

Further Reading
Haskins, James. *Profiles in Black Power.* New York: Doubleday, 1972.

1965 Cesar Chavez Leads Strike of Migrant Farm Workers

In 1965, labor leader Cesar Chavez organized a strike of Chicano migrant workers against California grape growers. He called the action La Causa—a movement aimed at changing the way Chicanos lived.

Cesar Chavez was born on March 31, 1927, near Yuma, Arizona, to Librado Chavez, the owner of a small grocery store and auto repair shop, and Juana Chavez. Cesar was forced to toil with the rest of his family as a migrant farm laborer, picking fruits and vegetables and living in tar paper and wood cabins. As a result, he attended school only through the seventh grade.

In 1952, the Community Service Organization (CSO) recruited Chavez to work among Mexican-Americans. Begun by Saul Alinsky, a Chicago labor activist, the CSO brought together poor people so they could win political and economic concessions from governmental agencies. As a CSO organizer, Chavez led a successful voter registration drive in San Jose, California, and founded chapters in Oakland and in towns throughout the San Joaquin Valley.

In 1962, Chavez quit the CSO over policy differences and founded the National Farm Workers Association (NFWA), a union for migrant farm laborers. Organizing, though, proved to be a tough uphill battle. Chavez had to overcome not only resistance from growers but also from farm workers who were demoralized by previous failed union efforts.

Nevertheless, by 1965 Chavez had enrolled 1,700 families in the NFWA, an action that provided enough clout to win pay raises from growers in the country around Delano, California. In addition, he began a credit union for the workers, along with a co-op store, newspaper, and insurance club. In fact, Chavez's vision was far broader than unionization: he called it La Causa, or the movement, an attempt to activate and uplift an entire community.

Chavez wanted no more labor battles until he could get better organized, but in September 1965, another union, the Agricultural Workers Organizing Committee (AWOC) led by Larry Itilong and representing migrant Filipino workers, went on strike over low wages, and Chavez listened to Itilong's plea for help and decided the NFWA should join them. What followed was a long strike against grape growers in California's San Joaquin, Imperial, and Coachella Valleys.

Chavez used tactics similar to those employed in the civil rights movement: sit-ins, marches, and support from the clergy. He even obtained help from activists sent in by the Congress of Racial Equality, and, as the strike against the grape growers continued, in 1966 he merged the NFWA with the AWOC, creating the United Farm Workers Organizing Committe (UFWOC).

The UFWOC won contracts from 11 major wine grape growers, but it failed to make headway against the table grape growers, those who provided the fruit sold in grocery stores and supermarkets. In the spring of 1968, Chavez launched a boycott of all table grapes grown in California. About 200 UFWOC members toured the United States and Canada, holding demonstrations to rally consumers and pressure city governments to join the boycott.

Chavez went on a 25-day hunger strike to gain national attention, and Massachusetts Senator Robert Kennedy boosted the protest when he made a public appearance with Chavez and announced that he firmly supported the principles that had led him to begin his fast. In reaction to this strike, the growers labeled Chavez a communist, recruited strikebreakers, and pressured the federal government to allow more Mexican immigrants into the nation so they could work the fields.

By the following year, the boycott had taken its economic toll. In July, several large growers who produced half the state's table grapes signed agreements with the UFWOC. Chavez followed that triumph with a lettuce boycott that also won concessions.

Chavez's efforts intensified Chicano awareness and contributed to the growth of "brown pride" in the late 1960s, but the transient and impoverished status of most migrant workers meant that only a small percentage of them were ever unionized. Chavez continued his work in what became the United Farm Workers (UFW) into the 1990s, and in spring 1993, he helped defend the UFW from a lawsuit filed against it by a large grower.

Chavez died in his sleep on April 23, 1993, in San Luis, Arizona. In tribute, union leader Lane Kirkland said "the improved lives of millions of farm workers and their families will endure as a testimonial to Cesar and his life's work." Yet the UMW had weakened during Chavez's last years, and protection for farm workers remained limited. The *Los Angeles Times* noted in April 1993 that "inadequate enforcement of labor and health laws, coupled with tumbling wages and backbreaking work amid toxic pesticides, have sentenced hundreds of thousands of farm workers and their children to a precarious existence from which they have little hope of escaping."

Further Reading

Davis, Lucile. *Cesar Chavez: A Photo-Illustrated Biography*. Mankato, Minn.: Bridgestone Books, 1998.

Griswold del Castillo, Richard, and Richard A. Garcia. *Cesar Chavez: A Triumph of Spirit*. Norman: University of Oklahoma Press, 1995.

1966   Huey Newton and Bobby Seale Found the Black Pantherss

Huey Newton and Bobby Seale formulated a 10-point program and founded the Black Panther Party for Self Defense, popularly referred to as the Black Panthers, in October 1966. With their fight for black power, the Black Panthers ranked among the more militant groups in the 1960s counterculture.

Newton (1942–89) grew up in a ghetto in Oakland, California, and attended Merritt College, a two-year school. It was there that his friend Seale introduced him to *The Wretched of the Earth* (1963), a book in which black psychologist Frantz Fanon argued that violence could awaken subjugated peoples to do something about their oppression and help them develop leadership. While at Merritt, Newton formed a gang and served six months in jail for felonious assault with a knife.

Seale (1937–) was born in Dallas, Texas, but grew up in Oakland. At Merritt College, he joined Newton in declaring his opposition to capitalism and argued that blacks should arm themselves for self-defense. In 1966, they formed the Black Panthers based on their 10-point program, which included demands for freedom, black self-determination, and the end of police brutality (see box).

They declared: "We believe that the federal government is responsible and obligated to give every man employment or a guaranteed income." And they said: "We believe that this racist government has robbed us, and now we are demanding the overdue debt of forty acres and two mules. Forty acres and two mules was promised 100 years ago as retribution for slave labor and mass murder of black people. . . . The Germans murdered 6 million Jews. The American racist has taken part in the slaughter of over 50 million black people; therefore, we feel that this is a modest demand that we make."

Several different Panther groups had already formed, such as the Black Panther Party of Northern California based in San Francisco. In beginning the Oakland organization, however, Newton and Seale

Black Panther poster, circa 1970. (Library of Congress)

Black Panther Manifesto

In forming the Black Panthers, Huey Newton and Bobby Seale wrote what they called a 10-point program. In tone, their demands echoed the pronouncement made some 60 years earlier by W. E. B. Du Bois in his Niagara Address (see entry, 1909), but the content of their demands was more extreme, expressing the seething resentment simmering in America's black ghettoes:

1. We want freedom. We want power to determine the destiny of our black community.
2. We want full employment for our people.
3. We want an end to the robbery by the white man of our black community.
4. We want decent housing fit for shelter of human beings.

5. We want education for our people that exposes the true nature of this decadent American society. We want education that teaches us our true history and our role in the present-day society.
6. We want all black men to be exempt from military service.
7. We want an immediate end to *police brutality* and *murder* of black people.
8. We want freedom for all black men and women held in federal, state, county, and city prisons and jails.
9. We want all black people, when brought to trial, to be tried in court, by a jury of their peer group or people from their black communities, as defined by the Constitution of the United States.
10. We want land, bread, housing, education, clothing, justice, and peace.

rejected cultural nationalism—the belief that whites should be condemned because of their race—and sought alliances with radical whites while promoting black self-determination. They supported Black Power, with its pride in African-American culture, and they claimed that the Panthers were not a racist organization "but a very progressive revolutionary party." By 1970, the group had numerous chapters and several thousand members largely in western and northern cities. Newton insisted the Panthers would create a "democratic socialist society free of racism."

The Panthers established various self-help programs for African-Americans in the ghettos, required strict discipline among their members—they forbade alcohol and drug use while doing party work—and ran candidates for political office. But their militancy gained them the most attention. The Panthers wanted a revolution to end political and economic oppression. They armed themselves with rifles, wore combat jackets, paraded militia-style, raised clenched fists, and shouted "Power to the people!" Riding in cars on armed patrol, they confronted police who arrested blacks, and they tried to prevent brutality.

In May 1967, while the California Assembly was debating a bill to make illegal the carrying of loaded guns in public, the Panthers staged a daring protest. They arrived at the state capitol, M-1 rifles in hand and pistols strapped to their hips, sent Governor Ronald Reagan scurrying from a meeting he was holding outdoors with several young people, and marched onto the floor of the legislature. While reporters looked on, Seale declared, "[As] the aggression of the racist American government escalates in Vietnam, the police agencies of America escalate the repression of black people throughout the ghettoes." Seale was quickly ushered out; with this event, however, the Panthers gained the notice of white America and earned the respect of many ghetto blacks.

Police harassment and internal problems soon hurt the Panthers. At various times, Newton and Seale were imprisoned, and the FBI and local police cooperated in extreme actions, such as raids on the homes of Panther leaders. On December 4, 1969, two prominent Panthers, Fred Hampton and Mark Clark, were killed during an attack by Chicago police. Indeed, in the words of a U.S. Senate committee, the FBI used its top-secret domestic spy program, called COINTELPRO, to "'neutralize' organizations which the Bureau characterized as 'Black Nationalist Hate Groups.'"

Soon after the killing of Hampton and Clark, a dispute between Newton and another Panther leader, Eldridge Cleaver, splintered the organization. Cleaver, meanwhile, fled arrest for his involvement in a shootout between several Panthers and the police. He went to Cuba and eventually to Algeria. He was expelled from the Panthers in 1971 after evidence suggested that he intended to kill Newton; it later came out that the "evidence" had been planted by the FBI.

Newton directed the Black Panthers to change tactics and pursue reform rather than violent revolution. As a result, they focused on such measures as economic boycotts. The Panthers continued as a localized Oakland group into the 1980s, providing school programs and other social services, but then passed from the scene. A successor group called the New Black Panther Party raised controversy in 2002. Its leader, Malik Zulu Shabazz declared: "You want to talk about terrorism? Come talk to the black people of America, because we have been terrorized by America for the last 400 years!" Writing in the *Christian Science Monitor* in March 2002, Alexandra Marks reported that former members of the 1960s-Black Panthers disliked the new group for what they called its anti-white and anti-Jewish hatred, and they charged them with exploiting the Panther name and ruining its legacy. Marks added that "the New Black Panthers insist they are neither racist nor anti-Semitic, but advocates for the downtrodden and the victims of racism, imperialism, and Zionism."

Further Reading

Churchill, Ward, and Jim Vander Wall. *Agents of Repression: The FBI's Secret Wars against the Black Panther Party and the American Indian Movement.* Boston: South End Press, 1990.

Cleaver, Eldridge. *Soul on Ice.* Reprint. New York: Delta Trade Paperbacks, 1999.

Foner, Philip S., ed. *The Black Panthers Speak.* New York: Da Capo Press, 1995.

1966 Timothy Leary Founds the League for Spiritual Discovery to Continue His LSD Experiments

When Timothy Leary founded the League for Spiritual Discovery in 1966, he intended it to be another step in his promotion of the drug LSD as a psychedelic route to a mystical transcendent experience.

A Harvard psychologist who became known as the "high priest of LSD," Leary (1920–96) first began his experiments with drugs in 1960. He had ingested the psilocybin found in "magic mushrooms" and experienced, he said, an enlightening, mystical revelation; now he wanted to see if psilocybin could alter personalities in profound ways by stimulating unconscious searches for a union with the greater universe, attaining a cosmic consciousness. So he began a psilocybin research project, using a chemical compound synthesized by Sandoz Laboratories. Leary discussed his research with Aldous Huxley, author of *The Doors of Perception* (1954). The men disagreed about how widely psychedelic drugs should be circulated, with Huxley arguing they should be restricted to an intellectual elite and Leary advocating their widespread use. Both men desired, however, to liberate society from its stifling conformity and barbaric violence, and both believed that psychedelics could lead the way.

Leary's research soon evolved into weekend gatherings where students and artists took psilocybin. As his work evolved into a holy crusade, his critics attacked him for sloppy procedures, and the psilocybin project split the Harvard psychology department into warring camps: those who supported Leary and those who opposed him.

On Good Friday 1962, Leary gathered 20 theology students together at Marsh Chapel and administered psilocybin to 10 of them (to the remaining 10 he gave a placebo) in an attempt to see if a mystical religious experience could be replicated. This experiment reinforced his belief in the positive benefits of psychedelics because, he reported, all but one of those who took the psilocybin reported deeply transcendent experiences that changed their view of life.

Wanting to proselytize his psychedelic message, Leary journeyed to Mexico later in 1962, where he and several followers gathered at a hotel situated along a dirt road in Zihuatanejo and took LSD to explore the unconscious. He hoped to create a community founded on spiritual brotherhood rather than individual egos, for he believed that once psychedelic substances could be handled without their damaging side effects, the human brain could be used to its fullest. Later that year, he founded the International Foundation for Internal Freedom (IFIF), a forerunner to the League of Spiritual Discovery, to train guides in psychedelic exploration, supply them with LSD (at that time, along with psilocybin, a legal drug), and get them to form small groups to continue the research.

In 1963, Harvard responded to the Marsh Chapel incident and Leary's continuing practice of supplying students with drugs by firing him. That summer, Mexican authorities ordered him and his IFIF to leave the country. Leary found a new home, however, when a wealthy benefactor allowed him to use an estate in Millbrook, New York. The land was dotted with woods, ponds, and streams; the 64-room house soon accommodated a research institute and monastery for mystics. Although the IFIF folded, Leary continued his experiments with LSD at Millbrook.

Leary traveled to India in 1965 and converted to Hinduism. The following year, he founded the League for Spiritual Discovery. He considered the League a religious sect dedicated to altering consciousness and exploring mysticism through LSD and other psychedelic drugs. Moreover, he intended the League to provide a rationale that would allow him to avoid conviction for a recent arrest for possessing marijuana; that is, he wanted to be able to argue that he used drugs as religious sacraments. The United States courts, however, rejected his argument.

In 1967, Leary, still at Millbrook but living in a teepee, claimed he had completely dropped out of society. Low on money, he presented lectures for a fee. He appeared barefoot and dressed in white trousers and Indian silk shirts, and as Beatles' music played in the background, he urged young people to "turn on, tune in, and drop out"—meaning, turn on to the mystical experience (likely through LSD), tune in to the message, and drop out of mainstream society. He proclaimed that the United States "will be an LSD country within fifteen years."

By 1968, Millbrook had deteriorated into an anarchic mix of drug escapists. The local police harassed the residents by setting up roadblocks and conducting raids. Following Leary's conviction on drug possession charges in California and Texas, the psychologist entered a minimal-security correctional facility located near San Luis Ibispo, California. A few weeks later, the Weatherman (see entry, 1969) helped him escape, and he fled to Algiers, where for a brief period he stayed with radical Black Panthers (see entry, 1966) who were living in exile. He then journeyed to Switzerland and lived there from 1971 to 1973 before traveling to Afghanistan. On his arrival, government officials in Kabul turned him over to the U.S. embassy. Leary spent the rest of that year and part of 1974 in Folsom Prison before being transferred to a facility in Vacaville, California. He remained incarcerated until 1976.

He held steadfast to his views about drugs into the 1980s; then in the 1990s, he declared that computers were the new way to expand the mind—"The PC," he said, "is the LSD of the '90s." Leary was, however, mainly a product of the 1960s with its countercultural challenge to mainstream morality and conformity, a rebel whose promotion of LSD scared middle America while encouraging many youths to try it as a means to enlightenment and other drugs as a means to escape.

Further Reading

Stevens, Jay. *Storming Heaven: LSD and the American Dream.* New York: Harper & Row, 1987.

"Eye! Eye!" "Pee! Pee!" The Yippies Are Formed

Formed on New Year's Eve 1967, the Yippies emerged from a marijuana haze as a partly serious, partly satirical group dedicated to revealing society's absurdities and staging a protest at the 1968 Democratic National Convention.

The idea for the Yippies germinated on December 31, 1967, when Abbie Hoffman and his wife Anita, along with Jerry Rubin, Nancy Kurshan, and Paul Krassner, gathered at the Hoffmans' apartment in New York City to smoke pot and have a good time. They started talking about putting together an event, some sort of protest, to be held at the Democratic National Convention in Chicago that coming August. Abbie Hoffman believed the under-30 generation needed something to watch and participate in that would transcend speeches. He began talking about a Festival of Life to contrast with what he called the political Convention of Death. When Krassner reacted to this idea by pointing out how, in making a peace sign to form a V, the arm extended beneath to really make it a Y, others in the group started shouting "Eye! Eye!," then "Pee! Pee!," and finally "Yippie!" They had inadvertently concocted the name for a group that could put together the Festival of Life.

To satisfy potential questions from the mainstream press about what Yippie meant, Anita Hoffman, or perhaps Krassner, came up with an officious-sounding title: Youth International Party. In January 1968, the Yippies began promoting their Chicago protest, releasing a call through the Liberation News Service: "Come all you rebels, youth spirits, rock minstrels, truth seekers, peacock freaks, poets, barricade jumpers, dancers, lovers, artisans." Abbie Hoffman cranked out flyers, posters, and 50,000 buttons bearing the word "Yippie!" in pink psychedelic letters against a purple background. Rubin explained the reason for the festival-protest, saying that because it was hard to reach people with words, the Yippies would do it with emotion. Writing in *Revolution for the Hell of It* (1968), Abbie Hoffman claimed that the Yippies had among their objectives:

1. The blending of pot and politics into a political grass leaves movement—a cross-fertilization of the hippie and New Left philosophies.
2. A connecting link that would tie together as much of the underground as was willing into some gigantic national get-together.
3. The development of a model for an alternative society.
4. The need to make some statement, especially in action-theater terms, about [President Johnson], the Democratic Party, electoral politics, and the state of the nation.

By March 1968, small Yippie groups had appeared in Washington, Philadelphia, Boston, Berkeley, San Francisco, Los Angeles, and Chicago. The New York City Yippies opened their meetings to anyone who wanted to come, and they held them at their office, at nearby Free University, and outdoors at Union Square. During their planning for Chicago, friction developed between Abbie Hoffman, who wanted only outrageous acts and fun, and Rubin, who wanted political content.

Nevertheless, the Yippies decided that to get needed recognition and show their true colors, they would hold several pre-Chicago events. So in March they announced a party, or "Yip-in," at Grand Central Station. More than 5,000 people turned out, but police attacked the revelers with clubs, sending Hoffman and several others to the hospital with bloodied heads.

With Chicago approaching and with it appearing that the authorities would use force to prevent any demonstrations, the Yippies encountered opposition from New Left groups that took politics seriously. Students for a Democratic Society called the Yippies irresponsible and stated that the group's "intention to

Radicalism and Humor

Radicals are sometimes criticized for being so dedicated to their causes that they lose their sense of humor. But history shows otherwise. We need only recall the words of IWW leader Joe Hill (see entry, 1915) as he was given the choice between execution by hanging or firing squad. "I'll take the shooting," he said. "I've been shot a couple times before, and I think I can take it."

In the 1960s and early 1970s, radical protest contained a keen sense of humor, often satirical in form, that was meant to underscore society's oppression and absurdities, or illuminate the culture that was peculiar to the protesters. In 1967, Abbie Hoffman threw dollar bills from the balcony of the New York Stock Exchange to the floor below, sending stockbrokers into a mad scramble for the money in a frenzy that paralyzed the Exchange for several minutes. Hoffman claimed that, by revealing greed, this act said "more than thousands of anti-capitalist tracts and essays."

About the same time, protesters challenged the mayor of Ithaca, New York, to an arm-wrestling match because they believed in "armed struggle," while elsewhere other protesters distracted ROTC cadets by playing leapfrog on training fields. When the National Organization for Women sponsored a Women's Strike for Equality in 1970, they used as their slogan "Don't Iron While the Strike Is Hot."

The drug culture that challenged mainstream society's values had its own underground humor expressed in folklore and jokes. "A concerned father came home to find his daughter and her friends smoking marijuana," went one joke. "Grabbing the pot out of her mouth, he exclaimed: 'What's a joint like this doing in a nice girl like you?'"

---

bring thousands of young people to Chicago during the DNC [Democratic National Convention] to groove on rock bands and smoke grass and then put them up against bayonets—viewing that as a radicalizing experience—seems manipulative at best." The National Mobilization Committee to End the War in Vietnam, or MOBE, the largest organization behind the political protests at Chicago, objected to the Yippies' plan, fearing it would detract from any antiwar message. With all these disagreements, and with the assassinations of Martin Luther King, Jr., in April and Robert Kennedy in June, Hoffman considered canceling the Festival of Life.

But the Yippies decided to forge ahead, and they rattled the media and Chicago's hard-nosed mayor, Richard Daley, by announcing they would drop LSD in the city's water supply; hijack the Chicago office of Nabisco and distribute free cookies; and rally young people to run naked through the streets. Perhaps the highlight for the Yippies occurred on August 23, the Friday before the convention opened. Marching in front of the Chicago Civic Center, Rubin introduced the Yippie presidential nominee: Pigasus, a 200-pound pig they had bought from a farmer. Rubin declared: "They nominate a president and he eats the people. We nominate a president and the people eat him." The police had other ideas, however, and they confiscated Pigasus and arrested Rubin.

As for the Festival of Life, violence ruined it. The Yippies tried to stage a rock concert at Lincoln Park on Sunday night, only to find the police opposing them and strictly enforcing a curfew. A melee followed. Other violent episodes erupted during the succeeding nights as militant radicals from several different groups battled angry cops.

Early in 1969, the federal government indicted Hoffman, Rubin, and six others, including officials with MOBE, for conspiring to riot. Known as the Chicago Eight, they were found guilty of rioting (though not of engaging in conspiracy). A higher court later overturned their convictions. The Yippies soon faded from the scene, but not without having contributed to the tumultuous developments of 1968 and having jabbed a satirical knife into the heart of mainstream society.

Further Reading

Albert, Judith Clavir, and Stewart Edward Albert, eds. *The Sixties Papers: Documents of a Rebellious Decade.* New York: Praeger, 1984.

Anderson, Terry H. *The Movement and the Sixties.* New York: Oxford University Press, 1995.

1967 The *SCUM Manifesto*

In 1967, as the women's movement radicalized, Valerie Solanas wrote the SCUM Manifesto. *She said that SCUM stood for the Society for Cutting Up Men and that the group would have as its goal eliminating men, whom she called vile oppressors and the source of humankind's major evils, such as war, conformity, prejudice, hate, violence, disease, and death.*

Valerie Solanas (1936–88) had grown up an abused child. That her father sexually molested her, and her grandfather whipped her, may well have influenced her views, establishing in her a distrust and even hatred of men. She graduated from college in the late 1950s and then earned money by panhandling and working as a prostitute.

The *SCUM Manifesto* gained considerable notice when it first appeared. At least in attitude, it fit the extreme feminist notions that men were not to be trusted and that women could gain their liberation only by working against them and never with them.

SCUM claimed that through modern technology it was possible to reproduce without males and to conceive only females. The male was "a biological accident," Solanas declared, and through the chance arrangement of chromosomes was "an incomplete female, a walking abortion, aborted at the gene state." Solanas declared that SCUM can take over the country by taking over jobs and then refusing to follow the rules: "SCUM salesgirls will not charge for merchandise. . . . SCUM office and factory workers will secretly destroy equipment." She declared also that SCUM will kill all men who refuse to join the SCUM Men's Auxiliary.

In an allusion to her belief that men should be controlled by neutering them, she said, "SCUM will not picket, demonstrate, march, or strike to attempt to achieve its ends. Such tactics are for nice, genteel ladies who scrupulously take only such action that is guaranteed to be ineffective. . . . If SCUM ever strikes, it will be in the dark with a six-inch blade."

In 1968, Solanas shot and wounded Andy Warhol, an avant-garde artist, for whom she had worked on occasion. "He had too much control of my life," she said. Solanas was placed on trial, during which feminist leader Ti-Grace Atkinson called her "the first outstanding champion of women's rights." She was sentenced to three years in prison and after her release spent time in several mental institutions. She claimed in the 1970s that SCUM was never really an organization, that it was really "a state of mind."

Further Reading

Morgan, Robin, ed. *Sisterhood Is Powerful: An Anthology of Writings from the Women's Liberation Movement.* New York: Vintage, 1970.

1967 Reies Lopez Tijerina Demands That Anglos Return Land Stolen from Hispanics

Born in a small town 40 miles southeast of San Antonio, Texas, Reies Lopez Tijerina rose above his dire migrant conditions to form the Alianza Federal de los Pueblos Libres (Federal Alliance of Free City States) that resorted to violence to fight the Anglo theft of Hispanic-American land grants in New Mexico and elsewhere. "Our people had not a guide, no light, no knowledge," Tijerina later explained, "and God therefore has chosen me."

In the early 1950s, Reies Tijerina (1926–), then a convert to a Pentecostal faith but preaching as a nondenominational minister, convinced 17 Spanish-American families to pool their finances and buy 160 acres of land in Pinal County, Arizona, where they could begin a community dedicated to justice and harmony. While he and his followers may have wanted togetherness, his neighbors destroyed the community by burning its buildings.

In July 1957, Tijerina was arrested for helping his brother break out of an Arizona jail. Before he went on trial, he jumped bail—his life, he claimed, was in danger—and fled to California. There he experienced messianic visions in which three personages appeared on a cloud and told him that God wanted him to lead the fight in restoring Spanish and Mexican land grants to Hispanic-Americans.

Tijerina had been to Mexico, where he had studied hundreds of land grant records. He claimed that over the years Anglos had illegally taken millions of acres from the descendants of Spanish settlers in the Southwest. The Treaty of Guadalupe Hidalgo that had ended the Mexican War in 1848 had guaranteed land titles held under Spanish and Mexican rule, but through thievery and shady deals, and through confiscation by the U.S. Forest Service, Anglos had acquired the land.

Tijerina joined an effort already begun by Hispanic-American farmers in northern New Mexico to regain some 600,000 acres, called the Tierra Amarilla tract, one of more than 1,700 land grants they, and other Hispanic-American settlers in the Southwest, had received prior to the advent of U.S. control. While a fugitive from the law, Tijerina operated underground to build his movement, and he returned to the Roman Catholic church so he could develop a stronger appeal among Hispanic-Americans.

When the statute of limitations in his bail-jumping case expired in 1962, he went public and the following year founded Alianza Federal de Mercedes (Federal Alliance of Land Grants). He declared that the group wanted the restoration of land grants to their Spanish descendants under the Treaty of Guadalupe Hidalgo.

Tijerina applied his talents as a preacher to his new mission and captivated audiences with a pounding, frenetic style filled with emotion. One observer said that "Tijerina's sturdy physique and unusually mobile face framed by coal black hair, combined with a tremendous range of vocal pitch and intensity, enable him to hold audiences spellbound for hours. His hands and arms . . . move constantly, fisting, clapping, wringing, waving, flying into the air."

In 1967, he founded Alianza Federal de los Pueblos Libres, and that June district attorney Alfonso Sanchez tried to arrest several of the group's members in Coyote, New Mexico, for raids against Anglo ranchers. About 20 *Alianzistas* retaliated by descending on Tierra Amarilla, a town in the tract of land claimed by Hispanic-Americans. They attempted to make a citizen's arrest of Sanchez but failed to find him and instead took over the Rio Arriba county courthouse. A gun battle ensued between the *Alianzistas* and the police; a jailer and a state trooper were wounded.

The *Alianzistas* then fled Tierra Amarilla, retreating into the mountains with some 400 soldiers, police, and state troopers, supported by 200 military vehicles, in pursuit. Tijerina was arrested in Albuquerque two weeks later with several other *Alianzistas*. When they appeared in court, the *Alianzistas* interrupted the legal proceedings with shouts of "Viva Tijerina!"

In November 1967, Tijerina was found guilty of assault in an earlier case. He had declared himself a candidate for governor under the banner of the People's Constitutional Party, but because of his felony conviction, the state supreme court disqualified him. Tijerina joined the Poor People's March (see entry, 1968) on Washington, D.C., and spoke at several college campuses, where he condemned the Anglo power structure and the Vietnam War.

Also in 1968, Tijerina went on trial in Albuquerque for his role in the raid at Tierra Amarilla. Charged with two counts of assault to commit murder, kidnapping, possession of a deadly weapon, and destruction of state property, he fired his attorney and defended himself. Tijerina argued that he had the right to attempt a citizen's arrest. As it turned out, only one person, Eulogio Salazar, the jailer at the Rio Arriba county courthouse, could positively identify Tijerina as among the 20 raiders, so the jury acquitted the defendant. Later, Salazar was found beaten to death in his car.

A showdown with forest service rangers in summer 1969 caused Tijerina to be charged with assault and destruction of property. He was found guilty that October and began a two-year prison term at the federal penitentiary in La Tuna, Texas. In a letter written that summer to his followers, Tijerina said, "What is my real crime? As I and the poor people see it, especially the Indo-Hispanos, my only crime is UPHOLDING OUR RIGHTS PROTECTED BY THE TREATY OF GUADALUPE HIDALGO."

Paroled in 1971, Tijerina was prohibited from holding any office in Alianza for five years. He subsequently pursued a more subdued approach and talked about building a brotherhood among people. At the same time, he tried to persuade the Mexican government to pressure the United States into abiding by the land grant clauses found in the Treaty of Guadalupe Hidalgo. Tijerina resumed his presidency of Alianza in 1976, and in the mid-1980s began blaming Jews for the loss of the land grants. He made several rambling and emotional statements to that effect while denying that he was anti-Semitic.

Earlier, former New Mexico governor David Cargo said about Tijerina and his movement: "This whole thing—*Alianza*—it had little to do with grants. Their real fight was poverty. The *Alianza* was a historical aberration. It was about their social condition. They were poor, dirt poor, and they had no opportunity." Cargo's analysis accurately summarized the dominant condition that had sparked Tijerina's movement. But to Tijerina his crusade meant more than economics. While the taking of the land grants from Hispanic-Americans had caused poverty, he believed it had done much more—it had robbed his people of their culture and decimated their spirit.

Further Reading

Gardner, Richard. *Grito! Reies Tijerina and the New Mexico Land Grant War of 1967.* New York: Harper & Row, 1971.

Nabokov, Peter. *Tijerina and the Courthouse Raid.* Berkeley, Calif.: Ramparts Press, 1970.

Vigil, Ernesto B. *The Crusade for Justice: Chicano Militancy and the Government's War on Dissent.* Madison: University of Wisconsin Press, 1999.

1967 Heavyweight Boxing Champion Muhammad Ali Refuses to Be Drafted into the Military

On April 28, 1967, world heavyweight boxing champion Muhammad Ali stood in front of officers at the U.S. Armed Forces Examining and Entrance Station in Houston, Texas, and announced he would refuse to be drafted to fight in the Vietnam War. "I refuse to be inducted into the armed forces of the United States," he wrote in an official statement, "because I claim to be exempt as a minister of the religion of Islam."

Born Cassius Clay, Ali (1942–) had won the heavyweight boxing championship by upsetting Sonny Liston in 1964 and had gone on to defend his title nine times. He had also become a Black Muslim, and that led to his claim that he was "a minister of the religion of Islam." But for Ali, his greater objection to the war came from his belief that it was unjust. "Man," he told one reporter several weeks before the military tried to induct him, "I ain't got no quarrel with them Vietcong." He insisted that the United States was wrong to be sending so many African-Americans to die overseas while oppressing black people at home.

In winter 1967, Ali appeared at antiwar rallies on college campuses, and he suffered severe recrimination for his outspokenness. The federal government spied on him and revoked his passport, hate mail poured in, and his popularity plummeted. The legislature in his home state of Kentucky called him a "discredit . . . to the names of the thousands who gave their lives for this country during his lifetime."

The adversity and pressure, however, stiffened Ali's resolve. He refused to take the easy way out and serve in the National Guard; he rejected calls that he accept a noncombatant role in the army. Instead, he said, "I either have to obey the laws of the land or the laws of Allah. I have nothing to lose by standing up and following my beliefs." Referring to what had happened to blacks in the past, he added: "We've been in jail for four hundred years."

But Ali had a lot to lose. He was sentenced to a five-year jail term, and the organizations that sanctioned boxing stripped him of his title and prevented him from fighting until, in a unanimous decision, the U.S. Supreme Court overturned his conviction and upheld his draft appeal on religious grounds.

Ali regained the heavyweight championship in 1974 when he defeated George Foreman in a fight in the African country of Zaire. Quoted by David Remnick in *King of the World* (1998), Ali recalled, "I was determined to be one nigger that the white man didn't get. One nigger that you didn't get, white man. You understand? One nigger you ain't going to get."

Further Reading

Marqusee, Mike. *Redemption Song: Muhammad Ali and the Spirit of the Sixties.* London and New York: Verso, 1999.

Remnick, David. *King of the World: Muhammad Ali and the Rise of an American Hero.* New York: Random House, 1998.

Muhammad Ali trains for a fight in 1966. (Hulton Deutsch Collection/CORBIS)

Blacks March for Economic Opportunity in Poor People's Campaign 1968

In 1967, civil rights leader Martin Luther King, Jr., stated that to eliminate inequality Americans would have to undertake a "radical reconstruction of society itself." With that in mind, he developed plans for a Poor People's Campaign, open to all races, that would begin in spring 1968 with a march to Washington, D.C., followed by an encampment there.

The Poor People's Campaign was marred with trouble from the start. A few weeks before it could get under way, an assassin killed King in Memphis, Tennessee. The assassination led to riots in many urban ghettos; the riots, in turn, caused a white backlash against the entire civil rights movement, making the environment for the campaign more hostile.

Dr. Ralph Abernathy, King's chief lieutenant in the Southern Christian Leadership Conference (SCLC), proceeded with the Poor People's Campaign. Pushing aside dissension within the SCLC, he led the protesters in May 1968. All told, about 50,000 people, mostly African-Americans, joined the campaign—a large number but considerably fewer than expected. They marched on Washington, D.C., to demand congressional action to help poor people—a goal that went well beyond the SCLC's previous civil rights program to promote racial integration. Now economic demands were being made with the goal of promoting a more equitable distribution of wealth. The *New York Times* said the protest "was planned to probe the essence of the American system, to see whether it could make a massive material and spiritual readjustment to change the lives of its poverty-stricken millions and construct a rational future where base poverty would not coexist with stupendous wealth."

The Poor People's Campaign failed miserably. The marchers set up a shantytown, called Resurrection City, near the Lincoln Memorial, but it turned into a muddy mess, complete with roving gangs, thefts, and muggings; the government arrested Abernathy—he spent 20 days in jail—and forced the demonstrators out. The ignominious defeat reflected the hardening of attitudes between whites and blacks and the increasing intolerance of many African-Americans for King's strategy of nonviolent protest. Many African-Americans began to look increasingly to the black power movement for inspiration and guidance.

Further Reading

Abernathy, Ralph. *And the Walls Came Tumbling Down: An Autobiography.* New York: Harper & Row, 1989.
Reef, Catherine. *Ralph David Abernathy.* Parsippany, N.J.: Dillon Press, 1995.

1968 Protests Shake the Nation

Shocking events shattered American society in 1968 and threatened to destroy it. In addition to the assassinations of Martin Luther King, Jr., and Democratic presidential candidate Robert F. Kennedy, protests and violence shook Columbia University in New York, the Democratic National Convention in Chicago, and San Francisco State College in California.

King's assassination in April so angered African-Americans that, in direct contradiction to the slain minister's commitment to nonviolent protest, thousands rioted in cities across the country. Many concluded that it was not just a lone gunman who had killed King, but all of white America. Tension increased to the point that soldiers were stationed atop the Capitol building in Washington, D.C., to protect it against a possible assault. Kennedy's assassination in June only reinforced the view that anyone prominent who spoke out against the Vietnam War and stood for the poor, blacks, ethnics, and the powerless in society would be killed.

The protest at Columbia began soon after King's murder; it was a product of the nationwide atmosphere of turmoil and distrust of authority and of conditions specific to the highly selective private college. First, traditional rules—the system of *in loco parentis* where college administrators assumed the role of parent and used regulations to treat students as children—still prevailed, allowing students little voice in campus affairs. Second, Columbia had contracted to engage in weapons research for the government through a program called the Institute for Defense Analysis (IDA). Third, for several years Columbia had been expanding outward from its campus at Morningside Heights into neighboring Harlem, and in the process acquired and leveled buildings that had housed blacks and Hispanics. Columbia now had plans to build a gym, a structure that many felt would scar the neighborhood, in Morningside Park. The plans were strongly opposed by Harlem residents, who believed the university cared little for their community. Finally, student activism had been increasing, with Students for a Democratic Society (SDS; see entry, 1960) demonstrating against the Vietnam War and the presence of military recruiters on campus.

Perhaps, then, no one should have been surprised when students began supporting local residents in a protest against Columbia. In April 1968, Mark Rudd, the college's SDS president, interrupted a memorial to Martin Luther King, Jr., to denounce Columbia's racist policies from the pulpit. Soon afterward, six radicals protested the college's affiliation with the IDA by demonstrating inside Low Library, where President Grayson Kirk had his office.

Then, on April 23, about 500 activists from SDS, from the Student Afro-American Society, and from more moderate groups held a rally on campus and marched to the gym construction site, which they proceeded to occupy. Presently, they descended on the administration building, Hamilton Hall, took a dean hostage, commandeered the offices, and renamed the structure Malcolm X Hall.

Other students entered President Kirk's office and went through his files, discovering papers that revealed details about the IDA. Over the next two days, 1,000 students joined the original protesters and took over additional buildings. On April 26, one of Columbia's vice presidents assured the students that there would be no attacks against them, but negotiations to end the protest collapsed, and President Kirk called in the police, who on April 30 charged into the buildings and bloodied students' heads.

While this response received widespread support from the college trustees and from enraged suburbanites who watched the confrontation on television, it polarized the campus. Angered by the bloodshed, moderate students and many teachers joined the protest, boycotting classes and shutting down most of the university. Columbia failed to resume a normal schedule that semester.

In the end, the protesters gained several concessions: President Kirk resigned, and Columbia severed its ties with the IDA and promised to get the consent of Harlem residents before building the proposed gym.

While events at Columbia raged, other groups planned to stage protests at the Democratic National Convention scheduled for Chicago in August. The plans came from two different sources, often at odds with each other. Radical political activists provided one source. They had formed a group called MOBE (National Mobilization Committee to End the War in Vietnam), which evolved from the November 8th Mobilization Committee that had been founded in 1966. MOBE included Rennie Davis, David Dellinger, Tom Hayden, and members of the liberal National Lawyers Guild, among them Bernardine Dohrn, a leader in the Columbia protest and soon-to-be leader of the terrorist group Weatherman. In October 1967, MOBE sponsored a March on the Pentagon that attracted 150,000 protesters. (MOBE split apart in 1969, reorganized later that year, and then dissolved in 1970.)

A second source for the protest emerged at the end of 1967 when Abbie Hoffman, his wife Anita, and three friends talked about staging a Festival of Life at the Democratic National Convention that would confront what they called the Democratic war party, or the Convention of Death. They named their organization the Youth International Party, or Yippies (see entry, 1967).

In the days before the convention, tension heightened. Mayor Richard Daley put all 12,000 Chicago police on 12-hour shifts; the government mobilized 5,000 National Guardsmen; the FBI assigned 1,000 agents to Chicago; and the army placed 6,000 troops in the suburbs. Meanwhile, radicals among the protesters itched for a confrontation, especially Hayden, who called the national government "an outlaw institution under the control of war criminals."

The Yippies began their Festival of Life at Lincoln Park, but it turned into a disaster. The next day, Chicago's police disrupted the festival's rock music by ordering the Yippies to remove a flatbed truck intended for use as a stage. Then, after a curfew took effect and many in the crowd refused to leave, the police charged, cracking heads with their nightsticks. Among the 2,000 demonstrators some relished the onslaught and fought back, and the cops responded with indiscriminate violence, clubbing a *Newsweek* reporter after he showed his credentials, beating an assistant U.S. attorney general dressed in a suit and tie, and attacking ministers.

On Monday, August 26, as the Democratic National Convention began, small groups reconvened at Lincoln Park and ran into the nearby streets, throwing rocks and bottles and smashing the windows of police cars. The cops closed the park that night, and when a hail of rocks greeted them, they assaulted the crowd—with badges and nametags removed so they could avoid identification.

That Wednesday, a protest crowd gathered around the band shell at Grant Park—an older group, many among them campaigners for presidential candidate Eugene McCarthy. When a teenage boy climbed a pole to lower the American flag, the police flailed away at the protesters, clubs again swinging.

Music and Radicalism

Much like earlier protests, such as IWW activist and songwriter Joe Hill (see entry, 1915), the countercultural upheaval of the 1960s and early 1970s found expression in music. Around 1960, many young people began rejecting packaged rock 'n' roll as irrelevant to the social issues confronting them. They turned instead to folk music, which had for years treated social problems and war as serious issues. Thus they listened to Pete Seeger, Joan Baez, Phil Ochs, and, most especially, to Bob Dylan.

Dylan infused popular music with a social consciousness. Political activist Todd Gitlin later recalled, "We admired Dylan's ability to smuggle the subversive into mass-culture trappings." By the late 1960s, rock music had hardened considerably with bands such as Steppenwolf and MC5 expressing a highly politicized, anti-capitalist message.

For young people in the 1960s, music was a vital part of daily life, and of almost every demonstration. Rock expressed a mentality that challenged the foundations of mainstream society. Activist John Sinclair said, "For our generation, music is the most vital force in most of our lives."

Popular music has continued to be associated with rebellion, protest, and counterculture. The gay rights movement of the 1970s, for example, was intimately associated with specific music, as were the feminist "riot grrls" of the 1990s. Gadfly activist Ralph Nader used his association with rockers such as Patti Smith and Eddie Vedder to boost attendance at rallies for his year 2000 presidential bid. Meanwhile, rock stars have used their status to oppose everything from apartheid to nuclear weapons to globalization.

Meanwhile, several young people, including, as it turned out, an undercover agent, attempted to raise a red T-shirt on the flagpole, once more enraging the police.

In the evening, protesters tried to march peacefully to the amphitheater where the convention delegates were meeting. The police, however, beat them and many bystanders. Television cameras broadcast the melee as the crowd chanted "The whole world is watching! The whole world is watching!" Tear gas used against the protesters drifted into the amphitheater, choking some delegates.

The violence in Chicago left the United States divided. On the one hand, public opinion polls showed most people siding with the Chicago police and condemning the protesters. (They did not know that one of every six protesters was an undercover agent.) On the other hand, many protesters considered the police violence a symptom of a sick and oppressive society.

With the gulf between extremists and mainstream America widening, violence erupted at San Francisco State College, where black students and their supporters clashed with a conservative administration. At least since the 1950s, San Francisco State had been a school that attracted bohemians and artists. But tension had begun to build in 1967, when several blacks physically attacked the white editor of the campus newspaper for having printed an article denigrating boxer Muhammad Ali (see entry, 1967). At the same time, the Black Student Union (BSU) announced its support of a third-world revolution in which all people of color would rebel and establish power in their own communities, separate from white influence.

In 1968, the BSU demanded a black studies program, the hiring of black professors, and open admissions for students of color (only 700 African-Americans attended the college), along with the waiving of tuition for them. The administration agreed to the black studies program, though on a more limited basis, and promised to change admissions standards, but it stopped short of establishing an open-door policy. These measures failed to satisfy the BSU, and a BSU leader advised black students to begin carrying guns on campus to defend themselves against racist administrators.

When the BSU called a student strike in November, the college board of trustees reacted by installing S. I. Hayakawa as president. A professor with no previous administrative experience, Hayakawa had impeccable conservative credentials and immediately announced he would defy the strikers and keep the college operating at all costs. He imposed stern measures and in January 1969 prohibited campus demonstrations. When protesters rallied anyhow, mass arrests ensued.

The strike continued, though; so did the violence that included several firebombings on campus. By the end of January, both sides were exhausted, and they decided to negotiate. The administration agreed to expand its plans for a black studies program, waive admissions requirements for "third world students," and appoint a black financial administrator. But Hayakawa refused to drop charges against 700 students arrested during the strike, and the college fired 24 professors.

The strike thus ended, after 134 days, leaving deep wounds on campus and throughout the country as activists called Hayakawa's actions excessive, and middle America hailed him as a hero. Along with the protests at Columbia and in Chicago and the other disconcerting events of 1968, the Third World Strike had polarized America and shaken society to its very foundations.

Further Reading

Caute, David. *The Year of the Barricades: A Journey through 1968.* New York: Harper & Row, 1988.

Farber, David. *Chicago '68.* Chicago: University of Chicago Press, 1988.

Gays Stand Up for Their Rights at Stonewall

1969

Much as the 1960s stirred many blacks, women, Chicanos, and Native Americans into action to protest injustice and oppression, so it did with gays. Widely discriminated against and relegated to a secretive existence, homosexuals clashed with police one summer night at a bar—Stonewall Inn— in New York City's Greenwich Village.

For several years prior to the Stonewall confrontation, some gays had been working for their liberation. One of the most notable incidents was in 1965 when activists staged a "sip-in" at nightclubs in New York to protest a rule established by the state liquor authority that no more than three homosexuals be allowed in a bar at any one time. Shortly afterward, Student Homophile Leagues were organized at Columbia University and at New York University. The 1960s countercultural promotion of the idea that individuals should be able to live as they wanted without harassment supported this expression of gay visibility and activism.

The showdown between police and gays in Greenwich Village occurred on the night of June 27, 1969. When cops moved against the Stonewall Inn, which was frequented by gays, they expected the bar's patrons to simply accept arrests without complaint, as they had usually done in the past. But this time gays fought back, and a melee resulted in injuries to four policemen. The Stonewall Inn closed, but when the police returned to the neighborhood the following night and made additional raids, a crowd of 400 young men and women hurled bottles and chanted "gay power!" The *Village Voice* newspaper called the events "a kind of liberation, as the gay brigade emerged from the bars, back rooms, and bedrooms of the Village and became street people."

Following Stonewall, gay activists formed the Gay Liberation Front (GLF) and demanded an end to discrimination based on sexual preferences. The GLF picketed companies that refused to hire homosexuals, and in June 1970 it organized Gay Pride Week to commemorate the first anniversary of Stonewall. About 10,000 gays marched in New York City while their liberation advanced elsewhere, evident in magazines and newspapers committed to gay life and in gays marching to protest the Vietnam conflict under banners proclaiming "Homosexuals against the War." Stonewall brought the gay rights movement out of the closet.

Further Reading

Clendinen, Dudley, and Adam Nagourney. *Out for Good: The Struggle to Build a Gay Rights Movement in America.*
    New York: Simon & Schuster, 1999.

Duberman, Martin. *Stonewall.* New York: Dutton, 1993.

Vine Deloria, Jr., Sides with Indian Activists in Writing *Custer Died for Your Sins*

In Custer Died for Your Sins: An Indian Manifesto, *Vine Deloria, Jr., expressed his Native American nationalism embedded in the belief that Indians should look to their own culture for guidance.*

Deloria (1933–) was born into a distinguished Indian family. His great-grandfather, Francois Des Laurias, had been a leader among the Yankton Sioux; an aunt, Ella C. Deloria, was a prominent anthropologist; and his father, Vine Deloria, Sr., held an executive post in the Episcopal church.

With that background of activism and social consciousness, Vine Deloria, Jr. spoke out on issues important to Native Americans. Given the roles of his aunt and father, however, his criticism of anthropologists and religious missionaries surprised many people.

In his youth, Deloria had thought about entering the ministry. He earned a bachelor's degree at Iowa State University in 1958, and received a theology degree from Augustana Lutheran Seminary in Rock Island, Illinois, in 1963. But instead of following in his father's footsteps, in 1964 he began serving as executive director of the National Congress of American Indians, an organization dedicated to addressing Indian problems.

Deloria earned his law degree from the University of Colorado in 1970 and then held various teaching positions. In the meantime, he had published *Custer Died for Your Sins*, a book that coincided with the rise of Indian activism evident in the occupation of Alcatraz Island (see entry, 1969) and in the formation of the American Indian Movement. Deloria argued that Indians should receive economic help from the federal government but that tribes should have sovereignty, and Native Americans should look to their traditional cultures for development because they were superior to white culture.

In *Custer Died for Your Sins*, Deloria attacked several white practices and institutions. He criticized government agencies, such as the Bureau of Indian Affairs, for their ineffective, misguided, and oftentimes cruel policies. He took religious missionaries to task for trying to rid Indians of their Indian ways, and despite his admission that Christian churches could still provide meaningful guidance to Native Americans, he urged Indians to turn to their own religions. "For me at least," he wrote, "Christianity had been a sham to cover over the white man's shortcomings."

He aimed a heavy criticism at anthropologists. "Every summer when school is out a veritable stream of immigrants heads into Indian country. . . ." he wrote. "From every rock and cranny in the East they emerge, as if responding to some primeval fertility rite, and flock to the reservations. 'They' are the anthropologists." Deloria claimed that reports issued by anthropologists led to misguided programs that worsened conditions for Indians. In one study, anthropologists concluded that Oglala Sioux lived in poverty because they were no longer able to follow their warrior instincts. Deloria wrote:

The question of the Oglala Sioux is a question that plagues every Indian tribe in the nation, if it will closely examine itself. Tribes have been defined as one thing, the definition has been completely explored . . . and finally the conclusion has been reached—Indians must be redefined in terms that white men will accept, even if that means re-Indianizing them according to a white man's ideas of what they were like in the past and should logically be in the future.

In short, Indians should not allow themselves to be defined by whites, nor should they accept white answers to their problems.

Deloria continued his critique in subsequent works. In *We Talk, You Listen: New Tribes, New Turf* (1970), he advocated a return to tribal social organization. In *God Is Red* (1973), he called Indian religions more attuned to the natural world than Christianity. His *Behind the Trail of Broken Treaties: An Indian Declaration of Independence* (1974) aligned him with the militant American Indian Movement by describing in sympathetic terms the events that had led to that group's occupation of Wounded Knee, South Dakota (see entry, 1973).

DeLoria's 1995 book *Red Earth, White Lies: Native Americans and the Myth of Scientific Fact* met with a generally hostile reception. Reviewer John C. Whittaker, called it "a wretched piece of Native American creationist claptrap that has all the flaws of the Biblical creationists [Deloria] disdains." Deloria wrote that Indian traditions provide a better way of understanding the world than does science, and then took this view to the extreme by condemning nearly all archaeological findings about Native American culture and placing his faith in tribal religious stories about how Indian culture had developed.

Through these works, but most especially through *Custer Died for Your Sins*, Deloria joined other Indian activists in stirring the cause of Native American nationalism and expressing pride in Indian culture.

Further Reading

Deloria, Vine. *Custer Died for Your Sins: An Indian Manifesto.* New York: Macmillan, 1969.

Warrior, Robert Allen. *Tribal Secrets: Recovering American Indian Intellectual Traditions.* Minneapolis: University of Minnesota Press, 1995.

Weatherman Seeks a Violent Revolution   1969

Amid the assassinations of Martin Luther King, Jr., and Robert Kennedy, the violence at the Democratic National Convention in Chicago, and the smoldering ruins from ghetto fires, some leaders within the leftist Students for a Democratic Society (SDS; see entry, 1960) formed a militant group in 1969 to hasten revolution: Weatherman.

Weatherman evolved from the Third World Marxists, a faction within SDS led by James Mellen, Bernardine Dohrn, and Mark Rudd. They advocated the use of street fighting to weaken U.S. imperialism, a rearguard action that would coincide with revolutions then under way in developing countries. Third World Marxists were in conflict with another SDS faction, Progressive Labor (PL), that believed street fights would only create a reactionary backlash among industrial workers, people crucial to any socialist revolt. At the SDS national convention in June 1969, the Third World Marxists presented a position paper, "You Don't Need a Weatherman to Know Which Way the Wind Blows," a title that came from the lyrics of a song by Bob Dylan. From that paper the group obtained its name.

SDS split apart at the national convention as Weatherman booted PL from the group. Known for its turgid doctrinal pamphlets, Weatherman nevertheless developed an intense militancy. To foster unity, it formed collectives aimed at eliminating individualism and destroying male dominance by ending monogamous relationships; couples, for example, could be broken up by a decision of the collective, with men ordered to sleep with men, women with women, men with a variety of women, and so on.

In summer 1969, Weatherman launched an offensive. In one action in the Northeast, it tried to recruit members at community colleges and high schools by marching into classrooms, tying up and gagging teachers, and presenting revolutionary speeches. At the Harvard Institute for International Affairs (suspect for its conservatism), they smashed windows, tore out phones, and beat up professors. In September, several women from Weatherman marched through a hippie neighborhood in Pittsburgh, carrying the flag of North Vietnam's National Liberation Front, and chanting "Ho Lives!" (referring to communist leader Ho Chi Minh).

Weatherman failed to gain many recruits, but it still wanted to foment revolution, so on October 8 it invaded Chicago to begin what it called National Action but what newspapers called the Days of Rage—

a direct assault on the police, or the "pigs." Weatherman declared: "The pigs are the capitalist state, and as such define the limits of all political struggles." Weatherman expected several thousand supporters to appear, but only a few hundred turned out, and during three days of street fighting, the police bloodied and arrested many of them.

Undaunted, Weatherman participated that November in the Moratorium, an anti–Vietnam War protest in Washington, that attracted at least 250,000 demonstrators. Fewer than 3,000 of them followed Weatherman, but the radicals attacked the South Vietnamese Embassy and assaulted the Justice Department with rocks, bottles, and smoke bombs. This violence only helped President Richard Nixon, who used it to prove his point that the antiwar movement was dangerous and un-American.

The Moratorium was the last major organized appearance by Weatherman. Disappointed by their failure to gain greater support, the core members, about 100 in all, decided at their national War Council in December 1969 to go underground, hence taking the name Weather Underground. In so doing they turned inward, convinced they needed neither the proletariat nor college students to make a revolution. Instead, they intended to weaken the government through terrorist acts.

Rudd, Dohrn, and others disappeared from view. Then on March 6, 1970, a townhouse in New York City collapsed in a huge explosion when Weather Underground members living there accidentally detonated a bomb. The blast killed three of the radicals, while two others escaped. Despite this setback, the Weather Underground continued its violent tactics by bombing several buildings, including the New York City police headquarters on Centre Street, and it issued threatening communiqués, such as one in July 1970 that declared: "The time is now. Political power grows out of a gun, a Molotov, a riot, a commune . . . and from the soul of the people."

Isolated even from fellow radicals who disliked Weatherman's tactics and its Marxist ideology, the group accomplished little. In the mid-1970s, the Weather Underground shattered into two quarreling factions. Some members drifted back into society, but in 1981, several former ones, reorganized as the May 19th Coalition, allied with the Black Liberation Army and robbed a Brink's armored car near New York City, killing a guard and two policemen. With the perpetrators behind bars in 1984, the revolutionary energy from Weather Underground dissipated, the group's activities a testament to an insular radicalism whose self-delusion produced only misguided actions rejected by nearly everyone else.

Further Reading

Jacobs, Ron. *The Way the Wind Blew: A History of the Weather Underground.* New York: Verso, 1997.
Sale, Kirkpatrick. *SDS.* New York: Random House, 1973.

1969 American Indians Occupy Alcatraz

When American Indians raised their flag—a banner displaying a red teepee under a broken peace pipe— above Alcatraz, the abandoned federal prison in California, they announced their desire for liberation and an end to government treachery. They awakened Americans to the mistreatment they had suffered, and were suffering, from years of neglect and oppression.

The protest began on November 9, 1969, when Richard Oakes chartered a boat and took with him a group of Indians who symbolically occupied Alcatraz Island. Oakes and his followers left Alcatraz, but he recruited a second, larger group of Indian students from the University of California at Los Angeles who returned to the island on November 20 and started the highly publicized occupation that would last into June 1971. This group took the title "Indians of All Tribes," to reflect its pan-Indian nature. The occupiers took over the island based on an old treaty that gave Sioux Indians the right to claim unused federal land. They wanted the U.S. government to surrender Alcatraz and provide money for an Indian cultural center to be built there.

The Indians organized themselves by forming an elected council and assigning jobs to each occupier. Some took part in security; others taught school; still others washed clothes and cooked. Over the next few months, about 10,000 Indians visited their embattled kinsmen, and the activist American Indian Movement gave its support. Some protesters began broadcasting "Radio Free Alcatraz" to reveal the dreadful conditions facing most Native Americans. In response to the protest, newspapers and magazines ran stories detailing life on the reservations—where unemployment exceeded 50 percent, most people lacked running water, and disease and alcoholism were overwhelming. In fact, the initial sympathetic reaction from the press fulfilled a goal of the occupiers to stir Americans into recognizing the Indian plight.

The Indians who occupied Alcatraz drew the connection between their action and conditions elsewhere when, satirically, they said the island fortress resembled most reservations in its isolation, inadequate sanitation facilities, unemployment, nonproductive land, and lack of schools. Further, those who had once lived there had "always been held prisoners and kept dependent on others."

The occupation continued into 1970, with the federal government showing little serious interest in negotiations; it wanted, instead, to stall so that the Indians would lose enthusiasm for their protest.

Indians protest at Alcatraz. (Bettmann/CORBIS)

The American Indian Movement

The strongest Native American protest group appeared in 1968 when several Indian leaders, among them Dennis Banks, formed the American Indian Movement (AIM). They modeled the organization on the Black Panthers (see entry, 1966), and, like the Panthers, they sought to prevent false arrests, harassment, and brutality by the police—but in this instance against Indians living in urban ghettos.

By 1970, AIM chapters had taken root in San Francisco, Los Angeles, Denver, Chicago, Cleveland, and Milwaukee. Their members came from many different tribes: Santee, Oglala Lakota, Ponca, Navajo, Oneida, Cherokee, Winnebago, and others. The inclusiveness reflected AIM's desire to surmount tribal differences and unite all Indians in an expanding effort to fight government oppression and protect Indian rights.

AIM gained national prominence in 1971 and 1972 with several daring protests. On July 4, 1971, AIM staged a "countercelebration" atop Mount Rushmore in South Dakota, a site they considered sacred and one that had been stolen from them in the 1800s. On Thanksgiving Day, AIM took over the Mayflower replica ship at Plymouth, Massachusetts, and painted Plymouth Rock red.

In February 1972, AIM staged a large protest in Gordon, Nebraska, when 1,000 marchers decried the refusal of local authorities to file charges against two white men implicated in the murder of an Oglala Lakota. A protest at Wounded Knee (see entry, 1973) would turn into a two-month stand-off between AIM members and federal agents. Unfortunately for AIM, their protests caused the FBI to infiltrate the group and mount a campaign to destroy it.

Indeed, during that year, a rift developed among the occupiers, and non-Indians settled on the island, bringing with them drug use and a general aversion to Indian leadership.

At the same time, the federal government shut off electrical power to the island and removed a barge that had provided fresh water to the occupiers. Finally, on June 10, 1971, federal marshals, FBI agents, and special forces police descended on Alcatraz and removed the few remaining Indians, thus ending the occupation.

The protesters at Alcatraz obtained no concessions. Yet they had demonstrated that Native Americans from different tribes could unite, at least for awhile, in fighting their oppression, and they sparked a larger wave of Indian protests in the early and mid-1970s, including the showdown at Wounded Knee (see entry, 1973).

Further Reading

Churchill, Ward. *Agents of Repression: The FBI's Secret War against the Black Panther Party and the American Indian Movement.* Boston: South End Press, 1988.

Johnson, Troy R. *The Occupation of Alcatraz Island: Indian Self-determination and the Rise of Indian Activism.* Urbana: University of Illinois Press, 1996.

Matthiessen, Peter. *In the Spirit of Crazy Horse.* New York: Viking Press, 1983.

1969   Feminists Form the Militant Group Redstockings

In 1969, Shulamith Firestone organized Redstockings, a militant feminist group espousing the idea that male supremacy rather than class exploitation accounted for women's oppression.

Redstockings was one of several radical feminist groups emerging as the 1960s counterculture gave birth to the women's liberation movement. One year before beginning Redstockings, Firestone (1945–) founded New York Radical Women (NYRW), and in January 1968 she led that group, which was preparing to protest the Vietnam War at the Capitol building in Washington, D.C., in a demonstration for women's liberation. She later recalled, "We staged an actual funeral procession with a larger-than-life dummy on a transported bier, complete with a feminine getup. . . . Hanging from the bier were such disposable items as . . . curlers, garters, and hairspray. Streamers floated off it and we also carried large banners, such as 'DON'T CRY: RESIST.'" At the gathering the NYRW distributed a pamphlet that read:

TRADITIONAL WOMANHOOD IS DEAD.
TRADITIONAL WOMEN WERE BEAUTIFUL . . . BUT REALLY POWERLESS.
"UPPITY" WOMEN WERE EVEN MORE BEAUTIFUL . . . BUT STILL POWERLESS.
SISTERHOOD IS POWERFUL!
HUMANHOOD THE ULTIMATE!

The NYRW action was intended to raise women's consciousness, and in so doing it foreshadowed Firestone's involvement with Redstockings.

The name Redstockings was a reference to "Bluestockings," a title once used to refer to nineteenth-century feminist intellectuals. The group's attachment to the idea that male supremacy rather than class exploitation explained women's oppression was reflected in its manifesto, issued in 1969: "We identify the agents of our oppression as men," they wrote. "All other forms of exploitation and oppression. . . .are extensions of male supremacy. . . . We call on all of our sisters to unite with us in our struggle."

The group disrupted hearings in the New York legislature on abortion reform after it learned that the legislative committee handling the matter put together a list of witnesses consisting of 14 men and one nun. One protester said to the legislature: "We are the ones that have had the abortions. . . . This is why we're here tonight. . . . We are the only experts." Where the legislators wanted to modify abortion laws, Redstockings wanted all such laws repealed.

Redstockings distributed feminist literature, and, perhaps most famously, staged a sit-in at the *Ladies' Home Journal* to protest the magazine's sexist content. But Firestone soon concluded that the Redstockings were too involved in consciousness-raising rather than in pursuing truly radical change. As a result, in 1970 she left the group. Redstockings continues in existence; today it describes itself as "a grassroots think tank established by movement veterans for defending and advancing the women's liberation agenda."

Further Reading

Morgan, Robin. *The Anatomy of Freedom: Feminism in Four Dimensions.* 2d ed. New York: W. W. Norton, 1994.

Morgan, Robin, ed. *Sisterhood Is Powerful: An Anthology of Writings from the Women's Liberation Movement.* New York: Vintage Books, 1970.

CHAPTER NINE

Contemporary United States

The period labeled "contemporary United States" spans from the mid-1970s, when most Americans were cynical and exhausted from the countercultural upheaval of the previous 10 years, through the 1990s, when arch-conservatives gathered in militias and a domestic terrorist bombed a federal building in Oklahoma City, into the twenty-first century, with the devastating terrorist attacks at the World Trade Center in New York City and the Pentagon near Washington, D.C.

Despite a conservative drive in the mid-1970s and the 1980s to roll back the counterculture and limit the power of the federal government, rebels and renegades from the left continued to push for change. They included the American Indian Movement, which staged a protest at Wounded Knee, South Dakota, in 1973; the Animal Liberation Front, which sought to end the mistreatment of laboratory, farm, and other animals; and the Guerrilla Girls, who formed in 1985 to fight sexism in the art world. On the right, Lyndon LaRouche organized the Revolutionary Youth Movement to fight Zionists and establish a dictatorship that would expel all Jews from the United States.

Differences between liberals and conservatives led to a political and culture war in which reactionaries complained about big government's violation of individual

> "In Ethiopia they have a saying, 'When spiders unite, they can tie down a lion.' . . . [I]f all of us small citizen forces come together, we can force these guys to change."
>
> Kevin Danaher, co-founder of Global Exchange, 1999

liberty and its promotion of ethnic and racial diversity. The battle between the two groups occurred as the United States quickly defeated Iraq in the Persian Gulf War of 1990 and entered a post–Cold War world following the 1991 collapse of the Soviet Union.

Conservatives argued that affirmative action had rewarded people for their skin color while oppressing whites; feminists had ruined families; and cultural malcontents—everyone from Hollywood filmmakers, to novelists, to rock stars—had corrupted society's values. Activists on the right fought these influences, and in one notable battle they condemned federal funding of the arts for promoting "immoral works." The dispute made clear that a "culture war" was under way, a vaguely defined but intense struggle between left- and right-wing beliefs that dominated the political scene throughout the 1990s.

The "culture war" stirred right-wing extremists who believed that an intrusive, powerful government threatened liberty. They assailed efforts to curtail gun ownership and spun stories about an impending police state. Some formed militias, and a handful resorted to terrorism; in April 1995, in an attack that killed more than 160 people, Timothy McVeigh bombed the Alfred P. Murrah Building in Oklahoma City.

That same year, racial divide widened when a largely African-American jury in Los Angeles acquitted black football and entertainment star O. J. Simpson of having murdered his former wife Nicole Brown Simpson and her friend, Ron Goldman. Because the evidence against Simpson appeared to be irrefutable, whites reacted to the verdict with disgust, while many African-Americans celebrated as they claimed that Simpson had beaten a racist police force and judicial system.

During the remaining years of the 1990s, several sensational events kept the culture war and racial tension alive. In August 1997, white police officers in New York City brutalized Abner Louima, a 32-year-old Haitian immigrant whom they had arrested. If more evidence was needed that racism was still a widespread problem, the actions of white supremacists in June 1998 made it clear. Three white men in Jasper, Texas, tied an African-American, James Byrd, Jr., to the back of their pickup truck and dragged him for three miles, tearing his body to shreds.

The cultural divide on the issue of sexual preference intensified early in 1998 when Russell Henderson beat and killed a homosexual, Matthew Shepard, in Laramie, Wyoming. Henderson's trial the following year, at which he was found guilty, brought cries of "God hates fags!" from one fundamentalist preacher, and homophobic statements from others on the far right.

But more than any other event, a scandal involving President Bill Clinton and White House intern Monica Lewinsky revealed the disturbing cultural divide. Special prosecutor Kenneth Starr charged that, in trying to hide an adulterous relationship with Lewinsky, Clinton had perjured himself and obstructed justice.

In December 1998, the House impeached Clinton for lying under oath to a grand jury and for obstructing justice. The majority counsel for the House Judiciary Committee, David Schippers, said,

> The President . . . has lied under oath in a civil deposition, lied under oath to a criminal grand jury. He lied to the people, he lied to his Cabinet, he lied to his top aides, and now he's lied under oath to the Congress of the United States. *There's no one left to lie to.*

Clinton became only the second president ever to be impeached (by the House of Representatives), leaving him with "a big, permanent stain on his record," according to one of his advisors. In January 1999, the Senate tried and acquitted him, and he remained in office. Clinton survived less because of what the evidence said than because public opinion polls (and his own, shrewd manipulation of the public) showed that most Americans still opposed his impeachment in a time of economic prosperity and thought that his crimes, while disgraceful, fell short of the severity needed to either place him on trial in the Senate or impeach him.

Nevertheless, the scandal had sullied Clinton's presidency and stoked debates about America's moral decline. To many conservatives, Clinton, the first president to have come of age during the countercultural 1960s, was a living symbol of the loose morals and hypocritical actions of that era. To them, Clinton proved that liberalism had led the country down the road of immorality.

The culture war cooled, however, as the scandal faded. Oddly, while the economy boomed in the mid- and late 1990s, left-wing radicals found they had something in common with the reactionaries: they, too, hated globalization, as evident in their protest in 1999 against the World Trade Organization meeting in Seattle, Washington. The left wing railed against globalization for its threat to individualism, though for them the belief was that this development would damage progressive programs, such as those concerned with protecting the environment, while the far right's belief was that globalization would create a one-world government that would restrict individual rights.

The smallness of an increasingly interconnected world took a tragic turn on September 11, 2001, when terrorists connected to the militant Islamic group Al-Qaeda killed approximately 3,000 people. Although the terrorist assault was staged by a foreign rather than domestic group, it so astounded liberals and conservatives alike that it left them scrambling to define the meaning of the horrific act for dissidents within the United States, and for the future of protest. Would the need for greater security limit free speech? Would the patriotic rally around a war on terrorism cause dissent to be characterized as un-American and subject to repression? In the year 2002, these questions remained to be fully answered, and dissent—clearly a vital part of America's history—existed in a tenuous state.

Native American Protesters Are Surrounded at Wounded Knee 1973

In February 1973, a violent confrontation erupted between members of the American Indian Movement (AIM) and the federal government at Wounded Knee, located on the Pine Ridge Reservation in South Dakota.

The American Indian Movement was founded in 1968 by Eddie Benton Banai, Dennis Banks, Clyde Bellecourt, and George Mitchell to protest the mistreatment of Native Americans by police in Minneapolis, Minnesota. AIM wanted to prevent false arrests, harassment, and brutality—many of the same issues that the Black Panthers (see entry, 1966) were facing and fighting in African-American neighborhoods. AIM pledged also to combat racial discrimination in housing, health care, and employment; and it wanted to address violations of Indian treaty rights.

In 1969, AIM began expanding into a national organization, sparked by the Indians of All Tribes (IAT) protest in California (see entry, 1969). IAT occupied Alcatraz Island, recently abandoned as a prison site, and demanded that existing treaty provisions be honored and that the site be turned over to them. IAT failed to achieve its demands, but the takeover encouraged younger Indians to expand their protests.

By 1970, AIM chapters had formed in San Francisco, Los Angeles, Denver, Chicago, Cleveland, and Milwaukee. Their members came from many different tribes, including the Santee, Oglala Lakota, Ponca, Navajo, Oneida, Cherokee, and Winnebago. The number of tribes reflected AIM's desire to unite all Indians.

In fall 1972, AIM organized the "Trail of Broken Treaties," a motorcade of about 2,000 Native Americans from more than 100 reservations that journeyed to Washington, D.C., where they held rallies and met with government officials to discuss Indian grievances. The protesters occupied the Bureau of Indian Affairs building for several days.

For Indians, the Wounded Knee site held special meaning; it was there in the late 1800s that the U.S. army massacred many Sioux—largely elderly men, women, and children. Now, in February 1973, AIM rallied at Wounded Knee to protest an alliance between tribal president Richard "Dickie" Wilson and the federal government that threatened to result in white ranchers gaining more rights to reservation lands and the government acquiring access to uranium deposits.

Wilson's police force reacted to the protesters by surrounding them, causing AIM activist Russell Means (1939–) and some 200 Indians to confiscate weapons from a trading post and erect barricades, thus creating a standoff. The federal government reacted by deploying marshals and enormous firepower, including armored personnel carriers, helicopters, and grenade launchers. Early in the showdown shots rang out—no one knows who fired first—and the government forces assaulted AIM; over the next few weeks, sporadic fighting left two Indians dead in the AIM compound and one FBI agent wounded.

When the government entered into talks with AIM, Means emerged as a negotiator, and, in meetings with the press, he strongly denounced federal actions. He joined six other AIM protesters in signing an agreement with federal officials, sealed with a traditional peace pipe ceremony, that called for a government investigation into the reservation leadership but provided no amnesty for the insurgents. He then surrendered to U.S. marshals and was arraigned before being released on bond so he could attend meetings with the Nixon Administration in Washington.

Means described the agreement as "a small victory, a preliminary victory, in our war with the U.S. over treaty rights," yet nothing came of a demand by AIM that the government recognize the Fort Laramie Treaty. This treaty had been signed in 1868 and, the Indians claimed, had been violated many times by the federal government, resulting in large losses of land. Means argued that the Wounded Knee occupation, which lasted from February 28 to May 7, 1973, taught Indian youths to take pride in their heritage. Several years later he said, "Wounded Knee woke up America. We're still here, and we're resisting. John Wayne did not kill us all."

In October 1973, Means stood trial in St. Paul, Minnesota, for his role at Wounded Knee. At the same time, he ran against Wilson for the Pine Ridge tribal presidency. Means lost, with the results widely viewed as tainted by Wilson's corrupt tactics; Means, however, won his case at St. Paul when the judge threw out the charges against him and another AIM leader, Dennis Banks, on grounds that the FBI had violated the wiretap law and that the federal government had engaged in illegal activities.

At the end of the 1970s, AIM disbanded as a national group, though it continued to operate in several localities; in the 1990s, it helped Indians in Wisconsin defend their traditional treaty rights. Means observed: "AIM never died. It only changed form."

Further Reading

Churchill, Ward, and Jim Vander Wall. *Agents of Repression: The FBI's Secret War against the Black Panther Party and the American Indian Movement.* Boston: South End Press, 1988.

Matthiessen, Peter. *In the Spirit of Crazy Horse.* New York: Viking Press, 1983.

Means, Russell. *Where White Men Fear to Tread: The Autobiography of Russell Means.* New York: St. Martin's Press, 1995.

1973 Lyndon LaRouche Organizes Right-Wing Street Gangs

In 1973, extremist Lyndon LaRouche ordered his National Caucus of Labor Committees (NCLC) to unite with urban street gangs and form political street-fighting units called the Revolutionary Youth Movement.

The NCLC emerged from the contorted transformation of its founder, Lyndon LaRouche (1922–). Originally a leftist who had been a member of the communist-affiliated Socialist Workers Party, he

Lyndon LaRouche. (Bettmann/CORBIS)

converted to the other extreme in the 1970s, accused the CIA of targeting him for assassination, and organized a far right militia movement. The CIA, he said, had been kidnapping his followers, brainwashing them, and changing them into killers who would be set into action by code words.

LaRouche's right-wing tactics remained largely the same as his left-wing ones, however, and ranged from TV advertising to violence. LaRouche directed members of the NCLC to disrupt Communist Party meetings and beat up its leaders (in what he called Operation Mop Up); he held ego-stripping sessions to rid members of their individuality and maintain their ideological purity; and he invented more stories of assassination plots to keep the group united through hysteria. By 1973, the NCLC had 600 members in 25 cities and was publishing a newspaper, *New Solidarity.*

That same year, LaRouche organized street-fighting units, or what he called a paramilitary structure, to unite urban gangs and politicize them. This Revolutionary Youth Movement, as he called it, collapsed after police arrested several gang members on weapons charges.

LaRouche infused the NCLC's paranoid political style with anti-Semitism. He declared that an evil dictatorship, dominated by international Zionist bankers, existed in the United States. He wanted this Zionist apparatus replaced by an authoritarian regime with a centralized, disciplined economy, led by engineers and scientists trained and totally committed to advancing United States world domination. In LaRouche's scenario, all political opposition would be purged by the police, and Jews would be expelled from the country. The Anti-Defamation League of B'nai B'rith accused him of injecting "anti-Semitic poison into the American political bloodstream."

To further his plan, LaRouche allied with the Ku Klux Klan. Michigan Klan leader Robert Miles praised him for "exposing the neo-atheist materialism of [secretary of state Henry] Kissinger." At the same time, in the late 1970s and early 1980s, LaRouche entered mainstream politics. He tried to win Democratic presidential primaries, but never received more than 2 percent of the vote. Political experts are uncertain about why LaRouche decided to run as a Democrat rather than a Republican. Some believe it was an opportunistic move—in the 1980s, the Democratic Party was struggling to reshape its identity in the wake of conservative Republican victories, thus LaRouche may have thought he could direct the party to embrace his ideas. Others believe he saw the Democratic Party as his greatest enemy and that he concluded he could more effectively defeat this enemy by infiltrating it and taking it over rather than by fighting it from the outside as a Republican.

Whatever the case, LaRouche supported Ronald Reagan's campaign to win the Republican presidential nomination, and though Reagan never publicly embraced LaRouche, the NCLC leader briefly wielded considerable influence within the Reagan Administration. Meanwhile, LaRouche established a secret paramilitary boot camp near Argyle, New York, where participants learned how to use rifles and explosives and formed several local militia units.

In 1988, LaRouche's political ambitions suffered a severe setback when he was convicted for loan fraud. The NCLC continued, but in diminished form. In 1996 LaRouche, out of prison, again entered the race for the Democratic presidential nomination and again lost. He entered and lost a third time in the year 2000.

LaRouche's brief fling as leader of the NCLC represented the assertion of a far-right ideology in the 1970s in reaction to liberalism and the upheaval from the counterculture in the 1960s. To offset the counterculture, LaRouche proposed an authoritarianism that would restore order to a badly divided and dispirited country suffering from increased crime and a loss of faith in leadership as a result of the Vietnam War.

Further Reading

King, Dennis. *Lyndon LaRouche and the New American Fascism.* New York: Doubleday, 1989.

LaRouche, Lyndon H. *Imperialism: The Final Stage of Bolshevism.* New York: New Benjamin Franklin House, 1984.

Radical Feminist Andrea Dworkin Publishes *Woman Hating*

"The New Porn Wars" was what at least one magazine labeled the battle between feminist antipornographers and civil libertarians in the 1970s and 1980s. It was a war ignited in large measure by Andrea Dworkin and her 1974 book Woman Hating *in which she insisted that, by degrading women sexually, pornography oppressed them socially and politically.*

In the 1960s, Dworkin (1946–) was an activist who marched against the Vietnam War while suffering in an abusive marriage (which ended in 1971). Before long her radical politics and her experience as a battered wife came together to produce *Woman Hating*. In that book she explored practices, traditions, and myths that had been harmful to women across cultures and throughout history. These included foot binding, female genital mutilation, and pornographic writings. She found that fairy tales rewarded female passivity while depicting women's assertiveness as evil or wrong.

Woman Hating received such widespread praise among feminists that Dworkin was invited to speak to many groups and further developed her themes through numerous articles and additional books. Dworkin asserted that pornography went beyond fantasy, that it turned women into sex objects for men to abuse, and in so doing it reinforced male domination in society at large. In a speech she presented in 1981, Dworkin stated: "Pornography exists because men despise women, and men despise women in part because pornography exists."

In 1983, she and Catharine A. MacKinnon, a feminist and a lawyer, drafted an ordinance passed by the Minneapolis (Minnesota) City Council that classified pornography as a form of sexual discrimination. They defined pornography as "the sexually explicit subordination of women, graphically depicted . . . as sexual objects, things, or commodities . . . who experience pleasure in being raped, or . . . as whores by nature, or . . . in scenarios of degradation, injury, abasement, torture, shown as filthy or inferior, bleeding, bruised, or hurt in a context that makes these conditions sexual."

Fearing that the ordinance would violate First Amendment guarantees of freedom of speech, the Minneapolis mayor vetoed it. His stand coincided with that of civil libertarians and feminists who opposed Dworkin's views. They argued that her campaign amounted to nothing less than censorship. Pornography, they pointed out, was difficult to define, and the description in Dworkin's proposed ordinance would leave a great number of books and articles, including many classic works, subject to being banned. The head of the American Civil Liberties Union called the feminist effort against pornography "the new censorship."

Dworkin, however, pushed onward with her work and picked up support from religious conservatives who were criticizing pornography for its assault on American morals. This produced an unusual alliance of left-wing feminists and right-wing Christians. Dworkin attacked the right-wingers, however, for an ideology aimed at keeping women subservient to men.

In 1984, conservatives in Indianapolis, Indiana, convinced the city council to pass a law similar to the one that had been passed in Minneapolis. A federal court later overturned that law, asserting that it violated the First Amendment protection of free speech.

Dworkin stirred controversy again in her book *Intercourse* (1987), in which she described the sex act as the "formal expression of men's contempt for women." Some feminists praised the book; critics labeled it as one-sided for portraying women merely as victims, with one feminist calling it "nonsense."

Dworkin combined several of her themes when she spoke to a conference in 1993. Scoffing at those who asserted that by censoring pornography the marketplace of ideas would be stifled, she said, "A

The Battle for Ideological Purity

When Theodore Roosevelt was president in the early 1900s, he feared that socialism would overtake America. His solution to the problem was to promote Progressivism and advance it as a moderate alternative that would defuse the radicals by showing that the country's political leaders could correct corporate capitalism's worst abuses. Other radical ideologies have met a similar fate—when the protests gain a substantial following, moderate groups confiscate their ideas. This does not necessarily mean that the original protest group disappears; the socialists, for example, continued their fight, though for the most part less effectively.

In the case of feminism, the National Organization for Women accomplished much. Corporations and colleges, for example, hired more women as professionals and revised their procedures to make promotions less sexist, while states changed their abortion laws, and more women ran for and won public office. For extremists among the feminist protesters, however, the gains were paltry when viewed in the face of the continuing exploitive, bourgeois system. While NOW won the respect of moderate protesters, it antagonized the radicals. The closer NOW moved to the mainstream by taking formerly extreme feminist positions and making them more widely acceptable, the more vociferous the radicals became, shifting the point for debate ever further to the left.

---

vagina doesn't have an idea; and the mouths of women in pornography do not express ideas. . . . I am talking . . . about pornography without visible violence. I am talking about the cruelty of dehumanizing someone who has a right to more." She added:

> Men use sex to hurt us. An argument can be made that men have to hurt us, diminish us, in order to be able to have sex with us . . . be invasive, push a little, shove a little, express verbal or physical hostility or condescension. An argument can be made that in order for men to have sexual pleasure with women, we have to be inferior and dehumanized, which means controlled, which means less autonomous, less free, less real.

For Dworkin, censorship of pornography would liberate women. Her critics argue that such censorship would invite similar proposals from other groups hurt by pictures or words, unleashing a dangerous cycle that would restrict people to "correct" speech as determined by those in authority.

Further Reading

Assiter, Alison. *Pornography, Feminism, and the Individual.* Winchester, Mass.: Pluto Press, 1989.

Dworkin, Andrea. *Woman Hating.* Reprint. New York: Dutton/Plume, 1991.

Jenefsky, Cindy. *Without Apology: Andrea Dworkin's Art and Politics.* Boulder, Colo.: Westview Press, 1998.

The Writings of Peter Singer Inspire the Animal Rights Movement

1975

In 1975, the philosopher Peter Singer introduced the word "speciesist" in his book Animal Liberation; *he used this word to define discrimination on a scale equal to that against races, ethnic groups, and women. In this case, it was discrimination against animals, mistreated by human beings who subjected them to pain solely based on their classification as "inferior" life forms.*

A utilitarian, Singer (1944–) was heavily influenced in his philosophy by the nineteenth-century English thinker Jeremy Bentham. In fact, Bentham provided the modern animal rights movement with its quintessential quotation: "The question is not, 'Can they reason?' Nor 'Can they talk?' But, 'Can they suffer?'" But where Bentham accepted human experimentation on animals, Singer rejected it.

Singer insisted that although extending complete equal rights to animals would be ludicrous, animals' ability to experience pleasure and pain, much as human beings do, must be recognized. To ignore this quality, simply because animals are nonhuman, discriminates against them based on categorization. Singer criticized scientific experimentation on animals as speciesist. He stated:

If an experimenter is not prepared to use an orphaned human infant, then his readiness to use non-humans is simple discrimination, since adult apes, cats, mice, and other mammals are more aware of what is happening to them, more self-directing and, so far as we can tell, at least as sensitive to pain, as any human infant.

He opposed even "painless" killing, stating that it violated an animal's best interests. As for the possibility that scientific experimentation might help save human lives, he insisted that "Many experiments inflict severe pain without the remotest prospect of significant benefits for human beings or any other animals."

Singer's ideas led to the emergence of the animal rights movement, particularly the group People for the Ethical Treatment of Animals (PETA), and as James Parker has written in an article for the animal rights network's web site, Singer and PETA's members found a receptive audience for several reasons. For one, Singer wrote during a period of increased activism concerning civil rights, peace, and environmental issues, allowing him to tap into social discontent and providing the animal rights movement with examples of tactics to emulate.

For another, many Americans had animals as pets, so they were sympathetic to the pleas for treating them more kindly and identified with the argument that animals had emotions. (PETA has, however, criticized the ownership of pets as creating a class of animals dependent on human beings for their survival.) Other people held to images of animals as presented in cartoons—lovable, Bambi-like creatures. Finally, many Americans saw only the results of scientific experimentation—drugs that fought diseases and extended human life—and failed to consider the laboratory work essential for their development.

To Singer, avoiding the infliction of pain on animals meant that human beings should refrain from eating meat. Furthermore, animals should not be subjected to squalid and barbaric living conditions. His ideas raised the point about whether human beings should avoid inflicting pain on all living things that experience pain, including insects. Critics insisted that his argument led to ridiculous, unreachable extremes, such as never stepping on an ant.

Singer went on to write *Practical Ethics* (1979); *Rethinking Life and Death* (1995); *Writings on Ethical Life* (2000); and *A Darwinian Left: Politics, Evolution, and Cooperation* (2000). In the 1990s, Princeton University appointed him a professor of bioethics.

His evolving ideas stirred tremendous controversy. He said that since the fetus is not a person, abortion is morally permissible, and may actually be a moral good if it increased human happiness. And he said that parents should have the right to use infanticide against severely impaired newborns (who lack feeling, reasoning, or self-awareness that would make them "persons"), and that adults suffering severe pain from disease should be able to choose euthanasia. In an essay for the *New York Times Magazine,* published in 2000, he argued that rich people in the developed world should give their excess wealth to the poor in other countries. "If . . . allowing someone to die is not intrinsically different from killing someone," he said, "it would seem that we are all murderers."

Critics attacked him for proposing ideas that would hobble scientific experimentation, promote abortions, and lead to doctors pulling the plug too quickly on ill patients. Moreover, they pointed out that while Singer advised giving away wealth, he lived in upper-class comfort.

Singer disliked being labeled an "animal rights advocate." He said that "while the language of rights has a use . . . I don't really like it as the foundation of moral argument, because it's too intuitive, and people's intuitions are different. People will say, 'I have the right to eat meat, I have a right to wear fur'. . . . Whatever they feel like doing, they've a right to do. I'd rather look at the interest of animals and the wrongness of ignoring those interests by inflicting suffering or death unnecessarily."

Despite his activism, he criticized those in the animal rights movement whose extremism allowed people "to write off the AR . . . as fanatics . . . or, worse still, terrorists." Groups such as the Animal Liberation Front used violent tactics; in 2001, they and their supporters firebombed a federal corral for wild horses in California, set fire to a primate research center in New Mexico, and broke into a fur farm in Iowa to release more than 1,000 mink.

Writing in *Reason* magazine in December 2000, Ronald Bailey said that Peter Singer's critics "call him 'the most dangerous man in the world,'" while the *New Yorker* "calls him 'the most influential living philosopher.'" Whatever the assessment, "speciesist" had entered the vocabulary as a controversial idea in the human debate surrounding ethics.

Further Reading

Hochsmann, Hyun. *On Peter Singer.* Belmont, Calif.: Wadsworth, 2002.

Jamieson, Dale, ed. *Singer and His Critics.* Malden, Mass.: Blackwell Publishers, 1999.

Singer, Peter. *Animal Liberation.* 2d ed. New York: Random House, 1990.

Louis Farrakhan Splits with Black Muslim Leadership 1977

Angered by the decision of Wallace Muhammad, leader of the Nation of Islam, or Black Muslims, to lead the organization away from its founding philosophy, Louis Farrakhan decided in 1977 to form a resurrected Nation of Islam.

Farrakhan (1933–) was born in Brooklyn and raised in Boston. He attended two of that city's outstanding high schools, Latin School and English High, where he earned academic honors. He enrolled at Winston-Salem Teacher's College in North Carolina in 1950, but left in 1953 without a degree.

Three years later, Farrakhan met Elijah Muhammad, the leader of the Nation of Islam, at Temple No. 2 on Chicago's south side. Shortly afterward, Farrakhan joined the Black Muslims. Impressed by the newcomer's intelligence and articulate manner, Muhammad made him a captain in the group's security detail, called the Fruit of Islam, and later promoted him to minister. When tension developed between Muhammad and the dynamic Black Muslim leader Malcolm X (see entries, 1948 and 1964), Farrakhan served as Muhammad's point man, condemning Malcolm X

Rev. Louis Farrakhan. (Bettmann/CORBIS)

and providing what Farrakhan later himself admitted were the conditions that led in 1965 to the assassination of Malcolm X.

Farrakhan expected to succeed Muhammad as head of the Black Muslims, but when Muhammad died in February 1975, Wallace D. Muhammad was chosen instead. Wallace appointed Farrakhan his special ambassador, but Farrakhan grew disenchanted when Wallace announced that the Nation of Islam would be radically changed. Wallace ordered that whites no longer be classified as devils and that they even be admitted to membership. He directed that the group accept a theology and belief system closer to that set forth in the Koran, the Muslim holy book. In October 1976, Wallace disbanded the Nation of Islam and formed a new group called the World Community of Al-Islam in the West.

A few months later, in September 1977, Farrakhan split with Wallace Muhammad and announced he would rebuild the Nation of Islam according to the ideas originally expressed by Elijah Muhammad. Operating out of Chicago, Farrakhan recruited African-Americans to the anti-white organization that extolled black pride and separatism. In 1979, he began publishing a newspaper with the same name as one previously published by Elijah Muhammad, *Final Call.*

In the ensuing years, membership in the Nation of Islam remained small, probably never exceeding more than 20,000, but Farrakhan built a substantial following in the black community. Some of his support was based in the controversial reputation he earned in 1984 when he backed African-American Jesse Jackson for the Democratic presidential nomination. Farrakhan attacked Milton Coleman, a reporter, for revealing that Jackson had once used anti-Semitic slurs when he called Jews "Hymies" and New York City "Hymietown." Farrakhan himself called Judaism a "gutter religion" and Israel an outlaw nation. He stated: "I say to the Jewish people, who may not like our brother, it is not Jesse Jackson that you're attacking. When you attack him, you attack the millions who are lining up with him. . . . If you harm this brother, I warn you in the name of Allah, that will be the last one you *do* harm." The outrage was so great in reaction to Farrakhan that the U.S. Senate unanimously passed a resolution censuring him.

Farrakhan had been elevated to the status of a major figure. In 1985, Chicago political consultant Don Rose observed that "two years ago, Louis Farrakhan couldn't fill a church in Chicago. Today, he can pack 25,000 into Madison Square Garden. He really is a creation of the media." Farrakhan remained influential with African-Americans for years afterward, as evidenced in 1995 when he organized a Million Man March (see entry, 1995) on Washington, D.C., to boost the standing of families in black communities. More than one million African-American men attended the rally.

In 2001, Farrakhan condemned the September 11 terrorist attacks on the World Trade Center in New York City and the Pentagon in Washington that killed more than 3,000 people. He labeled the terrorists "wild beasts" and said he agreed with President George W. Bush "that there must be an appropriate response." But he urged Bush to make public the evidence linking terrorist leader Osama bin Laden to the attacks. "Don't hide behind national security," he said in a speech. "The nation would be more secure if you give the American people a reason to fight." He insisted that the U.S. government had lied before and could be lying again. "There's nothing wrong with asking the American government to show us proof," he said. And he questioned the U.S.-led military action in Afghanistan, doubting whether it was the best way to defeat terrorism.

Some analysts have seen Farrakhan as a dangerous demagogue, ready to spread racist hatred against whites. Others have seen him as committed to rhetoric intended to raise passions rather than a vendetta intended to cause harm. Yet words can often create explosive conditions—as Farrakhan himself noted when he admitted he had poisoned the atmosphere in the days leading up to the killing of Malcolm X.

Further Reading

Farrakhan, Louis, with Michael Hardy and William Pleasant. *The Honorable Louis Farrakhan: A Minister For Progress.*
3d ed. New York: Practice Press, 1988.

Singh, Robert. *The Farrakhan Phenomenon: Race, Reaction, and the Paranoid Style in American Politics.* Washington, D.C.: Georgetown University Press, 1997.

White, Vibert L., Jr. *Inside the Nation of Islam: A Historical and Personal Testimony by a Black Muslim.* Gainesville: University Press of Florida, 2001.

William Pierce's *The Turner Diaries* Stirs Right-Wing Extremists

1978

In 1978, William Pierce, a member of the National Socialist White People's Party, a Nazi group, wrote The Turner Diaries, *a book considered a "revelation" to many right-wing extremists.*

Pierce (1933–2002) was highly educated. He grew up in Atlanta, Georgia, and in 1955 earned a bachelor's degree from Rice University in Houston, Texas. In 1962, he finished a doctorate in physics from the University of Colorado at Boulder and then worked as a science laboratory researcher. Later that year, he became an assistant physics professor at Oregon State University, but in 1965 he moved to Connecticut, where he worked in a science lab at Pratt and Whitney, an aerospace company. Pierce quit the company in 1966 to devote his energies to the American Nazi Party.

By the following year, he had become one of the main leaders in the Nazi organization, renamed the National Socialist White People's Party. In 1970 he began the National Alliance, which urged young people to protect the white race against Jews and what he called other "undesirables."

In 1978, Pierce published *The Turner Diaries* (under the pen name Andrew Macdonald), a novel derived from a series he had written for a tabloid. Steeped in anti-Semitism and racism, the book tells of a world ruined by a Jewish conspiracy, then saved by a fearless fighter who leads "the Organization," dedicated to killing Jews and nonwhites. On "Day of the Rope," the Organization hangs tens of thousands of white traitors who had associated with the members of other races. In the end, a New Era emerges, with society redeemed by white supremacy. In *The Turner Diaries* Pierce writes about a war between whites and Jews:

> If the white nations of the world had not allowed themselves to become subject to the Jew, to Jewish ideas, to the Jewish spirit, this war would not be necessary. We can hardly consider ourselves blameless. We can hardly say we had no choice, no chance to avoid the Jew's snare. We can hardly say we were not warned. . . .
>
> We had chance after chance to save ourselves—most recently 52 years ago, when the Germans and Jews were locked in struggle for the mastery of central and eastern Europe.
>
> We ended up on the Jewish side in that struggle, primarily because we had chosen corrupt men as our leaders. . . . We ignored the really important issues in our national life and gave free rein to a criminal System to conduct the affairs of our nation as it saw fit, so long as it kept us moderately well-supplied with bread and circuses.

The Turner Diaries gained a wide audience within the far right, selling more than 200,000 copies, and exerted influence among militia leaders in the 1980s and 1990s. Timothy McVeigh, who bombed the Murrah Federal Building in Oklahoma City (see entry, 1995), treated the book as his Bible. Most Americans had never heard of *The Turner Diaries* until the bombing, when observers pointed out the similarity between the explosion that leveled the office building and a tactic used by the main character in the book.

In the late 1990s, Pierce continued to write his extremist literature on a 400-acre farm near Hillsboro, West Virginia, and provided what he called a training ground for his followers to prepare for the great fight to save white civilization. "My purpose from the beginning has been the dissemination of ideas," Pierce told *Contemporary Authors*, "ideas about right and wrong behavior, about individual responsibility, about identity, about purpose, and about the significance of our lives in a cosmic context." For Pierce, individual responsibility meant the responsibility to hate, to build not an inclusive community of brotherly love, but an exclusive one where people who are different would be persecuted and where any group designated a threat would meet the destruction meted out by McVeigh at Oklahoma City.

Further Reading

Griffin, Robert S. *The Fame of a Dead Man's Deeds: An Up-Close Portrait of White Nationalist William Pierce*. Santa Clara, Calif.: MightyWords, 2001.

MacDonald, Andrew. *The Turner Diaries*. 2d ed. Washington, D.C.: National Alliance, 1980.

1979 Radical Environmentalists Resort to Violence

Angry about continued assaults on the natural environment and the failure of mainstream activist groups to stop them, a cadre of extremists affiliated with the group Earth First! resorted to violent actions, labeled by the federal government as "terrorist acts," to stop the exploitation.

David Foreman (1946–) founded Earth First! in 1979 out of frustration with what he perceived to be the ineffective environmental reform pursued by mainstream organizations such as the Sierra Club and the Wilderness Society, for which he worked as a lobbyist. Foreman believed in militant tactics and led his first Earth First! protest when he sabotaged the bulldozers being used in the building of a dam at Glen Canyon, Colorado. This type of action became known as "ecotage" or "monkeywrenching."

Foreman wanted to disrupt companies engaged in development to the extent that they would lose money and abandon their projects. Toward that end, Earth First! took on the forest industry, which was cutting down redwoods in the Pacific Northwest. The group drove metal spikes into the trees so that the equipment used in felling them would be wrecked. In 1986, Earth First! targeted the nuclear power industry by cutting down the transmission lines at a generating plant at Palo Verde, Arizona.

In the early 1990s, Earth First! began moderating its strategy, and this contributed to a rupture within the group. Much as Earth First! had been started as a radical alternative to mainstream environmental organizations, the Earth Liberation Front (ELF; see entry, 1998) emerged as a radical alternative to Earth First! The ELF formed as an underground group, loosely structured, with no public officials, but with a web site and with an informal connection to various other extreme environmentalist groups, such as the Liberation Collective in Portland, Oregon, and the Animal Liberation Front.

Further Reading

Scarce, Ric. *Eco Warriors: Understanding the Radical Environmental Movement*. Chicago: Noble Press, 1990.

Taylor, Bron Raymond. *Ecological Resistance Movements: The Global Emergence of Radical and Popular Environmentalism*. New York: SUNY Press, 1995.

Zimermann, Michael, ed. *Environmental Philosophy: From Animal Rights to Radical Ecology*. Upper Saddle River, N.J.: Prentice Hall, 2000.

1980 Identity Christianity and Aryan Nations Promote Racist and Anti-Semitic Beliefs

Richard Girnt Butler formed Aryan Nations as the political arm of Identity Christianity, a racist and anti-Semitic religious belief system that emerged among extreme rightists who were apprehensive about a perceived decline of American society.

Identity Christianity materialized as a full-blown ideology shortly after World War II, when Wesley Swift and William Potter Gale promoted it through the Christian Defense League, a religious group whose doctrine portrayed Jews as the devil's children engaged in a conspiracy to take over the world. In the 1980s, several small Identity churches emerged similar to Swift's own Church of Jesus Christ Christian, claiming they "identified" with the Ten Lost Tribes that had been conquered in 722 B.C.E. and dispersed from Israel. According to Identity belief, these tribes had journeyed during an ancient period to England, where they had developed a superior culture, one divinely inspired, and one that made Americans, at least those descended from British stock, the chosen people of God.

These new Identity churches sometimes downplayed the anti-Semitic emphasis in Swift's church and instead stressed the supremacy of the white race over "coloreds" or the "mud people" (as they called non-whites), who had no right to equality with whites. A primary Aryan characteristic, Identity Christians asserted, was the ability to blush, or as they put it, show "blood in the face."

The differences between anti-Semites and racists—Identity Christians preferred the term "racialists"—proved slight, however, and in most Identity churches the concepts intermingled and became indistinguishable. After all, Armageddon, the story had it, would in the end pit Aryans against both of their enemies, namely Jews and nonwhites.

Apocalyptic visions permeated Identity groups: they foresaw a showdown between Aryans and Jews (the latter working for Satan), at which time the U.S. government would collapse and a conflagration, a necessary prerequisite to the Second Coming of Christ, would begin. Unlike fundamentalist Christians (criticized as too pro-Israel), Identity Christians believed no one would escape the impending battle: there would be no rapture, no dwelling with Christ prior to his Second Coming, not even for the righteous. Regardless of faith or piety, the battle would be joined, and Aryans had to be mentally, physically, and morally prepared. One Identity group proclaimed: "We of the Nordic race who believe in Jesus Christ are determined this nation will remain ours."

The Identity movement took an ominous turn in the 1980s, when Richard Girnt Butler (1918–), a leader in the Christian Defense League, founded Aryan Nations, the political arm of Identity Christianity. Aryan Nations included Identity and non-Identity racists and considered itself engaged in a battle to protect and advance white power. One leader asserted, "We're racial brothers and sisters, struggling for the survival of the white race."

Aryan Nations was soon implicated in several plots to bomb businesses in Seattle, Washington. At about the same time, Butler tried unsuccessfully to build bond among Identity Christians, neo-Nazis, and the Ku Klux Klan and promoted the Northwest Territorial Imperative to make the Pacific Northwest a separate Aryan state, one in which only whites and Christians would be allowed to live. Butler said about this land: "All hybrids called Jews are to be repatriated from the Republic's territory, and all their wealth be redistributed to restore our people."

In 1987, a federal grand jury in Fort Smith, Arkansas, indicted Butler for his role in a plot to overthrow the U.S. government. He was acquitted the following year. Presently he had heart bypass surgery, and his deteriorating health diminished his influence within Aryan Nations.

Butler located the headquarters for Aryan Nations at Hayden Lake in Idaho, a place he described as the "international headquarters of the White race." In the 1990s, Aryan Nations experienced internal turmoil, with several of its members leaving to form new groups. Carl Franklin, named by Butler as his successor and carrying the official title of chief of staff for Aryan Nations, resigned in July 1993 as a result of disagreements with Butler. He and three other members moved to western Montana to begin their own white supremacist group called the Church of Jesus Christ Christian of Montana. Other defections also occurred, but in 2001, Aryan Nations remained in operation and continued to espouse its racist and anti-Semitic doctrine.

Further Reading

Aho, James Alfred. *The Politics of Righteousness: Idaho Christian Patriotism.* Seattle: University of Washington Press, 1990.

Walters, Jerome. *One Aryan Nation Under God: Exposing the New Racial Extremists.* Cleveland, Ohio: Pilgrim Press, 2000.

1983 Posse Comitatus Member Gordon Kahl Kills U.S. Marshals

In 1983, Gordon Kahl, a North Dakota farmer, encountered several U.S. marshals at a roadblock near the town of Medina. A gunfight ensued that left two of the marshals dead. Later that year, Kahl was killed by law enforcement officers. The two episodes occurred as right-wing extremists mobilized into a group called Posse Comitatus.

Founded several years earlier by Henry L. Beach, a retired dry-cleaning executive from Oregon, the Posse Comitatus condemned liberalism and a federal government that had trampled the individual. (The *Oxford English Dictionary* traces the Latin phrase *Posse Comitatus* back to the thirteenth century and defines it as "the force of the county; the body of men . . . whom the sheriff may summon or 'raise' to repress a riot or for other purposes.") A Posse-controlled radio station in Kansas declared: "[The Bible] didn't say you were going to vote them out—it said, 'thus with violence shall the great city Babylon—that international Communist system—be thrown down and shall be found no more. . . .' And all the disco bongo congo from the bong is gonna be gone. All the nigger jive and the tootsie wootsie is going to go."

Posse ideology recognized no governmental authority higher than the county sheriff. Everything above that position was invalid because the state and federal governments had usurped popular rights by taking power away from the local community. Consequently, Posse members refused to pay federal taxes—they even refused to have driver's licenses or license plates for their cars.

To the Posse, though, county sheriffs were not infallible; citizens in local communities had the ultimate power and responsibility to decide if the sheriffs were performing their duties properly. If the sheriff had failed, they were to bring him to the gallows and execute him in public at high noon, with his body remaining until sundown as an example to others who might subvert the law and defy the popular will.

The Posse cloaked itself in secrecy. It occasionally ran candidates for public office, but it believed that publicity only invited federal oppression. The group refused to divulge membership numbers; however, outsiders estimated that in the 1980s, 78 chapters existed in 23 states. In addition, the Posse often maintained close ties to other right-wing groups, including the Iowa Society of Education, the Montana Vigilantes, and the Christian Posse. One Posse leader publicly proclaimed that his organization had engaged in cooperative paramilitary training with members of the Ku Klux Klan (see entry, 1866).

The Posse believed that a Jewish conspiracy existed involving the FBI and the Central Intelligence Agency. Many in the Posse cherished William Pierce's book *The Turner Diaries* (see entry, 1978), and some advocated a race war to protect Aryan civilization. In 1982, the Posse issued arrest warrants against a sheriff and his deputy in a small Kansas town. The attempt to capture the sheriff fizzled, but the event sent shock waves across the midwestern countryside and showed the stridency within the Posse—its willingness to act forcefully against what it perceived as oppression.

The most prominent Posse incident, however, involved Gordon Kahl, who, as a member of Posse Comitatus, had established the Gospel Divine Doctrine Church of Jesus Christ as a ploy—which eventually failed—to help the Posse avoid income taxes. When hard times struck farmers, including himself, in the early 1980s, he spoke at rallies, portraying the federal government as Satan. At the time, he was on probation for failing to pay his income taxes. (He had served one year in prison.) He still refused to file; and, after he violated the terms of his probation, federal marshals tracked him down.

The Militia Movement and the Far Right

Throughout the 1980s and into the 1990s, militias organized to stand up to a federal government they believed had become oppressive. Some 224 militias operated in 39 states, with a total membership approaching 100,000. These militias appeared while right wingers vented their anger at politicians in Washington, D.C. They represented that strain of society, dating at least from the American Revolution, that distrusted central government. Some of the militias, however, also tapped into the country's racist and anti-Semitic heritage and attitudes.

Although the militia movement lacked a centralized structure, several common themes emerged. The militias opposed gun control; they insisted that the United Nations and treasonous leaders in the United States were cooperating to create a socialist One World government; and they claimed that the federal government had violated liberty.

Among the militias there appeared unnerving conspiracy theories: the federal government intended to import Nepalese Gurkhas and Hong Kong police as a fighting force to oppress Americans; highway signs displayed on their reverse side stickers that served as directions for the soon-to-be invading armies of the One World government; and internment camps were being set up by federal authorities to hold dissidents. As wild as some of the stories might appear, they found a considerable audience in a population made suspicious by the Vietnam War, the lies of Watergate, and the ever-expanding bureaucracies.

They set up a roadblock close to his farm near Medina, North Dakota. When Kahl and several others—one of them his 23-year-old son—encountered the roadblock, he refused to surrender and instead stood his ground, rifle in hand. Then someone, probably Kahl's son, fired a shot, and a bloody 30-second exchange followed.

Amazingly, Kahl escaped, leaving behind two dead and four wounded marshals. His son had also been shot, so he took him to the local hospital and then fled. Kahl made his way to Arkansas, where it took several months for federal marshals to find him. In early 1983, they surrounded his hideout, a house that had been converted into a fortified bunker. There Kahl shot a local sheriff who later died from his wounds, and marshals retaliated by firing into the bunker. They killed Kahl, but the episode made the Identity Christian a martyr, not only within the Posse Comitatus but also within the greater extreme right movement. To many radicals, Kahl's death reinforced their view that the federal government stood for oppression. He was killed, they said, for his belief in Identity Christianity, a murder intended to stifle freedom of speech.

Further Reading

Corcoran, James. *Bitter Harvest: Gordon Kahl and the Posse Comitatus, Murder in the Heartland.* New York: Viking, 1990.

Talk Show Host Alan Berg Is Murdered by the Order   1984

Founded by Robert Matthews, the secretive group called the Order advocated anti-Semitic views that led in 1984 to its members murdering Alan Berg, a liberal Jewish radio talk show host in Denver, Colorado.

In 1983 Robert Matthews began the Order, formally the Silent Brotherhood, in Metaline Falls, Idaho. Anti-Semitic and opposed to nearly all federal authority, including taxes, the Order, with about 40 members, plotted to overthrow the U.S. government, or what it called the Zionist Occupation Government (ZOG). In 1984, several Order members printed counterfeit money and robbed $3.8 million from a Brinks armored truck.

The group set its sights on Alan Berg, hated by right-wing extremists for his liberal opinions, Jewish background, combative style, and for his popularity—at one point his show was aired in 38 states—and murdered him. The *New York Times* reported the death scene:

The 50-year-old Mr. Berg, who in recent years angered and delighted nearly a quarter million listeners in a metropolitan area of 1.2 million people, was found in a pool of blood with his feet still in his parked automobile. Several bullet holes were in his garage door. Neighbors reported hearing shots shortly before midnight. The police found 10 .45-caliber shell casings on the ground at the scene of the murder. Mr. Berg, a former Chicago lawyer, apparently died instantly from wounds to the head and neck.

Later that year, the FBI tracked Matthews down and killed him in a shoot-out at Whidbey Island in Washington State. Over the next two years, the authorities arrested Matthews's accomplices, and the Order dissolved.

In its ideas about Zionist occupation, the Order had reflected the bigotry found in an early twentieth-century work, *The Protocols of the Meetings of the Learned Elders of Zion*, which had attained new-found popularity among right-wing extremists. Published in Russia sometime between 1903 and 1907, *The Protocols* purports to be minutes from a secret gathering of Jewish leaders in the late nineteenth century.

The 24 protocols outline a so-called Jewish conspiracy to dominate Gentiles and establish a world dictatorship. "Even now [control of the press] is already being attained by us, inasmuch as all news items are received by a few agencies," *The Protocols* proclaims. The "minutes" further reveal that Jewish conspirators directed the French Revolution, communism, and numerous upheavals to force the masses to accept authoritarian Zionist rule. In addition, Jews intended to control all money needed by businesses and to make materialism a cult, so that when economic troubles ensued, the lower classes would rise up against wealthy Gentiles. "All terror will emanate from us," pronounce the Elders. "Party conflict and paralysis in government will be orchestrated—there are no checks to limit the range of our activities."

The Protocols is a fake document, plagiarized from a pamphlet written by a Frenchman in the 1860s; nevertheless, right-wing extremist groups in the United States have treated *The Protocols* as truth. In its brief existence, the Order had taken the book's ideas to stir hatred and make itself into a terror organization aimed at fighting supposed Zionist rule.

Further Reading

Berlet, Chip, and Matthew N. Lyons. *Right-wing Populism in America: Too Close for Comfort.* New York: Guilford Press, 2000.
George, John, and Laird Wilcox. *American Extremists: Militias, Supremacists, Klansmen, Communists & Others.* Amherst, N.Y.: Prometheus Books, 1996.

1985 Guerrilla Girls Protest Sexism in the Art World

Angered by the paucity of female-created works on display in New York City art galleries, in 1985 a group of women artists formed Guerrilla Girls, whose members made speeches and pasted posters to walls while dressed in gorilla outfits.

What most stunned the future Guerrilla Girls in the early 1980s was the continuing discrimination against women in the New York City art world despite gains made by feminists in other pursuits. One Guerrilla Girl stated that "most young women who were in [art] school or getting ready to enter [art] school assumed the problem had been solved, so from the early to the . . . middle '80s they've been coming into the city, anticipating that, because of the quality of their work, they would be able to survive. They had a big surprise when they got here."

The Guerrilla Girls—whose numbers could never be precisely determined—owed their formation to the anger generated by the Museum of Modern Art when it displayed its "International Survey of

Contemporary Painting and Sculpture" in 1984 with 165 artists represented, only 19 of whom were women. The following spring, the Guerrilla Girls pasted posters on walls in the East Village that asked, "What do These Artists have in Common?" and provided the answer: "They All Allow Their Work to be Shown in Galleries that Show No More than 10% Women or None at All."

In a Catch-22 situation, art galleries usually displayed the works of the most salable artists, and the most salable had been men; but to become salable, artists needed to be represented by a gallery. It was a cycle that women found difficult to break. Guerrilla Girls claimed that about 70 percent of the artists in New York City were women, but that 95 percent of the work being shown was by white males. Others disputed the group's statistics, saying the situation was not nearly so dire.

In spring 1987, Guerrilla Girls held a substantial protest at the Whitney Museum of Art during its biennial show. They complained that the art being displayed had been chosen by the museum's trustees, overwhelmingly male executives from large corporations. The Guerrilla Girls staged an alternative display at a nearby gallery. There they hung huge posters that listed the corporate sponsors of art shows and presented statistics to show sexual discrimination in the arts.

Had the Guerrilla Girls affected the art world? In 1990, three gallery directors offered differing opinions to the *Christian Science Monitor.* Eugenia Foxworth of the Soho 20 gallery said, "I think they're the innovators in starting a movement to get women and minorities into galleries that have not shown them before." Bill Arning of the White Columns gallery agreed: "There's a lot of peculiarity about the numbers when people percentage out who gets shown and who doesn't. I think they have made a real difference." But another gallery director, Diane Brown, demurred, saying that gender considerations had no place in the arts: "I will never represent someone because they're a woman or not represent them because they're not a woman," she said.

In the 1990s, the Guerrilla Girls organized in cities outside New York, including overseas. In 2001 they attacked Hollywood, complaining about the movie industry's aversion to female directors, producers, cinematographers, and screenwriters. Of the 100 top-grossing films in 2000, the group claimed, only four had been directed by women.

In 2001, the Guerrilla Girls stated that "in 16 years we have produced over 70 posters, printed projects, and actions that expose sexism and racism in the art world and the culture at large. . . . The mystery surrounding our identities has attracted attention and support. We could be anyone; we are everywhere."

Further Reading

Chadwick, Whitney. *Confessions of the Guerrilla Girls.* New York: HarperPerennial, 1995.
Guerrilla Girls Staff. *The Guerrilla Girls' Bedside Companion to the History of Western Art.* New York: Penguin Putnam, 1998.

AIDS Activists Block Wall Street

1988

In 1988, members of ACT-UP blocked traffic along Wall Street in New York City, one of several protests they had sponsored over the years meant to call attention to inadequate government and corporate policies in the treatment of AIDS (acquired immune deficiency syndrome).

ACT-UP, an acronym for the AIDS Coalition to Unleash Power, was founded in 1987 by Larry Kramer (1935–), a playwright who first came to national attention in 1970, when his screen adaptation of D. H. Lawrence's *Women in Love* earned four Oscar nominations. His novel *Faggots*, published in 1978, satirized the gay demimonde.

Kramer's activism began in 1981, when at a meeting in his Manhattan apartment he founded Gay Men's Health Crisis (GMHC) to help homosexuals deal with the deadly disease AIDS. GMHC has grown to be the largest nonprofit group to serve those with AIDS, assisting 11,000 people in the year 2000 alone.

With the formation of GMHC, Kramer began a strident, vociferous campaign to awaken the public to the threat posed by AIDS. He found many gays ignorant on the subject, and many heterosexuals dismissing it as something peculiar to gays, with extreme conservatives even labeling it a just retribution for a sinful way of life. Kramer advised gays to practice safe sex and warned about the devastating effects from AIDS as a sexually transmitted disease.

In 1985, Kramer wrote *The Normal Heart*, a play that became an international hit. The drama depicted an abrasive gay activist waging war against the apathy and the political maneuvers hindering efforts to fight an unnamed plague.

As more AIDS patients died, Kramer demanded that political leaders pressure the medical community into finding a treatment for the disease. He resolved that a more radical group than GMHC was required and, in 1987, when about 350 people gathered at a meeting to hear Kramer speak, he founded ACT-UP. Shortly afterward, ACT-UP adopted as its logo the pink triangle, which the Nazis had forced homosexuals to wear in World War II concentration camps, accompanied by the words "Silence=Death." Kramer intended ACT-UP to engage in civil disobedience, such as picketing, marches, and sit-down demonstrations, to force research on AIDS and make drugs more readily available.

In March 1988, members of ACT-UP gathered along Wall Street. The newspaper *Newsday* reported the scene:

> The sun had just begun to glint off the worn edges of the tombstones at Trinity Church yesterday morning when the first 25 demonstrators sat down to pit their bodies against lower Broadway's traffic and started their chant: "Act Up. Fight back. Fight AIDS." The chant resonated off Trinity's façade just before the clock struck eight. The protest against the federal government's AIDS research policies had begun.

An ACT-UP demonstration in front of the White House, 1998. (Bettmann/CORBIS)

Within an hour, and the number of protesters reached 400, blocking traffic into the financial district, and forcing many workers along Wall Street to make their way on foot. Soon the protesters swelled to more than 700, of which the police arrested 100. The organizer of the protest, Ron Goldberg, said that ACT-UP wanted "a comprehensive national policy on AIDS," along with "increased drug research and testing."

The following year, ACT-UP staged a much bigger protest when at least 2,500 picketers surrounded New York's City Hall. One ACT-UP leader said, "There is a tidal wave of AIDS cases coming, and all the city has for sandbagging the steps of City Hall is a pile of reports—none of which has been acted upon." Some of the protesters displayed ACT-UP stickers that showed a reddened hand emblazoned with the words, "The government has blood on its hands. One AIDS death every half hour."

By the early 1990s, ACT-UP had expanded to 54 cities and nine other countries. Yet divisiveness soon hampered the group as its members argued over whether they had gone too far or not far enough with their tactics. ACT-UP suffered a serious split in 1990 when a breakaway ACT-UP/San Francisco group formed, asserting that HIV did not cause AIDS and that the drugs used to control the virus did more harm than good. They were supported in their position by Peter Duesberg, a virologist at the University of California at Berkeley. ACT-UP/San Francisco antagonized its opponents by using militant tactics to discredit ACT-UP and mainstream political leaders.

In 1997, ACT-UP celebrated its tenth anniversary by holding a protest outside the New York Stock Exchange. As in the past, the group hoped to draw attention to the high price of medicines used to fight AIDS and prolong life. But ACT-UP had changed. For one, many in the organization had been absorbed by mainstream government and private agencies. The *San Francisco Chronicle* reported that "people who used to scream in the street are now ensconced in a smooth-running AIDS machine, working as caregivers, lobbyists, heads of policy and service groups and even paid consultants to the drug companies they once denounced as 'AIDS profiteers.'"

In 2001, both ACT-UP and ACT-UP/San Francisco made news with their battles. That March, ACT-UP staged a "die-in" outside the headquarters of the Pharmaceutical Research and Manufacturers of America in New York City. The protesters demanded "medication for every nation," a reference to the AIDS crisis in other countries, especially in Africa. In November, police arrested David Pasquarelli, the spokesman for ACT-UP/San Francisco on charges that he and a colleague had stalked newspaper reporters and public health officials and had made terrorist threats against them.

ACT-UP made its mark on the nation. ACT-UP's protests caused the Federal Drug Administration to streamline procedures for approving drugs to treat AIDS and convinced pharmaceutical companies to lower prices for AIDS medicines. Writing in the *New Yorker* in 2002, Michael Specter said that "It is difficult to overstate the impact of ACT UP. The average approval time for some critical drugs fell from a decade to a year . . . ." He added that while "scores of drugs were made available and used widely before they had been tested long enough for scientists to know if they would ever work. . . sophisticated anti-retrovial medicines now make AIDS a chronic but relatively manageable disease for hundreds of thousands of Americans."

In 1989, one ACT-UP member said, "Yes we are rude. Direct action is rude. That's what gets attention. With us there screaming at the top of our lungs, and getting on the front pages—that's what these people respond to."

Further Reading

Cohen, Peter F. *Love and Anger: Essays on AIDS, Activism, and Politics.* New York: Haworth Press, 1998.

Kramer, Larry. *The Normal Heart and The Destiny of Me: Two Plays.* 1st Grove Press ed. New York: Grove Press, 2000.

Shepard, Benjamin, and Ronald Hayduk. *From ACT UP to the WTO: Urban Protest and Community Building in the Era of Globalization.* New York and London: Verso, 2002.

Shiltz, Randy. *And the Band Played On.* New York: St. Martin's Press, 1987.

Specter, Michael. "Public Nuisance." *New Yorker*, 13 May 2002.

1991 Black Bloc Engages in Violent Anarchistic Protest Against the Gulf War

From the 1990s into the year 2001, the anarchist movement rejuvenated itself in the United States with protests against globalization and with the use of a new tactic called the Black Bloc whereby anarchist groups, and those sympathetic to anarchy, coordinated their strategies to launch violent attacks against the authorities.

Anarchy has a long heritage in American society, dating back at least to the activities of Emma Goldman and Alexander Berkman (see entry, 1919). In the 1990s, anarchist groups protested the use of U.S. military power overseas and the movement toward globalization represented by the formation of the World Trade Organization (WTO).

With their intensified protests, the anarchists borrowed a tactic from European anarchists, called the Black Bloc. An article in the *Ottawa Citizen* said about the Black Bloc, "There are no official members . . . no headquarters, no general meetings, and no constitution. They are more technique than structure and come together only at public protests." When anarchist groups decide to stage a protest, they will unite into a bloc—joined by whatever non-anarchist groups support them—dress in black, including covering their faces with black masks, and take to the streets, attacking property and police. The *Ottawa Citizen* explained, "The Blocs will wear masks so no leader will be apparent. Decisions will be made by informal vote or spontaneously by the crowd. The Blocs may move together in a large mass of black, or break into smaller groups to outmaneuver security forces."

The Black Bloc appeared for the first time in the United States during protests against the Persian Gulf War in 1991. Its greatest exposure, however, came during protests in Seattle, Washington, in 1999 against a meeting of the WTO. There the black-hooded radicals smashed store windows, set garbage bins afire, and assaulted the police.

They appeared again in April 2000 in Washington, D.C., when they took to the streets to disrupt a meeting of officials from the World Bank. Anarchist Emil Zap said, "Our strength is that we can move however we want. We can freelance." He defended the smashing of windows and other vandalism by stating, "Communities are being destroyed all over the world, and we're showing . . . what an empowered community looks like: that it's strong, that it acts for the good of the people."

Such tactics, however, divided protesters. Some believed that the Black Bloc and its strategies added force in weakening the power structure; others believed that such tactics made all protesters appear to be unreasonable and caused the various protest messages to be lost in a sea of reports about the violence, accompanied by a mainstream reaction against attacks on property.

Further Reading

Green Mountain Anarchist Collective. *The Black Bloc Papers: An Anthology of Primary Texts from the North American Anarchist Black Bloc.* Oakland, Calif.: A K Press Distribution, 2002.

Shepard, Benjamin, and Ronald Hayduk. *From ACT UP to the WTO: Urban Protest and Community Building in the Era of Globalization.* New York and London: Verso, 2002.

1992– 1994 Showdowns at Ruby Ridge and Waco Lead to the Forming of the Militia of Montana

In 1992 and 1993, violent confrontations between extremists and federal agents gave rise to an increasing fear that individual liberty was under assault by the government. Thousands of Americans thought they could protect that liberty by joining militias, the most prominent of which was the Militia of Montana, organized in 1994.

In 1992, violence erupted at a cabin in Ruby Ridge, Idaho, the home of white supremacist Randy Weaver, which was then occupied by him, his wife, their children, and a friend. The federal government had begun pursuing Weaver soon after he had failed to appear at a court hearing related to charges against him for having sold illegal shotguns to undercover agents of the Bureau of Alcohol, Tobacco, and Firearms (BATF). Weaver's absence at the hearing was not necessarily intentional: the notice Weaver received instructing him to appear at the hearing had listed the wrong date. Nevertheless, the government issued a warrant for his arrest.

When federal marshals approached his cabin, a primitive dwelling with no electricity or running water, shots rang out. A BATF surveillance team had encountered Weaver's 14-year-old son, Samuel; Weaver's friend, Kevin Harris; and the family dog. The gunfire erupted after a federal agent shot the dog, and Samuel and Harris returned fire. In the exchange, both Samuel and a surveillance team member were killed.

The FBI dispatched a special Hostage Rescue Team to Ruby Ridge. One of its members, purportedly aiming for Weaver, instead shot and killed Weaver's wife, Vicki, while she stood at the cabin door holding her baby daughter. A 10-day siege ensued, during which Weaver and Harris, both wounded, remained in the cabin. The federal government brought in helicopters and armored personnel carriers. Weaver finally surrendered, and he and Harris were tried for the death of the federal agent. A jury acquitted them, and a government investigation subsequently found the FBI guilty of having violated long-standing rules of engagement, namely that shots be fired only at armed adults, and then only if life were endangered.

The investigation concluded that Vicki Weaver's civil rights had been violated. (The Justice Department finally agreed in August 1995 to settle civil damage claims Weaver had filed against the federal government; Weaver's family received $3.1 million.) The episode proved deeply embarrassing to the FBI and served to reinforce fears of a high-level government conspiracy among radicals.

Not long after Ruby Ridge, violence again involved federal agents, this time at the Branch Davidian compound near Waco, Texas. David Koresh had become leader of the Branch Davidians, an offshoot of the Seventh Day Adventist church that believed there would be an apocalypse followed by Christ's Second Coming. Koresh declared himself the "father" of all the Davidian children, insisted on Spartan living conditions, armed the compound, which they called Mount Carmel, and began daily paramilitary training as a defensive measure to prepare for the apocalypse.

The BATF believed Koresh had stockpiled illegal weapons, and on February 28, 1993, agents raided Mount Carmel. A gun battle ensued, resulting in deaths on both sides. The government then surrounded the compound, with the FBI employing the same special unit that had been used at Ruby Ridge.

In mid-April, the government decided to end the siege. Tanks punched holes in the walls of the compound and pumped tear gas inside. A fire then erupted, and Mount Carmel burned to the ground, killing Koresh and 74 others, including more than 20 children. Critics of the government said the FBI had caused the fire, but most of the evidence pointed to it having been set by the Davidians.

At the ensuing trial, 11 surviving Branch Davidians pleaded self-defense and were acquitted of killing four agents during the initial February raid (although seven were found guilty of aiding and abetting the voluntary manslaughter of a federal agent). The New York Times called the verdict a "stunning defeat" for the BATF and the Justice Department, and many right-wingers saw evidence in the federal actions of a police state with its sights set on crushing liberty.

Ruby Ridge and Waco convinced John Trochmann (1943–), a one-time auto parts distributor and resident of Noxon, Montana, that the country was under the thumb of government tyranny. So, in January 1994, he, his wife, Carolyn, his brother David, and David's son, Randy, joined him in forming the Militia of Montana, or MOM. Trochmann declared that the time had come to restore high moral values and gain control of the government from secular humanists and special interest groups. He warned that some federal officials intended to take guns away from the people and guide the United States into

Protesters at Ruby Ridge, 1992. (AP/Wide World Photos)

joining a "One World Government," under which national boundaries would become meaningless and socialism would prevail.

Literature issued by MOM avoided explicit racism or anti-Semitism, and Trochmann denied being a bigot. He claimed that he just happened to be born white and was not ashamed of his skin color. MOM's leader, however, engaged in prayer meetings with white supremacist Identity Christians and visited the Aryan Nations compound in Idaho on several occasions—a compound replete with pictures of Adolf Hitler and swastikas.

MOM had no more than 250 members, but Trochmann gave it a high profile by providing guidance to other militias and by distributing a mail-order catalog packed with videotapes and books about government conspiracies.

He issued his Blue Book, a loose-leaf binder filled with material to prove the government conspiracy under way against liberty, along with the *M.O.D. Training Manual* (it has never been clear what "M.O.D." stood for), a 200-page publication showing how to use explosives, engage in sabotage (to disrupt the economy), target government buildings (easy to attack), spread false rumors (to conduct a "war of nerves"), and raid armories (to gain weapons and ammunition). The manual stated that "the placement of a bomb or fire explosive of great destructive power, which is capable of effecting irreparable loss against the enemy . . . is an action the urban guerrilla must execute with the greatest cold-bloodedness."

MOM's extremism found a friendly environment in Montana. Journalist Donald Voll wrote about the state: "This place is the motherlode not only of the militia movement but also of the deepest, most unsettling paranoia I've felt anywhere in my own country." Racist and anti-Semitic groups, along with those opposed to federal authority, abounded, perhaps encouraged by the state's spaciousness, which gave a sense of anything goes; or by its largely white population; or by the difficulty law enforcement had in covering such a large territory. The presence of so many groups, including Identity Christians, Christian Patriots, Constitutionalists, Aryan Nations, the Posse Comitatus, the White Students Union, and the Church of Jesus Christ Christian, caused the Northwest Coalition Against Malicious Harassment to warn about increased attacks directed at Jews, Indians, ethnic minorities, and homosexuals.

The atmosphere in Montana and in many areas of the country had become tense. To the extremists, those who threatened mainstream white values had to be contained; and to extremists and many mainstream Americans alike, the episodes at Ruby Ridge and Waco reinforced the idea that the federal government was to be feared.

Further Reading

Reavis, Dick J. *The Ashes of Waco: An Investigation.* New York: Simon & Schuster, 1995.

Stern, Kenneth S. *A Force Upon the Plain: The American Militia Movement and the Politics of Hate.* New York: Simon & Schuster, 1996.

Thibodeau, David. *A Place Called Waco: A Survivor's Story.* New York: Public Affairs, 1999.

Walter, Jess. *Every Knee Shall Bow: The Truth and Tragedy of Ruby Ridge and the Randy Weaver Family.* New York: Regan Books, 1995.

Wright, Stuart, ed. *Armageddon in Waco: Critical Perspectives on the Branch Davidian Conflict.* Chicago: University of Chicago Press, 1995.

Physician David Gunn Shot and Killed

1993

On March 10, 1993, Michael Griffin stepped out from a group of protesters in front of an abortion clinic in Pensacola, Florida, and shot to death Dr. David Gunn (1946–93) in what is widely believed to be the first murder of an abortion provider in the United States.

Violence against abortion clinics had been increasing for years, hand in hand with increased extremism among pro-life groups, who view abortion as murder and link it to the Bible's stricture of "Thou shalt not kill." They placed the issue on the same uncompromising moral level as had abolitionists with slavery in the first half of the nineteenth century. On Christmas Day 1984, abortion opponents bombed two doctors' offices and a clinic in Pensacola. One survey revealed that the number of violent acts committed nationally against abortion providers between 1977 and 1993 reached 80 assaults, 441 vandalisms, 75 arsons, and 36 bombings.

Prior to the shooting, Gunn had been targeted by antiabortionists because of the clinics he operated in Alabama and Georgia. Operation Rescue, a pro-life group, circulated posters with his photo and phone number, reminiscent of the "wanted" posters distributed to capture criminals in the Old West.

On the Sunday before Gunn was killed, Griffin attended a service at the Whitfield Assembly of God Church and asked the congregation to agree with him that Gunn should sacrifice his life for Jesus Christ. Then on March 10, Griffin joined the protesters outside Gunn's clinic, which had opened just one month earlier. As Gunn made his way toward the clinic door, Griffin rushed up to him, pulled out a .38-caliber snub-nosed revolver, and shot the doctor three times in the back. Gunn died a short while later at a local hospital.

Reports differed over whether Griffin had said anything in the moments before he shot Gunn. One antiabortionist claimed Griffin had yelled to Gunn, "Don't kill any more babies." Another witness insisted that the assailant had committed the murder in silence. Steve Powell, who worked near the clinic, said that after the shooting the protesters "looked like they were just happy."

The intent of the pro-life extremists was to terrorize doctors into abandoning abortion clinics, making it difficult, if not impossible, for any woman to obtain an abortion despite the Supreme Court's ruling in *Roe v. Wade* that protected women's right to an abortion. One Florida doctor said after Gunn's killing that "I predicted what happened. It wasn't me, but it could have been. . . . I have to consider that somebody is systemically planning to assassinate me." Another physician said, "You got one doctor down. All they need to do is kill a couple more, and then everybody will quit."

Writing in the *Los Angeles Times*, reporter Dianne Klein said that "the inner voice that guides Griffin is not one that most Americans pay much heed. It is the voice of religious fanaticism, only it seems this man confuses it with God's. . . . [Dr. Gunn's] murder was not an isolated incident, but a byproduct of an organized harassment campaign."

Griffin was sentenced to life in prison. Writing to a friend, he said, "If only one little baby is saved, it is worth anything they can do to me." Curiously, he later claimed that he had been framed for the crime by a conspiracy among his friends in the antiabortion movement.

The killing of Gunn led to Congress passing legislation that restricted the blocking of abortion clinics by protesters. Moderate antiabortion groups decried the use of violence. Yet the doctor's death energized the extremists even more. Operation Rescue continued to stage an "impact training camp" in Florida, and more murders followed. In July 1994, a second doctor was shot and killed in Pensacola by another pro-life extremist, Paul Hill. That December, a gunman dressed in black fired a rifle into two abortion clinics in Boston, killing two staff workers and wounding several others. Massachusetts Governor William F. Weld called the attacker "a terrorist," and President Bill Clinton condemned what he called "domestic terrorism."

But to extremists, those who killed the doctors and their assistants who "murdered" the unborn were nothing less than martyrs. Hill, who was sentenced to death for his crime, said, "I know for a fact that I'm going to heaven when I die. . . . My actions are honorable." He added: "There's no question that what I did was a relatively new concept. Someday it will be commonplace and generally accepted as normal."

Further Reading
Baird-Windle, Patricia, and Eleanor J. Bader. *Targets of Hatred: Anti-Abortion Terrorism.* New York: Palgrave, 2001.
Gorney, Cynthia. *Articles of Faith: A Frontline History of the Abortion Wars.* New York: Simon & Schuster, 1998.

1995 Two Newspapers Publish the Unabomber Manifesto

For more than a decade, beginning about 1980, a shadowy figure known as the Unabomber was at work; he killed three people and maimed or injured 23 others. In 1995, he threatened more bombings unless a major publication, such as the New York Times, *published his manifesto.*

It would be hard to find a more unusual terrorist from the 1990s than Ted Kaczynski (1943–). The Unabomber, as Kaczynski was called, came from an intellectual family, dropped out of college, and lived in a tiny unheated cabin without electricity or plumbing, in the Montana wilderness. In this cabin, he made bombs that he sent through the mail or placed in locations to kill people who were linked, he claimed, to the technological world that was destroying individualism. In some instances, the bombs were defused with little incident. Kaczynski worked deliberately and wrote in his journal in 1982 that he found it "frustrating, but I can't seem to make a lethal bomb."

Acting on the recommendations of the FBI and Attorney General Janet Reno, the *New York Times* and *Washington Post* published the Unabomber's entire 35,000-word manifesto—which ran to seven full pages in the newspapers. Journalists debated the soundness of giving in to Kaczynski's demand, and readers pondered the meaning and accuracy of the manifesto itself. Writing in *U.S. News & World Report,* John Leo insisted that "a lot of people seem to think that giving all that space to the bomber will set a precedent. . . . [But] literary terrorists aren't very common. Killers who tap out 35,000-word manifestoes and force them on leading newspapers are even rarer." Bob Guccione, editor of the adult magazine *Penthouse*, even offered the Unabomber a monthly column in which to express his views.

Untold numbers of people read the Unabomber's manifesto and besieged the *Washington Post* with requests for extra copies of the work, titled "Industrial Society and Its Future." Yet many journalists thought the decision to publish opened up newspapers and magazines to being blackmailed by terrorists and dissidents. The *Baton Rouge Advocate* stated that "submission to blackmail only proves that it works, thus encouraging more of it, either by the blackmailer or someone else."

In his manifesto, Kaczynski condemned modern society. One historian called it "unoriginal," but parts of the work struck a responsive chord with some Americans disillusioned with the growth of impersonal technologies and a bureaucracy that threatened individualism and the quality of the natural environment. In separate passages, Kaczynski wrotefrom his primitive dwelling:

> The Industrial Revolution and its consequences have been a disaster for the human race. They have greatly increased the life-expectancy of those of us who live in "advanced" countries, but they have destabilized society, have made life unfulfilling, have subjected human beings to indignities, have led to widespread psychological suffering . . . and have inflicted severe damage on the natural world. . . .
>
> There is no way of reforming or modifying the system so as to prevent it from depriving people of dignity and autonomy. . . .
>
> We therefore advocate a revolution against the industrial system. This revolution may or may not make use of violence: it may be sudden or it may be a relatively gradual process spanning a few

---

Terrorism and Dissent: A Problem of Definition and Policy

Should some domestic protest groups be labeled terrorist? The question is more than a semantic one; the answer could determine the limits of free speech in the United States.

The attacks of September 11, 2001, prompted Americans to focus unprecedented attention on "terrorist" activity. But there has never been a consensus among either social scientists or political leaders about what specific actions constitute terrorism. One academic has defined terrorism as "an anxiety-inspiring method of repeated violent acts employed by a clandestine individual, group, or state." In 1937 the League of Nations defined terrorism as "all criminal acts directed against a State and intended or calculated to create a state of terror in the minds of particular persons . . . or the general public." The U.S. Department of Defense defines terrorism as "the calculated use of violence or the threat of violence to inculcate fear; intended to coerce or to intimidate governments or societies in the pursuit of goals that are generally political, religious, or ideological." Other definitions limit "terrorism" to attacks on civilian targets.

Using these definitions, several of the individuals and groups discussed in this volume are said to have committed acts of terrorism, including the Ku Klux Klan (see entry, 1866), Weatherman (see entry, 1969), Timothy McVeigh (see entry, 1995), and Earth First! (see entries, 1979 and 1998). Other cases may also be classified as "terrorist," though their status is more debatable. These include the Boston Tea Party (see entry, 1773; although the word "terrorism" postdates that event, not appearing until the 1790s), John Brown's raid at Harper's Ferry (see entry, 1859), and the anti–World Trade Organization protests in Seattle (see entry, 1999).

With several states passing antiterrorism legislation after September 11, Adam Schwartz, a staff attorney for the American Civil Liberties Union in Illinois, complained about a bill in his state. His objection summarized the danger to protesters: "The General Assembly should take their time and assure that any new legislation actually combats terrorism and does not subject an individual who engages in civil disobedience doing minor property damage to a long prison sentence." Civil libertarians fear that an overly broad definition of "terrorist" activity will stifle the very dissent on which American political development has thrived.

decades. . . . This is not to be a POLITICAL revolution. Its object will be to overthrow not governments but the economic and technological basis of the present society.

Kaczynski was captured in 1996 by the FBI, a result of his brother having recognized certain ideas expressed in the manifesto as peculiar to Kaczynski that led to turning him in. A psychological analysis found Kaczynski to be suffering from schizophrenia, an illness known for its delusions and the tendency of those afflicted to commit violent acts. In early 1998, Kaczynski reached an agreement with the government under which he pleaded guilty to 13 federal charges, involving the deaths of three people and the injury of two others from five of his bombings. He admitted also that he had placed or mailed an additional 11 bombs that had caused 21 more injuries. In return for his plea, he avoided the death penalty and received a sentence of life in prison without parole.

The Unabomber thought he could change public opinion with his manifesto by revealing the "truth" to a society bewildered and frustrated by modern technology. Kaczynski wrote in his journal: "Do not get the idea I regret what I did. I would do it all over again."

Further Reading

Gibbs, Nancy, et al. *Mad Genius: The Odyssey, Pursuit, and Capture of the Unabomber Suspect.* New York: Warner Books, 1996.
Graysmith, Robert. *Unabomber: A Desire to Kill.* Washington, D.C.: Regnery Publishing, 1997.

1995 Bomb Destroys the Murrah Federal Building

On April 19, 1995, a tremendous explosion ripped through the Alfred P. Murrah Federal Building in Oklahoma City, Oklahoma. The blast left a large portion of the nine-story structure a tangled, shattered mess of glass, concrete, metal support rods, and human bodies. Workers, visitors, and children in a day-care center were injured; 168 people died.

Within days after the blast, federal authorities arrested Timothy McVeigh, a 26-year-old army infantry veteran from New York State who had fought in the Persian Gulf War, and newspapers linked him to the militia movement. They claimed that McVeigh had associated with the Michigan Militia and navigated a subterranean world of armed malcontents who lived in places such as Kingman, Arizona, a desert center of antigovernment extremism. In fact, McVeigh had imbibed the words of militia advocate Mark Koernke, listening avidly to his short-wave radio broadcasts; associated with members of the Arizona Patriots, a militia group dating from the 1980s; watched videotapes produced by militia extremist Linda Thompson about the government raid on the Branch Davidian compound at Waco, Texas; and read and re-read William Pierce's white supremacist, anti-Semitic book, *The Turner Diaries* (see entry, 1978).

The bombing unleashed a media and government investigation of militias, putting the burgeoning militia movement on the defensive. Militia supporters, meanwhile, accused federal officials of using the Oklahoma City tragedy as a bogeyman through which to discredit them. To a certain extent they had a point, as the government and the media lumped all militias together as racist, anti-Semitic, and terrorist when many of them were not.

The point, though, became lost in the rash of comments offered by some prominent militia leaders and their supporters in the wake of the catastrophe. Bo Gritz likened the bombing to a work by Rembrandt, a masterpiece of art and science. Norm Olson claimed the Japanese had exploded the bomb in retaliation for the United States supposedly having committed a terrorist act in 1995 by detonating poison gas on a Tokyo subway. The New Jersey Militia called it strange that no one in the offices of the Bureau of Alcohol, Tobacco, and Firearms (BATF) on the ninth floor of the Murrah Building was killed. Some reports, said the militia, indicated that BATF workers were given the option to take the day off. The New Jersey Militia wondered, too, why no children of BATF agents were in the day-care center. Through its assertions, the group implied that the federal agency had been forewarned about the bombing.

Other militia leaders told of mysterious black helicopters circling the Murrah Building before the blast and claimed that the federal government had exploded the bomb to launch an offensive aimed at eliminating all militias. Linda Thompson claimed, "I definitely believe the government did the bombing. I mean, who's got a track record of killing children?" Frank Smith, head of the Georgia Militia, blamed the federal government, too. "We expected them to do something drastic," he said. "We didn't expect it to be that drastic." Vernon Weckner, leader of the Unorganized Militia of El Dorado County, California, pointed a finger at the CIA as the real culprit, and Randy Trochmann, a leader in the Militia of Montana, suggested that President Bill Clinton may have planned the bombing as a way to build support for his proposed Comprehensive Terrorism Protection Act and gun control legislation.

The federal government, however, insisted that McVeigh had destroyed the Murrah Building, and that he had only one accomplice, Terry Nichols. McVeigh was executed by lethal injection in 2001 for his crime; Nichols was sentenced in 1998 to a life term in prison.

Yet questions abounded about the case. Many analysts still believe that McVeigh and Nichols were not the only individuals involved in the blast. They point to eyewitnesses who implicated other mysterious figures. Writing in the periodical *In These Times* (2001) Martin A. Lee, an expert on neofascism, claimed that McVeigh may well have received help from the Aryan Republican Army, a Nazi group intent on overthrowing the U.S. government. In *Insight on the News* (2001), Kelly Patricia O'Meara discussed evidence that shows Nichols visited the Philippines shortly before the bombing and attended a meeting of fundamentalist Muslims that included Ramzi Yousef, who planned the 1993 bombing of New York City's World Trade Center. Another news report claimed that Nichols had Iraqi telephone numbers in his possession when he was arrested. The FBI, critics say, ignored information that conflicted with its theory so the agency could claim that the case had been wrapped up.

Prior to the destruction of the World Trade Center on September 11, 2001, the bombing of the Murrah Building was the most devastating terrorist attack in the history of the United States—one that displayed the depths to which some Americans hated the federal government.

Further Reading

Hamm, Mark S. *Apocalypse in Oklahoma: Waco and Ruby Ridge Revenged.* Boston: Northeastern University Press, 1997.

Jones, Stephen, and Peter Israel. *Others Unknown: Timothy McVeigh and the Oklahoma City Bombing.* New York: Public Affairs, 2001.

Michel, Lou, and Dan Herbeck. *American Terrorist: Timothy McVeigh and the Oklahoma City Bombing.* New York: Regan Books, 2001.

Louis Farrakhan Leads the Million Man March

1995

With the cry of "Clean up, black man, and the world will respect and honor you," Louis Farrakhan, leader of the Black Muslims (Nation of Islam), exhorted the participants in the Million Man March in Washington, D.C. He had organized the march to encourage African-American men to act responsibly toward their families and toward the black community, to show his own power as a leader, and to prove that blacks could gather en masse to promote a cause.

Not all blacks supported the Million Man March, and many white liberals, normally supportive of black civil rights, also opposed it. Their criticism was directly related to Farrakhan. As head of the Black Muslims (see entry, 1977), Farrakhan rejected racial integration in favor of black independence. Furthermore, his often scathing criticisms of Jews caused many to treat him as a bigoted outcast. Civil rights activist Julian Bond, a board member of the National Association for the Advancement of Colored People (NAACP), said that to earn respect Farrakhan must give up "the anti-Semitism, the homophobia, the white-bashing, the Catholic-bashing, the standard messages of hate that have been part and parcel of his for the last 30 years." President Bill Clinton halfheartedly supported the march, but criticized Farrakhan's role in it.

For Farrakhan, the march originated in the spiritual realm. He said that God had given him the idea and that "he didn't bring it through me because my heart was dark and I was filled with anti-Semitism." Where previous demonstrations in Washington by blacks had stressed civil rights and attacked conservative legislation, the Million Man March contained only some of that while it infused the participants—who numbered anywhere from 400,000 to 800,000—with a sense of togetherness and pride. Like a congregation at a revivalist's meeting, those who felt the spirit were expected to take it with them and change their lives and those of their neighbors. The march came amid the disturbing growth among African-Americans of single-parent families headed only by the mother, partly a result of nearly 70 percent of black births occurring out of wedlock.

With the march completed, one man from Montgomery, Alabama, returned home and expressed his commitment to family by marrying his longtime girlfriend, who was also the mother of his three sons. Another from Chesapeake, Virginia, said, "I . . . told my wife from this day forward I am going to be a better husband and that no matter what, through thick and thin, we are going to be together. I meant it from the bottom of my heart."

In the atmosphere of spirituality, poet Maya Angelou said to the throng gathered in front of the Capitol: "Save your race. You have been paid for in a distant place. The old ones remind us that slavery's chains have paid for our freedom again and again." Rev. Jesse Jackson declared: "How good it is to hear the sound of chains and shackles breaking."

But bigotry reared its head. A *Washington Post* survey of more than 1,000 participants showed that 4 in 10 had an unfavorable impression of Jews. And former Representative Gus Savage said to the crowd, "Blacks should atone not for our anger, but for not being angry enough, [and for not] taking control of our economy in defiance of white power, in defiance of Jewish influence." In a rambling two-and-a-half hour speech, Farrakhan declared: "The real evil in America is that idea that undergirds the setup of the Western world, and that idea is called white supremacy."

In short, the Million Man March left a legacy of hope for reform among African-American men, of anger over white racism, and a residue of anti-Semitism that nagged at the black conscience.

Further Reading

Alexander, Amy. *The Farrakhan Factor: African-American Writers on Leadership, Nationhood and Minister Louis Farrakhan.* New York: Grove/Atlantic, 1997.

Cottman, Michael H. *Million Man March.* New York: Crown Trade Paperbacks, 1995.

1996 Freemen and the FBI Engage in Showdown in Montana

In March 1996, FBI agents surrounded the right-wing Freemen at their ranch near Jordan, Montana, beginning a long showdown. Not wanting to repeat the violence and deaths that had occurred at Ruby Ridge, Idaho, and Waco, Texas, the federal government moved cautiously against the radicals.

The Freemen had adopted theories closest in content to Identity Christians and the Posse Comitatus. They feared a New World Order, disavowed the validity of the Constitution beyond the first 10 amendments, and believed that the national government had violated the document through policies that favored Zionists and nonwhites. The Freemen concluded that they did not have to abide by federal laws or pay income taxes. Nor did they have to recognize state governments, which they claimed had become corrupted by the federal system. Under their leader, LeRoy Schweitzer (1938–), the Freemen reached the point of separating themselves from society at large and retreating to their ranch, which they claimed was the independent "Justus Township."

John Bohlman, the county attorney in Musselshell County, Montana (where the town of Jordan was located), attested to the threat posed by the Freemen and the frustration in trying to contain them, when he said:

> There is the fear that should one speak out against these individuals, that one's property or person will be harmed. The liens filed by the "Freemen" [to harass those who oppose them] may seem like a joke unless you are the person attempting to sell your property and you learn you can't buy title insurance because a Freeman has a million dollar lien filed against [it]. The community is further aggravated because the most militant individuals are able to break laws without punishment. It is particularly frustrating to see some people continue to not pay taxes for many years with what appears to be impunity because those people threaten violence. If this trend continues, more and more people will believe that the Freemen interpretation of the law is correct; and even if they don't believe that they will at least see the obvious: that guns are cheaper than taxes!

Schweitzer and his Freemen colleagues had printed and circulated checks and money orders, passing them off as valid when, in fact, they were fraudulent. In all, from 1994 to 1996 they defrauded banks and businesses of some $1.8 million. During that period, they threatened the life of a U.S. district court judge, Jack Shanstrom of Billings, Montana. These actions caused the federal agents to surround the Freemen's ranch, and, when the Freemen refused to surrender, the FBI decided to implement what it called a "soft siege."

The siege lasted several weeks, with the FBI worried about the Freemen's stockpile of rifles, handguns, shotguns, and 11,000 rounds of ammunition, along with the presence of several children in the group of 20 people on the ranch. Local residents, meanwhile, urged action, expressed their disgust with the Freemen, and said they did not want any of the recently organized militias coming to their town to help the extremists.

At times it appeared the standoff would result in violence, especially when efforts by Bo Gritz and other far-right leaders to negotiate a compromise failed. Early in June, however, the FBI increased its pressure by cutting off electricity to the ranch and blocking the Freemen's cellular telephones. The Freemen finally surrendered on June 13, 1996. In 1999 Schweitzer, who said to his trial judge, "We are from the foreign country of Montana, not a state," was sentenced to more than 20 years in prison on 25 counts relating to attempting to undermine the U.S. banking system. Nine other Freemen were convicted on similar charges.

The Freemen had posed as a group fighting to protect individual rights. In actuality, they were armed thugs, hunkered down, dangerous, and criminal.

Further Reading
Berlet, Chip, and Matthew N. Lyons. *Right-wing Populism in America: Too Close for Comfort.* New York: Guilford Press, 2000.

Heaven's Gate Members Commit Mass Suicide to Join a Spaceship

1997

Outsiders called Heaven's Gate a cult; the group's members thought themselves a chosen people who on their death would ascend to a UFO traveling behind the Hale-Bopp comet to live in the Next Level. As the comet neared Earth in 1997, 39 Heaven's Gate members committed suicide so they could leave their bodies, or what they called their "earthly vehicles," and join the spaceship.

Heaven's Gate began in the early 1970s when Marshall Herff Applewhite (1932–97), a voice professor and the son of a Presbyterian minister, and Bonnie Lu Trusdale Nettles (1927–85), a registered nurse, claimed that God had come to them and given them a special mission, anointing them as his emissaries through which he would save the world. The Two, as they originally called themselves, began traveling the country, proselytizing and seeking recruits to their mission. They found few, and, according to a report in the *New York Times,* a frustrated Applewhite said, "Bonnie and I are discovering more and more that the 'religious' and 'loving' are the last to see or accept our truth."

The Two believed that UFOs had visited Earth and had in the distant past been mistaken for angels. Soon, they said, the world would come to an end, but before that day, they and their followers could prepare themselves for the "Next Level," when they would board a UFO that would take them to heaven.

Applewhite was arrested in 1974 for having stolen a rental car, and he served six months in jail. The Two then continued their work; at a meeting in Los Angeles in May 1975, they recruited several followers who were sent out as missionaries. At another meeting in Waldport, Oregon, that September, The Two convinced 20 people to abandon their possessions and families and join them as disciples. Like the other recruits, the 20 new members were required to sacrifice their individuality to the group and live a regimented life that included celibacy and restricted diets. Soon news reports were calling Heaven's Gate "the UFO cult." By 1976, Heaven's Gate had about 200 members, but that number declined because of internal dissension and the failure of a UFO to appear at a time forecast by The Two.

Undaunted, The Two took new names. Bonnie Nettles called herself Ti and Marshall Applewhite called himself Do, after the notes on the musical scale. Heaven's Gate kept nighttime vigils, looking up into the sky for the first sign of a UFO. Once more, Ti and Do forecast the imminent arrival of a spaceship, and once more, it failed to come. In 1985, Bonnie Nettles died of cancer at Parkland Hospital in Dallas.

Applewhite's message grew more strident—the devil now controlled the Earth, he said. The time to depart was drawing ever closer. He and seven disciples were castrated to enforce their dictum against sensuality.

Then, in July 1995, astronomers sighted the unusually large Hale-Bopp comet, about 25 miles wide. At the same time, a published photograph of Hale-Bopp showed a trailing shower of light, and rumors spread that it indicated a UFO was traveling next to the comet. Even if no UFO were present, the members of Heaven's Gate finally concluded, the prophecy was nearing reality. At their web site, the group posted a message stating:

> Whether Hale-Bopp has a "companion" or not is irrelevant from our perspective. However, its arrival is joyously very significant to us at "Heaven's Gate." The *joy* is that our Older Member in the Evolutionary Level Above Human (the "Kingdom of Heaven") has made it clear to us that Hale-Bopp's approach is the "marker" we've been waiting for—the time for the arrival of the spacecraft from the Level Above Human to take us home to "Their World"—in the literal Heavens. Our 22 years of classroom here on planet Earth is finally coming to conclusion—"graduation" from the Human Evolutionary Level. We are happily prepared to leave "this world" and go with Ti's crew.

By this time, members of the group were making money designing home pages for the Internet, and they had vacated their 40-acre ranch near Albuquerque, New Mexico, to live in an adobe mansion along winding, tree-lined roads in San Diego, California. Movie stars and wealthy businessmen were their neighbors.

Finally, in late March 1997, Applewhite and 38 of his disciples packed their bags to prepare for the arrival of the UFO. They concocted a formula of vodka and Phenobarbital (a sedative), and made videotapes of themselves. Dressed in all-black outfits and wearing newly purchased Nike tennis shoes, some of them giggled for the camera as they explained what they were about to do. Over the course of three or four days they drank their suicide formula. No one changed their minds or resisted, not even the last person to take the drink as the house became cluttered with dead bodies. Police found them on March 26.

On hearing about the suicides, most Americans scoffed at the notion that anyone could believe in finding salvation by killing themselves as a means to ascend to a UFO trailing a comet. Yet some questioned how different these beliefs were from Christian theology and other religious doctrine. Writing in the *Los Angeles Times*, Edward Tabash, an activist with the Council for Secular Humanism, said that many of the same Christians who scoffed at Heaven's Gate "uncritically believe that God turned Lot's wife into a pillar of salt for doing no more than observing the destruction of Sodom and Gomorrah." He added: "Humankind has always had a problem with irrational supernatural beliefs. Whether it is salvation through a UFO or salvation through some invisible and unproven god, it is time that we . . . begin to reexamine all of our superstitious beliefs, be they those of New Age sects or those of conventional religion."

No one knows the complete reason for Heaven's Gate's appeal. Beyond Applewhite's own persuasive and beguiling personality, the attachment to his irrational beliefs may have come from the insecurity and isolation felt by those adrift in a technologically driven society (ironically, by a people who worked with the Internet). The nearing of the millennium may have intensified the feelings of helplessness and impending apocalypse. Writing in *American Demographics* in December 1997, James R. Rosenfield stated that "death and rebirth are familiar millennial themes, highly prominent in '90s decades and other end-time periods."

The Heaven's Gate suicides continued after March 1997. That May, another member of the group, Wayne Cooke, despairing over the loss of his wife in the earlier suicides, killed himself at a hotel near San Diego; another Heaven's Gate member did the same the following February. Several weeks before his death, Cooke told a reporter: "I totally believe and support the group and what it stands for and has done. I believe they reached the point where word was given to depart from this world back to the mother ship. Now, they're on a craft somewhere."

Further Reading

Jackson, Forrest. *Cosmic Suicide: The Tragedy and Transcendence of Heaven's Gate.* Dallas: Pentaradial Press, 1997.

Jeurgensmayer, Mark. *Terror in the Mind of God: The Global Rise of Religious Violence.* Updated ed. Berkeley: University of California Press, 2001.

Earth Liberation Front Sets Fire to a Ski Resort in Vail, Colorado   1998

In October 1998, the wealthy ski town of Vail, Colorado, became the site of an "eco-terrorist" attack when radicals set seven fires that burned chair lifts and buildings at a resort, causing damage estimated at $12 million. Claiming responsibility for the attack was the Earth Liberation Front (ELF), a shadowy group stirred by the belief that the government had been ineffectual in protecting the natural environment from the ravages of a greedy, corporate America.

The ELF emerged from the extremist wing of the environmental movement that had earlier coalesced around the group Earth First! (see entry, 1979).

In a communiqué, the ELF described itself as "operating in cells" to protect the security of the entire group. "Each cell is anonymous not only to the public but also to one another," the ELF said. "This decentralized structure helps keep activists out of jail and free to continue conducting actions." In spring 1997, five ELF members were arrested in Michigan for breaking into a fur ranch in Canada to release mink. Later the same year, the ELF claimed that it had burned down a corral in Oregon to protest the confinement of wild horses.

The attack in Vail was intended to stop the expansion of a ski resort owned by Vail Associates into a forest inhabited by lynx, a wild cat. The corporation proposed an 885-acre expansion, which was much discussed and much debated at town meetings. In choosing Vail as a site for "ecotage," the ELF picked a high-profile town known for its wealth and its celebrities. Lear jets and Mercedes cars were as common as snowdrifts; movie stars owned houses in Vail. Paul Witt, a spokesman for Vail Associates, observed that "this is one of the most famous ski resorts in the world. I seriously doubt that an attack on, say, a small skiing area in Michigan would have got these sort of headlines."

In addition to the chair lifts, the fire destroyed a ski patrol center and a restaurant. It was set only three days after work had begun on expanding the ski facilities and only a week after a court had dismissed a suit filed by environmentalists to stop the proposed development. The ELF issued a statement: "On behalf of the lynx, five buildings and four ski lifts at Vail were reduced to ashes on the night of Sunday, October 18 [1998]. . . . Putting profits ahead of Colorado's wildlife will not be tolerated. This action is just a warning. We will be back if this greedy corporation . . . continues to trespass into wild and unroaded areas."

From 1998 into 2001, the ELF continued its attacks from the Pacific Northwest all the way into the Midwest and New York, causing damage that exceeded $30 million. Among its targets were a road construction site in Bloomington, Indiana, and a luxury home being built in Niwot, Colorado.

In 2000 and early 2001, the ELF set fire to new house constructions at several residential sites on Long Island, New York. The group wanted to alert the public to the effect of urban sprawl and halt the building projects. In Boulder, Colorado, the ELF burned a $2.5-million mansion. In a statement, ELF said, "We know that the real 'ecoterrorists' are the white male industrial and corporate elite. They must be stopped."

In spring 2001 the ELF set fire to an Oregon tree farm to protest genetic research on poplar trees. Following the attack, *U.S. News & World Report* stated: "Flummoxed law enforcement authorities say ELF and a sister organization, the Animal Liberation Front, have been behind the majority of terrorist acts committed on U.S. soil over the past two years. . . ."

But radical conservatives who oppose environmental regulations also have been using terrorist tactics. A February 2002 report in the *Christian Science Monitor* described the widespread theft of natural resources and attacks on government officials as a "more serious source of violence than periodic attacks

---

Tree Sitting

While the ELF gained attention for its destructive tactics, some activists took a different course. Earth First! member Julia "Butterfly" Hill resolved to protest the destruction of ancient giant redwoods by sitting atop one near the town of Eureka, California. By fall 1998, she had been living for 10 months on a 6-by-8-foot platform attached to the approximately 1,000-year-old, 200-foot tree as she sought to prevent it and other nearby redwoods from being harvested by the Pacific Lumber Company. She survived gale-force winds and torrential rains, thick fog and freezing temperatures. "It is vital that we start reconnecting again to the Earth," Hill said. "We are beginning to die because we've lost the connection."

Hill was not the first member of Earth First! to perch in the tree. In winter 1997, several others took turns living in the redwood that they had named Luna for the full moon that shone on the night they discovered it, when it was on the verge of being chopped down. Hill joined the activists in their initial protest and then announced she would stay in the tree for as long as it would take to save it. According to the *Los Angeles Times*, Hill explained, "I felt compelled that I was supposed to be a part of something bigger. I gave my word to the forest, to Luna, that until I felt I'd done everything I possibly could to help make people aware, I would not come down."

Hill ended her vigil in December 1999 when the Pacific Lumber Company agreed to spare Luna and the trees in a surrounding 200-foot buffer zone. Hill said, "I understand all of us are governed by different values. I understand that to some people I'm just a dirty tree-hugging hippie. But I can't imagine being able to take a chainsaw to something like this."

The redwood was attacked by vandals in 2000, who slashed its trunk. The tree was seriously damaged but, as of this writing, still survives.

by [the] ELF." The article quoted Michael Pendleton, a social scientist and former police officer: "While the 40 million dollars of damage attributed to ecoterrorist groups . . . is clearly unacceptable . . . it pales in comparison to the 100-million dollar annual loss attributed to timber theft from natural forests." On an even graver note, there has been an increase in fire bombings and shootings aimed at workers with the U.S. Forest Service and the U.S. Bureau of Land Management.

Congress, though, was focusing in 2002 on legislation to deal with the ecoterrorists. Unmoved by its detractors, an adamant ELF declared: "Economic sabotage is the only thing the earth-raping, animal-abusing scum will respond to."

Further Reading

Glick, Daniel, and Sarah Van Boven. "Fire on the Mountain." *Newsweek*, 2 November 1998.

Knickerbocker, Brad. "Eco-terrorists, Too, May Soon Be On the Run." *Christian Science Monitor*, 15 February, 2002.

Murr, Andrew, and Tom Morganthau. "Burning Suburbia." *Newsweek*, 15 January 2001.

Protesters Disrupt World Trade Organization Meeting in Seattle 1999

In recent years, the world has gotten smaller—obviously not in size but through the complexity of economic contacts and the rapidity of communication. To critics of the trend, the smaller world means more exploitation by countries and corporations, and a crushing of individualism. That conclusion inspired numerous groups to protest on the streets of Seattle, Washington, in late November 1999 as the World Trade Organization (WTO) met there to discuss additional ways to integrate economies.

The WTO evolved in the mid-1990s from a loose organization of 23 countries formed after World War II under the General Agreement on Tariffs and Trade (GATT), aimed at liberalizing international trade relations. Prior to Seattle, the GATT countries met several times, including in Uruguay in 1986. There the delegates worked in near anonymity to produce an agreement that lowered tariffs on many industrial goods. The agreement reflected the desire to expand free trade and foster a more global economy, in which goods would cross national boundaries based on market forces rather than artificial tax and regulatory barriers. Yet disputes among countries afraid to end protection for all goods made the 1986 agreement incomplete and produced the need for more meetings. So too did controversies over whether to monitor the environmental impact of trade agreements, along with their effects on wages and labor rights.

Near the top of the WTO agenda for Seattle was whether to lower agricultural tariffs and end export subsidies. *The Economist* revealed one of many sources of discord within the WTO when it reported: "America and the . . . group of leading farm exporters, which includes Australia, Canada and Brazil, are pressing for sweeping liberalization. . . . But the [European Union], Japan, South Korea, Norway, and Switzerland, all with highly sheltered farmers, are steadfastly opposed."

An anti-WTO protester in downtown Seattle, 1999. (AP/Wide World Photos)

Globalism: The Next Protest Frontier?

With protests in Seattle in 1999, Washington, D.C., in 2000; and Genoa, Italy, in 2001, the anti-globalism campaign was positioned to become the primary battleground for dissidents in the twenty-first century. For those opposed to globalization, the new wave of international economic relations had become the symbol of evil. In spring 2000, Medea Benjamin, director of the human rights organization Global Exchange, called the World Bank, the International Monetary Fund, and the World Trade Organization an "unholy trinity."

Globalization exhibited the power to compel a variety of radical groups into action. Environmentalists, for example, blamed the World Bank for financing projects that threatened the Yangtze River in China and rain forests in Brazil; human rights activists pilloried the same institution for supporting countries that exploited child labor. Robert Litan, director of economic studies at the Brookings Institution, said, "This is about more than trade. This is about globalization."

Had the protesters made any impact? "Some of the critics have a point," admitted Joseph Stiglitz, a former chief economist at the World Bank, in spring 2000. "Some of the conditions set for less-developed countries to receive loans were too harsh, too contradictory, and made tough economic conditions worse." Benjamin Barber saw a grand vision emerging; he wrote in *The American Prospect* in September 2000 that the protests were leading to a global civil society, a movement to "recreate on a global scale the normal civic balance that exists within democratic nations." While the globalization controversy took a back seat to the war on terrorism after September 11, 2001, it remained a potent issue with roots in the struggle for social justice that extended at least to the countercultural upheavals of the 1960s.

Yet to the protesters who gathered in Seattle, the WTO appeared to be a monolith. Typically, those who opposed free trade in the past had argued for protectionist economic policies. Some of that argument appeared at Seattle, particularly from U.S. unions that wanted to maintain tariffs in certain industries to prevent an influx of cheaper foreign goods, which would cause factories to close and put the employees out of work.

But the protests voiced by the groups in Seattle were much broader than the arguments against free trade voiced by unions and protectionists. They claimed that freer trade without constraints on businesses had caused a trend sometimes described as "a race to the bottom"—industries relocating from country to country in search of sites where they could pay the lowest wages, offer the fewest benefits, and escape environmental regulations. Furthermore, they argued that the WTO was a tool of multinational corporations that have profits as their only goal: sacrificing workers, the environment, and ethics; trampling on local economies and cultures; and promoting greater income inequality between the rich and the poor.

Moreover, the protesters attacked the WTO for using secret deliberations to make decisions that affect large numbers of people, including the adjudication of trade disputes among WTO member nations. Public Citizen, a consumer rights group established by Ralph Nader, called the WTO secretive and undemocratic. Environmentalists criticized a WTO decision in 1998 that caused the United States to retreat from its demands that foreign shrimp fleets use stricter methods to keep sea turtles from being caught in fishing nets.

Many of the Seattle protesters offered less a reasoned argument against the WTO than a visceral response to a world being shaped by impersonal corporations and bureaucracies—a world in which the individual meant little. *U.S. News & World Report* quoted Stewart Weschler of Public Citizen: "The WTO is a threat to life on earth." Union leader George Becker agreed: "People do not count in the WTO."

More than 50,000 protesters turned out in Seattle, ranging from the aforementioned unions and Public Citizen to the Free Rebels Coalition and the Eugene (Oregon) Anarchists. Most of them demonstrated peacefully, but hundreds of them prevented WTO delegates from getting to the Seattle Convention Center, and violence ensued; anarchist groups and their sympathizers organized into a Black Bloc (see entry, 1990) and smashed store windows and set fire to trash bins.

The mayhem temporarily shut down the meeting and forced Washington Governor Gary Locke to call in 200 National Guardsmen to supplement the 300 state troopers and local police already on duty. The *Los Angeles Times* reported "surreal scenes" in which "lines of police in full riot gear stood eye-to-eye with lines of demonstrators dressed as sea turtles and butterflies." Many of the protesters who originally wanted the limited reform of convincing the WTO to give representation to nonelite groups, became more radical with their demands. As Todd Tollefson of Jobs with Justice explained, "The goals changed. . . . Before the march it was mostly just to send a message, say that we need to have a seat at the table. Then after the march realizing that the WTO, you know, there's no reforming it, it is not going to be fixable, that's just saying that the 'WTO's got to go!'"

Some of the protesters in Seattle came from outside the United States; demonstrations also erupted in Europe. In London, protesters overturned cars before being subdued by riot police—all of which underscored an irony: while the protesters decried globalization, they too acted globally. They not only hailed from different countries and acted in concert, they also coordinated the Seattle protest through the Internet (as they would a subsequent protest in Genoa, Italy, in July 2001, that was much more violent than the one in Seattle).

For the protesters, it was a case of David taking on Goliath. Kevin Danaher, cofounder of the group Global Exchange, said, "In Ethiopia they have a saying, 'When spiders unite, they can tie down a lion,' and that's part of what's going on—people realizing that if all of us small citizen forces come together, we can force these guys to change and then go on to actually replace these institutions with more life-affirming institutions."

Further Reading

Cockburn, Alexander, et al. *Five Days that Shook the World: The Battle in Seattle and Beyond.* London and New York: Verso Books, 2001.

Dunkley, Graham. *The Free Trade Adventure: The WTO, the Uruguay Round and Globalism—A Critique.* New York: St. Martin's Press, 2000.

Elliott, Michael. "Lessons from the Battle of Seattle." *Newsweek*, 27 December 1999.

———. "The New Radicals." *Newsweek*, 13 December 1999.

Indians Protest White Control of Whiteclay, Nebraska   1999

The deaths of two Oglala Sioux men, Wilson "Wally" Black Elk, Jr., and Ronald Hard Heart, outside of Whiteclay, Nebraska, infuriated Native Americans who had long been subjected to violence against their people on and near the Pine Ridge reservation. On June 26, 1999, they decided to stage a "Rally for Justice" to challenge white control of Whiteclay and the sale of alcohol there to Indians.

The Rally for Justice began at a meeting inside Billy Mills Hall, where 500 Indians gathered, including leaders from the once-formidable but recently fractured American Indian Movement (AIM), namely Russell Means (an actor known for his role in the movie *Last of the Mohicans*), Dennis Banks, and Clyde Bellecourt. Means claimed that Whiteclay, an unincorporated town of 25 residents located on Highway 87 just across the state line from South Dakota and on the boundary of the Pine Ridge reservation, belonged to the Oglala Sioux largely based on the 1868 Treaty of Fort Laramie, which stipulated that much of South Dakota, Wyoming, and western Nebraska were to be under Indian control.

While few objective observers believed that the federal courts would ever recognize Indian authority over Whiteclay, some thought that the courts might agree that the town was part of a buffer zone set aside by Congress in the late 1800s to the south of the Pine Ridge reservation. In this buffer zone, white settlers were prohibited and alcohol was not to be sold. In 1904, President Theodore Roosevelt had arbitrarily yanked away from the Pine Ridge reservation that part of the zone located in Nebraska.

About 250 protesters left Billy Mills Hall and marched through Whiteclay. Means declared: "We're here to tell all Nebraska—from the governor on down and especially the commissioners of Sheridan County—that we're going back to our agreement. We're going to force the government to give back our land." The protesters were also concerned with the heavy sale of beer to Indians at Whiteclay, which contributed to alcoholism at Pine Ridge. They wanted the sales to stop.

One white resident observed about the Indians, however, that "It's their choice to come up here. Nobody makes them come up here. They have the state line. Why let it go on this long and then want it back if it does belong to them?"

As the Indians marched, they threw beer cans, watermelons, and rocks. Stores were looted and one grocery was set afire. Law enforcement officers from Nebraska and South Dakota then cleared the town.

One week later, the protesters returned, again led by Means, Bellecourt, and other AIM officials. The *Omaha World-Herald* described the group as a "colorful mix of men with red bandannas on pinto ponies, older men with the red berets of AIM, and young children carrying signs, including one that read: 'Stop Indian ethnic cleansing.'" The *St. Louis Post-Dispatch* quoted Bellecourt as saying, "If I had my way, we'd tear the damn town to the ground, but we can't do that."

The protesters attempted to march into Whiteclay, but state troopers emptied the town of its residents and set up a barricade. The Indians then debated whether to try to break through the barricade. Most of them decided to turn back, but Means marched forward, and he and eight other Native Americans were arrested when they reached the barricade.

Means challenged his arrest in court, claiming that the state of Nebraska had no jurisdiction over Whiteclay because Roosevelt's 1904 order was illegal. But in February 2000, a Sheridan County judge ruled against him.

Other Indians led yet another march on Whiteclay in June 2000. "It's for justice," Kills Black, an Oglala Sioux, said. "We really want something done."

Further Reading

Tysver, Robynn. "Second Whiteclay Protest Quieter." *Omaha World-Herald*, 4 July 1999.
Von Kampen, Todd. "Looting Ends Indian Rally." *Omaha World-Herald*, 27 June 1999.

2001 Terrorist Attacks on September 11 Leave Both the Right and Left Wings in Disarray

The September 11, 2001, terrorist attacks on the World Trade Center in New York City and the Pentagon near Washington, D.C., left many Americans at a loss for words to describe the devastation they had experienced or witnessed.

Both right wingers and left wingers scrambled to make sense of the tragedy, and for those who had previously criticized the federal government, disagreements arose over what motivated the attacks and how to interpret President George W. Bush's call for a war on terrorism. From his home in Lynchburg, Virginia, right-winger Jerry Falwell, the fundamentalist Christian preacher who had led the born-again political revolt of the 1980s, reacted to the terrorist attack a couple of days after it occurred by stating,

> I really believe that the pagans, and the abortionists, and the feminists, and the gays and the lesbians who are actively trying to make that an alternative lifestyle, the ACLU, People for the American Way, all of them who have tried to secularize America—I point the finger in their face and say "you helped this happen."

Falwell explained that the attack was retribution from God for throwing him "out of the public square, out of the schools. The abortionists have got to bear some burden for this because God will not be mocked." Later, Falwell apologized for having blamed people other than the terrorists for the tragedy, but he insisted that the movement to secularize the United States "created an environment which possibly has caused God to lift the veil of protection which has allowed no one to attack America on our soil since 1812."

A fellow fundamentalist, Pat Robertson, offered a similar view. On his Christian television program, the *700 Club*, he stated: "We have sinned against Almighty God, at the highest level of our government, we've stuck our finger in your eye. The Supreme Court has insulted you over and over again, Lord, they've taken your Bible away from the schools." Groups that had been singled out by Falwell objected strenuously to his comments. Lorri L. Jean, executive director of the National Gay and Lesbian Task Force, offered a counter view that many other Americans thought valid: that the terrorist attacks, which had been staged by Muslim fundamentalists, emanated from the hate and intolerance found among religious extremists. She said that "the terrible tragedy that has befallen our nation, and indeed the entire global community, is the byproduct of fanaticism." Where Falwell had pointed his finger at people such as her, she pointed her finger back at him. The terrorist attacks, she said, came from "the same fanaticism that enables people like Jerry Falwell to preach hate against those who do not think, live, or love in the exact same way he does."

Meanwhile, movie director Oliver Stone described the September 11 attacks as "a revolt" against the "New World Order" in which corporate conglomerates exerted oppressive power. He added: "This attack was pure chaos, and chaos is energy. All great changes have come from people or events that were initially misunderstood, and seemed frightening, like madmen."

In the 1980s and 1990s, extreme leftists and rightists had converged in their distrust of the federal government. Even though they proposed different solutions to Washington's encroaching power, they agreed that the government was an evil entity. But President Bush's call for a war on terrorism confused them. They debated how much the government should be supported in the military part of the war.

Leftist writer Christopher Hitchens, who had previously antagonized many liberals with his support for the impeachment of President Bill Clinton, now ignited another controversy with his fervent support for the military assault on the fundamentalist Islamic Taliban regime in Afghanistan. The regime had harbored Al Qaeda, the group headed by Islamic radical Osama bin Laden and considered to be the perpetrator of the September 11 attacks. Writing in the December 17, 2001, issue of *The Nation*, Hitchens said about the massive U.S. aerial attack on Afghanistan: "The United States of America has just succeeded in bombing a country back out of the Stone Age. . . . The nexus that bound the Taliban to the forces of Al Qaeda . . . has been destroyed. We are rid of one of the foulest regimes on earth, while one of the most vicious crime families in history has been crippled and scattered."

To those on the left who condemned the September 11 attacks but qualified their statements by alluding to U.S. imperialism as being partly responsible for the assault, Hitchens stated that while he agreed that in the past the United States "has been the patron of predatory regimes in five continents" and that it "exports violence by means of arms sales and evil clients," for Osama bin Laden these American actions were of secondary importance. In Hitchens's view, bin Laden was engaged in a holy war against a monolithic American society filled with infidels. "The struggle against theocratic fascism is one of the main struggles of our time," he said, adding that "it started long before 11 September 2001."

Leftist intellectual Noam Chomsky disagreed with Hitchens and claimed that the United States bore some responsibility for the September 11 attacks (though he considered them horrendous). In the past, he claimed, the CIA had backed Islamic extremists in Afghanistan and elsewhere. "They mobilized the best killers they could find from the Muslim world," he said, "who happened to be radical Islamists, and they created a powerful mercenary army" to fight the Soviet Union's occupation of Afghanistan in the 1980s. The CIA "armed them, trained them, gave them manuals, showed them how to carry out terrorist acts." Chomsky went so far as to claim that the U.S. attack on Afghanistan "is a major crime, in my opinion far worse than September 11."

Writer Susan Sontag complained that prominent leaders and TV commentators were misleading the public about the nature of the September 11 terrorism. In contrast to Hitchens, she said that "this was not a 'cowardly' attack on 'civilization' or 'liberty' or 'humanity' or 'the free world' but an attack on the world's self-proclaimed superpower, undertaken as a consequence of specific American alliances and actions." Alluding to both the United States and the terrorists, she said that "if the word 'cowardly' is to be used, it might be more aptly applied to those who kill from beyond the range of retaliation, high in the sky, than to those willing to die themselves in order to kill others."

Where many on the left did agree, however, was that parts of Bush's antiterror plan threatened civil liberties, especially his decision, one made without congressional approval, to use military tribunals rather than the judicial system to try foreigners in the United States suspected of terrorism. Even several leading conservatives joined the critical chorus, claiming that some of Bush's effort threatened to make big government bigger and oppressive.

Hitchens said that "military tribunals that take evidence in secret and that have the power to impose the death penalty are, by definition, not up to recognized international standards." Most chilling to defenders of civil liberties were comments by White House Press Secretary Ari Fleischer and Attorney General John Ashcroft. In September 2001, Fleischer admonished Americans "that they need to watch what they say, watch what they do." Ashcroft appeared before the Senate Judiciary Committee that December and said that criticism of the Bush Administration "gives ammunition to America's enemies, and pause to America's friends." Ashcroft added, "To those who scare peace-loving people with phantoms of lost liberty my message is this: your tactics only aid terrorists." Patriotism, he seemed to be saying, required unquestioning support for the administration. The *New Yorker* magazine reacted to Ashcroft's stridency by calling on Bush to oust him.

To those on the left who believed that the September 11 attacks and the subsequent war on terrorism would silence them by leaving them no room in which to pursue their proposals in a militaristic atmosphere, *The Nation* offered hope. Writing in November 2001, Joel Rogers and Katrina Vanden Heuvel said that war not only represses dissent but also "raises the stakes in politics and invites consideration of wider goals, including justice." They added:

War's mobilization of the populace against a shared threat also heightens social solidarity, while underscoring the need for government and other social institutions that transcend or replace the market. And war's horrors daily press the question of how military action can be avoided in the future without abandoning core principles of domestic order.

They concluded that trust in the federal government had increased and that "September 11 has made the idea of a public sector, and the society that it serves, attractive again." It is through the creative use of the public sector that reformers might yet achieve their goals.

Further Reading

Ali, Tariq. *The Clash of Fundamentalisms: Crusades, Jihads, and Modernity.* London and New York: Verso, 2002.

Chomsky, Noam. *9–11.* New York: Seven Stories Press, 2001.

Hitchens, Christopher. "Blaming Bin Laden First." *The Nation*, 22 October 2001.

Vanden Heuvel, Katrina, and Jonathan Schell, eds. *A Just Response:* The Nation *on Terrorism, Democracy, and September 11, 2001.* New York: Nation Books/Thunders Mouth Press, 2001.

Bibliography

For additional information about specific rebels and renegades, please also consult the Further Reading sections at the end of each entry.

Abbott, Philip. *Leftward Ho: V. F. Calverton and American Radicalism*. Westport, Conn.: Greenwood Press, 1993.

Abzug, Robert H. *American Reform and the Religious Imagination*. New York: Oxford University Press, 1994.

Acuna, Rodolfo. *Occupied America: A History of Chicanos*. 3d ed. New York: Harper & Row, 1988.

Albert, Michael. *Stop the Killing Train: Radical Visions for Radical Change*. Boston: South End Press, 1994.

Ali, Tariq, and Susan Watkins. *1968, Marching in the Streets*. New York: Free Press, 1998.

Anderson, Terry H. *The Movement and the Sixties*. New York: Oxford University Press, 1996.

Aptheker, Herbert. *Anti-Racism in U.S. History: The First Two Hundred Years*. New York: Greenwood Press, 1992.

Aronowitz, Stanley. *The Death and Rebirth of American Radicalism*. New York: Routledge, 1996.

Bacon, Margaret Hope. *Mothers of Feminism: The Story of Quaker Women in America*. San Francisco: Harper & Row, 1986.

Barrett, James R. *William Z. Foster and the Tragedy of American Radicalism*. Urbana: University of Illinois Press, 1999.

Baxandall, Rosalyn, Linda Gordon, and Susan Reverby, eds. *America's Working Women: A Documentary History, 1600 to the Present*. New York: Vintage, 1976.

Bennett, David H. *The Party of Fear: From Nativist Movements to the New Right in American History*. Chapel Hill: University of North Carolina Press, 1988.

Berman, Paul. *A Tale of Two Utopias: The Political Journey of the Generation of 1968*. New York: W. W. Norton, 1996.

Berry, Mary Frances, and John W. Blassingame. *Long Memory: The Black Experience in America*. New York: Oxford University Press, 1982.

Breitman, George, Paul Le Blanc, and Alan Wald. *Trotskyism in the United States: Historical Essays and Reconsiderations*. Atlantic Highlands, N.J.: Humanities Press, 1996.

Bristow, Nancy K. *Making Men Moral: Social Engineering During the Great War*. New York: New York University Press, 1996.

Bronner, Stephen Eric. *Moments of Decision: Political History and the Crises of Radicalism*. New York: Routledge, 1992.

Browder, Laura. *Rousing the Nation: Radical Culture in Depression America*. Amherst: University of Massachusetts Press, 1998.

Brownworth, Victoria A. *Too Queer: Essays from a Radical Life*. Ithaca, N.Y.: Firebrand Books, 1996.

Buhle, Mari Jo, Paul Buhle, and Harvey J. Kaye, eds. *The American Radical*. New York: Routledge, 1994.

Buhle, Paul, and Edmund B. Sullivan. *Images of American Radicalism*. Hanover, Mass.: Christopher Publishing House, 1998.

Castro, Ginette. *American Feminism: A Contemporary History*. New York: New York University Press, 1990.

Chafe, William H. *The Paradox of Change: American Women in the Twentieth Century*. New York: Oxford University Press, 1991.

———. *Women and Equality: Changing Patterns in American Culture*. Oxford: Oxford University Press, 1978.

Chepesiuk, Ronald. *Sixties Radicals, Then and Now: Candid Conversations with Those who Shaped the Era*. Jefferson, N.C.: McFarland, 1995.

Cohen, Ian. *Green Fire*. Sydney: Angus & Robertson; New York: HarperCollins Publishers, 1997.

Collier, Peter, and David Horowitz. *Deconstructing the Left: From Vietnam to the Clinton Era*. 3d ed. Los Angeles: Second Thoughts Books and Center for the Study of Popular Culture, 1995.

Coppola, Vincent. *Dragons of God: A Journey Through Far-Right America*. Atlanta: Longstreet Press, 1996.

Cott, Nancy F. *The Grounding of Modern Feminism*. New Haven, Conn.: Yale University Press, 1987.

Crunden, Robert M. *Ministers of Reform: The Progressives' Achievements in American Civilization, 1889–1920.* Urbana: University of Illinois Press, 1984.

Dahl, Goran. *Radical Conservatism and the Future of Politics.* London and Thousand Oaks, Calif.: Sage Publications, 1999.

Darsey, James Francis. *The Prophetic Tradition and Radical Rhetoric in America.* New York: New York University Press, 1997.

Davis, Allen F. *Spearheads for Reform: The Social Settlements and the Progressive Movement, 1890–1914.* New Brunswick, N.J.: Rutgers University Press, 1984.

Davis, Flora. *Moving the Mountain: The Women's Movement since 1960.* New York: Simon & Schuster, 1991.

Dees, Morris, with James Corcoran. *Gathering Storm: America's Militia Threat.* New York: HarperCollins Publishers, 1996.

Degler, Carl N. *At Odds: Women and the Family in America from the Revolution to the Present.* New York: Oxford University Press, 1980.

D'Emilio, John, and Estelle B. Freedman. *Intimate Matters: A History of Sexuality in America.* New York: Harper & Row, 1989.

Derber, Charles. *What's Left?: Radical Politics in the Postcommunist Era.* Amherst: University of Massachusetts Press, 1995.

Diggins, John P. *The Rise and Fall of the American Left.* New York: W. W. Norton, 1992.

Dinnerstein, Leonard, Roger L. Nichols, and David L. Reimers. *Natives and Strangers: Blacks, Indians, and Immigrants in America.* 2ᵈ ed. New York: Oxford University Press, 1990.

Dubofsky, Melvyn. *Industrialism and the American Worker, 1865–1920.* 2ᵈ ed. Arlington Heights, Ill.: Harlan Davidson, 1985.

Eichols, Alice. *Daring to Be Bad: Radical Feminism in America, 1967–1975.* Minneapolis: University of Minnesota Press, 1989.

Epstein, Barbara. *Political Protest and Cultural Revolution: Nonviolent Direct Action in the 1970s and 1980s.* Berkeley: University of California Press, 1991.

Evans, Sara M. *Born for Liberty: A History of Women in America.* New York: Free Press, 1989.

False Patriots: The Threat of Antigovernment Extremists. Montgomery, Ala.: Southern Poverty Law Center, 1996.

Farrell, James J. *The Spirit of the Sixties: Making Postwar Radicalism.* New York: Routledge, 1997.

Flexner, Eleanor. *Century of Struggle: The Women's Rights Movement in the United States.* Rev. ed. Cambridge, Mass.: Belknap, 1975.

Foner, Philip Sheldon. *History of the Labor Movement in the United States.* 10 vols. New York: International Publishers, 1947–92.

———. *Organized Labor and the Black Worker, 1619–1982.* 2ᵈ ed. New York: International Publishers, 1982.

Franklin, John Hope, and Alfred A. Moss, Jr. *From Slavery to Freedom: A History of Negro Americans.* 8ᵗʰ ed. New York: Knopf, 2000.

Frey, Sylvia R. *Water from the Rock: Black Resistance in a Revolutionary Age.* Princeton, N.J.: Princeton University Press, 1991.

Frisch, Michael H., and Daniel J. Walkowitz, eds. *Working-Class America: Essays on Labor, Community, and American Society.* Urbana: University of Illinois Press, 1983.

Fuchs, Lawrence H. *The American Kaleidoscope.* Hanover, N.H.: University Press of New England, 1990.

Gardner, James. *The Age of Extremism: The Enemies of Compromise in American Politics, Culture, and Race Relations.* Secaucus, N.J.: Carol Publishing Group, 1997.

Giddens, Anthony. *Beyond Left and Right: The Future of Radical Politics.* Stanford, Calif.: Stanford University Press, 1994.

Giddings, Paula. *When and Where I Enter: The Impact of Black Women on Race and Sex in America.* New York: Morrow, 1984.

Gitlin, Todd. *The Sixties: Years of Hope, Days of Rage.* Rev. ed. New York: Bantam Books, 1993.

Goodwyn, Lawrence. *Democratic Promise: The Populist Movement in America.* New York: Oxford University Press, 1976.

Gutman, Herbert G. *The Black Family in Slavery and Freedom, 1750–1925.* New York: Vintage, 1977.

———. *Work, Culture, and Society in Industrializing America: Essays in American Working-Class and Social History.* New York: Vintage, 1977.

Handlin, Oscar. *The Uprooted: The Epic Story of the Great Migrations that Made the American People.* 2ᵈ ed. Boston: Little, Brown, 1990.

Hofstadter, Richard. *The Age of Reform: From Bryan to F.D.R.* New York: Knopf, 1955.

Innes, Stephen, ed. *Work and Labor in Early America:* Chapel Hill: University of North Carolina Press, 1988.

Isserman, Maurice. *If I Had a Hammer . . . The Death of the Old Left and the Birth of the New Left*. New York: Basic Books, 1987.

Katz, Jonathan Ned. *Gay American History: Lesbians and Gay Men in the U.S.A.: A Documentary History*. Rev. ed. New York: Meridian, 1992.

Kerber, Linda K. *Women of the Republic: Intellect and Ideology in Revolutionary America*. Chapel Hill: University of North Carolina Press, 1980.

Klatch, Rebecca E. *Women of the New Right*. Philadelphia: Temple University Press, 1987.

Laslett, John H. M., and Seymour Martin Lipset, eds. *Failure of a Dream? Essays in the History of American Socialism*. Rev. ed. Berkeley: University of California Press, 1984.

Lerner, Gerda, ed. *Black Women in White America: A Documentary History*. New York: Vintage, 1992.

———. *The Female Experience: An American Documentary*. New York: Oxford University Press, 1992.

Lynd, Staughton. *Intellectual Origins of American Radicalism*. Cambridge, Mass.: Harvard University Press, 1982.

Macleod, Duncan J. *Slavery, Race, and the American Revolution*. London: Cambridge University Press, 1974.

Mandle, Jay R. *Not Slave, Not Free: The African-American Economic Experience since the Civil War*. Durham, N.C.: Duke University Press, 1992.

Marchand, C. Roland. *The American Peace Movement and Social Reform, 1898–1918*. Princeton, N.J.: Princeton University Press, 1973.

Montgomery, David. *Workers' Control in America: Studies in the History of Work, Technology, and Labor Struggles*. Cambridge: Cambridge University Press, 1980.

Munoz, Carlos, Jr. *Youth, Identity, and Power: The Chicano Movement*. London: Verso, 1989.

Norton, Mary Beth. *Liberty's Daughter: The Revolutionary Experience of American Women, 1750–1800*. Glenview, Ill.: Scott, Foresman, 1988.

Norton, Mary Beth. *Major Problems in American Women's History: Documents and Essays*. Lexington, Mass.: Heath, 1989.

Pessen, Edward, ed. *Three Centuries of Social Mobility in America*. Lexington, Mass.: Heath, 1974.

Pole, J. R. *The Pursuit of Equality in American History*. Berkeley: University of California Press, 1978.

Quarles, Benjamin. *The Negro in the Making of America*. 2^d rev. ed. New York: Collier, 1987.

Reichert, William O. *Partisans of Freedom: A Study in American Anarchism*. Bowling Green, Ohio: Bowling Green University Popular Press, 1976.

Rosenberg, Rosalind. *Beyond Separate Sphere: Intellectual Roots of Modern Feminism*. New Haven, Conn.: Yale University Press, 1982.

Sargent, Lyman Tower, ed. *Extremism in America: A Reader*. New York: New York University Press, 1995.

Shapiro, Herbert. *White Violence and Black Response: From Reconstruction to Montgomery*. New York: Oxford University Press, 1987.

Steinberg, Stephen. *The Ethnic Myth: Race, Ethnicity, and Class in America*. Rev ed. Boston: Beacon, 1989.

Tyler, Alice Felt. *Freedom's Ferment: Phases of American Social History to 1860*. Freeport, N.Y.: Books for Libraries Press, 1970.

Walters, Ronald G. *American Reformers, 1815–1860*. New York: Hill and Wang, 1978.

Young, Alfred F., ed. *Beyond the American Revolution: Explorations in the History of American Radicalism*. DeKalb: Northern Illinois University Press, 1993.

Zieger, Robert. *American Workers, American Unions, 1920–1985*. Baltimore: Johns Hopkins University Press, 1986.

APPENDIX

Primary Documents

1. For having upon specious pretenses of Publick works raised unjust Taxes upon the Commonalty for the advancement of private Favourits and other sinnister ends but noe visible effects in any measure adequate. For not having dureing the long time of his Government in any measure advanced this hopeful Colony either by Fortification, Townes or Trade.

2. For having abused and rendered Contemptible the Majesty of Justice, of advancing to places of judicature scandalous and Ignorant favourits.

3. For having wronged his Majesty's Prerogative and Interest by assuming the monopoley of the Beaver Trade. By having in that unjust gaine Bartered and sould his Majesty's Country and the lives of his Loyal Subjects to the Barbarous Heathen.

4. For having protected favoured and Imboldened the Indians against his Ma^{ts} most Loyall subjects never contriveing requireing or appointing any due or proper meanes of satisfaction for their many Invassions Murthers and Robberies Committed upon us.

5. For having when the Army of the English was Just upon the Track of the Indians, which now in all places Burne Spoyle and Murder, and when wee might with ease have destroyed them who then were in open Hostility for having expresly Countermanded and sent back our Army by passing his word for the peaceable demeanour of the said Indians, who immediately prosecuted their evill Intentiions Committing horrid Murders and Robberies in all places being protected by the said Engagement and word pass'd of him the said Sir William Berkley having ruined and made desolate a great part of his Ma^{ts} Country, have now drawne themselves into such obscure and remote places and are by their successes soe imboldened and confirmed and by their Confederacy soe strengthened that the cryes of Bloud are in all places and the Terrour and censteration of the People soe great, that they are now become not only a difficult, but a very formidable Enemy who might with Ease have been destroyed.

6. And lately when upon the Loud Outcries of Blood the Assembly had with all care raised and framed an army for the prevention of future Mischiefs and safeguard of his Ma^{ts} Colony.

7. For having with only the privacy of some few favourits without acquainting the People, only by the Alteration of a Figure forged a Commission by wee know not what hand, not only without but against the Consent of the People, for raising and effecting of Civill Wars and distractions, which being happily and wthout Bloodshed prevented. For having the second tyme attempted the same thereby, calling downe our Forces from the defence of the Frontiers, and most weake Exposed Places.

8. For the prevention of civill Mischief and Ruine amongst ourselves, whilst the barbarous Enemy in all places did Invade murder and spoyle us by his Ma^{ts} most faithfull subjects.

Of these aforesaid Articles wee accuse Sir William Berkley, as guilty of each and every one of the same, and as one, who hath Traiterously attempted, violated and Injured his Maties Interst here, by the losse of a great Part of his Colony, and many of his Faithfull and Loyall subjects by him betrayed, and in a barbarous and shamefull manner exposed to the Incursions and murthers of the Heathen.

And we further delare these Ensueing Persons in this List, to have been his wicked, and pernitious Councellors, Aiders and Assisters against the Commonalty in these our Cruell Commotions

Sr Henry Chicherly, Knt.,	Jos. Bridger,
Col. Charles Wormley,	Wm Clabourne,
Phil. Dalowell,	Thos. Hawkins, Juni'r,
Robert Beverly,	William Sherwood,
Robert Lee,	Jos. Page, Clerk,
Thos. Ballard,	Jo. Cliffe,
William Cole,	Hubberd Farrell,

Richard Whitacre,
Nicholas Spencer,

John West,
Thos. Reade,
Mathew Kemp.

And wee doe further demand, That the said Sir William Berkley, with all the Persons in this List, be forthwith delivered upp, or surrender themselves, within foure days, after the notice hereof, or otherwise wee declare, as followeth, That in whatsoever house, place, or shipp, any of the said Persons shall reside, be hide, or protected, Wee doe declare, that the Owners, masters, or Inhabitants of the said places, to be Confederates, and Traitors to the People, and the Estates of them, as also of all the aforesaid Persons to be Confiscated, This wee the Commons of Virginia doe declare desiring a prime Union among ourselves against the Common Enemye. And Let not the Faults of the guilty, be the Reproach of the Innocent, or the Faults or Crimes of ye Oppressors divide and separate us, who have suffered by theire oppressiions.

These are therefore in his Majesty's name, to Command you forthwith to seize, the Persons above mentioned, as Traytors to ye King and Countrey, and them to bring to Middle Plantation, and there to secure them, till further Order, and in Case of opposition, if you want any other Assistance, you are forthwith to demand it in the Name of the People of all the Counties of Virginia.

NATH BACON, General by the Consent of the People.

"Common Sense" by Thomas Paine (excerpt)

1776

THOUGHTS ON THE PRESENT STATE OF AMERICAN AFFAIRS

In the following pages I offer nothing more than simple facts, plain arguments, and common sense; and have no other preliminaries to settle with the reader, than that he will divest himself of prejudice and prepossession, and suffer his reason and his feelings to determine for themselves; that he will put on, or rather that he will not put off, the true character of a man, and generously enlarge his views beyond the present day.

Volumes have been written on the subject of the struggle between England and America. Men of all ranks have embarked in the controversy, from different motives, and with various designs; but all have been ineffectual, and the period of debate is closed. Arms, as the last resource, decide the contest, the appeal was the choice of the king, and the continent hath accepted the challenge. . . .

The sun never shined on a cause of greater worth. 'Tis not the affair of a city, a country, a province, or a kingdom, but of a continent—of at least one eighth part of the habitable globe. 'Tis not the concern of a day, a year, or an age; posterity are virtually involved in the contest, and will be more or less affected, even to the end of time, by the proceedings now. Now is the seed time of continental union, faith and honor. The least fracture now will be like a name engraved with the point of a pin on the tender rind of a young oak; The wound will enlarge with the tree, and posterity read it in full grown characters.

By referring the matter from argument to arms, a new era for politics is struck; a new method of thinking hath arisen. All plans, proposals, &c. prior to the nineteenth of April, i.e. to the commencement of hostilities, are like the almanacks of the last year; which, though proper then, are superceded and useless now. Whatever was advanced by the advocates on either side of the question then, terminated in one and the same point, viz. a union with Great-Britain; the only difference between the parties was the method of effecting it; the one proposing force, the other friendship; but it hath so far happened that the first hath failed, and the second hath withdrawn her influence.

As much hath been said of the advantages of reconciliation, which, like an agreeable dream, hath passed away and left us as we were, it is but right, that we should examine the contrary side of the argument, and inquire into some of the many material injuries which these colonies sustain, and always will sustain, by being connected with, and dependant on Great-Britain. To examine that connexion and dependance, on the principles of nature and common sense, to see what we have to trust to, if separated, and what we are to expect, if dependant.

I have heard it asserted by some, that as America hath flourished under her former connexion with Great-Britain, that the same connexion is necessary towards her future happiness, and will always have the same effect. Nothing can be more fallacious than this kind of argument. We may as well assert that because a child has thrived upon milk, that it is never to have meat, or that the first twenty years of our lives is to become a precedent for the next twenty. But even this is admitting more than is true, for I answer roundly, that America would have flourished as much, and probably much more, had no European power had any thing to do with her. The commerce, by which she hath enriched herself are the necessaries of life, and will always have a market while eating is the custom of Europe.

But she has protected us, say some. That she hath engrossed us is true, and defended the continent at our expence as well as her own is admitted, and she would have defended Turkey from the same motive, viz. the sake of trade and dominion.

Alas, we have been long led away by ancient prejudices, and made large sacrifices to superstition. We have boasted the protection of Great Britain, without considering, that her motive was interest not attachment; that she did not protect us from our enemies on our account, but from her enemies on her own account, from those who had no quarrel with us on any other account, and who will always be our enemies on the same account. Let Britain wave her pretensions to the continent, or the continent throw off the dependance, and we should be at peace with France and Spain were they at war with Britain. The miseries of Hanover last war ought to warn us against connexions.

It hath lately been asserted in parliament, that the colonies have no relation to each other but through the parent country, i.e. that Pennsylvania and the Jerseys, and so on for the rest, are sister colonies by the way of England; this is certainly a very round-about way of proving relationship, but it is the nearest and only true way of proving enemyship, if I may so call it. France and Spain never were, nor perhaps ever will be our enemies as Americans, but as our being the subjects of Great-Britain.

But Britain is the parent country, say some. Then the more shame upon her conduct. Even brutes do not devour their young, nor savages make war upon their families; wherefore the assertion, if true, turns to her reproach; but it happens not to be true, or only partly so, and the phrase parent or mother country hath been jesuitically adopted by the king and his parasites, with a low papistical design of gaining an unfair bias on the credulous weakness of our minds. Europe, and not England, is the parent country of America. This new world hath been the asylum for the persecuted lovers of civil and religious liberty from every part of Europe. Hither have they fled, not from the tender embraces of the mother, but from the cruelty of the monster; and it is so far true of England, that the same tyranny which drove the first emigrants from home, pursues their descendants still. . . .

As to government matters, it is not in the power of Britain to do this continent justice: The business of it will soon be too weighty, and intricate, to be managed with any tolerable degree of convenience, by a power, so distant from us, and so very ignorant of us; for if they cannot conquer us, they cannot govern us. To be always running three or four thousand miles with a tale or a petition, waiting four or five months for an answer, which when obtained requires five or six more to explain it in, will in a few years be looked upon as folly and childishness. There was a time when it was proper, and there is a proper time for it to cease.

Small islands not capable of protecting themselves are the proper objects for kingdoms to take under their care; but there is something very absurd, in supposing a continent to be perpetually governed by an island. In no instance hath nature made the satellite larger than its primary planet, and as England and America, with respect to each other, reverses the common order of nature, it is evident they belong to different systems: England to Europe, America to itself.

I am not induced by motives of pride, party, or resentment to espouse the doctrine of separation and independance; I am clearly, positively, and conscientiously persuaded that it is the true interest of this continent to be so; that every thing short of that is mere patchwork, that it can afford no lasting felicity,—that it is leaving the sword to our children, and shrinking back at a time, when, a little more, a little farther, would have rendered this continent the glory of the earth.

As Britain hath not manifested the least inclination towards a compromise, we may be assured that no terms can be obtained worthy the acceptance of the continent, or any ways equal to the expense of blood and treasure we have been already put to.

The object, contended for, ought always to bear some just proportion to the expense. The removal of North, or the whole detestable junto, is a matter unworthy the millions we have expended. A temporary stoppage of trade, was an inconvenience, which would have sufficiently ballanced the repeal of all the acts complained of, had such repeals been obtained; but if the whole continent must take up arms, if every man must be a soldier, it is scarcely worth our while to fight against a contemptible ministry only. Dearly, dearly, do we pay for the repeal of the acts, if that is all we fight for; for in a just estimation, it is as great a folly to pay a Bunker-hill price for law, as for land. As I have always considered the independancy of this continent, as an event, which sooner or later must arrive, so from the late rapid progress of the continent to maturity, the event could not be far off. Wherefore, on the breaking out of hostilities, it was not worth the while to have disputed a matter, which time would have finally redressed, unless we meant to be in earnest; otherwise, it is like wasting an estate on a suit at law, to regulate the trespasses of a tenant, whose lease is just expiring. No man was a warmer wisher for reconciliation than myself, before the fatal nineteenth of April 1775, but the moment the event of that day was made known, I rejected the hardened, sullen tempered Pharaoh of England for ever; and disdain the wretch, that with the pretended title of FATHER OF HIS PEOPLE, can unfeelingly hear of their slaughter, and composedly sleep with their blood upon his soul.

But admitting that matters were now made up, what would be the event? I answer, the ruin of the continent. And that for several reasons.

First. The powers of governing still remaining in the hands of the king, he will have a negative over the whole legislation of this continent. And as he hath shewn himself such an inveterate enemy to liberty, and discovered such a thirst for arbitrary power; is he, or is he not, a proper man to say to these colonies, "You shall make no laws but what I please." And is there any inhabitant in America so ignorant, as not to know, that according to what is called the present constitution, that this continent can make no laws but what the king gives it leave to; and is there any man so unwise, as not to see, that (considering what has happened) he will suffer no law to be made here, but such as suit his purpose. We may be as effectually enslaved by the want of laws in America, as by submitting to laws made for us in England. After matters are made up (as it is called) can there be any doubt, but the whole power of the crown will be exerted, to keep this continent as low and humble as possible? Instead of going forward we shall go backward, or be perpetually quarrelling or ridiculously petitioning. We are already greater than the king wishes us to be, and will he not hereafter endeavour to make us less? To bring the matter to one point. Is the power who is jealous of our prosperity, a proper power to govern us? Whoever says No to this question is an independant, for independancy means no more, than, whether we shall make our own laws, or, whether the king, the greatest enemy this continent hath, or can have, shall tell us, "there shall be no laws but such as I like."

But the king you will say has a negative in England; the people there can make no laws without his consent. In point of right and good order, there is something very ridiculous, that a youth of twenty-one (which hath often happened) shall say to several millions of people, older and wiser than himself, I forbid this or that act of yours to be law. But in this place I decline this sort of reply, though I will never cease to expose the absurdity of it, and only answer, that England being the King's residence, and America not so, make quite another case. The king's negative here is ten times more dangerous and fatal than it can be in England, for there he will scarcely refuse his consent to a bill for putting England into as strong a state of defence as possible, and in America he would never suffer such a bill to be passed.

America is only a secondary object in the system of British politics, England consults the good of this country, no farther than it answers her own purpose. Wherefore, her own interest leads her to suppress the growth of ours in every case which doth not promote her advantage, or in the least interferes with it. A pretty state we should soon be in under such a second-hand government, considering what has happened! Men do not change from enemies to friends by the alteration of a name: And in order to shew that reconciliation now is a dangerous doctrine, I affirm, that it would be policy in the king at this time, to repeal the acts for the sake of reinstating himself in the government of the provinces; in order that HE MAY ACCOMPLISH BY CRAFT AND SUBTILITY, IN THE LONG RUN, WHAT HE CANNOT DO BY FORCE AND VIOLENCE IN THE SHORT ONE. Reconciliation and ruin are nearly related.

Secondly. That as even the best terms, which we can expect to obtain, can amount to no more than a temporary expedient, or a kind of government by guardianship, which can last no longer than till the colonies come of age, so the general face and state of things, in the interim, will be unsettled and unpromising. Emigrants of property will not choose to come to a country whose form of government hangs but by a thread, and who is every day tottering on the brink of commotion and disturbance; and numbers of the present inhabitants would lay hold of the interval, to dispose of their effects, and quit the continent.

But the most powerful of all arguments, is, that nothing but independance, i.e. a continental form of government, can keep the peace of the continent and preserve it inviolate from civil wars. I dread the event of a reconciliation with Britain now, as it is more than probable, that it will followed by a revolt somewhere or other, the consequences of which may be far more fatal than all the malice of Britain. . . .

O ye that love mankind! Ye that dare oppose, not only the tyranny, but the tyrant, stand forth! Every spot of the old world is overrun with oppression. Freedom hath been hunted round the globe. Asia, and Africa, have long expelled her.—Europe regards her like a stranger, and England hath given her warning to depart. O! receive the fugitive, and prepare in time an asylum for mankind.

1813–1814 "A New View of Society, Or, Essays on the Principle of the Formation of the Human Character, and the Application of the Principle to Practice" by Robert Owen (excerpt)

The principle, then, on which the doctrines taught in the New Institution are proposed to be founded, is, that they shall be in unison with universally revealed facts, which cannot but be true.

The following are some of the facts, which, with a view to this part of the undertaking, may be deemed fundamental:

That man is born with a desire to obtain happiness, which desire is the primary cause of all his actions, continues through life, and, in popular language, is called self-interest.

That he is also born with the germs of animal propensities, or the desire to sustain, enjoy, and propagate life; and which desires, as they grow and develop themselves, are termed his natural inclinations.

That he is born likewise with faculties which, in their growth, receive, convey, compare, and become conscious of receiving and comparing ideas.

That the ideas so received, conveyed, compared, and understood, constitute human knowledge, or mind, which acquires strength and maturity with the growth of the individual.

That the desire of happiness in man, the germs of his natural inclinations, and the faculties by which he acquires knowledge, are formed unknown to himself in the womb; and whether perfect or imperfect, they are alone the immediate work of the Creator, and over which the infant and future man have no control.

That these inclinations and faculties are not formed exactly alike in any two individuals; hence the diversity of talents, and the varied impressions called liking and disliking which the same external objects make on different persons, and the lesser varieties which exist among men whose characters have been formed apparently under similar circumstances.

That the knowledge which man receives is derived from the objects around him, and chiefly from the example and instruction of his immediate predecessors.

That this knowledge may be limited or extended, erroneous or true; limited, when the individual receives few, and extended when he receives many ideas; erroneous, when those ideas are inconsistent with the facts which exist around him, and true when they are uniformly consistent with them.

That the misery which he experiences, and the happiness which he enjoys, depend on the kind and degree of knowledge which he receives, and on that which is possessed by those around him.

That when the knowledge which he receives is true and unmixed with error, although it be limited, if the community in which he lives possesses the same kind and degree of knowledge, he will enjoy happiness in proportion to the extent of that knowledge. On the contrary, when the opinions which he receives are erroneous, and the opinions possessed by the community in which he resides are equally erroneous, his misery will be in proportion to the extent of those erroneous opinions.

That when the knowledge which man receives shall be extended to its utmost limit, and true without any mixture of error, then he may and will enjoy all the happiness of which his nature will be capable.

That it consequently becomes of the first and highest importance that man should be taught to distinguish truth from error.

That man has no other means of discovering what is false, except by his faculty of reason, or the power of acquiring and comparing the ideas which he receives.

That when this faculty is properly cultivated or trained from infancy, and the child is rationally instructed to retain no impressions or ideas which by his powers of comparing them appear to be inconsistent, then the individual will acquire real knowledge, or those ideas only which will leave an impression of their consistency or truth on all minds which have not been rendered irrational by an opposite procedure.

That the reasoning faculty may be injured and destroyed during its growth, by reiterated impressions being made upon it of notions not derived from realities, and which it therefore cannot compare with the ideas previously received from the objects around it. And when the mind receives these notions which it cannot comprehend, along with those ideas which it is conscious are true and which yet are inconsistent with such notions, then the reasoning faculties become injured, the individual is taught or forced to believe, and not to think or reason, and partial insanity or defective powers of judging ensue.

That all men are thus erroneously trained at present, and hence the inconsistencies and misery of the world.

That the fundamental errors now impressed from infancy on the minds of all men, and from whence all their other errors proceed, are, that they form their own individual characters, and possess merit or demerit for the peculiar notions impressed on the mind during its early growth, before they have acquired strength and experience to judge of or resist the impression of those notions or opinions, which, on investigation, appear contradictions to facts existing around them, and which are therefore false.

That these false notions have ever produced evil and misery in the world; and that they still disseminate them in every direction.

That the sole cause of their existence hitherto has been man's ignorance of human nature: while their consequences have been all the evil and misery, except those of accidents, disease, and death, with which man has been and is afflicted: and that the evil and misery which arise from accidents, disease, and death, are also greatly increased and extended by man's ignorance of himself.

That, in proportion as man's desire of self-happiness, or his self-love, is directed by true knowledge, those actions will abound which are virtuous and beneficial to man; that in proportion as it is influenced by false notions, or the absence of true knowledge, those actions will prevail which generate crimes, from whence arises an endless variety of misery. and, consequently, that every rational means should be now adopted to detect error, and to increase true knowledge among men.

That when these truths are made evident, every individual will necessarily endeavour to promote the happiness of every other individual within his sphere of action; because he must clearly, and without any doubt, comprehend such conduct to be the essence of self-interest, or the true cause of self-happiness.

Here, then, is a firm foundation on which to erect vital religion, pure and undefiled, and the only one which, without any counteracting evil, can give peace and happiness to man.

It is to bring into practical operation, in forming the character of men, these most important of all truths, that the religious part of the Institution at New Lanark will be chiefly directed, and such are the fundamental principles upon which the Instructor will proceed. They are thus publicly avowed before all men, that they may undergo discussion and the most severe scrutiny and investigation.

Let those, therefore, who are esteemed the most learned and wise, throughout the various states and empires in the world, examine them to their foundation, compare them with every fact which exists, and if the shadow of inconsistency and falsehood be discovered, let it be publicly exposed, that error may not more abound.

But should they withstand this extended ordeal, and prove themselves uniformly consistent with every known fact, and therefore true, then let it be declared, that man may be permitted by man to become rational, and that the misery of the world may be speedily removed.

Having alluded to the chief uses of the playground and exercise rooms, with the School, Lecture Room, and Church, it remains, to complete the account of the New Institution, that the object of the drill exercises mentioned when stating the purposes of the playground, should be explained; and to this we now proceed.

Were all men trained to be rational, the art of war would be rendered useless. While, however, any part of mankind shall be taught that they form their own characters, and shall continue to be trained from infancy to think and act irrationally that is, to acquire feelings of enmity, and to deem it a duty to engage in war against those who have been instructed to differ from them in sentiments and habits - even the most rational must, for their personal security, learn the means of defence; and every community of such characters, while surrounded by men who have been thus improperly taught, should acquire a knowledge of this destructive art, that they may be enabled to over-rule the actions of irrational beings, and maintain peace.

To accomplish these objects to the utmost practical limit, and with the least inconvenience, every male should be instructed how best to defend, when attacked, the community to which he belongs. And these advantages are, only to be obtained by providing proper means for the instruction of all boys in the use of arms and the arts of war.

As an example how easily and effectually this might be accomplished over the British Isles, it is intended that the boys trained and educated at the Institution at New Lanark shall be thus instructed; that the person appointed to attend the children in the playground shall be qualified to drill and teach the boys the manual exercise, and that he shall be frequently so employed; that afterwards, firearms, of proportionate weight and size to the age and strength of the boys, shall be provided for them, when also they might be taught to practise and understand the more complicated military movements.

This exercise, properly administered, will greatly contribute to the health and spirits of the boys, give them an erect and proper form, and habits of attention, celerity, and order. They will, however, be taught to consider this exercise, an art, rendered absolutely necessary by the partial insanity of some of their fellow creatures who by the errors of their predecessors, transmitted through preceding generations, have been taught to acquire feelings of enmity, increasing to madness, against those who could not avoid differing from them in sentiments and habits; that this art should never be brought into practice except to restrain the violence of such madmen; and, in these cases, that it should be administered with the least possible severity, and solely to prevent the evil consequences of those rash acts of the insane, and, if possible, to cure them of their disease.

Thus, in a few years, by foresight and arrangement, may almost the whole expense and inconvenience attending the local military be superseded, and a permanent force created, which in numbers, discipline, and principles, would be superior, beyond all comparison, for the purposes of defence; always ready in case of need, yet without the loss which is now sustained by the community of efficient and valuable labour. The expenditure which would be saved by this simple expedient, would be far more than competent to educate the whole of the poor and labouring classes of these kingdoms.

1829 "The Working Men's Declaration of Independence" by George Evans

"When, in the course of human events, it becomes necessary" for one class of a community to assert their natural and unalienable rights in opposition to other classes of their fellow men, "and to assume among" them a political "station of equality to w hich the laws of nature and of nature's God," as well as the principles of their political compact "entitle them; a decent respect to the opinions of mankind," and the more paramount duty they owe to their own fellow citizens, "requires that they should declare the causes which impel them" to adopt so painful, yet so necessary, a measure.

"We hold these truths to be self evident that all men are created *equal*; that they are endowed by their creator with certain unalienable rights; that among these are life, liberty, and the pursuit of happiness; that to secure these rights" against the undue influence of other classes of society, prudence, as well as the claims of self defence, dictates the necessity of the organization of a party, who shall, by their representatives, prevent dangerous combinations to subvert these indefeasible and fundamental privileges. "All experience hath shown, that mankind" in general, and we as a class in particular, "are more disposed to suffer, while evils are sufferable, than to right themselves," by an opposition which the pride and self interest of unprincipled political aspirants, with more unprincipled zeal or religious bigotry, will willfully misrepresent. "But when a long train of abuses and usurpations" take place, all invariably tending to the oppression and degradation of one class of society, and to the unnatural and iniquitous exaltation of another by political leaders, "it is their right it is their due" to use every constitutional means to reform the abuses of such a government and to provide new guards for their future security. The history of the political parties in this state, is a history of political iniquities, all tending to the enacting and enforcing oppressive and unequal laws. To prove this, let facts be submitted to the candid and impartial of our fellow citizens of all parties.

1. The laws for levying taxes are all based on erroneous principles, in consequence of their operating most oppressively on one of society, and being scarcely felt by the other.
2. The laws regarding the duties of jurors, witnesses, and militia trainings, are still more unequal and oppressive.
3. The laws for private incorporations are all partial in their operations; favoring one class of society to the expense of the other, who have no equal participation.
4. The laws incorporating religious societies have a pernicious tendency, by promoting the erection of magnificent places of public worship, by the rich, excluding others, and which others cannot imitate; consequently engendering spiritual pride in the clergy and people, and thereby creating odious distinctions in society, destructive to its social peace and happiness.
5. The laws establishing and patronizing seminaries of learning are unequal, favoring the rich, and perpetuating imparity, which natural causes have produced, and which judicious laws ought, and can, remedy.
6. The laws and municipal ordinances and regulations, generally, besides those specially enumerated, have heretofore been ordained on such principles, as have deprived nine tenths of the members of the body politic, who are *not* wealthy, of the *equal means* to enjoy "*life, liberty, and the pursuit of happiness*" which the rich enjoy exclusively; but the federative compact intended to secure to all, indiscriminately. The lien law in favor of landlords against tenants, and all other honest creditors, is one illustration among innumerable others which can be adduced to prove the truth of these allegations.

We have trusted to the influence of the justice and good sense of our political leaders, to prevent the continuance of these abuses, which destroy the natural bands of equality so essential to the attainment of moral happiness, "but they have been deaf to the voice of justice and of consanguinity."

Therefore, we, the working class of society, of the city of New York, "appealing to the supreme judge of the world," and to the reason, and consciences of the impartial of all parties, "for the rectitude of our intentions, do, in the spirit, and by the authority of that political liberty which has been promised to us equally with our fellow men, solemnly publish and declare, and invite all under like pecuniary circumstances, together with every liberal mind, to join us in the declaration, "that we are, & of right ought to be," entitled to equal means to obtain equal moral happiness, and social enjoyment, and that all lawful and constitutional measures ought to be adopted to the attainment of those objects. "And for the support of this declaration, we mutually pledge to each other" our faithful aid to the end of our lives.

"Appeal to Christian Women of the South" by Angelina Grimké (excerpt) 1836

But some slaveholders have said, "we were never in bondage to any man," and therefore the yoke of bondage would be insufferable to us, but slaves are accustomed to it, their backs are fitted to the burden. Well, I am willing to admit that you who have lived in freedom would find slavery even more oppressive than the poor slave does, but then you may try this question in another form—Am I willing to reduce *my little child* to slavery? You know that *if it is brought up a slave* it will never know any contrast, between freedom and bondage, its back will become fitted to the burden just as the negro child's does—*not by nature*—but by daily, violent pressure, in the same way that the head of an Indian child becomes flattened by the boards in which it is bound. It has been justly remarked that "*God never made a slave*," he made man upright; his back was not made to carry burdens, nor his neck to wear a yoke. And the *man* must be crushed within him, before *his* back can be *fitted* to the burden of perpetual slavery; and that his back is *not* fitted to it, is manifest by the insurrections that so often disturb the peace and security of slaveholding countries. Who ever heard of a rebellion of the beasts of the field; and why not? simply because *they* were all placed *under the feet of man*, it was originally designed that they should serve him, therefore their necks have been formed for the yoke, and their backs for the burden; *not so with man*, intellectual, immortal man! I appeal to you, my friends, as mothers; Are you willing to enslave *your* children? You start back with horror and indignation at such a question. But why, if slavery is *no wrong* to those upon whom it is imposed? why, if as has often been said, slaves are happier than their masters, free from the cares and perplexities of providing for themselves and their families? why not place *your children* in the way of being supported without your having the trouble to provide for them, or they for themselves? Do you not perceive that as soon as this golden rule of action is applied to *yourselves* that you involuntarily shrink from the test; as soon as your actions are weighed in *this* balance of the sanctuary that *you are found wanting*? Try yourselves by another of the Divine precepts, "Thou shalt love thy neighbor as thyself." Can we love a man *as* we love *ourselves* if we do, and continue to do unto him, what we would not wish any one to do to us? Look too, at Christ's example, what does he say of himself, "I came *not* to be ministered unto, but to minister." Can you for a moment imagine the meek, the lowly, and compassionate Savior, *a slaveholder*? Do you not shudder at this thought as much as at that of his being a *warrior*? But why, if slavery is not sinful?

1873   Speech by Susan B. Anthony (excerpt)

Friends and fellow citizens: I stand before you tonight under indictment for the alleged crime of having voted at the last presidential election, without having a lawful right to vote. It shall be my work this evening to prove to you that in thus voting, I not only committed no crime, but, instead, simply exercised my citizen's rights, guaranteed to me and all United States citizens by the National Constitution, beyond the power of any state to deny.

The preamble of the Federal Constitution says:

> We, the people of the United States, in order to form a more perfect union, establish justice, insure domestic tranquility, provide for the common defense, promote the general welfare, and secure the blessings of liberty to ourselves and our posterity, do ordain and establish this Constitution for the United States of America.

It was we, the people; not we, the white male citizens; nor yet we, the male citizens; but we, the whole people, who formed the Union. And we formed it, not to give the blessings of liberty, but to secure them; not to the half of ourselves and the half of our posterity, but to the whole people—women as well as men. And it is a downright mockery to talk to women of their enjoyment of the blessings of liberty while they are denied the use of the only means of securing them provided by this democratic-republican government—the ballot.

For any state to make sex a qualification that must ever result in the disfranchisement of one entire half of the people is to pass a bill of attainder, or an ex post facto law, and is therefore a violation of the supreme law of the land. By it the blessings of liberty are forever withheld from women and their female posterity.

To them this government has no just powers derived from the consent of the governed. To them this government is not a democracy. It is not a republic. It is an odious aristocracy; a hateful oligarchy of sex; the most hateful aristocracy ever established on the face of the globe; an oligarchy of wealth, where the rich govern the poor. An oligarchy of learning, where the educated govern the ignorant, or even an oligarchy of race, where the Saxon rules the African, might be endured; but this oligarchy of sex, which makes father, brothers, husband, sons, the oligarchs over the mother and sisters, the wife and daughters, of every household—which ordains all men sovereigns, all women subjects, carries dissension, discord, and rebellion into every home of the nation.

Webster, Worcester, and Bouvier all define a citizen to be a person in the United States, entitled to vote and hold office.

The only question left to be settled now is: Are women persons? And I hardly believe any of our opponents will have the hardihood to say they are not. Being persons, then, women are citizens; and no state has a right to make any law, or to enforce any old law, that shall abridge their privileges or immunities. Hence, every discrimination against women in the constitutions and laws of the several states is today null and void, precisely as is every one against Negroes.

"Conservatism" by Daniel DeLeon

The scientific principle of the class struggle is a basic principle from which socialist tactics proceed.

The principle is denied, by the superficial and the vicious, as unsound and immoral. And, yet, hear them talk and you will find that, unconsciously, they act obedient to it. Like bees, who, without mathematical knowledge, build their cells mathematically, the adversaries of the theory of the class struggle frame their conduct obedient thereto.

"Conservatism" is the motto of the upholders of the present system. "Conservatism," as against "revolution," is what they recommend.

In the one word, the principle of the class struggle is ratified by its very denouncers.

The exploiting and idle class struggles upon the lines of their class interests. They aim to conserve the power they now enjoy to live in luxury without work, to ride the proletariat, to fleece the workers. That their aim should be such is not to be wondered at; it is natural. But for the very reason that "conservatism" is natural with the capitalist class, "revolution" is the natural principle to control the class struggle of the oppressed.

The working class of America has nothing, no economic or social powers, worth conserving. "Conservatism" can never mean the striving to conserve chains. When the lot of a class is thralldom, "conservatism" ceases to be a natural principle with it; revolution must become its moving spring. And that is the situation of more than one half of our population today.

Time was when the workers still held some economic power. They could combine in unions, and the force of their numbers in the shops and mills could ensure for them a certain amount of freedom. That was when machinery had not yet reached its present perfection, when capitalist concerns had not reached their present stage of concentration, when, consequently, there were not more applicants for jobs than there were jobs to be had.

Now all that has changed.

Owing to the stupendous army of the unemployed, coupled with the elimination of skill by the machine, the subdivision of labor, and the concentration of capital, the economic power once wielded by the workers is a thing of the past, and whatever little power they may still seem to possess in this respect, their bosses can at any moment shatter to pieces, as they have done again and again, with the aid of the public powers.

Stripped of all economic power, and thereby thrust into rags, squalid homes, dependence, with overworked wives and underfed children, to talk "conservatism" to the worker is irony, and to hear the labor misleaders recommend the thing to the toilers is insanity, where it is not rascality.

"Conservatism," by all means, if there is anything worth conserving, and everything not worth losing.

"Revolution," if there is nothing worth conserving, and everything worth gaining.

These are the class lines upon which the political battle is being fought, and is bound to be fought, to the end.

With the reactionary and therefore conservative ballot of the capitalist parties, backed by their guns, the oppressing class seeks to conserve its usurped position and continue to enjoy its stolen goods.

With the revolutionary and therefore socialist ballot, ready to be backed by all other means if the capitalist class rebels against the fiat of the suffrage, the wage slave class, the proletariat, seeks to rid itself of its chains, and to regain possession of its own!

Preamble to the Constitution of the Industrial Workers of the World

The working class and the employing class have nothing in common. There can be no peace as long as hunger and want are found among the millions of the working people and the few, who make up the employing class, have all the good things in life.

Between these two classes a struggle must go until the workers of the world organize as a class, take possession of the earth and the machinery of production, and abolish the wage system.

We find that the centering of the management of industries into fewer and fewer hands makes the trade unions unable to cope with the ever growing power of the employing class. The trade unions foster a state of affairs which allows one set of workers to be pitted against another set of workers in the same industry, thereby helping to defeat one another in wage wars. Moreover, the trade unions aid the employing class in misleading the workers into the belief that the working class have interests in common with their employers.

These conditions can be changed and the interest of the working class upheld only by an organization formed in such a way that all its members in any one industry, or in all industries if necessary, cease work whenever a strike or lockout is on in any department thereof, thus making an injury to one an injury to all.

Instead of the conservative motto, "A fair day's wage for a fair day's work," we must inscribe on our banner the revolutionary watchword, "Abolition of the wage system."

It is the historic mission of the working class to do away with capitalism. The army of production must be organized, not only for the every-day struggle with capitalists, but also to carry on production when capitalism shall have been overthrown. By organizing industrially we are forming the structure of the new society within the shell of the old.

1912 "Casey Jones, Union Scab" by Joe Hill

The Workers on the S. P. line to strike sent out a call;
But Casey Jones, the engineer, he wouldn't strike at all;
His boiler it was leaking, and its drivers on the bum,
And his engine and its bearings, they were all out of plumb.

> Casey Jones kept his junk pile running;
> Casey Jones was working double time;
> Casey Jones got a wooden medal,
> For being good and faithful on the S. P. line.

The workers said to Casey: "Won't you help us win this strike?"
But Casey said: "Let me alone, you'd better take a hike."
Then some one put a bunch of railroad ties across the track,
And Casey hit the river bottom with an awful crack.

> Casey Jones hit the river bottom;
> Casey Jones broke his blessed spine;
> Casey Jones was an Angelino,
> He took a trip to heaven on the S. P. line.

When Casey Jones got up to heaven, to the Pearly Gate,
He said: "I'm Casey Jones, the guy that pulled the S. P. freight."
"You're just the man," said Peter, "our musicians went on strike;
You can get a job a'scabbing any time you like."

> Casey Jones got up to heaven;
> Casey Jones was doing mighty fine;
> Casey Jones went scabbing on the angels,
> Just like he did to workers of the S. P. line.

They got together, and they said it wasn't fair,
For Casey Jones to go around a'scabbing everywhere.
The Angels' Union No. 23, they sure were there,
And they promptly fired Casey down the Golden Stairs.

Casey Jones went to Hell a'flying;
"Casey Jones," the Devil said, "Oh fine:
Casey Jones, get busy shovelling sulphur;
That's what you get for scabbing on the S. P. Line."

Speech in Canton, Ohio, by Eugene V. Debs (excerpt) 1918

Comrades, friends and fellow-workers, for this very cordial greeting, this very hearty reception, I thank you all with the fullest appreciation of your interest in and your devotion to the cause for which I am to speak to you this afternoon. [Applause.]

To speak for labor; to plead the cause of the men and women and children who toil; to serve the working class, has always been to me a high privilege; [Applause] a duty of love.

I have just returned from a visit over yonder [pointing to the workhouse], where three of our most loyal comrades are paying the penalty for their devotion to the cause of the working class. [Applause.] They have come to realize, as many of us have, that it is extremely dangerous to exercise the constitutional right of free speech in a country fighting to make democracy safe in the world. [Applause.]

I realize that, in speaking to you this afternoon, there are certain limitations placed upon the right of free speech. I must be exceedingly careful, prudent, as to what I say, and even more careful and prudent as to how I say it. [Laughter.] I may not be able to say all I think; [laughter and applause] but I am not going to say anything that I do not think. [Applause.] I would rather a thousand times be a free soul in jail than to be a sycophant and coward in the streets. [Applause and shouts.] They may put those boys in jail—and some of the rest of us in jail—but they can not put the Socialist movement in jail. [Applause and shouts.] Those prison bars separate their bodies from ours, but their souls are here this afternoon. [Applause and cheers.] They are simply paying the penalty that all men have paid in all the ages of history for standing erect, and for seeking to pave the way to better conditions for mankind. [Applause.]. . .

There is but one thing you have to be concerned about, and that is that you keep foursquare with the principles of the international Socialist movement. [Applause.] It is only when you begin to compromise that trouble begins. [Applause.] So far as I am concerned, it does not matter what others may say, or think, or do, as long as I am sure that I am right with myself and the cause. [Applause.] There are so many who seek refuge in the popular side of a great question. As a Socialist, I have long since learned how to stand alone. [Applause.] For the last month I have been traveling over the Hoosier State; and, let me say to you, that, in all my connection with the Socialist movement, I have never seen such meetings, such enthusiasm, such unity of purpose; never have I seen such a promising outlook as there is today, notwithstanding the statement published repeatedly that our leaders have deserted us. [Laughter.] Well, for myself, I never had much faith in leaders. [Applause and laughter.] I am willing to be charged with almost anything, rather than to be charged with being a leader. I am suspicious of leaders, and especially of the intellectual variety. [Applause.] Give me the rank and file every day in the week. If you go to the city of Washington, and you examine the pages of the Congressional Directory, you will find that almost all of those corporation lawyers and cowardly politicians, members of Congress, and misrepresentatives of the masses—you will find that almost all of them claim, in glowing terms, that they have risen from the ranks to places of eminence and distinction. I am very glad I cannot make that claim for myself. [Laughter.] I would be ashamed to admit that I had risen from the ranks. When I rise it will be with the ranks, and not from the ranks. [Applause.]. . .

Socialism is a growing idea; an expanding philosophy. It is spreading over the entire face of the earth: It is as vain to resist it as it would be to arrest the sunrise on the morrow. It is coming, coming, coming all along the line. Can you not see it? If not, I advise you to consult an oculist. There is certainly something the matter with your vision. It is the mightiest movement in the history of mankind. What a privilege to serve it! I have regretted a thousand times that I can do so little for the movement that has done so much for me. [Applause.] The little that I am, the little that I am hoping to be, I owe to the Socialist movement. [Applause.] It has given me my ideas and ideals; my principles and convictions, and I would not exchange one of them for all of Rockefeller's bloodstained dollars. [Cheers.] It has taught me how to serve—a lesson to me of priceless value. It has taught me the ecstasy in the hand-clasp of a comrade. It has enabled me to hold high communion with you, and made it possible for me to take my place side by side with you in the great struggle for the better day; to multiply myself over and over again, to thrill with a fresh-born manhood; to feel life truly worthwhile; to open new avenues of vision; to spread out glorious vistas; to know that I am kin to all that throbs; to be class-conscious, and to realize that, regardless of nationality, race, creed, color or sex, every man, every woman who toils, who renders useful service, every member of the working class without an exception, is my comrade, my brother and sister—and that to serve them and their cause is the highest duty of my life. [Great applause.]

And in their service I can feel myself expand; I can rise to the stature of a man and claim the right to a place on earth—a place where I can stand and strive to speed the day of industrial freedom and social justice.

Yes, my comrades, my heart is attuned to yours. Aye, all our hearts now throb as one great heart responsive to the battle cry of the social revolution. Here, in this alert and inspiring assemblage [Applause] our hearts are with the Bolsheviki of Russia. [Deafening and prolonged applause.] Those heroic men and women, those unconquerable comrades have by their incomparable valor and sacrifice added fresh luster to the fame of the international movement. Those Russian comrades of ours have made greater sacrifices, have suffered more, and have shed more heroic blood than any like number of men and women anywhere on earth; they have laid the foundation of the first real democracy that ever drew the breath of life in this world. [Applause.] And the very first act of the triumphant Russian revolution was to proclaim a state of peace with all mankind, coupled with a fervent moral appeal, not to kings, not to emperors, rulers or diplomats but to the people of all nations. [Applause.] Here we have the very breath of democracy, the quintessence of the dawning freedom. The Russian revolution proclaimed its glorious triumph in its ringing and inspiring appeal to the peoples of all the earth. In a humane and fraternal spirit new Russia, emancipated at last from the curse of the centuries, called upon all nations engaged in the frightful war, the Central Powers as well as the Allies, to send representatives to a conference to lay down terms of peace that should be just and lasting. Here was the supreme opportunity to strike the blow to make the world safe for democracy. [Applause.] Was there any response to that noble appeal that in some day to come will be written in letters of gold in the history of the world? [Applause.] Was there any response whatever to that appeal for universal peace? [From the crowd: "No!"] No, not the slightest attention was paid to it by the Christian nations engaged in the terrible slaughter. . . .

Wars throughout history have been waged for conquest and plunder. In the Middle Ages when the feudal lords who inhabited the castles whose towers may still be seen along the Rhine concluded to enlarge their domains, to increase their power, their prestige and their wealth they declared war upon one another. But they themselves did not go to war any more than the modern feudal lords, the barons of Wall Street go to war. [Applause.] The feudal barons of the Middle Ages, the economic predecessors of the capitalists of our day, declared all wars. And their miserable serfs fought all the battles. The poor, ignorant serfs had been taught to revere their masters; to believe that when their masters declared war upon one another, it was their patriotic duty to fall upon one another and to cut one another's throats for the profit and glory of the lords and barons who held them in contempt. And that is war in a nutshell. The master class has always declared the wars; the subject class has always fought the battles. The master class has had all to gain and nothing to lose, while the subject class has had nothing to gain and all to lose—especially their lives. [Applause.]

They have always taught and trained you to believe it to be your patriotic duty to go to war and to have yourselves slaughtered at their command. But in all the history of the world you, the people, have never had a voice in declaring war, and strange as it certainly appears, no war by any nation in any age has ever been declared by the people.

And here let me emphasize the fact—and it cannot be repeated too often—that the working class who fight all the battles, the working class who make the supreme sacrifices, the working class who freely shed their blood and furnish the corpses, have never yet had a voice in either declaring war or making peace. It is the ruling class that invariably does both. They alone declare war and they alone make peace.

Yours not to reason why; Yours but to do and die.

That is their motto and we object on the part of the awakening workers of this nation.

If war is right let it be declared by the people. You who have your lives to lose, you certainly above all others have the right to decide the momentous issue of war or peace. [Applause.]. . .

Now what you workers need is to organize, not along craft lines but along revolutionary industrial lines. [Applause.] All of you workers in a given industry, regardless of your trade or occupation, should belong to one and the same union.

Political action and industrial action must supplement and sustain each other. You will never vote the Socialist republic into existence. You will have to lay its foundations in industrial organization. The industrial union is the forerunner of industrial democracy. In the shop where the workers are associated is where industrial democracy has its beginning. Organize according to your industries! Get together in every department of industrial service! United and acting together for the common good your power is invincible.

When you have organized industrially you will soon learn that you can manage as well as operate industry. You will soon realize that you do not need the idle masters and exploiters. They are simply parasites. They do not employ you as you imagine but you employ them to take from you what you produce, and that is how they function in industry. You can certainly dispense with them in that capacity. You do not need them to depend upon for your jobs. You can never be free while you work and live by their sufferance. You must own your own tools and then you will control your own jobs, enjoy the products of your own labor and be free men instead of industrial slaves.

Organize industrially and make your organization complete. Then unite in the Socialist Party. Vote as you strike and strike as you vote.

Your union and your party embrace the working class. The Socialist Party expresses the interests, hopes and aspirations of the toilers of all the world.

Get your fellow workers into the industrial union and the political party to which they rightly belong, especially this year, this historic year in which the forces of labor will assert themselves as they never have before. This is the year that calls for men and women who have courage, the manhood and womanhood to do their duty.

Get into the Socialist Party and take your place in its ranks; help to inspire the weak and strengthen the faltering, and do your share to speed the coming of the brighter and better day for us all. [Applause.]

When we unite and act together on the industrial field and when we vote together on election day we shall develop the supreme power of the one class that can and will bring permanent peace to the world. We shall then have the intelligence, the courage and the power for our great task. In due time industry will be organized on a cooperative basis. We shall conquer the public power. We shall then transfer the title deeds of the railroads, the telegraph lines, the mines, mills and great industries to the people in their collective capacity; we shall take possession of all these social utilities in the name of the people. We shall then have industrial democracy. We shall be a free nation whose government is of and by and for the people.

And now for all of us to do our duty! The clarion call is ringing in our ears and we cannot falter without being convicted of treason to ourselves and to our great cause.

Do not worry over the charge of treason to your masters, but be concerned about the treason that involves yourselves. [Applause.] Be true to yourself and you cannot be a traitor to any good cause on earth.

Yes, in good time we are going to sweep into power in this nation and throughout the world. We are going to destroy all enslaving and degrading capitalist institutions and re-create them as free and humanizing institutions. The world is daily changing before our eyes. The sun of capitalism is setting; the sun of socialism is rising. It is our duty to build the new nation and the free republic. We need industrial and social builders. We Socialists are the builders of the beautiful world that is to be. We are all pledged to do our part. We are inviting—aye challenging you this afternoon in the name of your own manhood and womanhood to join us and do your part.

In due time the hour will strike and this great cause triumphant—the greatest in history—will proclaim the emancipation of the working class and the brotherhood of all mankind. [Thunderous and prolonged applause.]

"The Case for Birth Control" by Margaret Sanger

1924

Everywhere we look, we see poverty and large families going hand in hand. We see hordes of children whose parents cannot feed, clothe or educate even one-half of the number born to them. We see sick, harassed, broken mothers whose health and nerves cannot bear the strain of further childbearing. We see fathers growing despondent and desperate, because their labor cannot bring the necessary wage to keep their growing families. We see that those parents who are least fit to reproduce the race are having the largest number of children; while people of wealth, leisure and education are having small families.

It is generally concluded by sociologist and scientist that a nation cannot go on indefinitely multiplying without eventually reaching the point when population presses upon means of subsistence. While in this country there is perhaps no need for immediate alarm on this account, there are many other reasons for demanding Birth Control. At present, for the poor mother, there is only one alternative to the necessity of bearing children year after year, regardless of her health, of the welfare of the children she already has, and of the income of the family. This alternative is abortion, which is so common as to be almost universal, especially where there are rigid laws against imparting information for the prevention of conception. It has been estimated that there are about one million abortions in the United States each year.

To force poor mothers to resort to this dangerous and health-destroying method of curtailing their families is cruel, wicked and heartless, and it is often the mothers who care most about the welfare of their children who are willing to undergo any pain or risk to prevent the coming of infants for whom they cannot properly care.

There are definite reasons when and why parents should not have children, which will conceded by most thoughtful people.

First.—Children should not be born when either parent has an inheritable disease, such as insanity, feeble-mindedness, epilepsy or syphilis.

Second.—When the mother is suffering from tuberculosis, kidney disease, heart disease or pelvic deformity.

Third.—When either parent has gonorrhea. This disease in the mother is the cause of ninety percent of blindness in newborn babies.

Fourth.—When children already born are not normal, even though both parents are in good physical and mental condition.

Fifth.—Not until the woman is twenty-three years old and the man twenty-five.

Sixth.—Not until the previous baby is at least three years old. This gives a year to recover from the physical ordeal of the birth of the baby, a year to rest, be normal and enjoy her motherhood, and another year to prepare for the coming of the next.

We want mothers to be fit. We want them to conceive in joy and gladness. We want them to carry their babies during the nine months in a sound and healthy body and with a happy, joyous, hopeful mind. It is almost impossible to imagine the suffering caused to women, the mental agony they endure, when their days and nights are haunted by the fear of undesired pregnancy.

Seventh.—Children should not be born to parents whose economic circumstances do not guarantee enough to provide the children with the necessities of life.

A couple who can take care of two children and bring them up decently in health and comfort, give them an education and start them fairly in life, do more for their country and for mankind than the couple who recklessly reproduce ten or twelve children, some of them to die in infancy, others to survive but to enter the mill or factory at an early age, and all to sink to that level of degradation where charity, either state or private, is necessary to keep them alive. The man who cannot support three children should not have ten, notwithstanding all pleas of the militarists for numbers.

Eighth.—A woman should not bear children when exhausted from labor. This especially applies to women who marry after spending several years in industrial or commercial life. Conception should not take place until she is in good health and has overcome her fatigue.

Ninth.—Not for two years after marriage should a couple undertake the great responsibility of becoming parents. Thousands of young people enter marriage without the faintest idea of what marriage involves. They do not know its spiritual responsibilities. If children are born quickly and plentifully, people consider that marriage is justified. I claim that this is barbaric and wrong. It is wrong for the wife, for the man, for the children.

It is impossible for two young people to really know each other until they have lived together in marriage. After the closeness and intimacy of that relation there often comes to the woman a rude awakening; the devoted lover becomes careless and dissatisfied. If she becomes pregnant immediately she becomes physically disturbed, nervous and irritable. The girl has changed, and the boy who knew her as a happy smiling sweetheart finds her disagreeable and disgruntled. Of course thousands of people learn to adjust themselves. Nevertheless, I maintain that young people should marry early and wait at least two years to adjust their own lives to play and read together and to build up a cultural and spiritual friendship. Then will come the intense desire to call into being a little child to share their love and happiness. When children are conceived in love and born into an atmosphere of happiness, then will parenthood be a glorious privilege, and the children will grow to resemble gods. This can only be obtained through the knowledge and practice of Birth Control.

P. S.—The American Birth Control League desires that the instruction in Birth Control should be given by the medical profession. Only through individual care and treatment can a woman be given the best and safest means of controlling her offspring. We do not favor the indiscriminate diffusion of unreliable and unsafe Birth Control advice.

Nicola Sacco's Speech to the Court   1921

Clerk Worthington: Nicola Sacco, have you anything to say why sentence of death should not be passed upon you?

Nicola Sacco: Yes, sir. I am no orator. It is not very familiar with me the English language, and as I know, as my friend has told me, my comrade Vanzetti will speak more long, so I thought to give him the chance.

I never knew, never heard, even read in history anything so cruel as this Court. After seven years they still consider us guilty. And these gentle people here are arrayed with us in this court today.

I know the sentence will be between two classes, the oppressed class and the rich class, and there will be always collision between one and the other. We fraternize the people with the books, with the literature. You persecute the people, tyrannize them and kill them. We try the education of people always. You try to put a path between us and some other nationality that hates each other. That is why I am here today on this bench, for having been of the oppressed class. Well, you are the oppressor.

You know it, Judge Thayer—you know all my life, you know why I have been here, and after seven years that you have been persecuting me and my poor wife, and you still today sentence us to death. I would like to tell all my life, but what is the use? You know all about what I say before, that is, my comrade, will be talking, because he is more familiar with the language, and I will give him a chance. My comrade, the kind man to all the children, you sentenced him two times, in the Bridgewater case and the Dedham case, connected with me, and you know he is innocent.

You forget all this population that has been with us for seven years, to sympathize and give us all their energy and all their kindness. You do not care for them. Among that peoples and the comrades and the working class there is a big legion of intellectual people which have been with us for seven years, to not commit the iniquitous sentence, but still the Court goes ahead. And I want to thank you all, you peoples, my comrades who have been with me for seven years, with the Sacco–Vanzetti case, and I will give my friend a chance.

I forget one thing which my comrade remember me. As I said before, Judge Thayer know all my life, and he know that I am never guilty, never—not yesterday, nor today, nor forever.

"Have You Ever Been to Jail?" by Dorothy Day   1950

There is a fascination about prison literature, just as there is fascination and suspense in stories of pursuit. There is suspense in not knowing what is going to happen next, and anything can happen, and whether or not and when freedom will come. There is admiration, wonder and fear, too, that perhaps some day we will be in the same boat if it comes to standing up for principle.

During the war conscientious objectors, the absolutists, served sentences in Danbury, Lewisburg, Chillicothe, Ashland and other federal prisons, endured hunger strikes for long stretches, and forcible feedings and solitary confinement, overcame their fear, overcame also the world, and all in the name of freedom.

As Harold Robbins, the English Distributist, wrote: "Freedom is the primary and supreme reason for the existence of mankind. That He should be freely loved and served seems, so far as our thought can penetrate, to have been God's chief reason for calling us into being. At the cost of this freedom God could have established and maintained a world full of order, but not of justice, for free will is of the essence of human justice."

These men who have endured so much have borne witness to Truth and Justice, and so have served God, even those who denied Him. We can only say they have denied the God of the bourgeoise, the God of the materialists, their money or their belly or their lust.

A Field of Broken Stones, by Lowell Naeve, in collaboration with David Wieck, and published by the Libertarian Press, Glen Gardner, New Jersey ($3), and *Prison Etiquette, the Convict's Compendium of Useful Information*, edited and with an introduction by Holley Cantine and Dachine Rainer, Retort Press, Bearsville, New York ($2.50), are two books which have been published recently. Both are illustrated by Lowell Naeve, an artist who served five years in prison during the last war and who is co-author of the first book and has an excerpt in the second. The second book was hand set and printed on a Gordon upright foot pedal press by the editors.

COURAGE

To me these men have shown a tremendous courage which is hard to analyze and make understood in these days of mediocrity, the times of "the regular fellow." We talk about the saints and are thrilled by the idea of sanctity, but the question is, how would we react to a St. Francis, a St. Benedict Joseph Labre, a Cure of Ars? Human respect is one of the greatest stumbling blocks.

I repeat. We would not recognize the saint if we met him on the street corner today. He would be "the crank," the "unbalanced," the "trouble maker," etc.

The conscientious objector portrayed in these books is even willing to give up his dignity, his person, because of his fierce faith in the dignity of other men, their sacredness (and from whom do they derive this sacred character except from God—they are sons of God).

These men went on long hunger strikes because of injustices to their brother the Negro. Why is he their brother, unless God is their father? Of course they share a common humanity. It was not enough that they lost their liberty and were held confined behind bars, for long hours and days and months awaiting trial, and were sentenced to interminable stretches in prison. Have you been in jail, I repeat. Or have you been on retreat at some convent or monastery and began to feel the oppression of the walls, and to shudder at the voluntary giving up of freedom of those who have had this vocation. I have been in jail twice, in Washington and in Chicago, and I also felt that sense of oppression on the first retreat I made when I became a Catholic. I felt oppressed, closed in, hemmed in, breathing an air which was not natural to me so that I got the spiritual "bends," as men who work in compressed air sections in tunnels get "the bends" unless they go in and come out gradually, taking it little by little. We have to take our spiritual life in this way, and recognize we cannot impose on others, in our Houses of Hospitality or farms or retreat houses, a spiritual practice which they are not yet ready for. Even in this way these books may serve our readers as preparations for the times of trial to come, like the compression chambers into which the workers go before they get out under the river, or far into the tunnel under the mountain where they are called to their appointed task on which their life, their bread and butter depends.

These are books to be read with prayer in order to achieve understanding. For instance, do you know what it is to have your person violated, taken hold of, dragged, thrown, stripped and degraded? Jesus Christ knew these things and we view His way when we make the Stations of the Cross. These may seem extreme parallels, but St. Paul recalled that Trial as "the Folly of the Cross," and so indirectly referred to Christ as the Fool of His time. He loved even to folly. He said we should forgive seventy times seven. He said to love your enemies. He told that foolish tale of the prodigal son, which if you stop to think of it, is madness and folly on the part of the old man who showed such a lack of appreciation for the sturdy qualities of the older son and contributed so to the delinquency of the younger. Why did he give him his inheritance, knowing his temperament and that he would spend it on drink and women? And then to forgive him, to fall on his neck and embrace him, to feast with him and spend more money on him! No doubt the youth fell again and again and did the seventy times seven business work here? The folly of the Cross! The failure of the Cross!

I write these things because pacifism today seems just such folly. What good does a handful of men do?, everyone asks. How does one man going on hunger strike far away in a grey cell behind bars, mean laying down his life for his brother. And what good does it do?

One always is alone in doing these things. The revolution starts with oneself.

It is hard to see how men have the fortitude to endure the degradation of being mauled around when they make the gesture of refusing voluntarily to enter a jail and so force the guards to carry them, drag them, dump them on the floor of the jail. They endure this degradation in order that other men's bodies may be treated with respect. They have already paid a great penalty, being deprived of their liberty. But they continue their fight in jail by work strike and hunger strike and they win their fight again and again and win too the reluctant admiration of the other prisoners.

"Integrated Bus Suggestions" by the Montgomery Improvement Association — 1956

This is a historic week because segregation on buses has now been declared unconstitutional. Within a few days the Supreme Court Mandate will reach Montgomery and you will be re-boarding <u>integrated</u> buses. This places upon us all a tremendous responsibility of maintaining, in the face of what could be some unpleasantness, a calm and loving dignity befitting good citizens and members of our Race. If there is violence in word or deed it must not be our people who commit it.

For your help and convenience the following suggestions are made. Will you read, study and memorize them so that our non-violent determination may not be endangered. First, some general suggestions:

Not all white people are opposed to integrated buses. Accept goodwill on the part of many.

The <u>whole bus</u> is now for the use of <u>all</u> people.

Pray for guidance and commit yourself to <u>complete</u> non-violence in word and action as you enter the bus.

Demonstrate the calm dignity of our Montgomery people in your actions.

In all things observe ordinary rules of courtesy and good behavior.

Remember that this is not a victory for Negroes alone, but for all Montgomery and the South. Do not boast! Do not brag!

Be quiet but friendly; proud, but not arrogant; joyous, but not boistrous (*sic*).

Be loving enough to absorb evil and understanding enough to turn an enemy into a friend.

Now for some specific suggestions:

The bus driver is in charge of the bus and has been instructed to obey the law. Assume that he will cooperate in helping you occupy any vacant seat.

Do not deliberately sit by a white person, unless there is no other seat.

In sitting down by a person, white or colored, say "May I" or "Pardon me" as you sit. This is a common courtesy.

If cursed, do not curse back. If pushed, do not push back.

In case of an incident, talk as little as possible, and always in a quiet tone. Do not get up from your seat! Report all serious incidents to the bus driver.

For the first few days try to get on the bus with a friend in whose non-violence you have confidence. You can uphold one another by a glance or a prayer.

If another person is being molested, do not arise to go to his defense, but pray for the oppressor and use moral and spiritual force to carry on the struggle for justice.

According to your own ability and personality, do not be afraid to experiment with new and creative techniques for achieving reconciliation and social change.

If you feel you cannot take it, walk for another week or two. We have confidence in our people. GOD BLESS YOU ALL.

THE MONTGOMERY IMPROVEMENT ASSOCIATON

THE REV. M. L. KING, JR., PRESIDENT

THE REV. W. J. POWELL, SECRETARY

Life in this society being, at best, an utter bore and no aspect of society being at all relevant to women, there remains to civic-minded, responsible, thrill-seeking females only to overthrow the government, eliminate the money system, institute complete automation and destroy the male sex.

It is now technically feasible to reproduce without the aid of males (or, for that matter, females) and to produce only females. We must begin immediately to do so. Retaining the mail has not even the dubious purpose of reproduction. The male is a biological accident: the Y (male) gene is an incomplete X (female) gene, that is, it has an incomplete set of chromosomes. In other words, the male is an incomplete female, a walking abortion, aborted at the gene stage. To be male is to be deficient, emotionally limited; maleness is a deficiency disease and males are emotional cripples.

The male is completely egocentric, trapped inside himself, incapable of empathizing or identifying with others, or love, friendship, affection of tenderness. He is a completely isolated unit, incapable of rapport with anyone. His responses are entirely visceral, not cerebral; his intelligence is a mere tool in the services of his drives and needs; he is incapable of mental passion, mental interaction; he can't relate to anything other than his own physical sensations. He is a half-dead, unresponsive lump, incapable of giving or receiving pleasure or happiness; consequently, he is at best an utter bore, an inoffensive blob, since only those capable of absorption in others can be charming. He is trapped in a twilight zone halfway between humans and apes, and is far worse off than the apes because, unlike the apes, he is capable of a large array of negative feelings—hate, jealousy, contempt, disgust, guilt, shame, doubt—and moreover, he is aware of what he is and what he isn't. . . .

Eventually the natural course of events, of social evolution, will lead to total female control of the world and, subsequently, to the cessation of the production of males and, ultimately, to the cessation of the production of females.

But SCUM is impatient; SCUM is not consoled by the thought that future generations will thrive; SCUM wants to grab some thrilling living for itself. And, if a large majority of women were SCUM, they could acquire complete control of this country within a few weeks simply by withdrawing from the labor force, thereby paralyzing the entire nation. Additional measures, any one of which would be sufficient to completely disrupt the economy and everything else, would be for women to declare themselves off the money system, stop buying, just loot and simply refuse to obey all laws they don't care to obey. The police force, National Guard, Army, Navy and Marines combined couldn't squelch a rebellion of over half the population, particularly when it's made up of people they are utterly helpless without.

If all women simply left men, refused to have anything to do with any of them—ever, all men, the government, and the national economy would collapse completely. Even without leaving men, women who are aware of the extent of their superiority to and power over men, could acquire complete control over everything within a few weeks, could effect a total submission of males to females. In a sane society the male would trot along obediently after the female. The male is docile and easily led, easily subjected to the domination of any female who cares to dominate him. The male, in fact, wants desperately to be led by females, wants Mama in charge, wants to abandon himself to her care. But this is not a sane society, and most women are not even dimly aware of where they're at in relation to men.

The conflict, therefore, is not between females and males, but between SCUM—dominant, secure, self-confident, nasty, violent, selfish, independent, proud, thrill-seeking, free-wheeling, arrogant females, who consider themselves fit to rule the universe, who have free-wheeled to the limits of this 'society' and are ready to wheel on to something far beyond what it has to offer—and nice, passive, accepting 'cultivated,' polite, dignified, subdued, dependent, scared, mindless, insecure, approval-seeking Daddy's Girls, who can't cope with the unknown, who want to hang back with the apes, who feel secure only with Big Daddy standing by, with a big strong man to lean on and with a fat, hairy face in the White House, who are too cowardly to face up to the hideous reality of what a man is, what Daddy is, who have cast their lot with the swine, who have adapted themselves to animalism, feel superficially comfortable with it and know no other way of 'life,' who have reduced their minds, thoughts and sights to the male level, who, lacking sense, imagination and wit can have value only in a male 'society,' who can have a place in the sun, or, rather, in the slime, only as soothers, ego boosters, relaxers and breeders, who are dismissed as inconsequents by other females, who project their deficiencies, their maleness, onto all females and see the female as worm. . . .

SCUM will become members of the unwork force, the fuck-up force; they will get jobs of various kinds and unwork. For example, SCUM salesgirls will not charge for merchandise; SCUM telephone operators will not charge for calls; SCUM office and factory workers, in addition to fucking up their work, will secretly destroy equipment. SCUM will unwork at a job until fired, then get a new job to unwork at.

SCUM will forcibly relieve bus drivers, cab drivers and subway token sellers of their jobs and run buses and cabs and dispense free tokens to the public.

SCUM will destroy all useless and harmful objects—cars, store windows, 'Great Art,' etc.

Eventually SCUM will take over the airwaves—radio and TV networks—by forcibly relieving of their jobs all radio and TV employees who would impede SCUM's entry into the broadcasting studios.

SCUM will couple-bust—barge into mixed (male-female) couples, wherever they are, and bust them up.

SCUM will kill all men who are not in the Men's Auxiliary of SCUM. Men in the Men's Auxiliary are those men who are working diligently to eliminate themselves, men who, regardless of their motives, do good, men who are playing ball with SCUM. A few examples of the men in the Men's Auxiliary are: men who kill men; biological scientists who are working on constructive programs, as opposed to biological warfare; journalists, writers, editors, publishers and producers who disseminate and promote ideas that will lead to the achievement of SCUM's goals; faggots who, by their shimmering, flaming example, encourage other men to de-man themselves and thereby make themselves relatively inoffensive; men who consistently give things away—money, things, services; men who tell it like it is (so far not one ever has), who put women straight, who reveal the truth about themselves, who give the mindless male females correct sentences to parrot, who tell them a woman's primary goal in life should be to squash the male sex (to aid men in this endeavor SCUM will conduct Turd Sessions, at which every male present will give a speech beginning with the sentence: 'I am a turd, a lowly abject turd,' then proceed to list all the ways in which he is. . . .

It is most tempting to pick off the female 'Great Artists,' liars and phonies etc along with the men, but that would be inexpedient, as it would not be clear to most of the public that the female killed was a male. All women have a fink streak in them, to a greater or lesser degree, but it stems from a lifetime of living among men. Eliminate men and women will shape up. Women are improvable; men are not, although their behavior is. When SCUM gets hot on their asses it'll shape up fast.

Testimony of Abbie Hoffman, Chicago Eight Trial (excerpt) 1968

Prosecutor: Richard Schultz
Defense Attorneys: William Kunstler, Leonard Weinglass
The Witness: Abbie Hoffman
The Court: Judge Julius Hoffman

MR. WEINGLASS: Will you please identify yourself for the record?

THE WITNESS: My name is Abbie. I am an orphan of America.

MR. SCHULTZ: Your Honor, may the record show it is the defendant Hoffman who has taken the stand?

THE COURT: Oh, yes. It may so indicate. . . .

MR. WEINGLASS: Where do you reside?

THE WITNESS: I live in Woodstock Nation.

MR. WEINGLASS: Will you tell the Court and jury where it is?

THE WITNESS: Yes. It is a nation of alienated young people. We carry it around with us as a state of mind in the same way as the Sioux Indians carried the Sioux nation around with them. It is a nation dedicated to cooperation versus competition, to the idea that people should have better means of exchange than property or money, that there should be some other basis for human interaction. It is a nation dedicated to—

THE COURT: Just where it is, that is all.

THE WITNESS: It is in my mind and in the minds of my brothers and sisters. It does not consist of property or material but, rather, of ideas and certain values. We believe in a society—

THE COURT: No, we want the place of residence, if he has one, place of doing business, if you have a business. Nothing about philosophy or India, sir. Just where you live, if you have a place to live. Now you said Woodstock. In what state is Woodstock?

THE WITNESS: It is in the state of mind, in the mind of myself and my brothers and sisters. It is a conspiracy. Presently, the nation is held captive, in the penitentiaries of the institutions of a decaying system.

MR. WEINGLASS: Can you tell the Court and jury your present age?

THE WITNESS: My age is 33. I am a child of the 60s.

MR. WEINGLASS: When were you born?

THE WITNESS: Psychologically, 1960.

MR. SCHULTZ: Objection, if the Court please. I move to strike the answer.

MR. WEINGLASS: What is the actual date of your birth?

THE WITNESS: November 30, 1936.

MR. WEINGLASS: Between the date of your birth, November 30, 1936, and May 1, 1960, what if anything occurred in your life?

THE WITNESS: Nothing. I believe it is called an American education.

MR. SCHULTZ: Objection.

THE COURT: I sustain the objection.

THE WITNESS: Huh.

MR. WEINGLASS: Abbie, could you tell the Court and jury—

MR. SCHULTZ: His name isn't Abbie. I object to this informality.

MR. WEINGLASS: Can you tell the Court and jury what is your present occupation?

THE WITNESS: I am a cultural revolutionary. Well, I am really a defendant—full-time.

MR. WEINGLASS: What do you mean by the phrase "cultural revolutionary"?

THE WITNESS: Well, I suppose it is a person who tries to shape and participate in the values, and the mores, the customs and the style of living of new people who eventually become inhabitants of a new nation and a new society through art and poetry, theater, and music.

MR. WEINGLASS: What have you done yourself to participate in that revolution?

THE WITNESS: Well, I have been a rock and roll singer. I am a reporter with the Liberation News Service. I am a poet. I am a film maker. I made a movie called "Yippies Tour Chicago or How I Spent My Summer Vacation." Currently, I am negotiating with United Artists and MGM to do a movie in Hollywood. I have written an extensive pamphlet on how to live free in the city of New York. I have written two books, one called *Revolution for the Hell of It* under the pseudonym Free, and one called *Woodstock Nation*.

MR. WEINGLASS: Taking you back to the spring of 1960, approximately May 1, 1960, will you tell the Court and jury where you were?

MR. SCHULTZ: 1960?

THE WITNESS: That's right.

MR. SCHULTZ: Objection.

THE COURT: I sustain the objection.

MR. WEINGLASS: Your Honor, that date has great relevance to the trial. May 1, 1960, was this witness' first public demonstration. I am going to bring him down through Chicago.

THE COURT: Not in my presence, you are not going to bring him down. I sustain the objection to the question.

THE WITNESS: My background has nothing to do with my state of mind?

THE COURT: Will you remain quiet while I am making a ruling? I know you have no respect for me.

MR. KUNSTLER: Your Honor, that is totally unwarranted. I think your remarks call for a motion for a mistrial.

THE COURT: And your motion calls for a denial of the motion. Mr. Weinglass, continue with your examination.

MR. KUNSTLER: You denied my motion? I hadn't even started to argue it.

THE COURT: I don't need any argument on that one. The witness turned his back on me while he was on the witness stand.

THE WITNESS: I was just looking at the pictures of the long hairs up on the wall . . . .

MR. WEINGLASS: Now, will you read for the Court and jury the eighteen demands [of the Yippies] first, then the postscript.

THE WITNESS: I will read it in the order that I wrote it. "Revolution toward a free society, Yippie, by A. Yippie.

"This is a personal statement. There are no spokesmen for the Yippies. We are all our own leaders. We realize this list of demands is inconsistent. They are not really demands. For people to make demands of the Democratic Party is an exercise in wasted wish fulfillment. If we have a demand, it is simply and emphatically that they, along with their fellow inmates in the Republican Party, cease to exist. We demand a society built along the alternative community in Lincoln Park, a society based on humanitarian cooperation and equality, a society which allows and promotes the creativity present in all people and especially our youth.

"Number one. An immediate end to the war in Vietnam and a restructuring of our foreign policy which totally eliminates aspects of military, economic and cultural imperialism; the withdrawal of all foreign based troops and the abolition of military draft.

"Two. An immediate freedom for Huey Newton of the Black Panthers and all other black people; adoption of the community control concept in our ghetto areas; an end to the cultural and economic domination of minority groups.

"Three. The legalization of marijuana and all other psychedelic drugs; the freeing of all prisoners currently imprisoned on narcotics charges.

"Number four. A prison system based on the concept of rehabilitation rather than punishment.

"Five. A judicial system which works towards the abolition of all laws related to crimes without victims; that is, retention only of laws relating to crimes in which there is an unwilling injured party: i.e. murder, rape, or assault.

"Six. The total disarmament of all the people beginning with the police. This includes not only guns but such brutal vices as tear gas, Mace, electric prods, blackjacks, billy clubs, and the like.

"Seven. The abolition of money, the abolition of pay housing, pay media, pay transportation, pay food, pay education, pay clothing, pay medical health, and pay toilets.

"Eight. A society which works towards and actively promotes the concept of full unemployment, a society in which people are free from the drudgery of work, adoption of the concept 'Let the machines do it.'

"Number ten. A program of ecological development that would provide incentives for the decentralization of crowded cities and encourage rural living.

"Eleven. A program which provides not only free birth control information and devices, but also abortions when desired.

"Twelve. A restructured educational system which provides a student power to determine his course of study, student participation in over-all policy planning; an educational system which breaks down its barriers between school and community; a system which uses the surrounding community as a classroom so that students may learn directly the problems of the people.

"Number thirteen. The open and free use of the media; a program which actively supports and promotes cable television as a method of increasing the selection of channels available to the viewer.

"Fourteen. An end to all censorship. We are sick of a society that has no hesitation about showing people committing violence and refuses to show a couple fucking.

"Fifteen. We believe that people should fuck all the time, any time, wherever they wish. This is not a programmed demand but a simple recognition of the reality around its.

"Sixteen. A political system which is more streamlined and responsive to the needs of all the people regardless of age, sex, or race; perhaps a national referendum system conducted via television or a telephone voting system; perhaps a decentralization of power and authority with many varied tribal groups, groups in which people exist in a state of basic trust and are free to choose their tribe.

"Seventeen. A program that encourages and promotes the arts. However, we feel that if the free society we envision were to be sought for and achieved, all of us would actualize the creativity within us; in a very real sense we would have a society in which every man would be an artist."

And eighteen was left blank for anybody to fill in what they wanted. It was for these reasons that we had come to Chicago, it was for these reasons that many of us may fight and die here. We recognize this as the vision of the founders of this nation. We recognize that we are America; we recognize that we are free men. The present-day politicians and their armies of automatons have selfishly robbed us of our birthright. The evilness they stand for will go unchallenged no longer. Political pigs, your days are numbered. We are the second American Revolution. We shall win.

"YIPPIE."

1995   "Unabomber Manifesto" by Ted Kaczynski (excerpt)

. . . STRATEGY

180. The technophiles are taking us all on an utterly reckless ride into the unknown. Many people understand something of what technological progress is doing to us yet take a passive attitude toward it because they think it is inevitable. But we don't think it is inevitable. We think it can be stopped, and we will give here some indications of how to go about stopping it.

181. As we stated in paragraph 166, the two main tasks for the present are to promote social stress and instability in industrial society and to develop and propagate an ideology that opposes technology and the industrial system. When the system becomes sufficiently stressed and unstable, a revolution against technology may be possible. The pattern would be similar to that of the French and Russian Revolutions. French society and Russian society, for several decades prior to their respective revolutions, showed increasing signs of stress and weakness. Meanwhile, ideologies were being developed that offered a new world view that was quite different from the old one. In the Russian case, revolutionaries were actively working to undermine the old order. Then, when the old system was put under sufficient additional stress (by financial crisis in France, by military defeat in Russia) it was swept away by revolution. What we propose is something along the same lines.

182. It will be objected that the French and Russian Revolutions were failures. But most revolutions have two goals. One is to destroy an old form of society and the other is to set up the new form of society envisioned by the revolutionaries. The French and Russian revolutionaries failed (fortunately!) to create the new kind of society of which they dreamed, but they were quite successful in destroying the existing form of society.

183. But an ideology, in order to gain enthusiastic support, must have a positive ideals well as a negative one; it must be FOR something as well as AGAINST something. The positive ideal that we propose is Nature. That is, WILD nature; those aspects of the functioning of the Earth and its living things that are independent of human management and free of human interference and control. And with wild nature we include human nature, by which we mean those aspects of the functioning of the human individual that are not subject to regulation by organized society but are products of chance, or free will, or God (depending on your religious or philosophical opinions).

184. Nature makes a perfect counter-ideal to technology for several reasons. Nature (that which is outside the power of the system) is the opposite of technology (which seeks to expand indefinitely the power of the system). Most people will agree that nature is beautiful; certainly it has tremendous popular appeal. The radical environmentalists ALREADY hold an ideology that exalts nature and opposes technology. It is not necessary for the sake of nature to set up some chimerical utopia or any new kind of social order. Nature takes care of itself: It was a spontaneous creation that existed long before any human society, and for countless centuries many different kinds of human societies coexisted with nature without doing it an excessive amount of damage. Only with the Industrial Revolution did the effect of human society on nature become really devastating. To relieve the pressure on nature it is not necessary to create a special kind of social system, it is only necessary to get rid of industrial society. Granted, this will not solve all problems. Industrial society has already done tremendous damage to nature and it will take a very long time for the scars to heal. Besides, even pre-industrial societies can do significant damage to nature. Nevertheless, getting rid of industrial society will accomplish a great deal. It will relieve the worst of the pressure on nature so that the scars can begin to heal. It will remove the capacity of organized society to keep increasing its control over nature (including human nature). Whatever kind of society may exist after the demise of the industrial system, it is certain

that most people will live close to nature, because in the absence of advanced technology there is not other way that people CAN live. To feed themselves they must be peasants or herdsmen or fishermen or hunter, etc. And, generally speaking, local autonomy should tend to increase, because lack of advanced technology and rapid communications will limit the capacity of governments or other large organizations to control local communities.

185. As for the negative consequences of eliminating industrial society—well, you can't eat your cake and have it too. To gain one thing you have to sacrifice another.

186. Most people hate psychological conflict. For this reason they avoid doing any serious thinking about difficult social issues, and they like to have such issues presented to them in simple, black-and-white terms: THIS is all good and THAT is all bad. The revolutionary ideology should therefore be developed on two levels.

187. On the more sophisticated level the ideology should address itself to people who are intelligent, thoughtful and rational. The object should be to create a core of people who will be opposed to the industrial system on a rational, thought-out basis, with full appreciation of the problems and ambiguities involved, and of the price that has to be paid for getting rid of the system. It is particularly important to attract people of this type, as they are capable people and will be instrumental in influencing others. These people should be addressed on as rational a level as possible. Facts should never intentionally be distorted and intemperate language should be avoided. This does not mean that no appeal can be made to the emotions, but in making such appeal care should be taken to avoid misrepresenting the truth or doing anything else that would destroy the intellectual respectability of the ideology.

188. On a second level, the ideology should be propagated in a simplified form that will enable the unthinking majority to see the conflict of technology vs. nature in unambiguous terms. But even on this second level the ideology should not be expressed in language that is so cheap, intemperate or irrational that it alienates people of the thoughtful and rational type. Cheap, intemperate propaganda sometimes achieves impressive short-term gains, but it will be more advantageous in the long run to keep the loyalty of a small number of intelligently committed people than to arouse the passions of an unthinking, fickle mob who will change their attitude as soon as someone comes along with a better propaganda gimmick. However, propaganda of the rabble-rousing type may be necessary when the system is nearing the point of collapse and there is a final struggle between rival ideologies to determine which will become dominant when the old world-view goes under.

189. Prior to that final struggle, the revolutionaries should not expect to have a majority of people on their side. History is made by active, determined minorities, not by the majority, which seldom has a clear and consistent idea of what it really wants. Until the time comes for the final push toward revolution, the task of revolutionaries will be less to win the shallow support of the majority than to build a small core of deeply committed people. As for the majority, it will be enough to make them aware of the existence of the new ideology and remind them of it frequently; though of course it will be desirable to get majority support to the extent that this can be done without weakening the core of seriously committed people.

190. Any kind of social conflict helps to destabilize the system, but one should be careful about what kind of conflict one encourages. The line of conflict should be drawn between the mass of the people and the power-holding elite of industrial society (politicians, scientists, upper-level business executives, government officials, etc.). It should NOT be drawn between the revolutionaries and the mass of the people. For example, it would be bad strategy for the revolutionaries to condemn Americans for their habits of consumption. Instead, the average American should be portrayed as a victim of the advertising and marketing industry, which has suckered him into buying a lot of junk that he doesn't need and that is very poor compensation for his lost freedom. Either approach is consistent with the facts. It is merely a matter of attitude whether you blame the advertising industry for manipulating the public or blame the public for allowing itself to be manipulated. As a matter of strategy one should generally avoid blaming the public.

191. One should think twice before encouraging any other social conflict than that between the power-holding elite (which wields technology) and the general public (over which technology exerts its power). For one thing, other conflicts tend to distract attention from the important conflicts (between power-elite and ordinary people, between technology and nature); for another thing, other conflicts may actually tend to encourage technologization, because each side in such a conflict wants to use technological power to gain advantages over its adversary. This is clearly seen in rivalries between nations. It also appears in ethnic conflicts within nations. For example, in

America many black leaders are anxious to gain power for African Americans by placing back individuals in the technological power-elite. They want there to be many black government officials, scientists, corporation executives and so forth. In this way they are helping to absorb the African American subculture into the technological system. Generally speaking, one should encourage only those social conflicts that can be fitted into the framework of the conflicts of power—elite vs. ordinary people, technology vs nature.

192. But the way to discourage ethnic conflict is NOT through militant advocacy of minority rights (see paragraphs 21, 29). Instead, the revolutionaries should emphasize that although minorities do suffer more or less disadvantage, this disadvantage is of peripheral significance. Our real enemy is the industrial-technological system, and in the struggle against the system, ethnic distinctions are of no importance.

193. The kind of revolution we have in mind will not necessarily involve an armed uprising against any government. It may or may not involve physical violence, but it will not be a POLITICAL revolution. Its focus will be on technology and economics, not politics.

194. Probably the revolutionaries should even AVOID assuming political power, whether by legal or illegal means, until the industrial system is stressed to the danger point and has proved itself to be a failure in the eyes of most people. Suppose for example that some "green" party should win control of the United States Congress in an election. In order to avoid betraying or watering down their own ideology they would have to take vigorous measures to turn economic growth into economic shrinkage. To the average man the results would appear disastrous: There would be massive unemployment, shortages of commodities, etc. Even if the grosser ill effects could be avoided through superhumanly skillful management, still people would have to begin giving up the luxuries to which they have become addicted. Dissatisfaction would grow, the "green" party would be voted out of office and the revolutionaries would have suffered a severe setback. For this reason the revolutionaries should not try to acquire political power until the system has gotten itself into such a mess that any hardships will be seen as resulting from the failures of the industrial system itself and not from the policies of the revolutionaries. The revolution against technology will probably have to be a revolution by outsiders, a revolution from below and not from above.

195. The revolution must be international and worldwide. It cannot be carried out on a nation-by-nation basis. Whenever it is suggested that the United States, for example, should cut back on technological progress or economic growth, people get hysterical and start screaming that if we fall behind in technology the Japanese will get ahead of us. Holy robots! The world will fly off its orbit if the Japanese ever sell more cars than we do! (Nationalism is a great promoter of technology.) More reasonably, it is argued that if the relatively democratic nations of the world fall behind in technology while nasty, dictatorial nations like China, Vietnam and North Korea continue to progress, eventually the dictators may come to dominate the world. That is why the industrial system should be attacked in all nations simultaneously, to the extent that this may be possible. True, there is no assurance that the industrial system can be destroyed at approximately the same time all over the world, and it is even conceivable that the attempt to overthrow the system could lead instead to the domination of the system by dictators. That is a risk that has to be taken. And it is worth taking, since the difference between a "democratic" industrial system and one controlled by dictators is small compared with the difference between an industrial system and a non-industrial one. It might even be argued that an industrial system controlled by dictators would be preferable, because dictator-controlled systems usually have proved inefficient, hence they are presumably more likely to break down. Look at Cuba.

196. Revolutionaries might consider favoring measures that tend to bind the world economy into a unified whole. Free trade agreements like NAFTA and GATT are probably harmful to the environment in the short run, but in the long run they may perhaps be advantageous because they foster economic interdependence between nations. I will be eaier to destroy the industrial system on a worldwide basis if he world economy is so unified that its breakdown in any on major nation will lead to its breakdwon in al industrialized nations.

the long run they may perhaps be advantageous because they foster economic interdependence between nations. It will be easier to destroy the industrial system on a worldwide basis if the world economy is so unified that its breakdown in any one major nation will lead to its breakdown in all industrialized nations.

197. Some people take the line that modern man has too much power, too much control over nature; they argue for a more passive attitude on the part of the human race. At best these people are expressing themselves unclearly,

because they fail to distinguish between power for LARGE ORGANIZATIONS and power for INDIVIDUALS and SMALL GROUPS. It is a mistake to argue for powerlessness and passivity, because people NEED power. Modern man as a collective entity—that is, the industrial system—has immense power over nature, and we (FC) regard this as evil. But modern INDIVIDUALS and SMALL GROUPS OF INDIVIDUALS have far less power than primitive man ever did. Generally speaking, the vast power of "modern man" over nature is exercised not by individuals or small groups but by large organizations. To the extent that the average modern INDIVIDUAL can wield the power of technology, he is permitted to do so only within narrow limits and only under the supervision and control of the system. (You need a license for everything and with the license come rules and regulations). The individual has only those technological powers with which the system chooses to provide him. His PERSONAL power over nature is slight.

198. Primitive INDIVIDUALS and SMALL GROUPS actually had considerable power over nature; or maybe it would be better to say power WITHIN nature. When primitive man needed food he knew how to find and prepare edible roots, how to track game and take it with homemade weapons. He knew how to protect himself from heat, cold, rain, dangerous animals, etc. But primitive man did relatively little damage to nature because the COLLECTIVE power of primitive society was negligible compared to the COLLECTIVE power of industrial society.

199. Instead of arguing for powerlessness and passivity, one should argue that the power of the INDUSTRIAL SYSTEM should be broken, and that this will greatly INCREASE the power and freedom of INDIVIDUALS and SMALL GROUPS.

200. Until the industrial system has been thoroughly wrecked, the destruction of that system must be the revolutionaries' ONLY goal. Other goals would distract attention and energy from the main goal. More importantly, if the revolutionaries permit themselves to have any other goal than the destruction of technology, they will be tempted to use technology as a tool for reaching that other goal. If they give in to that temptation, they will fall right back into the technological trap, because modern technology is a unified, tightly organized system, so that, in order to retain SOME technology, one finds oneself obliged to retain MOST technology, hence one ends up sacrificing only token amounts of technology.

201. Suppose for example that the revolutionaries took "social justice" as a goal. Human nature being what it is, social justice would not come about spontaneously; it would have to be enforced. In order to enforce it the revolutionaries would have to retain central organization and control. For that they would need rapid long-distance transportation and communication, and therefore all the technology needed to support the transportation and communication systems. To feed and clothe poor people they would have to use agricultural and manufacturing technology. And so forth. So that the attempt to insure social justice would force them to retain most parts of the technological system. Not that we have anything against social justice, but it must not be allowed to interfere with the effort to get rid of the technological system.

202. It would be hopeless for revolutionaries to try to attack the system without using SOME modern technology. If nothing else they must use the communications media to spread their message. But they should use modern technology for only ONE purpose: to attack the technological system.

203. Imagine an alcoholic sitting with a barrel of wine in front of him. Suppose he starts saying to himself, "Wine isn't bad for you if used in moderation. Why, they say small amounts of wine are even good for you! It won't do me any harm if I take just one little drink . . ." Well you know what is going to happen. Never forget that the human race with technology is just like an alcoholic with a barrel of wine.

204. Revolutionaries should have as many children as they can. There is strong scientific evidence that social attitudes are to a significant extent inherited. No one suggests that a social attitude is a direct outcome of a person's genetic constitution, but it appears that personality traits tend, within the context of our society, to make a person more likely to hold this or that social attitude. Objections to these findings have been raised, but objections are feeble and seem to be ideologically motivated. In any event, no one denies that children tend on the average to hold social attitudes similar to those of their parents. From our point of view it doesn't matter all that much whether the attitudes are passed on genetically or through childhood training. In either case they ARE passed on.

205. The trouble is that many of the people who are inclined to rebel against the industrial system are also concerned about the population problems, hence they are apt to have few or no children. In this way they may be hand-

ing the world over to the sort of people who support or at least accept the industrial system. To insure the strength of the next generation of revolutionaries the present generation must reproduce itself abundantly. In doing so they will be worsening the population problem only slightly. And the most important problem is to get rid of the industrial system, because once the industrial system is gone the world's population necessarily will decrease (see paragraph 167); whereas, if the industrial system survives, it will continue developing new techniques of food production that may enable the world's population to keep increasing almost indefinitely.

1997 Communiqué from the Earth Liberation Front

Welcome to the struggle of all species to be free.

We are the burning rage of this dying planet. The war of greed ravages the earth and species die out every day. ELF works to speed up the collapse of industry, to scare the rich, and to undermine the foundations of the state. We embrace social and deep ecology as a practical resistance movement. We have to show the enemy that we are serious about defending what is sacred. Together we have teeth and claws to match our dreams. Our greatest weapons are imagination and the ability to strike when least expected.

Since 1992, a series of earth nights and halloween smashes has mushroomed around the world. 1000's of bulldozers, powerlines, computer systems, buildings and valuable equipment have been composted. Many ELF actions have been censored to prevent our bravery from inciting others to take action.

We take inspiration from the Luddites, Levellers, Diggers, the Autonome squatter movement, ALF, the Zapatistas, and the little people—those mischievous elves of lore. Authorities can't see us because they don't believe in elves. We are practically invisible. We have no command structure, no spokespersons, no office, just many small groups working separately, seeking vulnerable targets and practicing our craft.

Many elves are moving to the Pacific Northwest and other sacred areas. Some elves will leave surprises as they go. Find your family! And let's dance as we make ruins of the corporate money system.

Form 'stormy night' action groups, encourage friends you trust. A tight community of love is a poweful force.

Recon—check out targets that fit your plan and go over what you will do.

Attack—powerlines: cut supporting cables, unbolt towers, and base supports, saw wooden poles.

—transformers: shoot out, bonfires, throw metal chains on top, or blow them up.

—computers: smash, burn or flood buildings.

Please copy and improve for local use.

Document Sources

"Declaration of the People," *Virginia Magazine of History and Biography*, 1:1 (1893); "Common Sense," Bartleby.com, http://www.bartleby.com/133/ (June 24, 2002); *A New View of Society*, McMaster University Archive for the History of Economic Thought, http://socserv2.socsci.mcmaster.ca/~econ/ugcm/3ll3/owen (June 24, 2002); "Working Men's Declaration of Independence," Illinois Labor History Society, http://www.kentlaw.edu/ilhs/doc29.html (June 24, 2002); "Appeal to Christian Women of the South" New York: New York Anti-Slavery Society, 1836; Speech by Susan B. Anthony, Famous American Trials: The Susan B. Anthony Trial, http://www.law.umkc.edu/faculty/projects/ftrials/anthony/sbahome.html (June 24, 2002); "Conservatism," Daniel DeLeon Internet Archive, http://www.marxists.org/archive/deleon (June 24, 2002); Preamble to the Constitution of the IWW, Melvyn Dubofsky, *"Big Bill" Haywood*, New York: St. Martin's Press, 1987; "Speech in Canton, Ohio," Schlesinger, Arthur, ed, *Writings and Speeches of E.V. Debs*, New York: Hermitage Press, 1948; "The Case for Birth Control," *The Woman Citizen*, February 23, 1924; "Nicola Sacco's Speech to the Court," Marion Denman Frankfurter and Gardner Jackson, eds, *The Letters of Sacco and Vanzetti*, New York: Viking Press, 1928; "Have You Ever Been to Jail?" Dorothy Day Library on the Web, http://www.catholicworker.org/dorothyday/ (June 24, 2002); "Integrated Bus Suggestions" from the Montgomery Improvement Association, Alabama Department of Archives and History, Inez Jessie Baskin Papers, Montgomery, Alabama; "SCUM Manifesto" http://www.bcn.net/~jpiazzo/scum.htm (June 24, 2002); "Testimony by Abbie Hoffman," Famous American Trials: The Chicago Seven Trial, http://www.law.umkc.edu/faculty/projects/ftrials/Chicago7/chicago7.html (June 24, 2002); "Unabomber Manifesto," Critical Criminology Homepage, http://www.soci.niu.edu/~critcrim/uni/uni.html (June 24, 2002); Communiqué from the Earth Liberation Front, http://www.earthliberationfront.com (June 24, 2002).

Index

Notes: Page numbers in **boldface** refer to main entries.
Page numbers in *italics* refer to the Appendix.